PERSONNEL SERVICES
IN EDUCATION

Officers of the Society
1958-59
(Term of office expires March 1 of the year indicated.)

STEPHEN M. COREY

(1960)

Teachers College, Columbia University, New York, New York

ROBERT J. HAVIGHURST

(1960)

University of Chicago, Chicago, Illinois

NELSON B. HENRY

(1959) (Ex-officio)

University of Chicago, Chicago, Illinois

T. R. MC CONNELL

(1961)

University of California, Berkeley, California

ERNEST O. MELBY

(1959)

Michigan State University, East Lansing, Michigan

WILLARD C. OLSON

(1959)

University of Michigan, Ann Arbor, Michigan

RUTH STRANG

(1961)

Teachers College, Columbia University, New York, New York

Secretary-Treasurer

NELSON B. HENRY

5835 Kimbark Avenue, Chicago 37, Illinois

PERSONNEL SERVICES IN EDUCATION

The Fifty-eighth Yearbook of the National Society for the Study of Education

PART II

Prepared by the Yearbook Committee: MELVENE DRAHEIM HARDEE *(Chairman),* C. E. ERICKSON, DANIEL D. FEDER, NELSON B. HENRY, ARTHUR A. HITCHCOCK, *and* C. GILBERT WRENN

Edited by

NELSON B. HENRY

19 | NSSE | 59

Distributed by THE UNIVERSITY OF CHICAGO PRESS • CHICAGO, ILLINOIS

The responsibilities of the Board of Directors of the National Society for the Study of Education in the case of yearbooks prepared by the Society's committees are (1) to select the subjects to be investigated, (2) to appoint committees calculated in their personnel to insure consideration of all significant points of view, (3) to provide appropriate subsidies for necessary expenses, (4) to publish and distribute the committees' reports, and (5) to arrange for their discussion at the annual meeting.

The responsibility of the Yearbook Editor is to prepare the submitted manuscripts for publication in accordance with the principles and regulations approved by the Board of Directors.

Neither the Board of Directors, nor the Yearbook Editor, nor the Society is responsible for the conclusions reached or the opinions expressed by the Society's yearbook committees.

Published 1959 by

THE NATIONAL SOCIETY FOR THE STUDY OF EDUCATION

5835 Kimbark Avenue, Chicago 37, Illinois

The Society's Committee on Personnel Services in Education

C. E. ERICKSON
Dean, College of Education, Michigan State University
East Lansing, Michigan

DANIEL D. FEDER
Dean of Students, University of Denver
Denver, Colorado

MELVENE DRAHEIM HARDEE
(Chairman)
Coordinator of Counseling, Florida State University
Tallahassee, Florida

NELSON B. HENRY
Secretary, National Society for the Study of Education
Chicago, Illinois

ARTHUR A. HITCHCOCK
Executive Secretary, American Personnel and Guidance Association
Washington, D.C.

C. GILBERT WRENN
Professor of Educational Psychology, University of Minnesota
Minneapolis, Minnesota

Associated Contributors

MARGARET E. BENNETT
Formerly Director of Guidance, Board of Education
Pasadena, California

IRWIN A. BERG
Chairman, Department of Psychology, Louisiana State University
Baton Rouge, Louisiana

HENRY BOROW
Professor of Psychological Studies, University of Minnesota
Minneapolis, Minnesota

A. J. BRUMBAUGH
Vice-President Emeritus, American Council on Education
Washington, D.C.

v

PAUL L. DRESSEL
Director of Evaluation Services, Michigan State University
East Lansing, Michigan

RAYMOND N. HATCH
Assistant Dean for Continuing Education
College of Education, Michigan State University
East Lansing, Michigan

HARRY DEXTER KITSON
Professor Emeritus of Education, Teachers College, Columbia University
New York, New York

ERNEST O. MELBY
Distinguished Professor of Education, Michigan State University
East Lansing, Michigan

BLANCHE PAULSON
Director, Bureau of Counseling Services, Board of Education
Chicago, Illinois

HAROLD B. PEPINSKY
Supervisor of Research and Professor of Psychology
Ohio State University
Columbus, Ohio

FLOYD W. REEVES
Distinguished Professor of Education, Michigan State University
East Lansing, Michigan

HERMAN L. SHIBLER
General Superintendent of Education
Indianapolis, Indiana

Editor's Preface

Guidance has long been a subject of study on the part of faculties of the schools and colleges of America. It is of interest to note the early recognition of the significance of educational and vocational guidance in the series of yearbooks of which this Society is sponsor. Part II of the Fourth Yearbook, entitled *The Place of Vocational Subjects in the High-School Curriculum*, dealt with such topics as "selective guidance" for pupils seeking vocational training, more liberal training of vocational teachers, and the artificial distinction between vocational and cultural studies. Part I of the Sixth Yearbook was devoted to a consideration of *Vocational Studies for College Entrance*, and Part II of the Eleventh Yearbook described programs of instruction in *Agricultural Education in Secondary Schools*. Part II of the Twenty-third Yearbook, entitled *Vocational Guidance and Vocational Education for the Industries*, presented an interpretative analysis of data pertaining to vocational-guidance practices and existing programs of industrial education in representative school systems. Part I of the Thirty-seventh Yearbook, *Guidance in Educational Institutions*, was prepared with the view of depicting the changes in the theory and practice of guidance which were then developing in keeping with the increasing emphasis upon the social aims of education. *Vocational Education*, which is Part I of the Forty-second Yearbook, deals comprehensively with the various aspects of vocational education, including a substantial chapter on vocational guidance, its place in the program of vocational education, and its procedures.

The title of the present volume, *Personnel Services in Education*, directs attention, first, to the generally recognized concept of the pupil as a person to be cultivated rather than a peon to be molded by authoritarian regimentation and, secondly, signalizes that type of pupil-teacher rapport which is implicit in the readiness with which personnel workers in education "take their appropriate place in the process aimed at helping each student develop to the limit of his potential" (p. 10).

NELSON B. HENRY

Table of Contents

SECTION I

The Personnel Movement in the Changing Educational and Social Order

SECTION II

Personnel Services in Action

SECTION III

Frontiers

SECTION IV

Historical Backgrounds

Socioeconomic Development. Education for All People. Education and Individuality. Mental Health. Guidance as an Instrument of National Policy. Conclusion.

CHAPTER I

The Mission of the Yearbook

MELVENE DRAHEIM HARDEE

An Era of Great Promise

The Fifty-eighth Yearbook makes its advent at a propitious moment in the period of ascendancy of personnel work. Public interest and professional zeal are seemingly at their peak. Guidance activity has been challenged with new responsibilities: eliminating juvenile delinquency, identifying the gifted, motivating able students to seek further education, extending guidance downward to the elementary school, and attempting to individualize education at a time of mounting school enrolments.[1] The number of counselors in schools has been growing rapidly, with some states reporting increases of 25 per cent in a two-year period. Since 1951, some states have experienced increases of more than 100 per cent in numbers of counselors.[2] In public and private schools of many areas, additional staff will be appointed as soon as qualified personnel can be found or potentially good candidates trained.

At the level of higher education, the growth in enrolment in colleges and universities coupled with the growth in complexity of institutional organization and curriculum have necessitated the formulation of unified comprehensive programs of personnel administration.[3] In these institutions, numbers of specially selected

1. Ruth Barry and Beverly Wolf, *Modern Issues in Guidance-Personnel Work,* p. 32. New York: Bureau of Publications, Teachers College, Columbia University, 1957.

2. Arthur A. Hitchcock, "By What Means Can the Quality and Quantity of Guidance Services, Particularly in the High Schools, Be Increased?" *Current Issues in Higher Education, 1958.* Washington: Association for Higher Education, National Education Association, 1958.

3. Eugenie Andruss Leonard, *Origins of Personnel Services in American Higher Education,* pp. 106-14. Minneapolis: University of Minnesota Press, 1956.

faculty members are augmenting and supplementing the activities of professionally trained personnel workers, with a resulting integration in programs of personnel and of instruction.[4]

Appropriately, specific attention is being given to the need for providing enlarged and intensified programs of preservice and in-service education for personnel workers at all levels.[5] Timely recognition has been made by the federal government of the essential nature of adequate programs of training, with provision being made in the National Defense Education Act of 1958 for extending educational opportunities for prospective counselors.

Coming at this point of high tide in the affairs of student personnel workers, the Fifty-eighth Yearbook addresses itself to the chronicle of the past, the inventory of the present, and the anticipation of the perhaps-in-future of the profession. The pervasive purpose of the book is reflected in these specific objectives:

1. To relate developments in personnel work to major social, economic, and cultural changes that have taken place in America, pointing out the fundamental relationship between these and personnel work.

2. To demonstrate that personnel work is an important and integral part of the educational unit within which it operates, conforming to and supporting the objectives of that unit.

3. To trace the emerging profession of personnel work, noting the growing self-concept held by personnel workers relative to their status in the profession.

4. To show that there is a systematic and orderly body of functions now performing at all levels of education by personnel workers, these functions being of such sufficiently distinctive nature as to permit their differentiation as a specialization.

5. To enumerate and describe the philosophical principles as well as the psychological content upon which the various functions in personnel work are based.

4. Melvene Draheim Hardee, *The Faculty in College Counseling*. New York: McGraw-Hill Book Co., 1959.

5. E. G. Williamson, "Essentials of Professional Training for Student Personnel Workers in the South," *Report of the Southern College Personnel Association*, pp. 40-45. Frankfort, Kentucky: Southern College Personnel Association, 1952. Also, E. G. Williamson, "Professional Preparation of Student Personnel Workers," *School and Society*, LXXXVI (January 4, 1958), 3-6.

6. To develop and sharpen the reader's awareness of problems and issues at hand, thus alerting him to the challenge of personnel work in the future.

Some Earlier Basic Studies

The reader will recognize that these objectives are rooted in an earlier statement of professional philosophy and objectives which affirms that the personnel point of view encompasses the student as a whole.[6] This concept of education stresses attention to the total development of the student—physically, socially, emotionally, spiritually, and intellectually. He is viewed not as a passive recipient of a prescribed economic, political, or religious doctrine but as a responsible participant in his own development. The concept further contends that, in the societal processes of American democracy, the student's full and balanced maturity is considered to be (a) the major end-goal of education as well as (b) a necessary means for achieving the fullest potential of colleagues, friends, and neighbors.

Similarly, the objectives of this yearbook bear close relationship to the statement of basic philosophy and services outlined by the Council of Guidance and Personnel Associations of a decade earlier.[7] This group cited in their report fourteen specific objectives contributing to the growth of the individual student and, in addition, enumerated fifteen services to be provided for students in their achievement of the objectives. The services enumerated include: (a) the functioning of the school for the individual; (b) the maintenance of personnel records; (c) the provision of competent counseling; (d) physical and mental health services; (e) remedial services; (f) supervision and integration of housing and food services, wherever provided; (g) creation of an activities program; (h) supervision of group activities; (i) initiation of a program of recreational activities; (j) treatment of discipline as a learn-

6. Committee on Student Personnel Work, E. G. Williamson, Chairman, *The Student Personnel Point of View*, p. 1. Council Studies, Series VI, No. 13. Washington: American Council on Education, 1949.

7. "Educational Personnel Work: Basic Philosophy and Services." Report of Study Commission of the Council of Guidance and Personnel Associations. Washington: The Council, 1950.

ing experience; (*k*) provision of financial aid when needed; (*l*) assistance in securing part-time employment; (*m*) assistance in securing employment upon school termination; (*n*) provision of learning experiences in the area of spiritual and ethical values; and (*o*) provision for making desirable social adjustments.

In addition, the objectives of this yearbook have a kinship with the pronouncements of other groups, such as the group of college and university administrators discussing future needs in personnel work,[8] the planning group in guidance of the curriculum supervisors,[9] the committee of the Thirty-seventh Yearbook, Part I, of the National Society for the Study of Education,[10] the committees for two publications of the American Educational Research Association,[11] the report of the analyses of jobs held by personnel workers,[12] and the recent statement made by the Council of the American Personnel and Guidance Association relating to human resources.[13]

These references constitute but a few of the many serving to suggest challenging points of view and immediate and long-range goals of personnel service. Utilizing the comprehensive findings of these study and editorial groups, their own professional experiences, and those of others in allied disciplines, the contributors to the present yearbook portray personnel work of the present and make predictions about the functions of personnel workers in the coming quarter century.

8. *Future Needs in Student Personnel Work*. Washington: American Council on Education, 1948.

9. Camilla M. Low, *Guidance in the Curriculum*. 1955 Yearbook of the Association for Supervision and Curriculum Development. Washington: National Education Association, 1955.

10. *Guidance in Educational Institutions*. Thirty-seventh Yearbook of the National Society for the Study of Education, Part I. Chicago: Distributed by the University of Chicago Press, 1938.

11. Merle M. Ohlsen and Committee, "Guidance, Counseling, and Pupil Personnel," *Review of Educational Research*, XXIV (April, 1954). Also, Dugald S. Arbuckle and Committee, "Guidance and Counseling," *Review of Educational Research*, XXVII (April, 1957), 165-236.

12. "Job Analyses of Educational Personnel Workers" (Interim Report by the Study Commission of the Council of Guidance and Personnel Associations), *Occupations*, XXX (October, 1951), Part II, pp. 1-22.

13. "A Statement of Policy concerning the Nation's Human Resources Problems," *Personnel and Guidance Journal*, XXXVI (March, 1958), 454-55.

The Organization and Preparation of the Yearbook

In 1956, the committee on publications of the American Personnel and Guidance Association, with the writer as chairman, began an exploration of possibilities for producing a yearbook in cooperation with the National Society for the Study of Education. A proposed outline for the yearbook was submitted to the Board of Directors of the Society in February, 1957. The Board's approval of the general nature of the Association's outline assured mutual co-operation on the part of the two organizations.

The tentative outline for the yearbook was circularized in March, 1957, to approximately seventy readers—members of the American Personnel and Guidance Association, all of whom had had experience in writing and publishing. Critical comments from these readers were compiled by the writer for examination by the committee on publications and the Executive Council of the American Personnel and Guidance Association.

In April, 1957, at the Detroit meeting of the Association, the Executive Council designated a yearbook committee comprised of members of the Association, with the writer as chairman. At its meeting in May, the Board of Directors of the National Society concurred in the action of the Association and named one of its own members to serve as a member of the yearbook committee. The responsibility of this committee was to plan and produce the personnel yearbook. In July, 1957, members of the yearbook committee met in Chicago to outline the volume and to select contributors.

In two successive meetings, November, 1957, and April, 1958, the work of chapter authors was reviewed in detail by the yearbook committee. It is doubtless obvious to our readers that the committee faced a challenging task in the creation of a yearbook designed to meet the needs of some ten thousand members in the personnel ranks and the additional needs of a sizable number of administrators and teachers seeking to develop greater understanding about personnel work. Withal, the committee has envisioned a book which will be useful for at least the next twenty-five years.

One of the knotty problems in the creation of this volume has hinged upon the advisability of including a comprehensive survey of the many aspects of guidance—educational, industrial, governmental, military, community—all in one volume. The decision of the yearbook committee was to delimit the yearbook to aspects of *educational personnel work* with appropriate recognition being made of other aspects of personnel and guidance as instances arose. The decision was in no way designed to minimize the laudable work being done by personnel workers in industry, labor, government, military installations, and the community. It is the belief of the yearbook committee that a very considerable amount of the material herein, relating to principles, practices, functions, and roles, has merit for many groups and agencies, not alone those designated as "educational."

In addition, the book is intended to reflect educational personnel work in the United States. The committee has recognized that there is commendable work going on in the area of personnel work abroad. There is, however, considerable evidence to the effect that personnel work in our own schools and colleges springs from the democratic process and is peculiar to the educational system fostered in the United States.

Choice of terminology and consistency in the use of particular terms must be considered in launching any book which is the product of writers-in-combination. The committee has consciously chosen to emphasize the special service concepts included in guidance, referring to these as *personnel work* and to those who dispatch these services as *personnel workers*. Finally, the committee has attempted to circumvent the use of the word *training*, it being too narrowly conceived and too specifically directed toward technique orientation. The reference, by way of substitute, has been to the broad aspects of learning.

The Plan for the Yearbook

The six purposes of the yearbook, enumerated earlier, are achieved by the chapter writer in his or her adroit handling of the assigned topic. The reader will observe that the yearbook is divided into four sections. Section I, consisting of two chapters, bears the title "The Personnel Movement in the Changing Educational and Social Order." In chapter ii, writers Melby and Reeves address themselves to the first two objectives, calling attention to the impact of new energy concepts, the influence of great combines, of unparalleled prosperity, of accomplishments in health and sanitation—all with their resultant challenge to the schools and communities of America. The writers emphasize the responsibility of education for giving leadership to social change and for effecting solutions for problems in human relations. The personnel worker is charged with helping man better understand himself and his neighbor for the purpose of bringing greater good to a more creative society.

In chapter iii, Wrenn calls attention to the fact that the literature of personnel work reflects many philosophical and psychological assumptions which are neither examined nor tested and that few writers possess a consistently operating philosophy or systematic point of view regarding behavior. Describing a number of selected systems of philosophy, Wrenn concludes that personnel work is the child of two worlds—humanitarianism and the behavioral sciences. He reviews twelve major theories of personality, pointing up the elements which combine in organismic and field theories, psychoanalysis, self-theory, learning theory, and social psychology. Wrenn concludes his chapter with the admonition that the bases of our professional future reside in the approaching convergence of two streams of understanding, those labeled *philosophy* and *psychology*. He affirms that it is extremely important that knowledge of man's behavior be viewed within the framework of *his existence* in the universe.

Section II of the yearbook covers "Personnel Services in Action" and includes four chapters which contribute appropriately to this theme. In chapter iv, writers Erickson and Hatch present principles for programming personnel services in educational settings. Commenting on the "identifiable center" where there is power of decision, these writers suggest careful study of the basic phases of programming which include planning, organizing, staffing, directing, and evaluating. They make suggestions for involving staff, students, and community in achieving the maximum values with students for whom the personnel services have been designed.

Bennett, in chapter v, views the functions and procedures in personnel services in relation to individual development in a democratically oriented society. She centers attention on two types of services: (*a*) leadership in an evolving program, and (*b*) direct service to individuals. Considering the former, Bennett comments that shifts in emphasis in personnel work, from services to special groups to preventive work with all, have directed attention to the learning processes involved in adjustment and personal development. Concerning the second, she enumerates the direct services provided individuals on the various educational levels and specifies the needs met by each.

The aim of Berg in chapter vi is to identify and suggest means for mobilizing internal and external resources which may be used by the personnel worker. Defining *internal* resources as those available within the school system, he designates them as (*a*) informal and unstructured student groups, (*b*) partially structured groups under student control, and (*c*) structured and partially structured groups under school direction or affiliation. *External* resources are defined as those outside the school situation, including civic groups, professional and business organizations, federal, state, and municipal agencies, local groups of varied sponsorship, the home, and the neighborhood. Berg affirms the belief that to do the best personnel job, the personnel staff is, and will continue to be, dependent upon outside resources. Certain persons and agencies can handle some particular problems more efficiently and reach a better solution than can an educational personnel worker who, for obvious reasons, is operating on the marginal range of his training and experience.

Shibler, the author of chapter vii, in discussing the organization of personnel services, cites *flexibility* as an important aspect of organization, applicable both to the functions of personnel workers and to the types of personnel services offered by them. Citing the existence of three main plans for the organization of these services, he proceeds to view the role of the administrator, teacher, and personnel worker in institutions large and small, in elementary and secondary schools as well as in institutions of higher learning. Shibler reiterates the theme that current concepts of learning and the emerging role of the well-educated man in our society demand that the pupil not only be properly taught but also that his learning include a pattern of self-adjustment and a series of skills for attacking and solving his own problems.

The third section of the yearbook, "Frontiers," includes three chapters with topics as follows: "The Emerging Role of the Professional Personnel Worker," "Frontiers of Student Personnel Research," and "Personnel Work in Education as Related to Change." In chapter viii, Feder traces the climb of the personnel worker, up the years, to professionalism. He discusses the personnel worker in relation to areas of preparation, title and job description, affiliations with professional associations, and personal qualifications. With reference to roles and function, there is description given of the work of the generalist and the specialist and the resulting integration of personnel workers with other professional persons in education. Withal, Feder views the future of the personnel worker in terms of his ability to understand (*a*) society's needs, (*b*) individual needs and psychological processes, (*c*) education and its processes, (*d*) the world external to school, and (*e*) the utilization of professional techniques.

In chapter ix, writers Borow, Pepinsky, and Dressel delineate some new frontiers in research in student personnel work. Borow cites four dominant emphases in research, these including (*a*) social psychology of student groups, (*b*) group-mediated personnel work, (*c*) process-analysis in counseling, and (*d*) mental health in the educational setting. Pepinsky considers one of the most promising research frontiers to be that concerned with the process of the student's development in his educational environment. He presents the research task in terms of observable antecedent and mediating conditions, using a schematic presentation of major variables as a basis for reviewing selected contemporary research activities. Concluding chapter ix, Dressel addresses himself to the all-important task of interrelating student personnel work and instruction. He contends that the common pattern of organization which distinguishes between student affairs, on the one hand, and instruction, on the other, is in need of study. Dressel urges that personnel workers and teachers join forces in agreeing on educational objectives, in examining their roles, and in studying means of accomplishing their mutual objectives.

In chapter x, Feder views in retrospect the road which the profession of personnel work has traveled, examining briefly the scene upon which the profession has arrived and predicting some of the challenges and functions of personnel work of the future. He reaffirms a basic tenet which is that personnel work is integral to the educational process, that the basic mission of this process is the teaching-learning function. In this framework, he sees counseling and other phases of personnel work take their appropriate place in the process aimed at helping each student develop to the limit of his potential. Feder reminds his readers of the need for testing out the applicability of theoretical constructs developed in psychological laboratories and expounded in seminars. He believes it important for the personnel worker to make a clear distinction between his personal philosophical orientation to his work and the techniques of his operation on the job. Citing the need for members of the profession to engage in research, he urges that the research undertaken be productive of differences which are significant *individually* and *socially*, rather than purely statistically. Finally, Feder exhorts leaders in education, including those in personnel work, to refrain from abdicating the leadership role even in the face of disconcerting pressures.

A final section of the yearbook presents a historical tracing of the emerging profession of personnel work. Hitchcock, Kitson, Paulsen, Brumbaugh, and others enumerate the significant events which initiated or gave primary direction to the student personnel movement. Among the various forces, originating both inside and outside the field of education and having noticeable impact on the profession, were: the industrial revolution, the advent of testing for individual differences, the growing emphasis on mental health, the rediscovery of the individual in his environment, the co-operative action of citizens in planning for their schools, and the increasing urgency for students to prepare to live in one world.

A Word to the Individual Reader

The author of a text depicting the life and times of a group in the Wady Qunran, 100 B.C. to 70 A.D., prefaces his work with the following:

I have tried to write with a man's pen, so that he who runs may read. Even so, I fear an attempt to read these chapters on the run will prove to be quite an obstacle race. I could not level the hills and valleys and make all the rough places plain without giving up my main purpose in writing. . . . I hope he who starts to read will not run away. In this kind of race, after all, there is no rule against cutting across the course and skipping the rugged places. If the reader chooses to turn at once to the last chapter to see how the story comes out, there is nothing to prevent it.[14]

The authors of the yearbook have written with the expectation that many who run to keep up with the daily exactions of their work will read this volume. Some readers, however, will find portions of the book a bit too difficult to read decathalon-fashion. The deeper purposes of the work may be better understood by the quasi-ambulatory, those persons with somewhat more time available to meditate. It is hoped that those who begin the reading of this volume will not veer from their objective. Certainly it is recognized that a reader may wish to select for initial reading those chapters or parts of chapters which have greatest appeal.

Thus, there appears here, bound not in scrolls of leather but in the accoutrement of twentieth-century-printing bookmanship, a chronicle of the life and times of a professional group, known as personnel workers, with reflections of their role and function on the differing levels of educational activity, and covering the years 1870 to 1959.

14. Millar Burrows, *The Dead Sea Scrolls*, p. xv. New York: Viking Press, 1955.

THE PERSONNEL MOVEMENT IN THE CHANGING
EDUCATIONAL AND SOCIAL ORDER

CHAPTER II

Education and the Evolving Nature of Society

ERNEST O. MELBY and FLOYD W. REEVES

To American teachers and American citizens engaged in the task of developing the appropriate role of education in a free society, the events of the last three decades have been both challenging and revealing. Challenging, in that world events with their domestic counterparts have threatened the very life of freedom, and revealing, in that the magnitude of the task of giving continued life to freedom has been a mirror in which we can, with increasing clarity, see the shortcomings of our past and current educational efforts. Far-reaching social changes, new concepts of energy, community disintegration together with a waning faith in freedom, all present education with problems as urgent as those coming to us from world affairs. Even the educational proposals made in an effort to meet the challenges are in many cases dangerous or at least inadequate. As they are made they reveal the partial understanding of those who make them and often disclose enormous fallacies in broad policy-thinking in relation to both education and world affairs. If ever American educators, together with other American people, are to give thought to educational policy and to the role of education in relation to social change, the time is now. In fact, it is not an exaggeration to say that failure to do such policy-thinking and planning may well be fatal to the life of freedom.

The Challenge of World Affairs

We often blame the Communists for our difficulties, but we would probably have had nearly as many problems if Karl Marx had never lived. The complexities of the international picture have been with us ever since the end of World War II. In a larger sense they have been building up for several decades. The revolutionary process in Africa and Asia, the disintegration of the great colonial empires, the rise in the military and economic power of our own nation, the emergence of communism as a world force have all altered the role of America in world affairs. In turn, our changed world role has affected nearly every problem we face not only in international relations but in domestic affairs as well. In addition, our foreign and domestic policies have suffered from several fallacious assumptions. To use Harry Ashmore's phraseology, we "have miscalculated the past, misunderstood the present, and ignored the future." Because the Russians had in the past been a technologically underdeveloped country, we misjudged the power of their current efforts. Even though we should have known that if the Russians continued to make two or three times as great an educational effort as we do they would sooner or later defeat us in scientific programs, we have ignored the future results of their programs and continued to starve our own education.

FALLACIOUS ASSUMPTIONS

The first of our dangerous assumptions has been that we are always best, always first, and inevitably superior in technical advancement. This has led us to overestimate our own achievements and power and to underestimate our competitors. This leads to the dangerous belief that if only we can keep our secrets away from our enemies all will be well. In turn, our security efforts have hamstrung our own scientific efforts, annoyed our friends abroad, denied our own public the facts upon which it could make wise policy decisions, and in the aggregate played into the hands of our enemies. Most important of all, we have confused dissent and disloyalty, ushering in one of the worst periods of conformity and anti-intellectualism in our history as a nation. Orthodoxy replaced originality as a guiding star in many aspects of our life.

A second fallacious assumption has been that communism is the world's basic problem—that, accordingly, the great aim of our policies is to bring death to communism. This in turn has caused us to forget that communism is an idea and cannot be destroyed by military action or containment. The only real way to bring death to communism is to give life to freedom. This we have failed to do in sufficient degree, partially, at least, because we were so occupied fighting communism we gave little heed to our own weaknesses, such as the race problem. Closely associated is the assumption that our conflict with the Russians is primarily military, causing us to forget that the issues are moral and spiritual, scientific and cultural. This preoccupation with the military aspects of the conflict has given us an ambiguous position in the international scene, forcing us to make opportunistic choices of policy rather than to take action on the basis of principles that are harmonious with our traditions of freedom and human values.

Even in those instances in which our policies have been broadly sound, as in the case of technical assistance, we have lost much of the gain from our efforts because we put political price tags on our help and let military considerations outweigh those of international good will, as in the case of the emphasis placed upon the arming of Pakistan.

Perhaps there will be disagreement about the specific illustrations we have used in foreign policy. But there can hardly be disagreement that sound domestic and foreign policies depend on public information, understanding, and attitude. Our leaders under both parties have no doubt made errors, but they would have erred less dangerously had we, the American people, understood our problems more fully.

THE INTERDEPENDENCE OF DOMESTIC AND FOREIGN POLICIES

Probably our most serious fallacious assumption has been that foreign policy and domestic life and practice are two different things. This assumption permits us to spend huge sums in countries with dark-skinned peoples in an effort to prevent them from becoming communist while at the same time we make second-class citizens of our own dark-skinned people. We have in reality given our enemies a free propaganda ride which many hundreds of millions of dollars in propaganda could not have provided.

If, in the future, America is to avoid the serious fallacies of recent years, our total educational program must give our people more realistic knowledge and understanding of the world in which we live. It must change the attitudes of our people and provide them with the social and political competencies to deal effectively with domestic and world challenges as they develop. To discuss these in detail is beyond the scope of this chapter. However, a brief review of some of the issues which presently confront us will help us to visualize the role demanded of education.

Few informed observers of world problems would deny that the most crucial issues of our day are those in human relations. This is true here at home in America. It is true broadly in world affairs, in the Middle-East area, and in Asia and Africa. Unfortunately, it is on the human-relations front that our education has been least effective. We need an education that makes the individual aware of his oneness with the rest of humanity, that will vividly portray to him the worth, dignity, and sacredness of individual human beings regardless of race, color, or creed.

The process of education which makes the individual a member of the human race, which relates him to other men, is intellectual, emotional, and experiential. The facts about human differences must be known. Particularly important are the facts which show that the differences are of minor significance and the similarities are important. Good will is essential, but good will without a factual base and needed insights may become a mere sentimentality which will not stand the stresses and strains of world and community tensions nor equip the individual for social effectiveness. Since race prejudice is largely emotional, it is important that the emotional climate of school and community be wholesome.

More specifically, we in America must develop a more wholesome and humble view of ourselves. We must appreciate the contributions of other peoples and nations. We must not expect always to be first and most powerful in all areas. This does not mean we do not strive for excellence, or that we are not proud of our country, or that we do not convey our pride and our aspirations to those we teach. It does mean that we take pride in all human achievement, all creative works of art and science, no matter on what part of the globe they emerge. It means, too, that if other nations achieve what we have not as yet accomplished we do not suffer a devastating loss of ego. Education must thus help each of us to a balanced, wholesome, humble, yet self-respecting view of himself and his country and a real appreciation for other peoples and their accomplishments.

In the future such qualities may well be essential for a healthy attitude toward ourselves and others in America. Many presently underdeveloped countries have elements of culture that may well be superior to corresponding elements in our civilization. As these countries get education and industrial development, they are certain to equal us in many respects and, because of their vast populations, huge areas, and rich natural resources, pass us in other respects. Certainly we know that the white race is a minority in the total world population. It is not an exaggeration to say that the white race will not survive unless brotherhood is somehow taught to both the dark-skinned and the white-skinned peoples.

We must never forget that the underdeveloped areas, with their larger populations now on the march toward a more decent life for themselves, are every day watching developments in China, Europe, Russia, and the United States. The latter two countries have become symbols of progress to hundreds of millions of people. The teeming hundreds of millions in the underdeveloped areas are truly on the march. They will have a better life under freedom if freedom is true to its values and outlook. They will get what they think is a better life under the hammer and sickle if democracies behave so as to cause peoples in uncommitted areas to develop doubts as to the sincerity of those under the banner of freedom.

Clearly important changes in the scope, character, content, and human-relations aspects of our education will have to be made if education is to contribute materially to meeting the challenges of world affairs. No mere tinkering with the social-studies curriculums will suffice. The entire program, the teacher's preparation irrespective of his subject, the attitudes of teachers, their values, and their behavior must take cognizance of the world scene. We will return to this problem after viewing challenges essentially domestic.

The Challenge of Dramatic Social Changes

We began this discussion with a view of the current international scene because this is the backdrop before which the drama of our own life is being played. This does not mean an exclusive involvement with matters international, nor does it indicate that domestic social changes are less than dramatic. Were there fewer tensions in world affairs, our public attention might well be centered more upon domestic than upon world events.

Almost forty years have elapsed since the end of World War I. In terms of radical changes of a technological, social, and economic nature, this forty-year period goes beyond the wildest dreams of those whose horizon was that of 1918. It has been said that greater change has taken place in the last forty years than in the previous six thousand. What is perhaps more important, change is accelerating, taking place at a more rapid rate with each passing year. The acceleration of change alone, to say nothing of the impact of the changes themselves, poses a largely unsolved problem to education.

THE IMPACT OF NEW CONCEPTS OF ENERGY

The moment that Enrico Fermi was able to produce a chain reaction under the stadium at the University of Chicago, a new world came into being. Previous measures and concepts of power and energy had to be revised. Hitherto impossible tasks now became feasible. Speaking of these profound changes, Granville Read of the DuPont Company points out that, after the first atomic fission, "the nuclear physicists were no longer earthbound. They had transferred their thinking to the heavens above and were calculating how to duplicate the reactions of the stars, so as to create on earth—and make available to man under controlled conditions—the same sort of energy as that generated in vast amounts in these celestial bodies. The sun [alone] gives off energy by changing hydrogen to helium at the rate of 564 million tons per second which is approximately seven million billion times the rate at which electric power is generated in the United States." [1]

In an effort to show the impact of such concepts of energy on our society, Read describes the task of the Savannah River Project:

It is estimated that some 120 different skills and talents were combined into one technological effort to achieve the final design. We drew upon scientific talent from all of DuPont's research laboratories. We drew management, supervision, and operating personnel from across

---

1. Quoted from a special brochure published by the DuPont Company, Wilmington, Delaware.

company boards. We used professional consultants in special fields to make sure we were not missing a bet.[2]

We have here a dramatic example of the impact of the new concepts of energy on business, government, labor, and science. All of these facets of our life as a nation have become interdependent. No matter how their leaders may thunder at each other in political campaigns, in the realm of action, one cannot do without the other. The roles of all have changed. The new concepts of energy have demanded a new life for the nation and the world. Our current history is witnessing the forging of this new life. It is a history of dramatic changes only a few of which can be considered here.

INFLUENCES OF THE GREAT COMBINES

The development of vast corporate enterprise is, of course, no new problem in American society. Trust-busting is associated with Theodore Roosevelt. But in the earlier years of corporate concentration, major governmental attention was given to the impact of the corporations on small business, to corruption in politics, and the defrauding of the consumer through price control. All these are still problems in certain instances. In recent years, however, students of the impact of corporate forms of industry and business on our life as a nation have shifted much of their attention to matters of education and the control of public opinion.

One of the best examples lies in the area of mass communication. In the last two decades the number of daily newspapers has fallen with every passing year. In many large cities all the papers are owned by a single corporation. Moreover, large chains own papers in many cities. Thus, not only in a single city but for large regions only a single viewpoint is reflected. The selection of the facts, the overtones, the choice of what is reported—all these are controlled in many instances by a single business enterprise. There is no competition.

In radio and television a similar condition prevails. Large networks control the dissemination of news and viewpoints. This is not to overlook the many excellent instances of news reporting;

2. *Ibid.*

the fact remains, however, that a few large corporations control the enterprise.

But the mass media themselves have inherent dangers. As an example, the TV program, "$64,000 Question," has been estimated to have been viewed by as many as sixty million people. A medium which can make one-third of the total population sit down at one time to view its offering is somewhat terrifying in its potentialities.

Through our mass media we get news, general information, music, art, and advertising. But in a very subtle way values are also communicated. It may be that today our mass media are a greater educational force in our society than all our schools and colleges. Unfortunately, in many cases the values they teach, the type of conduct they laud, and the attitudes they appear to develop are exactly contrary to what is taught in these areas by our schools, churches, and homes.

It would be a mistake, however, to lay all the thought-control at the door of the communications industry. Other large business enterprises exert pressure for conformity; so do other agencies in society. The total force for conformity has led to such works as David Riesman's *The Lonely Crowd* and William Whyte's *The Organization Man*. Many of these forces in society seem to reward orthodoxy and penalize originality and creativity. The quest for orthodoxy comes to permeate even college and university campuses which have usually been thought of as sources of dedicated search for the new and different, at times even being accused of dangerous radicalism.

From an educational and broad social point of view, another effect of large aggregates must be noted. This comes about through the combination or collaboration of many large enterprises into associations. Thus, the steel companies join hands in the Steel Institute, the labor unions in the AFL-CIO, large-scale manufacturers in the National Association of Manufacturers. Through such associations the various enterprises, often large and powerful themselves, give a tremendous new dimension to their influence.

Perhaps the most potent control exercised by concentrated industry, labor, and mass media over the individual comes not from what these forces directly say one must believe and say. Within the large enterprises, within the community itself, the individual desires promotion, recognition, approval, and sense of belonging. In hundreds of ways he learns what is expected of him in belief, attitude, and action. In many instances he is not even aware that his thoughts are made for him by others and that he does what great forces want him to do.

Here is thought-control, American style. There is not a single dictator, few, if any, of the trappings of a totalitarian society. But in an almost omnipresent way the individual is having his wants, his tastes, his values, his standards of success, his political and social outlooks tailored for him by others, the process being so subtle he cannot name time and place for the origin of his views.

What then is the function of education? Of schools? Of informal agencies? More than ever the school must become the one place in the life of the individual where facts can be faced calmly, where people can differ with safety, where originality can be encouraged, rewarded, and prized by others. To have such schools, we must have teachers who have not succumbed to the conformist mood, who are still seeking the truth, who are more fearful of untruth and of unsound action than of nonconformity. We need careful studies of each child, each pupil, each student to help him grow in his own image and in terms of his own uniqueness, toward socially useful participation in society. Counseling, personnel work, here takes on a new meaning, a new urgency.

Ideally, all teachers should be (in reality are) personnel workers. They may be functioning at a very ineffective level, but we cannot do without them. We must educate them for their new role. The provision of such education is a great challenge to the professional personnel worker. It is well to remember, however, that many earlier assumptions in the guidance movement may not hold in the new social, psychological, and vocational conditions that are emerging. We must now fear and avoid waste of creative talent as never before. Self-knowledge for all takes on new importance. General education is raised in urgency as opposed to narrow specialization. Vocational choices may well be in terms of broad areas of endeavor rather than specific trades or processes. Creative development of individuals will take priority over the acquisition of skills. Capacity to learn, the attitude of wanting to learn, competence in knowing how to learn, all these will be more important than knowledge of facts or specific skills.

We must now view the capacities of those with whom we do personnel work from a different viewpoint. We will ask, in the case of a given person, not only or even so much what he knows or knows how to do but what kinds of learning is he most capable of carrying on, not what jobs he knows how to fill but which ones can he learn to fill.

There must be a new emphasis on the effect of the job on the man. In other words, if a man works as an engineer in a plane factory, what will such service do to his growth and development? There is a real danger that our belated recognition of our shortages in trained leadership may, in near panic, lead us to overlook our tradition that a human being is always an end and never a means. A crash program to produce scientists and technical personnel might easily do violence to persons by making scientists of people who should be artists or humanists. This would injure not only them but the nation. Never before in our history has it been so important to respect personality. Only by complete respect for personality can we raise the whole nation to the highest level of creativity. Personnel workers must, therefore, constantly seek the unique development of persons the more because they know the nation's need.

EFFECTS OF IMPROVED HEALTH AND LONGEVITY

Progress in the health sciences has made pronounced impact on society. Infant mortality is a small fraction of its earlier figure. Control of contagious disease and chronic ailments prolongs life in the more advanced ages. By 1970, it is estimated that one-tenth of the population of the United States will be sixty-five years of age or older. Greater longevity combined with early retirement creates a relatively new problem for society, giving rise to the new medical specialization known as geriatrics. This is not the place to consider all the social and economic problems stemming from the increasing number and proportion of aged, but many of these problems can be effectively solved only by education.

Occupational choice may for many persons be affected by the length of probable period of service. Besides, the mental hygiene of older persons is affected by their frequent lack of educational preparation for retirement years. This preparation cannot or at least should not be postponed until people are a year or two away from retirement age. Planning for retirement years, development of hobbies, wholesome attitudes toward life-problems, all need emphasis. Perhaps training for a new vocation to be undertaken with retirement must be a part of our education. Equally important is broad popular understanding of the problems of older people and the development of industrial and public policies which utilize the talents of the older individuals, talents which are now urgently needed.

Adult education, community organization, and curriculum content must all take account of the growing number of older persons in society. Personnel workers, especially, should be cognizant of their problems, sympathetic toward the persons involved, and competent to influence education in creative directions as it applies to older persons.

One aspect of geriatrics is the growing concern over the mental health of the older person. Personnel workers have, of course, been vitally concerned with mental health for decades. More recently, however, attention is being given to the social and economic factors in mental health, to the impact of industry, of conditions of living, of our value systems, and especially to the rapid changes occurring in all of these directions. It is obviously beyond the scope of this discussion to consider all of these factors. One thing is, however, clear. The personnel worker must be a more broadly prepared leader than we assumed at one time. True, he must be a student of the individual human being, but it is equally vital for him to be a student of society, of social, economic, and community affairs. To no group of educators is a wholesome philosophy of life with deep understanding and broad alertness more important than to the personnel worker.

THE IMPACT OF UNEXAMPLED PROSPERITY

Current prosperity in America has lifted production and increased consumption to levels undreamed of three decades ago. High wages and high productivity have brought economic well being and even luxury to a larger proportion of our society than the most sanguine socialists dared hope for at the turn of the century. While we can take satisfaction in having brought comfort and improved living conditions to so large a proportion of our people, our increased prosperity has taken its toll in the realm of values, in the spiritual and cultural areas. Moreover, our spiritual and value losses (or at least lags) have become a major problem in the area of national defense, especially in relation to education and our spiritual strength as a nation.

Thrift and saving had, until the last two decades, been seen as virtues to be cultivated by the vast majority of Americans. The good citizen was supposed to save his money and thus make himself a substantial citizen, building up capital for the development of his country. Recently, however, in an effort to expand markets, the virtuous citizen has come to be thought of as the one who *spends*, not the one who *saves*. The vast persuasive power of advertising and of "motivation research" have been harnessed to the mass media in a massive effort to subtly "brainwash" the American people into spending. Slogans like "Eat More Bread" have been applied to food, clothing, and cosmetics. Rapid obsolescence creates markets for new automobiles. Social prestige is attached to the second car and to the high-priced, powerful automobile as a mark of status.

There is, however, one kind of spending that is seen to be without virtue, and that is public spending. Such spending, far from being assumed to be virtuous, is held to be a waste if not socially damaging. We have, thus, for years been taught the enormous fallacy that the important element in the American way of life is the high consumption of material goods. This has brought near starvation to education and the many cultural aspects of life which depend upon public rather than private expenditure.

Only one city in America can support an extended opera season. Only one can maintain the legitimate theater in rich and extended season form. That city is New York. Even there, the opera and symphony have perilous existence. Several European countries support opera largely at public expense. This would be viewed as outrageous "boondoggling" in America. Even in education, a process has gone on for decades whereby in our publicly supported universities and colleges the burden of support has (by means of increasing tuition rates) been gradually but continuously shifted from the backs of the taxpayers to the backs of the students and their parents.

The net effect of this extreme emphasis on consumption goods is to make us more materialistic, to stress things rather than ideas— plunging us deeper into an anti-intellectualism in which the man who thinks, who has original ideas, is looked upon as an "egg-head."

The image of the successful man is more and more that of the one who makes money. This very trend makes it hard to get teachers and scientists. In so far as it is characteristic of our people and our leadership, it militates against us in the international scene and handicaps all public agencies that depend on public sources of funds.

It is the proper role of education to emphasize moral and spiritual values; to show that ideas, character, and sense of responsibility are more important than things. We must help our children and youth respect our government whether it be local, state, or federal. We must help them see how much our schools, colleges, and universities contribute to our society. They must understand fully that the money paid in taxes is an investment in a better life for all, not a waste or a mere drain on their finances.

Here teachers and counselors must be aware that in teaching our values, powerful and almost ever-present forces are arranged against them, making the school's contribution increasingly important.

The Challenge of Community Problems and Community Vitalization

The American local community has undergone such rapid changes that many persons act as if they still lived in the community of earlier periods, not realizing that the community has changed. In earlier periods of our history the community was a far different force in the life of the individual than is now the case. The close personal contacts, the fact that each person and often each child was known to nearly every neighbor, the transoccupational character of acquaintance and friendships, the close interdependence of families, the group feeling that, like a cement, held people together and acted as a moral force, all these are largely absent in most communities today. Now we often do not know our neighbors. We walk unrecognized on city streets, sit in church beside people whose names we do not know, buy in stores from salespeople we do not recognize. Dozens of other examples of the loss of intimate and continuing relationships could be mentioned.

But the fact that we have lost the earlier cement that held the local community together does not mean there is no "cement" at all. We live in an age of specialism. Thus, the teacher may think first of the National Education Association, the factory worker of the U.A.W., the factory owner of the N.A.M. Often these groups are in economic conflict with one another, serving to separate rather than to unite. In social contacts, the tendency for members of religious groups is to seek each other. The same thing happens to occupational and economic groups. The result is a community which often has little significance except in its areal sense.

The rapid concentration of population in the larger metropolitan areas, the outward movement of people within such areas, adds another divisive force. People in the suburbs live in a highly artificial situation in which they make their living in one place and live in another. Usually one works in the city and lives in the country, but in relation to the huge Ford plant at Mahwah, New Jersey, the country living is so expensive the workers find it necessary to live in New York City which costs less.

Decentralists feel that the disintegration of the community is responsible for most of the ills of human society. They display a nostalgia for the earlier close-knit community. Meanwhile the population continues to concentrate itself the more. At least for the foreseeable future, decentralization seems a vain hope, so that a more practical challenge seems to lie in vitalizing the new community with new dimensions of culture and human relations, made possible in many cases by the richer resources and the greater variety of cultural assets.

From an educational standpoint the trends in American community development present many problems and opportunities. There is, first of all, the community school which, in many places, bids fair to give a new meaning to the community as a group of people living near a school which brings people together not only around the education of their children but in terms of the education of the parents. One cannot visit community schools like those in Flint, Michigan, for example, without realizing that there is a fertile field for development in giving schools and community agencies new power and a more productive interrelationship.

The most dynamic possibilities, however, loom up when we consider the process of adult education and the needs for community vitalization. In a country as large as ours it is not easy for the citizen to participate in state and national government. Too often his participation is limited to voting and paying his taxes. But at the local level he can act not only alone but with his neighbors. He can join with others in activities which will make his community a better place in which to live. The exciting part about such activities is that they simultaneously improve the community and provide effective educational experience for those who participate.

Community development furnishes us with a striking example of urgent problems and urgently needed means of solution. As has already been pointed out, school education alone will not solve our problems in a rapidly changing society. There must be lifelong education. Moreover, it must be a kind of education in which one learns by *doing, doing* which builds the ego, self-respect, and effective functioning of the citizen. Only an energized creative community can supply such educational experience. Yet many communities have disintegrated. Their vitalization is a world-wide problem. It is here at the local community level that we have the deepest roots of freedom; here that freedom meets its final test. Therefore, our real educational problem is to build good communities. It is in good communities that boys and girls and men and women have an opportunity to become all they are capable of becoming.

Preparation for community leadership is not education of the very gifted alone, of the professional groups, or of the well to do. We do not know who the future leaders will be, how they will make their living. Recently the superintendent of schools in a fairly large city stated that his best school board member was a machinist in an automobile factory.

If personnel workers are to help our children and youth to effective participation in the vitalization of our community life, they must have a greater understanding of our community problems, of the forces at work in communities, of community struc-

ture and organization. The counselor's preparation must be sociological as well as psychological. The best way for a counselor to
maintain his own awareness and competence in the community
field is to participate actively himself in community affairs. He has
much to contribute to the community, and the community will
give him a testing laboratory for his ideas.

The Appropriate Role of American Education with Reference to Social Change

"Dare the school build a new social order?" This question,
asked by George Counts nearly three decades ago, has probably
provoked as much controversy as any educational question ever
asked in America. To some it meant, "Dare the school predict the
future nature of society and shape the thinking and attitude of its
pupils to meet the needs of the visualized future pattern?" To
others it aroused fears of subversion, of even paving the way for
state socialism or communism. So bitter has the conflict raged at
times that many teachers have feared to enter the realm of controversy at all, believing all controversial subjects "too hot to handle."
Within the general public, the McCarthy episode took its toll
in an insidious climate of conformism, superpatriotism, and anti-
intellectualism. The man who thought, whose opinions deviated
from the group, was often considered to be a "square" or at least
an "egg-head," an impractical theorist to be feared or, at best, ignored. So reactionary did the climate of fear and conformity become that many schools and teachers did not dare even to try to
build the old social order, let alone teach children, youth, and adults
for a new one.

Wiser councils are, however, beginning to be heard. Most
Americans, once they sense the problem, are willing that the schools
help their pupils understand society. They are willing to admit
that our society is in process of rapid change. They are beginning
to see that some kinds of education will not prepare people to face
changes. They would, we believe, welcome the kind of education,
which, while it did not predict the future pattern of society, would
at least equip the individual with the capacity to face changes when
they come and help him acquire the wisdom to influence changes in
needed and desirable directions.

Even Counts, when he asked his now famous question, could not have realized fully what would happen in the following thirty years. The phrase, "preparation for life," has new implications. What does "for life" mean? Surely not our present life. Surely not the life of the first-grade child today, not even the life he will face as he gets his high-school diploma, let alone the life he will enter, let us say, as a college graduate. Moreover, change has occurred so rapidly during our own life time that we do not as teachers fully understand the life of which we are a part. Perhaps for the first time in human history the adult is turning over to his children a world he does not himself understand.

What we often fail to see in viewing accelerating social changes is that they force us to change our basic assumptions as to the individual's need for educational equipment, so to speak. The fund-of-knowledge concept is definitely outdated. We can no longer depend on what we know—we are dependent on what we are learning.

It is really the individual's capacity to keep on learning that now equips him to face change with wisdom and to react in a socially desirable manner. An individual may have encyclopedic knowledge and yet not be equipped to face the current, rapidly changing scene. If he is a prisoner of his great knowledge, such knowledge may even be a handicap.

What is true for knowledge is true for social orientation, and especially for prediction as to the nature of society. Dogma and rigid, closed-system ideologies are obstacles to the citizen's effective action in seeking to meet the issues of his time. Here, too, we must remember that he will in all probability in the course of a single lifetime find it necessary not only to face changes but to meet them in different ways at different periods in his life. All rigid systems of economic and social life have broken down. Nowhere do private enterprise, socialism, or communism exist and operate in pure form. Even the Russians have employed the incentives of private endeavor and individualism in science and education.

The individual who tries to make up his mind about public issues in terms of dogma and closed ideology is under a severe handicap. He is starting with assumptions about his world that are almost certain to be, in part, false. We must, therefore, constantly re-examine our assumptions to determine their present validity. We must take account of new conditions and be ready to follow new paths toward solution.

This does not mean that we are without values or completely without sense of direction. We base our policies on a deep faith in human beings, on their capacity to develop their own criteria of truth, value, and beauty, and on their potentiality for creative development. Operationally in education and community life we increasingly seek to show greater respect for the worth, dignity, and sacredness of the individual. More effort, organizational and individual, is being put into furthering human brotherhood than ever before. Even our bad lapses in the area of civil rights and civil liberties serve to remind us that freedom is our most precious heritage. A totalitarian society may have high production of economic goods, heavy industry, and scientific accomplishment, but it does not produce truth, justice, and love. Our constant challenge is thus to give new meaning and new dimensions to freedom. For example, a much higher level of educational opportunity and creative teaching becomes essential in a period such as the present when we are challenged to mobilize all our resources in the struggle for freedom. Thus, the remedy for any ills of freedom is more freedom, not less. Our concept of freedom is growing as our human experience reveals new facets we had not earlier sensed.

In this process of expanding our conception of freedom, we do well not to become wedded to specific means of implementation. Our devices will and must of necessity change. We can discard them when no longer effective, the way we discard worn clothing. But we hold on more tenaciously to our value system, to respect for personality, to freedom of thought and expression, and to our concept of human brotherhood. It is important that we all be taught and all realize that we can change the implementation of our concepts not only without weakening them but often strengthening them. It is the reactionary's tendency to hang on to the machinery of freedom and to forget its spirit. The truly free man is stubborn about his values but seeks ever to give them new and larger meaning. He is experimental in seeking new and better implementation.

In some cases in the past, our education has attached people to the forms and failed to give them the spirit of freedom. Teachers, administrators, and counselors need to be aware of this problem and, by their own attitude and behavior, to influence children, youth, and adults in the creative attitudes which alone can provide the education needed by a rapidly changing society.

We cannot predict either the exact problems of the future or their solutions. To attempt to do so would mean applying today's knowledge and wisdom to the problems of tomorrow. Those who advocate an education designed for a kind of life they now predict lack faith in the capacity of people to apply ingenuity to problems as they confront them. Our children and grandchildren will be able to move creatively to the solution of the problems they will meet at every stage in their lives if we give them a creative education, for the only way to get ready to cope with a rapidly changing society in the future is to live creatively at each stage of one's life.

The Vital Importance of Faith in Freedom

Our faith in freedom and its many values and institutions appears to be strongest when we relax in the absence of external or internal threat. In the presence of such threats we seem to come rather quickly and easily to the view that, however desirable freedom may be, we cannot in a crisis depend upon it and its processes. Thus, in the McCarthy case we saw freedom of thought and expression as too dangerous, and, in our efforts to identify and remove those we thought security risks, we violated our traditions of civil rights and civil liberties. On another front it is well to recall that in the last forty years we have in America sought to extend education to all and to develop for each person the education best suited to his needs, interests, and capacities. We have also sought to give our democratic outlook an expression in humane treatment of the pupil in an effort to help the child grow up with a healthy body, a healthy mind, and a wholesome emotional development. Yet, in the near panic following the Sputniks we heard a raucous din of voices wanting to abandon what we had worked upon so long. We needed more scientists, hence there was a call for a larger science content in all education. Many proposed that we identify future scientists early in their school experience and rigorously undertake to shape them in scientific directions.

Since we felt we must somehow explain our lag in satellites, we found education a convenient whipping boy. Accordingly, so-called educational frills, attention to the pupils' individual needs, emotional growth, and health and physical education were now condemned as thieves that have taken the pupils' time—time that ought to have been spent on science and mathematics. We hear calls for a return to a tough education, for rigid discipline, and an emphasis on learning *subjects*. We heard some make fun of teachers who, in their concern for effective education, "teach children" rather than subjects.

Those who called for this reaction in education sounded as if they would rather have Russian education than American education. They turned their backs on a half-century of research by psychologists, pediatricians, and psychiatrists. Calling for more science, they turn their backs on those sciences which throw light on the human organism and on human growth and development.

In the last fifty years we have been working to develop an education that would help children, youth, and adults make the most of themselves and become responsible, productive citizens. We have not wholly succeeded. There are many weak spots, such as incompetent and too few teachers, inadequate financial support, and lack of facilities necessitating half-day sessions in many places. We have not yet learned how to meet the learning problems of every pupil. We have far to go in realizing our goals.

Is not the same thing true of every human enterprise? Shall we discontinue wonder drugs because some who take them die or become ill from allergies? Shall we return to crude, unscientific diets because many who follow good nutrition practice seem to gain little in health? In other words, shall we in education throw out the baby with the bath?

Attention to individual children is important because we owe it to the child, because it is right in terms of our values, but it is more important now than ever because we need creative scientists, humanists, and teachers. If we try to make a scientist out of a person who should be a musician, we shall not only fail to get a good scientist but may destroy a musician.

How can we expect the people in Viet Nam, for example, to acquire faith in the American way of life and in American education when in our press they read that we blame our education for our every ill? How can we commend freedom to others when we act as if we had little faith in it ourselves?

This is the time to reaffirm our faith in freedom to learn and in freedom for those who learn and those who teach. Building our faith in America and what America means is a task for all education and for the whole community.

We need to renew our acquaintance with and to re-enforce our understanding of the meaning of freedom. We would do well to recall that freedom is in many respects a difficult way of life. The processes of dictatorship, of direct, immediate, short-range action look inviting to us in a crisis. They do not, however, build solidly for the future and, in the long run, have a built-in mechanism for betrayal. Their use belies our own dedication to freedom and weakens the fabric of freedom.

Increased Urgency of a Creative Education

Even though educational and informed civic leaders have for years emphasized the need for more well-educated leadership personnel for our society, it has taken Russian scientific accomplishment to really alert the American people to the need for more educated personnel. Readily available facts concerning our needs here at home in America would be enough since serious shortages of scientists, teachers, doctors, and other highly educated professional personnel have been with us for some time. It is hardly a credit to our alertness as a nation when we have to be whipped into action by fear of the achievements of those we think are potential enemies.

A vague awareness of shortages, however, is not enough. Nor is it merely a matter of more education, that is, of getting more people to go to school and for more years. We are challenged both by international developments and by domestic changes to give dynamism and creativity to education. We need not only more highly educated people but more creative individuals. The demand is not met merely by education with high academic standards in the traditional sense for we need people with more than knowledge and skill. It is a high level of creativity, imagination, and inventive genius that is necessary.

Let us turn first to the modern industrial scene with increasing use of automation. As the number of men required in a given factory operation decreases, the competence they are required to have increases. The man who operates an automation set-up must understand a complicated machine and know what to do when something goes wrong. He must exercise judgment and show capacity to think quickly and logically. The earlier industrial revolution made a skilled worker out of the unskilled laborer and, in the process, greatly increased his earning power. The automation revolution is making a skilled technician of the skilled worker and again greatly increasing his income.

With every passing year a smaller proportion of the population is engaged in pursuits requiring little insight and preparation, and a larger proportion of the people is engaged in activities demanding skill and high level of competence. Eighty-five per cent of the American people in 1855 had to be at work producing our food. Today, only 15 per cent are so employed. The farm, which once was thought of as the place for people with little education, now calls for both broad and deep knowledges as well as for managerial competence.

It is a mistake, however, to view the need for higher levels of education only in terms of professional and occupational pursuits. Citizenship, parenthood, and community life make ever greater demands on the individual's creative capacities. No effective foreign policy is possible unless our citizens can think clearly and imaginatively in the area of international relations. Right now our foreign policy suffers severely because too few of our people can do such thinking. We are not able to get the educational program we need in most communities because our people are not giving creative thought to the community's educational needs.

The race problem is, in the last analysis, a problem to be solved largely by education. The supreme court has spoken, interpreting the meaning of our constitution. The vast majority of people in America agree with the court, but its decision is widely flouted. Real solutions await the changing of the minds and hearts of people in many areas. Education is our primary means for changing the minds and hearts of men.

There is a challenge to creative education that comes not only from the demands of a changed social and industrial world but from our highest human aspirations. The totalitarian regimes have offered economic security to the masses. To date, they have (from our point of view) failed. But even if they could succeed in the physical realm, human beings will not long be content to live by bread alone. Freedom should choose its battleground with dictatorship in the realm of the human spirit. For it is in this area we have greatest comparative potentiality. The ultimate triumph of the human spirit can come only through freedom, for only by being himself can any human being be creative and, in the process of creative living, become the highest expression of a complete man.

There is much talk about creative teaching, but, despite this, really creative education is not easy to find above the lowest grades of the elementary school. Nursery-school, kindergarten, and first-grade teachers appear to have moved farthest in education for creativity. As we move up the grades of the elementary school, through the high school, and into the college, we increasingly ask pupils to remember what others have created rather than encourage creativity on their own part. Even at the doctoral level, where originality is usually demanded (on paper at least), a creative thesis is sometimes specifically rejected in the rules and regulations. No doubt there are several reasons for our failure to develop a truly creative education. One is our preoccupation with subject matter, the acquisition of which is a task so time-consuming and deadening in its effect that little time remains for creative effort. If an individual spends sixteen years of his life mastering subject matter with no opportunity to practice his creative endeavors, we should not be surprised to find him both the recipient of a diploma and something of a slave to what has been produced by others.

Many teachers believe no outstandingly creative person can be kept from creative achievement. Such teachers and some creative artists hold that any budding artist whose creativity has been thwarted by lack of a sympathetic environment was not really creative anyway. This kind of viewpoint seems too "hard-boiled" to be supported by the facts concerning human development. It appears also to apply largely to the highly exceptional musical composer, poet, or painter rather than to education for creativity on the part of the average person. We need a creative education for all, not because we believe we can make great artists out of all children but because we believe education for creativity to be intrinsically good education for everybody. Only such education will advance our science and art to the highest levels.

Here we have at least one reason for the paucity of creative education, viz., that many teachers do not believe it is feasible. Such teachers hold creativity to be a quality possessed only by the very few. Education for creativity obviously does not seem important to teachers who believe only one person in ten thousand is creative. But many teachers are held back from creative teaching by a lack of understanding about it and by lack of skill in developing the required environment for creative living on the part of children, youths, and adults.

The present need for scientists and creative thinkers in every field highlights creative teaching. For one cannot deal with scientists and artists in quantitative terms. Ten scientists would not atone for the loss of an Einstein or a Urey. The only sure way to develop all our creative capacities is to give every individual a creative education.

Too often the word *creative* is seen to apply only to the arts. Similarly, we fail to see that teaching is an art and that the teacher, to be successful, is in truth an artist. The artist constantly seeks new reality. So does the teacher. His pupils must not be minor replicas of himself but artists in their own sphere and sight. Helping the child enter the unknown is an act of creative teaching. Helping the child free his own spirit is an act of creative teaching. The creative teacher should, therefore, be a bold, imaginative person who is not afraid of other people or of ideas other than his own, of those he does not readily comprehend. He is engaged in a constant search. But it is a disciplined search for both teacher and pupil. Freedom to be one's self cannot be attained without self-discipline.

It may be objected that we are here setting forth a concept of creative teaching unattainable except for a few artist teachers. This is no doubt true as long as most of our education seeks merely to transmit knowledge and skill. But once we comprehend the creative character of the human organism, once we understand the meaning of creativity, we can learn how to teach creatively. The technical side will present the least difficulty and will be of relatively minor importance. Our biggest challenge will be that of becoming the kinds of persons we must be to be truly creative teachers.

Finally, it is in furthering creativity that freedom and democracy have their greatest promise for mankind. To be sure, political freedom is inspiring. Economic freedom has been highly productive. Social freedom exercises a beneficial and ennobling influence on humanity. But man's freedom to become all he is capable of becoming in the creative sense is the ultimate flower of a free society. Only creative education can build a creative society.

When we visualize the meaning and potentiality of creative education, when we consider the demands of an automated industry and the challenges of the international scene, we are forced to take a new look at vocational competence. Preparation in skills may (beyond the purpose of general education) be a waste of time, of time that is needed for the general education of the individual in creative directions. Industry will increasingly train its own workers. But industry has a right to expect that those who have had the benefit of education can think straight, that their attitudes are socially desirable and vocationally productive, and that they have originality, inventiveness, good judgment, and resourcefulness.

We need a new and larger vision of the educational task, a vision commensurate with our new concepts of energy and the resulting complexities of world society. Man is greater in potentiality than our most ambitious hopes. Future scientific achievements will make even the striking events of this generation seem elementary. Mankind has yet to apply to its own life the creative genius that has flowered in knowledge of the atom and in the higher reaches of art. Here is the new frontier helping man to understand himself and his neighbor and teaching him how his life with his fellow men can bring about better life for the individual and a more creative society. The educational personnel worker occupies a key position in this sight-raising process. To the degree that he can see his techniques as tools and view creative individual human beings and a creative human society as ends, he will become a potent influence in providing the great education demanded by our expanding world.

REFERENCES

ALLEN, FREDERICK. *The Big Change*. New York: Harper & Bros., 1952.

BROWNELL, BAKER. *The Human Community*. New York: Harper & Bros., 1950.

COMMAGER, HENRY STEELE. *Freedom, Loyalty, and Dissent*. New York: Oxford University Press, 1954.

FOSDICK, DOROTHY. *Common Sense and World Affairs*. New York: Harcourt, Brace & Co., 1955.

JONES, HOWARD MUMFORD. *Education and World Tragedy*. Cambridge, Massachusetts: Harvard University Press, 1946.

LIPPMANN, WALTER. *The Public Philosophy*. Boston: Little, Brown & Co., 1955.

MEYER, AGNES. *Education for a New Morality*. New York: Macmillan Co., 1957.

POSTON, RICHARD WAVERLY. *Small Town Renaissance*. New York: Harper & Bros., 1950.

STALEY, EUGENE. *Creating an Industrial Civilization*. New York: Harper & Bros., 1952.

WHYTE, WILLIAM. *The Organization Man*. New York: Simon & Schuster, 1956.

CHAPTER III

Philosophical and Psychological Bases of Personnel Services in Education

C. GILBERT WRENN

Preamble

In a chapter of this nature it becomes important to define one's terms early. Thumbnail descriptions of selected philosophies and psychologies will be provided so that the contribution of each to personnel services in education can be examined. It would seem desirable for the writer to remain objective in this examination, but it is impossible. I cannot speak of the philosophies and psychologies which appear to hold most promise for this field without making this a matter of personal judgment in terms of what I personally consider the most important emphases in personnel work. To be implicit rather than explicit at this point appears almost dishonest. Furthermore, rather than say, "Personnel work is this . . ." and thus be truly dogmatic, would it not be better to say, "I believe this . . . ," which leaves the reader free to believe otherwise? There needs must be a considered humility in such an approach, for one person's highly fallible set of convictions are spread out for public view. They are bare and unprotected, fair targets for any who wish to take pot shots at them. The reader may have a set of "importances" that he prefers. All that can be said here is that it is *this* concept of personnel work about which I am talking when we later attempt to relate philosophies and psychologies to it.

WHAT IS IMPORTANT IN STUDENT PERSONNEL WORK:
A PERSONAL VIEW

1. Above all else, personnel service in education is predicated upon *seeing the learner totally*. We attempt to see him (a generic term) beyond the classroom, as a person with a life, present and

past, which is more heavily nonschool than school oriented. He has interests, associations, and motivations which have their origins in his family, his community, his age peers—in a total world of which the classroom and the school as a whole are only a part, often a minor part. This is a reality which all educators, but particularly counselors and other personnel workers, must accept although it be damaging to our egos. Other agencies contribute as well as the school. We must understand these, co-operate with them, integrate them with our efforts. This means that we should be sociologists as well as psychologists. Being educators means being both.

This wholeness concept has another dimension as well. Wholeness demands that we contribute to the pupil as a total organism, physical, intellectual, social, and spiritual. Our job is to provide the unique facilities of an educational system that will contribute to total development (not wholly, but in part) during his formative years.

2. We are dedicated *to treat the student with dignity*, to respect his integrity and his right to self-fulfillment. We are committed, to be sure, to assist in his socialization, to see that he understands and accepts as realities the requirements and limitations of society. We cannot ourselves be other than the products of our society so that we as professional adults have values and convictions that have deep meaning to us. We cannot separate ourselves from these values, but we can attempt to avoid imposing them upon children and youth because they have been an essential part of our ego development. We must accept students as learners having the same right to personal conviction that we cherish for ourselves. When we must, at times, impose limitations and restrictions to freedom upon them, it must be done with understanding of their natural resistance and resentment, the same resistance and resentment that we ourselves have often felt at the restrictions of our society.

3. Personnel work is concerned with *the student's plans for the future* as well as optimum living in the present. We may well believe that school is not primarily a preparation for the future but that it should focus upon adequate experience now and that the nature of this experience is one's best preparation for the future. We are, nevertheless, responsible to help the student appreciate and

clarify his aims, his understanding of himself, his visualization of himself as a contributing member of society. This means that we are responsible for assisting young people to apply experience gained, in school and out, to their personal-life situation, to a personalizing of their knowledge, to seeing the relationship of the here-and-now to the future.

4. We are the prime *advocates of individual differences* in the school. This does not mean that others are not responsible too but that we are *more* responsible for seeing that uniqueness is respected. The "molding of a child" may be thought of as the function of a school as an agent of society but "molding him in *his own image*" is our task. This means that we respect abilities and interests of a high order but are equally insistent that other aptitudes and interests of a moderate order are also essential to society.

5. *Personnel work depends upon a varied methodology*, one that is fitted to the ends to be served. This field currently has a focus in counseling. It is developing an equal concern for healthy and stimulating group experiences. It has begun to appreciate its responsibility for relating the school experiences to community and out-of-school experiences. Either individual or group approaches to the achievement of desirable growth ends may be used, but the means should be appropriate to the ends and be subordinate to them. The task is to assist the pupils to self-understanding, more mature purpose, improved skills in interpersonal relations, acceptance of the realities of societal limitations as well as opportunities. It is also to provide facilities for optimum development in the areas of financial planning, living arrangements, part-time employment with eventual job placement, and health facilities.

In this complex task the means should be seen as varied. There is no one road to any of these goals, whether it be counseling, student activities, a testing program, or group guidance classes. Nor should we put faith in a smooth-running program, professional titles, fine equipment, and office space. More important than any of these is lack of dogmatism about the "best" procedure, noncommitment to a one-way approach which is often merely the reflection of one person's ego needs.

6. Just as the best conception of counseling is that of a creative relationship between counselor and student, so *the important ele-*

ment in all personnel service is the quality of the relationship estab-lished between worker and learner, between worker and colleague. If we believe deeply in the importance of interpersonal relation-ships, in respect for each person, in a sensing of feeling as well as of fact, then we must stress this quality in *all* that we do. The effectiveness of what is done will depend equally upon skill and knowledge on the one hand and humaneness on the other. The best personnel service lies in the quality of a fine person. School personnel work needs knowledge and skills desperately, needs equipment and facilities, needs recognition from other educational workers of the significance of our part of the task, but, most of all, needs understanding and dedication of purpose on the part of the worker. Without attempting to be supermen or a priesthood, and in all humility, we need to be continually alert to the quality of our personal relationships to all in the school, need a sense of regard for and acceptance of all personalities with whom we work.

7. Finally, personnel service *must remain in the central stream of educational effort.* We are to be neither a fifth wheel nor a steering wheel, rather a part of the chassis. In our attempt to learn more about student needs, to stress purposes and values that seem important to us, to develop professional self-consciousness along with professional skills, we have frequently alienated the teaching and administrative colleagues with whom we must collaborate most closely. If we are to consider student personnel work as part of the major task of the school or college, that of instruction in many forms and settings, instruction defined in the sense of any planned facility which contributes to student learning and development, then we cannot "be apart" from that central focus. True, we can agree only in part at times with the philosophy (aims) and psy-chology (procedures) of our colleagues, yet our disagreement should be one only of emphasis, not of kind, not quality of effort. Educational workers have more aims and values in common than we are wont to perceive. We see so clearly our differences and fail to make use of our commonalities. Disagree, yes; there is little ad-vance in constant sweetness and light, but disagree each with mutual respect for the other and with a more frequent highlighting of the areas of agreement.

Much of what I have proposed as important in student personnel work could be said to be of equal importance for all of the educational effort. There is no quarrel with this proposal, rather, there is agreement. But our task is to keep our own corner of the house in order while, deftly we hope, we contribute to seeing that the rest of the house is functioning effectively. And, perchance, the decor of the rest of the house might be seen as contributing to and even changing our own corner. Personnel workers have no corner on either brains or ideals.

The Social Task of School Personnel Work

The relationship between this chapter and the preceding one seems quite apparent. The authors of chapter ii have stressed four points (among others perhaps) which have immediate philosophical and psychological implications. They have said that the educator of 1959 and beyond must see his world as:

1. *A world of rapid change* (". . . greater change has taken place in the last forty years than in the previous six thousand") that is taking place at an accelerating rate. The *fact* of rapid change, with tomorrow's thinking and patterns of adjustment making today's largely obsolete, is of greater significance than the facts of current knowledge.

2. The school, and all who work within it, *becoming an integral part of today's society* and of its own particular community in that society. Isolation is no longer possible; provincialism, space-wise, is as hazardous as it is in a temporal sense. The teacher and counselor must be sociologically as well as psychologically sophisticated.

3. A democracy in which there is *an elevation of spiritual values* above material progress. "A totalitarian society may have high production of economic goods, heavy industry, and scientific accomplishment but it does not produce truth, justice, and love." "Freedom should choose its battleground with dictatorship in the realm of the human spirit;" ours should be a world in which there is a distinction between (*a*) stable and immutable values and (*b*) the changing procedures used to translate these values into action. The nature of freedom must not be confused with the machinery of freedom. "The truly free man is stubborn about his values—[but] is experimental in seeking new and better implementation."

4. Schools in which there is *an encouragement of the creative*

person at all levels of accomplishment and in all areas of thought and action. This means change from the current tendency to become *less creative* and *more dependent* upon what others have thought and written as we move from the first years of the elementary school through high school and into college.

These are stirring words. The "practical man" will say they are idealistic, impossible of accomplishment. Who has said that the educator should not be an idealist, a dedicated champion of the impossible? In developing free and imaginative "hewers of wood and drawers of water" as well as creative scientists and artists, the danger is that we shall ourselves become earthbound and become hewers of wood in our own province.

What the Literature on Student Personnel Work Reveals

The transition is an abrupt one from these vital concerns of our country and its schools to the all too unimaginative literature on the personnel services of a school or college program. When one looks to the literature in the field of education for the objectives and procedures of personnel work, there appears to be no cement to bind the proposed objectives into a cohesive whole, no firm and consistent guide lines. There is unmistakably lacking any set of generally accepted value-oriented aims or scientifically based understandings of human nature. In short, student personnel work has philosophic and psychological foundations which have been only haltingly developed and are disturbingly incomplete.

Any careful reading of the extensive literature on personnel work in the schools and colleges is certain to leave the reader with two disquieting conclusions: (*a*) the authors involved make many philosophical and psychological assumptions, both explicit and implicit, which are neither examined nor tested; (*b*) few of these authors pretend to possess a consistently operating philosophy or a systematic psychological point of view. The philosophy and psychology are present, of course, but often in the form only of assumptions. Statements such as these are common:

"Student personnel work contributes to the objectives of higher education." What is the evidence for this statement? What are the specific objectives to which reference is made? To what degree is the philosophy of a given educational institution in harmony with the philosophy of a given student personnel program? What is the philosophy of the whole and of the part anyway?

"Every student should take some part in student activities." Why? What values are inherent in student activities? Do these values accrue to *all* students? What evidence is there, other than the logic of presumed cause and effect, that student activities contribute to institutional objectives—or to student growth?

"Counseling is more psychologically meaningful than group guidance." What kind of counseling—and what kind of group guidance? Do these two forms of student personnel work contribute to the same areas of human behavior—can they logically be compared?

Not all of the reasons for this unhappy state of affairs suggest culpability upon the part of either the practitioners or the textbook writers in this field. There has been a rapid increase in the service demands made of the personnel staff during the past three or four decades, and practice has moved far ahead of logical foundations. The writing has been technique-oriented, designed to give immediate and much-needed help to practitioners rather than to develop a substantial body of thought as a foundation.

A parallel might be drawn between this situation and the program of street development in the burgeoning suburbs of a large city. If home building is extensive and expansion rapid, the need for streets will be a demanding one. Concrete or asphalt roadways may be laid so rapidly that careful grading and the preparation of foundations is neglected. The streets may carry the traffic and keep people out of the mud, but they will soon break through in spots or fail to adapt to the runoff in time of heavy rainfall. Such streets may further lack consistency of material and structure—with one block of concrete and another of blacktop, gutters here but no gutters there, street signs on the curb in one block and on posts in another.

An observer viewing this system of streets might cry aloud "expediency," "opportunism," and even "graft," but of course such an observer is not likely to have been present when the pressure was on, when subdivision succeeded subdivision with appalling rapidity. Such a critic might be merely a critic. He would bewail the inefficiency of the past and call for the discharge of all street department employees. Such behavior is simple and calls for no intellectual effort. Its very nature makes it more unethical than the situation being criticized. What is needed are answers to these questions: *What* is the best engineering and architectual plan for the streets of this suburb? *What* is the best foundation material for good streets in this suburb? *What* can be done to help the street department employees become more professionally cautious while maintaining their strong sense of service, become more resistant to calls of expediency without losing the support of the community?

The parallel between the suburban streets system and the student personnel program of a school or college is a possible one. Both are operating too much in an atmosphere of emergency and pressure in the attempt to meet unplanned-for needs. In student personnel work this has affected both writing and practice.

Another reason for the paucity of careful psychological and philosophical thinking in this area is the scarcity of research specifically oriented to a personnel service model. Designs for student personnel research are largely borrowed, not indigenous to the field. The research upon which the field depends is behavior research from developmental, educational, or clinical psychology, group research from sociology or group dynamics, administrative models from business. This has high value, of course, but the literature is very short on student personnel research in which design and method grows out of the nature of the data involved. This is even true of counseling where many criteria of effective counseling are proposed—should the criterion be educational achievement, vocational satisfaction, modifications of self-concept, reduced emotional tension, the ratings of observers, or the judgment of the counselor? If not any one of these alone, then what combination of these in a multiple criterion?

Perhaps all of this is as it must be because student personnel work is too young as a self-conscious field of endeavor to permit a sophisticated research, a thoughtful integration with the broad aims of education, practice based upon tested procedures. The result is that we have all too few guidelines in planning, practice, and research. We must seek maturity through more effective integration with the great disciplines of thought and of science.

An Analysis of Philosophies

So far in this discussion there have been many references in a global sense to philosophy and psychology. What, specifically, is meant by these terms, and are there dimensions and subdivisions in each field of thought which might contribute to more exact thinking?

Philosophy and psychology may be thought of as complementary in that one contributes to an understanding of truth, meaning, and purpose and the other to an understanding of human behavior within the larger setting of total existence. *Psychology is, first of all, a science, a systematic ordering of observations of human behavior.*[1, 2] As in all sciences, it describes rather than explains. Where inferences are drawn from observations in the development of a law, principle, or explanation of behavior, this is an explanation within the strict boundaries of the man as an organism. The meaning of this behavior within the cosmos, the nature of the knowledge possessed, *the nature of behavior and of existence itself is the province of philosophy.* Psychology is thus seen as more exact but also more limited than philosophy—philosophy as more inclusive in subject matter but less exact in that it cannot be limited to empiric observations.

Some schools of psychology deal with inferences and assumptions which are far removed from observed fact, i.e., they are to this extent philosophical in nature. Some philosophies depend heavily upon empiric observations, and their logic and reality is the logic and reality of science. Philosophy, of course, antedated psychology and, indeed, all science as we now use the term. Philosophy, "love of wisdom or learning," is sometimes called the mother of sciences. Physics and chemistry were once branches of philosophy

1. Comparative psychology is the study of animal behavior undertaken primarily in the expectation that it will, comparatively, contribute to a better understanding of specific aspects of human behavior.

2. Psychology is also a practice, an application of what is known to a modification and integration of individual or group behaviors. When one *practices* psychology he utilizes not only a science but, knowingly or unknowingly, the meanings and values of a philosophy. He must do so because he is an interactive organism, contributing to and borrowing from the meanings and values of the other in the process of interaction.

and were known as "natural philosophy;" psychology began as "mental philosophy."

THE DIMENSIONS OF PHILOSOPHY

It may prove helpful to those who have read little in philosophy to consider (*a*) some of the dimensions of philosophy and (*b*) some of the systems of philosophy which have most relevance for education.[3] Whatever is done in this connection will appear abstract and technical to some readers and too unqualified and oversimplified to others. The one group is asked to consider these brief descriptions carefully for they may provide useful tools of thought for later use in the chapter, while the other is asked to be tolerant of semantic difficulties and to have patience. There is apparent agreement upon the fundamental dimensions or factors of philosophy.[4]

1. *Theory of Reality (Metaphysics)*. This deals with the nature of existence itself (ontology): of the nature and origin of the universe (cosmology), of the nature of man, his purpose, his free will; of the nature of God. Of these aspects of reality, the nature of man is the most significant for education. Human behavior is described by psychology, even though as yet in elemental terms, but its meaning and purpose are sought through philosophy and religion. Some aspects of the mind-body problem also may be best examined philosophically, as may freedom of the will and man's purpose in life, his *raison d' etre*.

2. *Theory of the Nature of Knowledge (Epistemology)*. This deals with the possibility of knowing reality; with the *importance* of knowledge; and with the *instruments* or ways of knowing. The latter is of great concern to education, with the empiricist's approach through observation and the experience of the senses being in sharp contrast to the rationalist's dependence upon reason as the source of knowledge.

3. Grateful acknowledgment is made to my colleague, Professor Robert H. Beck, for early assistance in the organization of this section and for a critical reading of this portion of the manuscript. Only I, however, can be held responsible for the descriptions involved. Only a philosophical amateur, indeed, would have attempted to combine brevity and accuracy in this field.

4. J. D. Butler, *Four Philosophies and their Practice in Education and Religion*. New York: Harper & Bros., 1957 (revised).

3. *Theory of Values (Axiology)*. This dimension of philosophy is concerned with the nature of values and with kinds of values. Are values subjective in nature, growing out of a person's interests and needs? Or are they external and objective, a quality of each thing or circumstance in the universe, possessing an existence independent of the experiencing person and his needs?

There are various kinds of values, aesthetic, religious, social, but central to any theory of values is the concept of ethics. What is good, how is good determined, is there any fixed hierarchy of values or of the goodness of any value relative to a given situation? For example, which of the following maxims can be best supported: (1) act only on those principles which you are willing should become universal moral laws—Kant; (2) assume that action to be right must be conducive to self-preservation—Spencer; (3) discover the probable consequences of what you consider doing—Dewey; (4) commit yourself to the fulfilment of God's purpose for yourself and the world—almost any religious leader.[5] In any system of philosophy affecting education, major consideration is given to values.

4. *Theory of the Relation of Ideas (Logic)*. Closely related to epistemology, this dimension is not always recognized as parallel in significance and discreteness to the other three dimensions named. Logic is sometimes called the science of thought or of reasoning. It is concerned with *methods* of thinking and the method, of course, is related to the nature of the reality dealt with. Logic is for many people identified with Aristotle and the *syllogism,* deductive reasoning in which major and minor premise are used. The *dialectic* is another form of reasoning in which contrast of ideas is used to detect the truth—Hegel's thesis, antithesis, and synthesis. *Inductive reasoning*—from the particular to the general— *deductive reasoning*—from a general principle to specifics that appear to fall within the scope of that principle, and *problem-solving* which uses inductive and deductive reasoning reciprocally, are known in all modern science and education.

The thumbnail definitions above concern factors that appear in almost any system of philosophy. They provide a brief vocabu-

5. Adapted from J. D. Butler, *ibid.,* pp. 17-38.

lary for the study of such systems. Their description was relatively easy.

Selecting the systems of philosophy that appear most significant for student personnel work is a different matter. As will be stressed upon various occasions in this yearbook, personnel work is most appropriately seen as an integral part of the total educational program, not as a function separate from other types of instructional activity. Instruction here is broadly conceived of as a planned function which contributes to learning wherever that learning may be and whatever the nature of the learning. It is infinitely more varied than classroom instruction, for example, even when that instruction is inclusive of more than the laymen's concept of teaching as lecture and drill. Instruction includes many forms of person-to-person and group situations in the personnel program which result in student learning. Since student personnel work is an integral part of the larger instructional function of education, it is concerned with philosophies which, generally speaking, are of most significance for formal education as a whole.

There are points of emphasis in personnel work, however, which may aid in the process of selection. Thus, personnel service is more heavily concerned with the *voluntary* aspects of the educational experience (a student is seldom required by the institution or some staff member to see a counselor, run for office in a student organization, or apply for a loan). It also deals with the student on matters which contain a large element of self-involvement and which call for *self-understanding and personal planning.*

It appears, also, to contribute more heavily than do other phases of the educational program to facets of life dealing with *social living and human interaction.* If kinds of learning should be specified, *self-learning* (nonimposed and autonomous learning about self and its relation to the world of outer reality), *social-interaction learning,* and *values learning* are contributed to most heavily by the personnel service program.

A simple grouping of systematic philosophies might be made

on the basis of (a) those considering reality as fixed and changeless, and (b) those which see reality as change itself. This is the to-be-known versus the knowing, the fixed versus the flexible. Another grouping might be made on the basis of those in which the focus is upon (a) that which is to be known or experienced, something outside of the learner as the true nature of reality, and (b) man as a learning organism. One broad grouping is the dichotomy into (a) a stable reality fixed in the nature of existence and/or of God; (b) a dynamic reality, bounded by time and rich in novelty and variation.[6] Still another grouping by Brubacher has the closest apparent relationship to education: (a) *essentialism* (idealism, realism, supernaturalism) and (b) *progressivism* (pragmatism, naturalism, etc.).[7]

Some of the most relevant specific philosophies are briefly described in the following paragraphs.

1. *Rationalism (Neo-Humanism, Rational Humanism).* This philosophy is one of the oldest of our western world philosophies, dealing more with the nature of man and the nature of knowledge than with the nature of reality itself. One of its earliest authors, if not its principal author, was Aristotle. With the advent of Christianity it was modified by St. Thomas Aquinas into a dualism of the natural and the supernatural—natural truth and revealed truth, the first being subordinate to the second. Rational humanism asserts that the essence of human nature is its rational character. Man is the only species endowed with reason, and his chief function is to use this reason in order to know the world in which he lives. Truth is universal and fixed, and man's destiny is to discover truth by distinguishing between the essential and the accidental.

The chief distinguishing characteristics of the rationalists are that (a) the essence of reality is a system of rational principles, everywhere the same, defining the nature of the universe and man's place in it (some would add man's relation to God), (b) the cultivation of reason is the chief aim of all education everywhere. The

6. John S. Brubacher, *Modern Philosophies of Education*, p. 40. New York: McGraw-Hill Co., 1950 (second edition).

7. *Ibid.*, chap. xiv.

rationalists of today hold that truth exists, in whole or substantial part, in the writings of classical thinkers so that man's intellectual task is to discover them and apply them to current situations. (This, of course, is the origin of the Great Books concept expounded by Adler, Hutchins, and Mark Van Doren.)

Modern interpretations of this point of view, neo-rationalists or neo-humanists, would admit present-day science and its discoveries but only as these empiric truths contribute to universal truths. Reason *per se* is still on the throne with empiric observations being of a second order variety. This almost parallels the Thomist's natural truth as opposed to revealed truth. Truth is fixed, not emerging. The essence of man is reason, not the complex of his total organism.

2. *Idealism.* "Idealism is the conclusion that the universe is an expression of intelligence and will, that the enduring substance of the world is of the nature of mind, that the material is explained by the mental. Idealism as a philosophy stands in contrast with all those systems of mind that center in nature (naturalism)[8] or in man (humanism)." [9]

This clear statement by a leading American idealist, now deceased, provides a good introduction. What is not clear, however, is that, in classical idealism at least, ideas are absolute, "the essences of archetypes which give form to the cosmos," [10] eternal. This absolutist aspect of idealism makes it akin to rationalism. On the other hand, the substance of existence is spiritual rather than mental in a restricted sense. This does not connote religion for "religion is man worshipping, and philosophy is man thinking." To an objective idealist the term "absolute mind" is a synonym for God. Since man strives to partake of the nature of the absolute, which is spiritual, the essence of man is spiritual too.

Theodore Greene writes on idealism in the Fifty-fourth Year-

8. Later it is clear that Horne approximates "naturalism" with "realism."

9. H. H. Horne, "An Idealistic Philosophy of Education," in *Philosophies of Education*, p. 139. Forty-first Yearbook of the National Society for the Study of Education, Part I. Chicago: Distributed by University of Chicago Press, 1942.

10. John S. Brubacher, *op. cit.* p. 310.

book [11] but he finds it necessary to make clear that he is an objective idealist, believing in objective reality as much as any realist; that he is in opposition to all authoritarianisms; that he is a Christian who believes in God as the source of all values although he repudiates all claims to infallible knowledge of God.

Idealists may conceive of themselves as "liberal" and "humanistic," they focus on the intellectual and the spiritual—yet they are absolutists in their ontology and mentalistic in their epistemology (i.e., their concept of reality and their concept of knowledge).

3. *Realism.* As a distinctive philosophy, realism is a twentieth century "scientific" product, yet it had its roots in Aristotle and Comenius and in some aspects of the thinking of Descartes, Spinoza, Locke, and Kant, who are otherwise classified as idealists.

As might well be guessed by any reader, ultimate reality to the realist lies in objects and situations external to the human mind, in the "real" or objective world. It is here, of course, where this philosophy differs most sharply from idealism, where ideas constitute reality, where the mental is more real than the objective world. For the realist, the universe is composed of substantial entities, existing in themselves whether they are known to man or not. This is called the "thesis of independence." The realist believes that objects can exist apart from the knowledge process, that objects are disclosed by acts of cognition (the pragmatist believes that they are *created* by the thought process—but more of that later).

Epistemologically, every concept is of something; knowing means developing a relationship with something existing outside of the mind. (This is sometimes called a "common-sense" view, a term repugnant to philosophers. In truth, common sense may be vague and hazy, full of lazy thinking and error.) Realism uses logic but also empiric and inductive reasoning. The scientist is likely to be a realist. Objects exist whether described accurately or not. Truth differs from reality in that "truth" is what reality is reported to be. Truth may be a product of the mind, reality is not. Reality simply is.

11. Theodore W. Greene, "A Liberal Christian Idealist Philosophy of Education," *Modern Philosophies and Education,* p. 91-136. Fifty-fourth Yearbook of the National Society for the Study of Education, Part I. Chicago: Distributed by University of Chicago Press, 1955.

Realism is admittedly dualistic or even pluralistic. Mind and external reality are not one; neither are mind and body. For most realists being and value are separated into two realms. Realism is objective, makes use of scientific findings, sees empiric truth as approximating but not necessarily equalling reality, but it differs markedly from the next system of philosophy to be presented.

4. *Experimentalism (Pragmatism, Instrumentalism)*. This most modern of philosophies is American in its development and emphasis although its roots go back to Francis Bacon and his *Novum Organum* and to Auguste Comte, the positivist. Its developers in this country are two of the best-known men in all American education, William James and John Dewey.

Essentially devoting its attention to a theory of knowledge and a theory of values, experimentalism has had a strong impact upon education. The key word for experimentalism is *continuity*, of knower and unknown, of object and observer. There is no dualism here. Geiger[12] comments upon the "cultural schizophrenia" of classic philosophy in the separation of fact from value, body from mind, the world to be known from the knower.

The scientist, say the proponents of this philosophy, shows small interest in a general theory of knowledge. He is concerned with phenomena, with a phenomenon. His context of knowing is fixed by a single problem or set of problems, and his most fruitful assumptions emphasize integration, not separation, of problem and solution. Problem-solving involves the solver as well as that which is to be solved. In the process of solution both become changed, experience affects both. Knowing is operational, not simply a beholding.

Anyone who takes evolution seriously must accept biological continuity. He becomes a naturalist in which man, his works and his values are a great transaction within the world, *of* it, and not outside it. A naturalistic and relativistic theory of knowledge will mean (*a*) knowledge can be neither discovery nor disclosure of a predetermined existence, for knowing depends upon a joint achievement of knower and environment; (*b*) the knower as well as the perceived environment, is part of his knowledge; (*c*) individual

12. George R. Geiger, "An Experimentalist Approach to Education," in *Modern Philosophies of Education, op. cit.*, pp. 137-74.

differences in knowldege among men can be detected, but the general human element in all that is known can neither be isolated nor eliminated; (d) what something may be when totally independent of any observer or personal reference, is meaningless.[13]

Experimentalism is not rationalistic. It does not begin with universal truths but with specific and particular experience. It is allergic to generalizations. The present and emerging future are stressed, not the past. Experimentalism uses the empiric method but is not under any illusion that observed facts are important in themselves. They are important only as they become a part of the experience of the observer and are made to yield desirable ends. "Is it true?" gives way to "Does it work?" The inductive, not the deductive, method is primary. The past becomes a humble servant of the present.

For the experimentalist, values have no existence in themselves; they are individual to the observer, an attribute of a particular experience by that observer. Values are the results of human choices made in a transaction involving a person and his environment, and their character must be found in that context and may not be imposed from the outside. Intentions and actions should both be appropriate to the situation, with each situation a new one. The experimentalist has no fixed and final values. *Truth is dynamic in a world which is constantly changing.*

5. *Existentialism.* This difficult-to-pronounce term has had a vogue of late, usage that is vaguely associated with the Bohemian, with those who inhabit the Left Bank of the Seine, with dissenters, sophisticates, cynics. It *is* true that this system of thought is a product of nineteenth-century Europe (its present literature is still heavily European in origin) and that its early followers were dissatisfied with middle-class morality, were the protesters, the lonely. Its early developers were Kierkegaard, Nietzsche, and Dostoyevsky, evangelists for a return to the inward man, for a concern with being one's self deeply and profoundly, for thinking of one's self as important, irreplaceable, with a mission to perform. In the nineteenth century this meant isolation, being different. Today, this hidden inwardness is a common concern of many.

13. Geiger, *ibid.,* p. 141.

If the key word of the last century was complacency, that of today is anxiety. Man needs recognition and a place in the scheme of things. To be is important—to be for something. What is it? *Existentialism is concerned with human longing—with man as seeking and needing importance in himself.* Many are existentialists today without knowing it—uncertain and seeking. Man now knows something of the true uncertain character of existence, and he seeks for his dignity, his sense of being irreplaceable. He wants life fully, completely, and with the purpose for *him* as a single creature. He believes in man's dignity, the completeness of education emotionally and spiritually as well as intellectually. He is a realist in a layman's rather than the philosophical sense, for he knows that his life can be tragically ended or thwarted at any moment. He faces this but he wants meaning for it. To the existentialist, man is a seeking and bewildered creature, but he is an individual man, a creation of the Infinite for some purpose.

Existentialism believes that pragmatism (experimentalism) lacks sufficient concept of the wholeness of man, that it is based upon the hope of an emerging ideal man. Ulrich writes: "The pragmatic concepts of trial, growth, the experimental method, and the test of the final outcome were conceived at a time when humanity was supposed to climb the last cliff of the mountain of progress. Mankind has behaved disappointingly, and we ourselves no longer feel secure about growth and perfection as the inevitable result of the experimental attitude." [14]

Existentialism may be religious or nonreligious. It ranges from devoutly religious leaders like Kierkegaard in the nineteenth century and Buber and Tillich in the twentieth to Jean Paul Sarte who asserts a positive faith in man and man alone. One would say that man's reason alone is insufficient, and the other would declare that rational man may stand alone and not be lonely. This is a courageous, realistic, many-faceted philosophy of man as he is—important and irreplaceable.

---

14. Robert Ulich, "Comments on Robert Harper's Essay, 'Significance of Existence and Recognition for Education,' " in *Modern Philosophies and Education, op. cit.,* p. 255.

Is There a Philosophy of Personnel Work in Education?

This sketching in of the outline of current philosophies has been most inadequate. The writer is as aware of this as most readers, yet somehow we must think our way through on what *is* the seeming philosophical basis of student personnel work. Can this be teased out?

The student personnel worker is deeply impressed with the present, with the uniqueness of individual experience, with the emerging. This would make him an experimentalist. He is likely to see change as central for he deals with individuals who change and who do so within the context of a changing society. He is impressed also with the dictum of knowledge and knower existing as a continuity, with perception being individual and unique so that the "reality" of a given situation is different for each person.

Being hard pressed at times, he may wonder how he can bring the other person around to "true" reality, his reality. Now he is behaving like a realist or an idealist. He may, on the other hand, accept the other's perception as right for him, as correct in his world as the counselor's is for *his* world. This puts him in the experimentalist camp. Is there *any* truth which is true for all, or is a truth true only for each knower?

The student personnel worker believes in the dynamic nature of human existence; but does he believe in the dynamic nature of all existence? Unless he does, he is not an experimentalist. He lives in a world of "real" objects, of scientific colleagues who are searching for the truth that exists in the world of objects and natural laws. He also lives in an intellectual world (perhaps an academic one) in which reason is the chief (or only) method of knowing. Perhaps this world too is one in which certain truths exist in and of themselves as abstractions, as immutable and unchanging, to be "known" with the mind through reasoning. If he reasons so, then he is a rationalist or an idealist.

In the world of values also he may not be consistent in a philosophical or systematic sense. He may see values as inherent in the experience of an individual, growing out of that experience and inseparable from it. He may have become resigned to the fact that if it works for a person it must be real and good for him. Yet he will stop at a point where the values of the other infringe too deeply upon his own sense of values and thus deny that the other's values are good for him—or for anyone. Some values, he will reason, are spiritual in nature, partaking of the infinite, good for all in their own rightness. Is the personnel worker *now* an instrumentalist or is he an idealist?

Student personnel work is the child of two worlds—humanitarianism and science. These are not necessarily discrete worlds for a man may attempt to be both. Yet their separate impact is different because their concepts of reality and of values are different. The humanitarian is likely to be an idealist (in both a colloquial and a philosophical sense), and the scientist to be a realist. The critical question that arises is simply stated: Is the much-heralded *experimentalism* (instrumentalism, pragmatism) the answer, denying as it does the absolutes of both idealism and realism? Or is the even more person-centered and much-less-certain *existentialism* a better faith for the future?

THE CURRENT FOCUS ON PSYCHOLOGY

The personnel worker of today, professor or administrator, writer or practitioner, is undoubtedly affected greatly by psychology as a science. He has had facts, objectivity, reliability, empiric validity, the scientific method fed to him in large doses, never fast enough, to be sure, to keep pace with the increasing thrust of his many complex and human relations. He never has enough facts, enough validated procedures or answers, and if he is urgently in need of more knowledge of human behavior, then psychology has much to offer him. For psychology contributes far more than philosophy to an understanding of human behavior, this is its chief end. It differs from philosophy in that it seeks the reality of human *behavior*, not human nature. Differently too, psychology may stress values as they affect behavior, but is less concerned with their essential reality. It uses the empiric method of observation and inference, and tests hypotheses in a world of operational truth and perceived reality. (In an examination of current psychologies, it might be significant to keep inquiring—"When psychology goes beyond empiric truth, does it remain a science or become a philosophy?")

The Contribution of Psychology to Personnel Work in Education

It will not be our purpose in this chapter to provide a systematic discussion of the psychological procedures used in student personnel work. Other chapters of this yearbook deal with procedures and techniques. Important to this chapter is that each procedure is based upon some set of postulates about the nature of human personality. In order to understand the things the personnel worker must do in order to carry out his task, the answers to two questions must be sought: (a) "What is the task, and what are to be sought as desirable outcomes in human behavior?" (b) "What is the nature of the human creature with whom we deal?" The answer to the first question is primarily in the realm of philosophy, while the answer to the second is certainly to be sought in psychology. It would appear to this writer that the basic answers to the psychological question proposed lie in the field of personality theory, in the psychologist's best thinking on the structure and function of the human personality.

SELECTED THEORIES OF PERSONALITY

To digest even the major theories of personality from the original sources is a formidable task, for this would encompass a good share of all existing psychological literature. Yet graduate students in many courses in psychology must attempt some portion of this, particularly those courses designed for the professional preparation of counselors at both the M.A. and Ph.D. levels. Almost always such programs include personality development as one major area.

The word "theory" will continue to plague some readers as impractical or even esoteric. Well, then, it may be called "a study of the different approaches to understanding personality" and this will seem reasonable and necessary to almost any educator. "What have different students of psychology and research workers in psychology found that would help me understand the students and colleagues with whom I must deal? What help can I get in developing my concept of the nature of human behavior since some clarity here is essential to my task?"

In broad outline one might dichotomize all theories of human behavior into *peripheralist* and *centralist* theories. The first deals with observed behavior, that which is peripheral or external to whatever may be the motivational core of behavior. From these accurately observed fragments of total behavior, sensory reactions or small units of total behavior, a principle or theory is advanced that is designed to explain what took place, the nature of the total of which this is a part. Hopefully, this will be cast in the form of a hypothesis which can be tested. This is largely an inductive process.

The centralist, on the other hand, starts with a concern for basic and internal motivation, for the drives and dynamics of behavior, and uses deductive method to explain observed behavior. The one is concerned to the greatest degree with the "what" and the other with the "why." The peripheralist can be more accurate in his descriptions, more objective and specific, and yet, says the centralist, is he more valid, can his explanations of parts be depended upon to contribute an understanding of the whole? The centralist deals with more basic and vital material regarding motivation, purpose, and meaning, and yet he currently appears to be much less accurate in his observations—even in his inferences, says the peripheralist. The one can deal more accurately with segments of behavior while the other describes in less verifiable terms psychological needs, behavior drives, motives.

In the development of student personnel work, and particularly of the counseling function, peripheralist theories of behavior have played the larger part. This is partly because psychology, as a study of behavior, and education, as an application of such studies, have been greatly influenced by the accumulated store of data about individual differences. The past half-century has been the "era of individual differences," and it is fortunate for all school children that this has been so. Another reason for the influence of this approach upon student personnel work has been that studies of differences in sensory motor patterns, kinds of intelligence, and aptitudes (defined as any measure of present behavior which is symptomatic of future behavior), have been essential to the counseling function. This is particularly so when counseling is seen as emphasizing educational and vocational planning.

Within the past two or three decades increasing attention in personnel work has been given to feelings, motivations, and self-awarenesses. These have been contributed to by both peripheralists and centralists, to be sure, but most heavily by the latter. Perhaps we are entering into the "era of personality dynamics."

If one were to look at the task of student personnel work in terms of what needs to be known about students, it would be easy to stress knowledge of (a) aptitudes of all kinds, (b) motivations, interests, and appreciations, (c) the nature of the learning process, with particular regard to self in its interaction with society. To be sure, it would not be difficult to make the same case for instruction in general, but here we are concerned with these particular educational functions. What theories or approaches to human behavior appear to throw most light upon these attributes and processes of personality?

A volume by Hall and Lindzey [15] examines twelve major theories of personality, examines each carefully and in terms of the same dimensions. The listing and treatment of these approaches to personality understanding seemed most pertinent to our present purpose, and it was decided to adapt from these rather than to seek somewhat self-consciously for a different treatment. Merely to list these theories would not be as helpful as to group them around some familiar concepts in education and psychology. This does violence to their historical sequence but may lend meaning.

One might first list two theories which derive from very familiar educational ideas:

1. *Factor theories of personality* revolve around the function of psychometrics, in particular that form of quantitative analysis known as factor analysis. The factors involved, those behavioral functions measured by the different tests, are not particularly different from the variables utilized in other theories. The distinctive contribution of this approach is the manner in which these factors (general, group, and specific) are derived and are then utilized in

15. Calvin S. Hall & Gardner Lindzey, *Theories of Personality*. New York: John Wiley & Sons, 1957.

a theory that attempts to account for the diverse complexity of varying elements of observed behavior. Such theorists are committed to a taxonomy of the dimensions of human behavior through the medium of factor analysis. Raymond Cattell is the outstanding "trait and factor" theorist in this country. His *common* traits and *unique* traits, *surface* traits and *source* traits are derived with exactness and woven with complexity into a theory of personality structure which includes concepts of self, dynamic learning, the impact of social institutions upon development, and so forth.

2. *Stimulus-response theories of personality* derive from theories of learning. Clearly a personality theory labeled S-R would lean heavily upon Hull, who, from the beginning, wished to develop a theory of human behavior but started with animal experimentation. Dollard and Miller developed a theory of personality based on stimulus-response (reinforcement) phenomena but which also used psychoanalytic and social learning concepts. In spite of these extensions, their theory of personality is based squarely upon the familiar learning concepts of primary drive, secondary drive, and habit.

Three chapters are given by Hall and Lindzey to psychoanalytic theories of personality.

3. *Freud's psychoanalysis*, called the first comprehensive theory of personality, is known to all and has influenced almost all later theories, whether acknowledged or not. In Freudian psychoanalysis the personality structure is a complex of three systems: (*a*) the Id, the reservoir of all psychic energy which contains all that is inherited and primitive and which operates under the "pleasure principle"; (*b*) the Ego, that portion of the personality which is in touch with the external world, which mediates between the Id and the external world through the operation of the "reality principle"; (*c*) the Superego which serves as the internal representative of societal expectations, punishing and rewarding through conscience and the ego-ideal. This operates under what might be called the "perfection principle." These three systems, the biological, psychological, and social are normally unified through the ego.

Although the more recent interpretations of psychoanalysis give less weight to the instincts as the source of psychic energy, to the oral, anal, and phallic stages of development, and to the dominance of the Id, such concepts of Freud as the psychogenesis of behavior, repression of emotion and resultant anxiety, and various "mechanisms" of behavior as outlets for repressed emotion are woven deeply into much psychological practice and many psychological theories.

4. *Jung's analytic psychology* is considered an offshoot of psychoanalysis because of its dependence upon the concept of the unconscious, but it actually bears little relation to Freudian analysis. Jung has a more comprehensive mind than Freud, and his theory is correspondingly broader. The foundation of the personality for Jung is the collective unconscious, an inherited store of latent memory traces from man's racial history. Upon it are erected the personal unconscious and the ego. Jung is best known in psychology for his concepts of introversion and extraversion, but beyond this many empiric-minded psychologists have looked askance at his collective unconscious or racial soul. As a result, this prodigious product of a lifetime of thought has not been given the attention it deserves. Jung's analytic psychology is, from an American viewpoint, more philosophy than psychology and has been less absorbed into psychological thinking than have Freudian concepts.

5. *The social psychoanalysts.* Starting with Adler we have a group of theorists, Fromm, Horney, Sullivan, and others, who part with Freud on his biological and instinctual genesis of behavior. They see man as a product of his society and of his interpersonal relations although they build upon concepts of the unconscious. For Freud's emphasis upon sex as the core of the libido, Adler substituted "the will to power" and a striving for superiority. This striving is an inherited core of personality, and through its operation one develops his own distinctive style of life. The drive toward individual self-realization (superiority) is through the operation of feelings of inferiority. A substantial continuing journal, the *Journal of Individual Psychology*, is dedicated to the development of Adlerian psychology.

The later neo-analysts have given even more attention than Adler to the social influences in personality development, although they may hold to an essential inborn human nature. Fromm is deeply concerned about man's relation to society, about the phenomenon of man's love for man, about his present loneliness. Horney has developed a concept of neurotic anxiety brought about by social pressures which result in a pattern of neurotic needs. Sullivan has developed his entire system of personality development around the individual's pattern of interpersonal relations. More than any other in this group, Sullivan has departed from Freud into the realm of social psychology.

Two theories are concerned with the relation of part to whole.

6. *Organismic theory* emphasizes the unity and wholeness of all experience. No part can be understood except in relation to the whole. The parts cannot be analyzed separately and then summed to represent the whole because the whole functions according to laws that are not found in the parts. A person sees, learns, exists as a meaningful whole. Organismic psychology is one expression of holism, a generalized doctrine that living matter has properties which pertain to the total organism rather than to its parts.[16] It is related to the philosophic concept of *holism* in which all interaction is with the total entity of the individual. Organismic psychology is also an extension to the total organism of the Gestalt principles which deal more specifically with the phenomena of consciousness and perception.

7. *Lewin's field theory* has points in common with general organismic theory. In a uniquely psychological manner, however, this theory contributes concepts of "the life space" (the person within his total psychological environment) and "valence" (the value to a person of a given region of his psychological environment), which have been applied both to the study of a person and to the study of group processes sometimes called group dynamics. Lewin's concepts grew out of Gestalt psychology's approach to perception, but he was influenced greatly also by mathematical models such as the geometric system of the properties of space called "topology." Field theory proposes that (*a*) behavior is a function of the field at the time the behavior occurs, (field meaning the

---

16. Horace B. English and Ava C. English, *A Comprehensive Dictionary of Psychological and Psychoanalytical Terms*, p. 241. New York: Longmans, Green & Co., 1958.

totality of coexisting facts seen as mutually interdependent); (b) the understanding of behavior begins with the situation as a whole and proceeds to its parts; (c) the individual is unique and exists in his own life space (psychological environment).

The next three theories bear little recognizable relationship to each other. Two of these are carefully developed individual theories with unique sets of assumptions and points of emphasis.

8. *Allport's psychology of the individual* is based solidly upon (a) the uniqueness of the individual and the need to study him with unique psychological methods, and (b) traits as the essential elements of personality structure. He is widely known as the developer of the personalistic psychology of William Stern, the *Study of Values* test, the functional autonomy of traits, the idiographic study of personality, etc.

9. *Murray's need-press personalogy* is holistic but accepts the importance of the unconscious. It also stresses the importance of the environment, yet places the physiological at the base of any motivation pattern. Murray accepts the full complexity of personality and has labored to devise careful methods of studying and classifying behavior, the final resultant being an elaborate taxonomy of needs. This is most heavily a theory of motivation compounded of psychoanalysis and cultural influences, but appraisal instruments such as the *Thematic Apperception Test* and Edward's *Personal Preference Inventory* have proved another valuable outcome of the theory and its taxonomic features.

10. *Self-theory*. Although Hall and Lindzey associate this theory in their chapter title with the name of Carl Rogers, their own review makes clear that many theorists have contributed to concepts of the *ego* which is a more inclusive concept than the *perceived self*, the person as seen by himself. There are many self-concepts to be considered—perceived self, esteemed self, ideal self, and many confusing situations where one theorist will call "self" what another calls the "ego." This confusing prevalence of treatment is illustrated by the fact that all but three of the twelve theories presented in these pages include concepts of the self and/or the ego as a factor, sometimes a major one. The three nonconformists are the factor and stimulus-response theories, earlier described, and Sheldon's constitutional psychology.

Rogers' self-theory provides for a concept of self (perceived self) which develops out of the person's interactions with his environment. This perception may be distorted from a true experience reality because others' values have been introjected. In the striving toward consistence in self-concept, a confusion arises between the "self I see myself to be" and the "self that I see others perceiving me to be." The resolution of this confusion is a major goal of psychotherapy. His complete statement of theory is contained in nineteen hypotheses which have generated a large quantity of research, all of which, to be sure, are based upon an assumption of the validity of the self-report itself.

One theory is unique in its dependence upon body build.

11. *Sheldon's constitutional psychology.* Based upon type psychology and difficult-to-support assumptions of the long-controversial physique-termperament relationship, this is an incompletely developed theory. It is unique in its complete dependence upon constitutional (body-type) factors as the basis for personality.

One theory is a careful synthesis of many.

12. *Murphy's biosocial theory* of personality was appropriately placed by Hall and Lindzey as the concluding theory statement. It is compounded of the basic elements of much modern psychology and many existing personality theories. This is not said to detract from its significance for only a man of Murphy's comprehensive scholarship in psychology could have developed a theory of this magnitude. If one accepts with Murphy that a constructive, creative electricism is a valuable approach to the understanding of personality, then his skilful compounding of organismic, psychoanalytic, physiological, and social psychology is to be admired rather than criticized.

More than any other theorist, Murphy satisfies psychologists with varied points of view. His theory is carefully and skilfully eclectic ("biosocial," for example, makes sense), functional in emphasis, strongly holistic, and field-theory based. The theory presents man as a biological organism who maintains a reciprocal relationship with his social environment. Personality development is a bipolar process, one pole lying within the body, the other in the environment of the body. Murphy writes that man is "an organized field within a larger field, a region of perpetual interaction. . . ." [17]

This, like Murray's, is a theory of motivation. With Murphy a motive is a tension gradient in a tissue, and tension reduction is sought, for it is generally satisfying. The elements of the theory involve physiological dispositions, canalizations, and conditioned responses which lead into each other and lead in turn to habits. Socialization, social role, and situationism are equally clear elements in his theory. Except for *canalization* (a channeling of the energy which is concentrated in one tissue—defined as a tension—into a particular pattern of behavior which is satisfying to that person) and *situationism* (a person responds as situations require him to respond—a changed situation calls for a changed role and consequently, a changed personality) the terms used have common significance and the theory is understandable. There is less need to wince at any point of this theory than where digestion is attempted of an idiosyncratic concept of any one of a number of other theories.

COMMON ELEMENTS IN PERSONALITY THEORIES

While not necessarily apparent in the concise theory descriptions of the preceding paragraphs, a few concepts of personality are common to many of the theories.[18] Most contemporary theorists accept the *organismic* view of personality as a total functioning unit. This is particularly true of Allport, Murphy, Murray, Rogers, Sheldon, and, of course, those classified more strictly as organismic. A smaller number stress the related *field* theory. It is not surprising, therefore, to find most theories accepting the importance of *group membership requirements*, although it is the theories affected most by sociology and anthropology that stress this factor—the neo-analysts, Miller and Dollard, Murray, and Murphy. As earlier stated, concepts of *self-awareness*, or simply of self, play a part in the majority of theories although the terms used may have a unique meaning for each author. *Unconscious determinants* of behavior

17. Gardner Murphy, *Personality: A Biosocial Approach to Origins and Structure*, p. 7. New York: Harper & Bros., 1947.

18. The final chapter of Hall and Lindzey, *op. cit.*, is drawn upon in the statements to follow.

are widely accepted, although with great variation in their relative importance to conscious determinants. The same is true of the principle of *reward or reinforcement* as a determinant of behavior, with some theories making it a central factor and some secondary, but all giving it attention.

Theories group at one of two poles, on the other hand, with respect to the importance of *events taking place early in development*—Dollard and Miller, Freud, Murray, Murphy, and Sullivan stressing their significance while Allport, Lewin, and Rogers are at the other pole. The same is true of emphasis upon *continuity of development*. Curiously enough, although personality theorists are concerned most vitally with motivation, only a few give full recognition to the *diversity and multiplicity of motivation* as do Allport, Cattell, Lewin, Murray, and Murphy.

Earlier it was said that the school personnel worker needs special help from psychological thought and research regarding "aptitudes of all kinds, interests and appreciation, motivations, the nature of the learning process with regard to knowledge of self, and, in particular, the nature of social learning and adaptation." How closely do the trends of agreement in personality theory—organismic concepts, field theory, social determinants of behavior, self-awareness, unconscious determinants of behavior, and the principle of reinforcement—relate to these areas of need for the personnel worker? Does any one theory of personality fit a major part or the whole of the need? Both of these questions and some regarding philosophy will be examined in the next section.

An Attempted Synthesis in Psychology and in Philosophy

THE PSYCHOLOGY OF PERSONNEL WORK IN EDUCATION

If the emphases in this field are, in reality, anywhere near those suggested earlier as the writer's personal view, then certainly the *organismic* and the *field theories* must be basic in our psychology. We believe in the wholeness, the indivisibility of experience. We use artificial classifications such as physical, mental, and emotional, but these are terms of convenience for analysis purpose and do not appear to be realistic in experience. There is a good bit of research supporting both holistic and field-figure concepts.

A digression on research evidence is appropriate here. All who have read research studies have been impressed with studies which refute other studies. We are impressed by one of two phenomena. One is the extent to which the design, sampling, and method used appear suitable to the data studied, the accuracy of the observations. The other is the relevance and psychological goodness of the conclusions drawn, the inferences from the observations. There is no space here to analyze these further, but it should be clear that acceptance of research depends upon (a) the sophistication of the reader in matters of adequacy of design and (b) the psychological point of view which he supports. It is the latter which is stressed in this chapter, but the former is at least equally important to the science of psychology. The nagging question is always present, "How much am I overlooking adequacy of design because the point of view expressed harmonizes with my own? Beyond this, how much is the research worker's inferences in the report that I am reading affected by this same uncertainty?"

The *point of view*, therefore, of the organismic-field theories appear to apply to our need. Mathewson has developed his thoughtful analysis of the guidance function upon a field-theory basis, of always a self-in-situation reality.[19] While the organismic theory takes in the total existence of the human creature as a unified organism, Lewin's field theory is more strictly the psychological phase of that totality wherein the wholeness is not only of man but of man in his psychological world.

If this point of view is accepted, then learning cannot be separated into classroom and nonclassroom, intellectual and affect, etc. The student personnel worker contributes to the same person who is the concern of the classroom teacher, the psychologist as scientist, the administrator, the parent. It behooves him, therefore, to see his work as inseparable in reality from the concerns of the others who deal with students. This has far-reaching implications for professional education, for personal attitudes, for program development.

It would seem difficult, also, to get away from some acceptance of a factor of *self-awareness* in our psychology. Granted that the

19. Robert H. Mathewson, *Guidance Policy and Practice*. New York: Harper & Bros., 1956 (revised).

concepts involved are "still in the making," and there is still confusion as to terms, an element of reality is involved. The research on this concept as applied to counseling is accumulating at a rapid rate.[20] How a student currently appears to himself is of primary importance, therefore, to a counselor who wishes to aid the student in greater self- and outer-reality awareness. Even a counselor who is certain that his, the counselor's, awareness of the student is more realistic than the student's own, must deal with the *reality* of the student's self-awareness. Counselors—as educators or psychologists —start from where the *student* is, not from where the counselor is, if student learning is to take place.

If counseling is a learning process, then the principle of *reinforcement* in learning appears too well established by both animal and human learning studies to be given other than respectful attention. What will happen to contiguity as a principle remains to be seen. In any event, learning psychology is currently being applied in personality study and may supply a key of as great significance to the student personnel worker as to the teacher of the world of reality in which the student exists.[21] (Whatever phrasing is used here to distinguish between counseling and teaching will cause concern to some. The writer has elsewhere suggested that the subject matter of the learning experience in counseling is the *learner*, his self, his ego, both present and future, and this distinguishes counseling from teaching as ordinarily conceived even though the learning process is the common element.)

It soon becomes apparent that the student personnel worker must draw elements from various existing theories of behavior if he is to develop a personality understanding that meets the needs of his task. This constellation of concepts will doubtless contain the following psychological elements as important to personnel work:

1. *Organismic*—the unity of experience
2. *Field theory*—figure-ground, self-in-situation

20. C. Gilbert Wrenn, "The Self Concept in Counseling," *Journal of Counseling Psychology*, V (Summer, 1958), 104-09.

21. See the symposium by Arthur W. Coombs, Franklin J. Shaw, and Joseph E. Shoben, Jr. for clear statements from three learning approaches, "Counseling as Learning," *Journal of Counseling Psychology*, I (Winter, 1954), 31-48.

3. *Psychoanalysis*—unconscious motivations as primary or secondary in behavior
4. *Self-theory*—the influence upon behavior of various concepts of self
5. *Learning theory*—some elements of the learning process such as the reinforcement principle
6. *Social psychology*—group membership determinants and the cultural impact

It remains the writer's conviction that educators need a personality theory more than a learning theory. On the one hand, the learning theories with which educators are familiar have grown out of animal studies or studies of limited types of classroom behavior while, on the other hand, the need is for a theory of behavior that encompasses the total behavior of a human being.[22] Educators may become weary of "the total child" phrase, and yet few would suggest that we are responsible only for an artificially classified segment of that whole, such as the intellect. For an understanding of the personality we must seek more than a learning theory per se just as Dollard & Miller had to go beyond Hull.

Will some existing theory supply most of the elements? The nearest to a satisfying eclectic approach is that by Murphy. He, of course, gives little attention to unconscious motivation, and his concept of the self is a specific one. He has, on the other hand, heavily emphasized two of the most critical groups of concepts, those of holism and field theory and those of social interaction and role theory. He has concepts of development and of learning that appear to stay close to basic research. He certainly includes physiological and constitutional determinants as well as those of social experience. In fact, the behavioristic "bio-" element in Murphy at times seems strained and cold-blooded. Yet Murphy in a great deal of his writing is fully aware of the nonphysical, the nonmaterial and spiritual. (It goes without saying that what is said here involves the writer's personal interpretation of what is "important" in personality theory as well as a personal interpretation of Murphy!)

This leads naturally to a statement of the conviction that no reader should accept someone else's interpretation. Tyler [23] writes

22. C. Gilbert Wrenn, "Counseling Theory," in *Encyclopedia of Educational Research*. New York: Macmillan Co., in press (third edition).

23. Leona Tyler, "Theoretical Principles Underlying the Counseling Process," *Journal of Counseling Psychology*, V (Winter, 1958), 3-8.

that each counselor (each personnel worker) should develop his own working theory. It does not matter too much what that theory is, within limits, but that he *have* one. The "within limits" means that the worker will not neglect the major sources of knowledge in the development of his theory. Just "any old theory" will not do if it is based upon whimsy and unexamined preconceptions. These sources, writes Tyler, are: (*a*) *the physiological and psychological laboratories* (homeostasis, the general adaptation syndrome, reinforcement and generalization concepts from stimulus-response studies, relationship, insight, and perception concepts from cognitive theory testing); (*b*) *psychoanalysis* (unconscious processes, motivation, anxiety, with socialization and the constructive unconscious from the neo-analysts); (*c*) *the social disciplines of anthropology, sociology, and personnel classification,* (biosocial systems, social role, trait); (*d*) *philosophy and religion* (the self, freedom, responsibility).

It is equally important that the theory he develops not be considered a final one. The *process* of theorizing is the major concern. Our current knowledge of behavior does not permit even the best of theorists to provide a completely defensible synthesis. No man can conceivably become final at this stage of development. The personnel worker may possess several varieties of theoretical concepts, but he should organize them in a fashion that will provide greater consistency and assurance in the performance of his task.

THE PHILOSOPHY OF PERSONNEL WORK IN EDUCATION

First of all, no one philosophy would appear to be sufficient. The experimentalist approach would appear the most sufficient of all those presented but not sufficient enough. The existentialist view might seem even better when the barriers are down. But then there are compelling elements in realism and idealism.

This appears to be a bad start, for the label of eclectic is already slapped on. Frankly, I can see no other way. Perhaps this is the result of the relative youth of our professional field of work. Perhaps, also, this is inevitable, even desirable, because of the nature of personnel work. We are also, as mentioned earlier, a child of two worlds. We are dependent upon scientific findings for much of our knowledge of human nature and our procedures. We are also dynamically and naturalistically oriented, and many of us are Judaeo-Christian idealists.

The emphases of student personnel work outlined in a prior section are clearly based upon assumptions of growth and process as opposed to fixed products, and this makes the concepts of experimentalism most applicable. We assume a monism or wholeness of personality, not a dualism. (Note the word *assume*, for practice may appear to be based upon a dualism in which reason is paramount.) We are also deeply concerned with growth as a process, one in which knowledge and knower are one. We are frankly pragmatic in that we are accepting of that which works. We watch method carefully, varying it to make it more effective, using method as modified by experience. We are certainly impressed with the continuity of experience even though we utilize what are thought of as stages of development. We apparently believe, too, that value and experience are inseparable, that one grows out of the other.

These are generalized statements, to be sure, but it appears that these concepts of reality underlie our personnel assumptions. There are two points at which our acceptance of experimentalism concepts cause us difficulty. We may accept *man* in the experimentalist sense, but are we truly experimentalist with regard to the nature of *knowledge* and the nature of *values?* In one we waver between rationalist and realist approaches while in the other we may act as though we were idealists. The setting of our professional preparation and the nature of our personal experiences may suggest why.

All of us are academically nurtured—with from sixteen to twenty or more years in school. In school our concepts of knowledge have been primarily rationalistic—great truths and the reason to apprehend them—or realistic in that our task is to understand the truth, the reality, that lies in the objective world about us. (*a*) The thesis of independence, of a world of objects outside of man's mind waiting to be understood by him, the thesis of truth as being one's perception of reality, the use of science to apprehend reality—these are all familiar emphases in schools and colleges. (*b*) If one's experience has stressed the humanities, then the abstraction of great truths that exist in a reality not tied to the objective world

are likely to have made rationalists out of us. (*c*) If we have studied
the social sciences, we will have been puzzled indeed by the attempts to apply realistic science methods to social and human
phenomena which are not objects but are relationship phenomena.

Most of us, also, are idealistically nurtured. Our totality of
religious and cultural experiences has left us with a deep feeling
of some eternal verities that exist in the world of man and God.
For some of us, some or a part of these have their origin in the
nature of God; for others they are simply ethical and humanistic
concepts. For both groups, they exist as realities; they *are* values.

This, then, is our dilemma. The task stresses experimentalist
assumptions of reality, of changing knowledge and knower, of relativistic and experience-centered values. The past which most student personnel workers bring to their field is rationalistic and
realistic with regard to knowledge, idealistic or realistic with regard
to values.

Past academic and cultural experience of student personnel worker	*Present task in light of psychological knowledge, personal experience and present values of worker*	*Future integration of aims and procedures*

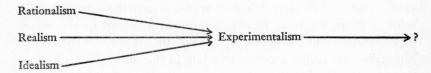

The future lies in a philosophy which is frankly agnostic with
regard to the adequacy of the experimentalist approach. We do not
know enough yet to know what we know. Much more knowledge
of human behavior, studied through the science of psychology and
through the art of various relationship experiences, will have to
accrue before we can be sure that the process-continuity-centered
concept of man and knowledge is one that we can live with. Right
now it appears to be our best bet.

The writer has no personal difficulty with accepting all knowledge and truth as relative and in the process of emerging. Since
whatever is known must be known by the mind of man, then
reality is affected by the changing knower. Truth is forever being
known, never completely known, as long as the experience of man

keeps apprehending new truths which modify what we already know—our current "truths."

On the other hand, I would appreciate the man who senses fixed truth as residing in the objective world of science about us, but would have to protest that this is not the only approach to fixed truth. Absolute truths exist in the idealist's world and the rationalist's world, and they are, philosophically speaking, as possible worlds as is the world of nature and objects. The crux of it lies in the difficulty of the apprehension of fixed truths by a creature whose experience, mentally and spiritually, is in a constant state of emergence. *What* is more real than man? "Oh," says the deeply religious, "God is." "Oh," says the scientific man, "the facts of the physical world." Well and good, but a school or college personnel worker is dedicated to a task in which the welfare of the human beings around him is central. If the focus of belief and assumptions of the religious worker is God and of the scientist is nature, might we not argue that, *for an educator, focus upon the nature of man is paramount?*

In the realm of values, however, I have more difficulty. I can accept the wisdom of not having final values or aims set in advance. At least if *all* values are to be so fixed, I would prefer the experimentalist belief in the instrumental, pragmatic, emerging nature of values. For *all* values to be fixed, either as abstractions or as inherent in the objects of nature, is a dangerous assumption when one must see them operating in an experience—that of man—which is not fixed. What is to control what? Rather, it is possible that *primary* values may exist in man's cosmos, although many values are always in a state of shifting emergence. This is not philosophical consistency, perhaps, but I personally can accept only that which lies within the limits of what I now am.

The primary values of which I speak—integrity of each man's personality, mercy which goes beyond facts, love as a positive quality of existence—are those which reside in Judaeo-Christian idealism, and I make no apologies for stating acceptance of them. They are "of the essence" of man's existence, it would seem. Whether their origin is of God, of man's experience alone, or of man's experience with God, they appear to exist as permeating realities of the spiritual phases of man's world.

Two Hopes

ESTABLISHMENT OF A PERSONNEL SERVICE CONTRASTED
WITH OPERATION

The first of these hopes is that the personnel worker will study the differences that may exist between the philosophical and psychological concepts involved in the *establishment* of his educational function and those that are apparently utilized in the *practice* of his work. The confusion exists in that the basic assumptions underlying the presumed *purpose* appear to be different from assumptions inherent in what *is done* in school or college. This is more than precept versus practice or aim versus achievement. It is that the philosophy and even psychology seem clear in what one is presumed to be responsible for doing, but personalities and the other exigencies of a given situation adulterate or even distort that purpose.

A student activity program is *designed* to provide opportunity for social learning, handling responsibility, and applying classroom learning to social situations. It may be so *organized and supervised* as to give the lie to all of these. The faculty adviser directs, sees that the outcome is good whether constructive learning takes place or not. The administration may hesitate to "take the rap" for learning that may result from failure or for mistakes that are made. The concepts in practice are not recognizable as those that were given as the reason for establishing the activity. Counseling for student self-learning becomes counseling for counselor learning or for counselor-approved outcomes. Group guidance designed to contribute to self- and social-understanding becomes didactic classroom teaching far removed from student motivation and application.

Some of this is inevitable. No performance is perfect. Rather than denying the poor wisdom of the practice because of the excellence of the reasons for establishment, one should admit the gap between theory and practice, or see that the concepts concerning purpose are modified to meet reality. To promise much and deliver little is poor professional practice; it may be either the practice or the purpose that needs attention. Of most importance is to distinguish between the two.

PHILOSOPHY AND PSYCHOLOGY IN THE DEVELOPMENT OF ENDS
THEORIES AND MEANS THEORIES

Psychometrics are a means to an end: To what end, and to give partial understanding to what kind of a person? Theories of personality growing out of psychometric-factor studies and out of learning studies are distinguished less by the inclusive concepts involved than by the *methods* used in the study. Very much of our attention is given to method, but basic to method is ends. And the ends phase of our professional development is immature as yet.

This leads us to the second hope that we will develop both ends theories and means theories. Theories as to ends and purpose are largely philosophical in nature—modified, it is true, by the knowledge of human beings that is gained through the studies of psychology, sociology, and anthropology. No matter how complete these studies, however, the nature of reality and of values will still draw heavily from studies of philosophy and religion. Man-on-this-earth must be seen more broadly than man as a biological-social organism, or so it seems to this writer. Man's purpose in the total scheme of existence calls for some postulates not covered by science. And the values of his existence may encompass more than the values of his daily evolutionary development.

Means theories, on the other hand, deal with procedures, with activities that can be observed and tested for their effectiveness, effectiveness in terms of criteria that are more than those self-contained in the procedure. If ends theories are philosophical, means theories for personnel workers are psychological and sociological. Here empiric testing and the use of the most careful measures of accuracy and validity are to be employed. Here there is little place for philosophic speculation, here a person is accurate or he isn't, and the procedure works or it doesn't. There is no excuse for poor technical skill or untested work. Here man must be scientific in a fairly careful use of the term. An ignorant or unskilled worker cannot be long tolerated.

Perhaps we can conceive of the "bases" of our professional future as residing in the approaching convergence of two streams of understanding, those now labeled philosophy and psychology. But it must be always only "approaching" convergence, for the streams are constituted of different elements. To say that the science of psychology cannot remain apart from the world of ends and values is not to say that it should blend its methods or lose its distinctiveness. It is of the utmost importance, however, that knowledge of man's *behavior* be seen within the framework of the *meaning of his existence* in the universe.

Student personnel workers and all educators must draw from these two streams. The goals of education must be realistic in terms of, both, what *man can do* and *who he is*.

Philosophical reasoning influenced by psychological fact

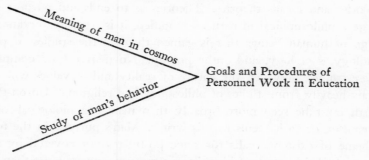

Goals and Procedures of
Personnel Work in Education

Psychological research interpreted within framework of philosophical meanings

Can we move ahead on these two fronts? We must, or we deny our usefulness and fail in our role as educators. Personnel workers believe in the integrity of each person, the importance of tolerance, the need for personal humility buttressed by self-respect. We believe much, and we know much, but how well do we do? Our performance is affected by so many factors—our unique experience pattern, personal satisfactions gained, type of supervision received, amount of encouragement and acceptance experienced, our personal values system. These are the measure of one's personal response to the total outer reality of his world. How well we do is often more a question of personal dedication and emotional maturity than of the concepts accepted in the abstract. To think through not only our task but ourselves as meaningful parts of the cosmos is the burden of this chapter.

REFERENCES

I. *Systematic Approaches in Counseling and in Student Personnel Work*

1. ARBUCKLE, D. S. *Student Personnel Services in Higher Education.* New York: McGraw-Hill Book Co., Inc., 1953.
2. MATHEWSON, R. H. *Guidance Policy and Practice.* New York: Harper & Bros., 1955.
3. PEPINSKY, H. B., and PEPINSKY, P. N. *Counseling: Theory and Practice.* New York: Ronald Press, 1954.
4. ROGERS, C. R. *Client-centered Therapy.* New York: Houghton-Mifflin Co., 1951.
5. *Student Personnel Work as Deeper Teaching.* Edited by Esther Lloyd-Jones and Margaret R. Smith. New York: Harper & Bros., 1954.
6. WARTERS, JANE. *High-School Personnel Work Today.* New York: McGraw-Hill Book Co., 1956.
7. WRENN, C. G. *Student Personnel Work in College.* New York: Ronald Press, 1951.

II. *Personality Development*

1. HALL, C. S., and LINDZAY, G. *Theories of Personality.* New York: John Wiley & Sons, Inc., 1957.
2. JOURARD, S. M. *Personal Adjustment: An Approach through the Study of Healthy Personality.* New York: Macmillan Co., 1958.
3. MURPHY, GARDNER. *Personality: A Biosocial Approach to Origins and Structure.* New York: Harper & Bros., 1947.

III. *Philosophies of Education*

1. BRUBACHER, JOHN S. *Modern Philosophies of Education.* New York: McGraw-Hill Book Co., Inc., 1950.
2. *Modern Philosophies and Education.* Fifty-fourth Yearbook of the National Society for the Study of Education, Part I. Chicago: Distributed by the University of Chicago Press, 1955.
3. *Philosophies of Education.* Forty-first Yearbook of the National Society for the Study of Education, Part I. Chicago: Distributed by the University of Chicago Press, 1942.
4. PARK, JOE. *Selected Readings in the Philosophy of Education.* New York: Macmillan Co., 1958.

SECTION II

PERSONNEL SERVICES IN ACTION

CHAPTER IV

Principles for Programming Personnel Services

C. E. ERICKSON and R. N. HATCH

Administrative Responsibility for Personnel Services

The progressive segments of our society are constantly seeking ways and means of maintaining and improving our way of life. It is obvious that if this is to come about, means must be found for the orderly transfer of social experience and for some projection into new frontiers. Educational programs have been the means by which society has not only transferred its culture to the next generation but has also gained new insights into a new way of life.

The complex nature of our modern society has led more and more to a dependence on the state and federal government for administrative direction and leadership. The public educational system is a primary agency of the modern state and, therefore, reflects the general purposes and objectives of the state. Since the form of government which we have in the United States has led us to a philosophy and practice consistent with democratic ideals, the framework within which educational programs function is democratic.

The philosophy of our culture and our heritage of freedom have served to encourage considerable autonomy in developing educational programs. There are those who would use this same heritage to plan programs completely apart from the general objectives of our society. There are others who in full cognizance of the objectives follow an orderly design in programming which meets the needs of the students, the community, and the state. The responsibility for meeting the needs of the clientele of schools and colleges is known as the administrative function in education.

Responsibility for the educational program, at all levels of education, rests with the governing board. This responsibility carries with it the requirement that the best program possible be provided within the broad regulations imposed by governmental agencies and the limits of available resources. Boards faced with a task of such magnitude try to build the best organizational framework to bring about the desired goals.

Governing boards in most phases of human endeavor find it impossible to perform the assigned duties unless an executive leader is charged with the responsibilities of the group. To such an officer goes the authority and responsibility for providing the framework within which educational leadership may labor with maximum results. The performance of such an assignment is again an example of administrative function. It is from this base that principles for the programming of any phase of personnel services must evolve.

UNIQUENESS OF EDUCATION

It has been a familiar observation that certain aspects of American education create unique problems in relation to various features of educational programs. Reference was made to the problems which spring from our democratic philosophy and precedents for local control of school systems. Such problems should not be thought of as obstacles but, rather, as opportunities which make it possible to develop the most acceptable program with a minimum of legislative or administrative restraint.

The purposes of the school are never very clearly defined. The administrator accepts this problem as a challenge to develop a set of tangible goals against which the program may be tested. If the educational leader sees the danger of an attack from every quarter in the absence of acceptable objectives, he may be moved to take the first step in the development of the educational program. Recent attacks on the reading and science programs only emphasize the validity of this point.

INDIVIDUALS AS CLIQUES OR STAFF

The educational staff is made up of individuals with their own personal perceptions of self in terms of competencies and limitations. The individuals represent different experience patterns, training, and emotional needs. The successful administrator accepts the differences and develops plans which utilize the best attributes of each individual. If the individual differences are ignored, the program will be fraught with dissension.

Related to the individuality of the staff members is the fact that our public schools are large, unwieldy, decentralized, and have few direct controls over staff members. The typical staff in an institution of higher education usually enjoys an even higher degree of independence. This results in an enormous amount of energy being spent in communicating, discussing, persuading, and planning. When this is added to the factors of individuality and the natural tendency of individuals toward independent work, the problem is compounded. Educational leadership must provide a means whereby the staff gains satisfaction from co-operative effort and skill in the techniques which make co-operation possible.

There is a tendency for groups or cliques to form in any staff. Groups form as the result of many factors and frequently function as an individual but with the added strength of numbers. Such groups may be vicious, arbitrary, and compulsive in relation to the staff as a whole. An understanding of why such groups are formed may aid in discovering ways of fitting the groups into the total program.

1. Groups form around an identifiable unit of the schools, such as a building, a congenial set of teachers at a certain grade level, or a particular curriculum area.
2. Groups form as the result of avocational or social interests having little to do with the professional ties originating in their daily work.
3. Groups form because the members wish to be identified with other members and not because they subscribe to the objectives of the group. Such "joiners" will give up their own ideas, beliefs, or activities to conform to the behavior of the selected group.
4. Groups form because it is felt that by this means the members gain through the principle of the "pressure group." Such a group may be held together by oppressive rules or dedication to a ritual. Historically, professional educators have not tended to form into such groups. It is logical, however, to expect that to a degree the motivations mentioned above are manifest in all individuals.

Individuals form groups for other reasons or from a combination of those which have been mentioned. This tendency is natural and is to be expected. The administrative staff members alert to the reasons for grouping, usually have ample opportunity to capitalize on those tendencies in organizing an educational program. Here again it is dangerous to write a recommended course of action; a knowledge of the dynamics of grouping and a generous amount of imagination should result in a favorable utilization of these group tendencies.

PERPETUATION OF PROGRAM

Programs usually begin with a small core of enthusiasts which generate interest that carries the program forward. Such a group may be likened to the proverbial "snowball" as it moves an idea or service into a position of significant stature in the total educational program. This phenomenon is essential to the development of the educational program, but it brings about a related problem.

As the program broadens and there is need to involve new people, the group is apt to weaken. The additions to the core group lack the orientation or experience of the original group and, therefore, fail to have the same dedication or understanding of the program. This represents a critical period in program development and accounts for much of the mortality of personnel services. An effective program will provide for continuous orientation to the goals and activities of the service.

POWER OF DECISION

Every organization must have an identifiable center where there is the power of decision. Anything short of this may result in chaos, mediocrity, or the maintenance of the *status quo*.

There may be an appearance of finality in administrative decisions, but this is largely an illusion. The real finality is in the soundness and wisdom of the decision. Administrative action should flow from those who know the entire situation as much as from those whose position determines their responsibilities for making decisions. Action judgments must be made at the point of greatest understanding. In education this means that decisions are made by different people on different issues and at different times.

An administrator can exert status leadership by virtue of his position, or he can exert executive leadership by virtue of demonstrated ability. In the latter he includes a review of the situation and confers with staff members of experience and discretion before a decision is announced.

In every educational situation there are important expectancy factors. The community, the students, the staff, and the alumni have certain understandings and desires regarding the kind of leadership they would consider most appropriate. At times this will call for strong and decisive action; at other times permissive, contemplative, and participative processes will work best.

Good administration requires a high quality of intellectual freedom and honesty. Ideas, not people, must play a central role. There is security for staff members if they know that ideas rather than their proponents finally determine a course of action. There is encouragement for creative effort; ideas are warmly greeted and intelligently considered. This leadership can emerge only when ideas precede, yet finally determine, administrative action.

Staff members have a multiple set of drives and aspirations. They want to attain selfhood in personal uniqueness and personal independence. They want to develop an effective relationship to their surroundings. They desire a feeling of progress and successful accomplishment. They want to enjoy the exhilarating experience of individual and personal growth. A stimulating environment must somehow harmonize these and many other drives and must, at the same time, help create a sufficient sense of frustration and dissatisfaction so that complacency, stagnation, and incompetence will not obstruct progress.

The administrator can never escape final and decisive responsibility. If he puts blame on others for an error, he weakens his own position and impairs the morale of the staff. He can set up committees, delegate responsibilities, or avoid issues, but in the end he must deal with any unfavorable situation. He can talk about democratic administration and sharing responsibility. These are methods for getting new ideas, collecting better judgments, or securing a balance of viewpoints. But these methods are not a means of escaping from personal responsibility. This ultimate responsibility is fair, just, and logical. The administrator is in a stronger position to resist pressures. He can initiate counter-movements, he can mobilize individuals in groups in support of a position, and he symbolizes the objectives of the enterprise. If he stands up to his full stature, refuses to bend with the wind, he strengthens and stabilizes the entire organization.

This center for decision-making does not need to be an obstacle in organizing; but it may prove to be just that, unless administrative leadership acts with discretion.

Developing Personnel Programs

PLANNING EDUCATIONAL PROGRAMS

The guides for administrative organization suggest a framework for the development of a set of general principles for organizing educational services.

The effective administrator is one who accepts and follows certain general but important steps of analysis in the accomplishment of the purposes of administration. Such phases may be taken in a definite sequence or may be altered as the situation dictates. The normal sequence is as follows:

Phase One. The identification of the purposes to be served by a given school. This is the framework within which the program, the facilities, and the personnel must function. Failure on the part of the educational leader to take this first and all-important step is a risk which will probably result in a minimum of positive programming.

Phase Two. The identification of strengths and weaknesses of present personnel. This type of information has a direct bearing on the initial program and serves as a guide for the recruitment of future staff.

Phase Three. The identification of appropriate functions of the administrative leader. The insight which an individual gains, consistent with the role of good administrative leadership, is in direct proportion to the continuing success of the total organization.

Phase Four. The identification of unique segments of the total educational program. The job descriptions which emerge from this analysis guide the executive in staff assignments and insures optimum staff utilization.

Phase Five. The identification of functions which call for executive leadership and those which require technical or academic leadership. The tendency of many educators is to lump all leadership into one category. This results in much confusion and ineffective performance. The administrators who identify their role as executive leaders and who utilize the academic or other competencies of the staff for technical leadership will provide a setting which should result in maximum growth.

Phase Six. The identification of logical assignment of staff to appropriate functions in the organization. In addition, there is the inherent need to develop a perception of the importance of the assignment and the responsibilities which the assignee must assume. An organization which has developed from the premise of most effective staff assignment is one which is fundamentally sound.

The above phases are not to be construed as a complete set of guideposts in the development of educational programming. They do represent, however, the key points of administrative analysis which have proved to be imperative if administrative leadership is to function at the optimum.

PROGRAMMING PERSONNEL SERVICES

The personnel program in the broader educational setting is subject to the guidelines which apply to the organization of the total educational program. The steps which have been suggested for the analysis of administrative organizing are mandatory to the component parts. There are, however, specific guides which apply to the personnel program and complement those suggested for the total organization. Many of these are adaptations of the general suggestions, since they serve to give depth to the analysis.

Many authorities have developed comprehensive lists of specific steps to be followed in the determination of program needs.[1, 2] All of these suggestions have merit, and all of the lists have certain unique characteristics. Rather than report several such lists, it seems advisable to suggest those steps which are the most common guides to be found in the professional literature.

1. Dugald S. Arbuckle, *Student Personnel Services in Higher Education,* pp. 33-35. New York: McGraw-Hill Book Co., Inc., 1953.

2. Edward C. Roeber, Glenn E. Smith, and Clifford E. Erickson, *Organization and Administration of Guidance Services,* p. 79. New York: McGraw-Hill Book Co., Inc., 1955.

Step I. The development of a readiness on the part of the total staff to accept responsibility for the programming of personnel services. This entails an identification of the role of such services and a review of the techniques used in such a program. A staff which has an emotional acceptance of the objectives, contributions, and staff responsibilities of personnel services is ready to launch an inspired personnel program.

Step II. A complete inventory of present services, facilities, and resources constitutes the second major step. This step includes several closely related parts, such as:

a) The educational objectives of the system to determine the consistency of the objectives with reference to the proposed role of personnel work.
b) The instructional and emotional needs of the pupils as perceived by the pupils, the staff, and the community.
c) An analysis of present activities carried on in the area of pupil personnel work. The goal of this analysis is twofold; to give recognition to those activities which now exist and to find the gaps which need to be filled for a complete program.
d) A review of present facilities and equipment for the same purpose as mentioned in item (*c*).
e) An evaluation of the interest of the school staff and the community in the development of the personnel program.
f) A program, to be successful, requires trained leadership.

The individuals responsible for programming personnel services should find out whether or not the information gained from the suggested inventory is sufficient for a positive program of action.

Step III. The development of staff experiences which may ultimately become a part of the on-going program is the next logical step. The variety of such experiences is limited more by time and imagination than by any other factors.

The goal of this step is to determine the amount of professional experience which will give the staff an understanding of the scope of the personnel program. A school staff with a general knowledge of the total program should be capable of programming personnel activities.

Step IV. The adoption of an informal design which permits constant appraisal of the program. There is a tendency on the part of educators to give careful study to a project, implement the activity, and place blind faith in the adopted program. A personnel program, like any other aspect of formal education, is vulnerable to this type of treatment unless appraisal procedures are established. Such activities need not be profound or difficult but they should be sufficiently complete so as to give an objective picture of the success or failure of the active program.

The guidelines which have been suggested here may be thought of as minimum in reviewing the initial considerations for the programming of personnel services. The effectiveness of the organization which eventually evolves will be in direct proportion to care exercised in following such a sequence.

Basic Aspects of the Administrative Process

The planning of any part of the educational program may be interpreted narrowly and terminated with the early planning which goes with the initial stages. It may be thought of in the broader context of the administrative process which affects the continuing educational program. The latter seems far more realistic, since a dynamic educational program is continually changing and being evaluated, although there may not be any identifiable point at which planning terminates. For this reason it is appropriate to discuss the basic aspects of the administrative process as they pertain to the programming of the personnel services.

Authorities differ somewhat as to the exact titles or divisions of the administrative process, but in general there is agreement as to the sequence. The five major functions are identified as: planning, organizing, staffing, directing, and evaluating. It seems advisable, therefore, to review the principles for administering the personnel services in the order of the normal sequence of administrative functions.

PLANNING PERSONNEL SERVICES

Planning is the first step of the administrative process. To plan in administration, one must find the answers to why, when, where, and how to perform certain activities. Many of the suggestions to be found earlier in this chapter are concerned with this phase of the programming sequence. If it can be remembered that this first phase is a means to an end and not in itself a final product, the organizing of personnel services is on solid footing.

The planning phase may be divided into several logical steps.

These steps follow a pattern commonly used in attacking a problem. The following aspects of analysis should be of assistance in the planning phase of programming personnel services:

a) Creation of a feeling on the part of individuals to be involved so that there is a *felt need* for personnel services.

b) An analysis of the situation for the purpose of identifying *obvious gaps* in the personnel services.

c) A careful review of the various ways by which the gaps of *time, facilities, resources,* and *staff* may be corrected.

d) The selection of a *course of action.* Such a course should include both immediate and long-term plans.

Planning which follows the logic suggested by this outline should be valid and result in a realistic personnel program.

ORGANIZING PERSONNEL SERVICES

The organizing phase of programming consists of two major parts: (a) grouping the various elements; (b) structuring the relationships within and among the groups. This phase is discussed in detail in a later chapter, but a few principles may be mentioned here for purposes of maintaining an analysis of the sequence.

The division of duties and responsibilities should result in the most effective effort of the total group. This being the goal, several assumptions may be made relative to the organizational structure. The effectiveness of the group is in direct proportion to the extent to which (a) the assignments are in accord with specialized skills; (b) all individuals have had an opportunity to participate in the planning aspect; (c) line and staff functions are identified and understood by the entire staff; and (d) administrative units are sufficiently small to permit maximum communication. The organization which emerges from these suggestions should be a healthy, self-energizing unit. The specific pattern may be different in each situation analyzed; but it should be a sound organization, capable of planning a complete program of personnel services.

STAFFING PERSONNEL SERVICES

The third aspect of programming is called staffing, or the identification of personnel for the program. This phase may be divided into several closely related parts: selection, development, assignment, and retention of capable individuals. There is little need to analyze these as separate parts, since the principles which underlie the total phase are similar.

Several assumptions serve as the basis for this phase of programming personnel services. Hatch and Stefflre have listed the following guides:

1. The effectiveness of personnel management is related directly to the extent to which individuals are recruited both for specific jobs and for the general contribution that they make to the effectiveness of the total program.
2. The effectiveness of personnel management is related directly to the degree to which individuals are selected for jobs only after consideration has been given to all available persons.
3. The effectiveness of personnel management is related directly to the extent to which personnel believes that salary scales are fair and just.
4. The effectiveness of personnel management tends to be related to the degree to which remuneration of staff is based primarily upon the importance of the duties they perform and the effectiveness with which those duties are performed. Seniority is thus placed in a secondary role of importance, but maintained to the degree necessary to develop morale among the staff at large.
5. The effectiveness of personnel management is related directly to the extent to which the executive encourages personnel to seek positions in which they can render maximum service.
6. The effectiveness of personnel management is related directly to the extent to which changes in the status of staff members are frequent enough to permit their development, yet not too often to cause instability in the organization.
7. The effectiveness of personnel management is related directly to the extent to which provision is made for gradual or partial retirement of the individual members of the staff.[3]

The individual responsible for the selection and assignment of the staff for the various positions in the personnel program should find the above assumptions most helpful. In some instances adaptations will be necessary for a given situation. The lesson to be learned here is that the assumptions have been designed as reliable guides for the educational leader so that he has a frame of reference within which he may perform the staffing function. Changes or adapta-

3. Raymond N. Hatch and Buford Stefflre, *Administration of Guidance Services, Organization, Supervision, Evaluation*, p. 62. New York: Prentice-Hall, Inc., 1958.

tions will result from his value judgments as dictated by circumstances.

DIRECTING PERSONNEL SERVICES

The phase of programming which is concerned with the coordination, control, and stimulation of others is presented here under the title of directing. This is a very broad phase, and some authorities prefer to divide the activities into several phases. This may be desirable because of the scope of the steps of administration, but the principles which may be followed permit all of the activity to be grouped under one heading.

The relationship of directing to the other phases of the sequence is sometimes misunderstood. Sears explains this as follows:

Direction as a part of the administrative process is not direction until there is action or, at least, a release of energy in a form calculated to start or to control or to guide action. When an executive faces a problem, he studies it, searching for and reviewing possible ways of meeting it, and finally, making up his mind what he will do. Strictly speaking, this activity is planning. Once he announces his decision, he thereby authorizes action or provides instructions that imply orders for action. This activity is direction. The problem in question may have had to do with policy, personnel, program, instruction, or anything else, so long as it called for decision and action.[4]

Several problems develop out of the directing phase which serve as obstacles to effective programming. The first of these relates to the meaning and use of the term *authority*.

Authority is created by law, and the laws may either authorize or prevent action. The authority of school law is quite restricted. First, it can only function within a stated purpose. Second, it is restricted because it is granted to certain officers and employees and not to all persons. The problems which develop from this phase can usually be traced to a failure on the part of the educational leaders to function within their power of authority and/or interpret the role of authority to the entire staff.

The ultimate source of authority is the true determinate of the exercise of the vested authority. The action of the executive leader

4. Jesse B. Sears, *The Nature of the Administrative Process*, p. 131. New York: McGraw-Hill Book Co., Inc., 1950.

and his administration is subject to the appraisal of the board, staff, customs, profession, and other variables which constitute the ultimate source of authority. This is a much broader interpretation of the source of authority than one which recognizes only the law or the governing board.

Adminstrative authority in this frame of reference is in direct proportion to educational leadership. The administrative leader gains his authority from his effectiveness in stimulating the staff and community, co-ordinating the total effort, and providing for dynamic appraisal. Directing in this context goes far beyond inspection and command.

Communication is the second major function of the directing phase. Inadequate communication may result from many causes, such as an extended span of control, failure to provide the mechanical processes, or incompetent personnel. To a major extent, the success of programming will be in direct proportion to the effectiveness of communication. The individual responsible for the personnel services has the obligation of providing the necessary channels of communication within the personnel staff. The same individual also has a related responsibility to initiate steps to correct communication omissions in the total administrative structure of the educational unit.

EVALUATING PERSONNEL SERVICES

The fifth and last phase of the programming sequence is the appraisal aspect. This is the final step, since it is the means by which those responsible for the personnel services may change those activities which might result in the most effective program. It may be said without reservation that the failure of the staff to include this part of programming is one way of signing the death warrant of the program.

Evaluation may be both formal and informal, but it should meet certain general criteria. The following are the most promising:

1. The appraisal program should be continuous.
2. The appraisal program should be systematic and in accordance with acceptable concepts of evaluation.
3. A major part of the program should be directed as a testing of the objectives which have been announced for the program.

4. A conscious effort should be made to test assumptions which have been made about the program.
5. The data collected should be used as the basis for staff analysis and for program planning.

Other guides could be added to the above list, but an appraisal program which achieves these criteria should insure adequate information for effective programming.

The five-phase sequence described above does not serve as an absolute guarantee of the implementation of a program of personnel services. It is a framework, however, which should prove adequate if the educational leaders involved allow themselves to enter into the spirit as well as the letter of the suggested phases. A program which evolves from this series, provided the phases have been followed, should be the very best program possible in light of all the related factors.

Some Specific Suggestions on Organizing

Implicit in all the principles and suggestions in the preceding pages are ideas for specific techniques to be used in developing a program of personnel services. It may be advisable to pinpoint a few ideas which have proved to be helpful in the accomplishment of a total program. For purposes of presentation these are divided into three categories: staff, students, and lay citizens. Many of the techniques may be used with more than one group and usually involve at least two of the groups.

SUGGESTIONS FOR INVOLVING STAFF

Staff members may become active contributors to the personnel program as the result of one of the following activities:

1. A structured survey of the present program with a frank recognition of acceptable personnel practices now being followed by certain staff members.
2. The use of the case study to relate the scope of the pupil information to possible classroom activity.
3. Reporting of a follow-up study of graduates and/or drop-outs, which reviews reasons for leaving school, problems of maladjustment, curriculum inadequacies, ineffective use of staff, and problems related to co-curriculum activities.
4. Visits to other schools and discussions with alert staff members who have experienced success in personnel programs.

5. Planned programs of in-service training of the staff with emphasis on how instruction may be made more effective as the result of better personnel programs.

SUGGESTIONS FOR INVOLVING STUDENTS

In many instances personnel programs are developed, but the students for whom these services are intended are ignored. A program which evolves in a sterile setting of this kind is apt to be just as sterile after its implementation. Some of the following suggestions may help to correct this omission.

1. A structured survey which permits the student to express his perception of the effectiveness of present services.
2. The inclusion of certain appropriate group activities in the curriculum so that the student is able to relate subject matter to his present and future goals.
3. Direct participation in personnel activities, such as a follow-up study, a community occupational survey, implementation of a placement service, student government, and resident-hall supervision.
4. Actual counseling contacts in the solution of a personal problem.
5. Role-playing activities which demonstrate improved social techniques as a part of the co-curriculum program, followed by an analysis of the roles played.

The extent of the activities in which students may be involved is conditioned more by the imagination of the staff than by any other criteria. Excellent suggestions for this aspect of organizing are to be found in the writing of Wrenn [5] and in most of the introductory books of the guidance field. The administrator responsible for the personnel services should experience no difficulty in identifying suggestions for involving students in personnel programs.

SUGGESTIONS FOR INVOLVING LAY CITIZENS

The educational program at the community level rests, in a large part, with the lay citizens of the community. The educational program in institutions of higher education is affected by the normal influences of the alumni and friends of the institution. These groups select the governing boards and vest them with the legal and administrative authority to draft the policies by which the

5. Gilbert C. Wrenn, *Student Personnel Work in College*, pp. 203-476. New York: Ronald Press Co., 1951.

school is governed. Thus, indirectly, the lay citizen is the individual in a position to accept or reject personnel services. The inherent value of involving such groups in the organizing of personnel services is obvious but is frequently omitted in the programming process.

Those responsible for the programming of various aspects of the educational endeavor have had a tendency to overlook the impact of citizen participation. It may be that the technical specialist thinks that the average citizen feels too inadequate to serve a useful role in planning and directing a given program. This is a fallacious assumption in most instances and especially so in the programming of personnel services. Not only is it important to have an understanding citizenry behind the program but some of the most constructive assistance available is to be found among the lay leaders.

The lay citizen may participate in groups of invited citizens, through the board of control, or by a combination of these groups. The last seems most desirable, since the members of the board of control should be able to expedite planning, and compromises can be reached in the context of discussion. This plan should prevent the contention which may develop as the result of separate recommendations from each group.

The board of control may become an active participant in the programming of personnel services in a number of different ways. The exact way in which it becomes involved is probably of less importance than the techniques used to inform it of personnel activities. The staff responsible for the personnel program should provide for the following orientation sessions for the members of the board of control:

1. A review of the objectives of the educational program and the role of personnel services in making it possible for the school to achieve those objectives.
2. Reporting the results of the staff and student surveys which identify the needs of the school.
3. Reporting the results of follow-up studies with all the data interpreted and suggestions for improvement recommended.
4. Presenting appropriate and accurate data regarding costs and staff needs of a personnel program.
5. Reviewing the results of personnel services so that the board member may be reassured that such a program pays dividends.

Parents, alumni, and other friends of the school will profit from much of the same information as that suggested for the board of control. This may be given to community groups or at meetings called for the purpose of discussing the information. The sharing of the information will usually encourage an interest in direct participation of individuals and groups in program developments. This is a rich resource and should not be permitted to go untapped.

Citizens may be able to participate in the organizing of personnel services in some of the following ways:

1. Serve on personnel councils which are advisory to the professional staff.
2. Act as club leaders and other resource persons in terms of a particular competency which they have and for which there is a need among the student body.
3. Assist with the implementation of the placement and follow-up services.
4. Provide educational and occupational information to supplement the school's offering.
5. Arrange for and provide out-of-school activities which are wholesome and educational.

The suggestions mentioned here for the involvement of staff, students, and lay citizens barely scratch the surface of the different possibilities. The personnel services will be as good as the total possibilities uncovered and utilized. It is to be hoped that those responsible for the program will wage an increasing campaign to involve all three groups so that the ultimate program will be one of maximum value to students for whom the activities have been designed.

The Continuing Task

Educational administration has enjoyed the growing pains of an evolving function during the last fifty or more years. The concepts of the role of the administrator have been located at both ends of a continuum from dictatorship to anarchy. The perception of the individual administrator as to his role is to be found at some point on that continuum but subject to the uncertainties of the tug of other points of view. It was into this administrative setting that the personnel movement was born. It is only to be expected, therefore, that much of the early organizational efforts should be seen to suffer the same growing pains as other phases of educational programming.

Today, as at no other time in recent decades, there is an emerging consensus as to the true role of the educational administrator. The administrative function, for which the executives are responsible, has become one of educational leadership of an educational unit. The unit is made up of a group of different services and functions, all striving to make the total educational offering most meaningful to the students, the perpetuators of our culture.

The organization of personnel services is subject to the same perceptives of the administrative function as all other aspects of administration. The perception of educational leadership is a healthy setting which should result in maximum growth. It is a position worth perpetuating if the students, staff, friends, and the world are to profit most from the contributions of education. Personnel workers are expected to shoulder their share of the responsibility for the continuation of our present point of view of educational administration.

SUGGESTED READINGS

ARBUCKLE, DUGALD S. *Student Personnel Services in Higher Education*. New York: McGraw-Hill Book Co., Inc., 1953.

EDMONSON, J. B.; ROEMER, J.; and BACON, F. L. *The Administration of the Modern Secondary School*. New York: Macmillan Co., 1948.

HAGMAN, HARLAN L. *The Administration of American Public Schools*. New York: McGraw-Hill Book Co., Inc., 1951.

HAGMAN, HARLAN L., and SCHWARTZ, ALFRED. *Administration in Profile for School Executives*. New York: Harper & Bros., 1955.

HATCH, RAYMOND N., and STEFFLRE, BUFORD. *Administration of Guidance Services, Organization, Supervision, Evaluation*. New Jersey: Prentice-Hall, Inc., 1958.

HULLFISH, H. GORDON. *Democracy in the Administration of Higher Education*. Edited by Harold Benjamin. New York: Harper & Bros., 1950.

MOEHLMAN, ARTHUR B. *School Administration*. Boston: Houghton-Mifflin Co., 1951.

MOONEY, JAMES D. *The Principles of Organization*. New York: Harper & Bros., 1947.

ROEBER, EDWARD C.; SMITH, GLENN E.; and ERICKSON, CLIFFORD E. *Organization and Administration of Guidance Services*. New York: McGraw-Hill Book Co., Inc., 1955.

SEARS, JESSE B. *The Nature of the Administrative Process*. New York: McGraw-Hill Book Co., Inc., 1952.

The Superintendent as Instructional Leader. Thirty-fifth Yearbook of the American Association of School Administrators. Washington: American Association of School Administrators, 1957.

WRENN, C. GILBERT. *Student Personnel Work in College*. New York: Ronald Press Co., 1951.

CHAPTER V

Functions and Procedures in Personnel Services

MARGARET E. BENNETT

Approaches in This Chapter

Personnel functions and procedures are considered here in relation to individual development in our democratically oriented society. Our knowledge of the growth and maturing process in human life suggests that personnel services are likely to become progressively differentiated at successive maturity levels and that co-ordination within the program becomes an increasingly complex task. Manipulation of the environment for the young child is a major emphasis in early school years, while guidance in learning to manipulate one's own environment in harmony with goals and life values becomes increasingly important at adolescent and adult levels. Services directed toward self-appraisal, self-direction, and adjustment gradually become wider in scope and deeper in meaning throughout the life span.

Many of the learnings needed by the young child to meet his developmental tasks successfully are provided without his conscious awareness of their fundamental purposes. But, as life presents more choices and adjustments, these learnings are approached more directly with conscious intent on the part of the learner to study alternatives and make wise choices and plans. Immediate adjustments merge with long-range perspectives on future living, and skills in self-direction are perfected if our goals for the personnel service are realized. A personnel program will thus be viewed not only as a central focus and pervasive aspect of a total educational program but as a continuous thread in the weaving of a human personality.

Personnel Functions

The functions of personnel work will be considered here from the viewpoint of two types of service: (*a*) leadership in an evolving program, and (*b*) direct service to individuals.

LEADERSHIP IN PERSONNEL WORK

The nature of personnel leadership depends upon the total organization of the educational institution, the available personnel workers, and the objectives and policies established for the personnel program. We are now thinking in terms of trained professional leadership, specialized services, responsibilities and contributions of the entire educational personnel and the students, contributions of home and community and their reciprocal interrelationships with the school. Such leadership anticipates also a plan for co-ordination of all the services, and facilities for continuous intercommunication that will implement the work of each participant, achieve articulation between levels, stimulate continuous professional growth, and allow for co-operative planning of the improvement of services. Specific organization may range from a simple committee or council in a small school where lines of communication within the staff can be kept open easily to a highly complicated organization of wheels within wheels in a large school system or university that seems to defy complete and accurate description.

Development and Co-ordination of Personnel Services. The rapid development over the past few decades of professional leadership in personnel work at national, state, county, and city levels has provided impetus to the expansion and improvement of services in the schools and the raising of standards for qualified personnel workers. A recent survey of the opinions of some 300 counselor-trainers, state supervisors of guidance, and directors of personnel programs yielded a high agreement that it was essential for successful functioning of a personnel program to have trained workers co-operating with the teachers and the community and carrying on an in-service training of the staff.[1] The rapid spread of state

---

1. George L. Keppers, "Organizing Guidance Services," *Clearing House*, XXXI (December, 1956), 216-20.

certification of counselors and the emphasis in professional organizations upon improved standards of counselor preparation attest to the widespread recognition of the need for this trained leadership. This does not negate the services rendered by all teachers who are quite generally recognized as focal personnel workers, particularly at the elementary-school level, but experience has demonstrated the need for certain special services to students and for leadership with the school staff in developing and co-ordinating all of the personnel services.

There is now quite general consensus that leadership in developing policy and program in personnel services should be achieved through the team-approach that pools and crystallizes the thinking of all who participate in the program—administrators, specialists, teachers, and, at strategic points, representatives of parents, community groups, business, industry, labor, and students served by the program. This facilitation of teamwork in policy and program planning, of the co-ordination among the various services, and of articulation between levels is one of the basic continuous responsibilities of a personnel leader in a central county or city-wide program or within a school or an institution of higher learning. The larger the unit to be served, the more complex becomes the task of co-ordination.

Provision of Physical Facilities and Equipment. The increase in school population has brought awareness of difficulties in personalizing the educational program.

1. *The school plant.* Some of the newer school plants are built in small grade-level or other units, with offices for unit administrators and counselors, to secure for a large school the advantages of small-school atmosphere. In Evanston (Illinois) Township High School, a reorganized plan divides the school population into four groups, cutting across grade-level units, with a large homeroom as the focal center of each division which has its own educational staff. Both pupils and parents can thus be identified with a group small enough to become acquainted and not lost in the complexities and the impersonal atmosphere of a large institution.[2] In some of

2. Frank S. Endicott, Camilla M. Lowe, *et al.,* "Report on Home Room Organization." Evanston, Illinois: Evanston Township High School, April 30, 1956 (mimeographed).

the larger colleges and universities, this personalization is achieved through units within large residence halls as well as smaller building units in the newer ones planned to conserve small-group values.

2. *Conference rooms*. Counselors' rooms are now often separated from administrative offices. Rooms for teacher conferences are recognized as essential but probably are not yet available in the majority of schools. Laboratory facilities for each department for special work with groups of students are increasing, as are clinic facilities for special remedial services.

3. *Personnel records*. Reports from twenty-one states indicate that continuous cumulative records are in use throughout the school years; eleven are specified as state-wide record systems.[3] Transfer of records with a student is a partially unsolved problem, but the newer duplicating processes should help eventually. Current opinion holds that records should be available readily to all who use them professionally. In some of the newer buildings an "island" area is provided for housing of records that makes them easily accessible from every office. Where office set-up makes the centralization of all major records of students impossible, the modern duplicating methods provide an inexpensive way of bringing together essential information about an individual for use by a counselor or adviser.

Leadership in Professional Growth. One of the most challenging aspects of in-service training within an educational setting is the fact that it can draw upon all of the firsthand experiences of trainees in a living laboratory as well as upon reported research and practices elsewhere. It can stimulate "action research" of an informal nature and, often, experimental research in co-operation with graduate schools offering personnel training. It can identify those individuals within an educational staff who can be encouraged to secure advanced training for more responsible positions within the personnel service—an emphasis in a long-term counselor-training program in the Los Angeles City Schools. A major objective is to raise the general level of personnel practices of everyone involved in the program—teachers, counselors, advisers, heads of residence,

3. Questionnaire replies to the writer from state supervisors of guidance in 1957.

student assistants, administrators, and the personnel leaders. The in-service training program at Stephens College, Columbia, Missouri, is one which actively involves the entire staff.[4]

In the Los Angeles County schools, the consultant services in the Research and Guidance Department are directed toward in-service training in the schools as teachers, counselors, and administrators are helped to study and work with individuals and to carry on group and individual services. The Maryland Child Study Program[5] conducted in numerous school systems for several years, is aimed at providing guided experience for teachers, with leaders and consultants, in learning to see school situations through the eyes of individual children. Parents can be helped to participate more effectively in co-operative home-school services not only through child study but also through study of interview techniques that will enable them to contribute more fully in teacher and counselor conferences. Training of students in secondary schools and colleges for their part in the orientation and adjustment of new students, for their leadership roles in school government and activities, and counseling roles in college residence halls is accepted practice at these levels and is increasing for pupil councils and other activities at the elementary-school level.

The picture would not be complete without noting the importance of mutual study by personnel workers in education, community agencies and organizations, business and industry, and employment services to develop common understanding and methods of exchange of information, referrals, and follow-up activities. Active participation in professional personnel associations affords splendid opportunities for valuable interdisciplinary perspectives.

The methods reported in in-service training programs run the gamut of possible techniques, such as directed reading, staff and case conferences, lectures, individual conferences, panels, discussions, demonstrations of interviews, and role-playing. It has been suggested that those that succeed best utilize the principles of learn-

4. Eugene L. Shepard, "A Three-level In-service Training Program for Advisers," *Personnel and Guidance Journal*, XXXVI (September, 1957), 48-50.

5. Daniel A. Prescott, *The Child and the Educative Process*. New York: McGraw-Hill Book Co., Inc., 1957.

ing and teaching through meeting felt needs and providing opportunities to put new ideas into practice.[6] Personal experience with
the same type of procedures used with students often increases
sensitivity to needs of counselees and to improved ways of meeting them.[7]

Co-operation in the Total Educational Program. Current emphasis upon personality development implies active participation
by personnel workers in the planning and continuous development
of the total educational environment. Knowledge about individuals in general at various age levels and information about a particular school population, such as social and economic factors,
abilities, interests, and educational and vocational objectives, are
essential for sound planning of an educational program. Personnel
workers are the logical resource people for such information, and
their membership on adminstrative and curriculum-planning committees is one effective means of sharing this information. Personnel
and curriculum teamwork facilitates exploration of various mental
hygiene, vocational guidance, and developmental aspects of every
subject in the curriculum, and, likewise, of all extracurriculum
activities. It can lead to fuller understanding of community needs
for general and vocational training. It can give counselors a richer
background for their programming services with students through
better understanding of curriculum offerings.[8] Such teamwork
opens the door to fuller opportunities for mutual study of individual students that will enhance both the teaching and the personnel
services.

Jersild's studies of interest manifested by pupils in classes have
impressed him with the fact that the traditional school program has
often failed to deal with real and fundamental interests of children
and youths. The areas of self-understanding and social relationships
figure largely in his surveys of these interests. He comments that

6. Clifford P. Froehlich, "In-service Training Programs that Succeed,"
Clearing House, XXIII (January, 1949), 259-62; and Barbara A. Kirk, "Tech-
niques of In-service Counselor Training," *Personnel and Guidance Journal,*
XXXIV (December, 1955), 204-07.

7. Margaret E. Bennett, *Guidance in Groups: A Resource Book for Teachers, Counselors, and Administrators.* New York: McGraw-Hill Co., 1955.

8. *Counseling and Guidance in General Education.* Edited by Melvene
Draheim Hardee. Yonkers-on-Hudson, New York: World Book Co., 1955.

to be interested in what is taught, students must find something of meaning and value related to personality development and self-fulfilment. Here is a meeting place for the goals of curriculum and personnel work.[9] Kelley [10] has collected many examples of team-work in guidance and curriculum to illustrate how this process can stimulate professional growth and bring the total educational environment into closer harmony with the personnel point of view. When this happens we move toward an educationally challenging environment in which developmental goals for all are more fully realized.

Leadership in Public Relations. Essential to the development and maintenance of a personnel program in the schools is the understanding and enthusiastic support of the service by the community and an organized plan of co-ordinating the work of school and community agencies. Interpretation of the program is a continuous responsibility of personnel leaders shared with all who participate in the program. Representatives of parents, social agencies, religious and recreational groups, employers, and labor on planning councils related to their interests are essential features of a program that is aimed not only at community support but also at improvement and full utilization of all environmental influences that affect the life of the individual.[11]

In both public schools and colleges the "community" serves as a laboratory for developmental experiences of individuals in social, civic service, and vocational areas. Personnel workers must be a functional part of this community life to utilize it fully for junior citizens. We are most likely to expand these co-operative community relationships in times of crisis, such as war, but, like all other phases of an evolving service, eternal vigilance and effort are needed to keep them at a high point of efficiency. Experiences in times of crisis have demonstrated great power potentials inherent in the integration of school and community.

9. Arthur T. Jersild, *In Search of Self.* New York: Bureau of Publications, Teachers College, Columbia University, 1953.

10. Janet A. Kelley, *Guidance and Curriculum.* Englewood Cliffs, New Jersey: Prentice-Hall, Inc., 1955.

11. Interesting illustrations have been described by Carrie R. Losi in the *1957 Report of Secondary-School Guidance* in Newark, New Jersey.

Leadership in Evaluation. This is a continuous function in a personnel program starting with appraisal of existing services when an initial organization or a reorganization is planned. It is a function in each new step ahead. Both informal "action research" and experimental research at crucial points provide guidelines for an emerging program. A few of the criteria for evaluation are the following: a definite organization for the personnel service understood by all with clearly defined functions and responsibilities; a clear-cut statement of purposes and objectives formulated co-operatively by the entire faculty with student and community participation in deliberations; co-ordination of services of administrators, personnel workers, and teachers to achieve efficiency without duplication of functions and without confusion for students; student understanding of available personnel services and how to secure them, and effective use of the services; evidence that various learnings are taking place in such areas as increased self-knowledge, good physical and mental health status, responsibility in school citizenship, and growth in self-direction; parent-school and community-school relations that utilize outside resources to the fullest extent; an in-service professional study program that keeps the staff alert to new developments and prepares them for each new step ahead.

DIRECT SERVICES TO INDIVIDUALS

The Major Focus. Shifts in emphasis in personnel work from services to special groups to preventive work with all and, eventually, to a developmental service permeating the entire educational program have directed attention to learning processes involved in personal development and adjustment. This word "adjustment" is used here to connote the achieving of harmony between inner and outer forces that may affect both the individual and his environment, not merely an acceptance of outer forces. Both, group activities and counseling, are required for this learning which is continuous throughout life. We have noted earlier that active, purposeful participation in this learning increases as the individual matures toward full self-direction.

Admissions and School Placement. Reports of research over the past twenty-five years suggest that emphasis in educational policy has been shifting from age-grade norms, which are notoriously unrelated to individual growth pattern, to concern with the holding power of the schools, achievement commensurate with ability, and the identification and fostering of all kinds of talent.[12] This trend toward individualization of education parallels the development of personnel services and has, without doubt, a cause-and-effect relationship with them.

Selection and admission policies at the college and university level are based in varying degrees upon tradition or experimentation with prediction studies of student characteristics important for success in a given institution. Firsthand study of the admission policies of many institutions by Fine [13] yielded the conclusion that trends were toward the following standards in the approximate order listed: grades or relative scholastic standing in class; results of college-entrance examinations; the high-school pattern of courses; principal's recommendation, more often on specific forms than in letters; extracurriculum record, less important than formerly but given consideration when candidates of otherwise equal standing are compared. The present highly competitive nature of selection has emphasized the importance of making the transition to college one phase of a long-term guidance process, including a thorough appraisal program, comprehensive cumulative records, intensive counseling with students and parents, and close co-ordination of school and college personnel workers. College guidance, like vocational guidance, is a long-term process, continuing throughout the school years and beyond admission to college.[14] Transitions from elementary or secondary schools to trade and vocational schools present problems similar to those of transition to colleges and universities, and often involve larger numbers of students.

With national policy tending toward the underwriting, when necessary, of a student's education through scholarships, loans, and

12. *Review of Educational Research*, III (June, 1933); IX (April, 1939); XII (February, 1942); XV (April, 1945); XVIII (April, 1948); XXI (April, 1951); XXIV (April, 1954); XXVII (April, 1957). Washington: American Educational Research Association.

13. Benjamin Fine, *How To Be Accepted by the College of Your Choice.* Great Neck, New York: Channel Press, 1957.

14. Arthur E. Traxler and Agatha Townsend, *Improving Transition from School to College: How Can School and College Best Co-operate?* New York: Harper & Bros., 1953.

expanded work-study programs, if both he and society stand to benefit from his training, personnel services are needed throughout the entire educational program to identify talents, provide opportunities for their development, and foster suitable work habits, study and social skills, and motivation in harmony with potentialities. Both parents and children must be served to bring those with suitable talent in line for admission to suitable schools. The four-year college-motivation program of the Chicago public schools illustrates personnel services to meet this need.

Personnel workers also face the task of preventing manpower demands from encroaching on the fullest development and utilization of all the potentials inherent in our human resources. One of our unsolved human engineering problems is that of providing opportunities for the full use of all our human resources. Here is where personnel services in education must reach out into the broader social scene if objectives are realized.

Orientation in Successive Educational Levels. It is a far cry from summer clinics for preschool youngsters and their parents to precollege clinics for prospective college students and their parents. However, all the new situations encountered between these two events and beyond these, in college or technical school, work life, and other phases of adult living, present problems of orientation through which self-directive skill in meeting new life situations is developed. This contrast of the preschool and precollege clinic tends to highlight the gradual increase in the active participation of an individual in the process by which he gains understanding of himself and his environment, formulates plans for school and later life, and learns how to utilize his chosen opportunities effectively.

Many of the preadmission orientation techniques used at several age levels are similar in acquainting parents and new students with the new institution and providing parent-student-counselor conferences. Television programs constitute one modern version used to acquaint parents and pupils with new opportunities ahead.[15] Since detailed descriptions of various methods cannot be included

15. New Jersey Personnel and Guidance Association, *Spotlight on New Jersey Guidance.* Rutherford, New Jersey: Fairleigh Dickenson Press, 1957.

here, the effort is made to stress the *continuity* of the *process* from level to level and to mention a few of the current promising practices and unsolved problems.

1. *Bridging the gap between school and home.* Kindergarten or first-grade children face the orientation task of adjustment from the protected home to the more complex school environment. Each new level presents new developmental tasks in physical, social, and academic skills and in orientation to new groups. Increased mobility of population brings many new children into groups during school terms, giving the group and teacher a reciprocal task of orientation with new members.

2. *A reciprocal process.* At all levels orientation should be a reciprocal process between old and new members of a school or college, in which each becomes acquainted with the other, and the adjustment process works both ways, resulting in dynamic changes in environment to meet the needs of all as fully as possible.

3. *Articulation between educational levels.* Planning for orientation to each successive level in the educational system, pupil visits to new schools, and exchange of personnel information are accepted practices from elementary school on. Some secondary schools offer opportunities in classes for intensive study of problems of selecting a college and preparing for successful college adjustment. College days or nights are increasingly becoming a series of meetings instead of a one-shot treatment. College clinics are offered by many colleges to provide parents and students with realistic views of college life and studies and to supplement high-school counseling on vocational and college potentialities. Some upper-elementary-school pupils must choose between types of high schools, such as academic and vocational or technical.

4. *Camps and small groups.* Many institutions provide an informal camp environment for preadmission orientation of student leaders to their responsibilities in the civic life of the campus. Students work actively with faculty as leaders in these Freshman camps and in residence halls and campus activities. Increased college enrolments have led to plans for small-group experience for new students. Among the attempts to meet the problems of large student populations are small campus-club groups with their own leaders, small living groups within residence halls, and small advisory groups

meeting with faculty advisers for discussions as well as interviews.

5. *Special classes.* Orientation courses or various courses in general education provide fundamental study of problems related to school or college experience and to social, economic, and personal development and adjustment throughout life. These courses are frequently taught by counselors or advisers who can follow through with students in applications to their own unique problems.

6. *Integrated and evolving programs.* All members of a school or college community—administrators, personnel workers, faculty, and students—co-operate in planning and evaluating an effective orientation program. Studies of orientation at the college level have indicated that some programs are too static and do not provide for this wide participation in the process and for its evaluation. Williamson [16] has said of their over-all orientation program at the University of Minnesota, "Regardless of whether we ever achieve optimum orientation, we have found that orientation efforts provide an excellent common interest around which to organize the efforts of nearly all members of the university community."

Assistance in Self-Understanding. Deepened awareness of the complexity of personality and increased emphasis upon the importance for life planning of the emerging self-concept have revealed the superficiality of many earlier measurement programs and have stimulated more comprehensive appraisal of individuals. Informal and more unstructured techniques are being used to supplement objective tests, and a few multi-factor test batteries are providing partial answers to difficulties of pattern analysis of tests and other appraisal data. Continuous research is needed to derive serviceable regression equations for probability prediction and to improve methods of clinical diagnosis.[17] There is need to understand the influence of the interaction of factors within a personality as well as their predictive validity.[18]

16. E. G. Williamson, "The Minnesota Program of Orientation," *Journal of Higher Education,* XXVI (November, 1955), 425-33.

17. Paul E. Meehl, "When Shall We Use Our Heads Instead of the Formula?" *Journal of Counseling Psychology,* IV (Winter, 1957), 268-73; and "Symposium on Clinical and Statistical Prediction," *Journal of Counseling Psychology,* III (Fall, 1956), 163-73.

18. Donald E. Super, *The Psychology of Careers,* p. 167. New York: Harper & Bros., 1957.

The wider use of cumulative records throughout the school years is evidence of recognition of the basic importance of long-range appraisal methods as compared with the use of cross-section data that formerly characterized, and still does, much vocational counseling and many group-appraisal projects in secondary schools and colleges.[19] Crucial aspects of any personnel record system relate to questions of how fully a true synthesized picture of each developing personality is being formulated by teachers and counselors and how much each individual is growing in awareness of his assets, liabilities, interests, and motivations and in the ability to use this understanding in planning and in living.

Frequent parent-teacher-counselor interviews, counseling with students, observation in varieties of school or college activities, and case conferences to pool viewpoints of teachers and personnel workers and co-ordinate their services make important contributions to realistic understanding of individuals. Intensive therapeutic counseling and group therapy by specialists may be needed in some instances to understand difficulties and release inner powers.

Elementary-school pupils need opportunities to come to grips with their emotions, to face fears, worries, and behavior difficulties, to recognize common problems, and to learn how to cope with them. Both group and individual guidance can help in this process. Adolescents in high school and college are ready to approach the task of self-appraisal directly and need adequate opportunity under trained leadership to study sound methods of appraisal, collect and organize information about themselves, interpret it cautiously with a counselor, and apply it in life planning. This self-appraisal should be based upon long-range data, both objective and informal. Autobiographies, analyses of school achievement, social and work experience, and varieties of projective techniques are helpful. It should reveal attitudes, motivations, life values, emotional and social maturity, conflicts, frustrations, and behavior patterns that may affect full self-realization through education, work, home, social, and civic life. With the increase in number of trained personnel workers conducting both group and counseling aspects of an ap-

19. *Manual of Instructions for Cumulative Records*, Maryland State Department of Education, 1957.

praisal program, there are indications that some of the informal approaches to self-understanding are achieving greater depth and subtlety of interpretation. For example, the autobiography which has frequently been merely a surface review of external events may with skilful guidance become one means of learning how an individual sees himself in relation to his life history, and how events may have influenced his personality.[20]

Understanding Environmental Opportunities and Demands. The natural curiosity of the young child will generally carry him avidly into his school work if it is adapted to his maturity and readiness and if any handicaps are overcome. The insightful teacher will take advantage of a multitude of opportunities to help each child wrest meaning from his work and play. For the child school is, to a degree, synonymous with living and needs but little interpretation. As "subjects" enter the program, the questions of purpose and value arise and the guidance-minded teacher will help children set tasks and develop plans that have real meaning even though they may be a few steps removed from immediate interests, such as skills that are means to desired goals.

As the curriculum becomes increasingly differentiated in high school and college, the educational guidance problem becomes twofold: first, to help the student understand the purposes of all the required subjects and his opportunities inherent in them, and, second, to help him select wisely from a bewildering array of electives those which will contribute most to his concept of the person he wishes to be and those which are essential to his future life work.

If the required subjects are part of a carefully planned program of general education designed to meet the needs of youth as maturing members of society, and if the purposes and values of this program are accepted enthusiastically by a faculty that has helped to develop it, the task of interpreting the opportunities therein to students will be a rewarding task for the counselor. Always there is the instructor's responsibility to explore all possible values of a subject with his students and to help each one formulate his own unique purposes within the general pattern of values for the course.

20. E. Evan Shaffer, "The Autobiography in Secondary-School Counseling," *Personnel and Guidance Journal,* XXXII (March, 1954), 395-98.

This is a personnel function, likewise, for the extracurriculum, but is not so widely and fully accepted and performed as in the curriculum.

In early school years, the individual is gaining a widened and deepened appreciation of his culture, the place of work therein, and its meaning to the worker and the consumer. Through his school activities, he is experiencing a variety of fundamental work processes, is trying out many of his latent powers, and is developing interests and attitudes concerning types of work that are important phases of his vocational maturing. The alert teacher and counselor at this level will observe and record evidences of aptitude in the work and play of children and will recognize the vocational significance of information and attitudes acquired about work and workers. Here is the ideal place to develop respect for all kinds of useful work and to foster self-respect and enjoyment in the things one can do best.

During high-school and college years, and on into graduate training and adult education, every subject has its implications for some phase of occupational life to which the faculty should be alert and for which they should assume responsibility for contributions to the vocational guidance or adjustment process. These will include direct services to students, co-operation with counselors in building up occupational files, and pooling information about interests and potentialities of students.

As in every other area of contemporary life, the occupational area has become too complicated for any one person to master in its entirety. The trained counselor will be responsible in co-operation with faculty and librarians for the collecting, filing, and general use of reliable occupational information and for its specific use in study and counseling with students at strategic points. These points are determined by the succession of choices and adjustments of students as they progress through general and vocational education and enter work life. Surveys of pupils' interests and problems suggest that direct study may be needed well before the time it usually begins.[21, 22]

21. Margaret E. Bennett, *op. cit.*, p. 88.

22. Robert Hoppock, *Occupational Information: Where to Get It and How To Use It in Counseling and Teaching.* New York: McGraw-Hill Book Co., 1957.

The group approaches range from surveys of broad fields to intensive examination of specific occupations and jobs. At near points of entrance into work, they deal with problems of job finding, adjustment, progress, and work satisfactions; in later years, with readjustments or new opportunities as the worker and conditions change.[23] Instructional methods are as varied, or more so, as in any other field.

The vocational counseling should be closely interrelated with group approaches, providing specific information when needed, correcting misconceptions, and guiding the counselee in thinking and feeling his way through all the mazes of uncertainty with respect to his developing career pattern. The interview provides opportunity to relate occupational information to the emotional life of the counselee and to relate worker trait-requirements to his specific self-knowledge.[24]

Making Life Plans and Adjustments. It is a common supposition that the American educational system may be relied upon to direct children and youth to appropriate goals and satisfying stations in life. To this end, schools and colleges provide counseling and guidance services of various types.

1. *Vocational guidance.* We seem to be in a transition stage in our thinking about sound methods of guiding vocational planning. Emphasis upon fostering the total personality is causing us to take a fresh and skeptical look at the time-honored process of matching traits or factors with jobs or the theory of individual adaptation to social and economic patterns. As yet we do not have adequate research and experiential background to proceed with full confidence in working with the complicated process of personality development recognized as the focus within which the maturing of vocational planning and adjustment occurs. We may be moving toward a synthesis of these various approaches.

23. *Earning Opportunities for Older Workers.* Edited by Wilma Donahue. Ann Arbor, Michigan: University of Michigan Press, 1955.

24. Herbert Rusalem, "New Insights on the Role of Occupational Information in Counseling," *Journal of Counseling Psychology,* I (Summer, 1954), 84-88. See also Sidney A. Fine and Carl A. Hienz, "The Estimates of Worker Trait Requirements for 4,000 Jobs," *Personnel and Guidance Journal,* XXXVI (November, 1957), 168-74.

There is fair agreement on two points: Vocational planning and adjustment are long-term processes that involve maturing and learning; and guidance must extend through the entire educational span. Super has redefined vocational guidance as ". . . the process of helping a person to develop and accept an integrated and adequate picture of himself and of his role in the world of work, to test this concept against reality, and to convert it into a reality, with satisfaction to himself and benefit to society." His theory of dimensions of vocational maturity includes: readiness to give concern to problems of vocational choice; degree of specificity of information and planning; degree of consistency of vocational preference; degree of crystallization of significant traits and aptitudes; and wisdom of vocational preferences that may lead to satisfactory vocational adjustment.[25]

If we could know what stage of maturity a person had reached in each of these dimensions at a particular time, we could understand his needs for vocational guidance. At present we use some shotgun methods in the scheduling of group approaches and counseling, but our accumulated research and experience can serve helpfully to estimate stages of readiness and to select pertinent techniques. It appears that vocational development, like reading or other types of learning, is always with us, and the problem is to discover where our techniques should be developmental and where they must be remedial in nature.

Rapidity of change in the nature of work-life, the decrease in working hours, and the increased span of life present the personnel service with two other major challenges: How can a sound vocational guidance and adjustment service be made available through adult years as an integral part of expanding adult education; and how can avocational guidance help individuals prepare for the creative and satisfying use of increasing leisure time throughout work-life and retirement years?

A few more of the crucial concerns in vocational guidance that call for dedicated effort are: the maintenance and extension of our democratic principle of freedom of vocational choice in a world of conflicting ideologies and in a culture where a degree of

25. Donald E. Super, op. cit., 183-97.

socioeconomic stratification still limits educational and vocational horizons of many citizens; the maintenance of a balanced program of service in all phases of personal development in a period of emphasis upon scientific and technological development for defense and for improved material living; the establishment of a wise balance in emphases upon technical competence, human relationships, and ethical standards in our guidance of youth toward vocational life; the identification of talents of some kind in every individual, and the utilization of all our human resources in the enrichment of our culture.

2. *Educational guidance.* For brevity's sake this term is used to cover assistance in making choices, plans, and adjustments in any phase of educational life and in evaluating educational experiences. It includes choice of subjects and activities and of participation in social, recreational, or cultural groups, school or college government, and citizenship. It would be impossible even to list here the personnel functions and procedures within the scope of this term. We shall consider a few of the implications of research in child and adolescent development and of the persistent and emerging trends and problems.

In earliest school years, guidance is directed to helping the young child develop useful habits, set limits for his behavior, solve problems suited to his maturity, explore his emotions, and find outlets for creative expression. A warm, accepting atmosphere created by the teacher is essential for this guidance. As he grows out of the egocentric period into the age of social co-operation, reason, and moral judgment, opportunities appear for the beginnings of inner discipline and participation in a democratic school life. Gradually, from the age of seven or eight, he is able to think somewhat critically about classroom and school procedures, is much interested in the rules of the game, and is ready for realistic practice in democratic citizenship.[26] Student councils and organized leadership-training in elementary schools attest to this maturing process.

3. *Planning educational programs.* In adolescent years, assist-

26. Jean Piaget, *The Language and Thought of the Child.* (New York: Harcourt, Brace & Co., Inc., 1926); *The Moral Judgment of the Child* (Translated by Marjorie Gabain. Glencoe, Illinois: Free Press, 1948); also, David H. Russell, *Children's Thinking* (Boston: Ginn & Co., 1956).

ance in long-range planning and the recurrent choices of subjects is a major personnel function of many counselors or faculty advisers. In some schools, this function has become a major task met through splintered interviews of five to fifteen minutes, followed by still shorter interviews to change programs made in the first brief conferences. Little significant guidance is likely to result from these brief contacts other than partial insurance that prerequisites are met for future training that may or may not be suitable for ultimate vocational pursuits unless careful re-evaluation of vocational goals is a preliminary to the programming function.

Some schools provide intensive group study of vocational- and educational-planning, conferences with students and parents, and opportunity to accumulate pertinent data on work sheets and to think through their implications for planning at points where decisions must be made ahead as to choice of school or college, course of study, or subjects.

4. *In extracurricular programs.* An important personnel function is that of guiding students in wise choices of activities among the many possibilities in a modern educational institution through awareness of their educational values. Advisers are increasingly helping students to formulate objectives, learn the arts of leadership, utilize sound principles of group dynamics, and evaluate the outcomes of their experiences. They are observing and recording evidences of individual growth through activities as bases for developmental counseling. Research is needed on the carry-over values into adult life.

5. *Students as junior citizens.* A personnel function that is assuming increasing attention, particularly at the college level, is that of bringing students into active co-operation with faculty in the governing bodies of institutions. Vassar has changed from "student" to "college" government. The University of Minnesota provides for student membership on a wide variety of committees and councils related to every phase of student activity and to curriculum evaluation and development.[27] A student at Brandeis Uni-

27. E. G. Williamson, "The Dean of Students as Educator," *Educational Record* XXXVIII (July, 1957), 230-40. Washington: American Council on Education.

versity comments, in a report of faculty-student co-operation in guiding the campus social structure, mores, and ideals, "What an exciting way to learn!" [28] A student report on similar developments throughout the country stresses the educational values of this trend and the emerging responsibilities of students rather than their *rights* in college government.[29]

6. *Housing.* Educators at all levels are interested in the physical and cultural surroundings of students in their homes. In colleges, the residence halls and other living quarters are major concerns of personnel officials either directly or through co-ordination with other offices. Counseling, government, study groups, organized social living, and referrals for special counseling are among the personnel functions that are aimed at making living quarters centers of learning and gracious living.[30, 31]

Achieving Physical and Mental Fitness. Administrators, teachers, and curriculum, personnel, and health workers need to combine forces to provide a healthful and safe environment; identify health assets and liabilities of individuals; adjust school or college programs to health resources of individuals; and foster the development of health regimens based upon knowledge by individuals of their health assets and liabilities and of physical and mental hygiene.

At all levels it is important that teachers detect evidences of need for referral to medical, psychiatric, or psychological services for study and planning with respect to special handicaps, such as vision, hearing, speech, and other medical or emotional problems. A major function of special personnel workers is to train teachers to identify those who need referral as well as to study and work therapeutically with some. There is little evidence as yet that students, generally, are receiving enough information about their own health resources to enable them to plan life regimens wisely to con-

28. Deborah Berman, "Evolving Patterns of Social Control at Brandeis University," *Journal of Educational Sociology*, XXVIII (April, 1955), 353-59.

29. *Student Government, Student Leadership, and the American College.* Edited by Eliot Freidson, Philadelphia: United States National Student Association, 1955.

30. Esther Lloyd-Jones and Margaret Smith, *Student Personnel Work as Deeper Teaching*, pp. 179-98. New York: Harper & Bros., 1954.

31. C. Gilbert Wrenn, *Student Personnel Work in College*, pp. 293-322. New York: Ronald Press, 1951.

serve and capitalize upon these resources. Health counseling is recognized as an essential part of a good college health service,[32] but not all colleges, and certainly not all public schools, have an adequate staff to make this possible.[33]

Guidance in Learning To Learn. There is evidence of a resurgence of efforts to improve learning methods. The newer approaches are on a broader basis than those that prevailed earlier. They include special classes in learning techniques that deal with motivation, study skills, effective reading, listening, thinking, and problem-solving and with evaluation of achievement. They relate this direct study to work in every class and enlist co-operation of all teachers. They are concerned with homework and parent participation in the process from early elementary-school years on through high school. At the college level, they include conditions in residence halls, special study-skills classes or units in orientation or general education, and laboratories or clinics for remedial work in reading and other techniques. These special services are also provided in public schools. Diagnostic and treatment services require the co-ordinated effort of health and personnel workers and the entire staff of an educational institution.[34]

Self-direction of a Life Plan. Vocational-planning and adjustment are major themes in an emerging life history, but they cannot be seen in true perspective except as part of a total life pattern including home, social, economic, civic, and religious aspects. For most students this pattern will include parent and sib relationships in the home; relationships with peers in work, play, organized groups, dating, and frequently marriage at the upper levels; economic problems of budgeting allowance, part-time work, or financial stringency in some instances; participation in school or college government and in community civic activities; religious affiliations; and, of course, their main job of study and class attend-

32. N. S. Moore and J. Summerskill, *Health Services in American Colleges and Universities.* Ithaca, New York: Cornell University Press, 1953.

33. Esther Lloyd-Jones and Margaret Smith, *op. cit.*, pp. 154-64; and C. Gilbert Wrenn, *op. cit.*, pp. 323-48.

34. Philip D. Cristantiello and James J. Cribben, "The Study-skills Problem," *Journal of Higher Education*, XXVII (January, 1956), 35-38; and "Homework" (Special Journal Feature), *National Education Association Journal*, XLVI (September, 1957), 365-74.

ance. For adults, the pattern encompasses the establishment of a home and the rearing of children; entrance into and progress in work; and the development of satisfying and creative outlets in civic, social, religious, and avocational activities. We should doubtless add continued education of some kind to keep abreast of change and certainly to plan for years beyond work life.

Frustrations and failures in meeting developmental tasks at any stage in life and innumerable crises and handicaps may result in difficulties that require special assistance to remove blocks to adequate self-realization. Experiences both within and outside the educational program contribute to growth in understanding of self and of life, in planning for balanced living, and in working out satisfying adjustments in all aspects of life.

The personnel service should function to help interpret all of these opportunities for understanding and for self-realization; help individuals formulate plans for achieving well-balanced lives; assist them to eliminate blocks and solve problems encountered in living. The first two types of service may be thought of as developmental, and the third as remedial. All three functions can serve as means of helping individuals develop sound techniques of studying and solving life problems and thereby acquire power in self-direction. Various group procedures and counseling are required at all levels to meet recurrent and emerging needs.

Fostering a Value System and Self-discipline. Longitudinal growth studies of children and adolescents have traced developmental patterns in ethical, religious, and philosophical outlook that afford significant clues to the importance of these growing value systems.[35] Psychological studies at various age levels yield different theories as to the sources of values but leave no argument as to their importance in personality development.[36] Intensive counseling with either youths or adults reveals the strong human desire to seek meaning in life through religious or secular paths.

The age-long argument as to whether character values can be

---

35. Arnold Gesell, Frances L. Ilg, and Louise Bates Ames, *Youth: The Years from Ten to Sixteen.* New York: Harper & Bros., 1956.

36. William F. Dukes, "Psychological Studies of Values," *Psychological Bulletin, LII* (1955), 24-50.

taught or caught should probably be answered, "Both." In early school years, there are innumerable opportunities to discuss the right and wrong, and the fair and unfair of realistic situations which may lead to guilt and anxiety or to unsocial attitudes and behavior if not faced in wholesome, accepting ways. Throughout high-school and college, there is need for discussion of perplexing personal and social problems, sometimes camouflaged to avoid undesirable embarrassment of individuals. These may take place in homerooms, guidance classes, informal advisory or residence-hall groups, and eventually in organized study of ethical, religious, and philosophical problems leading to the crystallization of a personal life philosophy that can grow with the years.

The growing value system is one essential consideration in the formulation of vocational and other life plans. When discipline problems are the focus of counseling with the purpose of searching for causes of misbehavior and planning a corrective program, the value system of the counselee as well as his frustrations and hostilities are involved. Rogers has observed that as a client with emotional problems becomes better adjusted, his attitudes toward his values change from rigidity through confusion to a realization that he may do much to shape his own values.[37] There is much difference of opinion regarding the desirable relationship of counselors to the discipline function. The view that discipline should be an educative, corrective, and growth-producing process seems to take root slowly. With self-direction a major goal of personnel work, we cannot fail to accept the challenge to foster self-discipline through growing value systems that harmonize individual and social welfare.

Identification and Treatment of the Exceptional. The term "exceptional" is applied here to all who do not benefit desirably from the usual educational procedures. Progress in identification of the mentally and physically handicapped as well as the gifted children and improved offerings of differentiated programs for all such pupils are now well under way. There is much less certainty as to methods of detecting, preventing, and treating the emotionally

37. Carl R. Rogers, *Client-centered Therapy: Its Current Practice, Implications, and Theory*, p. 31. Boston: Houghton-Mifflin Co., 1951.

handicapped. The solution of emotional and behavior problems is not merely referral to a specialist for diagnosis and therapy; it requires the "team approach" by personnel workers and the entire school staff. For some, direct services through psychological counseling or other therapeutic techniques are imperative and early treatment may prevent more serious difficulties later.

The study of *drop-outs*, such as the Holding Power Project in New York State, is identifying many vulnerables and intensifying preventive measures through personnel services and school-home-community team work. Programs at the college level often start with selective admissions and then run the gamut of general personnel services to remedial clinics, special counseling, and financial assistance.

The search for talent in scientific fields has aroused our awareness of the critical urgency of developing all talents inherent in our human resources. Studies of gifted individuals have yielded evidence that discrepancies between potentialities and achievement are often interrelated with personality trends that can be detected early in life.[38] Personnel services aimed at fostering wholesome personality growth may be the important link to insure that the talented are ready to benefit from their expanding opportunities in school and college programs.

Placement and Follow-up. These personnel functions not only serve students but help in the evaluation of training programs and in articulation between levels in the educational system. The U.S. Office of Education, in co-operation with an interdepartmental subcommittee on Transition from School to Work [39] has formulated a succinct statement of this transition process. It is described as extending over several years and as influenced by many forces in home, school, and community. It encompasses occupational planning and preparation, placement, adjustment, and progress in work.

38. Lewis M. Terman, "The Discovery and Encouragement of Exceptional Talent," *American Psychologist*, IX (1954), 221-30; Harry O. Barrett, "An Intensive Study of 32 Gifted Children," *Personnel and Guidance Journal*, XXVI (November, 1957), 192-94.

39. *Transition from School to Work.* Report of Subcommittee on Transition from School to Work of the Interdepartmental Committee on Children and Youth, and the Office of Education, U.S. Department of Health, Education, and Welfare. Washington: Government Printing Office, 1957.

It requires teamwork of all who contribute to these steps in the process. A comprehensive transition employment program is developing in the West Contra Costa Junior College and Richmond school districts (California) in co-operation with the state employment office, pertinent community agencies, employers, labor, and parents, directed toward common understandings, mutual services to youth, and the motivation of youth to prepare for participation in the work life of the community.

Follow-up is a time-consuming process that is not always a continuous, integral part of some personnel programs. Experimentation with a variety of techniques has shown some simple, impersonal procedures to be fairly effective, though interviews and fairly comprehensive questionnaires are usually considered more desirable. Experience has shown that preparation of graduates to understand the value of follow-up data through using information from former students about jobs and training opportunities ahead helps measurably to secure their co-operation in the follow-up process after leaving school.

Overview of Major Techniques

COUNSELING

The term *counseling* is used here to apply to all face-to-face relationships between two individuals in which one is performing a personnel role in relation to the other. These may range from brief, informal discussions to longer conferences in which the relationship is structured in some way. Wrenn had defined counseling as ". . . a dynamic and purposeful relationship between two people in which procedures vary with nature of the student's need but in which there is always mutual participation . . . with the focus upon self-clarification and self-determination by the student." [40]

Many aspects of counseling are being subjected to minute analysis and experimentation that are expanding the boundaries of scientific knowledge in a field that is still more of an art than a science. As we attempt to keep abreast of scientific contributions and use them in practice, we need caution to prevent preoccupation with

40. C. Gilbert Wrenn, *op. cit.*, p. 60.

the process and our roles in it from causing us to lose sight of the personalities we are serving.

Research has indicated that the personalities of the counselor and the counselee and the nature of their interactions in this communication process are important determiners of what happens and of the outcomes; [41] also, that the nature of the problems may influence the techniques used by the counselor. In an educational setting, any problem, such as choice of major, vocational planning, or some interpersonal difficulty, is likely to spread into other areas, and the technique may shift within a conference from one emphasis to another—directive or nondirective, informational, interpretive, or problem-solving. Perhaps the entire process should be considered as one of mutual problem-solving with an immediate goal the solution of a particular problem and the ultimate goal that of improved skill in tackling any problem. Counseling is recognized as an educational technique that should be available to all, not just those with special problems. Also, awareness is growing as to the close interrelationships between teaching in groups and counseling individually, each implementing the other, though the content of learning may be different—more objective in one and more subjective in the other.[42]

The personality of the counselor has been subjected to much study, and suggested requirements include emotional maturity; security; frustration-tolerance; loving concern for people; the understanding and objectivity that will enable him to enter naturally, spontaneously, and creatively into the situations met in counseling with attitudes of warm acceptance; and the desire to help the counselee explore and clarify his feelings and insights without threat of evaluation, to help him marshal, interpret, and synthesize needed information and new insights and gain perspectives to project planning toward solutions. It has been suggested wisely that the counselor must accept himself as an individual and project himself naturally into each situation rather than try arti-

---

41. "Symposium on Counselor Personalities in Counseling," *Journal of Counseling Psychology*, IV (Summer, 1957), 124-43.

42. C. Gilbert Wrenn, "Some Emotional Factors in Counseling," in *Guidance in the Age of Automation*, pp. 34-43. Edited by M. Eunice Hilton. Syracuse, New York: Syracuse University Press, 1957.

ficially to play varying roles. Co-operatively with the student, he must identify each problem and the factors that may be involved and structure the conference in the light of the problem, the expectations of the counselee, and his empathic awareness of the interpersonal relationships as the counseling proceeds. Tyler [43] has said aptly, "Each person constitutes for us a new adventure in understanding."

Preoccupation with the process of guiding learning in the counselee should not preclude that process of observation which may yield clues to problems that are not immediately evident in the intercommunication process. The good old case-study approach helps in noting evidences of need for referral to medical or other special services, or of new problems of which the counselee is unaware. All available, long-range cumulative records and data compiled in cross-section study will be brought into consideration by the trained counselor, regardless of how much is interpreted at any point with the counselee. The same theories of readiness applicable in teaching apply here, though technical terms are used in counseling and there is difference of opinion as to how far interpretation should go beyond the counselee's immediate awareness.

Units of discussion that appeared in recorded interviews in one research study [44] were classified in the following groups: (a) interpretation and discussion of test data; (b) interpersonal relations other than family; (c) family relations; (d) educational and vocational problems and planning; (e) self-reference—discussion of client attitudes, feelings, and concepts about himself; (f) study habits and skills. Analysis of the counseling methods employed in these units pointed to the possible differentiation of counselor style between two clusters: the *affective* composed of units b, c, and e; and the *cognitive* composed of units d and f. The researchers suggest that these differences in counselor style may offer a partial explanation of differences of opinion regarding "directive" and "nondirective" approaches. Research approaches to the evaluation

43. Leona Tyler, "The Initial Interview," *Personnel and Guidance Journal,* XXXIV (April, 1956), 466-73.

44. Robert Callis, Paul C. Polmantier, and Edward C. Roeber, "Five Years of Research on Counseling," *Journal of Counseling Psychology,* IV (Summer, 1957), 119-23.

of counseling have isolated numerous behavior variables that are being used to measure changes resulting from varied counseling techniques.

The tentative findings of research offer the busy counselor fruitful suggestions for evaluative observation. We need to keep abreast of research and theories, extract whatever leads we can from them and from our experience. In the uncharted areas we can only "plow in hope"—hope compounded of respect for each personality, integrity of desire to be helpful, faith in human potentialities for insight and growth, care not to unearth what is not yet ready for attention, and effort to shed light on those forces that are ready for healthy growth.

GROUP PROCEDURES

This term refers to any phase of personnel work carried on with groups of individuals rather than between counselor and counselee in the face-to-face interview. It includes instruction in classes, informal discussion groups, activities in extracurriculum and student-government areas as they relate to personnel objectives, and remedial and therapeutic services in groups. There is great diversity of organization and content but growing consensus as to the functions of group procedures in a personnel program.

These functions are: to provide opportunities for learning essential for self-direction in educational, vocational, and personal-social aspects of life; to provide opportunities for therapeutic effects of group experience through perspective gained from study of common human problems, and through the emotional release, increased insight into personality dynamics, and creative redirection of energy resulting from group study and experience related to these common problems in an atmosphere conducive to ease of communication and intragroup acceptance; and, to implement individual counseling through understanding of aspects of common problems, reduction of emotional barriers to facing of unique aspects, and preparation for effective participation in the counseling process. An important question is what can be done *only* or *more effectively* through counseling and group procedures, respectively, and how these two approaches can best be interrelated.

According to the judgments of state supervisors throughout

the country,[45] the homeroom set-up in public schools appears to prevail most widely as the medium for group services, with special classes ranking next, and core programs a close third. Estimates of programs that are emerging and that may prevail in the next ten or twenty years gave special courses the first rank, and comments in eleven cases emphasized the need for trained workers to carry on all phases of the group service. One described this trained worker as having interdisciplinary training in education, psychology, anthropology, sociology, and personnel and social work and visualized him as working with groups of thirty students in group and individual services.[46]

For *content* there is a wealth of material about common problems at various ages that should be supplemented by knowledge of the specific groups to be served. Many units or courses in general education deal with these human problems. Criticism has been directed to this so-called "life-adjustment" approach as being superficial and inconsequential as compared with acquisition of the heritage of the past. Actually, this service cannot function soundly without utilization of what we know about life, past and present, and some perspective on the future. Every area in the curriculum has implications for this life process. One personnel task is to help individuals apply knowledge of self and their world to the innumerable problems of living. This is no task for amateurs.

Social, student-body, and other extracurriculum activities provide many opportunities for living and learning democracy, fine human relations, and leadership and followership. Many so-called discipline problems involving groups and school regulations can be handled most effectively by group study in a well-organized guidance program. One of the most significant findings in group-dynamics research is that of the strong influence of group judgments upon individual attitudes and behavior. We can utilize profitably this important source of human motivation.

Methods in group guidance are as varied as teaching tech-

45. In questionnaire replies cited.

46. Donald J. Diffenbaugh, Director of Guidance Services, Division of Child Welfare and Guidance, State of Delaware.

niques.[47] They range from organized study to informal discussion, role playing, case conference, dramatics, play therapy, and group therapy. Many of these group procedures serve the personnel worker as well as the student. Play therapy, for example, provides a means of exploring attitudes and emotions of the young child who cannot yet verbalize his thoughts and feelings, of probing below the conscious level, as well as providing release of tensions and creative outlets for the child. Sociometric and observation techniques yield essential insights on group structure and individual roles.

These organized group procedures should be cumulative in nature, established at points where choices or adjustments are imminent, and should be closely tied in with counseling services. Outcomes in techniques of self-appraisal, planning, and self-direction may be more important than any specific information, choices, or plans that may accrue from the group experience. We have yet to test the full value of group experience combined with counseling throughout the entire educational span planned and conducted by trained workers.

Conclusions

Long-range perspective on personnel functions seems to resolve them into the task of facilitating a creative process, not just an educing of what is already there in each personality, nor just a feeding in of information with the expectation that the human thinking machine will click out answers. Rather, it is a slow process of nurturing a life about which we know only too little. We present this personality with opportunities, deduced from research and experience, to learn about human life and the surrounding world; we help him probe within himself to discover what we cannot reach from our external vantage point; we guide him in the development of skill in organizing and interpreting the resulting knowledge—awareness of his motivations, attitudes, feelings, his value standards and his perceptions of his environment, as well as objective facts about manifestations of self. We cannot follow in all its ramifications the process by which specific choices are made, life plans are formulated, and adjustments are projected. We can

47. Margaret E. Bennett, *op. cit.*, pp. 97-307.

find analogies in our own lives as we search for new lights on problems and find that solutions come often stealthily when we least expect them. Usually they do not seem to come without this intensive search. Perhaps this process within ourselves and those with whom we work is part of a universal creative process that goes on perpetually, and we are merely catalytic agents in keeping it moving ahead. If so, we need all the wisdom we can distill from research and experience and the humility that comes from awareness that we can neither determine nor know the ultimate direction of the process. Faith that there is meaning in every human life, hope that we can ever improve our services in fostering this emergent creative process, and a quality of charity with respect to our own and others' limited efforts are beacon lights that beckon us forward in the pursuit of our goals.

SUPPLEMENTARY REFERENCES

ARBUCKLE, DUGALD S. *Guidance and Counseling in the Classroom.* New York: Allyn & Bacon, 1957.

COTTINGHAM, HAROLD F. *Guidance in Elementary Schools: Principles and Practices.* Bloomington, Illinois: McKnight & McKnight, 1956.

FROEHLICH, CLIFFORD P. *Guidance Services in Schools.* New York: McGraw-Hill Book Co., Inc., 1958.

MARTINSON, RUTH A., and SMALLENBURG, HARRY. *Guidance in Elementary Schools.* Englewood Cliffs, New Jersey: Prentice-Hall, Inc., 1958.

MATHEWSON, ROBERT HENDRY. *Guidance Policy and Practice.* New York: Harper & Bros., 1955 (revised).

McDANIEL, H. B., and SHAFTER, G. A. *Guidance in the Modern School.* New York: Dryden Press, 1956.

OHLSEN, MERLE M. *Guidance: An Introduction.* New York: Harcourt, Brace & Co., 1955.

TYLER, LEONA. *The Work of the Counselor.* New York: Appleton-Century-Crofts, 1953.

WARTERS, JANE. *Personnel Work Today.* New York: McGraw-Hill Book Co., Inc., 1956 (revised).

CHAPTER VI

Internal and External Resources of the Personnel Staff

IRWIN A. BERG

Introduction

Before the personnel point of view takes root in an educational institution, the personnel staff often consists of one part-time person, who struggles to meet student needs by seeking help from a wide variety of outside sources. In these early stages of development the personnel job gets done, in one fashion or another, in so far as the lone personnel worker is effective in commandeering or cajoling aid from agencies or persons not directly identified with his professional function. But with acceptance of a personnel program there comes an increase in staff and facilities so that dependence upon outside agencies is reduced or, at times, virtually eliminated. Gradually, but inexorably, the personnel program becomes more self-contained.

Yet, to do the best personnel job, the personnel staff is, and will continue to be, dependent upon outside resources. This will be true no matter what the size of the personnel staff is. Certain persons and agencies can handle particular problems more efficiently and reach a better solution than an educational personnel worker, who, for certain problems, is operating at the marginal range of his training and experience. Thus, an effective personnel program cannot avoid dependence upon resources which are outside the local office. The burden of the present chapter is the *identification* and *mobilization* of these internal and external resources which may be utilized by the personnel staff. By using such resources, three significant advantages accrue:

1. There is direct benefit to the student. He receives competent assistance, and he usually receives it promptly without meaningless

side-excursions in areas unrelated to his needs. In a highly personal way, he sees his perplexities and uncertainties, which once loomed so large, gradually diminish to manageable proportions.

2. The personnel worker achieves breadth. He encounters new skills at work, fresh viewpoints, and different approaches with respect to student needs. To the extent that he uses resources outside his own office, he grows professionally because he must. Since he still has the responsibility for the student, he must keep informed of what is being done for the student and how it is being done. Thus, the increase in the student's capabilities is paralleled, to a degree, by an increase in the personnel worker's capabilities.

3. Liaison is effected between the community and the school and between administrative units within the school. School activities are community activities, but this fact is not realized until participation in school affairs by outside agency representatives creates a feeling of identification with the school. The personnel program is an ideal, constructive channel in this respect. Between units within the school administrative liaison exists, of course; however, the personnel program can provide a more functional and less formal means of meeting student needs. The other units of the school refer students to the personnel staff and, in turn, render assistance to certain students referred by the personnel staff.

Accordingly, the appropriate use of both internal and external resources can mean that more problems can be handled by the personnel staff, and they can be handled more effectively. Further, many little student problems never become big ones because, through interaction with the personnel staff, the referral sources become sensitive to student needs, and the student is often referred to the personnel staff before the problem gets out of hand. And there are always problems, problems in greater number than the personnel staff can comfortably handle.

In a review of studies concerned with the needs of students for guidance services, Mathewson noted that the results of a survey revealed that one grade-school pupil out of every three was regarded as a problem by his teachers. One out of every four was an intellectual misfit in his grade. Another study cited by Mathewson was concerned with high-school students. This group was deeply concerned with the future, with such problems as vocal expression, heterosexual adjustment, and social adequacy, among others. At the college level, similar problems existed. Thirty per cent of the students in various colleges desired but had not received help on personality problems; 23 per cent had similar, unsatisfied needs concerning vocational problems; while 18 per cent wanted but had not obtained help in choosing a program of study.[1] Beyond question, then, the problem of meeting student needs is poignantly with us, and it is with us at every educational level from first grade through college.

The problems of students will be with us, but it seems likely that during the next decade or so the activities of educational personnel workers will sporadically be called into question by the public press. There is hysteria on the educational horizon with respect to science training in America; however, sensible measures are being prepared on a national scale to remedy any inadequacies we may have in this respect. Nevertheless, as a result of the public anxiety, there may come a castigation of educational activities which are not directly immersed in the subject matter of the natural sciences. For example, at the close of 1957, Hale wrote, "This year they put the U.S.S. *Wisconsin,* the last of our battleships, away in mothballs, and the life-adjusters in education followed it soon after into oblivion." [2] It seems quite possible that *adjustment* will become a dirty word in the lay public's mouth. Any protests that life itself is a series of adjustments will not be heeded. The internal and external resources of the personnel staff may possibly come to be regarded as frivolities, not germane to the issues of intercontinental ballistics missiles. Beyond question, we need more science training, and we shall get it. Also, beyond question, people must learn to work together, whether in the laboratory or the legislature; and this learning experience is provided largely by the extracurriculum, wherein lies the major resources of the personnel worker.

For present purposes, the resources useful to the personnel staff may be summarized as follows:

1. R. H. Mathewson, *Guidance Policy and Practice,* p. 49 ff. New York: Harper & Bros., 1949.

2. William Harlan Hale, "This Year of Such Great Changes," *Reporter,* XVII, (December 26, 1957), 30.

1. Internal resources available to the personnel staff, i.e., those within the school situation.

   a) Informal and unstructured student groups, such as "cramming" sessions for tests, celebrity "fan" clubs, "listen to records" groups, "game of marbles after school."

   b) Partially structured groups primarily under student control, such as clubs, sand-lot ball teams, student councils, playground games, etc.

   c) Structured and partially structured groups under school direction or affiliation, such as the health service, the classroom, school plays, dormitories, YMCA, athletic and other teams, etc.

2. External resources available to the personnel staff, i.e., those outside of the school situation.

   a) Civic groups of varied aims and purpose, such as P.T.A., League of Women Voters, Rotary, Kiwanis, and similar clubs, chambers of commerce, etc.

   b) Professional and business organizations, such as medical societies, trade associations, unions, business and industrial firms, etc.

   c) Federal, state and municipal agencies, such as hospitals, employment offices, police departments, welfare offices, etc.

   d) Local groups of varied sponsorship and direction, such as United Givers, Red Cross, Boy and Girl Scouts, 4-H Clubs, churches, Salvation Army, etc.

   e) The home and neighborhood, such as family friends, relatives, and the parents themselves.

The remainder of the present chapter will center in a discussion of the various internal and external resources outlined above in terms of their value for the educational personnel worker. No attempt will be made to list all of the possible resources; for such a list, even without discussion, would be longer than the chapter itself. All resources are fluid, anyway, and they change in function with the passage of time. The Spanish Club one year may be excellent for practice in conversational Spanish, but the next year it may sponsor a series of flamenco-type dances but talk in English. Both last year's and this year's Spanish Club are good personnel resources but obviously do not serve the same student need. Thus, it is idle to assume that one can ever prepare a tabular list of student needs and then specify by name the resources which will meet each need. One can identify resources by function, but the functions will vary from group to group and from time to time within a group. It is at this point that the training and experience of the educational personnel worker has its *raison d'etre*. Were the personnel job merely one of consulting a printed table, only a clerk would be needed and the challenge of the personnel function would be lost for most present workers in the field.

In consequence, the significant task becomes one of illustrating the variety and kind of resources and how they may be useful to the personnel worker. No great concern need be attached to the name of a particular group or agency. Personnel resources, like roses, will smell as sweet if they serve student needs. Not every school, for example, will have an astronomy club, but every school has some similar student grouping which has equal value from the personnel point of view. The same applies, of course, to external resources useful to the personnel staff. A given town may not have a Kiwanis club, but it may have a civic development league, or something like it, which, from the standpoint of the school's personnel resource needs, can render the same service. A little ingenuity must sometimes be exercised by the educational personnel worker in order to identify the various internal and external resources since functions are sometimes obscured by names and titles. Be that as it may, there are resources in the school and the community; and the effort of seeking them out will be well repaid.

Internal Resources Available to the Personnel Staff

Within every educational organization there are a variety of internal resources, some of which are obvious in their usefulness to the personnel staff and some of which are equally useful but not obviously so. The obvious resources are usually those which are controlled by the school, such as the nurse's office or the health service; and the educational personnel worker is most likely to think of these first. Less often used, despite the fact that they may sometimes be more effective, are casual groups under student control. Often such student groups can make a contribution to the personnel program that agencies under school direction and control cannot make. For that reason it may be desirable to consider these somewhat neglected student groups first.

Informal and Unstructured Student Groups. Man is a social animal, and in a school setting some of the clearest evidence for the social nature of man is to be found in the casual groupings which students form. Some of these groups are so ephemeral that they hardly seem to be properly worthy of the name. The suggestion made in a high-school cafeteria or college dining hall, "Hey, guys, let's all go to the movie at the Palace tonight" results in a group, however kaleidoscopically transient it may be. The same is true of, "We're reviewing for the history test over at Ed's" or "Bridge game tonight at the center." The fact that such groups exist for but a single meeting and sometimes do not achieve their announced purpose does not mean they are useless from the personnel point of view. If the history-test review, for example, never gets around to history, it is unfortunate academically, but it may be quite valuable for the socially starved student. Thus, such casual groups with little or no structure must be considered a possible internal resource for the personnel staff in dealing with certain types of cases. Every school has its lonely ones, those students who wistfully linger on the social fringes, yearning to be one of the group but not quite knowing how. These casual groups often provide the first forward steps for improving social adjustment, since such groups typically make few demands upon their members, permitting each person to participate to the extent he wishes. Accordingly, when seeking to help such lonely ones, the personnel worker can first ascertain the extent to which the student enters into such casual groupings and then proceed to point out the value of being just one of the group.

Student Groups with Slight Degree of Structure. Besides these casual and informal student groups, which take temporary shape but once for some particular purpose, there are similar groups which are equally casual and equally informal; but they observe a fairly regular time and place of meetings during the school year. These groups usually make somewhat greater social demands upon their members, although no particular penalty is attached for non-participation. That is, rejection by such groups is rare, and, if it does occur, it does not commonly carry over to other groups nor is rejection irrevocable in the sense that blackballing by a fraternity is. These groups often have a descriptive phrase rather than a name for identification, i.e., "The Goal Post every day at 10 for coffee," "Jokes and cokes in the lounge on Mondays," "Tennis on Tuesdays," etc. Such groups are essentially centered around particular student interests; and, as Strang remarks, "Since groups such as these bear the strongest resemblance to the associations of adult life, they may be expected to be the best preparation for adult group living." [3]

While the present purpose is to indicate how certain informal student groups represent valuable internal personnel resources, it is probably worth while to mention, at least parenthetically, that some of these groups are capable of creating the very problems that bring the student to the personnel worker. The roots of academic failure and its ensuing problems may sometimes be found in the gang that gathers every evening in the neighborhood pool hall. More serious problems may develop from the "rock 'n' rollers" who learn to use marijuana or other drugs to heighten their responsivity. Beyond question, certain student groups can create problems, just as other groups may help alleviate them.

Most informal groups, of course, can be used constructively by the personnel worker. At first glance it may appear that the chief contribution of such groups lies in the acquisition of social competence. Yet the opportunities for personal growth are equally available. The same group may serve a variety of individual needs. For one student, listening to classical music on Sunday afternoons with a group of other "squares" means a chance to enjoy a situation which makes no demands beyond his social skill. For another student the same gathering is a means of broadening his intellectual horizons in a cherished area. For still another the music affords a welcome emotional release. In consequence, it matters little whether a particular informal group is concerned with art or athletics, with church-going or coffee-drinking. What does matter is whether the student can achieve, through the group, a measure of maturation in personal and social terms. If he can, the group has potential value as an internal personnel resource.

Usefulness of Student Groups Not Always Apparent. No informal student group should be dismissed as being without value to the personnel worker until a careful scrutiny has been made. A "jokes and cokes" group, for example, had as its announced purpose

3. Ruth Strang, "Education through Guided Group Experiences," in *Student Personnel Work in College,* p. 205. Edited by C. G. Wrenn. New York: Ronald Press, 1951.

the exchange of the so-called horror jokes currently popular with high-school and college students.[4] Despite the frivolity of purpose, this group was of real help to at least one person, a transfer student who had been experiencing an incipient depression, the causes of which were never clinically identified. Paradoxically, the horror jokes and the boisterous camaraderie were of direct assistance in enabling him to overcome a serious personal problem. Of course, this is not to say that the value of informal groups is limited to therapeutic benefit in the clinical sense. The chief contribution of such groups is the opportunity they afford for normal, personal, and social development. This is their greatest value as a resource for the personnel worker.

Partially Structured Groups Primarily under Student Control. In every school there is a variety of interest groups which have an announced purpose and a regular time of meeting. Such student groups have some structure in the sense that they select officers or committees and have specific duties assigned to certain members. The groups with relatively greater structure are those which have a continuing function during the school year. The student council, clubs, fraternities, and the like are examples. Other groups of less rigid structure are essentially task forces for a single occasion, such as a dance or picnic, and have no function which continues beyond the event. From the personnel worker's point of view, this distinction between different groups in terms of structure and continuing function, while not critical, is a useful one in that the different groups provide different learning opportunities. That is, different kinds of benefit accrue to the student from participating in each of the types of grouping.

All groups, of course, offer passive, spectator participation; how-

---

4. It is perhaps worth while reminding the educational personnel worker that such "horror stories" seem to appear in cycles and will probably continue to do so. About 30 years ago, they took the form of popular songs placed in a gruesome context—i.e., "What song did John the Baptist sing to Salome?" Answer, "I ain't got no body." Twenty years ago the "little Audrey" and "little moron" stories were cast in a similar mold. The current horror stories appear to be just as gruesome but no worse than those of previous decades. Example, "Mary, if you don't stop yanking your brother's arm, I'll close the coffin." The aghast adult may take what solace he can in the awareness that next year the fad will shift to absurd puns or something similar but less macabre.

ever, active participation in the affairs of the group is another matter. Those groups with a continuing function typically have duties that are carefully spelled out for the active participants, and the responsibilities are spread over a period of time. By contrast, the single-event type of student grouping usually offers more opportunity for exercising ingenuity and creative effort, but the work is concentrated, often hectic, during a relatively short time span. The secretary of the French club, for example, must keep the records of the club's activities, a task which involves no heavy burden in time for any one week, though the total number of hours for the school year may be considerable. On the other hand, the decorations committee for the Spring Dance will work at a frenzied pace for a few weeks, often ignoring class preparations or even cutting classes as a consequence. Obviously, a marginal student may be hurled into academic oblivion by the work of the decorations committee while active participation in the French or chemistry club may provide for social growth and also strengthen his work in those fields.

It is at such decision points where guidance from the educational personnel worker is most critical. He knows the student and his needs; and he is able, therefore, to be of direct assistance in helping the student arrive at a wise choice. Thus the basic concerns of the personnel worker with respect to such activities may be expressed as: What does the student need, and what can he handle without detriment?

One student may need to learn to accept continuing responsibility, but he is not ready for it. For him, appropriate guidance will center in making it possible for him to achieve success, first, with shorter-term tasks and, later, with longer-term responsibilities. In the case of another student the problem may be one of entry, that is, acceptance as an active rather than a passive member of a group. He is capable of doing a job for the group, but no one knows this, and he does not know how to make his talents visible. The guidance most likely to be profitable to him will involve an appreciation of entry tasks. The duties of a clean-up committee for a dance, for example, are prosaic in nature; yet volunteers are eagerly welcomed. Every student group has similar jobs which need doing but which are not eagerly sought after. Yet, they provide entering wedges for increased responsibilities for other tasks and, in consequence, for increased personal growth.

Structured and Partially Structured Groups under School Direction or Affiliation. Thus far consideration has been given to types of groups under student control. Such internal resources have varying degrees of school support, ranging from little or none to direct support in the form of money or faculty advisers. Yet the fundamental control of such group activities rests in the hands of the students themselves. There are a number of other internal resources for the educational personnel worker which are quite definitely under school direction. The full list of such school-directed agencies and activities would be very long; however, a few may be mentioned: new student orientation programs, the health service, the dean's office, the student union, dormitories, the school newspaper, dining halls, student placement and employment, classes, school athletics, debate and other teams, the student loan office. In addition, there are other agencies which have full school support in an affiliative sense; but final control rests elsewhere. Student religious centers, campus churches, YMCA, and YWCA are examples.

Of particular importance is the classroom teacher. Whether in first grade or the Senior year in college, the teacher commonly has more opportunity to observe the behavior of students under a variety of conditions. Thus, the teacher is a primary resource of the educational personnel worker. Parents are frequently defensive or oblivious with respect to difficulties their children are encountering. But the teacher usually is able to provide objective information and often can be the catalyst for working with the parents of a student where such action is essential.

The effectiveness of these internal personnel resources will vary in terms of how they are operated. In a college setting, for illustration, the dormitories may have proctors, whose duties are essentially custodial in nature. On other campuses dormitory supervision may center chiefly around the acquisition of social graces, recreational activities, and the like. Even in the educational personnel field, services may vary from "test 'em and tell 'em" in one school to a full counseling program, complete with follow-up, in another. Accordingly, the use a personnel worker can make of a given internal resource will be governed by how the agency or activity functions. This will necessarily vary from one school to another and from time to time in a particular school.

Variability in Structure of School Resources. Some school agencies are so specifically structured that nothing much need be said about them since their functions and resource value is perfectly clear to the personnel staff. The student health service is such an agency, although, as Farnsworth observes, there is room even here for considerable improvement in the extent of such services.[5] Much the same might be said of student loan or student employment offices. While such agencies vary in efficiency of operations, what they do and how they do it is usually well understood by the personnel staff. Further, such agencies usually are exclusive in function. If a student problem involves his health, a loan, or a job, he can be referred to only one agency within the school aegis. He goes to the health service if he is sick; to the speech clinic if he stutters. The only alternative is likely to be some private, nonschool arrangement. By contrast, a student with a social problem may have fifty or more school groups which can render aid. Therefore, attention may be most profitably turned to school agencies and activities of less limited function.

Certain school activities are of great significance for the personnel staff; for they can prevent some student problems or simplify early recognition of them, thereby easing the load of the personnel office. The orientation program is an activity of this sort. The student has an opportunity to learn what services are available to him beyond the classroom instruction he expects. Some schools, of course, use the orientation period merely to introduce the administrative bigwigs and then exhort the captive audience ". . . to seize the opportunity; the future is in your hands." But other institutions, of which the University of Illinois is an example, have a thoroughgoing introduction to school life, complete with a full testing and counseling program.[6] The advantage of such carefully thought-out programs is that they reduce the necessity of a student's

5. Dana L. Farnsworth, "College Health Services—Reality and Ideal," *Personnel-O-Gram*, XII, (October, 1957), 11-14.

6. H. W. Bailey, W. M. Gilbert, and I. A. Berg, "Counseling and the Use of Tests in the Student Personnel Bureau at the University of Illinois." *Educational and Psychological Measurement*, VI (Spring, 1946), 37-60.

waiting until he gets into serious trouble before he finds out what help he can get.

When the student does appear at the personnel office for help, the personnel worker must arrive at an understanding of the student's needs before he can make use of the internal resources available to him. A student may obviously gain from a particular activity; yet he may not be ready for it without some intervening experience. If a student is a poor dancer, for example, he had better acquire this particular skill before attending the winter formal. In other cases, too rapid entry into a particular activity may threaten the student and produce a setback. Some school teams, whether they be athletic, debate, or chess, may have such an effect, although the understanding of the team coach is the all-important variable. As in all such situations, the wisdom and the insight of the personnel worker is critical in determining how the personal growth of a given student may best be facilitated. Some students can plunge into any activity and profit thereby. If rebuffs come, they are taken in stride. Other students may be thrown into a panic or may withdraw unhealthily into a shell of isolation. It is in rendering the appropriate aid in such cases that the educational personnel worker justifies the provision for his professional appointment.

External Resources Available to the Personnel Staff

In all probability, the greatest waxing and waning in the availability of educational personnel resources occurs in the part played by agencies or institutions which are outside the school situation. The internal resources, such as the student- or school-directed activities described earlier, are conveniently at hand and play a fairly regular part in the lives of students and personnel staff alike. But external resources shift in emphasis, in availability, and in management, with the result that a given group which once was so helpful to the personnel staff now has nothing to contribute. The local community booster's club, for example, may have been previously immersed for five years in helping the physically handicapped, finding jobs, or raising funds for medical aid for these unfortunates. Now the same group is devoted to mobilizing community support for a city park, whereas its earlier interests in the physically handicapped may have subsided. While there are exceptions, this pattern is a common one. After a series of such experiences, the personnel worker tends to generalize the previous episodes and look more closely at the resources of his own office or his school on the logical premise that half a loaf is better than none.

But while external resources ebb and flow in their usefulness to the personnel worker, the broad configuration of service does endure, though not necessarily with the same group. When one resource ebbs, another flows, and it is up to the personnel worker to find out which group is in what stage. Sometimes a particular group can be aroused to help, especially if a project is presented in specific terms. Enthusiasm may lag, for example, with a general "Support Your School" campaign; but it may be a huge success when it is presented in concrete terms such as, "We need two dads for volunteer playground assistants" or "What mothers can help with costumes for the school play?" Indeed, many community groups are looking for just such projects. The members usually won't give support for an indefinite period of time; but when one group drops a project, another group can be found to pick it up.

Personnel Resources Found Everywhere. In any geographical area, the number of groups, agencies, and even individuals whose activities have relevance as personnel resources are myriad. Some of them will be civic groups of varied aims and purpose, such as the P.T.A., League of Women Voters, Chamber of Commerce, Taxpayers League, American Association of University Women, clubs like Rotary, Kiwanis, Lions, to mention but a few. There are also professional and business organizations such as medical, dental, law, and other societies as well as trade associations, unions, and the like. In addition, there are a host of other groups, including business and industrial firms, state and municipal agencies, federal agencies, among others. Finally, there are community groups of varied sponsorship and scope, such as the Boy or Girl Scouts, 4-H Clubs, United Givers, the Red Cross, Salvation Army, social welfare centers, local hospitals, summer camps, and many others. A mere listing of such organizations for a typical city could cover many pages. Beyond question, far more resources are available than the personnel staff can readily use in most sections of the country.

The task before the personnel staff lies in using the legion of possible resources effectively. The personnel worker must learn to thread the maze of resource utility and pertinence for his professional task, and this takes time. He learns which groups welcome unskilled volunteer workers such as students and which do not. Some outside organizations function as personnel resources by giving services, others by giving things. Most groups will do something when they understand a specific need and how they can help fill it. It may be furnishing a speaker on some specified topic, organizing a tour through an industrial plant, offering advice, or supplying something material. But whatever it is, it is a resource if it furthers the efforts of the personnel worker in helping students.

School and Community Groups Offering Mutual Assistance. It should be kept in mind that more than a benefit in the terms of personnel resources accrues from contact with community groups. Because of its participation, the outside group develops a degree of identification with the school, thereby promoting closer school-community relations. Some student activities which the educational personnel worker can foster are especially valuable in this respect. An excellent example is found in the projects organized by Cottingham in Paris, Illinois.[7] Groups of high-school students interviewed over two-hundred professional, business, and industrial leaders for the purpose of gathering information about jobs and job opportunities in their home-town area. Other groups of students, under Cottingham's direction, completed a survey of midwest post-high-school education at trade schools, business colleges, technical schools and universities. The students organized their data, wrote up summaries of their findings, and prepared a mimeographed book as a final product. Thus, friendly liaison with community leaders was established, the students who participated gained practical experience as well as job information, and the report of their survey was of immediate use to other students and to people in the community.[8] This is but one example of many possible projects that have distinct value as resources for the educational personnel worker.

Relating Personnel Resources to Student Needs

Integral with the discussion thus far has been the relationship of

7. Harold F. Cottingham, "Your Job." Paris, Illinois: The Author, 1941 (mimeographed).

8. Harold F. Cottingham, "Your College." Paris, Illinois: The Author 1941 (mimeographed).

personnel resources to student needs. Resources do not functionally stand apart from the needs they serve, nor does the consideration of the one appropriately stand apart from the other. Thus, the last section of the present consideration of internal and external personnel resources has significance for a final emphasis and elaboration of the relationship of resources and need.

Whatever the student does outside of his prescribed course of studies is, by definition, extracurricular and, by implication, a source of potential growth experience. He meets problems and usually solves them, sometimes alone and sometimes with help. But whether he soars lightly over the hurdles that his problems present or whether he limps over them, he is achieving personal growth and adding to his armory of useful skills. He is experiencing what Cowley calls "Social maturation through the extracurriculum." [9]

Student Needs Not Isolated. A safe generalization for the personnel worker is that, whatever needs a student has, they do not stand alone. The lack of academic competency has a direct bearing on the choice of vocation. A religious problem can affect social adjustment. Emotional upheavals can create needs in any area. So while we may talk of student needs as if only a single area were involved, this is only for the sake of convenience.

Most student needs may be satisfied in one or more of the following four ways:

1. By direct experience as an active participant, as getting a part-time job, joining a club or team, or working on the school paper.
2. By information supplied from various sources, as the library, interviews with a person of special competence, the classroom, or lectures.
3. By getting something done for him, as fitting a hearing aid, glasses, or prosthetic appliance; obtaining needed surgery, or a scholarship.
4. By personal counseling or psychotherapy as offered by a person of appropriate training for dealing with emotional problems of students.

Once a student need has been identified, the various resources can be appraised by the personnel worker in terms of what each resource can contribute. A problem of vocational choice, for ex-

9. W. H. Cowley, "Jabberwocky versus Maturity," in *Trends in Student Personnel Work*, p. 350. Edited by E. G. Williamson. Minneapolis: University of Minnesota Press, 1949.

ample, might sensibly begin with psychological interest and aptitude testing and be followed by reading about certain occupations. The student might then arrange for interviews with persons who are in the occupations he is interested in. Of course, the personnel worker might arrange such interviews; however, when possible, the student should be encouraged to do this himself since such experiences aid the maturation process. Finally, the student might, with the assistance of the school placement service, obtain a job which will provide at least peripheral contact with the occupations under consideration. Medical fields, for example, use orderlies, nurse's aides, attendants, clerks, and the like, all of which permit close observation of a variety of medical specialities. Other jobs, particularly trades, offer direct participation to varying degrees. The carpenter's or painter's helper actually does some of the work done by the master tradesman.

Direct experience is of inestimable value in eliminating or reducing prevalent warped ideas about jobs. The messenger in a law office doesn't see a lawyer as spending his days delivering impassioned speeches to a spellbound jury. Unlike the high-school debater who plans to enter law, the messenger *knows* that lawyers spend most of their days examining papers and talking privately to clients. The same holds true for any occupation; hence the soundest basis for a vocational decision includes the opportunity to acquire knowledge about a given job by reading and interviews and then by experience.

The Resource at Hand Not Necessarily the Best Available. At times, the problem of relating available personnel resources to student needs is deceptively simple. That is, certain resources are so plainly in view that, unwittingly, the personnel worker may choose what lies immediately at hand. Scholarship aid is a case in point. All colleges offer scholarships, as do various foundations and government agencies. Many of these are well advertised and so are likely to be familiar to the personnel worker. Yet often much more generous financial support, ranging from full tuition to tuition and all expenses, can be obtained from little-known sources. The problem is to ferret out such sources and relate them to the student's background. There are, in some areas for example, scholarships for ex-newsboys, for descendants of World War I veterans, for Indians, for students planning to enter missionary work; there are also scholarships offered by unions, business firms, fraternal lodges, and many others.[10] A little looking about can be highly rewarding.

A task of utilizing certain resources may be a delicate one because of the nature of a student's problems. Religious problems are frequently of this order. A student tormented by feelings of guilt or conflicts concerning his system of beliefs will need wise and patient help. Thus, a religious group which had a splendid social activity program nevertheless bungled the case of a student who was writhing in a slough of religious uncertainties. Instead of help, he was handed a *Bible* and sternly admonished to read it and forget his questions. His need was for tolerant understanding, not off-the-cuff exhortation. The personnel worker in this case should have had better knowledge of the resource person to whom he referred the student.

Marital problems among students, at least at the college level, have become increasingly common in recent years. These problems, like those involving religion, require great sensitivity on the part of the personnel worker. In most instances the external resource will be where specialized professional services are to be had, as a marriage counseling center, a psychological clinic, or the like. When such referral is not feasible, the personnel worker will have to employ the resources available to him. As is always the case, he will need first to obtain as thorough an understanding of the problem as possible. The difficulty is likely to be manifold, not due to a single cause. Finances will be a problem for some, and a job for either husband or wife or even both may be arranged through the placement office. Religion may be involved, and still another referral resource will be needed. Some of the difficulties may be symbolic of the real problem area. Poor academic performance, for example, may be consciously or unconsciously attributed to the marriage, representing a source of friction. Indeed, the possible complexities of such problems are such that if progress is not made in a reasonable length of time, the personnel worker should make a determined effort to locate a specialized professional resource.

Specialized Help Sometimes Necessary. Ordinarily, educational

10. Scholarships are available for nonsmoking girls, for boys with such surnames as Anderson, Baxendale, Borden, Bright, DeForest, Downer, Haven, Murphy, Pennoyer, and others, according to *Time*, February 24, 1958, page 85.

problems such as study skills are grist for the educational personnel worker's mill, since these involve his own area of special training. Available internal resources are quite familiar to the personnel worker, and referral, when necessary, for remedial reading or spelling, for example, is quickly made. Some educational problems, however, will involve obstacles that external resources can best remove. Where poor vision, hearing, or other physical handicaps influence poor academic performance, civic groups can usually be interested in supplying the funds for remedial treatment or equipment. Other educational problems are the outgrowth of a lack of motivation on the part of the student. Such problems are highly involved in a number of instances, and referral to a psychologist or psychiatrist may be necessary because the basic difficulty is rooted in a serious personality disorder. But it seems safe to say that in a majority of cases this is not true. For some students, poor academic performance is an expression of rebellion against parents, the school, and so forth. Often such students have not identified with their peers; and for them, participation in student-directed activities provides a channel for better academic as well as social adjustment. Other students may have academic difficulties as a consequence of too close identification with student groups. For them it is all activities and no study. Their need is for a sense of proportion which often can be supplied by a time budget. Here the personnel worker is not using internal resources; rather he is using his knowledge about such resources and how they may interfere with the academic adequacy of the student who participates in them.

Increase of Personnel Resources in the Future. The use of various resources is a test of the educational personnel worker's ingenuity and a sign of professional maturity. There was a time when the personnel worker often hesitated to employ such assistance on the false assumption that it was a sign of weakness and reflected discredit upon his competency. Now the opposite is true. The effective use of personnel resources has become a hallmark of the professionally trained person. The coming decades will see the use of personnel resources burgeon and their application become more precise and less characterized by global "cut-and-try" approaches. There are virtually no carefully designed researches on the use of personnel resources at present, but it seems a safe prediction that the next quarter-century will have hundreds of such studies. Some researches will enable us to understand scientifically the broad process of social interaction while others will enable us to fathom the physiological bases of both individual and social responses. This will not complicate the problem of the personnel worker, although it will increase his use of outside resources. It will also increase his understanding of people and his ability to help them when they need assistance.

All in all, the basic personnel function becomes one of *understanding*. There is first the understanding of the student's needs. Then there is the understanding of the nature and function of the various internal and external personnel resources. Finally, there is the understanding of how student needs and the available resources may be related smoothly and meaningfully.

REFERENCES

BERG, I. A. and GILBERT, W. M. "Discarding the White-Collar Halo," *School and College Placement,* IV (October, 1943), 57-60.

BORRESON, J. B. "The Application of Personnel Methods to University Housing Procedures," *Educational and Psychological Measurement,* VII (March, 1947), 583-93.

CALLIS, R.; POLMANTIER, P. C.; and ROEBER, E. C. *A Casebook of Counseling.* New York: Appleton-Century-Crofts, 1955.

CORNEHLSEN, VIRGINIA. "Overview of Orientation," *Journal of the National Association of Deans of Women,* X (January, 1947), 92-94.

GARDNER, D. H. "Student Personnel Work—Student Organizations" *in Encyclopedia of Educational Research,* pp. 1345-47. Edited by W. S. Monroe. New York: Macmillan Co., 1950.

HAHN, M. E., and MacLEAN, M. S. *General Clinical Counseling in Educational Institutions.* New York: McGraw-Hill Book Co., 1950.

HORROCKS, J. E. *The Psychology of Adolescence.* Boston: Houghton-Mifflin Co., 1951.

KITSON, H. D., and NEWTON, J. B. *Helping People Find Jobs.* New York: Harper & Bros., 1950.

PEPINSKY, H. B., and PEPINSKY, PAULINE N. *Counseling Theory and Practice.* New York: Ronald Press, 1954.

ROBINSON, F. P. *Principles and Procedures in Student Counseling.* New York: Harper & Bros., 1950.

STRANG, RUTH. *Group Activities in College and Secondary School.* New York: Harper & Bros., 1946 (revised).

SUPER, D. E. *Appraising Vocational Fitness.* New York: Harper & Bros., 1949.

TYLER, LEONA E. *The Work of the Counselor.* New York: Appleton-Century-Crofts, 1953.

WILLIAMSON, E. G. *Trends in Student Personnel Work.* Minneapolis: University of Minnesota Press, 1949.

WRENN, C. G. *Student Personnel Work in College.* New York: Ronald Press, 1951.

CHAPTER VII

Organization of Personnel Services

HERMAN L. SHIBLER

Introduction

In order to more clearly define elements of the following discussion, it is essential that the combination of the various services dealing with one or more aspects of pupil and student adjustment be specifically defined. Personnel services deal with the variety of services offered in elementary and secondary school systems and those offered to the student in institutions of higher learning.[1] The organization of these many services will stem from the similar pupil needs and from the same desire to help the teacher and the learner produce a more receptive atmosphere for learning. Whether the learner is an elementary-school child, a high-school student, or a college student will, in most cases, be immaterial to this discussion. The differences, which normally would involve the age and the level of education of the learner, are not being ignored but are merely being placed in the proper light in view of the intent of this discussion.

Many of the terms of this discussion will, for the most part, be simplified to include those persons who perform a similar service, whether to the younger pupil or to the older student. As the various topics are given some treatment, this similarity of function will tend to reveal itself and to point out the fact that need for and desire to render personnel services to the learner will usually evolve from the same motivations.

1. A. O. Heck, *Administration of Pupil Personnel.* Boston: Ginn & Co., 1929.

Patterns of Organization

THE PERSONNEL STAFF

Most personnel staffs dealing with the pupil are specially trained to operate within a specific area of need. This is not to say that a member of the personnel staff works independently of all other members of the staff. The qualifications and the training of such staff members are logically grounded and derive from a need for service rather than from historical reference. In every case, whether the basic organizational type is of the multiple or unit variety, there is a head, director, or administrative co-ordinator.[2] This staff member performs many functions, but his main orientation is toward administration of a division having as its basic task the rendering of one or more personnel services. The director of this division must deal with the interpretation of established policy and is the final authority for the determination of relative jurisdiction of the services offered by the division.

Included in the services of the personnel division is a function devoted to the suggested solutions and recommendations for action which will tend to alleviate mental or psychological conditions blocking learning or producing situations which tend to prevent others from learning.[3] The usual title of such a person is "psychologist," but he may also perform services under the general classification of "student counselor" or adviser. It is essential that the staff member be an integrated part of the division and not act entirely on his own. Actually, it would be impossible under current practices for the psychologist to function without direct referral from the teacher or for the recommendations of the psychologist to be carried out without the understanding and co-operation of all other members of the staff and the teaching service. As a further statement of his function and service, it is essential that the psychologist not be too closely oriented toward a clinical approach

2. C. E. Erickson and G. E. Smith, *Organization and Administration of Guidance Services.* New York: McGraw-Hill Book Co., 1947.

3. D. J. Wiens, "Organization of Pupil Personnel Services in City School Systems." Doctoral dissertation, Western Reserve University, 1941.

but that he have an understanding of the influence of education and its aims.

Closely connected with the function of a psychological service is the social service.[4] The social aspect and the psychological aspect of service frequently combine to deal with a specific case. The social service worker, who may be identified by a number of different names, e.g., "attendance officer," "home visitor," "truant officer," or "school social worker," deals with the needs which arise from problems exhibited by those pupils who, through various behaviors inside and outside of school, are not learning. Usually, the contacts made through the social worker will lead to the need for other personnel services. Many of the services which are rendered by the personnel service will frequently stem from a case under investigation by the social service section. Training of the worker must be of the highest standard. A specific professional course in social work leading to the Master's degree is considered a necessity.

A fourth aspect of the personnel staff may take a variety of forms, but basically it will include a supervisor who devotes time to the administration and functioning of classes for pupils who would not normally profit from regular class placement. These classes are usually designated "special education." This service staff is made up of teachers and principals specially trained for the task.

Having cared for the specific problems of the learning situation from a psychological standpoint, catered to the social service aspects of the pupils' life, and designated special classes for those pupils needing special care, another service of the personnel staff dealing with the medical and dental health of the pupil can be defined. This service is administered in a fashion to suit the needs and the limitations of the particular system. The "medical supervisor" is generally under the jurisdiction of both the school system and the local health authorities. At a higher level in education, the medical service may operate independently. Whatever the arrangement might be, the person so selected must be able to practice within a medical and dental framework. Frequently, state law governs this aspect of

4. *Visiting Teacher Service Today: A Study of Its Philosophy and Practice in the United States.* Washington: American Association of Visiting Teachers, 1940.

service, and limitations of the service will reflect these regulations. In most cases, these laws control the physical examination and immunization of the pupil.

The personnel staff will usually include a professional person whose main function is the gathering and analysis of various data, designed to aid in the planning for the future of the pupil. This member is commonly called a "director of research"; however, in the strictest sense of the word, he may be more devoted to the analysis of data and thereby closely resemble, in function, a specialized statistician. Pupil accounting, census, the evaluation and measurement of pupil achievement, pupil records, and the many aspects covered by the need for clear planning and those aspects of the pupil-accounting control covered by the legal requirements of state reimbursement will fall under the control of the research director.[5] The training and background of this member of the staff will not be governed by regulation but will be dictated by the needs of the particular school system. In some instances this staff member will act as assistant to the co-ordinator of the personnel services.[6]

Another staff member whose title is usually "guidance director" will function in co-operation with the psychologist and the social worker. A major portion of the guidance director's time is spent in direct contact with the pupil to help plan an educational and vocational program. This member of the personnel staff serves to integrate the services offered by many of the other members of the personnel staff. Training of this individual is clearly defined as guidance training by the institutions of higher learning. All aspects of this position will be direct guidance work. Learning problems of the mental, physical, and social type will come under his notice and, according to the severity of the problem, will be handled through the co-operation of the more specialized services of this division.

Rather than list further members of the personnel staff, it will be more expeditious to state that wherever and whenever a person-

5. A. E. Traxler, "A Cumulative Record Form for Elementary Schools," *Elementary School Journal*, XL (September, 1939), 45-54.

6. Joseph C. Payne, "The Responsibilities of a Research Director in a Public School System, *Educational Administration and Supervision*, XLII (November, 1956), 398-402.

nel problem arises, and depending upon the quantity and quality of such problems, a service should be formed. Flexibility, which is a necessity in the modern concept of personnel services, will be implied more than once in the body of this discussion. If the functions of personnel are not completely flexible and have a tendency to become rigid in their function, the service will lose its vitality and, hence, will cease to give the service for which it was originally intended. The description of the members of the staff of a personnel service will always include this quality and will dictate the need for complete and efficient multiple-communication channels whereby all the services rendered can be brought into play at the proper time and in the proper way.[7]

In regard to the formation of personnel services based upon need and urgency of the problem area, it is advantageous to illustrate the desirability to exercise flexibility of service. If, for example, it has been evident to those dealing with the learning situation that chronic reading problems have begun to occur and that the problems cannot be handled satisfactorily in the regular class situation, then a service may be formed which will deal with these problems efficiently and expeditiously. Such a service should be properly and professionally staffed. It might, to continue the illustration, be called "The Reading Clinic." If, in the course of dealing with these problems, the causes and sources of such problems are corrected, the service may then be discontinued.

Giving service in this fashion does demand flexibility of organization. The principle of flexibility can dictate a temporary mingling of the service function as, for example, when a special type of student has enrolled in the school and, in order to properly plan the program of the student, special evaluation, interpretation, and guidance is needed. Such involvement of service may be only temporary but should not be considered less important in function.

FUNDAMENTAL PATTERNS OF ORGANIZATION

Unit or Multiple Organization. The methods of organizing personnel services can broadly be grouped into three main plans:

---

7. *Encyclopedia of Educational Research.* Edited by W. S. Monroe. New York: Macmillan Co., 1950.

1. The totally disassociated set of services, each mutually exclusive in function and acting as completely autonomous units without reference to each other, can be considered as one extreme of the plans which one may observe in personnel organization.[8] It is true that no formally organized system will exhibit all the extremes dictated by such a plan but, in the light of function, institutions of higher learning may seem to follow some of the aspects of the unit plan.

2. The second type of plan can be described as a complete multiple plan.[9] This type, which utilizes the close-knit team system, treats each problem and case with a thoroughness that would be considered unusual by any evaluator of administrative systems. Unfortunately, this type of organization is rarely found, owing to a lack of talent, training, and resources. The size of such an operation necessary to maintain the complete functioning of the multiple-service-approach plan would dictate such costs and staff requirements as to make it impossible. Another difficulty which always arises in such close-knit systems is the overtreatment of problems which might otherwise be more efficiently and economically dealt with by a single, well-trained staff member. The multiple team-type organization of a personnel service is disposed to thoroughness but will tend to be inefficient and, in many cases, will not be able to accept or respond to co-ordinated administrative necessity. The multiple plan can be regarded as the other extreme of the continuum of personnel service plans of organization.

3. The third, more reasonable plan takes the middle way. In truth, it may be regarded as a hybrid of the two preceding plans, but this description may be an oversimplification. The development of this service plan does result from taking the best things from both, the unit and multiple plans, but the result is definitely more than the mere sum of such components. The system, when efficiently administered, is able to treat the proper problems with the team approach, while other more administratively oriented problems may be dealt with in an efficient manner. Whether this

8. J. LeM. Schultz, "An Analysis of Present Practices in City Attendance Work." Doctoral dissertation, University of Pennsylvania, 1938.

9. D. J. Wiens, *op. cit.*

be on a large or small basis, the semimultiple plan seems to function well.

The Directed and the Service Aspects. In order to expand the discussion of the basic organization of the personnel service, it is advisable to discuss some aspects of the directed and service functions of the personnel service.

The best example of a service function of the personnel section is the social service. This group provides a multiple service in that, from its findings and case studies, other services come into play. The psychological service which renders, upon referral, a distinct, highly technical service can be considered closely allied to the social service function.

The social service will deal basically with the individual case. Though there is a generalized policy and action for dealing with the practical aspects of adjustment problems which arise in the social service function, the operational aspects of this service are oriented to the individual. This point is made to emphasize the possible differences found in other directed and service functions.

Special education can be defined as a service which deals with individual cases. It does have some general directory aspects. Where the social service–psychological service team will deal directly with cases coming to their attention, the special-education service deals with the pupil through the teacher of special-education classes. At the organizational level, the supervisors and consultants function to aid all teachers in the proper education of pupils in the regular classroom situation. This consultant service, though minor in many respects, does provide the regular teaching staff with an ability to educate all pupils satisfactorily.

The research service renders a service to all pupils and, therefore, cannot be defined as a contact-service function but, rather, a generally directed aspect of service. Research, which usually involves data-gathering, interpretation of evaluations and measurements, and recommendations regarding general queries and programs, seldom deals with the individual pupil. In this regard the various aspects of the functions of this service fall into the directorate type of functional organization. Most of the functions are at the top administrative level, although as a result of the various evaluations and investigations, this directed service may influence every part of the particular system and hence affect each student in some way. If, for example, an investigation of the methods used to deal with overcrowded classes shows a necessary change in policy, the research service through its function may conclude and recommend the necessary changes in policy to alter and improve the methods used.

The function of dealing with the pupil's medical and dental condition is an individual service in all respects. Certain administrative qualities are inherent in this function; however, records, supplies, and procedures do require a director and administrator who must deal with policy and practices and the legal limitations which control the operation of this aspect of personnel service.

Guidance in all its aspects will and can be considered an individual service function. Here, the educational and vocational problems of the pupil are dealt with directly and with a maximum of personal application. The integration of other individual services come into play and illustrate again the necessary flexibility which must exist in the personnel division.

Other specialized services which result from the needs exhibited in the school system will usually be of an individual type, because the very nature of that service will derive from a clear and distinct student need. Variations of administrative details will merely be an expansion of the directed aspects of the personnel service. Administrative needs will usually be handled through the co-ordinator of all the services or through the director of research, who may act as an assistant to the co-ordinator of personnel.

Functional Patterns. The methods of function formed by the solution or resolution of conflicts arising in the educational and social life of the pupil are oriented in the pupil himself. Any pattern of operation which is adopted serves many ends but will always center in the pupil as the focal point. The solution of an educational problem for a pupil may involve several of the services of the personnel division. The basis of the development of the function is a referral from the teacher or other person who observes behavior signs indicating the need for help.[10] This referral will reach the

10. Commission on Teacher Education, *Helping Teachers Understand Children.* Washington: American Council on Education, 1945.

social, psychological, special-education services, or other services and be treated in such a manner that all will contribute to the building of a complete picture and possible solution of the pupil difficulty. If the problem is widespread, that is, observable in a large number of pupils, other services in the area of pupil personnel will begin to function. Necessarily continuous evaluation reveals the patterns of the pupil and his behavior. Research services will investigate to ascertain if some widespread change or variation in service function is needed.

If it is understood that all service is individual-centered, one may further develop the functional pattern by defining the age-level of best service. It is generally accepted that the best plan is to encourage referrals as early in the child's school career as possible. This attempt at preventive service will be richly rewarding if followed to the end. Practice has shown that the more simple problem observable in the primary-school child can develop into a full-blown, traumatic crisis in the adolescent. *It is essential that all personnel divisions, after locating the real trouble in any problem area, determine the future preventive aspects of the problem.*

PROGRAMMING IN ELEMENTARY AND SECONDARY EDUCATION

The Roles of the Administrator, Teacher, and Personnel Worker. Although programming is only one aspect of the organization of personnel services, it becomes a good example of the co-ordinated efforts necessary to provide the learner with a suitable learning situation. The function of programming eventuates in the process of individualizing each student's education. Procedures of elementary-level programming are fixed because of laws and procedures covering this level. Any variation in the elementary program will involve considerable study and adjustment on the part of the teacher, administrator, and personnel worker.

The role of the administrator in the programming procedure is confined to the provision of leadership and co-ordination with special reference to the pupils in school. The provision of actual room space and preparation of an equitable and realistic atmosphere for teaching and learning can also be attributed to the role of the administrator.

The teacher's role in the programming procedure is the direct contact with the needs of the pupil. Knowledge of courses and course sequence is mandatory for providing the pupil with a coherent education. The function of the teacher in so far as curriculum is concerned will not be discussed here. The *initiation* of curriculum change is not, nor should ever be, the function of a personnel service.

The personnel worker with a more realistic, intimate knowledge of the needs of the pupils will have the responsibility for *influencing* and *varying* curriculum offerings. However, it is essential that these adjustments be primarily individual in nature. The personnel worker can act as a valuable and successful resource person, who can aid those dealing with curriculum philosophy and offerings. However, as a personnel worker, the function does not imply the initiation of basic curriculum change.

The personnel worker has, perhaps, the most unique function in the programming procedure. Whatever procedures are generally accepted, the personnel worker must adjust the pupil's program to the actual, existing conditions in the pupil's life, both in and outside of school.

Trends in Large-School Organization. Programming methods in the large-school organizations generally center around the principal of the school or the administrator whose primary function is the development and planning of the school schedule. The function of personnel services in this planning is minor until the individual student begins to set up a program to serve his own needs. In this case, the personnel counselor will help the student adjust his program to provide for the most suitable learning situation. The basic trend in the large system is to provide more individualized service for every pupil. Such procedures will, if necessary, call into play all aspects of the personnel service. With the addition of staff members, a new approach or a more crystalized approach to personnel service and guidance can be observed.

The larger school system, in its own way, provides leadership in the organization of personnel services. The techniques of implementing the organization of personnel services can be original and, in some cases, experimental. Generally, however, the procedure must be based on (*a*) professionally trained staff members, (*b*) a staff-felt need for rendering the services, (*c*) the recognized need on the part of the pupils for such personnel services, and (d) a co-operative attitude on the part of the administrator, the teacher, and the personnel worker.

There are no basic differences at the various grade levels as to the essential qualities found in the above principles. A positive, communicative, co-operative atmosphere must pervade the entire organization, or all that is done will lose its effectiveness.

In order to clarify one of the more important trends in large-school organization, the reader's attention is directed to the differential diploma-plan recently adopted by the Indianapolis Public Schools.[11] This plan, which is designed to provide the maximum in service and curriculum to the pupil, is basically divided into four diploma-plans. Depending upon the needs of each pupil, an academic, a fine-and-practical-arts, a vocational, or a general diploma is offered. The variations in these plans depend upon the pupil's ability, his future occupational plans, and his initiative to learn and achieve. The over-all plan combines the effectiveness of good guidance and other vital personnel services, yet retains the flexibility necessary to a successful educational achievement. The important point in this illustration is that every step in this process has been carefully analyzed to make each personnel service operate to provide for all pupils, regardless of achievement, intent, or ability.

Trends in Small-School Organization. The trends toward more individualized programming is also observable in the smaller school systems. More testing and evaluation of the pupil and his grade placement are parts of the usual provisions of the smaller system. The limitations of money and actual space frequently cause the smaller system to make decisions that may not be completely in accord with the welfare of the individual pupil. Services that the personnel worker may render are small. But the homeroom teacher, who can also be considered a guidance person, can aid in the smooth function of this service. There is some trend in the area of consolidating personnel services through a larger administrative unit. The reasons for this trend are basically financial, but the plan does provide the opportunity for service where none formerly existed.

11. *Your Schools and You*, VIII, No. 8 (April, 1958). Indianapolis, Indiana: Indianapolis Public Schools.

Techniques of Co-ordinating Component Parts. The manner in which the various services may be co-ordinated to function coherently may vary with the type of organization that has been set up. Generally, co-ordination of the services is possible only in the multiple type of personnel organization. In the matter of programming, the co-ordination techniques which must be adopted should first consider the needs exhibited by the pupils. Depending upon the services which might be rendered, the plans, practices, and procedures necessary for the smooth functioning of this activity depend upon a staff person responsible for the final approval of the program. This person may be the principal, the supervisor of the personnel service, or some similar official. The procedure does not stop there. The application of the predetermined plans must be adapted to suit the individual needs of each pupil. Each guidance person must understand the limitations of the case. This will entail general seminars or meetings designed to orientate the personnel worker to these limitations. At this point, suggestions as to the improvement of the service may be offered. After the programming and placing of pupils in the program has begun, no variation of the plan may take place without approval by the person responsible for the entire procedure.

In the unit type of pupil personnel organization, it becomes necessary to set up check points at which the entire program may be evaluated.

PROGRAMMING IN HIGHER EDUCATION

Major Personnel Components. Personnel services at the college and university level exhibit many similarities to the services offered in the elementary and secondary schools. In order to clarify the components comprising most college personnel services, these similarities will be discussed, and a few of the variations necessary because of the educative level will be explained. Much of this discussion is based upon a recent publication of the American Council on Education which deals with personnel programs in American Colleges and universities.[12]

12. *The Administration of Student Personnel Programs in American Colleges and Universities.* Daniel D. Feder, Chairman, *et al.* American Council on Education Studies, Series VI, Student Personnel Work, XXII, No. 19. Washington: American Council on Education, February, 1958.

The organizational plans of the service take on aspects similar to those previously discussed. The unit plan, which is basically a college decentralized-plan, can be compared to the centralized college plan which is similar to the multiple organizational plan. The combination of these two extremes has been found to be more successful so that the centralized-decentralized plan has been generally adopted in most institutions. It is important, however, that the principle of flexibility be honored at this level. The college which finds a distinct need for a given service or set of services must, after proper investigation, organize these functions in such a way that the maximum service may be rendered to the student. If too much administrative detail is allowed to enter the organization, programming of personnel services, the records, registration, listings, and copies of documents tend to become an end in themselves.

The use of the student counselor represents one of the major functions of the college personnel service. In the organization of personnel services, the counselor function corresponds directly to the guidance service performed at the elementary and secondary levels. Usually a counselor is provided for each 500 students.

The health service of the college has the basic purposes and components of the medical-dental service of the public school system personnel service. There are some extensions of this service due to the characteristics of the college educational organization. Special health programs and some medical services, such as first aid or treatment of personal illness, may be considered as additional service.

The provision of food and housing for the students of a college illustrates the principle of flexibility in use at the college level. Because many students reside at the college away from their homes, it becomes a part of the personnel service to provide for food and housing. In this function, the colleges and universities are unique, and there is no basic comparable service offered at other levels. This function also provides an opportunity for extended guidance and counseling work.

In the colleges, student activities are usually defined as a personnel function. This service differs slightly from other educational levels but does make up a composite of all the extracurriculum work that will involve the individual. At other levels, this activity function is serviced on a more school-oriented basis and only utilizes the general personnel services where needed. Usually this function is administered by the deans of men and women.

Financial aid is a distinct college function, yet its components compare closely with the elements of the social service function of other educational levels. Need of service, value of educational experience, and a necessity that the student meet the obligation of the aid rendered are the basic principles existing in this function. Administration of this service is usually given to specially appointed committees who operate through an office set up for this purpose.

In the institutions of higher learning, a distinct and separate function for placement exists. This corresponds closely with a part of the secondary-school guidance program. Basically, the college placement service assists students in obtaining jobs during and after their college training. The placement service is usually centralized in one office and the number of personnel depends upon the needs exhibited.

The disciplinary function at the college level provides another illustration of the formation of a service based upon need. Whereas in other educative levels, this function is distributed among a number of services, it seems necessary at the college level to form a specific service for this activity. The formation and maintenance of personal, social, and educative standards at this level is the purpose of this function. Those who administer this function vary among the colleges. In some cases, a special disciplinary officer is appointed. Primarily, however, the function is basically one of special counseling.

In many colleges, there is a need for special clinics such as special remedial reading or the improvement of study habits. In many cases, this function correlates closely with the type of clinical service performed at other educational levels. Because need dictates the formation of such clinics, decentralization seems to be the most expeditious method of administering these services. It is essential that co-ordination be maintained in the instructional and other service functions.

Unique to colleges is the special-services function. Yet the elements of this function closely resemble the components of the special-education service. At the college level, there are many types of special students. Mainly, the classification of such students is not based upon ability or achievement but upon background and the social characteristics of the student. New student orientation or special advisory programs for foreign students are examples of this service.

Centralized or Decentralized Services. The organization and administration of the college-level personnel service is similar to the organization of personnel services at other levels. A combination of the centralized and decentralized philosophy seems to be the most feasible and flexible plan. This is the plan most commonly encountered. The decentralized plan lacks co-ordination and places a burden upon the staff members whose job is teaching. All services should be placed under an administrative head, and provision should be made for specialized staff members to administer each service. Special services or clinics may be decentralized; for example, the remedial reading clinic may be located and administered in the English department; however, referrals and final administrative authority should rest in one central administrative head. Commonly, this head is called a dean of students. No one basic plan can work in all colleges, but the principles of flexibility and the process of establishing need is vital to the programming of these services. As additional services are planned, it is essential to bear in mind that the student is the one who is being served; not the organizational program itself.

Trends in University Patterns. In larger institutions, centralization of personnel services is the distinct trend. The need for more efficient and economic operation is arising due to the anticipated increase in enrolment at this level. The urgency of this development demands that universities be far-sighted and prepare now for this influx of students. The functions listed above will be expanded to a great extent. Primarily, counseling and guidance services will be utilized to aid the university in the development of a method of screening and selection which will allow the more able, potentially-successful student to enter without restriction. More flexibility is definitely a "must," and recent trends show this development. Through a properly administered service, it is possible to create or disband services whenever the needs rise or diminish. On the more practical side, the use of data-processing machines have finally come into their own in the universities. Trends show that practically every function of personnel service can use this mechanization system to a distinct advantage.

One major trend, which although not now generally observable, is the development of a closer liaison of personnel services between the secondary level and those of the university level. Such examples are the formation of Grades XIII and XIV and the granting of college credit for certain secondary-school courses.

Trends in Small-College Patterns. Essentially, the same trends in the universities are evident in the smaller colleges. Variations, however, are being exhibited due to the size of the college. Where a large, centralized personnel service is developing in the university, the smaller colleges are slightly more decentralized, and, in many cases, staff members are being assigned additional duties. In many cases, however, a separate administrative head is appointed to co-ordinate the activities of the formerly completely decentralized services. It has become necessary for regular staff members to be skilled in counseling work and, thereby, provide a more individualized service for each student.

Data processing machinery can be found in most small colleges, and this development is being used to a distinct advantage.

Techniques of Co-ordinating Major Parts. Most plans at the level of higher learning, include a complete orientation for the instructor and the professor to the personnel services offered. Administratively, the counseling and advisory function of the college are dealt with at the dean's offices and a majority of the routine tasks are handled by his staff. One of the best, and perhaps the most clearly democratic, methods of integrating and co-ordinating the various parts of the variety of services designed to aid the student in college is through a council or standing committee of instructors, administrators, and professors whose main function is to examine and implement the services offered. Basically, communication should exist between all services. The need for service, which will first be recognized by the instructor, should, through the student's advisor, be provided by a referral system.

Basic needs governed by university regulation for all students become an administrative problem of co-ordination and record-keeping. Special-guidance health examination, student counseling of a psychological type, and any educational variation in the plans of the student will pivot on the advisor and his ability to refer the pupil to the proper service. Reports from these services to the advisor are essential. Hence, two basic techniques of co-ordination emerge. One, which may be defined as administrative co-ordination, centers in the administrative head and entails routine examination, evaluation, and record-keeping. The other, which may be described as individual student service co-ordination, centers in the advisory function where a student may be counseled and guided by an individual, well-qualified staff member.

Procedures of Implementation

DEVELOPING ATTITUDES FOR CHANGE

Staff, Student, and Public Readiness. Provision for change in any situation calls for an analysis of the needs of the specific condition. Usually pressure for change will be evident to those who will make the decision for the change. The readiness for change in the staff should usually include vertical committees designed to review and revise whatever plan is being considered. The changes in pupil personnel work must always include this form of two-way communication. Any changes taking place, which will affect the pupil directly, must take into account the feelings and ideas of the pupil. It has become a cardinal rule that the pupil must be protected from any administrative variation which might unnecessarily work a hardship on him. In regard to the public, it becomes mandatory that the parents and patrons of each system be given adequate orientation to the change. This approach should include announcements of discussion sessions or study groups which will review the details of the change. If the change or variation is an original one, that is, has never before been introduced in the particular system, it behooves the administration to include the public in its original planning. Interested parents provide a point of view that is not only interesting and necessary but valuable.

APPRAISING NEEDS

Evaluation of Staff, Student, and Public Opinion. The entire procedure of development of attitudes for change is dependent

upon the actual needs proclaimed by those who are vitally interested in the change. It becomes necessary, therefore, to evaluate
the actual opinion of the pupil, the teacher, and the public as to
exactly what attitudes exist and what changes are thought to be
necessary.

Although it would be an oversimplification to say merely that
the only way to obtain an opinion would be to ask for it, the procedure for evaluation is not much more complex than that. The
reactions of the public are reflected in a number of ways. The news
releases from various organizations give, to a limited extent, the
feelings of specific portions of the public. Pressure groups, which
attempt to persuade the leaders of the school system, indicate what
opinions might be representative of the population. The best way
available is opinion-polling, which involves the distribution and
tabulation of an opinionnaire. The opinionnaire, which will attempt
to assess the true feeling of the public, must be both objective and
representative.

Evaluation of pupil opinion and the needs of the pupil are
available through observation on the part of the staff. A simplified
version of an opinionnaire presented with the proper rapport will
produce what the pupil feels. It is important to remember, however, that student opinion, no matter how representative, generally
will contain indications of immaturity and must be interpreted
accordingly.

Staff opinion and evaluation of need will probably be no more
than an expansion of a normally continuous process. If the school
organization does not contain the elements of a two-way communication from administration to teacher, it should make an immediate attempt to provide such liaisons. If real evaluation of a
specific need or an attempt to determine the opinion of this professional group is required, it may become essential to construct and
administer an opinionnaire. Because professional questions are
asked, and professional answers are expected, the framing of the
questions will require extreme care. Under no circumstances
should the dignity of the professional person be questioned nor
should any element of threat or coercion to produce a given attitude
appear.

In the final evaluation, the assessment of staff opinion is and must be left to the administrator directing the service. Careful compiling and analyzing will aid in the conclusions drawn. If the democratic approach is to be maintained, the conclusions must be submitted for review to a group so designated for this purpose, but final administrative authority will always rest with the administrative head.

REPORTING RESULTS

The resources of the personnel services can be used in the reporting of any deliberation about a change in a personnel-service function. The research service will be able to supply the technical reporting necessary in the analysis of any problem which involves planning for change.

Of primary concern is the procedure of reporting any result which will not violate the principles of good communication. It is highly essential that all persons concerned in a decision or examination of a particular problem be kept informed of the results being reported.

Reporting results of the investigations of a specific functioning within a service follows the same basic principles. Clarity, permissiveness, and professionalism should pervade the entire procedure. As an illustration, let us consider the need for analyzing a specific case of truancy. Initiation of the referral will come from the social service and will be accompanied by a detailed explanation of the case to date. If the referral is to the guidance service, a request for psychological service may stem from this action. Each interplay of service carries detailed professional reporting. Final action is summarized and reported by the social service, which acts as the custodian of such reporting. Various records and reports of the entire case history are carefully and accurately filed in a pupil folder for future reference.

Again, good communication is essential to such a case. The obvious results of poor communication would be contradictory actions and recommendations.

EVALUATING PRESENT PROGRAMS

Maximum Participation. The proper programming of any personnel service organization will include provision for continuous evaluation of the achievement of the purposes stated in the policy of operation. The techniques of evaluation will vary according to the services rendered. Basically, the beginning is made by an annual examination of the actual achievements of each service. This annual report may not be literary in nature but must carefully describe the extent to which the purposes of the services were achieved. Charts and tables indicating the quantity as well as quality of service are included. It is essential that all personnel participate in this annual evaluation. The more involved the individual is in the process of evaluation, the better the evaluation will be. The annual-type report only serves as a basis for the continuous evaluative process. Included in the annual report are recommendations for the improvement of the service.

Other techniques for the continuous evaluation process will include re-evaluation checks at strategic times during the school year.[13] Verbal reports and unofficial statements of operation are to be encouraged in so far as they can be constructive. One of the qualities of a democratic operation of the series of services is two-way communication which is typified by the use of short, to-the-point memoranda which will speed the understanding of the particular case at hand.

DEVELOPING AND REPORTING RECOMMENDATIONS

As a final step in the evaluation of the services rendered to the student, and as a part of the annual report procedure, recommendations should be developed first at the teacher level, then at the counselor level, then at the supervisor level, and, finally, at the administrative level. The reporting procedure, which can be regarded as continuous on the part of the teacher, will necessitate the compilation of the consensus of teacher opinion. This is usually best developed through the use of representative committees. These committees which should be vertical in organization should analyze and summarize all recommendations in order to clearly state the best representation of the teacher's evaluation. The level of further co-ordination of this procedure is the review and expansion of the

13. S. E. Barber, *Evaluating School Guidance*. Buffalo: Foster & Stewart Publishing Co., 1946.

recommendations by the appropriate supervisor of each service. Further contacts with the teacher groups may be necessary. It is sometimes advisable for the supervisor of the service to be present in the development of the original teacher recommendations. This first-level analysis and evaluation, in order to develop recommendations, may be held during a teacher's professional day or similar function. It is important that each teacher be given the opportunity to express himself and that devotion to the task of evaluation and recommendations be unhampered by other duties.

After expansion and development of the original recommendations by the teacher, the supervisor will make a final report to the administrative head of pupil personnel, who then begins the process of implementing the approved recommendations.

Selecting the Action Program. After the development of the needed recommendations, a plan of implementation becomes necessary. Implementation will appear to be a reversal of the procedure used for arriving at the recommendations. Provision is made for implementation through the suggestions and co-operation of teacher committees. The decisions made are based upon the discussions of these implementation committees. Eventual action is taken by the administrative staff or the staff member directly responsible for the area in which the change is to take place. In the procedure for the selection of action to be taken, it is essential that an order of priority be developed and that financial and other practical considerations be taken into account. Before completion of the selection of the action program, final decisions must be reviewed and approved by the administrative head of the pupil personnel services. That is to say, no matter what developments take place in the area of the formation of recommendations or the suggested plan of action, the pyramid of committees formed are, at best, advisory and do not have the eventual administrative responsibility held by the administrative head. It is presumed that action-planning will deal only with administrative decisions and will not violate or supersede existing policy. If policy decisions are needed, the plan of action will always include the referral of the recommendation to a board of laymen who are responsible for policy-making. In each case, a fully documented analysis is necessary for the complete review of the request for revised or adjusted policy.

Selecting Leadership. The formation of the various technical and vertical committees requires extreme care in selection. It behooves the administrative head to be fully aware of the abilities and limitations of every participating member of his staff. The selection of a committee will involve utilizing those persons interested professionally in the problems under examination. Leadership of these committees will temporarily rest with the supervisor of the area in which the action is being taken. It is, however, the best policy to select and encourage the emergence of leadership from within the committee itself. Acceptable group processes are usually the best plan to follow.

Soliciting Staff, Board, and Public Support. Support for any major changes will, for the most part, be relegated to a specialized group whose main function will be to prepare the way for understanding and acceptance of the changes. In the case of staff members themselves, complete involvement in the original planning will aid materially in the acceptance of the program. Any indication of dissatisfaction or unusual disapproval on the part of the staff should appear during the deliberations of the original recommending group. In short, any action taken, will, for the most part, be anticlimactical for the members of the staff.

In the preceding section, small mention was made of the possibility that recommendations from the vertical and technical committees selected for the annual and continuous review of operation may involve a revision or creation of policies for which the school system would become bound. In this case, presentation of the investigations and the reasoning behind each section of each recommendation will need to be presented to the board of laymen who represent those who are supporting the particular school system. This presentation need not be simple because of the nature of the recipients. But, it must be clear, logical, understandable, and comprehensive. The final authority in the policy change will rest with this board of laymen.

Public support is essential to any major change within a school system. It is true that many minor administrative or highly technical changes need not be "checked" with the public to obtain their approval, but major changes which affect the educational product or the day-to-day operation of a system or institution will undoubtedly be more successful if they have public understanding. In many cases, disastrous results can occur if an administrator attempts to thrust an unimportant plan of a highly technical nature upon the public. As a general rule, public support is needed for basic policy change or major operational change, but if in the opinion of the professional administrative head, the matter is either too minor or too technical to be brought to the attention of the public, then public reaction should not be sought.

In so far as organizational provisions are concerned, in some of the larger organizations, a specific service may function as the agency to acquaint the public with the proposed ideas. In smaller units, however, variations of this more permanent service may emerge as a temporary committee whose function is the same as the permanent public relations service.

Usually the best means of communicating the plan or suggestions for which understanding is sought is to not digress too far from the usual means to which the public has become accustomed. In many cases, reaching the school-oriented public can be successful by contacting groups in the individual school units or through parent-teacher organizations.

If the plans for change in dealing with the pupil and his educational, emotional, and social development are reasonable, and if the public is fully informed of the need for such change as well as the facts leading up to the desirable action, no antireactions should appear. *It is a more or less consistent observation that public reaction against change is due to misinformation which leads to misunderstanding and complete misinterpretation of the original intent of the change.*

Implementation of the changes which will improve the learning situation must be cautious. The initial steps should always include a trial or experimental period in which the aspects of the results are evaluated constantly. Success or failure of a plan may depend entirely upon these actions. To launch into a new or revised program of change without first trying out the suggested plan of action is foolhardy, and the risks to future planning and action are increased.

PROVIDING FOR STAFF GROWTH

The staff of a personnel service is only as good as its ability to grow and change within itself. Without the ability to constantly learn and improve, the service is soon left behind by those it serves. A prominent part of the internal action program of the personnel service should be provision for professional improvement and reward. Most professionals can profit by participation in their own national organizations. This will presuppose a liberal and understanding attitude on the part of the administration of the school system concerning professional participation. Workshops designed for both professional growth as well as re-evaluation and examination of purposes and aims are essential. The lack of recognition by the administrative head of the personnel service of the advancement made within the staff in the profession itself can lead only to stagnation and large personnel turnover.

CONTINUOUS EVALUATION

The basic elements of annual and public re-examination of services provided have been discussed freely. Mention made of the necessary continuous evaluation has been slight, yet this is an essential part of a thinking, growing service. The concept of continuous self-evaluation should be fostered within each teacher, staff member, and administrator. Self-evaluation is where growth really starts. If the concept that education is guidance and that every teacher, staff member, and administrator is a personnel worker is to be believed, then continuous evaluation must be present.[14] If continuous evaluation is not observable in each member of the staff, then it will not be observable in the service itself. If each member of the staff practices continuous self-examination of the achievement of the purposes to which his service is committed, then the ground work is laid for the continuous evaluation of the service itself. Verbalization of this continuous evaluation need not take place at all times, but it does become important that ample opportunity be provided for the publishing or verbalizing of the results

14. Jane Warters, *High-School Personnel Work Today*. New York: McGraw-Hill Book Co., 1946.

of continuous evaluation. Communication again becomes an important part of the evaluative process.

A Look to the Future

Discussions of the current feelings about any organization are merely the sum of observations and the conclusions one may draw. Attempting to predict the future is, at best, risky. Yet, it is important that some statement be made regarding the future needs of the pupil and the implications of these needs for the personnel service. Current concepts of learning and the emerging role of the well-educated man in our society demand that the pupil not only be properly taught but that his learning include a pattern of self-adjustment and a series of skills for attacking and solving his own problems. The need for better and more precise guidance is immediately apparent, if one begins to examine the possibilities of the increasing population alone. By guidance we mean the broader, expanded concept of the term and imply specialized personnel whose task it will be to make learning more efficient through improvement of the teacher-learner relationship. Expansion and extension of the teacher's role as a personnel worker will include requirements of professional guidance training. Competition to enter college will undoubtedly increase. Each pupil, who feels the need for higher education or whose plans include further education in some other form, will find it necessary to bring into play the adjustment techniques acquired in the normal course of his schooling. Without adequate guidance, the learner will not be using his capacities to the fullest. In these days of satellites, escape velocity, and rocketry it is essential that every pupil be educated in accordance with his capacity to learn.

There undoubtedly will be an increased emphasis upon the personal attention given to each learner. Understanding learner behavior, discovering psychological bases for apparent abnormal behavior, increasing knowledge of preventive steps for eliminating antisocial behavior, and a careful analysis of where successful learners may use their abilities are all areas currently regarded as essential to the success of future educational programs.

The avowed purpose of any personnel service is to help the pupil or student help himself. Thus, as the complexity of the requirements for mere existence in our society increases, so must the precision with which the pupil must deal with these complexities increase.

The extent to which personnel services can provide maximum benefit to the learner is dependent upon the understanding and co-operation of the public, the learner, and the teacher. Any look to the future should include the statement that an increased under-standing of what the personnel services are actually able to do must be made clear to the public.

Although currently not much is said about preventive guidance and its advantages, it is necessary that personnel workers, through a carefully organized approach to their own methods of operation, provide an adequate amount of preventive guidance which will aid the pupil in coping with the pitfalls of everyday living.

SECTION III

FRONTIERS

CHAPTER VIII

The Emerging Role of the Professional Personnel Worker

DANIEL D. FEDER

Introduction

Ten years ago Lloyd-Jones, Wrenn, and Darley participated in a searching analysis of the status of personnel work as a profession.[1] The numerous references to the statements of these three highly creative contributors to our field in the decade which has elapsed are ample testimony to the guidance and stimulation which their statements have given to both research efforts and thoughtful evaluations of the problems they posed.

At the time of the University of Minnesota symposium, this writer was preparing his presidential address to the Council of Guidance and Personnel Associations. He proposed that the then-loose federation of ten organizations, some of which were not basically and directly concerned with educational personnel work per se, be restructured into a single national professional organization. This single organization would then operate with divisions in terms of functional interests and defined membership standards, which would involve specific education and training and which might ultimately lead to establishment of published standards of ethical practice and self-policing activities by the organization.[2] The subsequent development of the American Personnel and Guidance Association was an outgrowth of this proposal.

Of greater significance for the present yearbook was the com-

1. *Trends in Student Personnel Work*, Part IX, pp. 260-87. Edited by E. G. Williamson. Minneapolis: University of Minnesota Press, 1949.

2. D. D. Feder, "Next Steps in the Personnel Profession," *Occupations*, XXVII (October, 1948), 5-10.

prehensive report of a study commission of the Council of Guidance and Personnel Associations.[3] This document represented several years of co-operative study by the Council's Commission, the United States Employment Service, and a number of state employment offices. It still stands as the most comprehensive and objective effort to define and describe the various jobs in personnel work and the desirable levels of education, training, and experience. This study by no means exhausted the possibilities of the field, and it did not presume to cover all of the then-known specialties or predict some which might and have since developed. It was, nevertheless, a monumental effort and has served as a milestone for many subsequent developments.

It is beyond the scope of the present chapter to review the many developments which have been taking place and which continue to occur in this area of appraising student personnel work as a profession. By the same token, it would certainly be inappropriate to attempt to attach these developments to any one document, study, or proposal. Many references expressive of this concern are to be found. They appear in the minutes, discussions, and papers at meetings of various related professional organizations; there have been several major conferences which have devoted their attention exclusively to the standards of education and training for specifically named and described positions; there have been numerous research studies designed to examine what personnel workers are like and, in some cases, to obtain the judgments of recognized leaders as to what they ought to be; there has been an ongoing, searching self-analysis by organization leaders to appraise the place, purpose, and function of professional associations in the field.[4] All of these

3. Thelma Mills, Chairman, "Job Analyses of Educational Personnel Workers: Interim Report by the Study Commission of the Council of Guidance and Personnel Associations," *Occupations*, XXX (October, 1951), Supplement, pp. 1-22.

4. A few references are cited here. Their bibliographies will provide extensive leads for the reader interested in more detailed information.
Leonard M. Miller, Chairman, *Counselor Preparation*. Washington: National Vocational Guidance Assn., 1949.
Training of Psychological Counselors. Edited by Edward S. Bordin. Ann Arbor, Michigan: University of Michigan, 1951.
William C. Cottle, "Personal Characteristics of Counselors," *Personnel and*

activities culminate in one globar but many-faceted observation. The problem of achieving status as a profession, in some way meeting the standards, and hence enjoying the benefits accorded to other recognized professional groups continues to be a major concern of persons engaged in the various phases of student personnel work. There is, perhaps, no better illustration of the depth and breadth of this concern to be found than in the continuing effort to achieve recognition for the specialized activities of counseling which will provide both legal and professional controls in the public interest and which will simultaneously grant to the counselor the right of privileged communication now enjoyed in the professions of ministry, medicine, and law.

DEFINITIONS OF "PROFESSION"

A search for definitions of the term "profession" takes one on a varied and devious path. From the classic recognition of medicine, theology, and law which appears in the *Encyclopedia Americana*, one may find the other extreme expressed in the first edition of the *Dictionary of Occupational Titles*, which implies that any career or vocation which requires a college education or its equivalent may be regarded as a profession. Even Webster's *New International Dictionary* (second edition), as might be expected, refers to the classic illustrations of the three learned professions (theology, medicine, and law) but broadens the definition as follows: "The occupation, if not purely commercial, mechanical, agricultural, or the like, to which one devotes oneself; a calling in which one professes to have acquired some special knowledge used by way either of instructing, guiding, or advising others or of serving them in some art. . . ." Almost as broad as the latter definition and the conception of the *DOT* is the definition given in the *Encyclopedia of*

Guidance Journal, XXXI (April, 1953), 445-50.

"Certification," *Personnel and Guidance Journal,* XXXIII (February, 1955), 356-57.

Harold F. Cottingham, "Roles, Functions, and Training Levels for College Personnel Workers," *Personnel and Guidance Journal,* XXXIII (May, 1955), 534-38.

"Counseling Psychology as a Specialty," *American Psychologist,* XI (June, 1956), 282-85.

C. Gilbert Wrenn, "Status and Role of the School Counselor," *Personnel and Guidance Journal,* XXXVI (November, 1957), 175-83.

the Social Sciences which notes that a profession is characterized by "possession of an intellectual technique acquired by special training which can be applied to some sphere of every-day life."

SOME VIEWS ON PERSONNEL WORK IN EDUCATION AS A PROFESSION

Moving from the realm of broad definitions to the greater specificity of description, Wrenn and Darley proposed eight criteria specifically germane to the field of personnel work and by means of which they proposed to examine whether our field has acquired status as a profession. These criteria are: [5]

1. The application of standards of selection and training
2. The definition of job titles and functions
3. The possession of a body of specialized knowledge and skills
4. The development of a professional consciousness and of professional groups
5. The self-imposition of standards of admission and performance
6. Legal recognition of the vocation
7. The development of a code of ethics
8. The performance of a socially needed function

Wrenn and Darley disavowed any intent of protagonism for the concept of personnel work in education as a profession. They were, rather, attempting only to appraise the status of the field in terms of the criteria which they had derived. Other writers, on the other hand, having explored the developmental scene with comparable vigor, have not been so generous. In several statements over the past two decades, Cowley has moved from a once-optimistic hope that personnel service could develop into a profession to a more recently expressed belief that it probably never will.[6] Cowley's pessimism is supported by evidence that large numbers of persons occupying key personnel positions have attained these jobs by circumstance and accident rather than by specific education and preparation for their duties.[7] Certainly the picture is not made any brighter when one examines the loose usage of some of the titles

5. Williamson, *op. cit.*, pp. 264-87.

6. W. H. Cowley, "Student Personnel Services in Retrospect and Prospect," *School and Society*, XXCV (January 19, 1957), 19-22.

7. Clifford G. Houston, "Limited Survey of Professional Standards and Training of College Personnel Workers," *Educational and Psychological Measurement*, Vol. IX, pp. 445-46.

that we have come to regard as specific and professional in nature. Perhaps the best illustration of this is the widespread application of the term "counselor" to persons in all levels of education who seem to have any kind of extraclass contact with students on an individual, and sometimes even on a group, basis. To say that the title is here used to describe a function, without reference to the qualifications of the person, is even being generous. Many other illustrations can be cited. At the level of definition of duties performed, the use of the title "dean of boys" or "dean of girls" at the secondary-school level is another good illustration of the confusion and uncertainties in this area. For example, in one school such persons may be required to have a minimal of specialized education and training, serving as counselors for students with self-referred problems, or as referral resources for faculty. They preside over and give direction and guidance to broad activities programs and co-ordinate the over-all extraclass programs of the school. Yet, very close by, one may find persons bearing the same titles and serving primarily as attendance and disciplinary officers.

Professional Requirements for Personnel Worker in Education

It is recognized that a profession is made up of its practitioners and that, therefore, to talk of a profession is to talk of the persons who are involved in it. Such an approach, however, leads to a level of abstraction and, oftentimes, to fruitless debates about whether or not we are a profession or what kind of a profession we ought to be. Since the concern of this chapter by title and by purpose is to examine the professional personnel worker in education and his emerging role, we shall proceed on certain arguable assumptions. The full validity or the full realization of these assumptions may be several decades hence. Nevertheless, there is evidence of sufficient emergence of a representative group of practitioners in the various phases of personnel work who can be identified as having at least "the possession of an intellectual technique acquired by special training" to warrant our identification of them as professional personnel workers. By examining the current scene and attempting to project some future developments, it is our hope to be able to establish certain benchmarks which may be useful to those currently involved in student personnel work and such of those readers who may be searching for understandings and insights which may assist them in their decision to enter this field of service.

IN TERMS OF AREAS OF PREPARATION

Specific areas of preparation have been defined for only a relatively small number of the job titles which exist in this field. Unquestionably the most extensive consideration of education and training standards has been given to the field of counseling.[8] Through a series of conferences of counselor trainers, there is now a well-defined body of content in terms of such things as psychological measurement, interview procedures, diagnostic procedures, and basic psychological understandings so well defined as to be clarified in the standards adopted by the United States Civil Service Commission and numerous states in their establishment of certification standards for persons who will bear the title "counselor." [9]

Seeking to spur the entry of new persons into their field, the American Association of Collegiate Registrars and Admission Officers has set forth a recommended program of education and experience designed to prepare people for their specialization in the field of personnel service. It is noteworthy that in connection with their expression of the belief that their specialty should be identified as a phase of personnel service, the Association has set the content of its program in the same frame of reference that characterizes the preparation of counselors and student personnel workers in general.[10]

8. There is an inherent fallacy in the use of the words "training" and "trainer" which has come into such common usage. They imply schooling in a body of techniques rather than fundamental education in psychological, sociological, and educational content out of which the professional person becomes a practitioner. The writer objects to the implication that student personnel workers are subhuman animals who are "trained" rather than intelligent human beings learning to apply their education.

9. Royce E. Brewster, *Guidance Workers Certification Requirements*, U.S. Department of Health, Education, and Welfare, Bulletin, 1957, No. 22. Washington: Government Printing Office, 1957.

10. Ellen L. Deering, Chairman, *Professional Training Recommended for the Registrar and Admissions Officer*. Chapel Hill, North Carolina: American Association of Collegiate Registrars and Admissions Officers, 1956.

In the area of nursing and medical services, the basic programs of medical education are, of course, the essential beginnings. Yet it is interesting to note that there is a growing body of literature dealing with the health problems of the specific age groups dealt with at various educational levels. Similarly, there are increasing expressions of the belief on the part of persons in these fields that such specialists should have the special insights, personal characteristics, and even education and experience which will make them particularly effective in dealing with these special age groups and their special problems.

Borrowing techniques and understandings from group work and group dynamics and tying these to basic psychological understandings is leading to the creation of a new and significant pattern of preparation for persons who seek their expression in the fields called extracurriculum activities.

As one examines this whole broad field of educational programs, of efforts to establish standards on the part of professional organizations, and of the offerings of graduate institutions themselves, certain common elements become apparent. Almost without exception the educational personnel worker is first expected to have insight into and understanding of the characteristics of the educational level at which he is to work. This is, perhaps, only another way of saying that the personnel worker must comprehend the environment in which he works as well as the individual with whom he works. The depth of this conviction is expressed at many institutions in the requirement that the student who wishes to enter formal preparation must have had at least a minimal background of experience in teaching or some other phase of education before he may pursue the academic program. Oftentimes, the graduate student will be advised to interrupt his program and have an intervening period of experience. This phase of preparation may be expressed as the period of gaining understanding of the objectives and the dynamics of the educational framework in which student personnel work will be carried out.

Common also to every delineated professional program is the emphasis upon understanding of the individual. This is expressed variously in courses in personality dynamics, psychological measurement, the psychology of learning, the psychology of motivation, and other similar background designed to give understanding of the mainspring of human behavior.

Except for the field of counseling, supportive courses in techniques are not so clearly defined. In counseling one finds a plethora of offerings and sometimes a somewhat questionable fractionation of course offerings dealing with various techniques of diagnosis, interviewing, and therapy. The fractionation is illustrated by the study of the interview as a diagnostic technique on the one hand and separately as a therapeutic device. In this area, too, the clinical counselor will have his choice between the emphasis upon projective techniques for the understanding of personality dynamics or the perfection of their use and application as diagnostic devices.

With the increasing development of a series of pragmatically evaluated techniques and procedures, the field of group dynamics has begun to produce a series of technique courses. Just where such techniques should be applied and in what special fields of personnel operations they have special validity has yet to be determined experimentally. On the other hand, there are many specialties in the field of personnel service which have not yet developed any specific technique pattern as reflected in the catalogues of teaching institutions. The fields of placement and student aid are typical examples of this. Here, in common with many other areas, the personnel worker is expected to acquire technique understanding by experience, osmosis, or insight. In fact, many of these areas are excellent illustrations of the extent of "apprenticeship training" in student personnel work.

Supplemental to the personnel worker's knowledge of the specific milieu in which he performs his duties, is knowledge of interrelated functions or areas external to the educational institution. Thus, for example, the counselor must learn of the world of work, the psychology of occupations, and related backgrounds. Such delineated programs as one can identify in the fields of group work, student housing and feeding, and the more general administrative titles either require or recommend background in the social sciences, economics, in addition to the specific informational areas available for these fields in relation to the educational scene.

In summary then the personnel worker's preparation is characterized by the specific understanding of the field and level in which he is to work, intensive study of the psychology of the individual, a background of technique courses where these have been developed in a particular specialty, and the kind of general broad background which characterizes a liberal-arts education carried forward more specifically into informational areas which impinge upon the specialized field or which, in turn, are interrelated and served by the specialized functions performed.

IN TERMS OF TITLES AND JOB DESCRIPTIONS

Numerous efforts have appeared in the literature seeking more clearly and more narrowly to define and describe jobs and titles in the various phases of personnel work in education. The work of the Study Commission previously cited stands as the most comprehensive effort in this area.[11] Despite the various efforts to delineate personnel work as a distinctive phase of the total educational operation, the titles which are found in general use tend inevitably to identify student personnel work with administration. Thus, deans and directors abound at nearly all levels. Perhaps the only distinctive title which is unique to student personnel work and which is completely permissive in its semantic implications is that of "counselor." It is somewhat ironic that no distinctively unique and permissive titles have developed in student personnel work in view of the oft-repeated insistence of workers upon the essentiality of their separation from administrative, disciplinary, and other directive relationships with students. In this regard we are obviously the victims of our own habit patterns and find it easier to adopt conventionally recognized rubrics rather than to have to continually explain to our various publics the functions which are related to what may be new and unusual titles.

Within quite broad boundaries, job descriptions at various levels have appeared. What they lack in uniformity and universality, they make up in uniqueness. For example, designed originally to denote a position responsible for administrative co-ordination of a number of personnel services and workers, the title "dean of students" may now be found in institutions of various sizes wherein the individual is responsible only for the work of his own single office. This is even the case in noncoeducational schools. One cannot help but

11. Mills, *op. cit.*

wonder whether there is a perceived pattern of "the right thing to be" or "the right title to bear," which leads to such practices pretty much without regard to basic meanings.

IN TERMS OF PROFESSIONAL ASSOCIATION AFFILIATIONS

In terms of the professional associations with which he will affiliate, the personnel worker has a wide variety from which to draw. The largest and most inclusive of these is, of course, the American Personnel and Guidance Association. Here one finds personnel workers at all levels of education and in all phases of personnel work. However, the existing divisional structure of this large and sprawling association still continues to be based upon the original organizational identities of the affiliated associations rather than upon a functional division of personnel workers in terms of their actual duties and responsibilities. To give particular emphasis to service to women in all levels of education, the National Association of Women Deans and Counselors continues to maintain a separate integrity. Because of its age and tradition as a small and highly intimate body, the National Association of Student Personnel Administrators (formerly the National Association of Deans and Advisors of Men) continues to follow its traditional pattern. There are many overlapping memberships among these three organizations. In fact, this is essential if the individual is to keep himself abreast of the often overlapping and duplicative thinking of the three groups.

As might be expected, personnel workers engaged essentially in the elementary and secondary levels have found their professional identification in the American Personnel and Guidance Association. The possibility of identification with others whose functions tend to be of a more general nature makes this identification a natural one. At the level of higher education, however, the proliferation of specialized functions and the more nearly full-time concentration of persons in these specialties has led, as would be expected, to the formation of more specialized groups. Thus, one finds both regional and national associations, independent of any other affiliation, devoted to health services, housing, placement, admissions counseling, student unions, to name but a few of the larger and well-formed so-called professional groups.

There appears to be no end to the possibilities of developing "professional organizations" in education. The development from simple association of persons with common interests and problems into structured organizations is happening so nicely in our current generation as to provide the bases for interesting sociological studies. Barry and Wolf have dealt with the major developments in student personnel work organizations in their recent volume and find them seriously wanting in so far as meeting the essential criteria which are expected of "professional" associations.[12] The personnel worker is a happy prototype of Whyte's "organization man." He may find "togetherness" and "belongingness" in a host of overlapping affiliations. With only a few notable exceptions (the American Psychological Association, the American College Personnel Association, "professional" membership in the National Vocational Guidance Association, and the American School Counselors Association, which require varying degrees of graduate education and experience), about the only limits to the extent of joining he can do are those of his own personal budget.

IN TERMS OF PERSONAL QUALIFICATIONS

Collating studies of personal characteristics of counselors, Cottle recently concluded that these studies are sporadic and unrelated.[13] Yet more has been done to evaluate the personal characteristics of the personnel worker than those of almost any other professional group in education. Some efforts have been made in the employment of personality inventories and other methods of measuring personal adjustments of counselors. For the most part, we are restricted to objective interpretation on the part of persons who have gauged the personality requirements for their fields pretty largely in terms of their own self-percepts and self-concepts. The person who wishes to enter the fields of personnel work because "I just love to work with people" is apt to find doors barred on the suspicion that he may be a missionary-type of "do-gooder" rather than

12. Ruth Barry and Beverly Wolf, *Modern Issues in Guidance-Personnel Work*. New York: Bureau of Publications, Teachers College, Columbia University, 1957.

13. Cottle, *op. cit.*

having a genuine educational orientation toward the field. In contrast, some persons who enter counseling as a specialization sometimes are suspect, as are psychiatrists and clinical psychologists, of seeking solutions to their own problems through their professional participation in the lives of others. Regrettably it must be concluded that there is no respectable body of valid evidence which would suggest the personality nature and characteristics of persons who ought to consider personnel work as a career. It is probably fair to say that those people who find satisfaction of service a motivation in any phase of teaching would find similar satisfactions in various phases of personnel service. Inevitably, however, as such services are structured in education today, the personnel worker must also be a person who finds satisfaction in the less personal contacts of administrative work, because this appears to be an inevitable identification and necessity.

What a Professional Personnel Worker Does

ROLES AND FUNCTIONS

The Generalist and the Specialist. As in any area of professional practice, personnel workers may be broadly classified into "generalists" and "specialists." In education, major determinants of this development appear to be the size and/or the level of the institution at which the work is performed. As Bennett has pointed out, educational personnel work tends to move from the very broadly based generalized service at the elementary-school level into a series of highly differentiated and specialized services and functions at the college level. The workers who perform these functions reflect the essential level of generality or speciality which is appropriate to the educational milieu in which they work.

At the level of higher education, however, there is a most notable exception to this trend. Here, as Barry and Wolf point out, one finds many small institutions in which the essential need is for a person with a broad base of training and insights so that he or she may perform a variety of functions, all of them student personnel in nature.[14] The degree of generality or speciality found in higher

14. Barry and Wolf, *op. cit.*, pp. 80-96.

education is largely related to the size and complexity of the institution itself. As numbers of students to be served increase, and as functions performed by the institution on behalf of its students proliferate, various individuals become more specialized in their service. Often the generalist by training moves into specialized fields of service by virtue of interest and need as reflected in the institution. There is no real dichotomy here. The essential need is for recognition of the fact that when people undertake to perform specialized functions, it may be desirable for them to have had the kind of professional education and experience which is recognized as specifically related to the specialized functions being performed.

Multiple Roles of the Generalist. The generalist, of course, wears several hats in the student personnel parade. He may function as a counselor to a disturbed student; he may supervise dormitory housing on the campus; he may participate in or actually administer disciplinary functions; he may be deeply involved in the processes of stimulating student self-government and a host of extraclass activities. Where the institutional size and complexity do not require the services of a full-time person in any of the foregoing areas, obviously it is wasteful and inappropriate to insist upon them as specialized functions with specialized personnel. Frequently a compromise is developed in the smaller institution where such functions become a part-time responsibility of a person who is engaged primarily in teaching activities. A most common example of this is encountered in the professor of education who serves also as a placement secretary or director.

Unit Functions of the Specialist. In sharp contrast, of course, are the unitary functions of a specialist in the larger and more complex institution. Thus, in many high schools counseling divides itself into persons who specialize in the counseling of students with reference to college plans, vocational counselors whose chief concern will be with students who terminate their education after high-school graduation, and even in some cases personal problem counselors. The large high school which can afford this type of specialization may also expect the counselor to do a minimal amount of teaching but usually frees him or her from any other kind of administrative responsibility. Where such specialization is developed at the college level, one finds the person so employed devoting virtually full time to the unit functions with which he is identified.

Problems of Both the Generalist and the Specialist. Chief among the problems of the generalist is the conflict of roles which he may experience in any given situation. For example, strive as he will to create the permissive identification which he desires with reference to his counseling relationship with students, he may find himself seriously frustrated if he has to switch roles into that of a disciplinarian as well. Similarly, the dean of men who serves as residence-hall counselor must keep himself sharply aware of the distinction between the services he might perform in that capacity and the requirements he must exact as administrative officer in charge of the housing function. There is no easy solution for these dilemmas. The role of and need for generalists is an ever present reality. The major solution for the problem would seem to lie in the professional competence of the individual and the development of sufficient insight so that he is aware of the potential dangers in his multiple roles and makes conscious compensation for them.

Lest it be assumed that the preceding paragraph argues for a complete specialization of all student personnel functions and persons, we must cite the ever present danger that the narrowness of the specialist may prevent his perception of the student as a dynamic *gestalt* in any situation. Thus, the housing officer who disposes of minor behavior irregularities within a framework of rules and regulations may well be ignoring an incipient personality disorder. The officer who administers student loans may become so involved in the manipulation of papers as to miss the existence of a deep-seated family conflict which creates the student's precarious financial situation. Obviously the specialist can become too specialized. As noted above, basic to the personnel worker's training and orientation must be the essential understanding of the individual student and what "makes him tick." How the specialist sees him "ticking" and how he may interpret it in its isolated manifestations is, of course, the old story of the blind men and the elephant. Nevertheless, this is the great hazard of the specialist, and his great need is to avoid blind spots while dealing with the aspects specific to his competencies.

INTEGRATION OF PERSONNEL WORKERS WITH OTHER PROFESSIONAL PERSONS IN THE EDUCATIONAL SETTING

Whatever the degree of specialization of any personnel worker, the importance of integration of his efforts with those of other professional persons in the educational setting is obvious. The classroom teacher may refer a student for counseling because he is "lazy" and "inattentive" in the classroom. Before the counselor can accept this diagnosis, which at its best is only a description of a superficial behavior phenomenon, he may need medical advice to insure that there are no physical disorders causing the symptoms. The counselor, however, must refrain from making his own medical diagnoses. This is but another way of saying that one of the important characteristics of the personnel worker is a recognition of his own personal limitations. With this must come a willingness to consult with and work with other professional persons in the total setting to assist the student in finding solutions to his problems.

EMERGENCE OF THE PERSONNEL WORKER AS AN INTEGER IN THE EDUCATIONAL FORMULA

The Personnel Worker as "Teacher." The most exciting aspect of this period of development is the emergence of the personnel worker as an integer in the educational formula. This has been the subject of a great deal of discussion and writing. The essential element in this process is the increasing recognition by the personnel workers themselves of their functions as "teachers" in the broad educational program. The literature of the past decade reflects the rapidly growing recognition that any experience which is in any way geared to the educational program has in it the potential for new learning for the student. Whether it be at the level of the problem-solving counseling situation, or an extraclass activity, the personnel worker now seeks to identify the learning potentials available in each of these experiences. His next step is to so structure his operations as to insure the greatest possible chance that these learnings will be accomplished. Significantly, there is a growing concern and interest in evaluating the outcomes of these experiences in terms of the changes they make in the behavior and attitudes of the individual students thus affected.

Identification through Legal and Administrative Means. This development of the personnel worker in the role of a teacher is, in many ways, more exciting than the administrative legal and certification provisions which have spread throughout the United States so rapidly in the past decade.[15] To be sure, most of the certification provisions have been directed toward the recognition of the term "counselor" or "guidance specialist" or some very similar correlate. These have been somewhat limited in nature but are the natural outcome of more highly developed preparatory programs. The many other facets of personnel work which are currently performed, but which are not so recognized, are still as challenging and as meaningful in the educational pattern.

Self-Concepts of the Personnel Worker. If there is a distinctive uniqueness about the personnel worker, it is in his perception of the possibility of educational experience—of basic and important learnings—occurring outside as well as within the confines of the classroom. For the personnel worker, the learning experience goes very much deeper than the acquisition of skills, knowledge, and attitudes. He sees it as a co-ordination and correlation of all of these into a restructuring of behavior or a basic original learning of behavior which results in the greatest possible personal effectiveness for each individual student. Simultaneously, the personnel worker recognizes that there are unique and distinctive contributions from the classroom upon which the student bases his behavioral patterns. The personnel worker, however, is distinctively and especially concerned with the teaching of the student and not with the teaching of the subject matter.

The Role of the Professional Personnel Worker in the Future

THE STUDENT PERSONNEL POINT OF VIEW

It is apparent from Wrenn's presentation that personnel workers actually have an underlying and systematic philosophical and psychological orientation, although they may not always be conscious of what it is. The fact that there is not a conscious recognition of

15. Brewster, *op. cit.*

a point of view or orientation may often lead to inconsistencies of interpretation and approach in dealing with students and their problems. Nevertheless, the neo-humanistic emphasis on human values, the broad and eclectic drawing from the many fields of experimental psychology, and the conception of the human organism as a dynamic operating in a self-inclusive environmental *gestalt* are distinguishing characteristics of the personnel worker who has prepared himself for service in this field with specialized education and orientation.

Development of Individual Differences as Educational Goals. A basic derivate from this orientation is the personnel worker's effort to stimulate the structure of educational processes around the concept of the uniqueness of the individual. Schooled in the concepts of individual differences, the personnel worker is actually dedicated to the effort to help each individual recognize his uniqueness as such and to capitalize upon his strengths in the development of his personality. Here, though not often consciously recognized, is the antithesis to the "organization man." It is a basic dedication of the personnel worker whose goal is the establishment of the integrity of the individual in the midst of group pressures and group processes.

Deriving Learning Experiences from All Phases of Education. Concomitant with the concern of the personnel worker in aiding the student to derive learning experiences from all phases of the educational program is a constant and necessary search for the sources of student motivation. Although the classroom teacher may accept the search for knowledge or the desire for grade and credit and degree recognition as the motivation in the classroom, the personnel worker also seeks these as well as the deeper-lying mainsprings of behavior. He knows that, from the needs for status, prestige, a sense of belonging, and the like, the student may be motivated to levels of achievement and energy output far beyond normal expectancy. To the extent that the personnel worker is able to relate these need perceptions to the on-going educational life of the student, he may be able to influence the broad general educational output and achievement as well as the more subjective, but none the less important, personal satisfactions which the student achieves at any level of education.

There is still a pervasive inclination to regard extraclass activities indigenous to the educational program as being something different and, in fact, something less than a valid part of the educational process. Oftentimes these are given a sort of second-best place in the sun by being accepted as a form of preparation for life in whatever stage follows a particular level of educational experience. But, consistent with the philosophy which has been espoused in earlier chapters of this yearbook, this type of separation is not only invalid, it is impossible. Basically our concern with these activities is as with an integral phase of the constantly ongoing program. The learnings thus derived are not an esoteric preparation for some kind of "adult" life after conclusion of the educational experience. They are indeed life itself at the particular age and maturity level for which they are designed.

Personnel Work as Constructive Education in Problem-solving. The transition from thinking about "problem students" to a concern for students who have problems is one of the subtler but, nevertheless, positive and constructive shifts in the personnel-work emphasis. Only a few years ago derisive comments about counseling as "coddling" and "spoon-feeding" were heard with great frequency at every level of education and were seen even in the literature. Yet, most recently, major educational policy statements, emanating not from personnel workers or counselors but from administrators and in some cases persons not directly associated with education, have made reference to the needs in long-range educational planning for counseling and other types of personnel services as integral to the long-range development of American education.[16] The whole emphasis upon mental-hygiene needs of students in all levels of education and the urgent attention to the continuing need of structuring classroom and other educational experiences so as to produce maximum quality of learning and an atmosphere of good mental health are ample evidence of the recognition of the person as an affective as well as a cognitive being. Despite the current emphasis upon our national needs in terms of the production of scientists and technicians, there is a concomitant recognition of the importance of

16. Herman B. Wells, Chairman, *Higher Education in a Decade of Decision.* Washington: Educational Policies Commission, 1957.

enabling individuals to satisfy their emotional needs as well as their economic ones.

With this veering away from concern with "problem students," personnel workers will of necessity be expected to concentrate more of their interest and energy on the stimulation of superior students to greater self-realization. No one in the educational system is more aware of the individual differences among students than is the personnel worker. A special mission in this new societal acceptance of recognition of a creative and constructive approach to student personnel functions is the challenge of "creeping mediocrity" which threatens American democracy. Much time and energy in the past have been spent in the effort to raise the failing or potentially failing student to a minimum level of success. Relatively little attention has been given until just recently to the identification and stimulation of the student of superior potential. Herein lies a major challenge of the future for personnel work. Herein lies the answer to the leveling tendencies of organizationalism. Herein lies the personnel worker's challenge of the future as he identifies talent and devises ways and means of stimulating the holders of such talent to a desire to express it constructively.

The Development of the Individual in a Setting of Social Responsibility. The growth and maturation of the personnel process itself is reflected in many interesting ways. Perhaps most notable is the shift in attitude represented in a quarter century of thought and work. The first edition of the *Student Personnel Point of View,* as well as early statements of purpose by professional associations, expressed a major concern with the development and guidance of the individual.[17] In the revision of the *Student Personnel Point of View* some twelve years later, the individual is still the main concern, but now in a setting of social responsibility.[18] One might have thought that, in the highly individualistic statements which motivated early philosophical writings in this field, a genera-

17. Committee on Student Personnel Work, *The Student Personnel Point of View.* American Council on Education, Series I, No. 3. Washington: American Council on Education, 1937.

18. Committee on Student Personnel Work, *The Student Personnel Point of View.* American Council on Education, Series VI, No. 13. Washington: American Council on Education, 1949 (revised edition).

ton of anarchists would be produced. But actually, with the emphasis on social responsibility which has characterized the ongoing educational program in the past quarter-century, personnel workers have quite naturally phrased their concepts into the main stream of educational thought. In the light of such a major shift in emphasis in so relatively short a span, may we not, in a projective document of this type, indulge ourselves in the liberty of pondering the future? Must education and all of its related processes continue, for an indefinite future, to be concerned only with the objective realities of content and the subjective realities of personality? Is it not conceivable that, in this essentially social process with all of its socially significant ramifications, we may at some time arrive at the possibility of a systematic approach to human values? Must the counselor forever seek to retain his position of neutrality, or will he find an acceptable ground upon which he will be able to manifest his own values orientation without fear of violating his position of nonjudgmentalism? And finally, in this sequence of questions, is it not valid to query whether, in the overreaction toward permissiveness, we have not obscured the basic need in student personnel relations which is essentially the establishment of a nonjudgmental atmosphere rather than a purely freewheeling permissiveness? Perhaps these questions are phrased so as to reflect the writer's bias. This is a bias based, however, upon a sensing of the broad areas of concern which today are high on the discussion and thought lists of personnel workers. If their phrasing in this fashion stimulates discussion and disagreement and, ultimately, solution, then part of the function of this chapter as a searching for new horizons will have been accomplished.

RESPONSIBILITIES OF LEADERSHIP IN STRUCTURING EDUCATIONAL PROCESSES

To accomplish the major goals cited in the preceding section, personnel workers must take leadership in actively relating themselves and their services to their colleagues in the educational process. They must themselves seek active involvement in ongoing educational functions. The past quarter-century has seen the erection of many psychosocial barriers by personnel workers themselves as they sought to establish their professional status and integrity. Theirs has been a conscious endeavor to carve out a little segment of the educational empire which they could call their own. At least, this is the interpretation that has been placed upon the activities of personnel workers who have sought to impress upon their faculty colleagues the uniqueness of their functions and services and the necessity of protection from violation by the non-trained and non-student-personnel-minded.

It is no accident that in many schools and colleges personnel services are regarded as some kind of educational side show which could be discarded with little or no harm to the main educational circus. Counselors who have resisted any creative co-operation with teachers in the effort to assist individual students with their problems have contributed to this feeling. Activities programs conducted essentially for their self-contained values and aims inevitably separate themselves from the central purposes of education as seen by the teaching faculty. The housing program, which is merely the provision of "room and board" without concern for its impact upon the morale of students and their consequent performance in the classroom, might just as well be conducted off the campus and by persons who have no educational identification with the institution. Personnel workers, who have complained of lack of acceptance by their colleagues or lack of recognition by their colleagues of the functions they perform, must essentially look to themselves to place the blame for this development. The break-through in this relationship will come when personnel workers at all levels aggressively pursue active relationships with their educational co-workers; when they make it unmistakably clear by their actions, as well as their thoughts and words, that they perceive their functions to have the central purpose of enhancing the learning experience for the individual student; and when they actively involve their colleagues at every level in the determination of policies which guide their functions and the conduct of their daily services.

INTEGRATIVE FUNCTIONS ON BEHALF OF THE INDIVIDUAL STUDENT

As the unique functions of personnel services become more clearly delineated in the future, these operations will be perceived as a bridge between administration and instruction rather than as a part of administration. In such a balance of valences, personnel services will inevitably be drawn more intimately into the relationship between instruction and the student body rather than to a relationship with administration per se. In providing the structured and unstructured learning experiences which help translate classroom learning into daily living, student personnel workers will provide a bridge between school and community for the transition of the student from the process of formal education to his position of community participation. Of particular importance is the bridge which personnel workers can construct to provide a route for the meeting of parents and the schools and the meeting of other publics and the schools on behalf of the students being served. Examples of this construction are developing in high-school programs, which provide a new content for parent-teacher meetings, namely, the children of the parents, and a sharing of information which will help all parties to the educational process do their job better. An outstanding example of this is the annual meeting conducted by one high school in which parents are given the files of their respective children, a counselor discusses the meaning of the tests and other data recorded therein, with illustrative individual applications, and there then follows an opportunity for parents to ask questions and make comments. How different this is, and how much more constructive this is than the attitude which surrounds test scores with an aura of mystery and denies to parents essential understandings about their children. Even though the college student is in the throes of his struggle for emancipation and adulthood, nevertheless, the validity of the concept of partnership between his parents and the school still holds. Progressive leadership by personnel workers at all levels of education is essential to create the bridge of communication and, ultimately, of solidifying families as well as students into a community with their schools and colleges.

NEEDS WITHIN INSTITUTIONAL GRADUATE PROGRAMS

In the decade since LaBarre's study of graduate offerings in personnel work, the number of colleges and universities offering such graduate programs has more than quadrupled.[19] According to

19. Corinne LaBarre, *Graduate Training for Educational Personnel Work.* American Council on Education, Series VI, No. 11. Washington: American Council on Education, 1948.

Ross, who prepared the 1957-58 survey of such offerings for the United States Office of Education, thirty-two of these programs were developed and announced in the year preceding this publication.[20] He reports, further, an increase of approximately 20 per cent over the previous year's offerings of specific courses related to various phases of the field of student personnel work. With 215 institutions (by their own report) currently offering graduate programs in personnel work, it is inevitable that there will be many differences of program offerings, program structures, and even pervasive philosophies. This is certainly not undesirable in a field which is in a state of such dynamic flux. There is incumbent upon the educational institution, however, the responsibility for offering educational experiences which will be structured to accepted minimal standards at the very least. To be sure, not too much guidance is yet available in the various fields of personnel work or the structuring of educational programs. The minimum essentials for individual understanding, however, have been well described, and these must represent a valid starting point. Not only is a desirable individuality of program to be sought but, additionally, some institutions should be giving consideration to the development of unique and needed programs of specialization at the graduate level. There is a real danger that the certificating, *ergo* accrediting, activities of the Boards of Divisions 12 (clinical) and 17 (counseling) of the American Psychological Association may weave a straitjacket on the educational ingenuity of our graduate programs. The possibility has already been sensed within the Association itself. Aggressive and imaginative curriculum planning in terms of the broad educational needs of society is the only effective counteractant. The graduate institutions themselves will assist materially in the future development of the profession of educational personnel work by rigorous screening and evaluation of its products. If it is assumed that the members of the faculty involved are competent representatives of the profession, they must assume responsibility for at least

20. Roland G. Ross, *Course Offerings in Guidance and Student Personnel Work, Summer 1957 and Academic Year 1957-58.* U.S. Department of Health, Education, and Welfare, Circular No. 503, April, 1957, Washington: Government Printing Office, 1957.

some minimal screening of those upon whom they would confer professional status and the right to practice in their field.

Studies of the personal characteristics and personality qualifications of personnel workers are notably lacking. But there is a considerable body of published comment concerning the characteristics that personnel workers should have in order to profit from the type of preparatory programs which have been developed and in order to serve effectively once they have been qualified by education and experience.

It is generally assumed that the individuals who seek to enter this field are endowed with sufficient innate ability to be able to master the intellectual content and challenges of graduate programs which will lead ultimately to the doctorate, although the doctorate is not necessarily the requisite terminal degree for all levels and services. Therefore, these comments will concern essentially what are thought of as "personal characteristics."

The candidate should have the ability to maintain objectivity in interpersonal relationships. In a field of operation where the essential content or subject matter is human beings, the person who is prone to become highly ego-involved may find himself unable to function effectively as a catalyst or reagent. Whatever his age level, the candidate should be possessed of a reasonable level of maturity so that his own personal needs are satisfied from within himself. It should not be necessary for him to "live others' lives" to find self-satisfaction. He should be able to cultivate permissiveness, not merely as a technique but as an ingrained and values-oriented behavior pattern. This is, perhaps, another way of saying that personnel workers must not be rigid personalities. Yet, as any experienced person in the field has observed, even persons who have appeared to be most rigid at the outset of their preparation can acquire flexibility. And with this flexibility is a fourth requisite—of being able to accept others nonjudgmentally. Seen at its apex in the establishment of effective counseling relationship, the nonjudgmental attitude is essential in any interpersonal relationship, where the learning experience is individualized rather than structured to preconceived patterns of "rightness" or "wrongness." And, finally,

the individual entering this work must have an essential dedication
to it as a phase of education without being addicted to self-gratifi-
cation in "soul-saving" and "service to mankind." In the area of
service to mankind, the personnel worker has no particular corner
on the market. Everyone who finds his satisfactions in education
today does so in the face of generally unfavorable economic re-
wards, inadequate status recognition, and generally negative social
relationships. If a prospective personnel worker perceives himself
as something other than a teacher in a particularly specialized phase
of operation, then both his perception of the work and of himself
in relation to it are inadequate.

Needed Equipment of the Personnel Worker for His Role

UNDERSTANDING SOCIETY'S NEEDS

In the rapidly changing era of which we are a part, prediction
of future need in almost any field is a risky venture at best. Nevertheless, if the professional personnel worker is to be prepared for
his role in whatever relationship he occupies in future years, he must
have the broad understanding of society's needs and trends as outlined by Melby and Reeves in chapter ii of this yearbook. Students
do not develop *in vacuo*. Personnel workers do not work in
vacuums. Nor is it enough merely to be able to transmit the best
elements in the culture of the past when there is so crying a need
for the development of a new culture and civilization that will
intellectually and emotionally encompass men's conquering of new
and hitherto undreamed of universes.

UNDERSTANDING INDIVIDUAL NEEDS AND PROCESSES

The need for deep and thorough understanding of psychological
processes and the needs of individuals is an ever present one. As
the science of psychology and its related disciplines of education
and sociology push forward frontiers of man's understanding of
man, there must be an ever intensified search for new and better
ways of understanding man and his behavior. The next quarter-
century of educational program developments in the area of personnel work must see increased attention given to the study of
individual differences, motivation, and personality and behavior

patterns at various levels of work and career interest. Already significant research efforts are underway in areas of measurement and evaluation reflecting the influence of newer psychodynamic approaches to human understanding. These are but the beginning of the shift from the mechanistic measurement of the past twenty-five years to the implementation of dynamic psychology.

UNDERSTANDING EDUCATION

The competent personnel worker of the future will require a broad understanding of education and all of its processes. Exposure to the teaching experience and all of its correlates will give him a better appreciation of the central purpose of the educational process. To function effectively, he will need to develop an understanding appreciation of the goals and objectives of education at the level of his concern. Understanding of the classroom experience and its objectives and the relationship of the personnel functions to it will complete the depth of insight the personnel worker requires in order to be able to function effectively as an integer in the educational equation.

UNDERSTANDING THE "OUTSIDE WORLD"

The personnel worker must develop broad understanding of the world in which students with whom he deals will be projected at the various levels of their educational experience. New approaches to the understandings of vocational orientation and information are yet to be developed. Here, too, is a field as dynamically fluid as the field of human behavior itself. For, with the rapid societal changes which are ever present, there are equally rapid changes in the world of work. Effective student personnel work calls for extensive and knowledgeable use of resources beyond those immediately indigenous to the personnel worker and the school. Berg's chapter in this yearbook points the way to a host of external resources which oftentimes are left untapped. Counselors and other personnel workers must learn to recognize that ingenuity in the use of resources is not an admission of personal weakness but rather of strength in knowledge and precision in insight which enable them to capitalize upon all possible sources of assistance in problem-solving.

UNDERSTANDING TECHNIQUES

Left to the last, purposely, in this category of needed equipment of the professional personnel worker is knowledge of techniques. For, far more important than any category of techniques which a personnel worker can "shake out of his sleeve" are the deep psycho-social understandings of individuals and processes which will enable him to develop and devise techniques in his day-to-day relations and operations. Flexibility and individuality are the keynotes in technique utilization. The counselor must learn to adapt techniques to his own personality, interest, and needs. Highly individual in their nature and, in essence, reflective of the personality of the user, techniques in interpersonal human relations cannot be applied with a pipette, a Bunsen burner, or a series of pulleys and weights. To be sure, courses in techniques of various sorts will continue to be offered and taken. Exposure to such courses should have the effect of showing the individual what can be done but should never imply that the techniques thus learned are the only things that can be done.

The Future of Personnel Service in Education as a Profession

CONTINUING IN-SERVICE EDUCATION

Effective student personnel workers, like effective physicians, lawyers, and other professional persons, will soon recognize that in a field in which concepts, understandings, methods, and even techniques are constantly changing, they, too, must stay alive intellectually if they are to continue their effectiveness. Possession of the doctorate should not be an armor cloak against the development of new ideation. Rather, it should be merely a milestone along a highway of continuous growth which the individual travels throughout his lifetime of service. Identification with appropriate professional associations, continued in-service education through summer programs and seminars, expanded experience through opportunities to participate in programs external to educational institutions (industry, business, recreation, welfare) are all ways by which the personnel worker may keep intellectually alive and growing. Most particularly, since ours is an area so completely dependent upon developing social attitudes and mores, the necessity of keeping abreast of and even dynamically engaged in these developments is prescribed as an element of continuing professional growth.

PROFESSIONAL ASSOCIATIONS IN THE FUTURE

The future of professional associations in the area of personnel work is clouded, indeed, as Barry and Wolf have pointed out.[21] The delineation of membership standards, definitions of functions and descriptions of jobs, development of ethical standards, and self-policing in the public interest are all yet to be achieved. To be achieved, that is, if, in the best interests of the service of education, these are, in fact, desirable.

Conclusion

In closing this chapter it may not be amiss to return to the note on which it was opened. The effort to define the word "profession" either by illustration or function, or as better done in terms of criteria and the ultimate recognition that student personnel functions are desirably integral to the total educational process, leads one inescapably to the conclusion that there is not now and should never be a broad professional area designated as personnel work. Rather, to do our job properly in the fields of education in which we operate, it would appear to be more appropriate to think of personnel work as part of that larger and, yet, in some ways more defined professional area of teaching. Within this broad area, personnel workers have developed a number of specialties. At least one of these specialties, namely, the field of student health service, has professional status fully recognized by all standards and criteria; this is actually a transfer from the pre-existing status of medicine. Another, the field of counseling, seems to be well on its way toward the achievement of this goal. It is highly questionable whether there is actually any valid need for the according of professional status to the other phases of personnel services. Rather, it seems to us to have greater validity to establish these as specialized functions when it becomes apparent that there is a valid content of specialized education and experience to support them as such.

21. Barry and Wolf, *op. cit.*, pp. 97-112.

Specialization and professionalization are not necessarily synonymous. Certainly, there are entire fields of operations within the area of personnel work which rightfully need never be held to the restrictive criteria which would characterize a profession entitled to legal definition and support. Suffice it to say that if the next quarter-century sees our schools and colleges and universities staffed with personnel workers with minimum requisites of education in human understanding and appreciation, the personnel movement will have progressed immeasurably toward its goals of educational and human service. With this accomplished, the arguments about professions, professionalization, and professional associations will vanish as the mist in the light of a blazing sun of achievement.

SUGGESTED READINGS

Counseling and Guidance in General Education. Edited by Melvene D. Hardee. Yonkers-on-Hudson, New York: World Book Co., 1955. Pp. 444.

Encyclopedia of Educational Research. Edited by Walter S. Monroe. (See sections on Guidance, Counseling, and Student Personnel Work.) New York: Macmillan Co., 1950 (revised).

FEDER, D. D., Chairman. *The Administration of Student Personnel Programs in American Colleges and Universities.* American Council on Education, Series VI, No. 19. Washington: American Council on Education, 1958. Pp. 46.

MATHEWSON, ROBERT H. *Guidance Policy and Practice.* New York: Harper & Bros., 1955 (revised). Pp. 424.

Review of Educational Research. Washington: American Educational Research Association.

The following issues are devoted to guidance and counseling: Vol. III (June, 1933); Vol. VI (April, 1936); Vol. IX (April, 1939); Vol. XII (February, 1942); Vol. XV (April, 1945); Vol. XVIII (April, 1948); Vol. XXI (April, 1951); Vol. XXIV (April, 1954); Vol. XXVII (April, 1957).

CHAPTER IX

Frontiers of Personnel Research in Education

I. Modern Perspectives in Personnel Research

HENRY BOROW

THE EVOLVING NATURE OF PERSONNEL RESEARCH IN EDUCATION

The Character of Early Research. In 1925, Professor Clark Hull, whose enduring position in the annals of American psychology will, in all likelihood, be identified with his subsequent contributions to formal theory construction in learning, published an imaginative and radical proposal in quite a different branch of the field, that of aptitude testing and vocational guidance.[1] What Hull offered was a description of an automatic prediction machine into which would be fed a large quantity of aptitude testing data for a given subject on perhaps forty or fifty occupations. The machine was hardly a child of whimsy. Hull described the mechanical procedure in some detail and reported that three prototypes of the machine had actually been constructed. He envisaged the future of his proposal with bold optimism. "We may look forward with confidence," he wrote three years later, "to a day not far distant when some such system (as that proposed) will be operating in every large school system. Then, and not until then, will there be possible a genuine vocational guidance for all the masses of the people."[2]

In retrospect, we see Hull's prophecy as having brushed the two extremes of accuracy. His forecasting machine anticipated the central strategy of the automatic data processing systems which

1. Clark L. Hull, "An Automatic Machine for Making Multiple Aptitude Forecasts," *Journal of Educational Psychology*, XVI (1925), 593-98.

2. Clark L. Hull, *Aptitude Testing*, p. 490. Yonkers-on-Hudson, New York: World Book Co., 1928.

today serve research not alone in the natural sciences and engineering technologies but in the behavioral sciences as well. In conceiving vocational guidance as a straightforward problem in actuarial prediction,[3] however, he failed to share William James' sobering conviction that, whatever the advances in psychology, biographies were not likely to be written in advance. There is little similarity between Hull's assembly-line method and our current conceptions and practices of student counseling.

In an important sense, Hull's proposal was an accurate reflection of the temper of his day. At the time he announced his forecasting machine, applied psychology was still savoring its unprecedented triumph in developing an intelligence testing and selection program for American military personnel in World War I. Conscious of its status as a rising young empirical science, it chose to model itself after the older, more firmly rooted natural sciences. The conceptual world of this earlier psychology was an uncomplicated and neatly ordered one. Its watchword was objective measurement.

It was inescapable that the emerging student personnel work of the 1920's and 1930's, in form and spirit, would carry the imprint of the new psychology, the psychology of individual and group differences, in particular. The section of this volume titled "Milestones in the Development of Personnel Services in Education" documents some of the notable advances of this period. The preoccupations of personnel workers were primarily with problems of educational and vocational guidance. Indeed, as employed by some of the writers of the period, the terms "guidance" and "pupil personnel services" were virtually indistinguishable from educational and vocational guidance. In the college setting, emphasis centered upon the measurement and interpretation of individual traits believed important in making academic and occupational choices. Somewhat more attention was given in the secondary schools to the collection and organization of occupational and educational information and to its dissemination to students. In the elementary schools, a formally organized and professionally oriented group of pupil person-

3. Hull noted in passing that the subject would need to consider his interests and the available opportunities as well as the machine-given prediction in making his career choice but left little doubt that he considered the last-named datum of overarching importance in the decision-making process.

nel services hardly existed, except as proposals in some of the journals and textbooks of the day. Concerns about the scholastic and emotional handicaps of high-school and college students were commonly expressed in the language of clinical medicine. Writers spoke earnestly of the "treatment of educational problems," of the techniques of "diagnosis" and "remediation." Relatively minor roles were assigned to programs of personality development, mental health, and leadership training, to the study of noncognitive variables in student performance, and to the analysis of student peer culture.

What were the dominant research concerns of this earlier period? The trait-measurement psychology, which was so intimately linked to the study of individual differences, became the common working model of student personnel research. A prodigious amount of psychometric data on student behavior was collected and classified. A principal *modus operandi* of such studies was statistical correlation, and considerable effort was given over to studies of concurrent and predictive validity. Numerous journal articles appeared on the construction, validation, and norming of intelligence, scholastic aptitude, and vocational aptitude tests and, later, of interest and personality tests. Interest ran high in the prediction of scholastic performance, and literally hundreds of studies were published which reported the relationship of test scores to high-school and college grades. It was, all in all, a period in which the regression equation was tacitly assumed to hold the answers to the pertinent problems of student adjustment. If circumstances were such that actuarial prediction did not apply, then perhaps the matter was not a proper concern for student personnel research.

Expanding Conceptions of Student Personnel Service and Research. While the precursors of personnel research, strongly influenced by the behavioristic psychology of the day, were relatively content to operate within the comfortable confines of psychometric models, student personnel administrators and service workers ostensibly were not. Their philosophical commitments and the insistent practical demands of their occupation required that they come to grips with the problems of student welfare wherever they found them. Admittedly, their image of the tapestry of student life lacked the geometric orderliness of the research worker; yet it possessed a vividness and a life-in-the-round quality unmatched by research abstractions. Paradoxically, then, the student personnel movement, which had proclaimed its allegiance to the test of experiment, saw its practitioners make bold forays into fields of student service as yet uncharted by empirical investigators. Student personnel *practice* clearly outran research.

The broadening of the base of student personnel work began considerably before World War II. Late in 1947, a historic conference was held in Minneapolis to commemorate, in the words of President James L. Morrill, "a quarter-century of the evolving student personnel program of the University of Minnesota."[4] The forty-three papers delivered by forty contributors made it abundantly clear how the boundaries of the province had changed. There were descriptions of recent developments in counseling process and interviewing technique, in occupational analysis and occupational research methodology, and in the services performed by faculty counselors, student health centers, mental hygiene clinics, and housing bureaus. There were analyses of the personnel problems which characterize such subgroups of the student population as military veterans, foreign students, residence-hall occupants, the speech-handicapped, and the financially straitened. The frequent references to the contributions of clinical and social psychology, sociology, cultural anthropology, and psychiatric social work, taken together, represented an unmistakable index of the evolution of professional student personnel work. A few years later, the publication of the second edition of the *Encyclopedia of Educational Research* furnished additional evidence of the extent to which the movement had permeated the structure of education and made its aims more nearly consonant with those of institutional learning.[5]

As this chapter will later attempt to show, personnel workers have not always displayed sufficient sensitivity to the need to unify their objectives and practices with those of classroom teachers and school administrators. There are, nonetheless, encouraging signs

4. *Trends in Student Personnel Work*, p. 3. Edited by E. G. Williamson. Minneapolis: University of Minnesota Press, 1949.

5. *Encyclopedia of Educational Research*, pp. 909-48. Edited by Walter S. Monroe. New York: Macmillan Co., 1950 (revised).

that the maturing field is identifying itself more closely with the totality of the educational experience. The disciplinary function, for instance, is coming to be viewed less as a matter of particularized remedial and retributive work with offending students and increasingly as a matter of facilitating student growth in socially responsible behavior by providing more liberal opportunities for them to share in the assumption of group obligations. Ancient extra-academic practices, such as student activities and student employment, are being re-examined for their effect upon the personal development, welfare, and achievement of school youth. In fine, whatever humanizing and socializing vectors support the student in the mainstream of his institutional life have become the legitimate concerns of personnel work.

That this extension of the domain of service has necessitated a revamping of research strategy is obvious enough. The tidy and cautious trait-test correlational studies of an earlier time are insufficient for today's needs. A bolder and more intricate conception of student personnel work requires nourishment by an experimentation which is imaginative and resourceful. The hypotheses, criteria, and experimental designs of personnel research are undergoing critical scrutiny and change. The fact that the student is now more commonly studied in the flux of his social interactions rather than as a behavioral isolate has meant that personnel research has had to align itself more closely with the experimental social sciences. Field-theory research, in particular, has held a strong attraction. The true-to-life research models, however, have imposed a fearsome burden on investigators. Generally speaking, more interdependent variables have entered our research designs, and problems of experimental control and inference have grown more obstinate. Confident generalizations are rarely permitted by the results of research.

This is not to imply that significant strides have not been taken in the development of a more sophisticated and versatile experimental methodology. Current personnel research happens to be asking more difficult questions about students, about personnel practices, and about the relations between the two. It is well to remind one's self that simplicity of design is not a sufficient virtue of fertile and consequential research. The pregnancy and relevance of the questions which an experiment raises through the logical formality of its main and subsidiary hypotheses are at least of equal moment. The growing concern of personnel work with genuine and vital problems of student behavior is compelling attention to research questions of this character, however difficult they may prove to answer.

Impact of Behavior Theory Development upon Student Personnel Research. For many years, research in personnel services contented itself with empirical attempts to establish lawful relationships between the observables in student behavior. There were few serious efforts to build conceptual systems which might weld together and explain observed facts. More recently, we have witnessed the growing disposition of personnel research to anchor itself in behavior theory. Attempts of this sort have been tentative and halting, for there is no extant theory of behavior sufficiently robust and broad-gauged to generate a rich measure of productive research hypotheses in the applied behavioral disciplines. To date, most contributions to theory construction in counseling and personnel work have drawn upon miniature systems in the psychology of learning, motivation, and perception. While some workers insist that the chaotic state of current behavior theory renders such attempts premature, it would be difficult to deny that the newer strategy has borne fruit in the form of promising hypothetical constructs and fresh research conceptions.

It has become helpful to conceive of the counseling experience as a structured learning situation and, therefore, analyzable within a framework of learning theory. Shoben, who was one of the first to advance a detailed statement of this proposition, has more recently described the counselor's task as the creation of a setting in which the subject may profitably make over his distorted expectancies and perceptions and develop new learning sets.[6] Others view counseling as a problem in social relearning, with the client generalizing his newly acquired attitudes and skills to interpersonal relations beyond counseling. These reformulations have already altered the nature of the independent and dependent variables which are built into experiments in student personnel work. One clear

6. E. J. Shoben, "Counseling and the Learning of Integrative Behavior," *Journal of Counseling Psychology,* I (1954), 42-48.

illustration of this is the research of Cartwright and his associates, which has set out to isolate the substantive variables, that is, "the primary factors of personality change" that occur in counseling. This long-range research project illustrates one kind of overdue attack on the criterion issue in counseling.[7]

The current movement toward the unification of miniature theoretical systems in the interest of general behavior theory may ultimately furnish personnel research workers with a more hospitable climate for hypothesis formation and testing. The trend is best seen in published efforts to link learning theory to personality and motivation theory. Writers such as Mowrer and Rogers have gone a step beyond and have re-examined the strategies and operations of counseling per se within this framework of expanding theory. Their contributions, which are marked by much admirable creative thinking, have freshly illumined the character of the helping relationship in counseling and captured the serious interest of other workers in the field.

Despite these advances, the theorizing in counseling and personnel work does not make an unqualified success story. With the exception of the classical psychoanalysts, neo-analysts, and client-centered counselors (and in the strict sense most student personnel workers are none of these), there are few who operate out of an established theoretical system. This is partly because the training of personnel workers is likely to be eclectic rather than doctrinal and partly because they perceive the practical and urgent demands of their jobs as unmet by current theoretical models of behavior. Thus, the attractiveness of theory among those who *write about* students is unmatched by those who *serve* students. It has been noted here that the work of the theorists has already produced some shifts in our conceptions of personnel work and in the design of research. It remains to be determined how significant and enduring these changes are. Few will dispute the proposition that hope for an effective student personnel program, based in science, rests ultimately with the development of an encompassing and tenable theory of behavior. The serious question of the moment is whether

7. Desmond S. Cartwright, "Methodology in Counseling Evaluation," *Journal of Counseling Psychology*, IV (1957), 263-67.

current theory is sufficiently mature to generate the productive research hypotheses which are indispensable to the advancement of the field.

SOME DOMINANT EMPHASES IN EMERGING RESEARCH

The Social Psychology of Student Groups. Earlier research on student personnel problems emphasized the development of tests and record forms and the use of these devices in cataloguing the traits and achievements of the individual student. Much effort was centered upon enumerative and normative studies, which took simple behavior description as their objective. In recent years, there has been a transfer of interest to psychodynamic considerations, to needs and motives which have an explanatory role in student behavior. Attending the increased importance of behavior dynamics has been a growing research concern with the cultural determinants of student development and adjustment. The impact of social psychology, in particular, upon student personnel research has helped speed the recognition of student life as a complex, cultural phenomenon. The student presents many faces in institutional life, and we are better able to understand him when the research worker examines the student's behavior in relation to his group identifications and to the status, roles, and loyalties bound up with his group commitments.

Why are some intellectually superior students content with mediocre scholarship records? Why are the conventional systems of institutional reward and punishment, so characteristically the invention of middle-class culture, ineffective in winning from certain students acceptance of the school's code of conduct? Research is beginning to suggest some answers. McArthur's study of the personalities of boys in public and in private schools reveals, for example, that the former tend to view preparation for vocational life as the means to desired upward social mobility whereas the latter, perceiving themselves as members of a privileged class, exhibit less pronounced vocational striving.[8] Both the tentative hypothetical picture which the school counselor constructs of his counselee and

8. C. C. McArthur, "Personalities of Public and Private School Boys," *Harvard Educational Review*, XXIV (1954), 256-62.

the general strategy invoked in working with him can be sharpened by knowledge of such class differences in values.

Studies of peer-group standards, morale, and cohesiveness yield information which is useful to personnel workers, both in interpreting student attitudes and overt behavior tendencies and in grouping students for responsible and effective action. As an illustration, one study of charitable giving among campus groups led to the tentative conclusion that "the most highly and formally structured student organizations, involving emotional or moral commitment as requirements for membership, seem to provide the most effective media through which to secure financial response to charitable appeals.[9] The development of sociometric techniques, such as the social-distance scale and the sociogram, has furnished a fresh approach to the study of the psychological climate of student groups and, indirectly, to the analysis of group tensions, morale states, and leadership potential. Some elementary-school teachers already make use of sociometry to study their classes and to organize them for more effective group learning. It remains for personnel workers at all levels of education to avail themselves more fully of sociometric methods as aids to the understanding and effective management of students in the extracurriculum.

Group-mediated Personnel Work. While group procedures in school personnel work have had an extended history, the movement has not been a vigorous one, and it lacks an impressive research record. In the past, neither psychologists nor curriculum specialists have placed a high value on group personnel approaches, the former because they have tended to view group techniques as superficial in contrast to individualized methods of counseling, and the latter because they have frequently regarded personnel activities as peripheral to the cognitive-centered subject-matter requirements of the school program. Recently, however, there has been a quickening of interest in group procedures in school personnel work, traceable in part to conceptual and research developments in the independent fields of group psychotherapy and group dynamics.

Within the curriculum, group approaches to personnel work are

9. E. G. Williamson, B. J. Borreson, and Robert Irvine, "Learning Habits of Charitable Giving through the Extracurriculum," *Educational and Psychological Measurement,* XI (1951), 103-20.

employed in classes and course units on educational orientation, vocational planning, personality development, and courtship, marriage, and family life. In the extracurriculum, group methods are often used in inducting new students into the school community, in organizing and conducting student activities, and in training student leaders. While it was common at one time to plead the usefulness of group techniques largely on grounds of economy, proponents now claim certain substantial advantages for them which are presumably not offered by counseling. To the student, the group represents society, and the working through of human problems within the group setting is more faithful to problem-solving in out-of-school life than is the atypical surround of counseling. Also, in the group, the student's awakening recognition that many of his age-mates have similar personal concerns may have a salutary effect upon his accepting his feelings about his problems as normal and natural. Moreover, latent social motives, which are bound to the adolescent's search for maturity and increased personal autonomy (for example, vocational motives), may be activated and sharpened by peer-group focus upon common problems. But perhaps the most convincing defense of group-mediated personnel methods is that they are, after all, neither rivals to nor substitutes for individual procedures. They are seen increasingly as performing a complementary role in personnel work, and it is in this perspective that many research studies on group methods are now conceived.

Published research in this area falls into three categories: (*a*) the study of group methods as preparation for counseling; (*b*) the study of group and individual counseling methods as integral aspects of the total helping relationship; (*c*) the comparative study of outcomes of group and individual methods. Several workers have called attention to the need for supplementing research on interview process and counselor strategy with studies of client motives and perceptions in counseling. While findings have by no means been decisive, there seems now to be sufficient preliminary evidence at hand to support the belief that the inappropriate motives, perceptual sets, and expectations with which many students enter upon counseling can be modified by a group experience, either preparatory or parallel to individual work. There have, furthermore, been a number of research reports which suggest the increased effectiveness of combining individual and group techniques in student counseling at both the secondary-school and college levels. Such studies as have compared the independent effects of individual counseling and group work upon short-range educational and vocational outcomes have generally failed to confirm the presumed superiority of the former. On the strength of this sort of research activity, one may be encouraged to hope that the experimental attitude has finally taken root in the group-methods field. Yet, the research has not generally been of a high order, and much of the significance of currently available studies is negated by the stringent evaluation placed upon them by our changing research methodology, with its increasingly exacting requirements for acceptable experimental design.

Process Analysis in Counseling. Until about 1940, by far the majority of publications on counseling in educational settings presented a molar view. They spoke of counseling in monolithic terms as if it functioned as a unit character in its influence upon behavior. The advent of client-centered therapy and the almost simultaneous development of feasible mechanical recording techniques led to serious examination of the in-process substance and form of counseling. What really occurs in counseling? It now became possible to "freeze" the interview and to observe its details (i.e., verbal emissions) in comparative leisure as a means to objective description. Snyder made a pioneering contribution to the problem of analyzing the content of the interview by devising both a practical method for separating the protocols into verbal units and a system for classifying the units.[10] Numerous studies of counseling process, which have revealed something of the nature of the varying roles assumed by counselor and client in the interview, have followed. By no means have all of these been the work of client-centered counselors. Naturally interested in counseling as a complex independent variable in personality modification, research workers have plotted client movement in counseling in terms of frequency changes in negative and positive statements, insightful statements, and the like. It cannot, of course, be seriously argued that such verbal criteria of client

---

10. William U. Snyder, "An Investigation of the Nature of Nondirective Psychotherapy," *Journal of General Psychology*, XXXIII (1945), 193-223.

"improvement" may be substituted for the test of life. But studies of the interview process help us know better what counseling is, and we know now that it is many things. Process analysis has taught, for instance, that practicing educational counselors are not readily classifiable by textbook labels and descriptions of counseling systems, inasmuch as they tend to distribute themselves along a continuum with respect to the degree-of-lead variable in interviewing. At least one series of studies has suggested, too, that experienced counselors of different theoretical persuasions may bear a closer resemblance to one another in the manner in which they view and practice counseling than do experienced and novice practitioners trained in the same system.

Apart from their value in counselor training, the results of research on process analysis have permitted us to become increasingly explicit about the nature of counseling. Global assessments of the outcomes of counseling rarely suggest the specific means by which the efficacy of the procedure may be enhanced. What is needed is considerably more descriptive information about how counselors function and about the lawful relations which bind stimulus sets in counseling to changes in student behavior. There is enough significant work here to keep student personnel research workers occupied for a long time.

Mental Health in the School Setting. Despite the insistence of many critics that the functions of the schools be limited to the cultivation of the mind, American education has inevitably come to assume increased responsibility for fostering the emotional and social well-being of students. The nursery-school or primary-school teacher serves as a part-time parental surrogate in imbuing the child with important societal values and in providing the emotional support upon which the child's security feelings appear to depend. Gradually, the mothering role of the teacher is replaced by one which helps the child enlarge his capacity for accepting social responsibility and find socially approved techniques for expressing his feelings and achieving need gratification. Whatever the grade level, the effective teacher is properly sensitive to the student's needs for substantial self-regard and for group acceptance and status. Both in the classroom and out, vital considerations of mental health permeate the school's operations.

Personality theory in classical Freudian psychology had stressed the disintegrative and disabling consequences of the emotional trauma of early childhood. Under this influence and also because the problem child was seen as a disruptive force upon institutional orderliness, early concerns about mental health in school personnel work were centered very largely upon the behavior deviant and the need for corrective or psychotherapeutic services. Yet, by contrast, the mental-hygiene movement in the United States was inspired and nourished by a dedication to the importance of *preventive* principles of emotional living. Gradually, as a body of knowledge about personality formation and adjustment has been accumulated through experimental and conceptual research in the behavioral sciences, many schools have declared themselves responsible for providing the sort of hygienic psychological climate in which positive growth tendencies are believed to occur. Moreover, in increasing numbers they are establishing in-class and out-of-class opportunities for education in self-understanding and in the techniques of effective interpersonal relations. A wide assortment of instructional materials on mental health is now available for the secondary schools. These innovations, of course, have not been introduced without mounting concern and criticism within the ranks of educational fundamentalists.

The Committee on Preventive Psychiatry of the Group for the Advancement of Psychiatry has published a description and critical analysis of four promising and radically differing classroom projects in mental-health education which have been in operation in certain elementary and secondary schools.[11] All four of the projects are exploratory in nature, and two of them have been described as "developing in a research frame of reference." In its report summary, the Committee said,

These projects with the goals so clearly defined should be considered as one aspect of preventive psychiatry in action. They utilize techniques based upon mental hygiene principles that may be applied to large groups of children. They have developed within the framework of education, primarily by educators and sponsored by education. They

11. *Promotion of Mental Health in the Primary and Secondary Schools: An Evaluation of Four Projects.* Report No. 18, Committee on Preventive Psychiatry of the Group for the Advancement of Psychiatry. Topeka, Kansas: The Committee, 1951.

indicate the tremendous interest of the educator in the emotional development of the child and his total life adjustment, for education has shown itself ready to accept this responsibility.[12]

Much of the research in mental-health education has been of an informal, exploratory character. Student ratings of techniques such as the case conference, multiple counseling, and role-playing are a commonly used method of assessing the worth of school units on mental health. Attempts to demonstrate the merit of such units in terms of pre- to post-test changes on personality inventories have generally yielded results which are neither encouraging nor illuminating. More recently, however, a new and promising study approach has been taken by research which addresses itself to more basic questions, such as that which studies the impact of classroom climate or teacher personality upon pupil behavior. Harold H. Anderson and his co-workers performed a series of studies on the relation between the contrasting personalities of a pair of second-grade teachers and the classroom behavior of their children.[13] The students of the dominating teacher tended more to the extremes of resistance and conformity and they displayed less spontaneity and less courtesy. While Anderson's studies involved only two teacher pairs and used only one of many possible types of "dominative" and "integrative" teacher personalities, the conclusion that teacher attitudes sharply influence the personal and social behavior of the student in the classroom is supported by the research of others. A broader inference which may tentatively be drawn from work in this area is that the school contributes to the formation of positive student attitudes and effective personal interactions not alone by direct and deliberate teaching about human behavior but also by creating and maintaining a stable social microcosm in which wholesome human relations are the accepted order.

THE REVITALIZATION OF OCCUPATIONAL PSYCHOLOGY

Classical Conceptions of Vocational Guidance. Three relatively

12. *Ibid.*, p. 13.

13. Harold H. Anderson and Joseph E. Brewer, "Studies of Teachers' Classroom Personalities: II, Effects of Teachers' Dominative and Integrative Contacts on Children's Classroom Behavior," *Applied Psychology Monographs*, No. VIII. Stanford, California: Stanford University Press, 1946.

independent strategies are discernible in the history of American vocational guidance. In the secondary schools and social service agencies before World War II, it was commonly assumed that vocational-choice difficulties originated in information deficits. The solution, it was believed, lay in confronting the individual with accurate information about job characteristics and opportunities so that he might make an informed choice of vocation. The Smith-Hughes Act of 1917, which provided federal funds in support of vocational education, led to a second form of vocational guidance, one encompassing trade training, placement, and follow-up. This scheme emphasized youth's need for supervised exploratory work-experience and adopted the position that occupational adjustment was best attained through the job-training tryouts and placement aids available through programs of vocational education. The third approach to vocational guidance, centered in trait measurement, grew out of the psychology of individual differences. Although some of its early foundations had been laid by James McKean Cattell and others near the turn of the twentieth century, it did not come into ascendancy until the testing contributions by army psychologists of World War I, which were referred to earlier in the chapter, had made their influence felt. Within education, this psychometric concept of vocational guidance was embraced earliest by the colleges and only more recently by the secondary schools.

In one way or another, all three of the classical strategies which have been briefly described here employ the idea, generally attributed to Frank Parsons, that the making of an appropriate vocational choice requires the effective matching of personal traits to occupational characteristics. Each system, in actual practice, has made some use of counseling to mediate the transmission and interpretation of relevant information toward the end that the matching operation be properly performed. In each case, however, the emphasis has been different. The trait measurement approach, the most influential of the three, has stressed both the student's self-understanding of his trait composition and counseling as the locus of its development. By the same token, the trait-measurement scheme is the only one to boast a vigorous research tradition.

Reaction and Reformulation. None of the classical conceptions of vocational guidance appears ever to have attracted the serious attention of those doing research in the fields of learning, motivation, and personality. Indeed, as these domains of behavioral theory and research grew, psychology as science and vocational guidance as technology became more disparate. Even among research workers in counseling, the conceptually impoverished studies of the trait-measurement approach to vocational guidance found little appeal, and counseling research occupied itself increasingly with matters of psychodynamics, psychotherapy, and interview process. In the years immediately following World War II, there was real cause to doubt whether occupational psychology as a branch of behavior science would survive.

More recently, we have witnessed a resurgence of interest in occupational psychology and vocational counseling as proper spheres for theory formation and hypothesis testing within behavior science. While the roots of the renascence cannot be fully traced here, it is worthy of note that many workers had become prepared to renounce the sterile and confining view which held that the incident of choice-making was the supreme event in occcupational life and that the actuarial method was the vehicle by means of which that event could best be carried off. Occupational adjustment needed to be conceived in broader terms than an act of choice. It required understanding in the context of total behavior flux. If this be granted, the need for vocational psychology to attune itself more directly to significant research and theory developments in behavior science becomes evident enough.

Whether the use of currently available theoretical models of behavior can advance the cause of personnel work was questioned at an earlier point in this chapter. Nonetheless, vocational psychology is now beginning to adapt such models for its own purposes. Vocational interests, for instance, are being re-examined within the rationale of motivation theory. Recent writing and research in vocational psychology reflect the contributions drawn from the disciplines of social psychology, mental health, and occupational and industrial sociology. But, significantly, this now promises to become a two-way street. In some ways, the student's career will occupy center stage in his life drama. As much as or more than any other social role he will occupy, his career will mediate his style of life and furnish the conditions for the fulfilment or denial of his motives. Can occupational psychology, then, be expected to make a contribution to general behavior theory? In her book on occupational psychology, Anne Roe, a clinical psychologist, voices the conviction, "Any development of the theory of occupational choice and selection will go far beyond vocational guidance, as such, in its meanings for normative psychological theory generally and for personality theory in particular." [14]

Contributions from Developmental Psychology to Theory in Occupational Psychology. Much recent research in occupational psychology has centered on the genesis and development of vocational motives. In some instances, such studies examine the occupational history of persons as an aspect of developmental psychology. This position would seem to embody the hope that the laws of vocational development, if such exist, might ultimately be derivable from a full-blown general developmental theory.

The personal history approach to research in occupational psychology has been spurred by conceptions of human development as an orderly progression of life stages. Charlotte Buehler's well-known work in Europe is an excellent example. Miller and Form used the life-stages concept to postulate a five-period work history.[15] Super has used the same scheme to describe vocational development, cutting his pattern to fit Buehler's sequence of life stages. Super labels the stages of vocational life as follows: (*a*) exploration: developing a self-concept; (*b*) reality testing: the transition from school to work; (*c*) floundering or trial process: attempting to implement a self-concept; (*d*) establishment; (*e*) maintenance; (*f*) decline.[16]

Two promising programs of co-ordinated occupational research within a developmental framework have been launched. One is the "Harvard Studies in Career Development" currently in progress at the Graduate School of Education, Harvard University. The other

14. Anne Roe, *The Psychology of Occupations*, p. 315. New York: John Wiley & Sons, 1956.

15. D. C. Miller and W. H. Form, *Industrial Sociology*. New York: Harper & Bros., 1951.

16. Donald Super, *The Psychology of Careers*. New York: Harper & Bros., 1957.

is the program of "Career Pattern Studies" under the supervision of Professor Donald Super at Teachers College, Columbia University. The Harvard studies have identified several critical-choice points in the educational and work histories of students and, among other objectives, have attempted to predict the selection of options at these successive choice points from ability patterns and personal history items.[17] The Columbia studies, which are set in an ambitious longitudinal design, trace the vocational development of male subjects over a twenty-year period and relate career patterns to a wide assortment of psychometric, biographical and socioeconomic indexes. Tests, personal data blanks, student interviews, and parent interviews have been used in data collection. The original 1951 sample consisted of 276 eighth- and ninth-grade boys in the Middletown, New York, school system. A series of six research monographs has been projected, following the life-stages sequence employed by the "Career Pattern Studies." One monograph in the series has been published, and a second is in preparation.[18] A serious limitation upon progress both in vocational-guidance practice and in the realm of vocational-theory construction has been a paucity of dependable factual descriptions of career histories and of the variables which shape them. The Columbia and Harvard studies, and others like them, should help correct this deficiency.

Contributions from Personality Theory to Theory in Occupational Psychology. While the status of personality theory may yet be too uncertain to shed a substantial light on the nature of occupational choice and adjustment, an increasing number of contributions to occupational psychology have drawn upon personality systems for their conceptual models. Most of these resort to self-theory and need-gratification theory, making free use of such hypothetical terms as self-actualization, self-concept, and ego strength to account for vocational striving and the meaning of occupational experience. A studied attempt to identify the principal psychologi-

17. Harold B. Pepinsky, "Research Notes from Here and There," *Journal of Counseling Psychology*, III (1956), 67-68.

18. Donald Super and Associates, "Vocational Development: A Framework for Research." *Career Pattern Study*, Monograph No. 1. New York: Bureau of Publications, Teachers College, Columbia University, 1957.

cal systems to which current conceptions of vocational development and choice are tied grew out of the "Scientific Careers Project" sponsored by the National Science Foundation.[19] While vocational-counseling practices in our schools continue to operate largely out of trait measurement and actuarial strategy, we now have proposed approaches to occupational psychology which are centered in cultural theory, psychodynamics, psychoanalysis, and other personality systems. The "Scientific Careers Project," moreover, proceeded a step beyond and offered a tentative integrated view of the process of vocational development. It is clear that occupational psychology is drawing closer to the mainstream of theory in behavior science and that active concerns of student personnel work for the vocational problems of youth must sooner or later reflect this now significant trend.

Development of Psychologically Oriented Systems of Occupational Classification. For many years, vocational counselors had at their disposal mainly occupational classification systems which sorted jobs according to industry or the type of work operation. Even the *Dictionary of Occupational Titles*, the most fully developed and widely used of all systems to date, makes limited use of psychological criteria in grouping jobs and, consequently, cannot be directly fitted to student descriptions derived from testing and counseling procedures. While there have, of course, been occupational classification schemes based on dimensions of aptitude and interest, none has been comprehensive or detailed enough to represent the occupational universe accurately, and none has been undergirded by the sort of painstaking program of research and validation which the development of a broadly useful system requires.

The resurgence of occupational psychology as a domain of research has brought with it a sharpening of interest in the improvement of occupational classification techniques. Roe has proposed a psychologically based scheme involving a 6 x 8 table.[20] One major axis is defined as "primary focus of activity" and the other as

19. Donald E. Super, Paul B. Bachrach *et al., Scientific Careers and Vocational Development Theory,* pp. 100-122. New York: Bureau of Publications, Teachers College, Columbia University, 1957.

20. Roe, *op. cit.,* pp. 144-67.

"level of function" (i.e., degree of personal autonomy). Roe's system does not avoid the weaknesses mentioned above. What it does is to provide one kind of framework within which the vast literature of occupational research findings can be meaningfully organized and interpreted.

For several years, the United States Employment Service has had in progress an exhaustive study which will become the basis of a new multi-dimensional, psychologically oriented occupational classification method. Through a detailed system of rating procedures, American occupations are described in terms of the general educational level, specific vocational preparation, aptitudes, temperament traits, interests, physical capacities and working conditions which are believed to characterize them. While it is likely that several more years will be required to perfect the classification technique and to assign all occupations studied to appropriate categories, a preliminary document of significance to student personnel workers has already been published in which ratings of the forementioned worker-trait dimensions are presented for four thousand jobs.[21] The new United States Employment Service rationale, in adhering to the classical scheme of matching personal attributes to the worker characteristics of jobs, makes little or no use of the theoretical developments in occupational psychology which have been traced in this chapter. Perhaps the major potential advantage of the new system is that it makes available to counselor and student a much-improved means by which, together, in the setting of counseling, they may symbolically enter into and explore the world of work.

Implications for Personnel Work in Education. Many of the developments in occupational psychology which have been described here are of such recent origin that the precise nature of their impact upon student personnel services cannot yet be ascertained. That these advances will drastically modify certain personnel practices in the secondary schools and the colleges seems beyond doubt. One may hazard a set of general predictions about the form these changes will take.

21. United States Employment Service, *Estimates of Worker Trait Requirements for 4,000 Jobs.* Washington: Government Printing Office, 1956.

1. Vocational counselors and group guidance workers will be less inclined to interpret the vocational problems of students as discrete, single-instance choice situations and more disposed to view them as aspects of a crucial developmental task which ranges over adolescence and early maturity.

2. With increased emphasis upon vocational plans rather than vocational decisions, the schools will better marshal the resources of the classroom, the extracurriculum, and the personnel program so that the student's emerging vocational motives may be sharpened, rendered conscious, and reality tested at many points along the way.

3. In increasing measure, the view that effective vocational planning is largely a matter of discovering and exploiting one's intellectual assets and salable skills will be supplanted by the thesis that vocational planning is a quest for self-fulfilment, and its resolution represents one way in which the person comes to terms with himself. This will mean that, while counselors may continue to encourage students to examine their personal balance sheets in the light of the known worker characteristics of the vocations under consideration, they will place a higher premium than before on counseling as the kind of learning situation in which the student explores and interprets his personal values.

4. The now generally accepted emphasis on self-theory in counseling will modify our accustomed methods of assessing and using occupational information. Counselors will judge the utility of occupational monographs not alone by application of traditional factual and literary criteria but by the adequacy of the job images which such monographs create in students. How the counselee perceives occupational information will assume precedence over the sheer virtue of the facts with which he is presented. His affective responses to occupational stimuli—resistances, rejections, distortions, revisions in self-evaluation—will become at least as important to his learning in counseling as the cognitive aspects of the vocational analysis.

5. As they become more familiar with class differences in cultural values, personnel workers will cease to use a single common strategy in assisting students with their vocational problems. They will recognize the task of counseling a student with a high level of aspiration as drastically different from that of helping a student from a marginal family who contends he is hoping just to get "a job." More counselors will know, too, that both the meaning and significance of work and of job satisfaction are culturally determined and that they cannot assume that students bring a shared outlook on these concepts to the interview. Counseling on vocational problems will rely somewhat less upon the standard formula.

II. Research on the Student in His Educational Setting

HAROLD B. PEPINSKY

A POINT OF VIEW

One of the most promising frontiers of personnel research is that which deals with the process of student development in the educational setting. While research accomplishment in this area stands as a large and visible heritage of the past, such effort has been lacking, heretofore, in several important respects. First, it has not taken account, impartially, of the organized totality of experiences available to students in an educational setting. Studies—available in quantity—have attempted to evaluate particular aspects, or even the whole of a personnel program. Second, where large-scale research has been conducted, it has been either a massive kind of census-taking or has tended to assume that stated educational objectives are consonant with those upon which actual practice is based. Third, it has failed to take advantage of the ideas and methods of a variety of disciplines in a single, co-ordinated program of inquiry. This section of the present chapter will present what appear to be minimally essential ingredients of research on student development, a scheme for organizing the study of these ingredients, a review of selected contemporary research activity along these lines, a statement of research needs, and the exposition of an attitude, among workers in the area of personnel, that takes account of the problem of student development.

Personnel workers are accustomed to viewing their research tasks as limited to the study of what the personnel services themselves provide for students. These workers have little quarrel with the assumption that their principal clients are students; in fact, one infers from the writings of this group that they, more than other educators, have student welfare at heart. If the latter view is accepted as true, however, personnel workers must, in conscience, be willing to consider the possibility that other persons may have a substantial influence upon student attitudes and behavior. It is for this reason that personnel workers in education are urged to take a more expanded view of their research tasks. And it is in this spirit that a proposed framework is offered for research on the larger problem of student development in an educational setting. As will be shown, this is a task that the personnel worker can learn to share with others in the educational setting, a task from which the student consumer stands to gain.

THE RESEARCH TASK

Clearly, such a research task requires, first of all, an understanding of what the individual student is like in successive stages of his educational progress and for dealing with him now in a present setting and for helping him to predict what he is likely to become in future settings. Here, Super [1, 2] has given strong support to two arguments of major importance: (a) that helping an individual predict his own future performance is not synonymous with the process of making actuarial predictions about large numbers of cases, and (b) that the likelihood of predicting an individual's future performance is increased if one has learned a great deal about him in successive stages of his development. Impressions of the student gained from direct observation of him, test data about him, information derived from his responses to questionnaires and inventories, available school records, reports on him from other persons and agencies, sociometric choices given to others and received by him— all of these traditional devices can still be usefully brought together for the task of understanding the individual student. Williamson and Darley [3] described this task as the processes of analyzing and synthesizing data on the individual case. More recently, Pepinsky and Pepinsky [4] and McArthur [5] have described the task more ex-

1. Donald E. Super, *Appraising Vocational Fitness*. New York: Harper & Bros., 1949.

2. Donald E. Super *et al.*, "Vocational Development: A Framework for Research," *Career Pattern Study*, Monograph No. 1. New York: Bureau of Publications, Teachers College, Columbia University, 1957.

3. Edmund G. Williamson and John G. Darley, *Student Personnel Work: An Outline of Clinical Procedures*. New York: McGraw-Hill, 1937, 313 pp.

4. Harold B. Pepinsky and Pauline N. Pepinsky, *Counseling: Theory and Practice*. New York: Ronald Press, 1954.

5. Charles McArthur, "Analyzing the Clinical Process," *Journal of Counseling Psychology*, I (Winter, 1954), 203-207.

plicitly as that of using information about an individual to construct a hypothetical other person; this hypothetical person, in turn, is used to make predictions, which can be tested against the actual individual's behavior. Super's important emphasis, however, is that the individual is better understood if one has developmental information about him.

In these and other writings, Williamson, Darley, Wrenn, Super, the Pepinskys, McArthur, and others in the personnel area have indicated the necessity for understanding, concurrently, the society and the culture in which the individual student develops. Here, for example, Super[6] is systematically providing for personnel workers in education both a conceptual scheme and a wealth of information about the emergence of developmental patterns among selected individuals within an entire community. Cogent attempts to explain social and cultural phenomena as they affect individual development, to buttress Super's contribution to the organization, method, and content of developmental research, are offered by social theorists such as Parsons,[7] Gerth and Mills,[8] and Merton.[9] "Understanding" the society in which the individual student develops, as these social theorists make clear, implies the ability to analyze and synthesize data that are used to describe an evolving social structure.

The educational setting constitutes a specific and highly relevant example of social structure that must be considered in organizing a framework for research on student development. But the educational setting, like the individuals who comprise it, is best understood in the context of the culture and society in which it has developed. How a school, a community, and a culture are interrelated and how the school can be meaningfully accounted for through knowledge of its sociocultural setting has been described by Seeley, Sim, and Loosely.[10] On the basis of observations and

6. Donald E. Super et al., "Vocational Development," op. cit.

7. Talcott Parsons, The Social System. Glencoe, Illinois: Free Press, 1951.

8. Hans Gerth and C. Wright Mills, Character and Social Structure. New York: Harcourt, Brace & Co., 1953.

9. Robert K. Merton, Social Theory and Social Structure. Glencoe, Illinois: Free Press, 1957 (revised edition).

10. John R. Seeley, Alexander Sim, and Elizabeth W. Loosely, Crestwood Heights. New York: Basic Books, 1956.

interviews, the investigators concluded that the attitudes and behavior of pupils, school officials, and parents are strongly influenced by more general cultural and community attitudes. The very architecture of the community school building seemed to be a clear outgrowth of these social forces.

Finally, a framework for research on student development demands understanding of the transactions that occur between the student and the setting in which he is being educated. This kind of understanding implies knowledge of what the student does to the setting and of what the setting does to him—knowledge based upon a sampling of the everyday interactions between the student and his school environment. Moreover, such understanding implies the ability to explain and predict how student and setting are modified in the process of interacting with each other. As Seeley, Sim, and Loosely [11] point out, the community and the school influence the students in the school, but the students, in turn, influence the school and the community. Even the architecture of the school building, influenced as we have seen by social forces within the community, seems to exert a reciprocal influence on the community, according to these authors.

A SCHEMATIC PRESENTATION OF THE RESEARCH TASK

In order to conduct research on student development within an educational setting, it is important to keep in mind each of the relevant variables cited: (a) the developing individual student, (b) his cultural and social background, (c) the developing educational setting, in the context of (d) its cultural and social environment, and (e) interactions between student and setting. In the proposed framework for research on student development, the above variables are regarded as being logically antecedent to the conditions of the individual who emerges out of the setting, either as a graduate or as otherwise separated from it, after spending time there in the formal capacity of student. The condition of the emerging individual is assumed to be an outcome—therefore, *dependent* upon the specified antecedent conditions. The latter are thus to be regarded as *independent* variables; the outcome condition is to be regarded

11. *Ibid.*

as a *dependent* variable. Mediating conditions are used to explain
how the two sets of variables are related to each other. These relationships among antecedent, mediating, and consequent conditions are schematized in Figure 1.

Obviously, the contents of Figure 1 suggest only the minimal
essentials for research on student development in an educational
setting, and each of the variables listed in Figure 1 requires careful
and explicit empirical definition. The figure does suggest an administrative outline for such a research enterprise, however, in that
major independent variables to be considered are specified; also,
the possibility is suggested of making statements of relationship
among them, and of predicting their relationship to a major dependent variable, namely, the future behavior of the student. Incomplete as it is, the proposed framework provides a means by
which personnel workers can check on the scope and impact of their
own research contributions and those of colleagues. Empirical
definition and measurement of the major variables prescribed by
the framework constitutes a major research task. The purpose of the
research outline is not simply to list the variables but to provide a
basis for making sense out of the process of explaining the student,
the setting, and the transactions between them. "Making sense out
of" the individual student, for example, implies both understanding
his complexity as an individual personality and organizing what is
known of his activities into a meaningful and coherent system.
Without this kind of awareness, supported by empirical knowledge,
his contribution to his own development cannot easily be predicted
or assessed. Similarly, the complexity of the educational setting's
structure and functions must become known and, subsequently, be
organized into a coherent system to account for the behavior of
persons within it. This knowledge is needed in order to predict
and to assess the contribution of the setting to the student's development. But either kind of knowledge, alone, does not suffice; interactions between student and setting must also be observed and
interpreted. While this process will be facilitated by knowledge of
student and setting, the transactions between them, by which one
or both are modified, must be studied in their own right as possible
major contributors to the development of the student. Finally,
these transactions help to define the *inter*personal, as opposed to the

OBSERVABLE ANTECEDENT CONDITIONS (Independent Variables)	MEDIATING CONDITIONS		OBSERVABLE CONSEQUENCES (Dependent Variable)
	Observed	Inferred	
Characteristics of the student prior to, or at time of, entering the educational setting. Characteristics of the student on successive occasions while in the setting. Relationship to setting and to sociocultural conditions	Temporal sequence of characteristics. Relationship of above sequence to general social and cultural conditions and to condition within the setting	Inferred developmental pattern. Sociocultural and educational influences upon student's developmental pattern	Characteristics of the student (a) at any future time while he is in the setting, (b) at time of leaving the setting, and (c) on subsequent occasions and in other situations
Characteristics of the culture(s) and society(ies) in which he has developed. Current cultural and social conditions. Relationships to setting and to student	Temporal sequence of characteristics. Relationship of above sequence to sociocultural environment and to student conditions	Inferred developmental pattern. Sociocultural and student influences upon educational pattern	
Characteristics of the educational setting, including its sociocultural environment, prior to, or at time of, the student's entrance into it. Interactions between the student and the setting. Relationships to sociocultural environments, educational setting, and student	Temporal sequence of interactions. Relationships to sociocultural, educational, and student conditions	Inferred developmental pattern. Reciprocal influences between student and setting	

FIG. 1.—A proposed scheme for conceptualizing the processes and outcomes of student development in an educational setting.

*intra*personal development of the student. And knowledge of interpersonal behavior, in its reciprocal manifestations, has been shown
by Leary [12] to be highly important in revealing the extent to which
personal development has taken place.

SOME CURRENT STUDIES

Happily, it can be reported that research studies on the process
of student development in the educational setting are well under
way. The most striking of these, at the present time, are being conducted in college or university settings. Perhaps the most comprehensive study of the student dimension is being made by Sanford
and Associates,[13] who have combined in their study of Vassar College women students the personality assessment methods and
interpretations of depth psychology, the sociological study of the
structure and functions of a total educational community, and the
longitudinal, reassessment methods of developmental psychology.
What may turn out to be equally comprehensive in scope and
method is the study of Princeton undergraduates, yet to be reported
in detail, by Stephan [14] and his co-workers. The study has pur-
ported to look at "all aspects of resident university life . . . for their
effect on the student's intellectual, moral and physical development." [15] It consists of a number of loosely co-ordinated projects,
whose purpose and method vary widely. One of these, for example,
is an intensive case study of 36 students who were closely observed
throughout four years of undergraduate living. The project, directed by Heath [16] has resulted in the isolation of three distinct
personality types among the students, each of whom also was in-

12. Timothy Leary, *Interpersonal Diagnosis of Personality: A Functional
Theory and Methodology for Personality Evaluation.* New York: Ronald
Press, 1957.

13. Nevitt Sanford (Issue Editor), "Personality Development during the
College Years," *Journal of Social Issues,* XII (1956), 3-72.

14. Frederick F. Stephan, "Attitudes, Expectations, and Decisions during
the Undergraduate Years." Paper read at the Educational Records Bureau's
Twenty-second Educational Conference, New York City, November 1, 1957.

15. *Ibid.,* p. 1.

16. S. Roy Heath, Jr., "Personality and Student Development: Some Research Findings of the Princeton Study." Unpublished manuscript, 1957.

ferred to vary along a dimension of "ego-integration." Still another study of the student in his university setting, more limited in scope but highly inventive in its method, has been conducted by Stern, Stein, and Bloom [17] at the University of Chicago. Although further aspects of this research are reported in the next section of the present chapter, the reader's attention now is called to these investigators' work in developing "assessment models," with which the measured personalities of university students could be compared. "Models" of successful and unsuccessful students in various fields of study in the university were developed out of information provided by faculty members and were translated by the authors into personality descriptions of students.

The above studies are selected for special comment here because they are informative about the developing student in his educational setting and, to a much more limited degree, about the transactions that take place between student and setting as he progresses through it. Although the framework presented in Figure 1 calls for extensive research, if definitive questions about student development are to be asked and answered, the Vassar, Princeton, and Chicago research indicates that large-scale programs are possible and potentially useful. This statement is not intended to belittle less inclusive research; one only hopes that smaller chunks of inquiry will be accompanied by appropriately modest conclusions. Moreover, as will be emphasized in the following section, student personnel workers can become more catholic in their objectives and procedures as they become aware, through their own and others' research, that their contributions to student development are highly limited in comparison with the total impact of an educational program.

In yet another respect, the Vassar, Princeton, and Chicago studies have been deemed worthy of special mention. This is the imaginativeness and flexibility of methods used in the conduct of the research and in the very asking of questions. And finally, the studies illustrate a potential value of interdisciplinary teamwork in research, when there are common problems to be solved. Such

17. George G. Stern, Morris I. Stein, and Benjamin S. Bloom, *Methods in Personality Assessment*. Glencoe, Illinois: Free Press, 1956.

teamwork can contribute its fair share to breadth of inquiry, novelty of method, and increased awareness of competencies and contributions by other kinds of workers.

Let us examine the Vassar project more closely as a case in point. In this ambitious program of research, an entire college is made the subject of inquiry by a team consisting of an anthropologist, a sociologist, and several psychologists. Since the major published report on the project which is presently available has been made by the psychologists,[18] their view of the research and its results will be discussed here. The study takes for granted that the objectives of the liberal-arts college are to acquaint the student with his cultural heritage, to help him exercise his intellect, and to further his individual development as a whole person, and the authors think that these objectives are similar to the psychologist's concerns with an individual's "health," "maturity," or "optimum functioning." The purpose of the research, generally, is to provide knowledge about personality development after ages seventeen or eighteen, and, specifically, to study the impact of the environment of a liberal-arts college upon its students. I have attempted to schematize the research in Figure 2.

A comparison of Figure 1 with Figure 2 indicates that the Vassar project is hypothesis-seeking rather than predictive in its present stage. Moreover, although we are told that personality theory has been drawn upon in the building of a standard test battery, the theory, as such, together with its implications for cross-sectional or longitudinal measurement of student behavior is never made explicit. Also, though we are told that a sociological study of the college has been made concurrently with the collecting of data on individual students, we are informed only that the related organizational research is very helpful; we are not able to determine from the Sanford report what the social structure is like, nor how the structure itself is related to the development of the students within it. Though we are given hints that students have social histories antecedent to their entrance into the College, these histories and *their* relatedness to student development are not made explicit. We learn, too, that student-student and student-faculty transactions

18. Nevitt Sanford *et al., op. cit.*

OBSERVATIONS						INFERENCES
Of present or former Vassar Students						Developmental patterns of students
Entering Freshmen	Freshmen	Sophomores	Juniors	Seniors	Alumnae	Temporal sequences of student development (as individuals, sub-group, and total group)

Of the educational setting (generally described, but not specified)

Fig. 2.—An attempt to schematize the study of Vassar College students. (After Sanford et al.)

have been observed and interpreted, but the report does not deal explicitly with these transactions and their implications for student development.

Figure 3, which portrays the design for data collection in the Vassar project, however, indicates that a major and important task of gathering information about college students has been performed. In four successive years, a three-hour battery of tests has been administered to entire groups of Freshmen entering Vassar College, and in four successive years entire Senior-class groups have been tested with the same battery. Supplemental performance data available for all students include scores on Scholastic Aptitude Test and on tests of the College Entrance Examination Board, plus academic grades and reports from faculty members. Four primary performance dimensions were used to determine what measures should be included: (a) intellectual functioning and achievement, (b) immaturity-maturity (effectiveness of ego functioning), (c) femininity and masculinity, and (d) psychological and physical well-being. To help validate these measures, and to supplement inadequate measures in the last category, a sample of one of the Freshman groups was given intensive interviews and was reinterviewed in the Sophomore year. Group I in Figure 3, an alumnae group, was intensively "assessed," following the pattern of assessment used with candidates for the OSS during World War II. The "assessment" process also helped in the validation and reinterpretation of the test data. In addition, other groups of available alumnae have been given the standard test battery. Moreover, faculty and administration groups were "generally observed."

What all this adds up to, if my interpretation of the Sanford report is correct, is summarized in Figure 4. Here, it can be inferred that the repeated testing of the entering Freshman (five times) and Senior groups (four times) should yield highly stable measures of each class group. In 1956, when the Sanford report was published, however, only one valid developmental comparison of the Freshman (1952 entrants) and Senior (1956 group) groups could be made, and even this can be questioned since the 1952 Freshmen were tested with a preliminary form of the present standard battery. Only one other valid developmental study has been made, that of the sample interviewed as Freshmen (1954) and again as

Groups	Year					
	1952	1953	1954	1955	1956	19??
A	EF–pT				S–T	
B		EF–T (f–pI)				
C			EF–T (f–I)	(so–I)		
D				EF–T		
E					EF–T	
F		S–T				
G			S–T			
H				S–T		
I ('29–'35 grads)	(3-day "assessment" in groups of 10 each; times not specified)					
J ('04–'43 grads)	(T only; times not specified)					
K (administrators and faculty)	(I and GO; times not specified)					

EF = all entering Freshmen in fall of year

f = sample of Freshmen during year

so = sample of Sophomores during year

S = Seniors in spring of year

T = standard test battery

pT = pilot test battery

I = interview

pI = pilot interview

"Assessment" = paper and pencil tests, situational tests, group interaction, and interviews (after OSS pattern)

GO = "general observation," (includes student and faculty discussions, classroom sessions, etc.)

Fig. 3.—The design for data collection in the Vassar Project. (After Sanford et al.)

Sophomores (1955). All other comparisons necessitate two assumptions: (a) that different groups of students were identical with each other at the same points in their training (i.e., as Freshmen), and (b) that the College itself has remained static as a set of curricular and extracurricular experiences to which the different groups of students were exposed. Neither of these assumptions is warranted by available evidence.

Group	Year in College					
	Entering Freshman	Freshman	Sophomore	Junior	Senior	Post-College
A	pT				T	
B	T	(pI)				
C	T	(I)	(I)			
D	T					
E	T					
F					T	
G					T	
H					T	
I						(3 day "assessment")
J						T
K	(I & GO)					

pT = pilot test battery
T = standard test battery
I = interview

"assessment" = paper and pencil and situational tests, group interaction, and interviews

GO = "general observation"

Fig. 4.—Summary of data collected in the Vassar Project. (From data in Fig. 3.)

Nevertheless, we can see in outline form the beginnings of a comprehensive research program. What have been cited in this review as deficiencies in the present research can be remedied in future studies. As the blank spaces in Figures 3 and 4 are filled in, as the sociological and anthropological data now being gathered become more truly integrated with the psychological data, as explicit theories of student behavior become formulated and tested, we, as student personnel workers, stand to learn much that can guide us in our own research and in our personnel practices. Is the preliminary finding of the Sanford group (that Seniors at Vassar are more independent but less secure, less decided than Freshmen) a valid one for our own institutions? Do we want our Senior women to resemble the Vassar Seniors in their personality development?

Considerable space has been devoted to the Vassar project in this review. Is this a "good" research study? As the 1950's draw to a close, who can say? The mere fact that the research has been carried out with some preplanning, with intelligence and enthusiasm, with a "pay off" in information not previously available to those of us who work in educational settings is testimony to the "goodness" of the Vassar study. If it is to fulfil more of the requirements implied in the schema of Figure 1, the Vassar research must demonstrate that it is more than procedurally interdisciplinary; it must show the solid and, we can hope, the novel results of an explicit and valid integration of (e.g., sociological and psychological) theory and method.

SOME RESEARCH NEEDS

In retrospect, neither the Vassar College project nor any other past or current study begins to take adequate account of the broad range of variables schematized in Figure 1. Yet I have hesitated to label it or other student personnel research as "good" or "bad"—in respect to questions asked, design, or results. Such evaluation must be preceded, in every case, by such questions as, "Good in whose view?" and "For what purpose?" Yet student personnel workers persist in wanting others to provide such evaluations for them . . . like Paul Meehl [19] they want "good cookbooks" to guide them in their research and other personnel practices. Unlike Meehl, however, they tend to short-circuit the process of deciding for themselves whether a given "cookbook" is indeed "good" for them.

A primary need in student personnel research today is central to student personnel work in general—a need for persons in the field who are able to ask intelligent questions about their everyday practices, because they are informed about the alternatives open to them and thoughtful about the possible consequences of choosing among alternatives. The dilemma here is that there are consumer demands for quantity as well as quality of personnel services; with increased student enrolments at all educational levels, the pressure for quantity has increased disproportionately. The problem of student development in educational settings also becomes more

19. Paul E. Meehl, "Wanted a Good Cookbook," *American Psychologist,* XI (November, 1956), 263-72.

complicated under the stress of providing more service for proportionately less money and personnel time, however, and the "pay off" of alternative actions open to all educators is a matter of acute concern.

A second need is for methodological developments that will contribute to intelligent awareness of alternative routes to be followed in selecting students for particular educational experiences or in helping students make optimal use of such experiences. This need is intimately related to the first one, because it is under the pressure of making immediate, everyday, operating decisions that student personnel workers and other educators are apt to short-circuit the question-asking-and-answering phases of their work. We should not be surprised if we find that the kind of research produced under these circumstances has little more to contribute than census-taking or the advertizing of vested interests plus modes of procedure to enhance them.

A third need, also, is highly related to the first two. It is for programs of graduate education for student personnel workers that contribute to the selection and development of persons who are keenly aware of and able to integrate scientific and professional concerns with the process of educating students. Graduate education could contribute significantly to the development of attitudes and understandings that would prevent much of the short-circuiting and reliance on "cookbook" procedure that now takes place on the job among educators. Unfortunately for the meeting of the third research need, graduate faculty members in student guidance and personnel areas, like many of their colleagues in medicine, chemistry, psychology, and other programs of professional education, have been more preoccupied with satisfying on-the-job demands than with creating them.

A RESEARCH ATTITUDE

The foregoing summary of needs in personnel research has been presented with a view toward upsetting the notion that personnel workers can be provided with a set of ready-made procedures and techniques for accomplishing their educational tasks. What is needed in all personnel work, in fact, is a research attitude based on faiths in educational values which need to be made explicit, on knowledge and understanding of human organizational behavior in general and on students and educational settings in particular, and on an intelligent skepticism that allows operating decisions to be questioned and validated. This kind of research attitude is as useful to an assistant principal or dean of men as it is to a school counselor or a therapist in a central counseling agency. The attitude permits new and important educational tasks to be created and accomplished, just as it fosters assessment through research of what is accomplished. In the next portion of this chapter, we shall see how an informed and flexible research attitude can lead to a constructive liaison between personnel work and instruction.

III. The Interrelations of Personnel Services and Instruction

PAUL L. DRESSEL

Dichotomies are conveniences, but once introduced they may become stereotypes which interfere with clear thinking and thereby impede progress. The heading of this section involves such a dichotomy, one which has come to be widely used in education. The mere fact that there is need to discuss the interrelations of personnel work and classroom instruction suggests that their separation has proceeded too far.

The underlying purpose of all formal education is that of changing the behavior of people through a carefully planned sequence of experiences. Although behavior and experience are words with overtones which are not entirely acceptable to all classroom teachers, it is clear that every educational objective ultimately implies some change in students. Even if the objectives of a particular course be limited—as they seldom are—to an increase in knowledge, there is implied thereby an increase in ability to recall and relate facts. These are changes in behavior and the changes are brought about by curriculum experiences selected because the teacher sees them as conducive to the desired increase in knowledge. In this broad sense of providing experiences designed to produce changes in behavior, the personnel worker is engaged in instruction.

It is not always immediately apparent that this is the case. Some personnel programs appear primarily to offer activities and services sufficiently extensive to keep students busy and sufficiently controlled to keep them out of mischief. In such cases the experiences are planned, and behavior may be changed, but there is some doubt that the changes are clearly specified or that they are desirable ones. The objectives implicit in such a program may actually be contradictory to the avowed educational purposes of an institution.

Even if the purposes of a personnel program in education are clearly defined and quite consistent with the avowed educational goals of an institution, the planning often falls short of providing a sequence of experiences appropriately adjusted to the development of the different individuals. It is not desirable nor is it possible to so organize student activities that a Freshman enrols in student activities 1 and 2, a Sophomore in student activities 3 and 4, thereby achieving the superficial characteristics of sequences in academic fields. Nevertheless, personnel service can hardly be regarded as having achieved full educational status until it provides for each student a sequence of experiences of increasing complexity or responsibility which helps to interrelate all phases of the student's total educational experience.

Implied in the preceding remarks is the assumption of close similarity, even the actual identity of the objectives of classroom instruction and of personnel work. Every educational institution formulates a statement of its objectives. The level of generality of such explicit statements of objectives makes it easy for both personnel workers and the instructional staff to subscribe to them. It is not so evident that the objectives implicit in class experiences and extracurriculum activity are identical. In fact, both teachers and personnel workers have been known to suspect each other of having lost sight of the really significant educational goals. The dichotomy in function has, indeed, beclouded thinking and led to distinctions for which, in fact, there is little justification. Familiarity with our cultural heritage, awareness and acceptance of the values inherent in it, increased ability to do critical thinking and make wise judgments, and good citizenship are representative of the broad objectives accepted by all educators. All experiences planned within the framework of a formal educational program should contribute to these objectives and to the changes in behavior implied by them. There is need, to a far greater extent than has been done, to look for and develop interrelations of personnel service and formal instruction so that they supplement and re-enforce each other in fostering desired changes in students.

In this section a number of research studies which involve or point to such interrelationships will be mentioned and their implications explored. The particular examples of research used have not been chosen primarily because of their quality or lack of it; rather, they have been chosen because they investigate a problem or arrive at conclusions which suggest how meaningful relationships between instruction and student personnel work may be most advantageously developed.

INTEREST AND EXPERIENCE

The significance of interests in academic and vocational success has been a continuing problem upon which much research has been done, though with very little tangible result. For example, Brooks and Weynane [1] in a study made at Texas A. & M. College found that interest preference scores had little if any effect on academic success, although great variations in interest profiles were found among the students in the various fields. Many similar studies have been made and, in the main, similar results have been obtained. Curious it is that, although education exists to change people, the personnel worker, somehow, cannot quite resist the belief that interests ought to be fixed and that people ought to act in accordance with them.

In another study attacking a different aspect of the same problem, Weitz, Clarke, and Jones [2] investigated whether Freshmen who express a preference for a major field are better prepared when entering college and whether they perform better than those who have no such goals. Their conclusion was that students, both men

---

1. Melvin S. Brooks and Robert S. Weynane, "Interest Preferences and Their Effect on Academic Success," *Social Forces*, XXXII (March, 1954), 281-85.

2. Henry Weitz, Mary Clarke, and Ora Jones, "The Relationships between Choice of a Major Field of Study and Academic Preparation and Performance," *Educational and Psychological Measurement*, XV (1955), 28-38.

and women, who have identifiable goals appear to be better prepared for college than those who do not. They found also that male
students with well-defined educational goals do better in college
and that women students do about equally well whether they have
definite educational goals or not. They concluded that further
investigation is needed to see if preferences act as a motivational
device which aids students in integrating their learning experiences
more effectively. It is not clear from this study whether or not the
institution involved accepts the belief that indecision in regard
to an educational goal or vocational choice is a respectable state of
mind.

From other investigations it is evident that many girls go to
college without a definite vocation in mind, desiring only a general
education in contemplation of early marriage.[3] This being the
case, women very frequently find difficulty in choosing majors,
and the recognition of this phenomenon makes lack of educational
goals more accceptable in women than in men. Perhaps this is why
in the Weitz, Clarke, Jones study the lack of educational goals did
not affect the achievement of women. In some colleges and even
in some high schools, the student—especially the male student—
who cannot declare a definite goal is regarded as odd or immature.
It may be that conformity or lack of conformity to the expectations
of the institution is the significant factor rather than presence or
absence of a definite goal. At Michigan State University, where
30 per cent of the Freshmen regularly report "no preference" in a
program which makes special provision for them, this group has
been found, when account has been taken of intelligence, to perform as well or better than those who initially declare a major.
Similar studies have been reported elsewhere.[4]

In contrast with studies which arise out of the assumption that
interests are or should be reasonably stable and should become the
basis for planning an education, Matteson[5] undertook a study of

3. Kate H. Mueller, *Educating Women for a Changing World*. Minneapolis: University of Minnesota Press, 1954.

4. John D. Krumboltz, "Measuring Achievement Motivation—A Review,"
Journal of Counseling Psychology, IV (Fall, 1957), 191-98.

5. Ross W. Matteson, "Experience-Interest Changes in Students," *Journal
of Counseling Psychology*, II (Summer, 1955), 113-21.

the extent to which interests change and the extent to which these changes are related to the educational experiences of the students. He concluded that interests, defined in terms of reactions to experiences commonly available to students, are changed by experiences in a program of general education; that changes in interest vary according to the nature and extent of experience, and that gains in interest are associated with the extent of initial difference between interest and experience. In short, the broader patterns of experience available in the first two years of college can become the basis for the modification of students' interests. The difference between this approach and that of the other studies mentioned cannot be over-emphasized. In the first case there is the assumption of some degree of permanency of interests and the further assumption that the educational experiences of the individual should be based on the existing interest. In the latter case, the educational experiences available to the individual are seen as productive of changes in interests and ultimately in the behavior of the individual. In one case the research is concerned with proper classification of the individual and in the other it is concerned with the development of the individual. The latter would seem to have much more profound educational implications than the former. Indeed, the former conception is more suited to placement practices in business and industry than to an educational institution.

PREDICTION OF ACADEMIC SUCCESS

Personnel workers in institutions of higher learning have engaged in many studies of academic success and failure. Most all such studies have examined success and failure in terms of the personal characteristics of the individual students without relating these characteristics to the academic situation of which the students are a part. Such studies have often concentrated on correlations of academic aptitude test scores, personality test scores, and similar evidence with grades. Other studies of successful and unsuccessful students have tried to determine categories of characteristics or factors that make for success or failure, apparently assuming that the students of the successful and unsuccessful groups are largely homogeneous with each group. In contrast with this, recent research by Roth [6] suggests that the success or failure of a student may be as much a matter of the expectations and conceptions of the faculty of an institution as of the personal characteristics of the student. To use one of Roth's examples, he remarks that in one institution research-oriented students in sociology might be dismissed as ivory-tower theorists, while in another institution oriented to research, the sociology student with a marked interest in social service might be almost automatically a failure. In short, the success or failure of an individual is predictable only in terms of the kind of educational experiences available in the institution. In a doctoral dissertation at Harvard, Kimball [7] has examined the same issue. She, too, notes that guidance often stresses the notion that success and failure are determined by the make-up of the individuals involved, but that the role of the educational situation itself in creating success or failure tends to be ignored. This limited approach of concentrating on the reasons for the failure of the individual tends to neglect the possibility of changing the pattern of educational experience provided. It also ignores the possibility of improving the educational experience of successful students who may appear relatively happy and effective in the accomplishment of their tasks precisely because the experiences which they are having are not really making much difference in them. A degree of tension and of frustration is a necessary concomitant of a really significant educational experience.

NEEDED CHANGES IN VIEWS OF PERSONNEL WORKERS

The preceding studies and remarks suggest a dawning recognition that the personnel worker's awareness of and concern about students, individual and group, must be tempered by an awareness of the total educational experiences provided in an institution. However, the personnel worker's attempt to see his role as an educational one and co-ordinate with that of classroom instruction and

6. Julius Roth, "The Study of Academic Success and Failure," *Educational Research Bulletin*, XXXV (October 10, 1956), 176-82.

7. Barbara Kimball, "The Relationship between Nonintellective Factors and Scholastic Achievement." Unpublished doctoral dissertation, Harvard University, 1950.

his efforts to bring about a merger of the two, which would promote a sense of unity in the total campus educational experience, are hampered by his vocabulary and by his preoccupation with his place and prestige in the administrative organization. For example, a recent workshop report from Florida State University [8] speaks of the importance of the relationship of students with adults, relationship with peers through such media as resident-hall living and participation in student government, and the facilitation of friendships between students, faculty, and non-instructional staff members. Personal interrelationships and friendships are undoubtedly desirable and even necessary. Their immediate relationship to the goals of education is less clear, and the faculty member may be pardoned if he sees these emphases as competing with the academic aspect of the curriculum rather than supplementing it. The vocabulary of personnel work, with its superficial facade of educational and psychological jargon, is not well chosen to convey to the teacher the identity of its goals with those of instruction. The undergirding of psychological principles, applicable equally to personnel services and instruction, needs more attention, more study, and translation into language understandable to all teachers.

As personnel work in education has developed its own administrative organization separate from instruction, there has developed a self-righteousness arising out of its devotion to the needs of the individual student as a human being. An associated tendency has been to remark on the inadequacies and inconsistencies of academic instruction, which are relieved only by the presence of the personnel worker whose advice enables the student to negotiate successfully this mysterious maze of academic requirements. Fortunately, some of the research discussed in the preceding paragraphs suggests that a different view is developing. In time, the common pattern of organization, which so clearly distinguishes between student affairs and instruction, may itself need restudy.

STUDIES OF THE INSTRUCTIONAL PROCESS

If, on one hand, some of the research of personnel workers is

8. Robert B. Kamm, "The Unity of the Educational Program, with Special Reference to Student Personnel Services," *Personnel-O-Gram,* XII (October, 1957), 3-8.

bringing a new awareness of the curriculum and the instructional program, it is equally true that certain research initiated from the side of the instructional program is demonstrating the importance of student characteristics and of experiences commonly associated with personnel-program responsibilities. This is particularly evident in a large number of studies concerned with student-centered versus instructor-centered teaching. The incentive for such studies arises out of attempts to examine the relevance to teaching of Rogerian nondirective, client-centered counseling and of group dynamics. Student-centered teaching encourages the student to find the questions rather than posing them and encourages him to seek his own answers rather than learning those given to him. Accordingly, it has been hypothesized as more effective in changing attitudes and values than instructor-centered teaching, wherein the student may memorize the answers presented without becoming personally involved in them. Some studies have found evidence for the validity of this hypothesis. Wieder,[9] for example, using a nondirective group-therapy pattern of instruction, found measurable changes in social, religious, and ethnic prejudice, whereas the traditional lecture-discussion approach produced no change.

Many studies of student-centered instruction turn out to be nothing more than an inconclusive examination of the comparative merits of the lecture and of a type of discussion which might better be described as a recitation. As McKeachie [10] has pointed out, the student-centered and the instructor-centered types of instruction have become stereotyped. One is seen as democratic, permissive, and interesting; the other as authoritative, content-centered, and dull. One is regarded as suited to teaching the student how to think and to modify his attitudes and values; the other is seen as setting goals of knowledge for knowledge's sake. Shades of the directive-nondirective counseling controversy! Actually, the studies comparing the two methods have often been contradictory because different investigators have meant entirely different things by

9. Gerald S. Wieder, "Group Procedures Modifying Attitudes in Classroom," *Journal of Educational Psychology,* XLV (October, 1954), 332-44.

10. W. J. McKeachie, "Student-centered versus Instructor-centered Instruction," *Journal of Educational Psychology,* XLV (March, 1954), 143-50.

student-centered. Even when the definitions appear to be identical, the actual classroom situation may be quite different. Not all counselors can become nondirective, and not all instructors can become student-centered. Glib use of the phrase does not evoke the spirit.

Studies of instruction, like many of the research studies in the field of counseling, have often become concerned more with the process than with the outcome. In the early stages this may be necessary, because there is a need for identifying the variables which really distinguish between various types of instruction. Consider such questions as: "Does an increase in verbal participation on the part of students result in more significant changes in attitudes and values?" "Does the nature of the instructor's comment implying reward or correction have a significant impact on students?" Such questions cannot be even investigated until an answer is found to the prior question, "Do classes really differ quite measurably in the extent to which these variables are present?" Out of such studies, too, is developing a realization that permissiveness in the classroom with a group lacking previous experience in such situations may increase the student's frustration rather than his learning.

Further studies in this area of instructional techniques will also have to take into account the studies by Stern, Stein, and Bloom [11] which emphasize the significance of certain personality traits, such as rigidity or authoritarianism, in determining the way in which a student reacts to an educational experience. An individual with strong beliefs may not be able to tolerate certain types of classes in which these beliefs are brought into question. There is also evidence that, even after equating for intelligence, drop-out rates are higher among students with rigid personality characteristics. Such students usually prefer a type of classroom situation which is dominated by the instructor; they prefer to be told what to do and what to learn; they are troubled by tentativeness and by indecision. Such an individual wants definite questions and definite answers, which accord with his own biases and beliefs or are objectively handled so that

11. George G. Stern, Morris I. Stein, and Benjamin S. Bloom, *Methods in Personality Assessment*. Glencoe, Illinois: Free Press, 1956.

they can be intellectualized with a minimum of affective involvement. It is becoming evident, as it always should have been, that the
effectiveness of instructional methods cannot be studied without
considering differences in the personality of individual students. The
objectives of a course may not include objectives in the affective
domain, but the affective domain, nevertheless, has some effect on
the changes made in knowledge and in intellectual goals. Attitudes
and values, barred at the front door, come in the back.

The importance of such student personality characteristics has
been noted in numerous studies of teaching techniques. Wispe,[12] to
take another example, found three kinds of students: first, those
with the constant desire for more direction, who tended to be in-
secure, dependent, and intropunitive, critical of their sections, their
instructors, and their fellow students; second, those who are always
satisfied, relatively favorable toward their teacher and their associates; third, those who indicated a desire for more permissiveness,
more independence; who are less tense; and who are extrapunitive.
In the same study, Wispe noted that the preference of students for a
particular type of teaching cannot be separated from the total educational milieu. In institutions which are strongly oriented to examinations (particularly so, one might hypothesize, if the examinations are primarily factual in nature), students will prefer directive
teaching; and the teachers, for the same reason, will find their work
easier and will be more successful. The objectives, thus made explicit
in the examinations, may become more potent determiners of the
nature of the educational experiences than the educational objectives
which have been stated for the institution or the course. It becomes
clear, then, that instructional techniques cannot be adequately investigated unless the personality differences of students and the total
pattern of educational experiences are taken into account. The
teacher who attempts to use student-centered or nondirective teaching in an institution in which the prevailing orientation is otherwise
may create only frustration for his students and for himself.

The studies of instructional problems remarked on here by no

12. Lauren G. Wispe, "Evaluating Section-teaching Methods in the Introductory Course," *Journal of Educational Research*, XLV (November, 1951),
161-86.

means exhaust either the number or range of problems which have been investigated. These, however, serve the present purpose for they make the point that instruction and personnel services are confronted with the same problems. They need to join forces in the study of them.

A NEW UNITY THROUGH RESEARCH

In a recent book, Jacob [13] concludes (although on rather inadequate evidence) that students, in general, are a self-satisfied group, that they are not very deeply moved by their college experiences and that, in particular, their value system undergoes very little change. Such a characterization of students implies that, despite verbal reiterations of concern for good citizenship and values as outcomes of education, the experiences provided in our schools are not particularly relevant to these outcomes. In an age when emphasis for some time to come is likely to be heavily on scientific study, the importance of providing a counterbalance in our educational program by equal emphasis on attitudes and values should be apparent. It is less apparent how this is to be accomplished, particularly when much of the current criticism of the schools is aimed at *adjustment* in such a manner as to suggest that attention to anything other than the 3 R's is wasteful and un-American.

Concern with the relations of instruction and personnel services provides the basis for a strong emotional plea for co-operation between these two fields. This plea can be backed up by an attractive and rational analysis of the possibilities for co-operation in which, on one hand, the classroom furnishes a model of inquiry which is equally applicable to the solution of problems with which students are confronted in their extracurriculum groups and activities and, on the other hand, the extracurriculum activities furnish a laboratory in which classroom theory is put into practice. It *is* a little ridiculous that group dynamics and role-playing are being introduced into classrooms under highly artificial circumstances, when the realities are just outside the classroom door. However, the gap between curriculum and the co-curriculum is a difficult one to

13. Philip Jacob, *Changing Values in College.* New York: Harper & Bros., 1957.

bridge. Good will and co-operation are not enough; both theory and practical knowledge are presently insufficient to the task.

The failure of a student to interrelate his classroom and extra-classroom experiences may be a deficiency on his part, or it may be a deficiency in the faculty and in the program. Education may have little constructive effect on the attitudes and values of students because these qualities are accorded only indirect and incidental treatment in the program. Neither teachers nor personnel workers would doubt that students ought to become aware of the assumptions and the values underlying the kind of educational program which is provided for them nor that they ought to become aware of their own values and the values of their associates. Moreover, they would agree that the students ought to realize the way in which different value systems lead to different points of view and different solutions to problems, and that they need also to become aware of very different value systems which exist in other cultures and then come to re-examine their own. Such an educational experience, involving careful self-examination, requires the development of critical thinking and judgment; it requires the development of integrative skills in each individual, fostered by an educational program which is cumulative and which possesses a unity in purpose and in organization apparent to students, teachers, personnel workers, and administrators. This is the theme of a recent yearbook,[14] which also concludes that the means of attainment of this type of education are uncertain and even its exact nature unclear. Here, then, is the challenge facing teachers and personnel workers, namely, finding a common task in developing an educational program which provides an integrative experience. To do so, however, we need comprehensive research studies in which the intellect and the personality of both the teacher and the student are involved; in which the educational milieu itself is regarded as a set of experiences existing to bring about changes in the student; and in which ineffectiveness in the fostering of changes is regarded as a basis for changing the educational program rather than as a basis for finding fault with

14. *The Integration of Educational Experiences.* Fifty-seventh Yearbook of the National Society for the Study of Education, Part III. Chicago: Distributed by University of Chicago Press, 1957.

the student. If personnel workers and teachers can join hands in agreeing on educational objectives, in examining their roles in providing an interrelated pattern of experience relative to these objectives, and in studying the means of accomplishment of these objectives, the artificial barrier which has been reared between the two groups may disappear. The unity engendered by co-operating in research on common problems, in turn, can lead to a unity, perceptible even to the student, in a series of integrated experiences related to important educational goals.

CHAPTER X

Personnel Work in Education as Related to Change

DANIEL D. FEDER

Introduction

In this chapter it is proposed to review the gradual extension of personnel services in education in past years, to examine briefly the character of these services at present, and to predict some of the innovations in aims and procedures of personnel work in the future. To accomplish these purposes it is necessary to single out certain high lights of the foregoing chapters. In so doing, no effort will be made to present what could be considered a summary of any chapter. The reader who has digested the materials in preceding chapters may well take exception to some of the items singled out for special comment here. Choices had to be made from the wealth of reports and concepts that have been mentioned. It can only be hoped that the reader who turns to a "last chapter," looking for a summary, will find instead a stimulus to turn to the preceding chapters as "original sources" and derive from them his own appraisal of the significant elements in the development of personnel work in American education.

Some Historical Perspectives

Foremost among the impressions derived from historical perspective is recognition of the factors in the social and economic milieu which have given rise to educational change and hence to the development of personnel work in education as a factor in this change. The functions of vocational guidance or vocational counseling can be traced to the Industrial Revolution and to the resultant development of myriads of specialized jobs with concomitant education and training programs. As the science of psychology moved out of the laboratories to apply its understandings of individual differences it gave rise to a whole new movement of measurement of human characteristics. It was natural and inevitable that the definition and delineation of jobs and of worker requirements, refined by the science of measurement, would tie together these two fields of knowledge so as to help the individual appraise himself in terms of the world in which he might build a life career.

The complex factors of cause and effect are so inextricably entwined in any major social movement that it is frequently impossible to untangle all of these relationships. But there is no gainsaying the impetus which was given to the whole personnel movement by the development of public schools in America. The broadening of the base of American education in the latter part of the nineteenth century made secondary-school education a right of every American child instead of the special privilege of the economic elite and recognized higher education as the privilege of all who could profit from it and would seek it. Such liberalizing viewpoints have been major factors in contemporary times in intensifying the need for and interest in the personnel movement. Proliferation and differentiation of educational programs have only served to emphasize the increased need for better information about the world of work, of its many occupations and its improved ways of helping students evaluate themselves in the process of making occupational choices, which is their right.

With the ever increasing complexity of the social and economic structure of our society and all the uncertainties of a rapidly developing industrial technology, there has been a continuing challenge to those who would participate in education at the point of helping students understand and evaluate their potential for constructive participation in the social order of their day.

Intelligent perspective for the appraisal of the role of personnel work in American education of the future may be gained by extracting from the preceding chapters some basic concepts which will enable us to appreciate the significance of this movement in education in the current period. We may thereby gain a sense of the level of development of this professional field as it relates to education as a whole and to the selective advantages thereof as they stem from the broad societal developments of free enterprise.

Some High Lights of This Yearbook

RESPONSIBILITIES OF AMERICAN EDUCATION

In chapter ii, Melby and Reeves have focused attention upon the centrality of human relations as a major concern of education in the immediate future. They point out that America cannot maintain a position of world leadership in the solution of international and interracial tensions until we have settled our own internal problems in these areas. The countries of the free world look anxiously to America for guidance in the struggle to contain those forces which would subjugate human integrity to the rule of the self-designated elite. But America cannot assume this role in international affairs until there is unmistakable evidence of the fact that the principles upon which the American way of life was founded are given more than lip service within our own boundaries. Accordingly, Melby and Reeves visualize the educational system of our country as one which accepts the obligation of stimulating and giving leadership to social change. It is no longer enough to accept the obvious fact that education as we know it is a product of a developing society. If it is to serve its proper function, education must be a dynamic factor in determining the directions which that society shall take in order that it may adequately serve the needs of its members.

Wrenn sees personnel service as the child of humanitarianism and the behavioral sciences. That is, personnel work is both an expression of the applications and a result of the practices of human science in a framework of service orientation. Perhaps most fundamental to an appreciation of the philosophical orientation of the personnel worker is Wrenn's delineation of this movement as one which could not have developed in any social setting except that of a democratic society based upon the tradition of Judaeo-Christian idealism. He sees the personnel worker as essentially an experimentalist and an instrumentalist. Psychological orientation in the search for explanatory principles upon which behavioral predictions may be based is most satisfyingly found in a combination of organismic and field theories. These psychodynamic systems provide the most adequate bases for the development of the essentially psychological procedures employed in the wide variety of functions performed under the rubric of personnel work. Culminating a dispassionate examination of the best of current philosophical and psychological approaches, Wrenn concludes on a poignant personal note of integrity compelling him to make a choice, which, in the final analysis, is an expression of his own values, perceptions, and dedications. He concludes his analysis with the warning that personal evaluation and introspection must, of necessity, be reckoned with in the philosophic orientation (values orientation) which the personnel worker accepts as his own. This orientation, furthermore, inescapably colors the attitudes which characterize the personnel worker's performance as well as his choices of techniques and procedures in dealing with students and their problems.

GUIDELINES FOR ADMINISTRATION

Setting guidelines for the administrator who is faced with the necessity of either reviewing an existing system of personnel service or installing a new one, Erickson and Hatch define this administrative function as the programming of personnel services. They emphasize the necessity of adapting the program to the educational needs of the constituency which the school system serves. To accomplish the programming function they delineate the following four steps:

1. Education of staff in the understanding of the purposes of personnel functions and the development of their readiness to accept responsibility for the provision of such services;
2. Study of existing services in light of the educational objectives of the school system involved and the needs of the various constituencies to be served, including a careful analysis of available facilities and needed additions to accomplish the objectives perceived as essential;
3. Structuring a program of in-service, continuing development which will insure meaningful vitality in the operations performed;
4. Adoption of a plan of operation with built-in flexibility which will insure its adaptability to the changing needs of the school system.

Drawing upon a rich background of experience, these authors deal insightfully with the types of problem which may ensue from poor administration; and they offer many pointed suggestions for insuring stable staff relationships. Perceiving the personnel program as integral to the total educational process, they emphasize the unitary nature of the school system and the importance of each component's functioning in relation to the needs of every other part. They see the administrative process as consisting initially of planning—the process in which the administrator must explain why it is necessary to provide for certain activities and when, where, and how to perform them; the organizing phase consisting of the grouping of various elements and the structuring of relationships among these groups; the staffing function consisting of the selection and assignment of qualified personnel for the various functions; directing the program which consists of co-ordination, control, and stimulation to secure acceptable performance of functions; and the continuous process of evaluation of the program to insure the adequacy of the functions performed. Within their conception of administrative responsibility for programming personnel services, Erickson and Hatch would confront the key administrative officer of an educational institution with the challenge and responsibility of over-all leadership to insure the appropriate support of personnel services as integral parts of the total educational operation.

THE RANGE OF PERSONNEL SERVICES

Bennett has supplied a comprehensive cataloguing of various personnel services as performed at different levels of schooling. She points out that these services increase in both complexity and degree of specialization in direct relationship to the increasing maturity of the individuals served. As the areas of personal operation increase in number and specialization with increasing age, specialized services have developed to meet the induced needs. Thus, the counseling function at the high-school and college levels becomes more complex and more differentiated than that which serves the needs of elementary and junior high school students. The framework which Bennett provides is a valuable check list against which the administrator may evaluate the adequacy of a programming function.

RESOURCES OF THE PERSONNEL WORKER

The personnel worker tends to become so immersed in the intimacy of his relationship with the student in his office that he loses sight of the tremendous number and variety of additional resources available to him in the school and in the immediate community for the useful implementation of his work with the student. Berg's clues for the identification and mobilization of such resources into a state of continuing readiness obviously suggest this operation as a fundamental preparatory one in the establishment of any program of personnel work. That the same resource may have multiple utility in a variety of cases is often not recognized. It is a significant contribution to personal understanding for the personnel worker to realize that his strength as a person and as a professional worker may lie in his ingenuity in locating and using the resources which may be available to him in any community, rather than in his search for self-sufficiency.

PROGRAMMING PERSONNEL SERVICES

Shibler provides an interesting distinction between *directed* and *service* functions. It is obvious, of course, that there are certain essentially nonpersonal functions which must be performed in any school system. Many of these are of a clerical nature or of a type which is designed to bring the student into the school system and process him through successive levels. To Shibler these are the "directed functions" in contrast with the many others which the student may be allowed to seek on a voluntary basis or as personal needs arise. There is a valuable distinction in the use of such terminology which distinguishes between the types of function which are regarded as "housekeeping" and those which must be keyed individually to the personal needs, interests, and abilities of the student seeking a special type of assistance. The delineation of principles of organization for student personnel services reinforces the concept of continuity in education. It must certainly be clear to the reader that regardless of the level of education at which an operation is performed, the need for the central focus on the student himself results in a body of general principles and practices which, in a sense, become universals. The ultimate goal of these principles of organization, as Shibler succinctly points out, is the process of evaluating on-going services and planning for future needs.

PREPARATION FOR PROFESSIONAL PERSONNEL SERVICE
IN EDUCATION

In evaluating the emerging role of the professional personnel worker, Feder brings into sharp focus the distinction between technique and content orientations in the preparation process. This distinction is perhaps nowhere better illustrated than in his insistence upon elimination of the word "training" from our vocabulary in reference to the educational preparation and experience of professional workers. The properly prepared professional worker does not merely have a "bag of tricks" at hand which he opens when he needs to extract a specific technique or formula to cope with an emergent problem. He must, rather, be equipped with a depth of understanding of society in its broadest relationships and with intensive understanding of the human sciences which will enable him to interpret and predict individual behavior in relevant situations. The need for such preparation on the part of professional personnel workers is actually intensified by the ever increasing variety and complexity of the problems which individual students may present to them. Perhaps most important in the perception of the emergent role of the personnel worker in the total educational process is the conception that he too serves as a member of the educational team with a central integrated purpose—the development of the individual student in terms of his personal potentials.

RESEARCH AS BASIS OF PERSONNEL WORK IN EDUCATION

Changing Emphases in Research-Problem Interests. Although not intended to serve as a compendium of research in the field of personnel work, the chapter by Borow, Pepinsky, and Dressel provides an unusual historical perspective as well as a challenging research design for needed studies of the future. Triggered by the rapid development of the aptitude testing movement in the era following World War I, personnel practitioners quickly began making a wide variety of applications of the available tests and testing procedures to problems of practice. Oftentimes lacking the opportunity for experimentation and sensing the need for application, these extensions and applications soon expanded beyond the boundaries of research knowledge.

On the basis of his analysis of a wide sweep of research studies, Borow observes that personnel workers have not always integrated their "objectives and practices with those of classroom teachers and school administrators." He notes encouraging evidence that in the current era the recognized need for such integration is leading to a bolder and broader conception of personnel work which is resulting in its integration with the broad instructional objectives of education.

Of great interest and promise is the more recently developing research in methodology for evaluating the outcomes of counseling in terms of basic factors of personality change. Borow questions whether there is a fundamental substantive theory in the field of personnel work, and specifically in counseling, which can actually serve the function of "generating productive research hypotheses." In the more recently developing research patterns he notes that unusual attention is being given to the effects of group relationships upon individual behavior. He sees this as a maturation and extension of research interest going beyond the emphasis upon the analysis of the individual by means of aptitude tests, case studies, and the other methods which have been concerned chiefly with diagnostic analyses of the individual in essential isolation. Innovations in the use of tape recordings and sound moving pictures have permitted the more intensive and objective study of the interview and its role in counseling and other personnel procedures. Despite the fact that much of the research in mental hygiene has been of a very informal nature, recent studies reflect the impact of the psychodynamics of the classroom and the interplay of teacher and student personalities on the mental health of students involved. Out of this developing body of research, Borow offers the tentative conclusion that "the school contributes to the formation of positive student attitudes and effective personal interactions, not alone by direct and deliberate teaching about human behavior but also by creating and maintaining a stable social microcosm in which wholesome human relations are accepted."

From Vocational Guidance to Life Career Planning. Of particular significance to counselors in secondary and higher education is a new emphasis in the study of occupational information and guidance. The contributions of motivation research as well as the life-history approach have led to a concept of career-pattern studies by Super and others based upon the life development of the individual which Super classifies into the following stages: "(1) Exploration: developing a self-concept; (2) reality testing: the transition from school to work; (3) floundering or trial process: attempting to implement a self-concept; (4) establishment; (5) maintenance; (6) decline." In this development of occupational information and guidance there is a substantial core of psychological background in the study of personality theory as well as motivation. These developments have caused vocational counselors to adopt a new interpretation of this aspect of the counseling process, looking upon it not as a singular and discrete experience but, rather, as a phase or step in a developmental process. Borow predicts that the concept of life-career planning as against entrance job vocational guidance per se will result in the intensification of the approach to counseling as a learning process in which the student is aided in his search for better self-understanding and ultimate self-fulfilment.

Dynamics of Personnel Research—Methodology and Evaluation. Moving from the broad sweep of major perspectives in personnel research, Pepinsky deals with the research methodology for defining the nature of the student and analyzing the educational setting in which he operates. He envisages the student as one of the relevant variables and his condition as an assumed outcome of specified conditions, and, therefore, as the dependent variable. He sees the developing educational setting, the cultural and social environment and interactions between the student and the setting as the independent variables which condition behavior and development. He proposes a scheme for "conceptualizing the process and outcomes of student development in an educational setting" which provides a unique outline of independent and dependent variables against which a research worker may check the structure and design of any given problem in this field. He goes on to test some well-known studies in the field of student development against these criteria as a method of demonstrating their usefulness in evaluating the contribution of any given research project. Despite the observation that few, if any, research studies "take adequate account of the broad range of variables," Pepinsky points out the precautions that must be observed in labeling a study as good or bad. He emphasizes that there is increased need for sophisticated research evaluation of programs and procedures; a need for methodological developments which will "contribute to intelligent awareness of alternative routes to be followed in selecting students for particular educational experiences or in helping students to make optimum use of such experiences;" and most particularly a need that programs of graduate education contribute to the understandings of personnel workers so that they will approach problems in a questioning frame of mind and seek appropriate answers.

Personnel Research as Part of the Educational Process. Although the section by Dressel starts out with an implied dichotomy under the title "The Interrelations of Student Personnel Work and Instruction," he quickly points out that the dichotomy is not a real one and that the fundamental objectives of classroom instruction and of personnel work are actually identical. To this end he has reviewed a number of studies designed to reflect these essential interrelationships. In the area of interests, for example, he notes that research indicates that not only do interests affect student achievement and behavior as expressed in various academic ways but that they in turn may be modified by and influenced by the academic experience.

Turning to the area of the prediction of academic success, Dressel notes that a new dimension has been added to research in this area by the discovery that "the success or failure of a student may be as much a matter of the expectations and conceptions of the faculty of an institution as it is a set of personal characteristics of the student." Here again we see recognition of the psychodynamics of the environment being taken into account in the development both of methodology and criteria of evaluation for a new look at studies in the area of the prediction of achievement.

Coming at the central problem of learning and achievement from the viewpoint of classroom and other instructional procedures, Dressel again observes that there is a substantial body of research which indicates that no single methodology can be considered the "best" for any type of learning situation unless it takes into account the special characteristics of the learner and the significance of method to him in a particular relationship. Here again is evidence of the personnel worker's central concern for the individual and his development and the recognition of the fact that the application of any given method of instruction may be essentially meaningless unless it takes into account the individual differences of the learners.

Dressel ends his section with a plea for a more common understanding between personnel workers and teachers as to their common, central objectives. Like the other writers, he notes the need for much additional research which will take into account the psychosocial dynamics of the learning situation, the interactions of teacher and student personalities and intellects, and recognition of the fact that the student in the learning situation is not only an object to be acted upon but is, in truth, a dynamic element in effecting the total learning structure.

The Discipline of Personnel Work in Education. As one concludes the review of high lights of the preceding chapters, it is certainly evident that there is no air of self-satisfaction or complacency in the profession of personnel work. Stemming from the disciplines of psychology and the other behavioral sciences, and representing significant efforts to apply the findings of these sciences in the practices of counseling and other types of personnel service, there is a "hard core" of scientifically oriented practitioners who make most exacting demands upon themselves and their colleagues for the technical accuracy of their insights and practices. Though we reflect what may appear to be a hypercritical attitude, there is actually a thread of constructive optimism which pervades these critiques.

There is an unwillingness to accept the validity of practice because of historical precedent or authoritative pronouncement. There is a demand for development of new and better research methodology which will provide the foundation for evaluating existing practices and developing new ones in terms of the requirements of a dynamically developing field of service. Drawing as it does upon many other disciplines in order to form its own discipline, the field of personnel work inherits not only the values and difficulties of each but, in the process of integration, may actually seem to multiply some of the difficulties which inhere in the respective individual disciplines from which it draws. Most significantly it is important to note that this is a field in which there are no static developments. Responsive to the socioeconomic changes, which are concomitants of the constantly changing cultural pattern, are both the research orientations and the techniques of practice in personnel work. In this frame of reference it is proposed in the next section of this chapter to examine in broad strokes what may be some of the anticipated future developments in this field. Obviously, one cannot indulge in wishful thinking concerning the outcomes of research yet to be done. The effort will be, rather, to attempt to point out both future needs and anticipated developments as both research workers and practitioners working together push ahead the frontiers of this phase of educational practice in its research and data-based orientation.

Emerging Trends in Personnel Service in Education

As we attempt to envisage some of the possible future developments in the field of student personnel work, we are inescapably brought back to the essential components of this yearbook covered in the preceding chapters. Obviously, the global approach on many different axes which the committee has attempted to incorporate through the contributions of the several authors has resulted in a broad sweep of the field enhanced by the focus on specific major elements. Therefore, it is somewhat inevitable that in the "look ahead" we are geared to the essential content of what has gone before.

THE FUTURE OF PERSONNEL WORK AS INTEGRAL TO THE EDUCATIONAL PROCESS

The steady surge of philosophical comment and research interest presages a future that will see the development of an appropriate relationship between personnel work and the broad functions of education. As in the case of any new discipline, its practitioners naturally seek to establish their special integrity and right to a "place in the sun." Undoubtedly, it will take considerable time and education before there is full recognition and acceptance of the fact that such specialized functions as counseling require a basic preparation in point of view, content, and techniques. Pending such full recognition, much will undoubtedly be said and written until this special discipline is clearly recognized. In this developmental process, many leaders will feel the necessity of continuing to emphasize the differences and special missions rather than the similarities and common mission. But the pathway is clearly marked. The evidence is unmistakable that there is a growing and valid recognition of the fact that the basic mission of the educational process is the teaching-learning function. In this frame of reference, counseling and other phases of personnel work take their appropriate place as phases of the total process designed to help each student develop to the limit of his potential. Whether this development takes place in the classroom, in the informal activities outside the classroom, in the privacy of a counselor's office, or in any other education milieu is relatively unimportant. What is important is that all of the workers in the educational vineyards have a clear realization that theirs is a common goal with the student as the central focus of their efforts.

THE DISTINCTIVE THEORY AND PHILOSOPHY OF PERSONNEL WORK IN EDUCATION

Need for a Research Theory. It may be predicted safely that there will be continuing discussion and argument concerning the possibility that personnel work may be able to develop a distinctive theoretical basis of its own. At this juncture it seems doubtful that what is essentially an applied discipline which makes its primary expression in the form of practice can ever make a fundamental contribution to the advancement of psychological theory as such. To be sure, personnel workers may perform distinctive research in the years ahead. Essentially, however, this research is based upon existing psychological theories and, in effect, is designed to test them in application to the unique problems of personnel work. The same fundamental problem inheres in the field of clinical psychology. In any applied field, the essential purpose of research is to test the applicability of the theoretical constructs developed in the "pure" laboratory situation and determine whether they can provide useful bases for behavior predictions in the more complex organizations of behavior found in the psychodynamics of daily life.

Whether or not the research and thinking in personnel service can ever make a fundamental contribution to the psychological theory upon which it is based seems, to the writer, to be a largely academic question. It is certainly clear that a distinctive type of research orientation and philosophy will be developed and that this will give increasing attention to the multiple and complex factors and interrelationships which exist in the behavioral situations with which personnel workers must deal. Some of these trends already have been indicated in the preceding chapter on research frontiers. There is, however, a more urgent and significant need for personnel workers in the development of their psychological and philosophical sophistication.

The Personnel Worker's Personal Philosophy. The expression that a given situation is to be "played by ear" is frequently heard among personnel workers. Frequently, it is applied to a situation in which discipline may be involved. The implication of the expression when applied in such a situation is that because the ultimate social consequences of the violator's action may not yet be fully revealed or the implications completely discerned, those who are involved in the administrative decision may wish to delay action. The further implication is that if the school does not run the risk of serious embarrassment it may be willing to retain the offender in its midst and carry forward some type of therapeutic activity on his behalf. On the other hand, if it appears that the school is likely to suffer in its "public relations," there is a greater likelihood that the offender will be dealt with more severely. In actuality, if the school involved espouses a counseling or educational approach to problems of discipline, its officials must perforce dedicate themselves to the principle that the welfare of the individual and, hence, the ultimate welfare of society requires a courageous and forthright stand. Thus, if re-education and therapy are the constructive indications, a concern for public relations will be secondary. Certainly this is not an easy position for the personnel worker or the school administrator. Nevertheless, it does call for a basic philosophical dedication and the recognition that once taken it ought to be practiced with a reasonable consistency which gives assurance that educators actually know the directions of their actions.

The other side of this same coin is the failure on the part of many of our schools to explain their basic "ground rules" to both students and patrons. Thus, one frequently encounters the plaintive confusion on the part of students expressed as, "We just don't know where we stand with the faculty and administration." In such instances, one encounters decisions being made on the basis of personal considerations without reference to any kind of basic principles. Oftentimes in such situations, what appear to be contradictory decisions may be made in two situations which seem to have like characteristics. When this occurs, the insecurity induced in the student body is obvious, and it is often manifest in the kind of poor morale which can ultimately lead to open rebellion.

Inherent in healthy and creative social development is the regard for orderly and constructive social interrelationships. The philosophy of permissiveness which was developed as the basis for grounding the techniques of counseling therapy may, when overextended into areas for which it was never intended, imply an anarchistic kind of individualism in behavior standards. In such an overextension of the theory, it is readily conceivable that the original usefulness of the theoretical construct may be lost. Thus, it seems entirely conceivable that the personnel worker may need one set of constructs when dealing with the individual qua individual as he attempts to work out his intimately personal attitudes and adjustments and quite a different set of constructs when operating in the area of group dynamics and interrelationships. Yet in both cases there may be (in fact, should be) a consistent philosophical and motivational core.

What we are talking about here is the need for the personnel worker to make a clear distinction, albeit a very fine and delicate one, between his personal philosophical orientation and his techniques of operation. As one works through this duality, it becomes increasingly clear that "permissiveness" or the "creation of a non-judgmental atmosphere" is essentially a technique of operation which the personnel worker should develop in his own working relationships, whether they be with an individual in the intimacy of a counseling situation or with a group in the planning of its programs of operations or its self-government. The real difficulties which have arisen in this connection may be traced to the erroneous belief that permissiveness is a philosophy of life rather than an operational technique. It is this confusion which has given many counselors difficulty as they have attempted to examine their "position of neutrality" in the counseling relationship. This is still one of the controversial viewpoints to be explored by research and subjected to more penetrating philosophical analysis. Nevertheless, the challenge to the personnel worker in this area is to clarify the distinctions between what may be thought of as operational techniques and one's personal philosophy or living ethic.

There is no simple unilateral solution to the problem of the personal philosophy of the personnel worker that will be expressed in his daily operations. To be sure, ultimately he must become conscious of what constitutes the central integrating orientation of his own life patterns. Wrenn has presented a variety of choices available on the contemporary scene. The introspective reader will have paused in the attempt to identify his own orientation and to determine whether it is actually serving his needs.

There is another and highly important axis upon which one's personal philosophy must hinge and this is the philosophy of the school or college with which one is identified. This need comes sharply into focus as one examines the possibility of effective operation when a personal philosophy is at variance with the central dedication of a school or college. The possibilities of both personal and personal-institutional conflicts in such situations would seem to be manifold. It is obvious too that even though a school or college may not have a manifest theological identification, the pervasive climate of opinion in such an area, even in a tax-supported institution, may be such as to create a subtle and pervasive philosophy against which the practices of classroom and extraclassroom activities will be projected. Awareness of the need for developing and expressing such broad philosophical orientations on the part of all kinds of educational institutions has begun to appear in the literature. For the most part, such expressions have dealt with the need for the institution to recognize its own personality in terms of whether it is essentially Deweyian in nature or espouses some other philosophy of education. Educational philosophy will inevitably reflect societal philosophy and organization. In addition, it has the responsibility of broadening the understanding of those affected in order that the highest integration in the cultural tradition of the Judaeo-Chrstian ethic may be realized.

Choice of a Psychological Basis. At the level of the psychological theory there is quite another problem. Here the personal wishes and cultural orientation of the individual ought to give way to the necessity of accepting "best knowledge" as the basis upon which to structure one's theoretical approach to student personnel practice. Obviously, as long as there are areas of valid difference in so far as basic theory is concerned, the individual has to rely upon his own knowledge and insights for his choices. Basic to all of this is the recognized search for explanatory principles which is the chief mission of any psychological theory. To the extent that we are able to derive more adequate explanations of behavior we shall be able to make more accurate predictions of it. It is the avowed goal of every science to perfect predictions of behavior in its particular phenomenological field. The psychologist's concern with the prediction of human behavior, which is the basic concern of any personnel worker, must not be construed as the effort to accomplish subconscious or subliminal controls of behavior in the sense of social manipulation. It is, rather, the effort to develop in each individual those personal insights and understandings of his own potentials which enable him to effect appropriate adjustive behavior in his personal goal seeking. As the personnel worker confers with his school charges, his need is to gain the kind of individual understanding which will enable him to assist them in either the restructuring of their own attitudes or their operational environments in such a way as to gain maximum life satisfactions. An adequate psychological approach to these problems requires a theory which takes into account the individual as an active element in the operative dynamics of a social structure. This requirement does not demand that psychological theory be ethically or philosophically oriented, but it does assume that the individual operates in a social environment of which he is an active, dynamic element.

As this broader psychological understanding is achieved, it does not seem likely that adequate explanatory principles will be found in the conditioned-reflex experiments of the laboratory. The complexity of human behavior and its sensitivity to external sociopsychodynamics presages the increased interest in and attention to more dynamic theories in which the totality of the organism operating in a dynamic social field will be the central focus of theoretical constructs.

Self-concept and Perceptual Internalization. Broadened meanings attached to the concept of perception will undoubtedly play a most important role in the future development of technical insights into the field of personnel operations. At the level of the individual, explorations on a scientific and experimental level of the self-concept and other internalized perceptions give promise of becoming important clues for evaluating the character of both educational and counseling experiences. In group relations, perceptions of roles of self as well as roles of others must be studied in order to determine the potentialities of group impact upon individual behavior. For example, in the area of student government, the perception of functions to be served by those being governed as contrasted with perceptions of service of those doing the governing may actually be quite different. As we seek to understand the successes and failures of individuals and groups in their operations, it may well be that our most important understandings will come not from the static analysis of individuals and their personal characteristics but, rather, from dynamic analysis of individuals and their perceptions of themselves and their roles in the groups of which they are a part.

Although there would seem to be some socioethical influence upon these predicted developments in psychological theory, we would prefer to believe that they are a reflection of the increased maturity and insight which recognizes that individual behavior cannot be understood, explained, and predicted except as the individual is studied as a dynamic element in the social setting in which he lives. Inevitably, out of such a theory there appears to be a sense of social responsibility. This is more truly an element of philosophical orientation and value judgment which must be left to the broad sociocultural ethics in evolution.

The Profession and Its Workers. Looking ahead to future developments in terms of present needs and anticipated demands in the field of personnel work, it appears that more professional workers will be drawn from the fields of the behavioral sciences. The mere "liking to work with people" or "getting along well with others" will not be enough assurance of the possession of scientific understandings and insights necessary for effective operation in the fields of personnel work. Possession of a solid body of psychological understandings, translatable into usable techniques which the personnel worker may consciously adapt to his own personality and to the needs of any given situation, will provide the hard core of a truly scientific basis for personnel work.

The professional personnel worker will emerge as a person possessing professional information and appropriate skills; he will operate as a mature, independent person, not necessarily directly supervised; he will read appropriate professional literature; he will identify with his profession as well as with his employer and will participate in the development of his profession.

It may be germane to observe here that a well-recognized personality characteristic of the personnel worker is his willingness to try changes as they give promise of improvement. But, with this courage is also a searching attitude of self-criticism and process evaluation which causes the personnel worker to approach such changes always in an evaluative frame of mind. Change for the sake of change is certainly not the goal; the goal is change for the sake of discovering a new and better way of functioning. This attitude calls for a willingness to make the change under conditions which permit evaluation of outcomes in as close to a valid and controlled research atmosphere as can possibly be developed and yet meet the needs of service demands.

Research That "Makes a Difference." Another characteristic which has been receiving much attention recently and which may be expected to condition personnel research of the future is the attitude that the personnel worker must be concerned with practices and the evaluation of practices that make a "difference" which is not just a statistically significant difference but one which has both individual and social significance. His concern will focus upon the intensive analysis of much larger segments of behavior as seen in their normal environmental and dynamic functioning. And the search here will be for methods of creating differences in behavior which have significance for the adaptive effectiveness of the individual in his social milieu. This is not to imply that the two methods of research are mutually incompatible but, rather, that in the shifting emphasis statistical significance, which is derived from the mere size of samples, will inevitably give way to a new evaluation of significance which is derived from the validity of differences.

PROBLEMS OF ADMINISTRATION AND INTEGRATION

As enrolments continue to rise in all levels of education with continuing shortages of professional personnel, the field of personnel work in education, like all other phases of education, will be challenged to develop new patterns of administrative operation. The essential characteristic of such patterns will be seen in the creation of plans which are indigenous to the school system in which the services are functioning rather than the result of questionnaire surveys of so-called "best" practices. Helpful as such surveys may be for the creation of temporary stop-gaps, rarely if ever can they develop the needed answers for a specific local situation. Although there is a large body of evidence indicating that the most commonly encountered pattern is that of centralized control in a single individual with departmental organization stemming from the central administrator, it must be recognized that such a system may call for more people with a higher level of educational preparation and experience than may be available in the years ahead. Careful attention to the principle of administrative grouping of related functions will make it possible, particularly in large and complex systems, to operate with a smaller number of persons having the high professional preparation, to reduce the number of persons involved in purely administrative functions, and to make available more specially qualified persons for performance of the actual service functions.

In the development of formulas for the financial support of personnel services, the essential element must be a rational evaluation of the part which such services play in the total educational process. Such evaluation will point out the fact that some of these functions cannot be made collateral duties of the classroom teacher but will increasingly require persons who have the desirable educational orientation. As the need for increased funds continues, budget requests will still be challenged. The personnel worker must be willing to defend his role in education without becoming defensive and must be objective without becoming objectionable. All persons engaged in education must recognize their responsibility to provide leadership to community thinking with regard to the needs of education and the needs of youth who participate in the educational program. A great danger with which we are currently confronted is the tendency of those in positions of responsibility to abdicate their leadership role in the face of community pressures. If those who have made education their professional career do not actively and aggressively speak out for what their education and experience has taught them to be the vital needs of American youth, then educational practice will fall prey to those special-interest groups which have the ability to generate the greatest amount of pressure at any given period or in any given direction.

The concern of the classroom teacher obviously is with subject matter, which is the central content of instruction. The concern of the personnel worker is a focus on the student as his subject matter and the educational process by means of which the student comes to greater self-understanding and acceptance of his appropriate roles in vocational, familial, and community life. Common to both of these broad areas of operation as well as all other phases which contribute to the educational program will be an increased emphasis upon the importance of adequate self-determination for every individual in a democratic society and the development of a sense of responsibility for creativity in appropriate learning situations. Regardless of the subject matter or the methodology, if our way of life is to be strengthened and extended, the concept of striving for the norm must give way to that of discovering each individual's maximum potential and providing the motivation to an expression of this potential on his part in his day-to-day achievements. Not all the choices which lie ahead in this era are so unmistakably clear as is this one. To continue down the pathway of acceptance of the norm as desirable is to encourage mediocrity and inhibit achievement. To throw aside the normative limitations and to lay before each individual student the challenge to operate to his maximum creative potential is to give that recognition to the individual which is philosophically and socially basic to the democratic way of life. The central problem of personnel work in education is not only the development of scientific and technological proficiency but also the development of skill and understanding in dealing with problems of human relations. Such effectiveness in social relations must start with self-understanding. Herein lies the special province of personnel service in education: to nurture the maturing student personality in its search for integrity, understanding, satisfactions, and creative operation in the cosmos.

SECTION IV

HISTORICAL BACKGROUNDS

CHAPTER XI

Milestones in the Development of Personnel Services in Education

ARTHUR A. HITCHCOCK

in collaboration with

HARRY D. KITSON, BLANCHE W. PAULSON, and A. J. BRUMBAUGH

A milestone is a "significant point in any course." In setting forth ideas, social developments, educational movements—in fact, any of the great changes that have affected personnel work in education—it is clear that, with rare exceptions, the developments under consideration here are not discrete points. These great forces can be delineated. They occurred over a period of time. They are great movements and gradual changes. These great, significant forces constitute the milestones in the course of personnel work in education. This chapter is not, therefore, a history of personnel work in education. Such histories of personnel work at all levels of education are available elsewhere. This chapter is a statement of the great forces that have shaped personnel work in education during modern times and to which personnel work in education has responded.

Socioeconomic Development

The American economy today is a product of the industrial revolution and the services that are needed to feed an industrial society. Since 1850 this nation has moved from the farm to the city, and from agriculture to a rapid industrialization. In 1850, six out of seven people lived on the farm; in 1900, about two out of three; and in 1950, one out of three.

This shift in the working force from agriculture to the diversified and specialized trades, factories, and businesses of the city altered the traditional mode of life and selection of an occupation. It created a shift in the economic sources of true family income and produced a climate for child labor, often oppressive. These causes and effects rendered the traditional educational pattern of the country as obsolete as its rural way of life for hundreds of thousands of young people, and so constitute a milestone.[1]

This situation led to the earliest attempts at diversifying the school curriculum, as the schools have always responded to the educational needs of the times. When only prospective ministers, lawyers, and the leisure classes attended school for any period of time, classical subjects seemed appropriate, but it was soon apparent that Latin grammar was of little use in factories and trades. Schools, which had always included the "vocational" training of teachers, now began to experiment with manual training as did George Arthur Merrill at the Cogswell School in San Francisco in 1888, and as did leaders in other cities during the next decade. The need for this kind of diversification represented a new pressure upon education but by no means the heavier one.

In addition to changes from the farm to the city, there is now developing also the phenomenon of large metropolitan areas which have multinucleated centers. Several of these are apparent in the East, South, Midwest, and Far West. It is apparent that most of the jobs of the working force will continue to be in and related to the industrialization that centers in large metropolitan areas.

The industrialization has been more than simply a shift of population from farm to city. It has entailed increasing specialization of job functions. This has two implications.

The first implication is in the preparation of young people for a specialization of job function in a setting in which it is necessary to have a great deal of flexibility in moving during one's working years from one specific job to another as industrial forces change. That is, with greater specialization it may be anticipated by anyone entering the job market that the particular kind of job he enters may shift during the years. This has created an especially significant condition for personnel work in education. It accentuates the great necessity for intelligent planning in order to equip one's self properly with the background to enter a constellation or family

1. *Road Maps of Industry.* National Industrial Conference Board Study No. 892. New York: The Conference Board, January 30, 1953.

of occupations at the same time that one becomes fitted to enter a particular specialized job.

The other implication is in the level of jobs. For some years there has been a trend, that now appears to be accentuated, toward a higher proportion of professional, technical, and managerial positions and a smaller proportion of unskilled and agricultural types of position in the labor force. This means that young people entering the job market must do so with a greater background of education than had been true earlier in the history of this nation. Such a continually increasing premium being placed upon education means that student personnel work in education must bring its forces to bear upon both the actual educational and career planning on the one hand and motivation and stimulation toward greater development of one's potentialities on the other.

The change in the socioeconomic life also has had repercussions in the role that members of minority groups may play in the economy. It has become evident that those members of minority groups that have contributed to the economy largely on the level of unskilled and semiskilled occupations, cannot possibly expect to make their contribution in the future of an economy that becomes more and more specialized and that tends to a larger and larger proportion of higher level positions that require more education.

The changes in the ways in which people earn their livings in this country have been coupled with significant changes in the aspirations of individuals and families in this society. It would indeed be difficult for a highly industrialized, highly specialized society to feed its economy were it not for the response of the individuals in that society. The geographical movement of the American population today is joined also by a social and economic movement that is best characterized by the movement of sons up the job ladder from the positions of their fathers. This type of movement has occurred not alone because the economy needs it but also because individual and family aspirations make it possible to support the economy by this type of social and economic movement. Great dramatic events such as World War II and such as the release of atomic energy have pointed up the conditions under which vast changes can be met by a population that has high aspirations. It becomes the "accepted" activity in a society of this nature for the children to acquire more education than the parents and to move farther up the ladder than the parents. It is this combination of industrial need and human response that have made the economy possible.

It is in this setting, too, that personnel work in education obviously bears a tremendous responsibility. It would, indeed, be difficult for human talents to grow and contribute were it not for the unusual place of personnel services in education. Through these services the individual finds his place in the kind of socioeconomic setting that is characteristic of this country.

Education for All People

Education is a hallmark of democratic peoples. Communities, colonies, and states within the earliest history of this nation recorded in words and in educational institutions the beliefs of the founding pioneers that education is important for the kind of life that people would live in this nation. It is true that many of the early educational institutions were highly selective. At the same time, however, even in the earliest colonies, certain basics were deemed to be important and, in fact, essential for young people growing up in the world of that time.

As states developed, they began to enact laws that had the effect of requiring all young people to attend school. Although this fact is tied in closely with social and economic problems relating to child labor, nevertheless the fact is also tied closely to the belief that education is essential to the well-being of all young people in our kind of society.

Following the establishment of schools and regulations that were designed to assure that all young people in the nation have at least a basic and fundamental education, the same concept was extended into the high-school level. Statistics on education constantly attest to the fact that more and more students attended high school each year even though they had passed the legal requirement for attendance at school. There was, therefore, born in this country the idea that a high-school education is expected of all students.

If a bench mark is taken at the year 1850, it is found that the northern states generally had free schools at the elementary-school level. It was not until modern industrial America emerged after the Civil War, however, that the schools were really transformed. The graded elementary schools spread widely. Compulsory education laws developed, and between 1860 and 1890, twenty-seven states had such laws. By the turn of the century, the elementary school had become recognized both as a right of all children and as a necessity for the nation's welfare. During the second quarter of the twentieth century, the same necessity for a high-school education developed. Tied to the belief in greater education for all people as a natural right and to the needs of the economy for better trained persons, the education through the high-school level has become very largely an accepted fact.

Beginning in 1880 and continuing for fifty years, school enrolments doubled each decade. During the same period of time, and especially since 1930, young people have also remained in school for a longer period of time. In 1955, 97 per cent of the age group of fourteen and fifteen were in school; 87 per cent of those sixteen and seventeen; and over 78 per cent of those eighteen and nineteen. Of the total college-age group, better than 33 per cent were in college that year. The nearly absolute character of universal education is the most significant single characteristic of the contemporary American public school system and the most potent influence upon its program and its methods of fulfiling our national values. Needless to say, universal education has directly given rise to pupil personnel services and is, therefore, to be recognized as another milestone.

At first glance, the universal acceptance of educational opportunity may seem to result from compulsory education laws, industry's demand for diplomas, and economic abundance. Actually the habit of sending children to school is an expression of the aspirations of our society and the application of our democratic principles of individual worth and of social mobility. This pressure, too, was exerted upon the curriculum, with a new dimension added, namely, range of ability as well as variety of interest.

The first differentiation in the organization of the school to care for individual differences in ability came in the 1890's with classes, first, for the blind, then for the crippled, and, finally, for the mentally handicapped. These earliest, gross differentiations have been refined and modified since, but the beginnings mark education's first organized attempt to adjust the school to the needs of its pupils, thus putting philosophy into practice.

Now, at the time of this yearbook, it is very apparent that the

nation is experiencing a further extension of the idea of education
for all people, namely, into the levels beyond high school. The
National Defense Education Act of 1958 has, in fact, indicated this
in law by designating area vocational education for those who can
profit by training beyond the high school in technical and scientific
areas but not necessarily training through four years of college.

There are other aspects of education beyond the high school
that accentuate the place of education for the people. Adult education continues each year to engage a larger proportion of the population. This is one of the great phenomena of American education.
It testifies to the belief of the nation in the educational process.

Through its history, the nation has exhibited a belief in education for all people. In the early days of the nation, education beyond
the rudiments of the three R's was the particular province of a
specialized few. But with the extension of the concept of education
for all people into the high-school level, many persons were brought
to the high-school scene who in earlier years would not have been
considered qualified for further education beyond the three R's.
This brought educational experiences that were different from the
strictly academic. With the advent of different kinds of curriculums
for different kinds of needs for all people, the problems of the right
education for the right people became apparent. Education for all
people has, therefore, emphasized the guidance function as an essential of American education. One cannot have differential potentialities on one hand and differential educational opportunities on
the other without introducing the element of guidance into the
scene.

But, it is more than simply the matter of helping young people
into the right educational experiences that has become necessary
from the point of view of education of all people. It is also the
concept of education to develop the maximum potentialities of all
young people regardless of the exact nature of those potentialities.
When the nation went to a belief in education of high-school grade
for all people, it recognized the fact that there are many different
kinds of potentialities in young people of any particular generation
and that the nation needs to capitalize upon them through the educational process. It has become apparent in more recent years that
in order to maximize potentialities through education, it is necessary

to know as much as possible about those potentialities. It has, therefore, become essential for American education to have the guidance process within it in order to help young people see and understand more about themselves and how their particular potentialities can be developed.

Education and Individuality

The "mass" versus the "person" or "homogeneity" versus "individuality" point up the sharp difference between that education which presumes that all persons have similar talents and interests and should, therefore, be developed in a common mold and the concept of education which presumes that the only way people can be expected to develop is in terms of their own peculiarities and individualities. It is apparent, moreover, that development along lines which emphasize individual skills and interest in accordance with common social necessities will eventuate both in the greatest individual satisfactions and the greatest contributions to the entire society.

In its political, social, religious, and economic life, this nation has been the refuge of those who have believed in the individual. Yet, it is difficult to carry the concept of the individual into its psychological connotations. It is much easier to place a "value" on the individual. A "common school" suggests the difficulty. It indicates a commonality that tends to decry the very marks of individuality that other parts of the national life tend to accentuate. In its impact upon personnel work in education, therefore, the developments that have come broadly from psychology are extremely important.

It is in the achievements of Binet [2] that the history of work with children received its first great impetus in the realization that when a person can actually be tested, it is found that he is different from others. It was the work of Binet that brought forth the concept of individual differences and made it possible for education generally to develop the unusual strengths of each individual instead of having education try to make all persons similar.

The work of Binet had been preceded by other attempts at test-

2. Anne Anastasi, *Psychological Testing*, pp. 10, 11. New York: Macmillan Co. 1954.

ing. The setting of Binet's work, however, tended from the outset to emphasize individual differences. The French Ministry of Public Instruction appointed a commission in 1904 "to study procedures for the education of subnormal children attending the Paris schools." From this emergency grew the Binet-Simon Scale. The emergency was in a setting in which there was a desire to learn more about the differences of certain children.

Through the years since the work of Binet, contributions of the testing movement have continued to accentuate individuality. A most startling spotlight was placed upon the individual by the wide testing carried out in the armed forces during World War I. This, again, was in response to a pressing need for information about individuals. The advent of this testing made it possible to see that the concept of the individual Binet Scale, which is necessarily limited in application because of time and expense involved, can be applied to certain types of group testing.

During the years since World War I, the testing movement has experienced both surges of popularity and declines. With the development of other methods of assessment and standardized testing, it became possible for schools to accentuate individuals within rather limited frameworks. With the advent of World War II, great strides were made in testing for the assessment of potentialities to carry out both routine and highly unusual operations during the war.

Following World War II, one of the great marks in testing has been the large scholarship programs that have tended to set off individuals within a group who gave particular promise of making marked contributions to the society.

Through these various stages during the years since the early work of Binet, there has been no diminution in attention given to means of looking at the individual student as an individual. The guidance movement in education has always been a movement concentrated on individuals. It is to the initial work of Binet that personnel workers in education today still must look for the beginnings of the great movement that set up clearly the focal point of personnel work in education, namely, the individual. This became the "break through" on the psychological front that was so essential before education, and before personnel work in education, could focus upon the individual as a psychological being. It became possible to bring into action in education the value of the individual that has been so apparent in other areas of the national life.

Mental Health

The force of mental health in this nation already has affected the educational setting in which pupil personnel work occurs. As a movement, it has had a profound influence upon the views that are held about the best atmosphere and conditions for human development. This great force, that still is in its formative stages, bears several great names.

Chronologically, Phillippe Pinel stands first, since, as a psychiatrist in the days of the French Revolution, he called attention to the deplorable conditions in insane asylums and gave positive suggestions for alternative methods to that of controlling dangerous patients by indiscriminate use of the strait jacket.

Nevertheless, conditions improved so little between his work in 1801 and Clifford Beers' experiences as a patient a hundred years later that Beers, more than Pinel, can be called the founder of the mental-hygiene movement. Released from an institution in 1903, this remarkable man recounted his experiences in *The Mind that Found Itself,* published in 1908, and pleaded for more understanding of the mentally ill. Adolph Meyer, the psychiatrist, and William James, the psychologist, endorsed Beers' book, thus helping to give it influence and to bring it to public attention. Meyer had suggested the term "mental hygiene" to Beers, and within a few months, with the help of his father and brother and a dozen other men of New Haven, Beers succeeded in organizing the Connecticut Society for Mental Hygiene. Their statement of the purpose of the Society includes not only raising the standards of care for the mentally ill but also conservation of mental health, the prevention of mental illness, and co-operation with other agencies working in the field.

A year later, in 1909, with money from the Rockefeller Foundation, Beers organized the National Committee for Mental Hygiene and began the publication of a journal. Other societies were soon organized, and in 1919 an International Committee for Mental Hygiene was established. At the first international meeting in Washington in 1930, fifty-three countries were represented, and, with the founding of the World Federation for Mental Health in the United Nations in 1948, world-wide co-operation was underlined.

Rivlin [3] points out that, in the beginning, the mental-hygiene movement tended to emphasize correction of conditions in institutions, and that the big impetus toward the conscious use of mental-hygiene principles and practices in school settings came from child guidance clinics and from the teamwork of psychiatrists, psychologists, and social workers. Rivlin feels that such clinics were highly instrumental in alerting teachers to the school setting as a source of tensions in children, aggravating if not causing some mental-health problems.

Without question the work of such clinics was instrumental in furthering the effectiveness of the movement within the schoolroom, but psychologists, educators, and the medical profession must be given a fair share of the credit for illuminating the dark corners. Regardless of major and minor credit, all pupil personnel workers will agree with Rivlin that "if we are to deal adequately with the mental health of all children, it becomes increasingly clear that the teacher has a major role." [4]

According to Klein,[5] mental-hygiene practices in the classroom and in guidance programs have been introduced into the schools to the extent that the schools have become child-centered as opposed to curriculum-centered. He says, in this respect, "In the last analysis both education and mental hygiene are concerned with the enrichment of life by self-fulfillment. This is their common goal, and how to reach it continues to be their common quest."

There is a peculiar combination of mental health and testing because both actually accentuate the individual, his needs and potentialities. But particularly related to the mental-hygiene movement has been the growth of psychology which, in earlier days in the twentieth century in this nation, tended to accentuate a some-

3. Harry N. Rivlin, "The Role of Mental Health in Education," *Mental Health in Modern Education*. The Fifty-fourth Yearbook of the National Society for the Study of Education, Part II. Chicago: University of Chicago Press, 1955.

4. *Ibid.*, p. 9.

5. D. B. Klein, *Mental Hygiene*. New York: Henry Holt & Co., 1956 (revised).

what mechanistic view of individuals. It was in the advent of Gestalt psychology and its modifications during the later years that "the whole individual" was recognized in a setting of the psychologically functioning individual. From this background has now come the rediscovery of the individual in his environment, namely, as an organism interacting with his environment. The connotations of the individual, on the one hand, and the possibilities in the environment, on the other, have made a circumstance in which personnel work in education finds a particular role.

In the first paragraph of this section, there was an allusion to the formative stage of mental hygiene. This has been emphasized by Jahoda, who explains the difficulty as follows:

. . . the survey of the literature does not resolve the complex problem of clarifying the psychological meaning of positive mental health. Indeed, the review makes it quite clear that the least fruitful approach to the subject consists in assuming that anyone has *the* answer to the problem. We shall have to be content with recognizing that there are many tentative answers or approaches available and that none of them is as yet based on so solid a body of knowledge and facts that it can definitely be singled out as the most promising approach.

To say that there is as yet no entirely satisfactory approach available in the conceptualization of mental health is one thing. To conclude from this state of affairs that all further clarification has to await the results of empirical research is quite another matter. To be sure, empirical research is urgently required. Its success, however, will to no small degree depend on further clarification of some general ideas in the mental health field.[6]

It seems very probable, in the immediate years ahead, that the various parts of personnel work in education must join their forces to investigate the mental-health roles that each of the parts should take in order to bring this great force into its fullest bearing upon the development of students.

Guidance as an Instrument of National Policy

In the 1950's the nation became gravely concerned about its place in the future of a technological world and in the defense of the nation in that kind of world. The word "technology" and the word

6. Marie Jahoda, *Current Concepts of Positive Mental Health*, pp. 65, 66. New York: Basic Books, Inc., 1958.

"defense" focused the nation's attention on manpower. It became obvious through many studies and particularly through Wolfle's study of specialized talent that the nation was not gaining the advantage that it should realize from the individuals who make up the population.[7] Countless human resources were being lost because talents were not being developed. At the same time, a major criticism of education swept across the nation, and this criticism concentrated in the same point, namely, whether or not the potentialities of individuals were being developed. From the concern and controversy grew the very widespread belief that the guidance function in education is essential if human resources are to be developed through educational processes.

The concern of the nation was undergirded with the idea that the function of guidance is essential if human resources are to be developed *in a democratic setting*. This was pointed up most sharply in the statement of policy issued by the American Personnel and Guidance Association on December 12, 1957:

Faced by a tragic shortage of scientists and technologists, we are strongly tempted to solve the manpower problem by channeling outstanding high school and college students into scientific and technical careers. Here lies the danger of tampering with freedom of choice. If the top academic potentiality of this nation were to be forced into a single, selected pattern, generations of youth would lose the privilege of freely choosing their life careers—a privilege cherished by youth throughout the history of this nation. Such a course of action might not solve even part of the problem, for a lack of educated talent persists in all areas of our national life. The solution, therefore, must be viewed from a broader perspective, and we must aim toward utilizing *every available* talent. Only then will the demand for scientists and technologists be met, along with the demand for educated talent in all fields.

Utilization of human potentialities depends upon two factors: one, the nation's decisions to turn needed educated talent to national uses; two, the maximum growth of human talent through our educational processes. This statement concerns only the latter.

Through education, it is possible to alleviate the present manpower shortage without damaging freedom of choice. This freedom can instead be enriched through the educational process, for persons can grow to the height of their potentialities when:

7. Dale Wolfle, *America's Resources of Specialized Talent*. New York: Harper & Bros., 1954.

1. They know their potentialities, interests, and values.
2. They have the opportunity to develop them through education.
3. They know about the complex, rapidly changing career picture.
4. They are motivated to develop their potentialities and to relate them to the opportunities in our society.[8]

The nation had recognized that the soundest educational curriculums could be developed but that they would amount to far less than they should for the growth of human resources unless the guidance function were exercised strongly as a part of the entire educational process.

In response to this concern and controversy, the Eighty-fifth Congress debated long and studiously the problem of improving the educational experience in ways that the federal government could exercise. The result is Public Law 85-864, which declares in part that:

The Congress hereby finds and declares that the security of the Nation requires the fullest development of the mental resources and technical skills of its young men and women. The present emergency demands that additional and more adequate educational opportunities be made available. The defense of this Nation depends upon the mastery of modern techniques developed from complex scientific principles. It depends as well upon the discovery and development of new principles, new techniques, and new knowledge.

We must increase our efforts to identify and educate more of the talent of our Nation. This requires programs that will give assurance that no student of ability will be denied an opportunity for higher education because of financial need; will correct as rapidly as possible the existing imbalances in our educational programs which have led to an insufficient proportion of our population educated in science, mathematics, and modern foreign languages and trained in technology.

In this law the nation has declared that guidance is an instrument of national policy. The law states in effect that in a democracy, the growth of human resources is dependent upon guidance to identify able students and to assist them in their fullest possible development. This underlying belief is stated specifically in two provisions of the bill that set forth federal support for the improvement of programs of guidance, counseling, and testing in the states and in

8. American Personnel and Guidance Association, "A Statement of Policy Concerning the Nation's Human Resources Problems," *Personnel and Guidance Journal*, XXXVI (March, 1958), 454, 455.

the provision for universities and colleges to conduct institutes for the education of counselors in order to provide more and better qualified counselors for work in the schools.

Several other parts of the bill are designed to create those conditions under which it will be possible for counselors working with students in schools to help them enter the best possible educational experiences for them. A rather substantial loan fund for undergraduate students in college is a case in point.

There are several important implications from this legislation. These implications are:

1. If a nation is to develop its human resources in a democratic setting, it must have the guidance function as a significant part of the entire educational process. In fact, this implies that the kind of curriculum experiences that are necessary to furnish the content for developing human resources cannot work unless there are strong programs of guidance and counseling in the schools.

2. The identification of talents starts at an early age, and, by the time a student is at the seventh-grade level, he must be acquiring a fairly clear insight as to whether or not he will go on through college beyond the high school. The identification occurs in many ways, but the point is that, without this function in education, such identifications will not take place and students who normally deteriorate in school will not be saved from that deterioration unless educational systems throughout the country have good student personnel work.

3. Career-planning should actually start at a rather early age and should be a continuous process with special emphasis at points of decision. The unity of educational planning and career-planning is obvious. In setting guidance as an instrument of national policy, however, the nation has declared it important that the planning ahead of broad avenues of development be started at a rather early age.

4. The fourth implication is, in effect, a negative one. The Congress clearly implied its belief that human resources can be developed in our educational processes, provided the guidance function is present. On the reverse, however, is the fact that if it is impossible to utilize the guidance function in American education to develop human resources, then we must face the fact that proc-

esses that are known as democratic today will have to be abandoned. This would leave the nation in an impossible dichotomy with human development through guidance and free choice, on the one hand, and human development through dictation, on the other. The impossibility of this dichotomy is the fact that this nation cannot possibly believe in the second part. It can believe only in the possibilities of free choice in an atmosphere of intelligent understanding about one's self and his possible futures.

It seems very clear that this great milestone in the development of personnel services in education has placed guidance in a highly strategic situation and has brought to recognition the deep significance of student personnel work in education as the great essential to make education work in a democracy in a world in which technology and defense are important.

Preceding sections of this chapter have pointed up the very natural role of guidance in its response to the great forces in this nation. This section, however, has emphasized that the nation has declared a recognition of this function in the laws that it has passed. The nation has, therefore, endeavored not only to recognize the place of personnel work in education but also has endeavored to expand it greatly through the nation's financial facilities.

Conclusion

This has not been a history of personnel work in education.[9] Personnel work in education shows in its history a remarkable confluence with the rise of the great forces in this nation that have been mentioned in this chapter. At the same time, that confluence is not remarkable because it is to these forces that personnel work in education has responded. It is highly arresting, however, to note the similarity in time between the rise of the great movements that have been pointed out in this chapter and the beginnings of guidance work in the schools and of student personnel work in the colleges.

9. For historical background, see Ruth Barry and Beverly Wolf, *Modern Issues in Guidance-Personnel Work* (New York: Teachers College, Columbia University, 1957); John M. Brewer, *History of Vocational Guidance* (New York: Harper & Bros., 1942); Robert Hendry Mathewson, *Guidance Policy and Practice* (New York: Harper & Bros., 1955, revised); and Willa Norris, "The History and Development of the National Vocational Guidance Association" (unpublished dissertation, George Washington University, 1954).

The timing is not accidental. The fact of student personnel work in education simply accentuates it as a response to the great needs of the nation and its people.

The same element that this nation has found in personnel work in education is repeated in other countries throughout the world. It is undeniably true that those nations that today are struggling toward the realization of democratic forms of government are realizing the significance of personnel work in their educational systems. They are developing with the understanding that the workings of a democratic nation with its accent upon the individual is inextricably tied to the success of personnel work throughout the educational experiences of its people.

The response of personnel work in education to the needs of this nation and to the needs of other nations throughout the world is far more than a response of a collection of techniques and instruments. It is the response of a way of looking at people, of a way of working with people, of a way of stimulating people, so that there can emerge individuals who have the strength that comes from having understood one's possibilities and can develop them to the fullest for one's own satisfaction and for the greatness of the nation and the world in which he lives.

Today's world is one in which the changes in technology and changes in ways of living are at a pace considerably faster than has ever been known before. Throughout these changes one verity remains, namely, the individual and his ability to handle himself with greatness in the face of change. Undoubtedly, there will be many changes in personnel work in education, but it is certainly also a verity that personnel work in education will continue always to be concerned with the greatness of the individual.

Index

CONSTITUTION AND BY-LAWS
OF
THE NATIONAL SOCIETY FOR THE STUDY OF EDUCATION

(As adopted May, 1944, and amended June, 1945, and February, 1949)

ARTICLE I

NAME

The name of this corporation shall be "The National Society for the Study of Education," an Illinois corporation not for profit.

ARTICLE II

PURPOSES

Its purposes are to carry on the investigation of educational problems, to publish the results of same, and to promote their discussion.

The corporation also has such powers as are now, or may hereafter be, granted by the General Not For Profit Corporation Act of the State of Illinois.

ARTICLE III

OFFICES

The corporation shall have and continuously maintain in this state a registered office and a registered agent whose office is identical with such registered office, and may have other offices within or without the State of Illinois as the Board of Directors may from time to time determine.

ARTICLE IV

MEMBERSHIP

Section 1. *Classes.* There shall be two classes of members—active and honorary. The qualifications and rights of the members of such classes shall be as follows:

(*a*) Any person who is desirous of promoting the purposes of this corporation is eligible to active membership and shall become such on payment of dues as prescribed.

(*b*) Active members shall be entitled to vote, to participate in discussion, and, subject to the conditions set forth in Article V, to hold office.

(*c*) Honorary members shall be entitled to all the privileges of active members, with the exception of voting and holding office, and shall be exempt from the payment of dues. A person may be elected to honorary membership by vote of the active members of the corporation on nomination by the Board of Directors.

(*d*) Any active member of the Society may, at any time after reaching the age of sixty, become a life member on payment of the aggregate amount of the regular annual dues for the period of life expectancy, as determined by standard actuarial tables, such membership to entitle the member to receive all yearbooks and to enjoy all other privileges of active membership in the Society for the lifetime of the member.

Section 2. *Termination of Membership.*

(*a*) The Board of Director by affirmative vote of two-thirds of the members of the Board may suspend or expel a member for cause after appropriate hearing.

(*b*) Termination of membership for nonpayment of dues shall become effective as provided in Article XIV.

Section 3. *Reinstatement.* The Board of Directors may by the affirmation vote of two-thirds of the members of the Board reinstate a former member whose membership was previously terminated for cause other than nonpayment of dues.

Section 4. *Transfer of Membership.* Membership in this corporation is not transferable or assignable.

ARTICLE V

BOARD OF DIRECTORS

Section 1. *General Powers.* The business and affairs of the corporation shall be managed by its Board of Directors. It shall appoint the Chairman and Vice-Chairman of the Board of Directors, the Secretary-Treasurer, and Members of the Council. It may appoint a member to fill any vacancy on the Board until such vacancy shall have been filled by election as provided in Section 3 of this Article.

Section 2. *Number, Tenure, and Qualifications.* The Board of Directors shall consist of seven members, namely, six to be elected by the members of the corporation, and the Secretary-Treasurer to be the seventh member. Only active members who have contributed to the Yearbook shall be eligible for election to serve as directors. A member who has been elected for a full term of three years as director and has not attended at least two-thirds of the meetings duly called and held during that term shall not be eligible for election again before the fifth annual election after the expiration of the term for which he was first elected. No member who has been elected for two full terms as director in immediate succession shall be elected a director for a term next succeeding. This provision shall not apply to the Secretary-Treasurer who is appointed by the Board of Directors. Each director shall hold office for the term for which he is elected or appointed and until his successor shall have been selected and qualified. Directors need not be residents of Illinois.

Section 3. *Election.*

(*a*) The directors named in the Articles of Incorporation shall hold office until their successors shall have been duly selected and shall have qualified.

Thereafter, two directors shall be elected annually to serve three years, beginning March first after their election. If, at the time of any annual election, a vacancy exists in the Board of Directors, a director shall be elected at such election to fill such vacancy.

(b) Elections of directors shall be held by ballots sent by United States mail as follows: A nominating ballot together with a list of members eligible to be directors shall be mailed by the Secretary-Treasurer to all active members of the corporation in October. From such list, the active members shall nominate on such ballot one eligible member for each of the two regular terms and for any vacancy to be filled and return such ballots to the office of the Secretary-Treasurer within twenty-one days after said date of mailing by the Secretary-Treasurer. The Secretary-Treasurer shall prepare an election ballot and place thereon in alphabetical order the names of persons equal to three times the number of offices to be filled, these persons to be those who received the highest number of votes on the nominating ballot, provided, however, that not more than one person connected with a given institution or agency shall be named on such final ballot, the person so named to be the one receiving the highest vote on the nominating ballot. Such election ballot shall be mailed by the Secretary-Treasurer to all active members in November next succeeding. The active members shall vote thereon for one member for each such office. Election ballots must be in the office of the Secretary-Treasurer within twenty-one days after the said date of mailing by the Secretary-Treasurer. The ballots shall be counted by the Secretary-Treasurer, or by an election committee, if any, appointed by the Board. The two members receiving the highest number of votes shall be declared elected for the regular term and the member or members receiving the next highest number of votes shall be declared elected for any vacancy or vacancies to be filled.

Section 4. *Regular Meetings.* A regular annual meeting of the Board of Directors shall be held, without other notice than this by-law, at the same place and as nearly as possible on the same date as the annual meeting of the corporation. The Board of Directors may provide the time and place, either within or without the State of Illinois, for the holding of additional regular meetings of the Board.

Section 5. *Special Meetings.* Special meetings of the Board of Directors may be called by or at the request of the Chairman or a majority of the directors. Such special meetings shall be held at the office of the corporation unless a majority of the directors agree upon a different place for such meetings.

Section 6. *Notice.* Notice of any special meeting of the Board of Directors shall be given at least fifteen days previously thereto by written notice delivered personally or mailed to each director at his business address, or by telegram. If mailed, such notice shall be deemed to be delivered when deposited in the United States mail in a sealed envelope so addressed, with postage thereon prepaid. If notice be given by telegram, such notice shall be deemed to be delivered when the telegram is delivered to the telegraph company. Any director may waive notice of any meeting. The attendance of a director at any meeting shall constitute a waiver of notice of such meeting, except where a director attends a meeting for the express purpose of objecting to the transaction of any business because the meeting is not lawfully called or convened. Neither the business to be transacted at, nor the purpose of, any regular or special meeting of the Board need be specified in the notice or waiver of notice of such meeting.

Section 7. *Quorum.* A majority of the Board of Directors shall constitute a quorum for the transaction of business at any meeting of the Board, provided, that if less than a majority of the directors are present at said meeting, a majority of the directors present may adjourn the meeting from time to time without further notice.

Section 8. *Manner of Acting.* The act of the majority of the directors present at a meeting at which a quorum is present shall be the act of the Board of Directors, except where otherwise provided by law or by these by-laws.

ARTICLE VI

THE COUNCIL

Section 1. *Appointment.* The Council shall consist of the Board of Directors, the Chairmen of the corporation's Yearbook and Research Committees, and such other active members of the corporation as the Board of Directors may appoint.

Section 2. *Duties.* The duties of the Council shall be to further the objects of the corporation by assisting the Board of Directors in planning and carrying forward the educational undertakings of the corporation.

ARTICLE VII

OFFICERS

Section 1. *Officers.* The officers of the corporation shall be a Chairman of the Board of Directors, a Vice-Chairman of the Board of Directors, and a Secretary-Treasurer. The Board of Directors, by resolution, may create additional offices. Any two or more offices may be held by the same person, except the offices of Chairman and Secretary-Treasurer.

Section 2. *Election and Term of Office.* The officers of the corporation shall be elected annually by the Board of Directors at the annual regular meeting of the Board of Directors, provided, however, that the Secretary-Treasurer may be elected for a term longer than one year. If the election of officers shall not be held at such meeting, such election shall be held as soon thereafter as conveniently may be. Vacancies may be filled or new offices created and filled at any meeting of the Board of Directors. Each officer shall hold office until his successor shall have been duly elected and shall have qualified or until his death or until he shall resign or shall have been removed in the manner hereinafter provided.

Section 3. *Removal.* Any officer or agent elected or appointed by the Board of Directors may be removed by the Board of Directors whenever in its judgment the best interests of the corporation would be served thereby, but such removal shall be without prejudice to the contract rights, if any, of the person so removed.

Section 4. *Chairman of the Board of Directors.* The Chairman of the Board of Directors shall be the principal officer of the corporation. He shall preside at all meetings of the members of the Board of Directors, shall perform all duties incident to the office of Chairman of the Board of Directors and such other duties as may be prescribed by the Board of Directors from time to time.

Section 5. *Vice-Chairman of the Board of Directors.* In the absence of the Chairman of the Board of Directors or in the event of his inability or refusal to act, the Vice-Chairman of the Board of Directors shall perform the duties of the Chairman of the Board of Directors, and when so acting, shall have all the powers of and be subject to all the restrictions upon the Chairman of the Board of Directors. Any Vice-Chairman of the Board of Directors shall perform such other duties as from time to time may be assigned to him by the Board of Directors.

Section 6. *Secretary-Treasurer.* The Secretary-Treasurer shall be the managing executive officer of the corporation. He shall: (*a*) keep the minutes of the meetings of the members and of the Board of Directors in one or more books provided for that purpose; (*b*) see that all notices are duly given in accordance with the provisions of these by-laws or as required by law; (*c*) be custodian of the corporate records and of the seal of the corporation and see that the seal of the corporation is affixed to all documents, the execution of which on behalf of the corporation under its seal is duly authorized in accordance with the provisions of these by-laws; (*d*) keep a register of the postoffice address of each member as furnished to the secretary-treasurer by such member; (*e*) in general perform all duties incident to the office of secretary and such other duties as from time to time may be assigned to him by the Chairman of the Board of Directors or by the Board of Directors. He shall also: (1) have charge and custody of and be responsible for all funds and securities of the corporation; receive and give receipts for moneys due and payable to the corporation from any source whatsoever, and deposit all such moneys in the name of the corporation in such banks, trust companies or other depositories as shall be selected in accordance with the provisions of Article XI of these by-laws; (2) in general perform all the duties incident to the office of Treasurer and such other duties as from time to time may be assigned to him by the Chairman of the Board of Directors or by the Board of Directors. The Secretary-Treasurer shall give a bond for the faithful discharge of his duties in such sum and with such surety or sureties as the Board of Directors shall determine, said bond to be placed in the custody of the Chairman of the Board of Directors.

ARTICLE VIII

COMMITTEES

The Board of Directors, by appropriate resolution duly passed, may create and appoint such committees for such purposes and periods of time as it may deem advisable.

ARTICLE IX

PUBLICATIONS

Section 1. The corporation shall publish *The Yearbook of the National Society for the Study of Education,* such supplements thereto, and such other materials as the Board of Directors may provide for.

Section 2. *Names of Members.* The names of the active and honorary members shall be printed in the Yearbook.

ARTICLE X

ANNUAL MEETINGS

The corporation shall hold its annual meetings at the time and place of the Annual Meeting of the American Association of School Administrators of the National Education Association. Other meetings may be held when authorized by the corporation or by the Board of Directors.

ARTICLE XI

CONTRACTS, CHECKS, DEPOSITS, AND GIFTS

Section 1. *Contracts.* The Board of Directors may authorize any officer or officers, agent or agents of the corporation, in addition to the officers so authorized by these by-laws to enter into any contract or execute and deliver any instrument in the name of and on behalf of the corporation and such authority may be general or confined to specific instances.

Section 2. *Checks, drafts, etc.* All checks, drafts, or other orders for the payment of money, notes, or other evidences of indebtedness issued in the name of the corporation, shall be signed by such officer or officers, agent or agents of the corporation and in such manner as shall from time to time be determined by resolution of the Board of Directors. In the absence of such determination of the Board of Directors, such instruments shall be signed by the Secretary-Treasurer.

Section 3. *Deposits.* All funds of the corporation shall be deposited from time to time to the credit of the corporation in such banks, trust companies, or other depositories as the Board of Directors may select.

Section 4. *Gifts*. The Board of Directors may accept on behalf of the corporation any contribution, gift, bequest, or device for the general purposes or for any special purpose of the corporation.

ARTICLE XII

BOOKS AND RECORDS

The corporation shall keep correct and complete books and records of account and shall also keep minutes of the proceedings of its members, Board of Directors, and committees having any of the authority of the Board of Directors, and shall keep at the registered or principal office a record giving the names and addresses of the members entitled to vote. All books and records of the corporation may be inspected by any member or his agent or attorney for any proper purpose at any reasonable time.

ARTICLE XIII

FISCAL YEAR

The fiscal year of the corporation shall begin on the first day of July in each year and end on the last day of June of the following year.

ARTICLE XIV

DUES

Section 1. *Annual Dues*. The annual dues for active members of the Society shall be determined by vote of the Board of Directors at a regular meeting duly called and held.

Section 2. *Election Fee*. An election fee of $1.00 shall be paid in advance by each applicant for active membership.

Section 3. *Payment of Dues*. Dues for each calendar year shall be payable in advance on or before the first day of January of that year. Notice of dues for the ensuing year shall be mailed to members at the time set for mailing the primary ballots.

Section 4. *Default and Termination of Membership*. Annual membership shall terminate automatically for those members whose dues remain unpaid after the first day of January of each year. Members so in default will be reinstated on payment of the annual dues plus a reinstatement fee of fifty cents.

ARTICLE XV

SEAL

The Board of Directors shall provide a corporate seal which shall be in the form of a circle and shall have inscribed thereon the name of the corporation and the words "Corporate Seal, Illinois."

ARTICLE XVI

WAIVER OF NOTICE

Whenever any notice whatever is required to be given under the provision of the General Not For Profit Corporation Act of Illinois or under the provisions of the Articles of Incorporation or the by-laws of the corporation, a waiver thereof in writing signed by the person or persons entitled to such notice, whether before or after the time stated therein, shall be deemed equivalent to the giving of such notice.

ARTICLE XVII

AMENDMENTS

Section 1. *Amendments by Directors.* The constitution and by-laws may be altered or amended at any meeting of the Board of Directors duly called and held, provided that an affirmative vote of at least five directors shall be required for such action.

Section 2. *Amendments by Members.* By petition of twenty-five or more active members duly filed with the Secretary-Treasurer, a proposal to amend the constitution and by-laws shall be submitted to all active members by United States mail together with ballots on which the members shall vote for or against the proposal. Such ballots shall be returned by United States mail to the office of the Secretary-Treasurer within twenty-one days after date of mailing of the proposal and ballots by the Secretary-Treasurer. The Secretary-Treasurer or a committee appointed by the Board of Directors for that purpose shall count the ballots and advise the members of the result. A vote in favor of such proposal by two-thirds of the members voting thereon shall be required for adoption of such amendment.

MINUTES OF THE ST. LOUIS MEETING
OF THE SOCIETY

FEBRUARY 22 AND 25, 1958

This report describes the programs presented by the Society at St. Louis, where the first of the three regional conferences of the American Association of School Administrators was held. In addition to the conference at St. Louis, similar meetings were scheduled by the Association at San Francisco and Cleveland. The three volumes comprising the Society's Fifty-seventh Yearbook were presented at each of the three conferences. The programs dealt with the same topics in each city, while the speakers were selected from the region in which the city is located.

The Society usually presents two programs in connection with the convention of the American Association of School Administrators, one program each for the two volumes of the current yearbook. It happened that three volumes were ready for publication by the time of the 1958 Annual Meeting in February and the Board of Directors authorized publication of the three volumes as Parts I, II, and III of the Fifty-seventh Yearbook. In order to adapt our programs for presentation of these three volumes at the two sessions the Society usually holds, Parts I and III were included in the program of the Saturday evening session, and Part II was presented at the second session, which was held Tuesday morning.

The first session was held in the Crystal Room at the Sheraton-Jefferson Hotel at eight o'clock Saturday evening, February 22. This discussion of Parts I and III of the Fifty-seventh Yearbook was planned as a joint meeting of the National Society with the American Association of School Administrators and the American Educational Research Association. The meeting was called to order by the presiding officer, Dean Stephen M. Corey, Chairman of the Society's Board of Directors. The following program was presented.

I. Basic Concepts in Music Education

(Part I of the Society's Fifty-seventh Yearbook)

Introducing the Yearbook

THURBER H. MADISON, Associate Professor of Music Education, Indiana University, Bloomington, Indiana; Chairman of the Yearbook Committee

Evaluation of the Yearbook

LEIGH GERDINE, Chairman, Department of Music, Washington University, St. Louis, Missouri

Informal Discussion

Led by Chairman of the Yearbook Committee

II. *The Integration of Educational Experiences*

(Part III of the Society's Fifty-seventh Yearbook)

Introducing the Yearbook
> PAUL L. DRESSEL, Professor of Education, Michigan State University, East Lansing, Michigan; Chairman of the Yearbook Committee

Evaluation of the Yearbook
> B. OTHANEL SMITH, Professor of Education, University of Illinois, Urbana, Illinois

Informal Discussion
> Led by Chairman of the Yearbook Committee

The second session of the 1958 meeting was held in Room 8 of the Sheraton-Jefferson Hotel at 9:30 A.M., Tuesday, February 25. This session dealt with Part II of the Fifty-seventh Yearbook, entitled *Education for the Gifted,* and the program was planned as a joint meeting of the National Society with the American Association for Gifted Children. Paul A. Witty of the American Association for Gifted Children and member of the Yearbook Committee presided over the meeting. The following program was presented.

Introducing the Yearbook
> ROBERT J. HAVIGHURST, Professor of Education, University of Chicago; Chairman of the Yearbook Committee

Evaluation of the Yearbook
> EARL G. HERMINGHAUS, Research Consultant, St. Louis Public Schools, St. Louis, Missouri

Informal Discussion
> Led by Chairman of the Yearbook Committee

SYNOPSIS OF THE PROCEEDINGS OF THE BOARD OF DIRECTORS OF THE SOCIETY FOR 1958

1. Meeting of February 22 at St. Louis

The Board of Directors met at the Statler Hotel, the following members being present: Corey (Chairman), Havighurst, McConnell, Melby, Olson, Witty, and Henry (Secretary).

1. The Secretary reported that the election for members of the Board of Directors in November resulted in the re-election of T. R. McConnell for a second term of three years and the election of Ruth Strang for the three-year term beginning March 1, 1958.

2. Officers of the Board of Directors for the year ending February 28, 1959, were selected as follows: Mr. McConnell, Chairman; Mr. Havighurst, Vice-chairman; Mr. Henry, Secretary.

3. The Secretary described the plans made for the presentation of the three volumes of the Fifty-seventh Yearbook in each of the three cities in which the Society participates in the programs provided under the auspices of the American Association of School Administrators. These three events are the programs to be presented in St. Louis, February 22 and 25; in San Francisco, March 8 and 11; in Cleveland, March 29 and 31. The preparations for the Society's annual meeting were somewhat complicated this year because of the unusual event of including three volumes in the yearbook for the year 1958, instead of the usual practice of issuing a yearbook comprising two volumes.

4. Mr. Corey reported on the deliberations of the committee for the preparation of the yearbook on "Fundamental Education," including a statement presented by Professor Arndt, chairman of the committee. Mr. Corey expressed confidence in the plans effected by the committee but indicated some apprehension over suggestions that might lead to the attempt to define fundamental education too rigidly to be representative of practices recently employed.

5. The Secretary, reporting as the representative of the Board of Directors for the committee on "Personnel Services in Higher Education," stated that the several chapters of the proposed plan for this yearbook have been assigned to the contributors selected. The schedule of meetings and deadlines for manuscripts as announced by Dr. Hardee, chairman of the committee, was considered favorable in light of the date of publication in 1959.

6. Mr. Olson reported on the progress of the committee for the yearbook in the field of group dynamics, tentatively entitled "The Class as a Group." Consideration is being given to other titles that have been suggested with the view of selecting a phrasing of the title that would

be more in keeping with the content of the volume. At the recent meeting of the committee in New York when the chapter allocations were reviewed, the committee reduced the number of chapters to fourteen.

7. Mr. Havighurst, representing the Board of Directors as a member of the committee for the yearbook on "Science in Elementary and High Schools," reported that the committee is making satisfactory progress. In the consideration of possible improvement of the manuscripts to be prepared for this yearbook, the committee decided to explore possible collaboration with the Institute of Textbook Publishers in the form of a critical review of appropriate members of their staffs prior to acceptance of the individual chapters as submitted. The Board of Directors considered the plan worth trying experimentally, although some doubts were expressed about the value of the procedure from the point of view of established procedures and policies of the Society.

2. MEETING OF JUNE 6 AND 7 AT CHICAGO

The Board of Directors met at the Conrad Hilton Hotel, the following members being present: Corey, McConnell (Chairman), Melby, Olson, Strang, and Henry (Secretary).

1. Reports of satisfactory progress by the committees engaged in preparation of the two volumes of the Fifty-eighth Yearbook scheduled for publication in advance of the Society's annual meeting in February, 1959, were received. Manuscripts of all but one of the chapters for the yearbook on "Fundamental Education" have been submitted. The Secretary reported on a communication from the chairman of the committee indicating a desire on the part of members of the committee to change the title of that yearbook. Although the matter was not finally adjusted at that time, an agreement was reached subsequently, as is reported in the proceedings of the meeting of the Board, October 31 and November 1. The yearbook dealing with personnel work, originally listed under the title of "Personnel Services in Higher Education," will be published as *Personnel Services in Education*, to allow for modifications of the original plan to include elementary- and secondary-school practices.

2. Mr. Jensen, chairman of the committee for the proposed yearbook in the field of group dynamics, reported to Mr. Olson that all outstanding contributions will be submitted by September 15. It is expected that the committee's review of the manuscripts and the time required for authors to make desired revisions will make it possible for the committee to submit the yearbook to the Board by March, 1959. This volume is scheduled for publication in 1960.

3. Professor Witty recently submitted a proposal for a yearbook entitled "Developmental Reading." This report was reviewed by the Board with suggestions for further consideration but approved Mr. Witty's recommendations for membership of the committee, the question of the title to be considered again in the future.

4. The American Educational Research Association recently announced a conference to be held in Washington, D.C., to consider the possible desirability of establishing a council comprising delegates of perhaps twenty interested educational organizations for such purposes as promoting research projects, reviewing proposals for such, and securing financial aid therefor. The Research Association invited the Board of Directors of the Society to send a representative to participate in discussions designed to promote interest and participation in the activities of the proposed council. The Board requested Mr. Corey to represent the Society in the organizing conference.

3. MEETING OF OCTOBER 31 AND NOVEMBER 1 AT CHICAGO

The Board of Directors met at the Conrad Hilton Hotel, the following members being present: Corey, Havighurst, McConnell (Chairman), Melby, Olson, Strang, and Henry (Secretary).

1. Professor Arndt, chairman of the committee for the yearbook originally entitled "Fundamental Education," attended this meeting for the purpose of formulating plans for the presentation of the yearbook at the convention of the American Association of School Administrators in Atlantic City and for further consideration of the title of this yearbook. The title agreed upon is *Community Education: Principles and Practices from World-wide Experience.*

The discussion of the Society's presentation of the two parts of the Fifty-eighth Yearbook led to a decision to present both parts of the yearbook at our Saturday evening session. The program was planned to allow one hour for the discussion of each volume. The program is to consist of a very brief introduction by the chairman of the committee in each case, namely, Dr. Arndt for Part I and Dr. Hardee for Part II. A selected speaker will then present a critical evaluation of the book, after which the discussion will be open to members of the audience for questions or comments.

2. Mr. Havighurst reported on the status of the yearbook on the teaching of science, noting that the various chapters are being mailed to the committee chairman according to schedule. It is assumed that the completed manuscript will be ready for publication in 1960.

3. Mr. Olson presented the report of the chairman of the committee studying problems of group dynamics. The new title now under consideration by the committee is stated as "The Dynamics of Instructional Groups." The work of the committee indicates that the manuscript will be completed in accordance with the original schedule.

4. The outline of a proposal under consideration by the Board of Directors is concerned with problems relating to professional education. This proposal was presented by Dean G. Lester Anderson of the University of Buffalo. The Board has suggested that Dean Anderson invite several consultants to meet with him for discussion of some of the

features of his proposal. The Board authorized payment of the expenses of persons participating in the conference.

5. Ralph W. Tyler, Director of the Institute for Advanced Study in the Behavioral Sciences, has accepted the Board's invitation to meet with the Board on Sunday, February 15, in Atlantic City to discuss the subject, "Forces Influencing Education."

REPORT OF THE TREASURER OF THE SOCIETY

1957-58

Receipts and Disbursements

Receipts:
Membership dues	$25,305.75
Sale of yearbooks	30,328.38
Interest and dividends on securities	271.70
Miscellaneous	228.71
	$56,134.54

Disbursements:
Yearbooks:
Manufacturing	$17,842.85
Reprinting	16,485.56
Preparation	4,227.43
Meetings of the Society	2,283.09

Secretary's Office:
Editorial, secretarial, and clerical services	12,265.09
Supplies	3,493.42
Telephone and telegraph	215.40
Miscellaneous	406.78
	$57,219.62

Cash in bank at beginning of year	$ 972.43
Receipts, 1957-58	56,134.54
Transfer from Reserve Fund to checking account, June 30, 1958	4,500.00
Total cash in checking account	$61,606.97
Total disbursements	57,219.62
Cash in bank at end of year	$ 4,387.35

STATEMENT OF CASH AND SECURITIES
As of June 30, 1958

Cash:

University National Bank, Chicago, Illinois—

Checking Account .... $ 4,387.35

Securities:

Bonds:

$12,200.00 United States of America Savings Bonds,

Series "G", 2½%, due 12 years from issue date......... 12,200.00

$ 700.00 dated May 1, 1944

2,000.00 dated February 1, 1945

1,000.00 dated March 1, 1945

3,500.00 dated November 1, 1945

5,000.00 dated February 1, 1949

Stock:

27 shares First National Bank of Boston, Capital Stock...... 1,035.75

Total securities $13,235.75

Total assets $17,623.10

MEMBERS OF THE NATIONAL SOCIETY FOR THE STUDY OF EDUCATION

(This list includes all persons enrolled November 15, 1958, whether for 1958 or 1959. Asterisk (*) indicates Life Members of the Society.)

Aarestad, Amanda B., Winona State College, Winona, Minn.
Aaron, Ira E., College of Education, University of Georgia, Athens, Ga.
Abate, Harry, Principal, Niagara Street School, Niagara Falls, N.Y.
Abbott, Samuel Lee, Jr., Plymouth Tchrs. College, Plymouth, N.H.
Abel, Frederick P., Principal, East High School, Aurora, Ill.
Abelson, Harold H., College of the City of New York, New York, N.Y.
Abraham, Willard, Arizona State College, Tempe, Ariz.
Abrahamson, Stephen, Sch. of Educ., Univ. of Buffalo, Buffalo, N.Y.
Acharlu, K. S., Sevagram P.O., Warda DT, Bombay State, India
Adams, Agnes L., National College of Education, Evanston, Ill.
Adams, Mrs. Daisy Trice, Principal, Charles Sumner School, Kansas City, Mo.
Adams, Fern Burnett, Los Angeles County Schools, Los Angeles, Calif.
Adams, Robert G., Principal, Lincoln School, Oakland, Calif.
Adams, Wanda N., 2602 La Madera Dr., Tucson, Ariz.
Adamson, Oral Victor, Principal, Highland Elem. School, Evansville, Ind.
Adelberg, Arthur J., Supt., School Dist. No. 3, Elmhurst, Ill.
Adell, James C., 16723 Fernway Rd., Shaker Heights, Ohio
Aden, Robert C., Dept. of Educ., Bethel College, McKenzie, Tenn.
Adler, Charles S., Principal, Lincoln Elem. School, Roseville, Mich.
Adolphsen, Louis John, Director, Secondary Educ., Davenport, Iowa
Aggens, Lorenz W., 5626 N. Francisco Ave., Chicago, Ill.
Agnone, Anthony F., Superintendent of Schools, South River, N.J.
Ahrens, Dolores F., Supv., Elem. Student Teachers, Champaign, Ill.
Akins, Harold S., 626 No. Mt. Carmel, Wichita, Kan.
Alawi, A. H., Dept. of Educ., Univ. of Peshawar, Peshawar, West Pakistan
Albin, Floyd B., Oregon College of Education, Monmouth, Ore.
Albohm, John C., Superintendent of Schools, York, Pa.
Albrecht, Carl H., Superintendent of Schools, Norwood, Ohio
Albrecht, Milton C., Col. of Arts and Sci., Univ. of Buffalo, Buffalo, N.Y.
Albright, Frank S., 37 Yale Terrace, West Orange, N.J.
Alcorn, Marvin D., San Diego State College, San Diego, Calif.
Alcorn, Maurice, Principal, Hyatt Park School, Columbia, S.C.
Aldrich, Frederic D., Dept. of Educ., Chatham College, Pittsburgh, Pa.
Aldrich, Julian C., School of Educ., New York University, New York, N.Y.
Aleck, Adolph W., Mississippi State University, State College, Miss.
Alexander, Jean H., Col. of Educ., University of Minnesota, Minneapolis, Minn.
Alexander, William M., George Peabody College, Nashville, Tenn.
Allbee, Lewis, Superintendent of Schools, Town of Groton, Poquonnock Bridge, Conn.
Allen, Beatrice Ona, Principal, Waters Elementary School, Chicago, Ill.
Allen, D. W., Assoc. Supt., Ohio State Reformatory, Mansfield, Ohio
Allen, Edward E., Supv. Principal of Schools, Akron, N.Y.
Allen, James Robert, 4631 S. Second St., Louisville, Ky.
Allen, James R., Superintendent, Harmony School, Belleville, Ill.
Allen, Ross L., State University Teachers College, Cortland, N.Y.
Allen, Warren G., State Teachers College, Minot, N.D.
Allen, W. Paul, Principal, Fox Meadow School, Scarsdale, N.Y.
Allman, Reva White, Dept. of Educ., Alabama State College, Montgomery, Ala.
Almcrantz, Mrs. Georgia, Box 87, Marseilles, Ill.
Almroth, Frank S., Principal, Public Schools, Westfield, N.J.
Aloia, Alex D., 7101 West 80th St., Loyola University, Los Angeles, Calif.

Alpren, Morton, Tchrs. College, Temple University, Philadelphia, Pa.
Alsup, Robert F., 1712 Farmers Ave., Murray, Ky.
Alt, Pauline M., Teachers Col. of Connecticut, New Britain, Conn.
Altieri, Dolores M., New Haven State Teachers College, New Haven, Conn.
Amar, Wesley F., 8036 S. Green St., Chicago, Ill.
Amberson, Jean D., Home Econ. Bldg., Pa. State Col., State College, Pa.
Ambrose, Luther M., USOM/Paraguay, Dept. of State Mail Room, Washington, D.C.
Amidon, Edmund J., 707 University Ave., No. 102, S.E., Minneapolis, Minn.
Amidon, Edna P., Office of Educ., Dept. of Health, Educ., and Welfare, Washington, D.C.
Amos, Robert T., Rhode Island College of Education, Providence, R.I.
Anderson, Mrs. Annie Lou, Principal, Alamo School, El Paso, Tex.
Anderson, Bernard, Principal, John Spry Elementary School, Chicago, Ill.
Anderson, C. R., Superintendent of Schools, Helena, Mont.
Anderson, Clarence K., Prin., Amundsen High School, Chicago, Ill.
Anderson, Dorothy May, Gustavus Adolphus College, St. Peter, Minn.
Anderson, Edmond C., Prin., George W. Carver School, Dallas, Tex.
Anderson, Ernest M., Kansas State Teachers College, Pittsburg, Kan.
Anderson, Evelyn, Otterbein College, Westerville, Ohio
Anderson, G. Lester, Dean, University of Buffalo, Buffalo, N.Y.
Anderson, Harold A., Dept. of Educ., Univ. of Chicago, Chicago, Ill.
Anderson, Harold H., 340 Wildwood Ave., East Lansing, Mich.
Anderson, Harry D., Supt., Maine Township High School, Des Plaines, Ill.
Anderson, Howard R., 50 Pelham Road, Rochester, N.Y.
Anderson, Jack O., 2067 Oakdale Dr., Drayton Plains, Mich.
Anderson, James W., 742 Ashland Ave., St. Paul Park, Minn.
Anderson, John E., Inst. of Child Welfare, Univ. of Minn., Minneapolis, Minn.
Anderson, Kenneth E., Dean, Sch. of Educ., Univ. of Kansas, Lawrence, Kan.
Anderson, Lester W., 4017 University High School, Ann Arbor, Mich.
Anderson, Marion, Ginn & Company, Boston, Mass.
Anderson, Philip S., State Teachers College, River Falls, Wis.
Anderson, Robert, 93 Village Dr., Columbus, Ohio
Anderson, Robert H., Lawrence Hall, Harvard University, Cambridge, Mass.
Anderson, Rodney, Northern Illinois State Tchrs. Col., DeKalb, Ill.
Anderson, Ruth, 274 West 127th St., New York, N.Y.
Anderson, Stuart A., Asst. Supt. of Schools, Niles Twp. High School, Skokie, Ill.
Anderson, Vernon E., Dean, Col. of Educ., Univ. of Maryland, College Park, Md.
Anderson, Walter A., Sch. of Educ., New York University, New York, N.Y.
Anderson, William F., Jr., Psych. Res. Center, Syracuse Univ., Syracuse, N.Y.
Anderson, William P., Teachers College, Columbia University, New York, N.Y.
Andes, John D., Asst. Supt. in Chg. of Instruction, Richmond, Calif.
Andree, R. G., Rich Twp. High School, Dist. 227, Park Forest, Ill.
Andregg, Neal B., Provost Marshal General's School, Camp Gordon, Ga.
Andrews, Clay S., San Jose State College, San Jose, Calif.
Andrews, Murray L., Supv., Library Service, Bd. of Educ., Rockville, Md.
Andrews, Wendell B., Director of Instruction, Public Schls., Schenectady, N.Y.
Angelini, Arrigo Leonardo, University of Sao Paulo, Sao Paulo, Brazil
Angell, George W., Pres., State Univ. Teachers College, Plattsburg, N.Y.
Angelo, Rev. Mark V., Siena College, Loudonville, N.Y.
Ansel, James O., Western Michigan University, Kalamazoo, Mich.
Antell, Henry, 120 Kenilworth Pl., Brooklyn, N.Y.
Antonacci, Robert J., Supv., Health and Phys. Educ., Pub. Schls., Gary, Ind.
Anyaegbunam, Okagbue, 5C Ogbendida, Onitsha, Nigeria, West Africa
Apple, Joe A., San Diego State College, San Diego, Calif.
Applegate, Stanley A., Curric. Serv. Center, Plandome Rd. Sch., Manhasset, N.Y.
Appleton, David, Superintendent of Schools, Conway, N.H.
Aramvalarthanathan, M., Tchrs. Col., S.R.K.M., Vidyalaya, Coimbatore Dist., Madras State, South India
Archer, Clifford P., Col. of Educ., Univ. of Minnesota, Minneapolis, Minn.

Armstrong, Grace, State Teachers College, Mankato, Minn.
Armstrong, Hubert C., Claremont Graduate School, Claremont, Calif.
Armstrong, Hubert E., Superintendent of Schools, Myrtle Point, Ore.
Armstrong, V. L., 6230 Crestview, Littleton, Colo.
Arnaud, E. E., Dept. of Educ., St. Mary's Univ., San Antonio, Tex.
Arndt, C. O., New York University, New York, N.Y.
Arndt, H. M., Supt., Catawba County Schools, Newton, N.C.
Arnesen, Arthur E., Supv., Curriculum and Research, Salt Lake City, Utah
Arnold, Earl A., North Texas State College, Denton, Tex.
Arnold, J. E., Dean, Univ. Ext., Univ. of Tennessee, Knoxville, Tenn.
Arnold, Mabel, Dept. of Educ., Earlham College, Richmond, Ind.
Arnold, Marshall, East Central State College, Ada, Okla.
Arnold, William E., Dean, Sch. of Educ., Univ. of Pennsylvania, Philadelphia, Pa.
Arnsdorf, Val, 101 Pattee Hall, University of Minnesota, Minneapolis, Minn.
Arnspiger, Varney C., East Texas State College, Commerce, Tex.
Arnstein, George E., *NEA Journal,* 1201 Sixteenth St., N.W., Washington, D.C.
Arny, Clara Brown, University Farm, Univ. of Minnesota, St. Paul, Minn.
Artley, A. Sterl, School of Educ., Univ. of Missouri, Columbia, Mo.
Arveson, Raymond G., 315 Logan Dr., Fremont, Calif.
Ash, Ruth E., Prin., Fifth and Spring Elem. School, Reading, Pa.
Ashe, Robert W., Arizona State College, Tempe, Ariz.
Ashland, Homer B., Superintendent of Schools, Rutland, Vt.
Ashton, Ralph W., Coronado High School, Coronado, Calif.
Aslin, Neil C., Supt., Public Schools, Columbia, Mo.
Assmus, Edward F., Principal, Nutley High School, Nutley, N.J.
Atkinson, William N., Pres., Jackson Junior College, Jackson, Mich.
Auble, Donavon, Western College for Women, Oxford, Ohio
Aukerman, Robert C., University of Rhode Island, Kingston, R.I.
Aurand, O. H., Superintendent of Schools, Lancaster, Pa.
Aurand, Wayne O., Iowa State Teachers College, Cedar Falls, Iowa
Austin, David B., Teachers College, Columbia University, New York, N.Y.
Austin, Martha Lou, P.O. 382, Sarasota, Fla.
Austin, Mary C., Grad. Sch. of Educ., Harvard University, Cambridge, Mass.
Ausubel, D. P., Bur. of Research & Serv., Univ. of Illinois, Champaign, Ill.
Avegno, T. Sylvia, Sch. of Educ., Fordham University, New York, N.Y.
Avery, George E., Educ. Dept., Arizona State College, Flagstaff, Ariz.
Avril, Edwin F., 219 Blaker St., Marquette, Mich.
Avtalion, Shimon, Pedagogic Cen., Ministry of Educ., Jerusalem, Israel
Aycock, Howard A., Dir., Jefferson Intermed. and Senior High Sch., El Paso, Tex.
Ayer, Joseph C., Cincinnati Public Schools, Cincinnati, Ohio

Baar, Lincoln F., Prin., Junior High School 3, Manhattan, New York, N.Y.
Babcock, Dorothy Boyeé, 610 East 19th St., Oakland, Calif.
Bachman, Ralph V., Principal, South High School, Salt Lake City, Utah
Backus, Thomas A., 736 West Lafayette St., Tallahassee, Fla.
Bacon, Mrs. Ruth N., Supt., St. Clair County Schools, Port Huron, Mich.
Bacon, William P., Hdqtrs. USAFE, APO 12, New York, N.Y.
Bagley, Clarence H., Stone Hall, Cornell University, Ithaca, N.Y.
Bahn, Lorene A., 32 South Elm Ave., Webster Groves, Mo.
Bahner, John M., Prin., Englewood Elem. School, Englewood, Fla.
Bailer, Joseph R., Dept. of Educ., Western Maryland College, Westminster, Md.
Bailey, Francis L., President, State Teachers College, Gorham, Me.
Bailey, Lucile, Prin., Wm. T. Machan School, Phoenix, Ariz.
Bailey, Mildred L., Dept. of Vocal Music, Public Schools, New Bedford, Mass.
Baird, Forrest J., San Jose State College, San Jose, Calif.
Baker, Bradley, Prin., Melbourne High School, Melbourne, Fla.
Baker, G. Derwood, New York University, New York, N.Y.
Baker, Harry J., Dir., Psych. Clinic, Detroit Public Schools, Detroit, Mich.
Baker, Harry L., Head, Dept. of Educ. & Psy., State College, Manhattan, Kan.
Baker, Ira Young, 1619 North George St., York, Pa.
Baker, I. D., Greenville College, Greenville, Ill.

Baker, Ralph W., Music Dir., Los Altos High School, Los Altos, Calif.
Baker, Rebecca, Southern Illinois University, Carbondale, Ill.
Baldwin, Robert D., West Virginia University, Morgantown, W.Va.
Baldwin, Rollin, 924 West End Ave., New York, N.Y.
Balian, Arthur, Southern Colony and Training School, Union Grove, Wis.
Ball, George G., Iowa State Teachers College, Cedar Falls, Iowa
Ballantine, Francis A., Dept. of Educ., San Diego State Col., San Diego, Calif.
Baller, Warren R., Teachers College, Univer. of Nebraska, Lincoln, Neb.
Ballou, Stephen V., Div. of Educ., Fresno State College, Fresno, Calif.
Balow, Bruce E., Psycho-Educ. Clinic, Univ. of Minnesota, Minneapolis, Minn.
Balsam, Mrs. Bertha, Julia Richman High School, New York, N.Y.
Balzer, David M., Col. of Educ., Univ. of Minnesota, Minneapolis, Minn.
Bancroft, Roger W., State University Tchrs. College, Cortland, N.Y.
Banfield, R. A., Taylor Hall, U.C.W.I., Mona, St. Andrews, Jamaica, B.W.I.
Banner, Carolyn, Critic Teacher, Langston University, Langston, Okla.
Bannon, Michael F., State Teachers College, West Chester, Pa.
Banta, Arthur E., 82-200 San Jocinto Ave., Indio, Calif.
Bany, Mary, Los Angeles State College, Los Angeles, Calif.
Barber, Anson B., 125 Alexander Ave., Nutley, N.J.
Barber, Joseph E., Bureau of Naval Personnel, Washington, D.C.
Barden, John G., Appalachian State College, Boone, N.C.
Barlow, Joseph T., Prin., Oakleigh Elem. School, Baltimore, Md.
Barlow, Melvin L., Dept. of Educ., Univ. of Calif., Los Angeles, Calif.
Barnard, Ethel M., Consultant, In-service Tchr. Educ., Bowling Green, Ky.
Barnard, J. Darrell, Sch. of Educ., New York University, New York, N.Y.
Barnard, William H., Dept. of Educ., Miss. State Col., State College, Miss.
Barnes, Cyril W., Supervising Principal, Waterford, Wis.
Barnes, Cyrus W., Beachlake, Pa.
Barnes, Fred P., Col. of Educ., University of Illinois, Urbana, Ill.
Barnett, Glenn E., Col. of Educ., University of Texas, Austin, Tex.
Barr, Charlotte A., 4950 South Archer Avenue, Chicago, Ill.
Barrett, Thomas C., 2153 Green Ave., Anoka, Minn.
Barrie, Margaret J., Principal, Lincoln School, Hawthorne, N.J.
Barros, Rev. Raymond, S.J., Catholic Univ. of Valparaiso, Valparaiso, Chile
Barry, Florence G., Adjustment Teacher, Lawson Elem. School, Chicago, Ill.
Barry, Robert F., Board of Education, Rochester, N.Y.
Bartels, Isabella, 3024 Fairway Drive, Dayton, Ohio
Bartlett, Roland O., Principal, Westmount Sr. High School, Westmount, Que.
Barton, George E., Jr., Tulane University, New Orleans, La.
Bash, Abraham, 792 E. Carl Ave., Baldwin, L.I., N.Y.
Bass, Floyd L., Div. of Educ., LeMoyne College, Memphis, Tenn.
Batchelder, Howard T., Dept. of Educ., Indiana University, Bloomington, Ind.
Bateman, E. Allen, Supt. of Public Instruction, Salt Lake City, Utah
Batha, Robert, Principal, Junior-Senior High School, Chester, Calif.
Battle, John A., 11 Jones St., New Hyde Park, N.Y.
Battle, William L., Dir., Albany State College, Columbus Center, Ga.
Battram, John V., 2363 North Cedar Rd., Holt, Mich.
Bauer, Harold C., Superintendent of Schools, Fond du Lac, Wis.
Baugher, James K., Prin., Wilday and Washington Schls., Roselle, N.J.
Baughman, Shirley, Westminster College, Salt Lake City, Utah
Baum, Paul B., LaVerne College, LaVerne, Calif.
Bauman, Frank O., Minot State Teachers College, Minot, N.D.
Baumann, Margaret L., Principal, Mason Elem. School, Chicago, Ill.
Baumgartner, Reuben A., Senior High School, Freeport, Ill.
Baxter, Marlin B., Moline Public Schools, Moline, Ill.
Bay, James F., Principal, Seabrook Elem. School, Seabrook, Tex.
Beach, Lowell W., University of Michigan, Ann Arbor, Mich.
Beadles, William T., Dean, Illinois Wesleyan Univ., Bloomington, Ill.
Beahm, W. I., Supv. Prin., Donegal Area Joint Sch. Sys., Mount Joy, Pa.
Beall, Harold, Superintendent of School, Springfield, Ore.
Beall, Ross H., Dept. of Educ., University of Tulsa, Tulsa, Okla.

Beamer, George C., North Texas State College, Denton, Tex.
Beamish, J. K., Supt,. Westchester Public Schools, Westchester, Ill.
Beane, Donald G, 2500 Park St., Rolling Meadows, Ill.
Bear, David E., 3226 Brown St., Alton, Ill.
Beard, Richard L., 1621 Bruce Ave., Charlottesville, Va.
Beardsley, Florence E., State Dept. of Education, Salem, Ore.
Beattie, Alfred W., Supt., Allegheny County Schools, Pittsburgh, Pa.
Beatty, Dorothy M., Broadview Apts., Baltimore, Md.
Beatty, Walcott H., 30 Tapia Dr., San Francisco, Calif.
Beaty, Betty, Teachers College, Univ. of Cincinnati, Cincinnati, Ohio
Beaubier, Edward W., 2431 Rockinghorse Rd., San Pedro, Calif.
Beauchamp, George A., School of Educ., Northwestern Univ., Evanston, Ill.
Beaumont, Urville J., Prin., Tenney High School, Methuen, Mass.
Beaver, Eugene H., Prin., James R. Doolittle School, Chicago, Ill.
Bebb, Aldon M., Kansas State Teachers College, Pittsburg, Kan.
Bebb. Randall R., Iowa State Tchrs. College, Cedar Falls, Iowa
Bebell, Clifford S., Dir., Div. of Curric., State Dept. of Educ., Denver, Colo.
Bechtel, Blair B., Moorestown High School, Moorestown, N.J.
Beck, Alfred D., N.Y.C. Board of Educ., New York City, N.Y.
Beck, Hubert Park, Sch. of Educ., City College, New York, N.Y.
Beck, John M., Chicago Teachers College, Chicago, Ill.
Beck, Norman W., Superintendent, Monroe County Schools, Waterloo, Ill.
Beck, Ralph Lea, Bowling Green State University, Bowling Green, Ohio
Becker, George, Prin., Public School 199, Brooklyn, N.Y.
Becker, Harry A., Superintendent of Schools, Norwalk, Conn.
Becker, Millie, 8012 Ellis Ave., Chicago, Ill.
Beckstead, Reed H., Supt., Jordan School Dist., Sandy, Utah
BeCraft, Gertrude, Genl. Supv. of Instruction, County Schools, Welch, W. Va.
Bedell, Ralph, U.S. Office of Education, Washington, D.C.
Beecher, George, Goddard College, Plainfield, Vt.
Beery, Althea, Supv., Elem. Educ., Public Schools, Cincinnati, Ohio
Beery, John R., Dean, Sch. of Educ., University of Miami, Coral Gables, Fla.
Behrens, Herman D., Dept. of Educ., State Teachers College, Oneonta, N.Y.
Behrens, Minnie S., Elem. Educ. Dept., East Texas Tchrs. Col., Commerce, Tex.
Belcher, Eddie W., Div. of Curric., Louisville Public Schls., Louisville, Ky.
Bell, Dorothy M., President, Bradford Junior College, Bradford, Mass.
Bell, Keith A., Psych. and Educ. Dept., Cascade College, Portland, Ore.
Bell, Laurence M., Teachers College, Victoria, Australia
Bell, Millard D., Superintendent. School Dist. 39, Wilmette, Ill.
Bell, Robert M., Prin., Pulaski Elementary School, Chicago, Ill.
Bell, Wilmer V., Acting Dean, Baltimore Junior College, Baltimore, Md.
Bellack, Arno A., Teachers College, Columbia University, New York, N.Y.
Bellis, Bertha, McMurry Lab. School, State Tchrs. College, DeKalb. Ill.
Beltramo, Louise, Col. of Educ., State Univ. of Iowa, Iowa City, Iowa
Bemis, Eaton O., Principal, Millikan High School, Long Beach, Calif.
Bemis, Maynard, Exec. Secy., Phi Delta Kappa, Bloomington, Ind.
Benben, John S., Head, Dept. of Educ., Northern Ill. Univ., DeKalb, Ill.
Bender, Celia, Creative Arts Center, 64 East Van Buren St., Chicago, Ill.
Bender, Lauretta, Children's Unit, Creedmoor State Hosp., Queens Village, N.Y.
Benneche, Merle, 231 Fairlawn Dr., Berkeley, Calif.
Benner, Charles H., Sch. of Music, Ohio State Univ., Columbus, Ohio
Bennett, H. K., Deputy Supt., Dearborn Public Schools, Dearborn, Mich.
Bennett, Marjorie, Principal, Kent Elem. School, Englewood, Colo.
Bennett. Robert, Supv. Prin., Greene Central School, Greene. N.Y.
Bennie, William A., Dir., Student Tchg., Miami University, Oxford, Ohio
Bentley, Harold. Director, Worcester Junior College, Worcester, Mass.
Bentley, Harold W., Dean, Ext. Div., University of Utah, Salt Lake City, Utah
Bentzen, Mrs. Mary M., Univ. Elem. School, Univ. of California, Los Angeles, Calif.
Benz, H. E., Col. of Educ., Ohio University, Athens, Ohio
Beran, D. L., USOM/L, Box B, c/o American Embassy, APO 231, New York, N.Y.

Berg, Arthur D., Principal, Bellevue Community High Schol, Bellevue, Mich.
Berg, Selmer H., Superintendent of Schools, Oakland, Calif.
Berge, Marvin L., Superintendent of Schools, DeKalb, Ill.
Berger, Arthur W., Dept. of Music, Trenton State College, Trenton, N.J.
Berger, M. I., State College for Teachers, Albany, N.Y.
Bergesen, B. E., 180 Nassau St., Princeton, N.J.
Berkson, I. B., 39 Claremont Avenue, New York, N.Y.
Berlin, Pearl W., 415 Abemarle Rd., Brooklyn, N.Y.
Berman, Samuel, Prin., FitzSimons Junior High School, Philadelphia, Pa.
Bernard, Alpha E., State Teachers College, Clarion, Pa.
Bernard, Harold W., Portland State Extension Center, Portland, Ore.
Bernard, S. J., Superintendent of Schools, Easthampton, Mass.
Berning, Emanuel F., 2107 East Hawthorne Ave., St. Paul, Minn.
Bernstein, Abbot A., 104 Edwards Rd., Clifton, N.J.
Bernstein, Abraham, Dept. of Educ., Brooklyn Col., Brooklyn, N.Y.
Bernstein, Mrs. Elizabeth, Prin., H. A. Hyde School, Watsonville, Calif.
Bernstein, Louis, Principal, Lefferts Junior High School, Brooklyn, N.Y.
Bertermann, Helen A., Prin., L. M. Schiel School, Cincinnati, Ohio
Berthold, Charles A., Prin., Clifton High School, Clifton, N.J.
Bertness, Henry J., 1316 North 10th St., Tacoma, Wash.
Bertrand, John R., President, The Berry Schools, Mt. Berry, Ga.
Bethel, Hollie, Dept. of Educ., University of Omaha, Omaha, Neb.
Betts, Emmett A., 830 Chauncey Road, Penn Valley, Narberth, Pa.
Beverly, Mrs. Austin C., Prin., Spicer Demonstration School, Akron, Ohio
Beyer, Fred C., County Superintendent of Schools, Modesto, Calif.
Bhaerman, Robert D., Wilkes College, Wilkes-Barre, Pa.
Bickel, L. G., Dean, Concordia Teachers College, Seward, Neb.
Bieber, Ida P., 7357 Cornell Ave., University City, Mo.
Biester, Lillian L., Arizona State College, Flagstaff, Ariz.
Bigelow, Karl W., Teachers College, Columbia University, New York, N.Y.
* Bigelow, Merrill A., Principal, Franklin School, Bloomfield, N.J.
Bigelow, Roy G., Div. of Educ. & Psych., Miss. Southern Col., Hattiesburg, Miss.
Biggy, M. Virginia, 227 Independence Drive, Chestnut Hill, Mass.
Bigsbee, Earle M., Dean, Junior College of Connecticut, Bridgeport, Conn.
Biles, Raymond, Dept. of Educ., Baylor University, Waco, Tex.
Bilhorn, J. Chester, 3846 North Kedvale Avenue, Chicago, Ill.
* Billig, Florence G., 2008 Melrose St., Rockford, Ill.
Billings, Mrs. Helen., Educ. Dept., College of St. Teresa, Kansas City, Mo.
Bills, Mark W., Superintendent of Schools, Peoria, Ill.
Bilterman, Kathryn S., San Diego State College, San Diego, Calif.
Binford, George H., Principal, Central High School, Charlotte Courthouse, Va.
Bingham, Alma, Portland State College, Portland, Ore.
Bird, Charles A., 23 Fraser Pl., Hastings on Hudson, N.Y.
Bird, Donald H., Prin., Adrian School, South Euclid, Ohio
Birkhimer, R. O., Dean, Centralia Twp. Junior College, Centralia, Ill.
Birkley, Rev. James I., Dir., St. Joseph's Col., Calumet Ctr. Ext., Whiting, Ind.
Birkmaier, Emma, Univ. High School, Univ. of Minnesota, Minneapolis, Minn.
Birks, Mrs. Edna J., 328 E. Washington, Villa Park, Ill.
Bishop, C. L., Chm., Dept. of Educ., State Tchrs. College, Cedar Falls, Iowa
Bishop, Eunice E., 108 Union St., Schenectady, N.Y.
Bishop, Frank E., Dept. of Educ., University of Redlands, Redlands, Calif.
Bishop, S. D., Principal, Community High School, West Chicago, Ill.
Bishop, W. E., Superintendent of Schools, Englewood, Colo.
Bittick, Edsell F., Dir. of Curriculum, Public Schools, Port Arthur, Tex.
Bivins, Mrs. Lewis M., La Salle Laboratory School, Washington, D.C.
Bixler, Lorin, Dept. of Educ., Muskingum College, New Concord, Ohio
Bixler, Ray H., Dept. of Psych., Univ. of Louisville, Louisville, Ky.
Black, E. H., Superintendent, LaMarque Independent School, LaMarque, Tex.
Black, H. B., Prin., Signal Hill School, East St. Louis, Ill.
Black, Leo P., Asst. Commissioner of Education, Denver, Colo.
Black, Mrs. Marian W., Sch. of Educ., Florida State Univ., Tallahassee, Fla.

Black, Millard H., Curriculum Supv., L.A. City Schools, Los Angeles, Calif.
Blackburn, Cleo W., Exec. Dir., Flanner House, Indianapolis, Ind.
Blackburn, Clifford S., North Texas College, Denton, Tex.
Blackledge, Mrs. Helen V., Principal, Southern Heights School, Fort Wayne, Ind.
Blackman, Charles A., Michigan State University, East Lansing, Mich.
Bladen, Cecilia W., 81-10 135th St., Kew Gardens, New York, N.Y.
Blaha, M. Jay, Curric. Co-ord., Los Angeles County Schools., Los Angeles, Calif.
Blair, Alexander, Teachers College of Connecticut, New Britain, Conn.
Blake, Paul C., San Jose State College, San Jose, Calif.
Blank, James D., Principal, Mark Twain Elem. School, Iowa City, Iowa
Blankenship, A. H., Superintendent of Schools, Gary, Ind.
Blanton, Roy R., Jr., Appalachian State Tchrs. Col., Boone, N.C.
Bledsoe, Ernestine, Dir., Tchr. Educ., Wesleyan College, Macon, Ga.
Bliesmer, Emery P., McGuffey Read. Clinic, Univ. of Virginia, Charlottesville, Va.
Bligh, Harold F., 217 S. Broadway, Tarrytown, N.Y.
Blodgett, Darrell R., Superintendent of Schools, Wheaton, Ill.
Blommers, Paul, Col. of Educ., State University of Iowa, Iowa City, Iowa
Blood, Don F., West. Washington Col. of Education, Bellingham, Wash.
Bloom, Royal F., Bethel College, St. Paul, Minn.
Blount, W. Archie, Agricultural and Technical College, Greensboro, N.C.
Blyth, Donald J., Principal, Skinner Elem. School, Chicago, Ill.
Boardman, Charles W., Col. of Educ., Univ. of Minnesota, Minneapolis, Minn.
Boeck, Clarence H., Col. of Educ., Univ. of Minnesota, Minneapolis, Minn.
Boekelheide, Viola, Music Educ. Dept., Sacramento State Col., Sacramento, Calif.
Boger, D. L., Asst. Dir. of Personnel, Morehouse College, Atlanta, Ga.
Boggs, Doyle W., Principal, Hartsville High School, Hartsville, S.C.
Bogle, Frank P., Superintendent of Schools, Morristown, N.J
Bogoslovsky, Christina Staël v. H., Director, Cherry Lawn School, Darien, Conn.
Boland, Michael P., St. Joseph's College, Philadelphia, Pa.
Bolar, Richard Allen, R.R. 4, Liberty, Ind.
Bolles, Robert, Department of Music, University of Florida, Gainesville, Fla.
Bolton, Dale L., Dir., Metro. Detroit Bur. of Coop. Sch. Studies, Detroit, Mich.
* Bolton, Frederick E., University of Washington, Seattle, Wash.
Bond, George W., State Teachers College, New Paltz, N.Y.
Bond, George W., Box 612, Harding College, Searcy, Ark.
Bond, Guy L., Col. of Educ., Univ. of Minnesota, Minneapolis, Minn.
Bond, Horace M., Dean, Sch. of Educ., Atlanta University, Atlanta, Ga.
Bond, Jesse A., Dir., Tchr. Trg., Univ. of California, Los Angeles, Calif.
Bondley, G. B., 1406 Griffith Ave., Las Vegas, Nev.
Bone, Paul L., Superintendent of Schools, Princeton, Ill.
Bonk, Edward C., North Texas State College, Denton, Tex.
Bonsall, Marcella Ryser, 137 Warwick Pl., South Pasadena, Calif.
Booker, Ivan A., National Education Association, Washington, D.C.
Bookwalter, Karl W., Sch. of Educ., Indiana University, Bloomington, Ind.
Boos, John R., 4 Grant Ave., Dundas, Ontario, Canada
Booth, Delores C., 6604 Tremont St., Oakland, Calif.
Booth, Glen W., Principal, Oakville School, Cleveland, Ohio
Boothroyd, Joseph E., 166 Great Rd., Maynard, Mass.
Borah, Ralph A., 6405 Brairwood Lane, Oklahoma City, Okla.
Boros, Arnold L., 396 East 170th St., New York, N.Y.
Borneman, G. H., Superintendent of Schools, Tracy, Minn.
Bos, Edward, Curric. Coordinator, Proviso Twp. High School, Maywood, Ill.
Bossier, Antonia M., 1661 North Roman St., New Orleans, La.
Bossing, Nelson L., Col. of Educ., Univ. of Minnesota, Minneapolis, Minn.
Bothell, John E., Colorado State College, Greeley, Colo.
Bottrell, Harold R., Col. of Educ., University of Houston, Houston, Tex.
Bouchard, John B., State Teachers College, Fredonia, N.Y.
Bourgue, Rev. Edgar A., Assumption Prep. School, Worcester, Mass.
Bowden, M. G., 2710 Exposition Blvd., Austin, Tex.
Bowen, Glenn W., Superintendent of Schools, River Rogue, Mich.
Bower, Robert K., 1905 East Loma Alta Dr., Altadena, Calif.

Bower, Von Durbin, Central P.O. Box 74, Kingston, N.Y.
Bowers, Norman D., Dir. of Tchr. Educ., Vanderbilt University, Nashville, Tenn.
Bowman, George A., President, Kent State University, Kent, Ohio
Bowman, Raymond B., 498 College Dr., Ventura, Calif.
Bowyer, Vernon O., 225 Millbridge Rd., Riverside, Ill.
Boyce, Floyd A., Principal, Becker Elem. School, Austin, Tex.
Boyd, Elizabeth Marie, 4146 West 63rd St., Los Angeles, Calif.
Boyd, Laurence E., Sch. of Educ., Atlanta University, Atlanta, Ga.
Boyd, Rachel E., Supv. of Home Economics, Elkton, Md.
Boyd, Richard S., 1530 S.W. Taylor St., Portland, Ore.
Boydston, Robert S., 2801 Castro Rd., San Pablo, Calif.
Boye, Charles L., Col. of Educ., Wayne State University, Detroit, Mich.
Boyer, C. E., Superintendent of Schools, Boonton, N.J.
Boykin, Leander L., Dir., Div. of Educ., Southern Univ., Baton Rouge, La.
Bracewell, George, Southern Illinois University, Carbondale, Ill.
Bracey, Mrs. Helen H., Dept. of Educ., Howard University, Washington, D.C.
Brachtl, Ellen L., Principal, McCormick School, Chicago, Ill.
Bradley, Carlos D., Principal, Lakeview Elem. School, Miami, Fla.
Bradley, Helen P., Prin., Cameron School, Chicago, Ill.
Bradley, Raymond J., Chm., Div. of Educ., Macalester College, St. Paul, Minn.
Brady, Elizabeth H., Los Angeles State College, Los Angeles, Calif.
Brady, John C., Bemidji State College, Bemidji, Minn.
Bragdon, Clifford Richardson, Dept. of Educ., Smith College, Northampton, Mass.
Bragdon, Helen D., Genl. Dir., American Assn. of Univ. Women, Washington, D.C.
Brandenburg, K. C., 110 Pine Avenue, Long Beach, Calif.
Brandon, Mrs. Bertha M., Waco Public Schools, Waco, Tex.
Brandt, Willard J., University of Wisconsin-Milwaukee, Milwaukee, Wis.
Branom, Wayne T., Superintendent of Schools, Hillside, N.J.
Brasted, F. Kenneth, Pres., University of Dallas, Dallas, Tex.
Braswell, Charles, Dir., Dept. of Music Therapy, Loyola Univ., New Orleans, La.
Brauer, Walter L., Principal, Rufus King High School, Milwaukee, Wis.
Braun, Gertrude, Danbury State Teachers College, Danbury, Conn.
Brazier, Mrs. E. E., Principal, Dorseyville School, Donaldsonville, La.
Breaux, Jerome E., Principal, J. C. Ellis Elem. School, Metairie, La.
Breen, Lelwyn C., Dept. of Educ., University of Alaska, College, Alaska
Brennan, A. F., Prin., Regina Regional High School, Corner Brook, Newfoundland
Brennan, Thomas G., Superintendent, Catholic Schools, Saginaw, Mich.
Brenner, Anton, Merrill-Palmer School, Detroit, Mich.
Bretsch, Howard S., Sch. of Educ., University of Michigan, Ann Arbor, Mich.
Bretz, Frank H., Dir. of Research, U.R.C.A., Philadelphia, Pa.
Brewer, Karl M., Superintendent of Schools, DuBois, Pa.
Brewer, Wenonah G., Indiana State Teachers College, Terre Haute, Ind.
Brickman, Benjamin, Dept. of Educ., Brooklyn College, Brooklyn, N.Y.
Brickman, William W., Dept. of Educ., New York University, New York, N.Y.
Bridge, Mrs. Merrill H., Teachers College of Connecticut, New Britain, Conn.
Bridges, Lonnie H., Southern University, Baton Rouge, La.
Bridges, Raymond H., Southern University, Baton Rouge, La.
Brieland, Donald, Dir., Eliz. McCormick Mem. Fund, 155 E. Ohio St., Chicago, Ill.
Bright, John H., 628 Cuesta Ave., San Mateo, Calif.
Bright, O. T., Jr., Superintendent of Schools, Lake Bluff, Ill.
Brimley, Ralph F. W., East Carolina College, Greenville, N.C.
Brink, William G., School of Educ., Northwestern University, Evanston, Ill.
Brinker, Robert D., Prin., Anacostia Evening H.S., Washington, D.C.
Brinkley, Sterling G., 419 Emory Dr., N.E. Atlanta, Ga.
Brinkman, A. John, 9929 S. Maplewood Ave., Chicago, Ill.
Brish, William M., Superintendent, Washington County Schls., Hagerstown, Md.
Brislawn, Maurice J., Dept. of Educ., Los Angeles State College, Los Angeles, Calif.
Bristol, Benton K., Pennsylvania State University, University Park, Pa.

Bristol, Stanley T., Principal, Washington School, Wheaton, Ill.
Bristow, Mrs. Norma S., 305 So. Lawrence St., Montgomery, Ala.
Bristow, W. H., Dir., Bur. Cur. Res., NYC Bd. of Educ., 130 W. 55 St., New York, N.Y.
Britt, S. S., Jr., Wofford College, Spartanburg, S.C.
Britton, Edward C., 1429 El Tejon Way, Sacramento, Calif.
Britton, Ernest R., Superintendent of Schools, Midland, Mich.
Broadhead, Edward H., Librarian, Hillyer College Library, Hartford, Conn.
Broadhead, Russell H., Col. of Educ., Wayne State University, Detroit, Mich.
Broening, Angela M., Dir. of Publications, Public Schls., Baltimore, Md.
Bronars, Joseph C., 2233 North Kenmore Ave., Chicago, Ill.
Bronfeld, J. William, State University Teachers College, Geneseo, N.Y.
Bronson, Moses L., 104 West 70th St., New York, N.Y.
Brooker, Jeanne E., Dept. of Educ., Mount Mercy College, Pittsburgh, Pa.
Brooks, John J., Dir., New Lincoln School, New York, N.Y.
Brooks, Mary B., Georgia State College for Women, Milledgeville, Ga.
Brostoff, Theodore M., Hunington Park High School, Hunington Park, Calif.
Brother Adelbert James, F.S.C., Head, Educ. Dept., Manhattan College, New York, N.Y.
Brother B. Joseph, F.S.C., Prin., St. Austine High School, Brooklyn, N.Y.
Brother John M. Egan, Iona College, New Rochelle, N.Y.
Brother Julius Edgar, F.S.C., Dean of Studies, St. Mary's Col., Winona, Minn.
Brother Leopold Taillon, Dean of Educ., St. Joseph Univ., Moncton, N.B., Canada
Brother Luke, Dir., Institut Pedagogique St. Georges, Laval-Rapids, Que., Canada
Brother Omer Cormier, C.S.C., St. Joseph's University, New Brunswick, Canada
Brother Timothy, O.S.F., Prin., St. Francis Prep. School, Brooklyn, N.Y.
Brother U. Cassian, F.S.C., Dean, St. Mary's College, St. Mary's College, Calif.
Brother William C. Penny, Principal, Brother Rice High School, Chicago, Ill.
Brother William Mang, St. Edward's University, Austin, Tex.
Brougher, John F., Principal, Woodrow Wilson High School, Washington, D.C.
Browder, I. J., Superintendent of City Schools, Gadsden, Ala.
Brower, George, Eastern Michigan College, Ypsilanti, Mich.
Brown, Aaron, Phelps-Stokes Fund, 101 Park Ave., New York, N.Y.
Brown, Alma J., 6301 West 78th St., Overland Park, Kan.
Brown, C. Victor, Dean, Elmira College, Elmira, N.Y.
Brown, Charles I., Sch. of Educ., Tuskegee Inst., Tuskegee, Ala.
Brown, Clyde M., Col. of Engr., University of Wisconsin, Madison, Wis.
Brown, Cynthiana E., Univ. Elem. Schl., Univ. of Calif., Los Angeles, Calif.
Brown, Douglas M., Superintendent of Schools, Shorewood, Wis.
Brown, E. W., Headmaster, Calvert School, Baltimore, Md.
Brown, Florence H., 824 Columbus St., Ottawa, Ill.
Brown, Francis J., 2500 Que St., N.W., Washington, D.C.
Brown, Fred A., State Teachers College, Lock Haven, Pa.
Brown, G. W. C., Dir. Evening Col., Virginia State Col., Norfolk, Va.
Brown, George I., Harvard Graduate School of Education, Cambridge, Mass.
Brown, George W., Supt., Riverside-Brookfield High School, Riverside, Ill.
Brown, Gerald W., Los Angeles State College, Los Angeles, Calif.
Brown, Grant, Editor-in-Chief, American Book Co., New York, N.Y.
Brown, H. D., Prin., Ecole de Pasteurs, Kimpses, via Matadi, Belgian Congo
Brown, Harold, Mansfield State Teachers College, Mansfield, Pa.
Brown, Harold N., Sch. of Educ., University of Nevada, Reno, Nev.
Brown, Howard L., Supv., Tchg. Materials, Public Schools, Springfield, Ohio
Brown, Hugh S., Pennsylvania State University, University Park, Pa.
Brown, I. C., Prin., Perrin-Thomas School, Columbia, S.C.
Brown, Josephine H., State Teachers College, Bowie, Md.
Brown, Kenneth G., Mankato State College, Mankato, Minn.
Brown, Kenneth R., Dir. of Research, Calif. Tchrs. Assn., San Francisco, Calif.
Brown, LeRoy, Superintendent of Schools, Anniston, Ala.
Brown, Mahlon C., Marshall College, Huntington, W. Va.
Brown, Mrs. Marjorie Dowling, Manual Arts High School, Los Angeles, Calif.
Brown, Perry, Principal, 93rd Street School, Niagara Falls, N.Y.

xxvi   MEMBERS OF THE NATIONAL SOCIETY

Brown, Thomas, Hofstra College, Hempstead, N.Y.
Brown, William H., Dir., Bur. of Educ. Research, North Carolina Col., Durham, N.C.
Browne, Rose Butler, North Carolina College, Durham, N.C.
Brownell, S. M., Superintendent of Schools, Detroit, Mich.
Brownell, W. A., Dean, Schl. of Educ., Univ. of California, Berkeley, Calif.
Browning, Bruce C., Texas Technological College, Lubbock, Tex.
Browning, Mary, Supv., Kdg.-Primary Educ., Board of Educ., Louisville, Ky.
Browning, Roy W., Ottawa University, Ottawa, Kan.
Browning, Mrs. Virginia W., Central Missouri State College, Warrensburg, Mo.
Bruce, Aldon J., Psychologist, Public Schools, Markham, Ill.
Bruce, William C., Editor, Bruce Publishing Co., Milwaukee, Wis.
Brubaker, Leonard A., 121 West Frambes Ave., Columbus, Ohio
Bruce, Imon E., Superintendent of Schools, Hot Springs, Ark.
* Bruck, John P., 218 Potters Corners Road, Buffalo, N.Y.
Brueckner, Leo J., 10790 Clarmon Pl., Culver City, Calif.
Brumbaugh, A. J., 4911 Flint Dr., N.W., Washington, D.C.
Brumbaugh, W. Donald, University of Utah, Salt Lake City, Utah
Brunner, Henry S., Head, Dept. of Agr. Educ., Penn. State Univ., University Park, Pa.
Brunner, Howard B., Superintendent, Public Schools, Scotch Plaines, N.J.
Brunson, Mrs. DeWitt, Ellis Avenue School, Orangeburg, S.C.
Bry, Neil William, 54 Gooseneck Point, Oceanport, N.J.
Bryan, Ray, Head, Dept. of Voc. Educ., Iowa State College, Ames, Iowa
Bryant, Hayden C., Dir., Teacher Educ., Mercer University, Macon, Ga.
Bryant, Ira B., Prin., Booker T. Washington High School, Houston, Tex.
Bryant, Merle L., Laboratory Sch., University of Minnesota, Duluth, Minn.
Bryant, Spurgeon Q., Alabama State College, Montgomery, Ala.
Bryce, Mayo J., San Francisco State College, San Francisco, Calif.
Bryner, James R., Superintendent of Schools, North College Hill, Ohio
Buchanan, Alfred K., Mulberry St., Plantsville, Conn.
Buchanan, James H., Kansas State Teachers College, Emporia, Kan.
Buchanan, Paul G., 19 Elmdale St., Dorchester, Mass.
Buckingham, Guy E., Division of Educ., Allegheny College, Meadville, Pa.
Buckingham, Mrs. Maude A., 512 Sixth St., Lafayette, La.
Buckley, J. L., Superintendent of Schools, Lockhart, Tex.
Buckner, W. N., Armstrong Tech. High School, Washington, D.C.
Buckton, La Verne, Dept. of Educ., Brooklyn College, Brooklyn, N.Y.
Buda, Mrs. Mary C., Principal, Julia Richman High School, New York, N.Y.
Budde, Dolores M., 3635 Aberdeen Ave., Alton, Ill.
Budde, Harold H., Southwestern State College, Weatherford, Okla.
Bueker, Armin H., Superintendent of Schools, Marshall, Mo.
Buelke, John A., Western Michigan College, Kalamazoo, Mich.
Buell, Madeline A., 59 Wells Ave., East Hartford, Conn.
Bull, Stanley, P.O. Box 1077, College Place, Wash.
Bullock, Arnold H., Arizona State College, Tempe, Ariz.
Bullock, Harrison, 815 Coventry Rd., Berkeley, Calif.
Bullock, W. J., Superintendent of Schools, Kannapolis, N.C.
Bunch, Marion E., Washington University, St. Louis, Mo.
Bunker, James G., Superintendent, Secondary Schools, Coalinga, Calif.
Burch, Charles H., Principal, Wiley School, Urbana, Ill.
Burch, Robert L., Ginn and Company, Boston, Mass.
Burdick, A. E., Dean, Arkansas State Tchrs. College, Conway, Ark.
Burdick, Richard L., Carroll College, Waukesha, Wis.
Burdine, D. I., Prairie View A. & M. College, Prairie View, Tex.
Burgdorf, Otto P., 40-20 77th St., Elmhurst, N.Y.
Burgess, James R., Jr., President, Reinhardt College, Waleska, Ga.
Burgess, Thomas C., Dept. of Psych., Montana State Univ., Missoula, Mont.
Burk, R. Burdett, Long Beach State College, Long Beach, Calif.
Burke, Arvid J., New York State Teachers Assn., Albany, N.Y.
Burke, Gladys, 244 Outlook Ave., Youngstown, Ohio

Burke, Henry R., 180 Prospect St., East Orange, N.J.
Burke, Thomas S., 6926 S. Wolcott Ave., Chicago, Ill.
Burkett, Mrs. Cecile C., Principal, Drew Elem. School, West Monroe, La.
Burkhardt, Allen P., President, Norfolk Junior College, Norfolk, Neb.
Burlingame, Anna Louise 7148 Jeffrey Ave., Chicago, Ill.
Burnham, Archer L., Nebraska State Teachers Assn., Lincoln, Neb.
Burnham, Marguerie, 2331 Okobee Dr., Sarasota, Fla.
Burns, Ralph L., Superintendent of Schools, Scarborough, Ont., Canada
Burns, Robert L., 1063 Palisade Ave., Palisade, N.J.
Burns, S. T., 2305 Arboretum Dr., Madison, Wis.
Burns, Thomas W., Principal, Woodstock Elem. School, Woodstock, Ala.
Buros, Francis C., Asst. Superintendent of Schools, White Plains, N.Y.
Burr, Elbert W., Monsanto Chemical Co., St. Louis, Mo.
Burrell, Anna P., State College for Teachers, Buffalo, N.Y.
Burrows, Alvina Treut, 117 Nassau Ave., Manhasset, N.Y.
Burt, Lucile, Principal, Lincoln School, Fond du Lac, Wis.
Burton, Alma P., Superintendent, Alpine School Dist., American Fork, Utah
Burton, Floyd H., Superintendent of Schools, Humble, Tex.
Burton, Robert L., Sch. of Sacred Music, Southwestern Sem., Fort Worth, Tex.
Burton, William H., 3512 Willamette Ave., Corvallis, Ore.
Bush, Clifford L., Newark State College, Union, N.J.
Bushnell, Allan C., 1815 Altschul Ave., Menlo Park, Calif.
Bushnell, Almon W., P.O. Box 35, Castleton, Vt.
Bussell, Lyell, Prin., Stevenson Elementary School, Muncie, Ind.
Buswell, G. T., School of Educ., University of California, Berkeley, Calif.
Buswell, Margaret M., Iowa State Teachers College, Cedar Falls, Iowa
Butler, Judson R., Dean, Boston Univ. Col. of Gen. Education, Boston, Mass.
Butler, Paul W., Dean-Registrar, Roosevelt Jr. Col., West Palm Beach, Fla.
Butler, Warren N., Superintendent of Schools, Metuchen, N.J.
Butterweck, Joseph S., Dir., Div. of Sec. Educ., Temple Univ., Philadelphia, Pa.
Butts, Franklin A., Principal, Clinton School, Poughkeepsie, N.Y.
Butts, L. A., Educ. Dept., McKendree College, Lebanon, Ill.
Butts, R. Freeman, Teachers College, Columbia University, New York, N.Y.
Buyse, R., School of Educ., University of Louvain, Tournai, Belgium
Byerly, Carl L., 14213 Woodmont Ave., Detroit, Mich.
Byerly, Mrs. Hilda, Forest Hills School Dist., Pittsburgh, Pa.
Byram, Harold M., Michigan State University, East Lansing, Mich.
Byrne, Mrs. Helen C., 726 So. York St., Denver, Colo.
Byrne, James A., Div. of Adult Educ., Marquette University, Milwaukee, Wis.
Byrne, Richard Hill, Col. of Educ., University of Maryland, College Park, Md.

Caccavo, Emil, 123 Willow St., Roslyn Heights, N.Y.
Cadwell, Herbert M., 3921 Division St., Los Angeles, Calif.
Cahan, Ruth, 12342 Milbank St., Studio City, Calif.
Cahill, Frederick P., 9801 Shore Rd., Brooklyn, N.Y.
Caird, Mrs. Florence B., Principal, Joyce Kilmer School, Chicago, Ill.
Caldwell, Cleon C., Lewis-Clark Normal School, Lewiston, Idaho
Caldwell, O. K., Prin., Fostoria High School, Fostoria, Ohio
Calhoon, A. Ray, Principal, Utica Free Academy, Utica, N.Y.
Call, Mary Ann, 1295 Mulvane, Topeka, Kan.
Callan, John H., Dean, Sch. of Educ., Seton Hall University, Newark, N.J.
Callas, Eliza E., Supv. Principal, Elem. Schools, Kensington, Md.
Callaway, Byron, Alabama Polytechnic Institute, Auburn, Ala.
Callis, Mary Aline, Northwestern University, Evanston, Ill.
Calvin, James S., Head, Dept. of Psych., Univ. of Kentucky, Lexington, Ky.
Cambron, Emmett F., North Texas State College, Denton, Tex.
Camien, Laiten L., P.O. Box 157, State College, N.M.
Cammarota, Gloria. Child Development Center, 280 Red Cedar Dr., Levittown,
  Pa.
Campbell, Joe W., Prin., L. S. Rugg School, Alexandria, La.
Campbell, Jay J., Chm., Div. of Fine Arts, Adams State College, Alamosa, Colo.

Campbell, Ronald F., Midwest Adm. Center, Univ. of Chicago, Chicago, Ill.
Campbell, T. J., 109 Hughes Ave., Attalla, Ala.
Canar, Donald A., Supt., Central YMCA Schools, 19 South LaSalle St., Chicago, Ill.
Canfield, James K., Long Beach State College, Long Beach, Calif.
Canning, Mrs. Bernice, Philip Sheridan Elem. School, Kenmore, N.Y.
Cannon, W. E., School of Educ., Univ. of Southern California, Los Angeles, Calif.
Canuteson, Richard, State Teachers College, Brockport, N.Y.
Capehart, Bertis E., Educ. Dept., Hill & Knowlton, Inc., New York, N.Y.
Capobianco, R. J., Dir. Research in Spec. Educ., Syracuse Univ., Syracuse, N.Y.
Cappa, Dan, Los Angeles State College, Los Angeles, Calif.
Capps, Lelon R., 4340 Jefferson St. N.E., Minneapolis, Minn.
Capps, Mrs. Marian P., Virginia State College, Norfolk, Va.
Capron, Clara, 301 No. Olive, West Palm Beach, Fla.
Carbaugh, Gaile A., Dir., Holcomb Campus Sch., Teachers College, Geneseo, N.Y.
Cardina, Philip J., 6 Rustic Dr., Lakewood, N.J.
Cardwell, Robert H., Prin., Park Junior High School, Knoxville, Tenn.
Carey, Elizabeth B., Supv., Elem. Educ., State Educ. Dept., Albany, N.Y.
Carey, E. Niel, 2A Dutton Ave., Baltimore, Md.
Carey, Justin P., 110 Echo Ave., New Rochelle, N.Y.
Carin, Arthur, University of Utah, Salt Lake City, Utah
Carlson, C. E., Superintendent of Schools, Ramsay, Mich.
Carlson, Mrs. Evelyn F., Superintendent, Dist. 13, Pub. Schls., Chicago, Ill.
Carlson, Ruth Kearney, 1718 LeRoy Ave., Berkeley, Calif.
Carlson, Thorsten R., Prin., Lab. Sch., San Diego State Col., San Diego, Calif.
Carmichael, Omer, Superintendent of Schools, Louisville, Ky.
Carne, Vernon E., Prin., Hooper Alexander School, Decatur, Ga.
Carnochan, John L., Jr., Principal, Williamsport High School, Hagerstown, Md.
Carpenter, Aaron C., Alcorn A. & M. College, Lorman, Miss.
Carpenter, W. W., Dept. of Educ., University of Missouri, Columbia, Mo.
Carper, M. L., Superintendent of Schools, Martinsville, Va.
Carr, Edwin R., Col. of Educ., University of Colorado, Boulder, Colo.
Carr, John W., Jr., Sch. of Educ., Duke University, Durham, N.C.
Carr, Louis D., Principal, Public School 23, Jersey City, N.J.
Carrithers, Lura M., University of Wisconsin-Milwaukee, Milwaukee, Wis.
Carroll, John B., Grad. Sch. of Educ., Harvard University, Cambridge, Mass.
Carroll, John S., Univ. of California, Santa Barbara Campus, Goleta, Calif.
Carron, Malcolm, S. J., Col. of Arts and Sci., Univ. of Detroit, Detroit, Mich.
Carruth, Irby B., Superintendent, Public Schools, Austin, Tex.
Carstater, Eugene D., Rte. 1, Falls Church, Va.
Carter, Gordon, Superintendent, School Dist. 501, Bellingham, Wash.
Carter, Harold D., Sch. of Educ., University of California, Berkeley, Calif.
Carter, Mrs. Hermione H., Virginia State College, Petersburg, Va.
Carter, Richard C., Supt., Territorial On-Base Schls., APO 949, Seattle, Wash.
Carter, R. L., Head, Dept. of Educ., Stetson University, De Land, Fla.
Carter, Ruby, Dir. of Child Study, Harlan, Ky.
Carter, Sims, Headmaster, Rhodes School, 11 West 54th St., New York, N.Y.
Carter, Thomas M., Head, Dept. of Educ. and Psych., Albion College, Albion, Mich.
Carter, Vincent, 221 North Bland Ave., Campbell, Calif.
Carter, William L., Tchrs. Col., University of Cincinnati, Cincinnati, Ohio
Carter, W. R., University of Missouri, Columbia, Mo.
Cartwright, H. William, Chm., Dept. of Educ., Duke Univ., Durham, N.C.
Carver, Velda, University of Toledo, Toledo, Ohio
Cash, Harry T., Prin., Hamilton High School, Memphis, Tenn.
Caskey, Helen C., Tchrs. Col., University of Cincinnati, Cincinnati, Ohio
Cassidy, Rosalind, University of California, Los Angeles, Calif.
Cassler, G. Winston, St. Olaf College, Northfield, Minn.
Castelli, Albert, 14922 Sussex Ave., Detroit, Mich.
Caswell, Hollis L., President, Teachers College, Columbia Univ., New York, N.Y.
Caton, W. Barnie, Superintendent of Schools, Alamogordo, N.M.

Catrambone, A. R., Superintendent of Schools, Camden, N.J.
Caughran, Alex M., 113 S. Ninth St., Lafayette, Ind.
Caulfield, Patrick J., Chm., Dept. of Educ., St. Peter's Col., Jersey City, N.J.
Cavan, Jordan, Dept. of Education, Rockford College, Rockford, Ill.
Cavanaugh, Alfred D., Dept. of Educ., University of Detroit, Detroit, Mich.
Cawrse, Robert C., Principal, Rocky River High School, Rocky River, Ohio
Cawthon, John A., Louisiana Polytechnic Inst., Ruston, La.
Cayco, Florentino, President, Arellano University, Manila, Philippines
Cayne, Bernard S., 11 Wildwood St., Winchester, Mass.
Center, Aaron M., 922 Queen Ave., North, Minneapolis, Minn.
Centuori, Carmine, 2116 Central Ave., Yonkers, N.Y.
Cerbus, Betty L., 7918 Kingsbury, Clayton, Mo.
Chadderdon, Hester, Iowa State College, Ames, Iowa
Chaffee, Charles E., Superintendent of Schools, Bethlehem, Pa.
Chaffee, John B., Superintendent of Schools, Wellesley Hills, Mass.
Chall, Jeanne, 218 East 12th St., New York, N.Y.
Chalmers, James F., Principal, High School, Perth Amboy, N.J.
Chaltas, John George, 20 D. Manheim Gardens, Philadelphia, Pa.
Chambers, J. Richard, Sch. of Educ., University of Miami, Coral Gables, Fla.
Chambers, W. Max, President, Central State College, Edmond, Okla.
Champlin, George R., State Department of Education, Hartford, Conn.
Chandler, H. E., Dept. of Educ., University of Kansas, Lawrence, Kan.
Chandler, John, Jr., Hdmr., Grosse Pointe Univ. Schools, Grosse Pointe Woods,
  Mich.
Chang, Jen-chi, Claflin College, Orangeburg, S.C.
Chao, Sankey C., Fla. Normal and Ind. Mem. College, St. Augustine, Fla.
Chapline, Allen W., Temple University, Philadelphia, Pa.
Chapman, Catherine, Weatherford College, Weatherford, Tex.
Chappell, Bartlett E. S., Dean, New York Military Acad., Cornwall-on-Hudson,
  N.Y.
Charles, Ramon L., State Department of Education, Topeka, Kan.
Charles, Victor, President, Lamar Junior College, Lamar, Colo.
Charnock, Leonard W. H., Eureka College, Eureka, Ill.
Charry, Lawrence, 5746 N. Camac St., Philadelphia, Pa.
Charters, Alexander N., University College, Syracuse Univ., Syracuse, N.Y.
Chase, Francis S., Dept. of Educ., University of Chicago, Chicago, Ill.
Chase, Naomi C., University of Minnesota, Minneapolis, Minn.
Chase, W. Linwood, Sch. of Educ., Boston University, Boston, Mass.
Chasnoff, Robert, Newark State College, Union, N.J.
Chauncey, Marion, Mary Washington College, Fredericksburg, Va.
Cheek, N. A., Principal, W. G. Pearson Elementary School, Durham, N.C.
Cheeks, L. E., 213 McFarland St., Kerrville, Tex.
Chellevold, John O., Dean of Faculty, Wartburg College, Waverly, Iowa
Chenault, R. N., Principal, Warner School, Nashville, Tenn.
Cheney, Robert B., Principal, Classen High School, Oklahoma City, Okla.
Chenoweth, Margaret, Janesville Public Schools, Janesville, Wis.
Cherry, J. H., Asst. Supt., Joliet Township H. S. & Jr. Col., Joliet, Ill.
Cherry, Ralph W., Sch. of Educ., Univ. of Virginia, Charlottesville, Va.
Chidekel, Samuel J., Principal, Nettelhorst Elem. School, Chicago, Ill.
Chidester, Albert J., Head, Education Dept., Berea College, Beara, Ky.
Chievitz, Gene L., Counseling and Test. Serv., Univ. of New Mexico, Albuquerque,
  N.M.
Childress, Jack R., Dir., Univ. Col., Northwestern University, Chicago, Ill.
Ching, J. Frederic, Superintendent of Schools, Salinas, Calif.
Chipman, R. S., Superintendent of Schools, Coalville, Utah
Chipps, Mrs. Dicie B., Alderson-Broaddus College, Philippi, W. Va.
Chiverton, William S., Prin., Cedar Road School, Philadelphia, Pa.
Choate, Ernest A., Principal, Roosevelt Jr. High School, Philadelphia, Pa.
Christensen, Arnold M., Long Beach State Col., Long Beach, Calif.
Christenson, Bernice M., 9601 S. LaSalle St., Los Angeles, Calif.
Christianson, Bertha, Bemidji State College, Bemidji, Minn.

Christman, Paul S., Superintendent of Schools, Schuylkill Haven, Pa.
Chudler, Albert A., 3812 Longview Valley Road, Sherman Oaks, Calif.
Chun, Dai Ho, University of Hawaii, Honolulu, Hawaii
Churchill, Ray L., Principal, Harrison Elementary School, Cedar Rapids, Iowa
Cinotto, Fred, Dean, Independence Community College, Independence, Kan.
Cioffii, Joseph M., 123 Palisade Ave., Garfield, N.J.
Clabaugh, R. E., Superintendent of Schools, Arlington Heights, Ill.
Clarizio, Harvey F., 1914 Orange Ave., St. Paul, Minn.
Clark, Catherine, Middle Tennessee State College, Murfreesboro, Tenn.
Clark, Rev. Edward F., Academic Vice-Pres., Fordham University, Bronx, N.Y.
Clark, Elmer J., Indiana State Teachers College, Terre Haute, Ind.
Clark, Mrs. Esmer Knudson, 2274 Cedar St., Berkeley, Calif.
Clark, F. B., Dist. Superintendent of Schools, Athens, N.Y.
Clark, Francis E., St. Olaf College, Northfield, Minn.
Clark, J. O., Superintendent of Schools, McGehee, Ark.
Clark, John F., Superintendent of Schools, Dist. 45, Villa Park, Ill.
Clark, Leonard H., 22 Burgoyne St., Elmwood, Conn.
Clark, Lois M., National Education Association, Washington, D.C.
Clark, Maurice P., Superintendent of Schools, Western Springs, Ill.
Clark, Max R., Superintendent of Schools, Dubuque, Iowa
Clark, Richard M., Col. of Educ., Univ. of Delaware, Newark, Del.
Clark, Stephen C., Dept. of Psych., Los Angeles State College, Los Angeles, Calif.
Clark, Thomas H., 622 Plymouth St., Missoula, Mont.
Clark, Mrs. Willa B., 1224—16th St., Parkersburg, W. Va.
Clark, Woodrow Wilson, 101 W. Leake St., Clinton, Miss.
Clarke, Stanley C. T., University of Alberta, Edmonton, Alba.
Claxton, Clarence C., Prin., Steinmetz High School, Chicago, Ill.
Clayton, Thomas E., 7 Kelly Dr., Manilus, N.Y.
Cleary, Rev. Vincent P., Supt., Diocese of Bridgeport, Stanford, Conn.
Cleeton, Kenneth, Head, Educ. Dept., Eastern Michigan College, Ypsilanti, Mich.
Cleland, Donald L., School of Educ., University of Pittsburgh, Pittsburgh, Pa.
Cleminson, Geraldine, Principal, Walnut School, Cranford, N.J.
Clemons, Clare, Bank Street College of Education, New York, N.Y.
Cleveland, E. D., Superintendent of Schools, Palestine, Tex.
Clewell, Geraldine, Dept. of H.E., State Univ. of Iowa, Iowa City, Iowa
Clifford, Paul I., Sch. of Educ., Atlanta University, Atlanta, Ga.
Clish, Herbert C., Superintendent of Schools, New Rochelle, N.Y.
Cloues Paul, Headmaster, Harvard School, Charlestown, Mass.
Clouthier, Raymond P., Dept. of Educ., Lewis College, Lockport, Ill.
Clugston, Herbert A., Dean, State Teachers College, St. Cloud, Minn.
Clymer, T. W., Col. of Educ., University of Minnesota, Minneapolis, Minn.
Cobb, J. E., Indiana State Tchrs. College, Terre Haute, Ind.
Cochran, J. Chester, Dept. of Educ., Univ. of Houston, Houston, Tex.
Codd, William J., Dir., Educational Library, Seattle, Wash.
Codwell, John E., Principal, Phillis Wheatley High School, Houston, Tex.
Coen, Alban Wasson II, Sch. of Educ., Northwestern University, Evanston, Ill.
Coetzee, J. Christian, University College, Potchefstroom, South Africa
Cofell, William L., St. John's University, Collegeville, Minn.
Coffey, Charles C., San Jose State College, San Jose, Calif.
Coffey, Warren, 1189 Walnut St., Berkeley, Calif.
Cohen, George, 1450 Jesup Ave., New York, N.Y.
Cohen, Samuel, Superintendent's Office, 60 Everit Ave., Hewlett, N.Y.
Cohen, Saris, 825 West End Ave., New York, N.Y.
Cohen, Rabbi Victor, 110 Cedar Hill Ave., Belleville, N.J.
Cohler, Milton J., 532 Madison Ave., Glencoe, Ill.
Colbath, Edwin H., 101-40 117th St., Richmond Hill, N.Y.
Colburn, A. B., Vice-Prin., Everett Senior High School, Everett, Wash.
Cole, Glenn A., Dept. of Educ., University of Arkansas, Fayetteville, Ark.
Cole, James C., 5421 Callister Ave., Sacramento, Calif.

Cole, Mary I., Western Kentucky State College, Bowling Green, Ky.
Coleman, F. Basil, 435 W. 119th St., New York, N.Y.
Coleman, Mary Elizabeth, Dept. of Educ., Univ. of Penn., Philadelphia, Pa.
Collett, Mrs. Roma, 542 N. Main St., Ada, Ohio
Colley, J. C., Chm., Dept of Educ. & Psych., Elon College, Elon College, N.C.
Collier, Calhoun C., Michigan State University, East Lansing, Mich.
Collier, Juanita, Dept. of Educ., Wayne University, Detroit, Mich.
Collier, Richard E., Sch. of Educ., Oklahoma State Univ., Stillwater, Okla.
Collings, Miller R., Cincinnati Public Schools, Cincinnati, Ohio
Collins, Carrie Lee, Radford College, Radford, Va.
Collins, Kathleen M., Dean of Women, Lewis College, Lockport, Ill.
Collins, Ralph C., 126 Del Norte Way, San Luis Obispo, Calif.
Conaway, Mrs. Freda Y., Dir., Elem. Educ., State Col., West Liberty, W.Va.
Conaway, Mrs. Winifred V., Bowling Green State Univ., Bowling Green, Ohio
Condit, Harold L., Dean, Student Personnel, Graceland Col., Lamoni, Iowa
Condon, Jean F., 23 Roosevelt Rd., Weymouth, Mass.
Conley, William H., Marquette University, Milwaukee, Wis.
Connell, John T., Superintendent, Butler County Schools, Butler, Pa.
Connelly, George W., 6201 S. Richmond St., Chicago, Ill.
Connor, E. Faye, Huntington College Library, Huntington, Ind.
Connor, Frances P., Teachers College, Columbia University, New York, N.Y.
Conrady, Kenneth, 705 West Pecan St., Carbondale, Ill.
Conway, Marie M., 4925 Saul St., Philadelphia, Pa.
Cook, Raymond M., Dean, Chicago Teachers College, Chicago, Ill.
Cook, Ruth Cathlyn, Supv. Lab. Sch., State Teachers College, Mankato, Minn.
Cook, Walter W., Col. of Educ., University of Minnesota, Minneapolis, Minn.
Cooke, Dan B. 1801 White Ave., Knoxville, Tenn.
Cooke, Dorothy E., State Education Department, Albany, N.Y.
Cool, Dwight W., 827 East Oakwood, Glendora, Calif.
Cooling, Elizabeth, Rhode Island College of Education, Providence, R.I.
Coon, Alice B., 303 West North St., Manteca, Calif.
Coon, Beulah I., U. S. Office of Education, Washington, D.C.
Coon, W. Edwin, Prin., Academy High School, Erie, Pa.
Cooper, Bernice, Peabody Hall, University of Georgia, Athens, Ga.
Cooper, George H., 2913 Washington Blvd., Chicago, Ill.
Cooper, James W., 205 Scott Street, Audubon, Iowa
Cooper, Lewis B., Texas Technological College, Lubbock, Tex.
Cooper, Russell M., University of Minnesota, Minneapolis, Minn.
Cooper, Shirley, American Assn. of School Administrators, Washington, D.C.
Cooper, William H., Col. of Educ., Ohio University, Athens, Ohio
Corbally, John E., Dept. of Educ., University of Washington, Seattle, Wash.
Corcoran, Mary, 211 Burton Hall, Univ. of Minnesota, Minneapolis, Minn.
Corey, Stephen M., Teachers College, Columbia University, New York, N.Y.
Corinti, Jo Kathryn, 1324 Cherry Ave., Muskegon, Mich.
Corley, Clifford L., Col. of Educ., University of Washington, Seattle, Wash.
Cornell, Francis G., 221 West 57th St., New York, N.Y.
Cornish, Dale, 5770 Dudley St., Arvada, Colo.
Cornwell, G. E., Supt., Taylorville Community Unit School, Taylorville, Ill.
Cortage, Cecelia, 2053 Illinois Ave., Santa Rosa, Calif.
Cory, N. Durward, Superintendent of Schools, Muncie, Ind.
Coss, Arthur F., 130 East Vine St., Oxford, Ohio
Coss, Mrs. Carrie B., Prairie View A. & M. College, Prairie View, Tex.
Cossa, John A., Dean, Dept. of Educ., Manhattan College, New York, N.Y.
Cotter, Katharine C., Dept. of Educ., Boston College, Osterville, Mass.
Couche, Martha E., Rust College, Holly Springs, Miss.
Coughlin, Rev. James H., S.J., Fairfield University, Fairfield, Conn.
Coulson, John R., Principal, Parkside School, Chicago, Ill.
Courter, Claude V., Superintendent of Schools, Cincinnati, Ohio
* Courtis, S. A., 9110 Dwight Ave., Detroit, Mich.
Courtney, Robert W., 10 Olcott St., Middlebush, N.J.
Cousins, E. H., 8 Upper Sandringham Ave., Jamaica, British West Indies

Cousins, John, Principal, High Street School, West Chester, Pa.
Covey, Lola B., Bristow High School, Bristow, Okla.
Cowan, M. H., Principal, Public School 45, Brooklyn, N.Y.
Cowan, Persis H., 1513 Laurel St., South Pasadena, Calif.
Cowan, William A., San Francisco State College, San Francisco, Calif.
Cowley, W. H., Cubberley Hall, Stanford University, Stanford, Calif.
Cox, Edwin A., Superintendent of Schools, Stratford, Conn.
Cox, Johnnye V., University of Georgia, Athens, Ga.
Cox, Muriel M., Dir., Chamberlain Sch. of Retailing, Boston, Mass.
Cozine, June, Head, H. E. Educ., Oklahoma A. & M. Col., Stillwater, Okla.
Crackel, Verne E., Superintendent, Will County Schools, Joliet, Ill.
*Craig, Gerald S., Teachers College, Columbia University, New York, N.Y.
Craig, James C., University of Pittsburgh, Pittsburgh, Pa.
Craig, Robert C., Dept. of Educ., Marquette University, Milwaukee, Wis.
Cramer, Beatrice E., Post Road Junior High School, White Plains, N.Y.
Cramer, Bessie W., Dir., Elem. Educ., Public Schools, Washington, D.C.
Crawford, David, Superintendent, Elem. Schools, Dist. No. 231, Rochelle, Ill.
Crawford, J. R., Sch. of Educ., University of Maine, Orono, Me.
Crawford, Robert T., 713 Maple Ave., Rockville, Md.
Crawford, T. James, Sch. of Business, Indiana University, Bloomington, Ind.
Crawshaw, Clyde, Superintendent of Schools, Marseilles, Ill.
Creason, Frank, Principal, Sequoyah School, Overland Park, Kan.
Crescimbeni, Joseph, 10 Grove St., New Paltz, N.Y.
Cressman, George R., Villanova University, Villanova, Pa.
Creswell, Mrs. Rowena C., Prin., A. & M. Cons. Elem. Sch., College Station, Tex.
Crews, Roy L., Aurora College, Aurora, Ill.
Crewson, Walter, 9 Brookside Dr., Delmar, N.Y.
Crissey, Kermit H., Principal, Philip Sheridan School, Kenmore, N.Y.
Critser, Porter L., Box 8, Hayfork, Calif.
Crocker, Richard F., Jr., Superintendent of Schools, Caribou, Me.
Crocker, Ruth, Dept. of Music, Westmar College, Le Mars, Iowa
Cromartie, Mrs. Sue W., College of Education, University of Georgia, Athens, Ga.
Cross, C. Willard, Superintendent of Schools, Faribault, Minn.
Cross, Charles H., Dir., Univ. Trg. Sch., Univ. of Arkansas, Fayetteville, Ark.
Crossley, John B., Dist. Supt., Ventura Union H.S., Ventura, Calif.
Crosslin, Barbara, 1116 South Third Ave., Yakima, Wash.
Crosson, Robert Henry, 4327 Grammarey Lane, Concord, Calif.
Crow, A. L., Superintendent of Schools, Kirkwood, Mo.
Crow, Lester D., Brooklyn College, Brooklyn, N.Y.
Crowder, Ariel, 7251 Champlain Ave., Chicago, Ill.
Crowder, William Waldrop, Col. of Educ., Univ. of Arizona, Tucson, Ariz.
Crowe, James W., Dir., Chicago Vocational High School, Chicago, Ill.
Crowley, W. B., Beaufort County School Dist. 1, Beaufort, S.C.
Crowlie, Mrs. Leone B., 215 W. Minnehaha Parkway, Minneapolis, Minn.
Crozier, Hubert R., Prin., Gen. Rosecrans Elem. School, Compton, Calif.
Crull, Howard D., Superintendent of Schools, Port Huron, Mich.
Crum, Clyde E., Div. of Educ., San Diego State College, San Diego, Calif.
Crumb, Frederick W., President, Potsdam State Teachers Col., Potsdam, N.Y.
Crutsinger, George M., Howard Payne College, Brownwood, Tex.
Cruz, Emilio Ramos, Direccion de Educacion Federal, Mexicali, Bajo California, Mexico
Culbertson, Jack A., 800 Mill Race, Eugene, Ore.
Culotta, Joseph S., Counselor, Patterson Park High School, Baltimore, Md.
Culver, Mrs. Erleen, Consult. Washington Union Sch. Dist., West Sacramento, Calif.
Cumbee, Carroll F., Col. of Educ., University of Florida, Gainesville, Fla.
Cumming, John R., Western Montana College of Education, Dillon, Mont.
Cummings, Mable E., 326 Indianola, Rapid City, S.D.
Cummings, Matthew G., 131 Kensington Ave., Jersey City, N.J.
Cunningham, J., Cossitt Library, Memphis, Tenn.
Cunningham, Mrs. Gwendolyn D., Principal, Double Oaks Elem. Sch., Charlotte, N.C.

Cunningham, Myron, Col. of Educ., University of Florida, Gainesville, Fla.
Currier, Mrs. Lynor O., 713 Giddings Ave., Annapolis, Md.
Curry, Guy A., Jr., Natl. Com. on Tchr. Educ. and Prof. Standards, N.E.A.,
 Washington, D.C.
Curry, John F., 1715 Linden Dr., Denton, Tex.
Curtin, James R., Col. of Educ., University of Minnesota, Minneapolis, Minn.
Curtin, James T., Supt., Diocesan High Schools, 4371 Lindell Blvd., St. Louis,
 Mo.
Curtin, Wylma R., 1908 Erie St., Hyattsville, Md.
Curtis, E. Louise, Macalester College, St. Paul, Minn.
Curtis, H. A., Florida State University, Tallahassee, Fla.
Curtis, James E., San Jose State College, San Jose, Calif.
Cushman, Grace Newsom, Peabody Conservatory, Baltimore, Md.
Cutts, Warren G., Jr., Dept. of Educ., Kent State University, Kent, Ohio

Dabney, Lillian G., Dir., Stud. Tchg., Coppin State Tchrs. Col., Washington,
 D.C.
Dahle, C. O., Superintendent of Schools, Highland Park, Ill.
Daines, Delva, McKay Bldg., Brigham Young University, Provo, Utah
Dale, Arbie Myron, Sch. of Commerce, New York Univ., New York, N.Y.
Dale, Edgar, Col. of Educ., Ohio State University, Columbus, Ohio
Dallmann, Martha, Dept. of Educ., Ohio Wesleyan University, Delaware, Ohio
Daltry, Joseph S., Dir., Summer School, Wesleyan University, Middletown, Conn.
Daly, Edmund B., Principal, Sullivan High School, Chicago, Ill.
Dandoy, Maxima A., Fresno State College, Fresno, Calif.
Daniel, George T., 123 N. Wilbur St., Walla Walla, Wash.
Daniel, J. McT., University of South Carolina, Columbia, S.C.
Daniel, Theodora H., 74 Silver St., Waterville, Me.
Daniels, Paul R., 100 Maple Ave., North Hills, Pa.
Danielson, Paul J., Col. of Educ., University of Arizona, Tucson, Ariz.
Darcy, Natalie T., Dept. of Educ., Brooklyn College, Brooklyn, N.Y.
Darnell, Mrs. Myra C., P.O. Box 5811, Milwaukie, Ore.
Darnell, Robert E., Frank Phillips College, Borger, Tex.
Darroch, Frank W., 27 Princeton Rd., Toronto, Ontario, Canada
Davenport, William R., Col. of Educ., Butler University, Indianapolis, Ind.
Davidson, Mrs. Evelyn K., Kent State University, Kent, Ohio
Davies, J. Leonard, East Hall, State University of Iowa, Iowa City, Iowa
Davies, Mrs. Lillian S., Curric. Consult., Rich Twp. High Sch., Park Forest, Ill.
Davis, Charles H., P.O. Box 80, Anchorage, Alaska
Davis, Courtland V., R. D. No. 1, Box 380, Metuchen, N.J.
Davis, David C., 101 Riverside Park, Iowa City, Iowa
Davies, Don, Col. of Educ., University of Minnesota, Minneapolis, Minn.
Davies, Gordon F., 1316 Harley Dr., Woodland, Calif.
Davis, Dwight M., Dean, Moline Community College, Moline, Ill.
Davis, Floyd A., Supt. of Schools, Knoxville, Iowa
Davis, Frances M., University of Nebraska, Lincoln, Neb.
Davis, Guy C., President, Trinidad State Junior College, Trinidad, Colo.
Davis, H. Curtis, Asst. Supt., Unified School District, San Jose, Calif.
Davis, J. Pinckney, Prin., Haut Gap High Sch., John's Island, Charleston, S.C.
Davis, Joseph H., Normandy Junior High School, University City, Mo.
Davis, Milton J., Principal, Gurnee Grade School, Gurnee, Ill.
Davis, O. L., Jr., Assn. for Supv. and Curric. Develop., N.E.A., Washington, D.C.
Davis, Paul F., Prin., Manatee County High School, Bradenton, Fla.
Davis, Robert L., Principal, Wilmington Manor Schol, New Castle, Del.
Davis, Ron W., Principal, John Fitch Elem. School, Levittown, Pa.
Davis, Sydney C., 3 Pine Street, Oneonta, N.Y.
Davis, Warren C., Rochester Inst. of Technology, Rochester, N.Y.
Dawald, V. F., Dept. of Educ., Millikin University, Decatur, Ill.
Dawsey, Sarah, Colegio Bennett, Rio de Janeiro, Brazil
Dawson, Dan T., Dept. of Educ., Stanford University, Stanford, Calif.
Dawson, W. Read, Sch. of Educ., Baylor University, Waco, Texas
Day, James F., Dept. of Educ., Texas Western College, El Paso, Tex.

Day, John Lee, 31651 Jewell Ave., Laguna Beach, Calif.
Deam, Calvin W., Col. of Educ., University of Colorado, Boulder, Colo.
DeBernardis, Amo, Supv., Audio-visual Educ., Public Schools, Portland, Ore.
Debin, Louis, Junior High School, Brooklyn, N.Y.
DeBoer, John J., Col. of Educ., University of Illinois, Urbana, Ill.
DeBros, Alice Marie, St. John's University, Brooklyn, N.Y.
Debus, Raymond L., 666 Malabar Rd., Maroubra, N.S.W., Australia
DeCamp, Mrs. Hazel N., Essex County Voc. & Tech. High School, Bloomfield,
    N.J.
Deer, George H., Col. of Educ., Louisiana State University, Baton Rouge, La.
DeHaven, Sula M., Junior High School, Martinsburg, W.Va.
Deighton, Lee C., Macmillan Co., 60 Fifth Ave., New York, N.Y.
DeJung, John E., 12408 Dalewood Dr., Silver Spring, Md.
DeKeni, Sara L., State Education Department, Tallahassee, Fla.
DeKock, Henry C., Col. of Educ., State Univ. of Iowa, Iowa City, Iowa
Delaney, Eleanor C., School of Educ., Rutgers University, New Brunswick, N.J.
DeLong, Arthur R., University of Delaware, Newark, Del.
DeMand, J. W., Dept. of Educ., Kansas State College, Manhattan, Kan.
Demoney, N. E., Box 14, Estherville, Iowa
Denecke, Marie G., University of Maryland, College Park, Md.
Dennison, Mary C., Principal, George Gray School, Wilmington, Del.
Denniston, A. Bruce, Superintendent of Schools, Altoona, Pa.
Denny, Robert, 1115—45th St., Des Moines, Iowa
Denny, Terry, Col. of Educ., University of Illinois, Urbana, Ill.
Deno, Mrs. Evelyn, 3224 East Minnehaha Pkwy., Minneapolis, Minn.
DeProspo, Chris J., Dept. of Educ., City College, New York, N.Y.
Derby, Orlo L., State University Teachers College, Brockport, N.Y.
DeSanctis, Pat, Principal, John C. Strather School, Louisville, Ky.
DeShane, Roy, County Superintendent of Schools, Wheaton, Ill.
DeShazo, Willard, 6117 Brookside Dr., Alexandria, Va.
Deutschman, Mrs. Marilyn L., 41-06 Denman St., Elmhurst, Queens, N.Y.
DeVault, M. Vere, University of Texas, Austin, Tex.
Devine, Thomas F., College of Our Lady of the Elms, Chicopee, Mass.
Devor, J. W., 6309 E. Halbert Rd., Bethesda, Md.
Deyell, J. Douglas, Master, Provincial Tchrs. Col., North Bay, Ontario
DeYoung, Chris A., USOM, c/o American Embassy, Phnom Penh, Cambodia
D'Heurle, Adma, 5727 Dorchester Ave., Chicago, Ill.
Dick, Mrs. Elizabeth Macy, 184 Marlboro St., Quincy, Mass.
Dickerson, James L., Prin., University Demonstration School, Athens, Ga.
*Diederich, Rev. A. F., St. Norbert College, West De Pere, Wis.
Diekhoff, John S., 13670 Cedar Rd., University Heights, Ohio
Diener, Russell E., Kent State University, Kent, Ohio
Dierenfield, R. B., Macalester College, St. Paul, Minn.
Dieterle, Louise E., 10700 S. Avenue F, Chicago, Ill.
Diffley, Rev. Jerome, P.O. Box 49, Notre Dame, Ind.
DiGiacinto, Rose D., 68 Pilgrim Ave., Yonkers, N.Y.
DiLeonarde, Joseph H., Principal, Hendricks School, Chicago, Ill.
Dillinger, Claude, Illinois State Normal University, Normal, Ill.
Dillon, Frances H., Moorhead State College, Moorhead, Minn.
Dimond, Stanley E., University of Michigan, Ann Arbor, Mich.
Di Napoli, Peter J., Principal, Public School 90, New York, N.Y.
DiNardo, V. James, State Teachers College, Bridgewater, Mass.
Dingus, Lona G., H.O.W. Staff Quarters 20, Kingsport, Tenn.
Dion, Rev. Louis F., Registrar, Assumption College, Worcester, Mass.
Di Pietro, Mrs. A. E., Apt. 22C, Veterans Housing Project, Carbondale, Ill.
Dittmer, Daniel G., Research Psychol., United States Air Force, Alexandria, Va.
Dixon, Mrs. Helen, Shimer College, Mt. Carroll, Ill.
Dixon, James T., 634 South Princeton Ave., Villa Park, Ill.
Dixon, W. Robert, School of Educ., University of Michigan, Ann Arbor, Mich.
Doak, Helen, 124—26th St., Santa Monica, Calif.
Doane, Kenneth R., Head, Educ. Dept. Hamline University, St. Paul, Minn.

Dobbs, Louis H., Dir., Evening Col., Midwestern Univ., Wichita Falls, Tex.
Dodd, John M., Bur. of Child Res., University of Kansas, Lawrence, Kan.
Dodds, A. Gordon, Superintendent of Schools, Edwardsville, Ill.
Dodds, J. H., Res. Dir., Illinois Assn. of Sch. Boards, Springfield, Ill.
Dodson, Dan W., New York University, New York, N.Y.
Dolan, Francis, Superintendent, LaSalle-Peru Twp. High School, LaSalle, Ill.
Dolch. E. W., Col. of Educ., University of Illinois, Urbana, Ill.
Doll, Ronald C., Sch. of Educ., New York University, New York, N.Y.
Dolton, Leonard J., Los Angeles County Dental Society, Los Angeles, Calif.
Domian, O. E., 1595 Northrop, St. Paul, Minn.
Dominick, Leo H., Superintendent of Schools, International Falls, Minn.
Dominy, Mrs. Mildred, Educ. Div., State Univ. Tchrs. College, Plattsburgh, N.Y.
Donley, Donald T., New York State College for Teachers, Albany, N.Y.
Donnels, Elliott H., Ouachita College, Arkadelphia, Ark.
Donner, Arvin N., Dir., Col. of Educ., Univ. of Houston, Houston, Tex.
Donohue, Francis J., Pres., St. Mary of the Plains College, Dodge City, Kan.
Donovan, Charles F., Dean, Sch. of Educ., Boston Col., Chestnut Hill, Mass.
Dorsinville, Fritz, Dept. of Education, Port-au-Prince, Haiti
Doster, Osie, Dorsey High School, Miami, Fla.
Dotson, John M., 154 Jones Dr., Pocatello, Idaho
Doty, Gerald, Sch. of Music, Montana State University, Missoula, Mont.
Dougherty, Marguerite C., State Teachers College, Towson, Md.
Douglas, Lillian N., 919 Hillary St., New Orleans, La.
Douglass, H. R., Dir., Col. of Educ., University of Colorado, Boulder, Colo.
Douglass, Malcolm P., Claremont Graduate School, Claremont, Calif.
Doyle, Andrew McCormick, 1106 Bellerive Blvd., St. Louis, Mo.
Dowling, Thomas I., Supt., Greenwood City Schools, Greenwood, S.C.
Dozier, V. E., Supv. Principal, Bartow School Area, Bartow, Fla.
Drag, Francis L., Asst. Superintendent, County Schools, Napa, Calif.
Dragositz, Anna, 39-80 52nd St., Woodside, L.I., N.Y.
Dramer, Daniel S., 101 Rockland Gardens, Nyack, N.Y.
Drees, Frank J., Department of Public Instr., Honolulu, Hawaii
Dreier, William H., Dept. of Educ., Iowa State Teachers Col., Cedar Falls, Iowa
Dreikurs, Rudolf, 6 North Michigan Ave., Chicago, Ill.
Dresden, Katharine, Chico State College, Chico, California
Dressel, Paul L., Head, Off. of Eval. Serv., Mich. State Univ., East Lansing, Mich.
Drew, Robert E., Principal, Steuben Elem. School, Kankakee, Ill.
Drews, Elizabeth M., Col. of Educ., Michigan State Univ., East Lansing, Mich.
Driscoll, Mary Fay, Principal, Robert Emmet School, Chicago, Ill.
Drobka, Frank J., Dept. of Educ., Catholic Univ. of America, Washington, D.C.
Dropkin, Stanley, Queens College, Flushing, N.Y.
Drubeck, Mrs. Pearl B., Principal, Richard Yates Elem. School, Chicago, Ill.
Drummond, Harold D., George Peabody College for Teachers, Nashville, Tenn.
Drummond, William H., Head, Educ. Div., East. Washington College, Cheney, Wash.
Dubocq, Mrs. Lucille, Parent Educ. Project, Univ. of Chicago, Chicago, Ill.
Duckworth, Alice, Curriculum Consultant, Board of Education, Fairfield, Conn.
Duerksen, George L., Dept. of Music Educ., Univ. of Kansas, Lawrence, Kan.
Duffey, Robert V., 611 Sheffield Dr., Springfield, Pa.
DuFour, Stuart, Vice-President, Hartnell College, Salinas, Calif.
Dunathan, Homer, University of Toledo, Toledo, Ohio
Duncan, Leonard S., Head, Dept. of Educ., Geneva College, Beaver Falls, Pa.
Dunham, Lance, 20 East Osborn Rd., Phoenix, Ariz.
Duncan, Neal, 810 North Spring St., LaGrange, Ill.
Duncan, W. E., Principal, El Paso Junior High School, El Paso, Tex.
Duncan, William B., Principal, Miami Edison Senior High School, Miami, Fla.
Dunham, Ralph E., 1302 Popkin Lane, Alexandria, Va.
Dunigan, David R., College of the Holy Cross, Worcester, Mass.
Dunkel, Harold B., Dept. of Education, University of Chicago, Chicago, Ill.
Dunkle, Maurice Albert, Supt., Calvert County Schools, Prince Frederick, Md.

Dunlap, E. T., Pres., Eastern Okla. A. & M. College, Wilburton, Okla.
Dunlap, John T., Superintendent of Schools, Pueblo, Colo.
Dunlop, G. M., Chm., Div. of Educ. Psych., Univ. of Alberta, Edmonton, Alberta
Dunn, W. H., Whitman College, Walla Walla, Wash.
Dunsmore, Philo C., 121 Southard, Toledo, Ohio
Dupee, C. W., State Teachers College, East Stroudsburg, Pa.
Durant, Adrian J., Jr., State Department of Education, Jefferson City, Mo
Durante, Spencer E., Principal, Second Ward High School, Charlotte, N.C.
Durlinger, Glenn W., Santa Barbara College, Santa Barbara, Calif.
Durkee, Frank M., General Supervisor, Public Schools, Belleville, N.J.
Durost, Walter N., 2045 Bay Blvd., Indian Rocks Beach, Fla.
Durr, William K., Col. of Educ., Michigan State Univ., East Lansing, Mich.
Durrell, Donald D., Sch. of Educ., Boston University, Boston, Mass.
Dutton, Wilbur H., 1913 Greenfield Ave., Los Angeles, Calif.
Dwyer, Roy E., Principal, Pineda Elementary School, Cocoa, Fla.
Dyde, W. F., Vice-Pres. and Dean of Fac., Univ. of Colorado, Boulder, Colo.
Dyer, Frank E., Delano Jt. Union High School, Delano, Calif.
Dyke, Elwood E., Principal, Southport Elem. School, Kenosha, Wis.
Dykes, Mrs. Alma, 1418 East St., Reading, Ohio
Dypka, Jessie B., University School, Univ. of Michigan, Ann Arbor, Mich.

Eads, Laura K., 141 Joralemon St., Brooklyn, N.Y.
Early, Margaret J., Sch. of Educ., Syracuse University, Syracuse, N.Y.
Early, William A., 208 Bull St., Savannah, Ga.
Eash, Maurice J., 509 West 121st St., New York, N.Y.
Eason, Leo A., Dept. of Educ., Washington University, St. Louis, Mo.
Ebel, Robert L., Educational Testing Service, Princeton, N.J.
Eberle, August William, University of Chattanooga, Chattanooga, Tenn.
Eberly, J. Wilgus, Texas Women's University, Denton, Tex.
Eberman, Paul W., Sch. of Educ., Univ. of Wisconsin, Madison, Wis.
Eckert, Ruth E., Col. of Educ., Univ. of Minnesota, Minneapolis, Minn.
Eckhardt, John W., 2914 Sunset Ave., Bakersfield, Calif.
Edelfelt, Roy A., Col. of Educ., Michigan State University, East Lansing, Mich.
Edgar, Robert W., Queens College, Flushing, N.Y.
Edgerton, D. R., Superintendent, Sch. Dist. 110, Overland Park, Kan.
Edmiston, R. W., Dir. of Extension, Miami University, Oxford, Ohio
Edson, Gilmore L., 229 Lexington Ave., East Lansing, Mich.
Edson, William H., Col. of Educ., Univ. of Minnesota, Minneapolis, Minn.
Edstrom, A. E., Principal, Senior High School, Hopkins, Minn.
Edwards, Arthur U., Eastern Illinois University, Charleston, Ill.
Edwards, Gerald F., 717 East Fifth St., Marshfield, Wis.
Edwards, G. N., Inspector of Schools, Stratford, Ont.
Edwards, H. T., Principal, Athens High and Industrial School, Athens, Ga.
Edwards, Marcia, Col. of Educ., University of Minnesota, Minneapolis, Minn.
Edwards, Nathan A., Bakersfield College, Bakersfield, Calif.
Edwards, T. Bentley, Sch. of Educ., University of California, Berkeley, Calif.
Edwards, William B., Superintendent of Schools, Lakewood, Ohio
Effron, Michael P., Principal, East Technical High School, Cleveland, Ohio
Egdorf, M. F., Superintendent of Schools, Garden City, N.Y.
Ehlers, Henry J., Duluth Branch, Univ. of Minnesota, Duluth, Minn.
Ehrenfeld, A., 50 West Ninety-sixth Street, New York, N.Y.
Ehrlich, Emanuel, 622 East Twentieth St., New York, N.Y.
Eikaas, Alf M., Bur. of Educ. Res., Univ. of Minnesota, Minneapolis, Minn.
Einolf, W. L., Birchrunville, Pa.
Eisenbise, Merlin E., Dir., Citrus Junior College, Azusa, Calif.
Eiserer, Paul E., Teachers College, Columbia University, New York, N.Y.
Eklund, Paul A., Principal, Lake View School, Zion, Ill.
Elder, Ruth E., Dept. of Elem. Educ., Univ. of Oklahoma, Norman, Okla.
Elkin, Sol, 3410 West Chicago Ave., Detroit, Mich.
Elkins, Deborah, Dept. of Educ., Queens College, Flushing, N.Y.

Ellerbrook, Louis William, Stephen F. Austin State Col., Nacogdoches, Tex.
Ellingson, Mark, Rochester Institute of Technology, Rochester, N.Y.
Ellington, Gene, Principal, Eaton High School, Eaton, Ohio
Elliott, Arthur B., President, Lyndon Teachers College, Lyndon Center, Vt.
Elliott, Lloyd H., Stone Hall, Cornell Univ., Ithaca, N.Y.
Ellis, Celia Diamond, 6362 W. 6th St., Los Angeles, Calif.
Ellis, Frederick E., University of Minnesota, Col. of Educ., Minneapolis, Minn.
Ellis, G. Gordon, Iowa State College, Ames, Iowa
Ellis, Joseph R., Col. of Educ., University of Texas, Austin, Tex.
Ellis, Robert Lawrence, 6362 W. 6th St., Los Angeles, Calif.
Ellison, Alfred, Sch. of Educ., New York University, New York, N.Y.
Elmer, Mrs. Marion Short, 20 Belmont Street, Buffalo, N.Y.
Elsbree, Harold M., Prof. of Education, State Teachers Col., New Paltz, N.Y.
Emig, Dorothy, Principal, Bonham School, El Paso, Tex.
Endres, Mary P., Dept. of Educ., Purdue University, Lafayette, Ind.
Engelhardt, Jack E., 44 Spencer St., Battle Creek, Mich.
Engelhardt, N. L., 221 West 57th St., New York, N.Y.
England, Byron, Asst. Superintendent, Public School, El Paso, Tex.
Engle, Arthur W., Exec. Head, Maplewood School, Elyria, Ohio
English, John W., 1015 Krings Lane, Joliet, Ill.
English, Mildred, P.O. Box 722, Milledgeville, Ga.
Enzinger, Philip, Jr., Genl. Consultant, Public High Schools, St. Louis, Mo.
Epstein, Bertram, City College of New York, New York, N.Y.
Erdman, Robert L., University of Wisconsin-Milwaukee, Milwaukee, Wis.
Erickson, C. E., Dean of Educ., Mich. State Univ., East Lansing, Mich.
Erickson, Carlton W. H., Audio-visual Center, Univ. of Connecticut, Storrs, Conn.
Erickson, Harley E., Dept. of Educ., Wisconsin State College, Superior, Wis.
Erickson, Ralph, Box 56, State College, Mankato, Minn.
Erickson, Ralph W., College Station, Columbus, Miss.
Erskine, Mildred R., 2096 Watson Ave., St. Paul, Minn.
Ervin, John B., Chairman, Educ. Div., Stowe Teachers College, St. Louis, Mo.
Ervin, William B., 1 Midland Place, Newark, N.J.
Erzinger, John F., 6600 North Campbell Ave., Chicago, Ill.
Eskridge, T. J., Jr., Dept. of Educ. & Psych., Newberry College, Newberry, S.C.
Eson, Morris E., New York State College for Teachers, Albany, N.Y.
Espy, James A., 243 20th Ave. South, Minneapolis, Minn.
Ethridge, Samuel B., 2431 Ridge Road So., Mobile, Ala.
Ettinger, Bernadette C., Dir. of Curriculum, Public Schools, Copiague, N.Y.
Eurich, Alvin C., 477 Madison Ave., New York, N.Y.
Evans, A. R., Dir. of Finance, Board of Education, Springfield, Ill.
Evans, Edgar Ernest, Alabama State College, Montgomery, Ala.
Evans, Ellsworth J., Principal, Cupples School, St. Louis, Mo.
Evans, Harold J., 608 South 118th St., Tacoma, Wash.
Evans, Howard R., Dean, Col. of Educ., University of Akron, Akron, Ohio
Evans, John C., Asst. Superintendent of Schools, Ogden, Utah
Evans, John W., Superintendent of Schools, Lorain, Ohio
Evans, Mary C., 8645 Washington, La Mesa, Calif.
Evans, Ralph F., Head, Dept. of Educ., Fresno State College, Fresno, Calif.
Evenson, Warren L., Midwest Adm. Center, Univ. of Chicago, Chicago, Ill.
Everett, Millard S., Oklahoma A. & M. College, Stillwater, Okla.
Ewing, Parmer L., New York University, Washington Sq., New York, N.Y.

Faeber, Louis J., Dean of Educ., University of Dayton, Dayton, Ohio
Fahey, George L., University of Pittsburgh, Pittsburgh, Pa.
Fairbanks, Gar, Col. of Educ., University of Rochester, Rochester, N.Y.
Falk, Conrad, Conception Seminary, Conception, Mo.
Falk, Philip H., Superintendent of Schools, Madison, Wis.
Fallon, Berlie J., Dept. of Educ., Texas Technological Col., Lubbock, Tex.
Fane, Arthur, Principal, Public School 150, Brooklyn, N.Y.
Farber, Evan Ira, Main Library, Emory University, Ga.
Farber, Nathan, 38 Church St., Cortland, N.Y.

Farley, Edgar S., Asst. Supt. in chg. of Instruction, Adm. Bldg., Garden City, N.Y.
Farley, Gilbert J., University of Miami, Coral Gables, Fla.
Farley, H. Kent, Oregon College of Education, Monmouth, Ore.
Farley, John A., University of Detroit, Detroit, Mich.
Farnsworth, R. Earl, Principal, Senior High School, Fort Smith, Ark.
Farr, John C., Superintendent of Schools, Southington, Conn.
Farr, S. David., Educ. Research Center, University of Buffalo, Buffalo, N.Y.
Farrell, Edmund J., James Lick High School, San Jose, Calif.
Farrell, Emma, East Tennessee State College, Johnson City, Tenn.
Fasan, Walter R., 7736 Sangamon St., Chicago, Ill.
Fattu, Nicholas, 921 Sheridan Drive, Bloomington, Ind.
Fawley, Paul C., USAOM/ICA, APO 928, San Francisco, Calif.
Fay, Leo C., School of Education, Indiana University, Bloomington, Ind.
Fea, Henry Robert, University of Washington, Seattle, Wash.
Fearing, Joseph L., Principal, Lutz School, Lutz, Fla.
Feelhaver, Carl T., Supt. of Schools, Ft. Dodge, Iowa
Feingold, S. Norman, Exec. Dir., Jewish Voc. Service, Boston, Mass.
Feller, Dan, 9951-B Robbins Dr., Beverly Hills, Calif.
Felsinger, Margaret J., Ohio University, Athens, Ohio
Feltman, Irene, New Haven State Tchrs. College, New Haven, Conn.
Felton, Ralph D., 35 High St., Montrose, Pa.
Femyer, Alice, 1820 South Sixth St., Terre Haute, Ind.
Fenollosa, George M., Houghton-Mifflin Co., Boston, Mass.
Fenske, Arthur S., Principal, Columbus Elem. School, Kenosha, Wis.
Fergen, Geraldine K., Sch. of Educ., University of Missouri, Columbia, Mo.
Ferguson, W. Stewart, Santa Monica Schools, Santa Monica, Calif.
Feroze, Hyat, Kabal Road, Sialkot Cantt, Pakistan
Ferran, Rose M., Dir., Elem. Grades, Public Schools, New Orleans, La.
Ferrier, William Kenneth, 6517 S.W. 35th Ave., Portland, Ore.
Ferris, Donald R., San Jose State College, San Jose, Calif.
Fessier, Mrs. Margery, 3336 Josephine St., Lynwood, Calif.
Ficken, Clarence E., Vice Pres. & Dean, Ohio Wesleyan Univ., Delaware, Ohio
Fiedler, E. L., Superintendent of Schools, Abilene, Kan.
Fiedler, William G., Asst. Superintendent of Schools, Union City, N.J.
Field, Robert L., Vice-Prin., North High School, Sheboygen, Wis.
Fields, A. J., Jr., Principal, Sanford High School, Opelika, Ala.
Fields, Clarence J., Coppin State Teachers College, Baltimore, Md.
Fields, Ralph R., Teachers College, Columbia University, New York, N.Y.
Fielstra, Clarence, Sch. of Educ., University of California, Los Angeles, Calif.
Fielstra, Mrs. Helen, 1125 Ravoli Dr., Pacific Palisades, Calif.
Fierman, Rabbi Morton C., 206 East Eighth St., Santa Ana, Calif.
Figuerel, J. Allen, The Sunwood, Buckboard Trail, Allison Park, Pa.
Finch, F. H., Col. of Educ., University of Illinois, Urbana, Ill.
Finck, Edgar M., Dickinson College, Carlisle, Pa.
Findlay, Stephen W., O.S.B., Headmaster, Delbarton School, Morristown, N.J.
Findley, Warren G., Board of Education, Atlanta, Ga.
Fine, Huldah, 2970 Blaine Ave., Detroit, Mich.
Fink, Abel K., Educ. Dept., College for Teachers, Buffalo, N.Y.
Fink, Martin B., 1808 Aloha Way, Modesto, Calif.
Fink, Paul S., 31 South Penn St., Allentown, Pa.
Fink, Stuart D., Prin., Lab. Sch., No. Illinois State College, DeKalb, Ill.
Finlay, Mrs. Helen K., Supv., Secondary Educ., County Schls., Arlington, Va.
Fischoff, Ephraim, 299 Edwards St., New Haven, Conn.
Fish, Allan, Supv. Prin., Oakwood Public Schools, Oakville, Ontario
Fishback, Woodson W., Southern Illinois University, Carbondale, Ill.
Fisher, Hazel, Harford County Bd. of Education, Bel Air, Md.
Fisher, Helen H., San Diego County Schools, San Diego, Calif.
Fisher, James A., Boston University Junior College, 688 Boylston, Boston, Mass.
Fisher, Joseph T., University of South Dakota, Vermillion, S.D.
Fisher, Lawrence A., Sch. of Educ., Univ. of South Carolina, Columbia, S.C.
Fisher, Lois, 123 Pike St., Reading, Ohio

Fisher, Marie R., Supv. Tests and Meas., Dept. of Educ., St. Paul, Minn.
*Fisher, Mrs. Welthy H., Dir., Literacy Village, Lucknow, U.P., India
Fisk, Robert S., Dean, Sch. of Educ., University of Buffalo, Buffalo, N.Y.
Fite, Kenneth A., Chm., Music Dept., Northwestern State College, Alva, Okla.
Fitz, John Allen, USOM/Iran, APO 205, New York, N.Y.
Fitzgerald, Edward J., Superintendent of Schools, Bristol, R.I.
Fitzgerald, Eloise R., State Teachers College, Boston, Mass.
Fitzgerald, J. C., Oklahoma A. & M. College, Stillwater, Okla.
Fitzgerald, James A., Scranton University, Scranton, Pa.
Fitzgerald, N. F., Dean, Col. of Educ., Univ. of Tennessee, Knoxville, Tenn.
Fitzpatrick, E. D., Dept. of Guidance, Southern Illinois Univ., Carbondale, Ill.
Fitzsimons, Frank P., Dept. of Educ., Brooklyn College, Brooklyn, N.Y.
Fitzwater, James P., Dir., Div. of Visual Educ., Public Schools, Chicago, Ill.
Flamand, Ruth K., 72 Goldenridge Dr., Levittown, Pa.
Flamme, Wayne H., Principal, Junior High School, Antigo, Wis.
Flanagan, John C., Dir., Amer. Inst. for Research, 410 Amberson, Pittsburgh, Pa.
Flanagan, Scott E., Principal, Union High School, Huntington Beach, Calif.
Flanagan, William F., Dir., Aldrich Junior High School, Warwick, R.I.
Flanders, Ned A., Col. of Educ., Univ. of Minnesota, Minneapolis, Minn.
Fleck, Henrietta, Chm., Home Econ. Dept., New York Univ., New York, N.Y.
Fleming, C. M., Inst. of Educ., University of London, London, England
Fleming, Harold D., Chm., Div. of Educ., State Tchrs. College, Bemidji, Minn.
Fleming, Robert S., Sch. of Educ., New York University, New York, N.Y.
Flesher, Mrs. Marie A., Ohio State University, Columbus, Ohio
Flesher, William R., Sch. of Educ., Ohio State University, Columbus, Ohio
Fliegler, Louis A., Syracuse University, Syracuse, N.Y.
Fligor, R. J., Southern Illinois University, Carbondale, Ill.
Flintom, Margaret, Supervisor of Elementary Education, Charlotte, N.C.
Flippen, John T., Bluefield State College, Bluefield, W. Va.
Flores, Vetal, Box 287, Bronte, Tex.
Flournoy, Frances, Dept. of Curric. and Instr., Univ. of Texas, Austin, Tex.
Flower, George E., Ontario College of Education, Toronto, Ont., Canada
Floyd, Mrs. Dorothy H., Principal, Edward S. Cook School, Atlanta, Ga.
Flug, Eugene R. F., Unit 333, University Village, Minneapolis, Minn.
Focht, James R., Education Dept., State Teachers College, Salisbury, Md.
Folger, D. F., Chm., Div. of Tchr. Educ., State Col. for Women, Milledgeville, Ga.
Fonacier, Andres Medina, Ilocos Norte Normal School, Laoag, Ilocos Norte,
    Philippines
Foot, Edwin L., Jr., 210 Sunnyside, Lawrence, Kan.
Foote, Lawrence E., Superintendent, Allen County Schls., Fort Wayne, Ind.
Foran, Thomas G., Seigniory Club, Province of Quebec, Canada
Forcinelli, Joseph, F.B.F.M.S. Vanga, Sur Kwilu par Kikwit, Congo Belge, Africa
Ford, Edmund A., 46 Monterey, Terre Haute, Ind.
Ford, Paul L., Illinois Children's Hospital, Chicago, Ill.
Ford, Roxana R., Sch. of Home Econ., Univ. of Minnesota, St. Paul, Minn.
Fordyce, W. G., Superintendent of Schools, Euclid, Ohio
Fornaciari, Earl F., Dept. of Math., Chicago Teachers College, Chicago, Ill.
Forney, E. B., Ginn & Company, 1932 Princeton Ave., St. Paul, Minn.
Forrester, Gertrude, 71 Overpeck Ave., Ridgefield Park, N.J.
Forsgren, Afton, State Dept. of Public Instruction, Salt Lake City, Utah
Forsman, C. T., Asst. Principal, Pontiac Senior High School, Pontiac, Mich.
Fortess, Lillian, 96 Bay State Rd., Boston, Mass.
Foshay, Arthur, Teachers College, Columbia University, New York, N.Y.
Foss, Elaine, 3109 Fremont St., Minneapolis, Minn.
Fossieck, Theodore H., Principal, Milne School of Practice, Albany, N.Y.
Foster, E. M., Dept. of Educ., Coe College, Cedar Rapids, Iowa
Foster, Grace L., Principal, Beveridge School, Gary, Ind.
Foster, Harry K., State Teachers College, Fredonia, N.Y.
Foster, Inez, Asst. Supt., Elem. Div., Public Schools, San Antonio, Tex.
Foster, Phyllis, 404 S. University St., Carbondale, Ill.
Foster, Zeph H., Prin., Walla Walla Col. Campus School, College Place, Wash.

Fougner, Herbert M., San Francisco State College, Santa Rosa, Calif.
Fournier, Edmond A., Registrar, Sacred Heart Seminary, Detroit, Mich.
Fowlkes, John Guy, Dean, Sch. of Educ., Univ. of Wisconsin, Madison, Wis.
Fox, James H., 2556 N. Upland St., Arlington, Va.
Fox, Robert S., Univ. Elem. Sch., Univ. of Michigan, Ann Arbor, Mich.
Fox, Willard, Wayne State University, Detroit, Mich.
Franklin, J. E., 1602 Cooper St., Commerce, Tex.
Franks, Milford, Dept. of Educ., Montana State College, Bozeman, Mont.
Franson, Arthur H., 337 N. Brainard Ave., La Grange Park, Ill.
Franz, Evelyn B., State Teachers College, Trenton, N.J.
Franzblau, Abraham N., Dean, Hebrew Union Sch. of Educ. & Sacred Music, New York, N.Y.
* Franzen, Carl G. F., School of Education, Indiana University, Bloomington, Ind.
Fraser, Dorothy McClure, City College, New York, N.Y.
Frazier, Eva, 4313 Wallace Lane, Nashville, Tenn.
Frazier, James R., Superintendent of Schools, Okmulgee, Okla.
Frederick, Orie, Western Michigan University, Kalamazoo, Mich.
Frederick, Robert W., Jr., Bakersfield College, Bakersfield, Calif.
Freeman, Frank N., Dean Emeritus, Univ. of Calif., Berkeley, Calif.
Freeman, M. Herbert, State Teachers College, Upper Montclair, N.J.
Freeman, Ruges Richmond, Jr., 4582 Aldine St., St. Louis, Mo.
Fred, Bernhart G., Iowa State Teachers College, Cedar Falls, Iowa
Freeman, Kenneth H., 403 Christian College Ave., Columbia, Mo.
French, Joseph L., University of Nebraska, Lincoln, Neb.
French, William M., Muhlenberg College, Allentown, Pa.
Fretwell, Elbert K., Jr., Asst. Commissioner for Higher Educ., Albany, N.Y.
Fretz, Floyd C., Superintendent of Schools, Bradford, Pa.
Freund, Evelyn, 5954 Guilford, Detroit, Mich.
Frieberg, Carter N., Loyola University, Chicago, Ill.
Friedman, Marcella F., Chicago Teachers College, Chicago, Ill.
Fristoe, Wallace H., Prin., Kelvyn Park High School, Chicago, Ill.
Fritschel, A. L., Dept. of Educ., Western Illinois University, Macomb, Ill.
Fritzsche, Bertha M., Mississippi Southern College, Hattiesburg, Miss.
Froelich, Gustav J., Bur. of Inst. Res., Univ. of Illinois, Urbana, Ill.
Froog, Arthur, 2560 Kessler Blvd., Lincoln, Neb.
Frost, George E., Dir., Holyoke Junior College, Holyoke, Mass.
Frost, S. E., Jr., Dept. of Educ., Brooklyn College, Brooklyn, N.Y.
Frutchey, Fred P., Ext. Serv., U.S. Dept. of Agriculture, Washington, D.C.
Fugate, Mamie L., Principal, Conway Elem. School, Orlando, Fla.
Fuglaar, Ollie B., Southwestern Louisiana Institute, Lafayette, La.
Fullagar, William A., Chm., Div. of Educ., Univ. of Rochester, Rochester, N.Y.
Fullerton, Craig K., 2712 North 52nd St., Omaha, Neb.
Fullmer, C. E., Principal, Wadsworth Elem. School, Chicago, Ill.
Fultz, Dan A., 1250 Stanford Ave., Santa Monica, Calif.
Furbush, Lawrence M., Jr., Prin., River Road Elem. School, Wilmington, Del.
Futch, Olivia, Dept. of Educ., Furman University, Greenville, S.C.

Gabbard, Hazel F., U.S. Office of Education, Washington, D.C.
Gabel, O. J., Northern Illinois University, DeKalb, Ill.
Gabler, Earl R., Sch. of Educ., New York University, New York, N.Y.
Gadbury, Mrs. Nada M., Ball State Teachers College, Muncie, Ind.
Gaffney, Matthew P., Spaulding House, 20 Oxford St., Cambridge, Mass.
Gaffney, Philip D., Arizona State College, Tempe, Ariz.
Gaiser, P. F., President, Clark College, Vancouver, Wash.
Gale, Ann, Principal, Edison School, Chicago, Ill.
Gallagher, Dora Agnes, 400 South Hauser Blvd., Los Angeles, Calif.
Gallagher, Margaret M., 412 South Bristol Lane, Arlington Heights, Ill.
Gallen, Albert A., Reading Consult., West Chester Public Schls., West Chester, Pa.
Gallicchio, Francis A., Box 34, Rome, Pa.
Galloway, O. F., Head, Dept. of Educ., MacMurray Col., Jacksonville, Ill.

Gambert, Charles A., Sch. Psychologist and Supv. of Spec. Educ., Niagara Falls, N.Y.
Gamble, LeRoy T., Principal, High School, Forest Grove, Ore.
Gambrill, Bessie Lee, Dept. of Educ., Yale University. New Haven, Conn.
Gamelin, Francis C., 4054 Quail Ave., Robbinsdale, Minn.
Gammon, Delore, Asst. Supt. in chg. Elem. Educ., Public Schools, Wichita, Kan.
Gans, Leo, American Book Co., 55 Fifth Ave., New York, N.Y.
Gansberg, Lucille, County Superintendent of Schools, Susanville, Calif.
Garbe, Lester, 1503 W. Hopkins St., Milwaukee, Wis.
Garbel, Marianne, 6732 Crandon Ave., Chicago, Ill.
Garber, M. Delott, Principal, Burr Junior High School, Hartford, Conn.
Garder, Clarence E., Central State College, Edmond, Okla.
Gardiner, Marian Juanita, Bishop College, Marshall, Tex.
Gardner, Laurence R., Superintendent, Parochial Schools, Manchester, N.H.
Garinger, Elmer H., Superintendent of Schools, Charlotte, N.C.
Garlin, R. E., Dept. of Educ., Texas Technological College, Lubbock, Tex.
Garness, Gerhardt, 1845 Wauwatosa Ave., Wauwatosa, Wis.
Garnett, Ray L., Wisconsin State College, River Falls, Wis.
Garrett, Charles G., 2 Ruth Street, Hammond, Ind.
Garrett, Cyril D., Chm., Dept. of Educ., Wheaton College, Wheaton, Ill.
Garrett, Mrs. Lettie D., Principal, Ingleside School, Norfolk, Va.
*Gates, Arthur I., Teachers College, Columbia University, New York, N.Y.
Gates, Charles D., Vice-Prin., Charlotte High School, Rochester, N.Y.
Gates, Mrs. Grace W., Supv., Elementary Education, Clarence, N.Y.
Gathercole, F. J., Superintendent, Public Schools, Saskatoon, Sask., Canada
Gauerke, Warren E., Dept. of Teacher Educ., Emory University, Ga.
Gauger, Paul W., Sch. of Educ., University of Wisconsin, Madison, Wis.
Gaunt, W. F., 8309 McKenzie Rd., Affton, Mo.
Gauvey, Ralph E., Director, Urbana Junior College, Urbana, Ohio
Gazelle, Mrs. Hazel N., 277 W. Poppyfields Dr., Altadena, Calif.
Gebbart, James W., Montana State University, Missoula, Mont.
Gebre-Hewet, Mengesha, c/o University College, Addis Ababa, Ethiopia
Geer, Owen C., 176 Los Robles Dr., Burlingame, Calif.
Gelerinter, Alfred, 232 Linden Ave., Ithaca, N.Y.
Gemeinhardt, William C., Northern State Tchrs. College, Aberdeen, S.D.
Geng, George, Paine College, Augusta, Ga.
Genter, Robert F., Box 365, Lawndale, Calif.
Gentleman, Florence L., Prin., Barton Elem. School, Chicago, Ill.
Gentry, George H., Supt. of Schls., Pres., Lee Jr. Col., Baytown, Tex.
Gentry, Ira A., Jr., Tennessee A. & I. State University, Nashville, Tenn.
Georgiades, William, Whittier Union High School Dist., Whittier, Calif.
Georgiady, Nicholas P., Principal, Lydell School, Whitefish Bay, Wis.
Gephart, Woodrow W., 451 Columbia St., Leetonia, Ohio
Geraty, T. S., President, Middle East College, Beirut, Lebanon
Gerberich, J. R., Dir., Bur. of Educ. Research, Univ. of Conn., Storrs, Conn.
Gergely, E. J., Brooklyn College, Brooklyn, N.Y.
Gerletti, John D., University of Southern California, Los Angeles, Calif.
Gernert, H. F., Jr., 522 North 24th St., Allentown, Pa.
Gesler, Harriet L., 21 Green Gardens Ct., East Haven, Conn.
Gest, Mrs. Viola S., P.O. Box 254, Seguin, Texas
Getzels, J. W., Dept. of Educ., University of Chicago, Chicago, Ill.
Ghalib, Hanna, American Mission, Beirut, Lebanon
Giannuzzi, John P., 482 Iris St., Los Alamos, N.M.
Gibbs, E. Delmar, College of Puget Sound, Tacoma, Wash.
Gibbs, Elsie, Dir., Secondary Educ., City Schools, San Bernardino, Calif.
Gibbs, John E., Principal, Courtenay Elem. School, Charleston, S.C.
Gibert, James M., Randolph-Macon Woman's College, Lynchburg, Va.
Gibson, Bernice B., Supt., Sutter County Schools, Yuba City, Calif.
Gibson, Christine M., Pres., Language Research, Inc., Cambridge, Mass.
Gibson, Mrs. Kathryn S., Prairie View A. & M. College, Prairie View, Tex.
Gibson, Mrs. Norma, 902 South Manhattan Place, Los Angeles, Calif.

Gibson, Mrs. Stuart, St. Catherine's School, Richmond, Va.
Gibson, Walter E., Prin., Lafayette School, Lincoln Park, Mich.
Giddings, Philip E., Oakwood College, Huntsville, Ala.
Gilbert, Eula Lee, Alabama State College, Montgomery, Ala.
Gilbert, Floyd O., Professional Studies Div., State College, St. Cloud, Minn.
Gilbert, Harry B., Bur. of Child Guidance, New York City Schls., New York, N.Y.
Gilbert, Ira, 225 Twenty-seventh St., Manhattan Beach, Calif.
Gilbert, Jerome H., 11155 South Depot St., Worth, Ill.
Gilbert, Lee R., Principal, Froebel School, Gary, Ind.
Gilbert, Luther C., Sch. of Educ., University of California, Berkeley, Calif.
Giles, Lawrence E., University of South Carolina, Columbia, S.C.
Giles, LeRoy H., Dean of Students, Carthage College, Carthage, Ill.
Gill, Bernard I., Librarian, State Teachers College, Moorhead, Minn.
Gill, Margaret, A.S.C.D., 1201 Sixteenth St., N.W., Washington, D.C.
Gilland, Thomas M., 327 Wood St., California, Pa.
Gillaspie, Howard H., Indiana State Teachers College, Terre Haute, Ind.
Gillespie, Paul C., Principal, Monte Vista School, Phoenix, Ariz.
Gillham, Vera M., Principal, Horace Mann School, Minneapolis, Minn.
Gilliam, Camp, Texas Wesleyan College, Fort Worth, Tex.
Gilligan, Michael B., State Teachers College, Jersey City, N.J.
Gilmore, John E., Superintendent of Schools, Wellsville, N.Y.
Ginger, Lyman V., Dean, Col. of Educ., University of Kentucky, Lexington, Ky.
Gilson, Harry V., Superintendent of Schools, Winchester, Mass.
Gipson, Theodore H., Box 9871, So. Branch P.O., Baton Rouge, La.
Glaeser, Mrs. Louise M., Clara Barton School, Alton, Ill.
Glasow, Ogden L., Western Illinois State College, Macomb, Ill.
Glasser, Mrs. M. Lawrence, 9201 Coral Way, Miami, Fla.
Glaza, Stephen M., Superintendent of Schools, Marshall, Mich.
Gleason, Gerald T., Sch. of Educ., University of Wisconsin, Madison, Wis.
Glenn, J. Curtis, Chicago Teachers College, Chicago, Ill.
Glock, Marvin D., Bur. of Educ. Research, Cornell University, Ithaca, N.Y.
Glogau, Arthur H., Dean of Men, Oregon College of Education, Monmouth, Ore.
Gobetz, Wallace, 540 East 22nd St., Brooklyn, N.Y.
Goble, Robert I., Miami University, Oxford, Ohio
Godfrey, Mary E., Pennsylvania State University, University Park, Pa.
Godfrey, Rollin E., 2003 Dellwood Drive, Greensboro, N.C.
Godwin, W. E., Principal, Union Bowen, Irving, Tex.
Godwin, Wendell, Superintendent of Schools, Topeka, Kan.
Goebel, Edmund J., Supt., Archdiocesan Schools, Milwaukee, Wis.
Goedert, William O., 730 N. Wabash Ave., Chicago, Ill.
Goewey, Gordon Ira, State University Teachers College, Geneseo, N.Y.
Goff, Mrs. Arnold E., Forest Grove, Ore.
Gold, Milton J., Dept. of Educ., Hunter College, New York, N.Y.
Goldberg, Joseph W., Principal, Public School 20, Paterson, N.J.
Goldberg, Nathan, 75-47 196th Street, Flushing, N.Y.
Goldhammer, Keith, Sch. of Educ., University of Oregon, Eugene, Ore.
Goldstein, Herbert, 1003 West Nevada, Urbana, Ill.
Goltry, Keith, Dean, Dept. of Educ., Parsons College, Fairfield, Iowa
Gomon, Neal S., Nebraska State Teachers College, Peru, Neb.
Gonnelly, Ellen M., Principal, James R. Lowell School, Chicago, Ill.
Good, Carter V., University of Cincinnati, Cincinnati, Ohio
Good, Richard M., 6814 Tenth Ave., Takoma Park, Md.
Good, Warren R., 1604 Stony Run Drive, Northwood, Wilmington, Del.
Goodlad, John I., Dept. of Educ., University of Chicago, Chicago, Ill.
Goodman, John O., University of Connecticut, Storrs, Conn.
Goodrich, Mrs. Lucile, County Superintendent of Schools, Pontiac, Ill.
Goodside, Samuel, Supv., Ramaz Lower School, New York, N.Y.
Goossen, Carl V., Prin., Univ. Elem. Sch., Univ. of Minn., Minneapolis, Minn.
Gordon, Alice S., Principal, Drummond School, Chicago, Ill.
Gordon, Ira J., Col. of Educ., University of Florida, Gainesville, Fla.
Gordon, Ted, 317 North Lucerne, Los Angeles, Calif.

Gorman, Frank H., University of Omaha, Omaha, Neb.
Gorman, William J., Registrar, St. John's Prep. School, Brooklyn, N.Y.
Gormley, Charles L., Chm., Dept. of Educ., Alabama College, Montevallo, Ala.
Gorton, Harry B., 6 Ross Ave., New Cumberland, Pa.
Goslin, Willard E., George Peabody College, Nashville, Tenn.
Gossard, Paul, Superintendent of Schools, Quincy, Mass.
Gottfried, F. J., Superintendent of Schools, Elyria, Ohio
Gould, Blanche B., 1032 North Hudson Ave., Hollywood, Calif.
Gould, George, University of Pittsburgh, Pittsburgh, Pa.
Gould, W. S., Vice-President-Dean, Graceland College, Lamoni, Iowa
Gowin, Mrs. Dorothy B., 70 Starr St., New Haven, Conn.
Graber, Eldon W., Head, Dept. of Educ., Bethel College, North Newton, Kan.
Grabowski, A. A., 2512 Southport Ave., Chicago, Ill.
Grace, Alonzo G., Sch. of Educ., New York University, New York, N.Y.
Grado, Louis M., Eastern Illinois University, Charleston, Ill.
Grady, Joseph E., St. Bernard's Seminary, Rochester, N.Y.
Graebner, Oliver E., Valparaiso University, Valparaiso, Indiana
Graetz, Ralph C., Long Beach State College, Long Beach, Calif.
Graff, George E., Supt., Rural Educ., State Dept. of Educ., Rockville, Conn.
Graff, Orin B., Dept. of Sch. Adm. & Supv., Univ. of Tenn., Knoxville, Tenn.
Graffam, Donald T., Dickinson College, Carlisle, Pa.
Graham, Thomas D., Principal, Willis High School, Delaware, Ohio
Graham, Willis Gayer, Instructional Materials Coord., Mukilteo, Wash.
Grant, Eugene B., Northern Illinois University, DeKalb, Ill.
Granzow, Kent R., 1117 South York St., Denver, Colo.
Grau, Mary L., Supv., Elementary Educ., Montgomery County, Towson, Md.
Grau, R. T., Director of Curriculum, Public Schools, Clinton, Iowa
Graves, Linwood D., Morris Brown College, Atlanta, Ga.
Gray, Archie L., University Station, Grand Forks, N.D.
Gray, Dorothy, Dept. of Educ., Queens College, Flushing, N.Y.
Gray, Mrs. Loretta, Dir., Elem. Educ., Public Schools, Burlington, Iowa
Gray, Merle, Dir., Elem. Educ., Public Schools, Hammond, Ind.
* Gray, William S., Dept. of Educ., University of Chicago, Chicago, Ill.
Graye, Mytrolene L., Principal, Fairview Elem. School, High Point, N.Y.
Green, Harold W., Utah School for the Blind, Ogden, Utah
Green, Donald Ross, 1419 Cornell Rd., N.E., Atlanta, Ga.
Green, John A., Educ. Field Service, Univ. of Idaho, Moscow, Idaho
Greenberg, Joseph, Principal, Public School 238, Brooklyn, N.Y.
Greene, Charles E., 1703 East Cliff Dr., Santa Cruz, Calif.
Greene, Harry A., 10575 Wyton Dr., Los Angeles, Calif.
Greene, John G., 6 Chestnut St., Boston, Mass.
Greene, Maxine, Sch. of Educ., New York University, New York, N.Y.
Greene, Mrs. Minnie S., Southwest Texas Junior College, Uvalde, Tex.
Greenfield, Curtis O., Principal, Percy L. Julian School, Phoenix, Ariz.
Greenwood, Edward D., Menninger Clinic, Topeka, Kan.
Greenwood, Roy, Broome County Technical Institute, Binghamton, N.Y.
Greer, John T., 1680 Landwehr Rd., Northbrook, Ill.
Gregerson, Grace, State Teachers College, Moorhead, Minn.
Gregg, Dorothy V. W., 13 Washington Lane, Orinda, Calif.
Gregg, Russell T., Dept. of Educ., Univ. of Wisconsin, Madison, Wis.
Gregory, Carl R., Principal, Roxana High School, Roxana, Ill.
Greif, Ivo P., Wayne State University, Detroit, Mich.
Greivell, Richard, Curric. Coord., Public Schools, Fort Atkinson, Wis.
Grey, Mrs. Emylu D., 2565 Duke Ave., Richmond, Calif.
Gribble, S. C., Washington University, St. Louis, Mo.
Griffin, Lee H., Ginn and Company, Chicago, Ill.
Griffin, Margaret T., Principal, Warner Elementary School, Springfield, **Mass.**
* Griffin, Margery M., 5778 DeGiverville, St. Louis, Mo.
Griffith, Coleman R., University of Illinois, Urbana, Ill.
Griffiths, Daniel E., 54 Clarendon Rd., Scarsdale, N.Y.
Griffiths, Ruth, 184 Middlesex St., North Andover, Mass.

Grigsby, Paul A., Superintendent, Com. Unit School Dist., Granite City, Ill.
Grillo, Mrs. Marguerite M., New Haven State Tchrs. Col., New Haven, Conn.
Grimes, Leslie K., Superintendent of Schools, Greeley, Colo.
Grispino, Rev. J. A., Marist College, Harewood Rd., N.E., Washington, D.C.
Gritzner, Leland J., Elem. Prin., Public Schools, Osage, Iowa
Grizzard, Mabel Youree, 711 West Main, Waxahachie, Tex.
* Grizzell, E. D., Dean, Sch. of Educ., Univ. of Pennsylvania, Philadelphia, Pa.
Groce, J. Verl, 3232 Titanic Ave., El Paso, Tex.
Groesbeck, Lue, Brigham Young University, Provo, Utah
Groeschell, Robert, Curric. Dir., School Dist. No. 17, Port Angeles, Wash.
Groff, Frank E., Reg. Supt., New Hope-Solebury Jt. Sch. Dist., New Hope, Pa.
Grogan, M. Lucille, 7638 South Wood St., Chicago, Ill.
Grogan, Vada, Prin., Clifton L. Ganus School, New Orleans, La.
Gronlund, Norman E., Col. of Educ., University of Illinois, Urbana, Ill.
Grose, Robert F., Psych. Dept., Amherst College, Amherst, Mass.
Grose, Wilma, Weber College, Ogden, Utah
Gross, Lydia, Lock Haven State Teachers College, Lock Haven, Pa.
Gross, Marie L., Principal, Central School, Evanston, Ill.
Gross, Neal, Harvard University, 20 Oxford St., Cambridge, Mass.
Gross, Richard Edmund, Sch. of Educ., Stanford University, Stanford, Calif.
Gross, Robert Dean, Sacramento State College, Sacramento, Calif.
Grossnickle, Foster E., State Teachers College, Jersey City, N.J.
Grotberg, Mrs. Edith H., Northern Illinois State College, De Kalb, Ill.
Grubbs, Hazel A., College of Educ., University of Nevada, Reno, Nev.
Gruber, Frederick C., University of Pennsylvania, Philadelphia, Pa.
Grundemann, Norma M., 3617 North 13th St., Milwaukee, Wis.
Gruner, Mrs. Mildred N., 16844 Beaverland Ave., Detroit, Mich.
Guess, George T., Principal, Picadome Elementary School, Lexington, Ky.
Guiles, R. E., Dean of Educ., Wisconsin State Col., Platteville, Wis.
Guinnane, Jane E., Newark State College, Union, N.J.
Gulick, Frank, Asst. Supt., Ventura Union H. S. Dist., Ventura, Calif.
Gullickson, Agnes, Iowa State Teachers College, Cedar Falls, Iowa
Gullo, Christopher J., 44 Ontario St., Rochester, N.Y.
Gulutsan, Metro, 53 Stadacona West, Moose Jaw, Sask., Canada
Gumm, Boyce L., Box 103, Athens, W.Va.
Gunn, Henry M., Supt. of Schools, Palo Alto, Calif.
Guss, Carolyn, Audio-visual Center, Indiana University, Bloomington, Ind.
Gussner, William S., Superintendent of Schools, Jamestown, N.D.
Guy, George Vance, Portland State College, Portland, Ore.
Guy, R. C., Principal, Senior High School, Hutchinson, Kan.
Gwynn, J. Minor, University of North Carolina, Chapel Hill, N.C.

Haaby, Lawrence O., Dept. of Educ., Univ. of Tennessee, Knoxville, Tenn.
Haas, Raoul R., Dir., No. Side Branch, Chicago Tchrs. Col., Chicago, Ill.
Haas, Richard J., Jr., 119 Stubbs Dr., Trotwood, Ohio
Habte, Aklilu, 2164 Tuller St., Columbus, Ohio
Hadley, S. Trevor, State Teachers College, Indiana, Pa.
Hagen, Elizabeth, Teachers College, Columbia University, New York, N.Y.
Hager, Walter E., Pres., Dist. of Columbia Tchrs. College, Washington, D.C.
Hagerman, Helen L., Col. of Educ., Univ. of Florida, Gainesville, Fla.
Haggerty, Helen Ruth, Adj. Gen'ls. Office, Dept. of the Army, Washington, D.C.
Haggerty, William J., Pres., State University College, New Paltz, N.Y.
Hagglund, Oliver C., Registrar, Gustavus Adolphus College, St. Peter, Minn.
Hagman, Harlan L., 1017 Kensington Rd., Grosse Pointe Park, Mich.
Hahn, Albert R., Clinical Psychologist, V. A. Hospital, Tucson, Ariz.
Hahn, Harry T., Dir., Reading Clinic, Oakland County, Pontiac, Mich.
Haight, Wilbur T., Guidance Counselor, Milford High School, Milford, Del.
Hailer, Harold H., San Jose State College, San Jose, Calif.
Haizlip, G. W., Principal, Hill Grade School, Marion, Kan.
Halberg, Anna D., District of Columbia Tchrs. College, Washington, D.C.
Halbert, Bernice, Eastern Texas Baptist College, Marshall, Tex.

Hale, R. Nelson, State Teachers College, Slippery Rock, Pa.
Haley, Elizabeth, 1938 Channing Ave., Palo Alto, Calif.
Haley, Gerald J., Principal, Medill Elem. School, Chicago, Ill.
Haley, Margaret T., State Department of Education, Richmond, Va.
Hall, Barbara C., 910 Normal Ave., Normal, Ill.
Hall, James A., Superintendent of Schools, Port Washington, N.Y.
Hall, M. E., Sch. of Music, Northern Texas State College, Denton, Tex.
Hall, Robert King, Trng. Dept., Arabian Am. Oil Co., Dhahran, Saudi Arabia
Hall, Ruel, County Superintendent of Schools, Kankakee, Ill.
Hall, Truman L., State University Teachers College, Geneseo, N.Y.
Hall, Viola, Principal, Seymour School, Syracuse, N.Y.
Hall, William Frank, Dir., Child Study Serv., Elem. Dist. 1, Phoenix, Ariz.
Hallenbeck, Edwin F., Com. to Study Higher Education, Providence, R.I.
Halleron, Mary, Principal, Public School 105, New York, N.Y.
Hallgrimson, Benedict T., Dean, Centralia Junior College, Centralia, Wash.
Halliwell, Joseph, St. John's University, Brooklyn, N.Y.
Hallman, George H., 520 N. Fairbanks Ave., Clarksville, Ind.
Halverson, Paul M., Sch. of Educ., Syracuse University, Syracuse, N.Y.
Hamalainen, Arthur E., Principal, Plandome Road School, Manhasset, L.I., N.Y.
Hamilton, Mrs. Charles W., Jr., Dept. of Educ., Creighton Univ., Omaha, Neb.
Hamilton, DeForest S., Superintendent, Sonoma County Schls., Santa Rosa, Calif.
Hamilton, Mrs. Dorothy W., Milford High School, Milford, Conn.
Hamilton, Homer H., Consultant, Dallas County Schools, Dallas, Tex.
Hamilton, Lester L., Box 5285, North Charleston, S.C.
Hamilton, Robert J., Principal, Julian Curtiss School, Greenwich, Conn.
Hamlin, Elizabeth, Elem. Supv., Memphis City Schools, Memphis, Tenn.
Hammack, Mary L., 540 Norway St., Salem, Ore.
Hammer, Eugene L., Chm., Dept. of Educ., Wilkes College, Wilkes-Barre, Pa.
Hammer, Irwin A., Western Washington College of Education, Bellingham, Wash.
Hammock, Robert C., University of Pennsylvania, Philadelphia, Pa.
Han l, Mrs. Doris Ruth, Elementary Supervisor, Public Schools, Merriam, Kan.
Hand, Harold C., Col. of Educ., University of Illinois, Urbana, Ill.
Handley, Owen B., Jr., Principal, Whittier School, LaJolla, Calif.
Hanigan, Levin B., Elem. Supv., Arlington County Schls., Arlington, Va.
Hanitchak, John Joseph, Sch. of Educ., Univ. of Kansas City, Kansas City, Mo.
Hankerson, M. R., Superintendent of Schools, Mapleton, Minn.
Hanna, Ben M., Dept. of Educ., Baylor University, Waco, Tex.
Hanna, Geneva, University of Texas, Austin, Tex.
Hanna, Paul R., Dept. of Educ., Stanford University, Stanford, Calif.
Hanscom, James H., 90-20 52nd Ave., Elmhurst, N.Y.
Hansen, Abner L., Florida Southern College, Lakeland, Fla.
Hansen, Carl W., Teachers College, University of Cincinnati, Cincinnati, Ohio
Hansen, G. G., County Superintendent of Schools, Aurora, Neb.
Hansen, Helge E., Dir., Audio-Visual Center, Public Schls., Dearborn, Mich.
Hansen, R. G., Asst. Supt., Elem. Educ., Public Schools, St. Paul, Minn.
Hanson, E. H., Superintendent of Schools, Rock Island, Ill.
Hanson, Gordon C., University of Wichita, Wichita, Kan.
Hanson, John W., Michigan State University, East Lansing, Mich.
Hanson, Robert J., Guidance Counselor, High School, Grosse Pointe, Mich.
Hanway, Hannah F., 8011 Eastern Ave., Silver Spring, Md.
Harbaugh, John W., Sch. of Educ., Univ. of Pittsburgh, Pittsburgh, Pa.
Harbert, Wilhelmina K., College of the Pacific, Stockton, Calif.
Harbin, Calvin E., Ft. Hays Kansas State College, Hays, Kan.
Harbo, L. S., Superintendent of Schools, Austin, Minn.
Hardesty, Cecil D., Supt. of County Schools, San Diego, Calif.
Hardy, B. B., Dean, Stillman College, Tuscaloosa, Ala.
Hardy, J. Garrick, Alabama State College, Montgomery, Ala.
Harmer, William R., 162 University Village, Minneapolis, Minn.
Harnack, Robert S., Sch. of Educ., University of Buffalo, Buffalo, N.Y.
* Harney, Julia C., 302 Pavonia Ave., Jersey City, N.J.
Harney, Paul J., University of San Francisco, San Francisco, Calif.

Harney, Thomas E., Superintendent of Schools, Dunkirk, N.Y.
Harnly, Paul W., Asst. Supt. in chg. Sec. Educ., Public Schools, Wichita, Kan.
Harper, George Leslie, Supv. Prin., Person County High School, Roxbard, N.C.
Harper, James R. W., Box 128, Baylor University Sta., Waco, Tex.
Harrington, Edna B., 901 Savannah Road, Lewes, Del.
Harrington, E. Ross, Asst. Supt., Taft City Elem. Sch. Dist., Taft, Calif.
Harrington, Edward, Box 267, Ozark, Ark.
Harrington, Frances J., 12½ Lafayette St., Attleboro, Mass.
Harrington, Johns H., Los Angeles City College, Los Angeles, Calif.
Harris, Albert J., Dir., Educ. Clinic, Queens College, Flushing, N.Y.
Harris, Albert T., Dir., Sch. of Educ., Virginia State Col., Petersburg, Va.
Harris, Mrs. Alta, Asst. Superintendent, Elem. Schools, San Francisco, Calif.
Harris, Charles H., Director, Austin High School, El Paso, Tex.
Harris, Chester W., Sch. of Educ., University of Wisconsin, Madison, Wis.
Harris, Claude C., Asst. Superintendent of Schools, Muskogee, Okla.
Harris, Dale B., Inst. of Child Welfare, Univ. of Minn., Minneapolis, Minn.
Harris, Florence R., Inst. of Child Develop., Univ. of Washington, Seattle, Wash.
Harris, Fred E., Baldwin-Wallace College, Berea, Ohio
Harris, John H., Superintendent of Schools, Des Moines, Iowa
Harris, Lewis E., Exec. Secy., Ohio Sch. Board Assn., Columbus, Ohio
Harris, Nelson H., Shaw University, Raleigh, N.C.
Harris, Raymond P., Dir., Sec. Educ., Public Schools, Mt. Vernon, N.Y.
Harris, Ruby Dean, Agric. Extension Serv., Univ. of California, Berkeley, Calif.
Harris, Theodore L., Sch. of Educ., Univ. of Wisconsin, Madison, Wis.
Harris, Wylie V., Supt., Westwood View School, Kansas City, Kan.
Harrison, George R., Head, Dept. of Elem. Educ., Bradley Univ., Peoria, Ill.
Harry, David P., Jr., Grad. Sch. Western Reserve University, Cleveland, Ohio
Harshman, Hardwick W., Community College, Muskegon, Mich.
Hartley, Joseph J., Superintendent of Schools, London, Ohio
Hartman, A. L., Principal, Edgemont and Watchung Schls., Upper Montclair, N.J.
Hartsell, Horace C., Audio-Viz. Center, Michigan State Univ., East Lansing,
    Mich.
Hartshorn, Herbert E., Dir., Elem. Educ., Edina-Morningside Sch., Minneapolis,
    Minn.
Hartshorn, William C., Supv., Music Educ., City Schools, Los Angeles, Calif.
Hartsig, Barbara, Curric. Consult., Orange County Schls., Santa Ana, Calif.
Hartstein, Jacob I., Dean, Grad. Sch., Long Island University, Brooklyn, N.Y.
Hartung, Helene, 2549 Decatur Ave., New York, N.Y.
Hartung, Maurice L., Dept. of Educ., University of Chicago, Chicago. Ill.
Hartvigsen, Elmer J., Superintendent, Granite School Dist., Salt Lake City, Utah
Harvey, A. D., Asst. Supt. of Schools, Kingsville, Tex.
Haskew, Laurence D., Col. of Educ., University of Texas, Austin, Tex.
Hasman, Richard H., 7 McAllister Dr., Saratoga Springs, N.Y.
Hass, C. Glen, 1920 N.E. Seventh Terrace, Gainesville, Fla.
Hassel, Carl W., Asst. Supt., Liverpool Central Schools, Liverpool, N.Y.
Haste, Maurice E., Tennessee Polytechnic Institute, Cookeville, Tenn.
Hatch, John S., Bus. Manager, Northwestern University, Evanston, Ill.
Hatch, Robert C., Supv., State Dept. of Education, Montgomery, Ala.
Hatchett. Ethel L., Dept. of Educ., Hardin-Simmons University, Abilene, Tex.
Hauer, William H., 106 Ninth Ave., Folsom, Delaware Co., Pa.
Hause, Enid M., Supv. of Elem. Education, Chula Vista, Calif.
Hauser, L. J., Superintendent of Schools, Dist. No. 96, Riverside, Ill.
Haven, Julia M., Sch. of Educ., University of Miami, Coral Gables, Fla.
Havighurst, Robert J.. Dept. of Educ.. University of Chicago, Chicago, Ill.
Hawes, Homer H., 1185 Mission St., S.E., Salem, Ore.
Hawes, Mrs. Opal R., Director of Education, Upland, Calif.
Hawley, Ray C., Superintendent of County Schools, Ottawa, Ill.
Haws, Nina, Principal, Sunnyside School, Wichita, Kan.
Hawthorne, Mark F., Superintendent of City Schools, Anderson, S.C.
Hay Charles K., Principal, John Bartram High School, Philadelphia, Pa.
Hayden, Alice H., Dir., Educ. Research, Univ. of Washington, Seattle, Wash.

Hayden, S. F., Principal, Houston School, El Paso, Tex.
Hayden, Velma D., State Teachers College, Trenton, N.Y.
Hayes, Dale K., Teachers Col., University of Nebraska, Lincoln, Neb.
Hayes, Denis A., Supt., Paterson Diocesan Schools, Paterson, N.J.
Hayes, Mrs. Betty M., 725 Hawthorne Dr., Tiburon, Calif.
Hayes, Paul C., 1024 North Wooster Ave., Dover, Ohio
Hays, Harry N., Supv. Principal, Philipsburg, Pa.
Hayward, W. George, Prin., Stockton and Eastern Schls., East Orange, N.J.
Hazen, Oliver M., Superintendent, District No. 403, Renton, Wash.
Hazleton, Edward W., Principal, Myra Bradwell School, Chicago, Ill.
Head, Marvin L., Kentucky State College, Frankfort, Ky.
Heagney, Genevieve, Principal, Lida Lee Tall School, Baltimore, Md.
Heald, James E., 1921 Lake St., Evanston, Ill.
Healy, Mary, 8459 Dante Ave., Chicago, Ill.
Heaps, Sarah B., 1364 E. Cavanaugh Rd., Okemos, Mich.
Heard, Charlsye Mae, 615 Jennette St., Memphis, Tenn.
Hearn, Arthur C., Sch. of Educ., University of Oregon, Eugene, Ore.
Hearn, Edell M., University of Tennessee, Martin Branch, Martin, Tenn.
Hearn, Edell M., 4412 High School St., Fountain City, Tenn.
Hearne, William P., Prin., Gage Park High School, Chicago, Ill.
Heavenridge, Glen G., Principal, Memorial Elem. School, Garden City, Mich.
Hebeler, Jean R., 805 South Crouse Ave., Syracuse, N.Y.
Hecht, Irvin Sulo, Prin., Girls High School, Brooklyn, N.Y.
Heck, Theodore, Head, Dept. of Educ., St. Meinrad Seminary, St. Meinrad, Ind.
Hecker, Izora, 1486 Woodrow, Wichita, Kan.
Hedden, Gerald W., Asst. Prin., South High School, Bakersfield, Calif.
Heding, Howard W., Oklahoma A. & M. College, Stillwater, Okla.
Heffernan, Helen, State Department of Education, Sacramento, Calif.
Heffernen, Martha M., State Department of Public Instruction, Dover, Del.
Hegman, M. Marian, 322 South Ave., Medina, N.Y.
Heise, Bryan, Eastern Illinois State College, Charleston, Ill.
Heisner, H. Fred, Superintendent of Schools, Redlands, Calif.
Heist, Paul A., Haviland Hall, University of California, Berkeley, Calif.
Hellman, Walter, Asst. Supt. of Schools, Fairfield, Conn.
Helmer, Robert D., Superintendent of Schools, Fredonia, N.Y.
*Helms, W. T., 1109 Roosevelt Ave., Richmond, Calif.
Hemington, Mrs. Mabel G., Chicago Teachers College, Chicago, Ill.
Hemingway, William C., Northern State Tchrs. College, Aberdeen, S.D.
Hemink, Lyde H., State University Teachers College, Cortland, N.Y.
Henderson, Algo W., Sch. of Educ., University of Michigan, Ann Arbor, Mich.
Henderson, Edward, Col. of Educ., University of Tennessee, Knoxville, Tenn.
Henderson, Kenneth B., Col. of Educ., University of Illinois, Urbana, Ill.
Henderson, Leon N., Head, Dept of Sec. Educ., Univ. of Florida, Gainesville, Fla.
Henderson, Richard Lee, Agnes Scott College, Decatur, Ga.
Hendrickson, Gordon, University of Cincinnati, Cincinnati, Ohio
Hengesbach, Alice R., Supv., Willoughby-Eastlake Schools, Willoughby, Ohio
Henion, Ethel S., 435 N. Central Ave., Ramsey, N.J.
Henle, R. J., Dean, Grad. Sch., St. Louis University, St. Louis, Mo.
Henry, George H., Alison Hall, Univ. of Delaware, Newark, Del.
* Henry, Nelson B., Dept. of Educ., University of Chicago, Chicago, Ill.
Henslee, U. D., Principal, W. B. Ray High School Corpus Christi, Tex.
Hensley, Iven Howe, Stephen F. Austin State College, Nacogdoches, Tex.
Henzlik, Frank E., Dean, Teachers College, Univ. of Nebraska, Lincoln, Neb.
Herbster, William E., 1419 Argonne Dr., North Chicago, Ill.
Herge, Henry C., Dean, Sch. of Educ., Rutgers University, New Brunswick, N.J.
Herr, Ross, District Supt., Chicago Public Schools, Chicago, Ill.
Herr, William A., 536 W. Maple St., Hazleton, Pa.
Herrick, Theral T., Dir. of Curric., Public Schools, Kalamazoo, Mich.
Herrick, Virgil E., Sch. of Educ., University of Wisconsin, Madison, Wis.
Herrick, Walter B., Steinmetz High School, Chicago, Ill.
Herrington, Mrs. Evelyn F., Texas Col. of Arts & Industries, Kingsville, Tex.

Herriott, M. E., Prin., Airport Junior High School, Los Angeles, Calif.
Herring, Helen, 512 Bellerive Blvd., St. Louis, Mo.
Herrmann, D. J., College of William and Mary, Williamsburg, Va.
Hertzberg, Oscar E., State Teachers College, Buffalo, N.Y.
* Hertzler, Silas, Goshen College, Goshen, Ind.
Hess, Clarke F., Marshall College, Huntington, W.Va.
Hess, Glenn C., Supv. Prin., Richland Township Public Schools, Johnstown, Pa.
Hess, Odean L., University of Utah, Salt Lake City, Utah
Hesse, Alexander N., 90 Salisbury Ave., Garden City, L.I., N.Y.
Hester, Kathleen B., Michigan State Normal College, Ypsilanti, Mich.
Hetenyi, Laszlo, University of Florida, Gainesville, Fla.
Hetzel, Walter L., Superintendent of Schools, Ames, Iowa
Heussman, John W., Concordia Seminary, Springfield, Ill.
Hibbs, M. Gregg, Jr., Supt., Red Bank Senior High School, Red Bank, N.J.
Hickerson, J. Allen, New Haven State Teachers College, New Haven, Conn.
Hickey, John M., Superintendent of Schools, Erie, Pa.
Hickey, Philip J., Superintendent of Inst., Public Schools, St. Louis, Mo.
Hicks, Mrs. Aline B., Booker T. Washington High School, Norfolk, Va.
Hicks, Samuel I., Superintendent of Schools, Pearl River, N.Y.
Hicks, Victor H., Dir., Stud. Tchg., East Central State College, Ada, Okla.
Hidy, Mrs. Elizabeth Willson, Box 287, Gila Bend, Ariz.
Hieronymus, A. N., Col. of Educ., State Univ. of Iowa, Iowa City, Iowa
Higgins, Mrs. Ardis, Santa Barbara Junior College, Santa Barbara, Calif.
Higgins, Harold H., Principal, Waco Elem. School, Wichita, Kan.
Hild, William C., Principal, Lander School, Cleveland, Ohio
Hildebrandt, William, 17 Barbara Drive, Syosset, N.Y.
Hilgard, Ernest R., Dept. of Psych., Stanford University, Stanford, Calif.
Hill, Alberta D., University of Connecticut, Storrs, Conn.
Hill, Arthur D., Indiana State Teachers College, Terre Haute, Ind.
Hill, Charles E., Dean, Rochester Junior College, Rochester, Minn.
Hill, Edwin H., 2628 Cathedral of Learning, Univ. of Pittsburgh, Pittsburgh, Pa.
Hill, Elizabeth F., Bur. of Child Study, Chicago Public Schools, Chicago, Ill.
Hill, George E., Ohio University, Athens, Ohio
Hill, Joseph K., Downstate Medical Center, Brooklyn, N.Y.
Hill, Katherine E., Sch. of Educ., New York University, New York, N.Y.
Hill, Mrs. Margaret Ford, 32 South Patterson Ave., Santa Barbara, Calif.
Hill, O. E., Superintendent of Schools, Cleveland Heights, Ohio
Hill, W. W., Head, Dept. of Educ., Berry College, Mt. Berry, Ga.
Hill, Walker H., Michigan State University, East Lansing, Mich.
Hill, Walter R., 321 Finkbine Park, Iowa City, Iowa
Hillerby, Ruth C., Principal, Robert Hill Lane School, Los Angeles, Calif.
Hillerich, Robert L., Principal, Elementary School, Glenview, Ill.
Hillier, Elizabeth C., Pennsylvania State University, University Park, Pa.
Hilton, Lewis B., Washington University, St. Louis, Mo.
Himler, Leonard E., 1225 Fair Oaks Pkwy., Ann Arbor, Mich.
Himmele, Irvin H., Asst. Superintendent of Schools, Buffalo, N.Y.
Hinds, Hazel Lee, 1354 West McKinley Ave., Pomona, Calif.
Hinds, Mrs. Lillian Ruth, Dir., Read. Clinic, Central High School, Phoenix, Ariz.
Hinkley, William C., Superintendent of Schools, Aurora, Colo.
Hinze, Richard H., Asst. Supt. of Schools, Phoenix, Ariz.
Hirschbeck, Loretta M., Principal, Murray Avenue School, Larchmont, N.Y.
Hites, Christopher, 302 Portola Rd., Portola Valley, Calif.
Hix, R. M., Principal, Crockett School, Abilene, Tex.
Hixon, Lawrence, Dir., Stud. Tchg., Cornell University, Ithaca, N.Y.
Hoag, Jack, 1863 Almaden Ave., San Jose, Calif.
Hobart, H. Bentley, Teachers College, Columbia University, New York, N.Y.
Hobbie, Katherine E., State Teachers College, Oneonta, N.Y.
Hochmuth, Joseph H., R.F.D. 2, Box 19, Dunbar, Pa.
Hodge, Mrs. Marian W., Asst. Supt., Whittier Union H. S. Dist., Whittier, Calif.
Hodge, Mrs. Rose M., P.O. Box 478, Grambling, La.
Hodgins, George W., Superintendent, Paramus High School, Paramus, N.J.

Hodgkins, George W., 1832 Biltmore St., N.W., Washington, D.C.
Hodgman, Crosby, Headmaster, Beaver County Day School, Chestnut Hill, Mass.
Hoeft, Norman R., Adm. Asst., Board of Education, Springfield, Mo.
Hoehn, H. Harry, 3051 Edwin Ave., Fort Lee, N.J.
Hoffman, Charles L., Principal, East High School, Waterloo, Iowa
Hogarth, Charles P., Pres., Mississippi State Col. for Women, Columbus, Miss.
Holbel, Rt. Rev. Msgr. Sylvester, Supt., Catholic Schools, Buffalo, N.Y.
Holdsworth, Willie, Div. of Ext., University of Texas, Austin, Tex.
Holland, Benjamin F., University of Texas, Austin, Tex.
Holland, Donald F., 11320 South Prairie Ave., Chicago, Ill.
Hollaway, Otto, Alabama Polytechnic Institute, Auburn, Ala.
Holliday, Jay N., P.O. Box 568, Canoga Park, Calif.
Hollingsworth, Henry T., Superintendent of Schools, Bloomfield, N.J.
Holloway, George E., Jr., University of Buffalo, Buffalo, N.Y.
Holloway, George L., 19462 Hatton St., Reseda, Calif.
Holman, W. Earl, Jackson High School, Jackson, Mich.
Holmblade, Amy Jean, Home Econ. Educ., Univ. of Minnesota, St. Paul, Minn.
Holmes, A. D., Emmanuel Missionary College, Berrien Springs, Mich.
Holmes, Chester W., Superintendent of Schools, Malden, Mass.
Holmes, Daniel L., Supervising Principal, North District, Braintree, Mass.
Holmes, Doris F., 88 Morningside Dr., New York, N.Y.
Holmes, Jack A., Sch. of Educ., University of California, Berkeley, Calif.
Holmes, Jay William, 350 Castlewood, Dayton, Ohio
Holmgren, Marvin E., State Teachers College, St. Cloud, Minn.
Holmquist, Emily, Indiana Univ. Sch. of Nursing, Indianapolis, Ind.
Holmstedt, Raleigh W., President, Indiana State Tchrs. Col., Terre Haute, Ind.
Holroyd, Flora E., Kansas State Teachers College, Pittsburg, Kan.
Holsinger, Clyde W., Manchester College, North Manchester, Ind.
Holstein, Louise V., 7130 South Union Ave., Chicago, Ill.
Holstein, Marion F., 7130 South Union Ave., Chicago, Ill.
Holston, M. J., 1128 Valley Dr., Borger, Tex.
Holt, Helen J., University of Toledo, Toledo, Ohio
Holtz, H. Arnold, Macalester College, St. Paul, Minn.
Holwerda, Raymond, Prin., Holland Christian High School, Holland, Mich.
Homburg, William, Supv. Prin., Union Grove High School, Union Grove, Wis.
Homer, Francis R., 4800 Conshohocken Ave., Philadelphia, Pa.
Homfeld, Melville J., Superintendent of Schools, Menlo Park, Calif.
Hood, Edwin Morris, 101 Old Mamaroneck Rd., White Plains, N.Y.
Hood, James R., 1405 Gattegno St., Ypsilanti, Mich.
Hooper, George J., Sidney Lanier and Eisenhower Schools, Tulsa, Okla.
Hoops, Robert C., Adm. Asst., Berkley Street School, New Milford, N.J.
Hooton, C. E., Principal, High School, Bessemer, Ala.
Hoover, Elmer B., Dept. of Educ., Elizabethtown College, Elizabethtown, Pa.
Hoover, Louis H., 152 New Hampshire South, Los Angeles, Calif.
Hoover, Norman K., Dept. of Agric. Educ., Pennsy. State Univ., University Park, Pa.
Hopkins, Monroe, Hannibal-LaGrange College, Hannibal, Mo.
Hopman, Anne B., 5935 Hohman Ave., Hammond, Ind.
Hopmann, Robert P., 2137 North 58th St., Lincoln, Neb.
Hoppes, William C., Northern Mich. College of Education, Marquette, Mich.
Hoppock, Anne, State Department of Education, Trenton, N.J.
Horn, Ernest, Prof. Emeritus of Educ., State Univ. of Iowa, Iowa City, Iowa
Horn, Ernest W., Dean, Seattle Pacific College, Seattle, Wash.
Horn, Thomas D., Dept. of Curric., University of Texas, Austin, Tex.
Horowitz, I. Lewis, Principal, Ben Franklin High School, Philadelphia, Pa.
Horsman, Ralph D., Superintendent, Mt. Lebanon Public Schools, Pittsburgh, Pa.
Horwich, Frances R., 910 Lake Shore Dr., Chicago, Ill.
Hoskins, G. C., Southern Methodist University, Dallas, Tex.
Hottenstein, Gerald G., Supt., Montgomery County Schls., Norristown, Pa.
Hough, Robert E., Principal, A. L. Johnson Regional High School, Clark, N.J.
Houk, Laura L., Principal, Jefferson Elementary School, Wichita, Kan.

Houlahan, F. J., Catholic University of America, Washington, D.C.
Houle, Cyril O., Dept. of Educ., University of Chicago, Chicago, Ill.
House, Ralph W., State Teachers College, Kirksville, Mo.
Houser, Winifred E., 107 North Collingsworth, El Paso, Tex.
Houston, James, Jr., Paterson State Teachers College, Paterson, N.J.
Houston, Mrs. Ruth R., Principal, Central School, Middlesex, N.J.
Houston, W. Robert, Principal, James Bowie School, Midland, Tex.
Hovet, Kenneth O., University of Maryland, College Park, Md.
Howard, Alexander H., Jr., Cen. Wash. College of Educ., Ellensburg, Wash.
Howard, Daniel D., Dean, Pestalozzi-Froebel Teachers College, Chicago, Ill.
Howard, Elizabeth Z., Dept. of Educ., University of Chicago, Chicago, Ill.
Howard, George, Chm., Dept. of Sch. Adm., Univ. of Alabama, University, Ala.
Howard, Glenn W., Queens College, Flushing, N.Y.
Howard, Homer, Philos. and Educ. Depts., Radford College, Radford, Va.
Howd, M. Curtis, Principal, Burris Lab. School, Muncie, Ind.
Howe, Henry W., Dept. of History and Pol. Sci., Alma College, Alma, Mich.
Howe, Joseph W., Superintendent of Schools, Burlington, N.J.
Howe, Kenneth E., Dean, Sch. of Educ., Woman's Col., Univ. of N.C., Greens-
    boro, N.C.
Howe, Walter A., Secy., Dept. of Educ., Cen. Union Conf. of S.D.A., Lincoln,
    Neb.
Howell, Miriam, Emory University, Emory University, Ga.
Howk, Charles D., Principal, Willard School, Pasadena, Calif.
Hoyle, Dorothy, Dept. of Educ., Temple University, Philadelphia, Pa.
Hoyt, Cyril J., Bur. of Educ. Res., Univ. of Minnesota, Minneapolis, Minn.
Hubbard, Mary K., 2 Longfellow Dr., New Hartford, N.Y.
Huber, Frederick, Dir., Palo Verde College, Blythe, Calif.
Hubert, Frank W. R., Superintendent of Schools, Orange, Tex.
Huckaby, Arthur L., Asst. Prin., Booker T. Washington Schl., Houston, Tex.
Hucksoll, William J., 3510 Woodlea Ave., Baltimore, Md.
Hudelson, Earl, Col. of Educ., West Virginia Univ., Morgantown, W.Va.
Hudson, Margaret, George Peabody College, Nashville, Tenn.
Hudson, Ruth, State Department of Education, Columbus, Ohio
Huebner, Mildred H., Western Reserve University, Cleveland, Ohio
Huelsman, Charles B., Jr., 120 East Chestnut St., Oxford, Ohio
Huesers, Donald J., Superintendent of Schools, Medford, Minn.
Hughes, McDonald, Principal, Industrial High School, Tuscaloosa, Ala.
Hughes, Vergil H., Div. of Tchr. Educ., San Jose State College, San Jose, Calif.
Hughson, Arthur, 470 Ocean Ave., Brooklyn, N.Y.
Hull, Marion, Dept. of Educ., Northern Illinois University, DeKalb, Ill.
Hullfish, H. Gordon, Sch. of Educ., Ohio State University, Columbus, Ohio
Hult, Esther, Iowa State Teachers College, Cedar Falls, Iowa
Hultgren, Robert B., Principal, Culbertson School, Joliet. Ill.
Humelsine, Martha, Roberts Wesleyan College, North Chili, N.Y.
Humphrey, Charles, 6001 Berkeley Dr., Berkeley, Mo.
Hunt, Mrs. Anne Brown, Elem. Supv., Mahoning County Schools, Youngstown,
    Ohio
Hunt, Dorothy D., Supv., Elem. Educ., Norclay School, North Kansas City, Mo.
Hunt, Herold C., Grad. Sch. of Educ., Harvard University, Cambridge, Mass.
Hunt, Lyman C., Jr., Pennsylvania State University, University Park, Pa.
Hunt, William A., Dept. of Psych., Northwestern University, Evanston, Ill.
Hunter, Harry W., P.O. Box 597, Ocala, Fla.
Hunter, James J., Jr., San Diego State College, San Diego, Calif.
Hunter, Lavinia, Western Kentucky State College, Bowling Green, Ky.
Hunter, Robert W., Grambling College, Grambling, La.
Hunter, William A., Sch. of Educ., Tuskegee Institute, Tuskegee, Ala.
* Huntington, Albert H., 736 Fairview Ave., Webster Groves, Mo.
Huntington, Elizabeth A., 45 Morris Ave., Springfield, N.J.
Hurd, Blair E., 4900 Heatherdale Lane, Carmichael, Calif.
Hurd, Paul DeH., Sch. of Educ., Stanford University, Stanford, Calif.
Hurdle, W.W., 122 Lincoln Court, Raleigh, N.C.

Hurlburt, Allan S., Dept. of Educ., Duke University, Durham, N.C.
Hurley, Mrs. W. C., Tennessee A. & I. State University, Nashville, Tenn.
Huss, Francis G., Dir., Lansdale Vocational School, Lansdale, Pa.
Husted, Inez M., Dir., Special Educ., Luzerne County, Wilkes-Barre, Pa.
Hutaff, Lucile W., Bowman Gray School of Medicine, Winston-Salem, N.C.
Hutchison, James M., 4231 West Fifty-ninth St., Los Angeles, Calif.
Hutson, P. W., University of Pittsburgh, Pittsburgh, Pa.
Hutzler, Damon, Supv. Prin., Junior-Senior High School, Fort Myers, Fla.
Hyde, Edith I., Phys. Educ. Dept., Univ. of California, Los Angeles, Calif.

Imes, Orley B., 3985 La Cresenta Rd., El Sobrante, Calif.
Imhoff, Myrtle M., Dept. of Educ., Long Beach State College, Long Beach, Calif.
Inabnit, Darrell James, 32 Sherman Terrace, Madison, Wis.
Ingalls, K. Elizabeth, State Teachers College, Jersey City, N.J.
Ingebritson, Kasper I., Humboldt State College, Arcata, Calif.
Ingersoll, George S., El Camino College, El Camino, Calif.
Ingerson, Gordon H., Dir., Henry Abbott Tech. School, Danbury, Conn.
Ingham, Roy J., University College, Syracuse University, Syracuse, N.Y.
Ingles, Edwin T., 804 Hackberry St., Modesto, Calif.
Ingram, Mrs. Mildred, Danville High School, Danville, Ill.
Ingrelli, Anthony V., University of Wisconsin-Milwaukee, Milwaukee, Wis.
Inlow, Gail M., Sch. of Educ., Northwestern University, Evanston, Ill.
Inskeep, James E., Jr., University of Minnesota, Minneapolis, Minn.
Ireland, Dwight B., Superintendent of Schools, Birmingham, Mich.
Ireland, Everett W., Superintendent of Schools, Somerville, Mass.
Ireland, Robert S., Superintendent of Schools, Concord, Mass.
Irish, Elizabeth, Univ. of Calif., Santa Barbara College, Goleta, Calif.
Irsfeld, H. L., Principal, Lamar Elementary School, Mineral Wells, Tex.
Irving, J. Lee, Bluefield State College, Bluefield, W.Va.
Irwin, Alice M., Supv., Dept. of Spec. Classes, Public Schls., New Bedford, Mass.
Irwin, Forrest A., Fairleigh Dickinson University, Rutherford, N.J.
Isaacs, Ann F., 409 Clinton Spring Ave., Cincinnati, Ohio
Isenberg, Robert M., Asst. Dir., Div. of Rural Service, N.E.A., Washington, D.C.
Isenogle, Laird, Principal, Avondale School, Canton, Ohio
Isley, Thurston, William Jewell College, Liberty, Mo.
Israel, Saul, Principal, Haaren High School, New York, N.Y.
Iversen, Mrs. Dorothy, Nebraska State Teachers College, Peru, Neb.
Iverson, Maurice T., UNC OEC(TC-AV), APO 301, San Francisco, Calif.
Ivie, Claud, Asst. Superintendent, Public Schools, Meridian, Miss.
Ivins, George H., Dept. of Educ., Roosevelt University, Chicago, Ill.
Ivok, Leo, Asst. Superintendent, Public Schools, Worcester, Mass.

Jackson, Frank M., Dir., Teacher Retirement System, Austin, Tex.
Jackson, Lowell M., Dir., Inf. and Educ. Sec., APO 74, c/o P.M., San Francisco, Calif.
Jacobs, Grace H., Coppin State Teachers College, Baltimore, Md.
Jacobs, Mrs. Lucy T., Teaching Principal, Bandon Heights, Bandon, Ore.
Jacobs, Ralph L., Dept. of Educ., Univ. of Cincinnati, Cincinnati, Ohio
Jacobs, Robert, Educ. Div., International Cooperation Adm., Washington, D.C.
Jacobson, George H., School of Music, Yale University, New Haven, Conn.
Jaeger, Alan Warren, P.O. Box 385, Pixley, Calif.
Jaeger, Herman F., Superintendent of Schools, Pasco, Wash.
James, Mrs. Bernice O., Central High School, Galveston, Tex.
James, Carl A., Superintendent of Schools, Emporia, Kan.
James, Newton Elder, 3537 California Ave., N.E., Albuquerque, N.M.
James, Preston E., Chm., Dept. of Geog., Syracuse University, Syracuse, N.Y.
James, Virginia White, University of Alabama, University, Ala.
James, W. Raymond, State Teachers College, Plattsburgh, N.Y.
Jamrich, John X., 1024 Sparrow, Lansing, Mich.
Jansen, William, Superintendent, New York City Schools, New York, N.Y.
Jansic, Anthony F., Educ. Clinic, City College of New York, New York, N.Y.

Jardine, Alex, 228 South St. Joseph St., South Bend, Ind.
Jarman. B. H., George Washington University, Washington, D.C.
Jarvis, Galen, Principal, South Elem. School, Des Plaines, Ill.
Jayne, Clarence D., University of Wyoming, Laramie, Wyo.
Jedrzejewski, Clement, St. Francis College, Brooklyn, N.Y.
Jehnek, James J., Sch. of Educ., Arizona State College, Tempe. Ariz.
Jenkins, David S., Superintendent, Anne Arundel County Schools, Annapolis, Md.
Jenkins, Earl J., Superintendent, Three Rivers School, North Bend, Ohio
Jenkins, John F., Portland State College, Portland, Ore.
Jenkins, Martin D., President, Morgan State College, Baltimore, Md.
Jenkins, Robert E., Superintendent of Schools, Ridgewood, N.J.
Jenkins, T. C., Spanish Dept., Univ. of Corpus Christi, Corpus Christi, Tex.
Jenkins, William A., University of Wisconsin-Milwaukee, Milwaukee, Wis.
Jensen, Gale E., 3055 Lakewood Dr., Ann Arbor, Mich.
Jensen, Grant W., South High School, Bakersfield, Calif.
Jensen, Harry T., San Jose State College, San Jose, Calif.
Jensen, Louis B., 12 Hamilton Place, Garden City. N.Y.
Jenson, T. J., Ohio State University, Columbus, Ohio
Jerrems, Raymond L., 9741 South 54th Ave., Oak Lawn, Ill.
Jewell, Marc E., 5291 Morning Sun Road, Oxford, Ohio
Jex. Frank B., Dept. of Educ. Psych., Univ. of Utah, Salt Lake City, Utah
Jochsberger, Tzipora H., 46 West 86th St., New York, N.Y.
Johns, Edward B., Dept. of Phys. Educ., Univ. of California, Los Angeles, Calif.
Johns, O. D., Superintendent of Schools, Seminole, Okla.
Johnson, B. Lamar. Sch. of Educ., Univ. of California, Los Angeles, Calif.
Johnson, Carl E., 420 N. Elmhurst Ave., Mt. Prospect. Ill.
Johnson, Charles E., Col. of Educ., University of Illinois, Urbana, Ill.
Johnson, Charles E., 722 South Van Ness St., San Francisco, Calif.
Johnson, Charles W.. Teachers College, Univ. of Cincinnati, Cincinnati, Ohio
Johnson, Dale C., West Union, Iowa
Johnson, Dorothy C., 2862 Gonzaga Dr., Richmond, Calif.
Johnson, Douglas Andrew, 14568 Ashton Rd., Detroit, Mich.
Johnson, Eleanor M., American Education Publications, Middletown, Conn.
Johnson, Elizabeth, Western Michigan University, Kalamazoo, Mich.
Johnson, Ellen V., State Teachers College, Minot, N.D.
Johnson, Eric H., Illinois State Normal University, Normal, Ill.
Johnson, Evelyn Lawlah, Soc. Sci. Dept., North Carolina College, Durham, N.C.
Johnson, G. Orville, Sch. of Educ., Syracuse University, Syracuse. N.Y.
Johnson, Gladys Viola, 3229 Fourth Ave., South, Great Falls, Mont.
Johnson, Harry C., Duluth Branch, Univ. of Minnesota, Duluth, Minn.
Johnson, Harry O., Supt., Livonia Twp. Sch. Dist., 11411 Ingram, Livonia, Mich.
Johnson, J. B., Superintendent of Schools, Alton, Ill.
Johnson, Leighton H., San Francisco State College, San Francisco, Calif.
Johnson, Lois V.. Los Angeles State College. Los Angeles, Calif.
Johnson, Louis H., Principal, Elementary School, Seymour, Tex.
Johnson, Margaret E., Interm. Grade Supv., Alpine School Dist., American Fork,
    Utah
Johnson, Mrs. Marjorie S., Supv., Read. Clinic, Lab. Sch., Philadelphia, Pa.
Johnson, Mauritz, Jr., New York State College for Teachers, Albany, N.Y.
Johnson, Palmer O., Col. of Educ., Univ. of Minnesota, Minneapolis, Minn.
Johnson, Philip G., 3 Stone Hall, Cornell University, Ithaca, N.Y.
Johnson, Ray W., Supt., Riverside County Schools. Riverside, Calif.
Johnson, Robert K., 913 Nelbar St., Middletown. Ohio
Johnson, Robert L., 513 Gascoigne Dr., Waukesha, Wis.
Johnson. Roberta A. E.. Dept. of Educ.. Univ. of Rochester. Rochester, N.Y.
* Johnson, Roy Ivan, 2333 Southwest Eighth Dr., Gainesville, Fla.
Johnson, Theodore D., 8914 Lamon. Skokie, Ill.
Johnson, W. L. D., Jr., Principal, B. H. Grimes Elem. School, Houston, Tex.
Johnson, Walter C., Jr., Alderson-Boarddus College, Philippi, W. Va.
Johnson, Walter F., Michigan State University, East Lansing, Mich.
Johnston, Aaron Montgomery, University of Tennessee, Knoxville, Tenn.

Johnston, Edgar G., Wayne University, Detroit, Mich.
Johnston, Eula A., Elem. Supv., Hamilton County Schls., Signal Mountain, Tenn.
Johnston, Joseph M., Assoc. Superintendent, Public Schools, Chapel Hill, N.C.
Johnston, Lillian B., 538 West Vernon Ave., Phoenix, Ariz.
Johnston, Mildred R., State Teachers College, Jacksonville, Ala.
Johnston, Ruth V., 125 Owre Hall, Univ. of Minnesota, Minneapolis, Minn.
Joll, Leonard W., State Department of Education, Hartford, Conn.
Jonas, Richard O., University of Houston, Houston, Tex.
Jonas, Russell E., President, Black Hills Teachers College, Spearfish, S.D.
Jones, A. Quinn, 1013 N.W. Seventh Ave., Gainesville, Fla.
Jones, Aaron E., President, Carbon College, Price, Utah
* Jones, Arthur J., University of Pennsylvania, Philadelphia, Pa.
Jones, C. E., Superintendent, Public Schools, Beloit, Wis.
Jones, C. H., Jr., Superintendent of Schools, Nevada, Mo.
Jones, Charles L., Principal, Gullett School, Austin, Tex.
Jones, Dilys M., 316 South Fayette St., Shippensburg, Pa.
Jones, Dixie M., Union University, Jackson, Tenn.
Jones, Douglas R., George Peabody College, Nashville, Tenn.
* Jones, Mrs. Elizabeth P., 422 Osceola St., Tallahassee, Fla.
Jones, Elvet Glyn, Western Wash. College of Education, Bellingham, Wash.
Jones, Eulalia B., Box 310, Cedar City, Utah
Jones, Harold E., Dir., Inst. of Child Wel., Univ. of Calif., Berkeley, Calif.
Jones, Howard R., School of Educ., Univ. of Michigan, Ann Arbor, Mich.
Jones, James Joseph, Sch. of Educ., Univ. of Virginia, Charlottesville, Va.
Jones, Kenneth G., Oswego State Teachers College, Oswego, N.Y.
Jones, Lee P., Principal, Loyall High School, Harlan, Ky.
Jones, Lloyd M., State Univ. College for Teachers, Buffalo, N.Y.
Jones, Olwen M., Hudson House, Ardsley-on-Hudson, N.Y.
Jones, Richard N., 6 Wolf Ave., Reistertown, Md.
Jones, Ronald D., Dean, Malone College, Canton, Ohio
Jones, T. B., President, Harbison Junior College, Irmo, S.C.
Jones, Vernon, Clark University, Worcester, Mass.
Jones, Vyron Lloyd, Principal, Fontanet High School, Fontanet, Ind.
Jones, Wendell P., Educ. Policies Commission, Washington, D.C.
Jonsson, Harold A., San Francisco State College, San Francisco, Calif.
Jordan, A. B., Central High School, St. Louis, Mo.
Jordan, Floyd, Co-ord. of Atlanta Area Tchr. Educ. Serv., Emory Univ., Ga.
Jordan, Howard, Jr., Dean, Sch. of Educ., So. Car. State Col., Orangeburg, S.C.
Jordan, Lawrence V., West Virginia State College, Institute, W.Va.
Jordan, Marion, Superintendent of Schools, Palatine, Ill.
Jorgensen, Elin K., Music Dept., University of Kansas, Lawrence, Kan.
Joslyn, Alvin L., Asst. Principal, High School, Ypsilanti, Mich.
Journey-McCarty, Hurshelene, Frank Phillips College, Borger, Tex.
Joyce, Bruce R., Wayne State University, Detroit, Mich.
Judenfriend, Harold, 23 Pleasant St., Colchester, Conn.
Juergenson, Elwood M., Dept. of Educ., Univ. of California, Davis, Calif.
Julstrom, Eva, 7647 Colfax Ave., Chicago, Ill.
Junge, Charlotte W., College of Educ., Wayne University, Detroit, Mich.
Junge, Ruby M., Michigan State College, East Lansing, Mich.
Justin, John R., 415 Townsend Rd., Newark, Del.
Justman, Joseph, Bur. of Research, Board of Educ., Brooklyn, N.Y.
Juvancic, William A., 1800 Hull Ave., Westchester, Ill.

Kaar, Mrs. Galeta M., Principal, Peabody Elementary School, Chicago, Ill.
Kaback, Goldie Ruth, Sch. of Educ., City College, New York, N.Y.
Kaiser, L. I., 1616 Queen Ave. No., Minneapolis, Minn.
Kalin, E. S., Dir., Isidore Newman School, New Orleans, La.
Kallen, H. M., 66 West Twelfth St., New York, N.Y.
Kalmon, Mrs. Sadie K., Principal, Haugan School, Chicago, Ill.
Kalupa, Mrs. Marie, 2527 South Thirteenth St., Milwaukee, Wis.
Kandyba, Bernard S., 8703 Nashville Ave., Oak Lawn, Ill.

Kantor, Bernard R., University of Southern California, Los Angeles, Calif.
Kaplan, Louis, Univ. Col., University of Southern Calif., Los Angeles, Calif.
Kara, Stephanie A., 14305 Blaine Ave., Posen, Ill.
Karason, Halldor C., Western Washington College of Education, Bellingham, Wash.
Karlin, Robert, Sch. of Educ., New York University, New York, N.Y.
Karnes, M. Ray, Col. of Educ., University of Illinois, Urbana, Ill.
Karrel, Oscar, Lord & Taylor, Fifth Ave., New York, N.Y.
Kasdon, Lawrence, Department of Public Instruction, Honolulu, Hawaii.
Kata, Joseph J., Principal, Red Bank Valley High School, New Bethlehem, Pa.
Katz, Joseph, Faculty of Educ., Univ. of British Columbia, Vancouver, B.C.
Kauffman, Merle M., Supt., Waukegan Twp. High School, Waukegan, Ill.
Kaump, Gladys L., Dir., Elem. Educ., Public Schools, Dodge City, Kan.
Kauth, William M., Dept. of Math., Fordson High School, Dearborn, Mich.
Kavanaugh, J. Keith, 29 Grust St., Battle Creek, Mich.
Kawin, Ethel, Plaisance Hotel, Chicago, Ill.
Kearl, Jennie W., Dir., Elem. Educ., State Dept. of Educ., Salt Lake City, Utah
Kearney, George G., Route 2, Box 221A, Morgan Hill, Calif.
Kearney, Leo I., Fordham University, New York, N.Y.
Kearney, Nolan C., Asst. Supt., Res. & Curric., Dept. of Educa., St. Paul, Minn.
Keaveny, Rt. Rev. Msgr., T. Leo, Supt., Diocese of St. Cloud, St. Cloud, Minn.
Keck, Winston B., Curric. Coord., School Dept., New Britain, Conn.
Keehn, Haden B., Jr., Principal, Sunnyside School, Burlington, Iowa
Keenan, Robert C., Supt., District 11, Chicago Public Schls., Chicago, Ill.
Kegler, John, Supv., Acad. Educ., City Schools, Los Angeles, Calif.
Keith Daun E., New York University Camp, Sloatsburg, N.Y.
* Keller, Franklin J., 6 East 82nd St., New York, N.Y.
Keller, Fred L., Tarkio College, Tarkio, Mo.
Keller, Raymond E., 1421 Plum St., Iowa City, Iowa
Keller, Robert J., Educ. Research Office, Univ. of Minn., Minneapolis, Minn.
Kelley, Beaman, Dir. of Inst., Harnett County Schools, Lillington, N.C.
Kelley, Claude, Col. of Educ., University of Oklahoma, Norman, Okla.
Kelley, Dorothy G., Indiana University, Bloomington, Ind.
Kelley, Mrs. Dorothy J., Principal, Willard School, Chicago, Ill.
Kelley, Janet A., Dept. of Educ., City College of New York, New York, N.Y.
Kelley, Victor H., University of Arizona, Tucson, Ariz.
Kelley, William F., Dean, Col. of Arts and Sci., Creighton Univ., Omaha, Neb.
Kellogg, E. G., Supt. of Schools, West Allis, Wis.
Kelly, Dean, 149 Parkwood Dr., Avon Lake, Ohio
Kelly, Edward J., Colorado State College of Education, Greeley, Colo.
Kelly, Mrs. Erma P., Principal, Capital Hill School, Little Rock, Ark.
Kelly, Warde, 2425 Ojibway Trail, Fort Wayne, Ind.
Kelner, Bernard G., 1804 Ashurst Rd., Philadelphia, Pa.
Kelsey, Roger R., Registrar, Kansas State Teachers College, Emporia, Kan.
Kemp, Edward L., Sch. of Educ., New York University, New York, N.Y.
Kennard, Andrew J., Texas State University, Houston, Tex.
Kentner, Harold M., Rochester Inst. of Technology, Rochester, N.Y.
Keppel, Francis, Dean, Grad. Sch. of Educ., Harvard University, Cambridge, Mass.
Kerbow, A. L., University of Houston, Houston, Tex.
Kerr, Everett F., Superintendent of Elem. Schools, Blue Island, Ill.
Kerr, Willard E., Dir. of Curric., Public Schools, Tyrone, Pa.
Kersh, Bert Y., Sch. of Educ., University of Oregon, Eugene, Ore.
Keshian, Jerry G., 10 Kilburn Rd., Garden City, L.I., N.Y.
Kesselring, Ralph, Principal, Methodist School, Sibu, Sarawak, Borneo
Ketcham, M. Kathleen, 201 Broad St., Tonawanda, N.Y.
Kettelkamp, Gilbert C., College of Educ., Univ. of Illinois, Urbana, Ill.
Khleif, Bahjab B., 827 West 39th St., Kansas City, Mo.
Kiah, Calvin L., Chm., Dept. of Educ., Savannah State College, Savannah, Ga.
Kidder, William W., 216 Walton Ave., South Orange, N.J.
Kiely, Margaret, Dean, Queens College, Flushing, N.Y.
Kies, Michael S., Supt. of County Schools, Milwaukee, Wis.

Kilbourn, Robert W., 4902 Argyle St., Dearborn, Mich.
Kilgus, Mrs. Helen J., 181 Audubon Dr., Bowling Green, Ky.
* Kilpatrick, William H., Teachers College, Columbia University, New York, N.Y.
Kincheloe, James B., Superintendent, Fayette Co. Schls., Lexington, Ky.
Kindred, Leslie W., Temple University, Philadelphia, Pa.
King, Mrs. A. W., Kimball, W. Va.
King, John R., East Bakersfield High School, Bakersfield, Calif.
King, Kent H., 103 Thayer Ave., Mankato, Minn.
King, Lloyd H., College of the Pacific, Stockton, Calif.
King, Lloyd W., Exec. Secy., Amer. Textbook Publ. Inst., New York, N.Y.
King, Thomas C., Dean, Col. of Educ. & Nurs., Univ. of Vermont, Burlington, Vt.
Kingdon, Frederick H., Kent State University, Kent, Ohio
Kinsella, Bernard W., Principal, Allen Creek School, Rochester, N.Y.
Kinsella, John J., Sch. of Educ., New York University, New York, N.Y.
Kinsellar, Frances M., Rye St., Broad Brook, Conn.
Kinsman, Kephas Albert, Long Beach State Col., Long Beach, Calif.
Kinzer, John R., 829 Eleventh St., Santa Monica, Calif.
Kircher, Everett J., Dept. of Educ., Ohio State University, Columbus, Ohio
Kirk, Samuel A., Col. of Educ., University of Illinois, Urbana, Ill.
Kirk, Mrs. Wanda M., Box 15, Rosamond, Calif.
Kirkland, J. Bryant, Sch. of Educ., North Carolina State College, Raleigh, N.C.
Kirkpatrick, J. E., Black Hills Teachers College, Spearfish, S.D.
Kirkpatrick, Lawrence A., Atherton Hall, Union Grove, Wis.
Kirkwood, Mrs. Gertrude S., Asst. Prin., McKinstry School, Detroit, Mich.
Kitch, Donald E., 721 Capitol Ave., Sacramento, Calif.
Klaus, Catherine, Box 268, West Union, Iowa
Klausmeier, Herbert J., School of Educ., Univ. of Wis., Madison, Wis.
Kleinmann, Jack H., 514 West 122nd St., New York, N.Y.
Kleinpell, E. H., President, Wisconsin State College, River Falls, Wis.
Klevan, Albert, 9218 California St., Livonia, Mich.
Kleyensteuber, Carl J., University of Wisconsin-Milwaukee, Milwaukee, Wis.
Kline, Frances F., Fordham University, New York, N.Y.
Klopfer, Leopold E., Regional School Dist. No. 8, Hebron, Conn.
Klopp, Donald S., Principal, Franklin School, East Orange, N.J.
Kluwe, Mary Jean, Supv., Language Educ. Dept., Public Schools, Detroit, Mich.
Knapp, Royce H., Dir., Educ. Res., F. E. Compton & Co., Chicago, Ill.
Knight, George S., Superintendent of Schools, Valley Park, Mo.
Knight, R. W., 3909 East Fifth Pl., Tulsa, Okla.
Knight, Reginald R., 4338 Heather Rd., Long Beach, Calif.
Knox, William F., Central Missouri State Teachers College, Warrensburg, Mo.
Knuti, Leo L., Montana State College, Bozeman, Mont.
Koch, H. C., University of Michigan, Ann Arbor, Mich.
Koch, Norman Edward, 510 North Kent, Kennewick, Wash.
Koch, Raymond H., Superintendent, Columbia High School, Columbia, Pa.
Koch, Wayne S., University of New Hampshire, Durham, N.H.
Koehler, Earl L., Principal, Walsh School, Chicago, Ill.
Koehring, Dorothy, Iowa State Teachers College, Cedar Falls, Iowa
Koeneman, Mrs. Adele S., 100 East Mountain View Ave., Barstow, Calif.
Koenig, Adolph J., Temple University, Philadelphia, Pa.
Koerber, Walter F., Scarborough Board of Education, Toronto, Ont., Canada
Koffman, Gladstone, 1610 Walnut St., Hopkinsville, Ky.
Kohs, Samuel C., 620 Plymouth Way, Burlingame, Calif.
Konen, Robert C., 1537 Monroe Ave., River Forest, Ill.
Kontos, George, Jr., Principal, Eastgate Elem. School, Bellevue, Wash.
Koos, Leonard V., Route 2, Newago, Mich.
Kopel, David, Chicago Teachers College, Chicago, Ill.
Kops, Walter E., Montclair State Teachers College, Upper Montclair, N.J.
Korey, Harold, Principal, Washington Irving School, Chicago, Ill.
Korntheuer, Gerhard A., St. Johns College, Winfield, Kan.
Kough, Blanchford, Principal, Hayes School, Chicago, Ill.
Koy, Arnold C., Principal, Little Fort School, Waukegan, Ill.

Kozak, Andrew V., Pennsylvania State University, University Park, Pa.
Kraeft, Walter O., Concordia Teachers College, River Forest, Ill.
Kraft, Milton Edward, Earlham College, Richmond, Ind.
Krathwohl, David R., Bur. of Educ. Res., Mich. State Univ., East Lansing, Mich.
Kraus, Howard F., Principal, Louis Barrett School, Belmont, Calif.
Kraus, Philip E., 215 West 78th St., New York, N.Y.
Krautle, Hilda E., 3599 Werk Road, Cincinnati, Ohio
Kravetz, Nathan, USOM to Peru, c/o U.S. Embassy, Lima, Peru
Kravetz, Sol., 1357½ South Cloverdale Ave., Los Angeles, Calif.
Krawitz, Harris, 1039 Hollywood Ave., Chicago, Ill.
Kreitlow, Burton W., Dept. of Educ., Univ. of Wisconsin, Madison, Wis.
Kress, Roy A., Sch. of Educ., Syracuse University, Syracuse, N.Y.
Krippner, Stanley, R.R. 1, Fort Atkinson, Wis.
Kroenke, Richard G., Dir., Elem. Educ., Valparaiso University, Valparaiso, Ind.
Kromann, Inga, University of Minnesota, Minneapolis, Minn.
Krueger, Lawrence, Supt., Pittsfield Sch. Dist. No. 9, Ann Arbor, Mich.
Krug, Edward, Sch. of Educ., University of Wisconsin, Madison, Wis.
Krug, Helen Esther, Defiance College, Defiance, Ohio
Kubik, Edmund J., Principal, Owen School, Chicago, Ill.
Kuehner, Kenneth G., Coker College, Hartsville, S.C.
Kugler, Mrs. Ida C., 7 South Sixth St., Minneapolis, Minn.
Kuhnen, Mrs. Mildred, 2106 Park Ave., Chico, Calif.
Kulieke, Alvin L., 801 West Foundry Rd., Mt. Prospect, Ill.
Kullman, N. E., Jr., 153 Murray Ave., Delmar, N.Y.
Kulp, Claude L., Rand Hall, Cornell University, Ithaca, N. Y.
Kumpf, Carl H., Principal, Mt. Vernon and Lincoln Schls., Newark, N.J.
Kurtz, Alton R., Head, Dept. of Educ., Defiance College, Defiance, Ohio
Kurtz, John J., Inst. for Child Study, Univ. of Maryland, College Park, Md.
Kusmik, Cornell J., Concordia Teachers College, River Forest, Ill.
Kutz, Frederick B., Principal, Newark High School, Newark, Del.
Kutz, R. M., Hanover College, Hanover, Ind.
Kvaraceus, W. C., Sch. of Educ., Boston University, Boston, Mass.
Kyle, C. J. M., Div. Supt. of Schools, Orange County, Orange, Va.
Kyle, Helen F., Col. of Educ., Univ. of Colorado, Boulder, Colo.
Kyme, George H., 304 Haviland Hall, University of California, Berkeley, Calif.
Kyte, George C., Sch. of Educ., University of California, Berkeley, Calif.

LaBlonde, Jeanne, College of St. Teresa, Winona, Minn.
LaBrant, Lou, 14 Chatham Rd., New Orleans, La.
Lacey, Maura Pat., 6835 South Winchester Ave., Chicago, Ill.
Lacy, Susan M., Principal, Whitworth School, Spokane, Wash.
Lafarelle, G. G., Principal, Morehead School, El Paso, Tex.
Lafferty, H. M., East Texas State Teachers College, Commerce, Tex.
LaForce, Charles L., Principal, Pope Elem. School, Chicago, Ill.
Laidlaw, John, President, Laidlaw Brothers, River Forest, Ill.
Laird, Byron F., Indiana University, Jeffersonville, Ind.
Laird, Dorothy S., Col. of Educ., University of Florida, Gainesville, Fla.
Lake, Barbara, Sch. of Educ., Fordham University, New York, N. Y.
Laky, Rev. John J., Supt., Cathedral High School, St. Cloud, Minn.
Lam, James H., Principal, Camp Taylor School, Louisville, Ky.
LaMal, Rev. E. J., Educ. Dept., St. Norbert College, West DePere, Wis.
Lambert, Hazel M., Fresno State College, Fresno, Calif.
Lambert, Pierre D., Sch. of Educ., Boston College, Chestnut Hill, Mass.
Lambert, Sam M., Dir., Research Division, N.E.A., Washington, D.C.
Lampard, Dorothy M., Faculty of Educ., Univ. of Alberta, Edmonton, Alberta
Lampkin, Richard H., State University Col. for Teachers, Buffalo, N.Y.
Lammel, Rose, Wayne State University, Detroit, Mich.
Lancaster, Christine, Keene Teachers College, Keene, N.H.
Landau, Elliott D., University of Utah, Salt Lake City, Utah
Landskov, N. L., Mississippi Southern College, Hattiesburg, Miss.
Lance, Gerald, Supt., Union High School Dist., Huntington Beach, Calif.

Lane, Elizabeth Miller, 4390 Hyland Ave., Dayton, Ohio
Lane, Frank T., 42 St. Clair Dr., Delmar, N.Y.
Lane, John J., Principal, Coolidge Junior High School, Natick, Mass.
Lane, Mrs. Ruth, 1144 North Church St., Rockford, Ill.
Lane, Wilson H., Principal, Emerson Elementary School, Amarillo, Tex.
Lang, Carl D., College of the Pacific, Stockton, Calif.
Lange, Phil C., Teachers College, Columbia Univ., New York, N.Y.
Langenbach, Louise, Government Center, c/o Co. Supt. of Schls., Placerville, Calif.
Langeveld, M. J., Dir., Educ. Inst., State's University, Utrecht, Holland
Langford, James A., California State Polytechnic Col., San Luis Obispo, Calif.
Langland, Lois E., 235 Montana Ave., Santa Monica, Calif.
Langston, R. G., Los Angeles State College, Los Angeles, Calif.
Langwith, J. E., Superintendent of Schools, Terrell, Tex.
Lanham, Frank W., Sch. of Educ., Univ. of Michigan, Ann Arbor, Mich.
Lant, Kenneth A., Principal, Jericho School, Jericho, N.Y.
Laramy, William J., Principal, Haverford Jr. High School, Havertown, Pa.
Larkin, Joseph B., San Jose State College, San Jose, Calif.
Larkin, Lewis B., Col. of Educ., Wayne State University, Detroit, Mich.
Larsen, Arthur Hoff, Illinois State Normal University, Normal, Ill.
Larson, Clint, Delta, Utah
Larson, Clifford E., Dean, Bethel College, St. Paul, Minn.
Larson, Eleanore E., Dept. of Educ., Univ. of Wisconsin, Madison, Wis.
Larson, Ira E., Superintendent of County Schools, Osage, Iowa
Larson, Irene M., Board of Education Office, Green Bay, Wis.
Larson, L. C., Dir., Audio-visual Center, Indiana University, Bloomington, Ind.
Larson, R. H., Dir. of Indian Educ., State Dept. of Educ., St. Paul, Minn.
Larson, Rolf W., Sch. of Educ., University of Connecticut, Storrs, Conn.
Lass, Abraham H., Prin., Abraham Lincoln High School, Brooklyn, N.Y.
Lassanske, Paul A., 35 Passaic Ave., West Paterson, N.J.
Latimer, James, State College, Orangeburg, S.C.
Laub, Norman A., Prin., Junior and Senior High School, Northampton, Pa.
Laughlin, Butler, Asst. Supt., Cook County Schools, Chicago, Ill.
Laughlin, Hugh D., Ohio State University, Columbus, Ohio
Lauria, Joseph L., 6401 Shoup Ave., Canoga Park, Calif.
Laurier, Blaise V., 1145 ouest, rue Saint-Viateur, Montreal, Quebec
LaVanture, Robert, Principal, High School, Morristown, N.J.
Lavell, Robert J., Dept. of Educ., Xavier University, Cincinnati, Ohio
Lavender, Harold W., Superintendent of Schools, Raton, N.M.
Law, Reuben D., 831½ Heliotrope Dr., Los Angeles, Calif.
Lawhead, Victor B., Ball State Teachers College, Muncie, Ind.
Lawler, Marcella R., Tchrs. College, Columbia University, New York, N.Y.
Lawnick, Mrs. Patricia G., University of Missouri, Columbia, Mo.
Lawrence, Mrs. Bessie F., Principal, LeMoyne School, Chicago, Ill.
Lawrence, Clayton G., Dir., Tchr. Educ., Marion College, Marion, Ind.
Lawrence, R. J., Supt., Bullock County Bd. of Educ., Union Springs, Ala.
Lawrence, Richard E., Div. of Sum. Sessions, Syracuse Univ., Syracuse, N.Y.
Lawrence, Ruth E., Music Consultant, Board of Educ., Fargo, N.D.
Lawton, John W., Principal, Willow Hill Elem. School, Statesboro, Ga.
Lazar, May, Bur. of Research, Board of Educ., Brooklyn, N.Y.
Leach, Kent W., Sch. of Educ., University of Michigan, Ann Arbor, Mich.
Leach, Marian Edith, 744 Albemarle St., El Cerrito, Calif.
Leaf, Curtis T., University of Dubuque, Dubuque, Iowa
Leahy, Dorothy M., Dept. of H.E., Univ. of California, Los Angeles, Calif.
Leamy, Cora M., Gardner Junior High School, Gardner, Mass.
Leavell, Ullin W., McGuffey Read. Clinic, Univ. of Virginia, Charlottesville, Va.
Leavitt, Jerome, Portland State College, Portland, Ore.
Lee, Annabel, College of Puget Sound, Tacoma, Wash.
Lee, Charles A., Washington University, St. Louis, Mo.
Lee, Dorris May, Portland State College, Portland, Ore.
Lee, Ernest C., Toorak Teachers College, Toorak, S.E. 2, Australia
Lee, Harold Fletcher, Dept. of Educ., Lincoln Univ., Jefferson City, Mo.

Lee, Howard D., Principal, Atwater School, Shorewood, Wis.
Lee, J. Murray, Southern Illinois University, Carbondale, Ill.
Lee, John J., Dean, Col. of Educ., Wayne University, Detroit, Mich.
Lee, John R., Sch. of Educ., Northwestern University, Evanston, Ill.
Leeds, Don S., 612 Argyle Rd., Brooklyn, N. Y.
Leeds, Willard L., San Francisco State College, San Francisco, Calif.
Leese, Joseph, State College for Teachers, Albany, N.Y.
Leeseberg, Norbert H., 663 Manor Rd., Staten Island, N.Y.
Lefever, D. W., University of Southern California, Los Angeles, Calif.
*Lefforge, Roxy, 1945 Fruit St., Huntington, Ind.
Leggett, Stanton, 221 West 57th St., New York, N. Y.
Lehman, Harvey C., Ohio University, Athens, Ohio
Lehmann, Irvin J., Michigan State University, East Lansing, Mich.
Lehmann, William, Jr., Concordia Teachers College, River Forest, Ill.
Leib, Joseph A., 2416 Summit Terrace, Linden, N.J.
Leibik, Leon J., Principal, Nobel School, Chicago, Ill.
Leichtweis, Charles F., University of Detroit, Detroit, Mich.
Leiman, Harold I., Prin., Hebrew Inst. of Long Island, Far Rockaway, N.Y.
Leister, Leroy L., Willimantic State Teachers College, Willimantic, Conn.
Leland, Simeon E., Dean, Col. of L.A., Northwestern University, Evanston, Ill.
Lemmer, John A., Superintendent of Schools, Escanaba, Mich.
Lennon, Joseph L., Dean, Providence College, Providence, R.I.
Lennon, Lawrence J., Head, Dept. of Educ., Univ. of Scranton, Scranton, Pa.
Lensmire, Warren J., Pres. Wood County Tchrs. Col., Wisconsin Rapids, Wis.
Lepera, Alfred G., Nakes Fdn. for Soc. Sci. Res. for Aged, Tyngsboro, Mass.
Lepthien, Mrs. Emilie V., 4019 North Long Ave., Chicago, Ill.
Lerner, Joseph S., 1103 Goden State Highway, Bakersfield, Calif.
Lessenberry, D. D., University of Pittsburgh, Pittsburgh, Pa.
Letson, J. W., 413 East Eighth St., Chattanooga, Tenn.
Letson, Robert J., Col. of Educ., University of Arizona, Tucson, Ariz.
Letton, Mildred C., Dept. of Educ., University of Chicago, Chicago, Ill.
Levin, J. Joseph, 8 Meadowbrook, Corning, N.Y.
Levin, Robert, 9932 South Yates Ave., Chicago, Ill.
Levine, Herbert, Rutgers University, New Brunswick, N.J.
Levine, Stanley L., 950 Embury St., Pacific Palisades, Calif.
Levit, Martin, University of Kansas City, Kansas City, Mo.
Levy, Sidney, 1205 Avenue R, Brooklyn, N. Y.
Lewis, Carleton Kenneth, Box 443, Route 1, Annandale, Va.
Lewis, Dwight P., Dir. of Curric., Imperial County Schls., El Centro, Calif.
Lewis, Edward R., 6354 Bernhard Ave., Richmond, Calif.
Lewis, Elizabeth V., Dept. of Educ., Huntingdon College, Montgomery, Ala.
Lewis, Gertrude M., U.S. Office of Education, Washington, D. C.
Lewis, Mrs. J. R., Elementary School Principal, Batesville, Miss.
Lewis, Maurice S., Payne Trg. Sch., Ariz. State College, Tempe, Ariz.
Lewis, Philip, Chm., Dept. of Educ., Chicago Tchrs. College, Chicago, Ill.
Lewis, William Paul, Utah State University, Logan, Utah
Lichty, E. A., Illinois State Normal University, Normal, Ill.
Lichty, John C., Principal, Paradise Twp. Elem. School, Paradise, Pa.
Liddle, Clifford S., University of Wisconsin, Madison, Wis.
Lidikay, D. R., Superintendent, Public Schools, Pratt, Kan.
Lien, Arnold J., Whitewater State College, Whitewater, Wis.
Lieuallen, R. E., President, Oregon College of Education, Monmouth, Ore.
Lifton, Eli, Principal, Junior High School 142, Brooklyn, N.Y.
Light, Alfred B., 6 University Place, Plattsburgh, N.Y.
Liljeblad, Maynard T., Reading Consultant, Public Schools, Barstow, Calif.
Limpus, Robert M., Western Michigan University, Kalamazoo, Mich.
* Lincoln, Edward A., Thompson Street, Halifax, Mass.
Lind, Arthur E., Asst. Superintendent of Schools, Richland, Wash.
Lindahl, Hannah M., Supv. of Elem. Educ., Public Schools, Mishawaka, Ind.
Lindberg, Lucile, Sch. of Educ., Queens College, Flushing, N. Y.
Lindeman, Richard H., 4936 Penn Ave. South, Minneapolis, Minn.

Lindemann, Erich, Psychiatrist-in-Chief, Mass. General Hospital, Boston, Mass.
Lindgren, Henry Clay, San Francisco State College, San Francisco, Calif.
Lindquist, E. F., Col. of Educ., State University of Iowa, Iowa City, Iowa
Lindvall, C. Mauritz, Sch. of Educ., University of Pittsburgh, Pittsburgh, Pa.
Linneman, Jessica, Dean of Col., Finch College, New York, N.Y.
Lino, Frank D., Principal, Volta School, Chicago, Ill.
Lipscomb, George, 608 Post St., Gladewater, Tex.
Lipsitz, Herbert J., Principal, Public School 21, Paterson, N.J.
Lipsky, Celia, Asst. Prin., John Ericsson Junior High School, Brooklyn, N.Y.
Lisle, Mrs. H. G., 1559 Kinney Ave., Cincinnati, Ohio
Liss, Nina E., 700 Clinton Ave., Newark, N.J.
Little, Evert T., USOM, APO 319, New York, N.Y.
Little, J. Kenneth, University of Wisconsin, Madison, Wis.
Little, Mrs. L. H., Principal, Glendale School, Nashville, Tenn.
Little, Lawrence C., Sch. of Educ., Univ. of Pittsburgh, Pittsburgh, Pa.
Littlefield, Lucille J., State Teachers College, Indiana, Pa.
Litzky, Leo, West Side High School, Newark, N.Y.
Livingood, F. G., Dept. of Educ., Washington College, Chestertown, Md.
Livingston, Thomas B., Box 4060, Texas Tech. College, Lubbock, Tex.
Lloyd - Jones, Esther, 525 West 120th St., New York, N.Y.
Lobdell, Lawrence O., Principal, Clear Stream Ave. School, Valley Stream, N.Y.
LoBuglio, Armand S., 132-16 North Hempstead Turnpike, Flushing, L.I., N.Y.
LoCicero, Benedict, Principal, Verona High School, Verona, N.J.
Lodeski, Frank J., Principal, Mulligan Elem. School, Chicago, Ill.
Lodine, Robert E., 1228 Hinman Ave., Evanston, Ill.
Loeb, Joe H., Kansas State College, Manhattan, Kan.
Loew, C. C., Superintendent of Schools, Urbana, Ill.
Lofgren, Mrs. Marie L., 61 Crestwood Dr., Daly City, Calif.
Lofthouse, Yvonne M., Chm., Div. of Educ., Mercy College, Detroit, Mich.
Logan, Jack M., Superintendent of Schools, Waterloo, Iowa
Loggins, W. F., Superintendent, County School Dist., Greenville, S.C.
Logsdon, James D., Supt., Thornton Twp. High Sch. and Jr. Col., Harvey, Ill.
Lohmann, Mrs. Ethel, Principal, Milan Local School, Monroeville, Ohio
Lohmann, Victor Louis, Dir., Psycho-Educ. Clinic, State Tchrs. Col., St. Cloud, Minn.
Lohnes, Paul R., Dept. of Educ., Univ. of New Hampshire, Durham, N.H.
Lola, Justita, Guinobatan, Albay, Philippines
Lomax, J. L., Principal, Lomax Junior High School, Valdosta, Ga.
Lomax, Paul S., Sch. of Bus., Southern Illinois Univ., Carbondale, Ill.
London, Jack, Sch. of Educ., University of California, Berkeley, Calif.
Long, Charles M., Pennsylvania State University, University Park, Pa.
Long, F. P., Jr., R.D. 1, Valencia, Pa.
Long, Isabelle, 4343 Harriet Ave. South, Minneapolis, Minn.
Lonsdale, Mrs. Maxine deLappe, 1405 Campbell Lane, Sacramento, Calif.
Lonsdale, Richard C., Sch. of Educ., Syracuse University, Syracuse, N.Y.
Looby, Arthur J., Iowa State Teachers College, Cedar Falls, Iowa
Loomis, Arthur K., Suite 11, 16 Fernold Dr., Cambridge, Mass.
Looney, William F., Pres., Boston Teachers College, Boston, Mass.
Loop, Alfred B., 2619 Franklin St., Bellingham, Wash.
Loos, Leonard E., Principal, Shore School, Euclid, Ohio
Loree, M. Ray, Louisiana State University, Baton Rouge, La.
Lorenz, Donald, Concordia College, Portland, Ore.
Lorge, Irving, Teachers College, Columbia University, New York, N.Y.
Lorusso, Rocco E., 2386 Knapp Dr., Rahway, N.J.
Loughead, George R., Superintendent of Schools, Poplar Bluff, Mo.
Loughrea, Mildred, Asst. Dir., Elem. Educ., City Schools, St. Paul, Minn.
Love, Curtis C., Principal, High School, Pine Bluff, Ark.
Low, Camilla M., Dept. of Educ., University of Wisconsin, Madison, Wis.
Lowe, Alberta, College of Educ., University of Tennessee, Knoxville, Tenn.
Lowe, Mrs. Herman, Western Kentucky State College, Bowling Green, Ky.
Lowe, Paul F., New Haven State Teachers College, New Haven, Conn.

Lowe, R. N., Sch. of Educ., University of Oregon, Eugene, Ore.
Lowes, Ruth, Prof. of Educ., West Texas State Col., Canyon, Tex.
Lowry, Carmen, Huston-Tillotson College, Austin, Tex.
Lowry, V. A., President, General Beadle State Tchrs. College, Madison, S.D.
Lowther, William L., Prin., Livingston High School, Livingston, N. J.
Lubell, Richard M., Principal, Public School 92, Brooklyn, N.Y.
Lucas, Rev. Ernest A. J., St. Joseph's College, Collegeville, Ind.
Lucas, John J., 300 East 159th Street, New York, N.Y.
Lucash, Benjamin, 1219 Robbins Ave., Philadelphia, Pa.
Lucio, William H., Sch. of Educ., Univ. of California, Los Angeles, Calif.
Luckey, Bertha M., Psychologist, Board of Education, Cleveland, Ohio
Ludes, Fr. Titus H., O.F.M., Quincy College, Quincy, Ill.
Ludington, John R., U.S. Office of Education, Washington, D.C.
Ludwig, Adela E., Principal, Greenfield School, Milwaukee, Wis.
Ludwig, Lois K., 661 South Cassingham Rd., Columbus, Ohio
Luebke, Paul T., Senior Elem. Editor, Webster Publishing Co., St. Louis, Mo.
Luecke, Mrs. Carl L., 411 Sergeant Ave., Joplin, Mo.
Lukas, John, Principal, Edison Elementary School, Rochester, Minn.
Luker, Arno H., Colorado State College, Greeley, Colo.
Lund, S. E. Torsten, Haviland Hall, Univ. of Calif., Berkeley, Calif.
Lundy, Mrs. Marguerite, Principal, Putnam Elem. School, El Paso, Tex.
Lunt, Robert, Supt., School Union Ten, Scarborough, Me.
Lurton, Sallie E., Headmistress, Holton-Arms Schools, Washington, D.C.
Lusk, Mrs. Georgia L., Supt. of Public Instruction, Santa Fee, N.M.
Lutes, Olin S., 141 Joralemon St., Brooklyn, N.Y.
Luvaas, Clarence B., Principal, Hayes Elementary School, Cedar Rapids, Iowa
Lynch, James M., Superintendent of Schools, New Brunswick, N.J.
Lynch, John C., Dept. of Educ., DePaul University, Chicago, Ill.
Lynch, Joseph, 541 Oberdick Dr., McKeesport, Pa.
Lynch, Katharine D., Bur. for Child. with Ret. Ment. Develop., New York, N.Y.
Lynch, Mary Elizabeth, State Tchrs. Col. of Boston, Boston, Mass.
Lyons, John H., Dir., Guid. and Audio-Vis. Aids, Pub. Schls., Thompsonville,
    Conn.

Macbeth, Ruby, 69 Cannon St., Charleston, S.C.
Macdonald, Leland S., Emory and Henry College, Emory, Va.
MacDonald, Nellie V., 2770 Yonge St., Toronto, Ontario, Canada
MacFee, Mrs. Winifred C., Western Mich. College, Kalamazoo, Mich.
Mack, Esther, State College of Washington, Pullman, Wash.
Mackay, G. Gordon, 2121 Staunton Ct., Palo Alto, Calif.
MacKay, James L., 2205 West Mistletoe St., San Antonio, Tex.
MacKay, Vera, Sch. of Educ., Ohio State University, Columbus, Ohio
MacKay, William R., 4067 Wesley Way, El Sobrante, Calif.
MacKenzie, Barbara, Dept. of Educ., Brooklyn College, Brooklyn, N.Y.
Mackenzie, Donald M., Dept. of Educ., University of Chicago, Chicago, Ill.
MacKenzie, Elbridge G., Grad. Inst. of Educ., Washington University, St. Louis,
    Mo.
Mackenzie, Gordon N., Teachers College, Columbia Univ., New York, N.Y.
Mackintosh, Helen K., U.S. Office of Education, Washington, D.C.
MacLean, Malcolm S., Sch. of Educ., Univ. of Calif., Los Angeles, Calif.
MacLeod, Kenneth M., Asst. Supt. of Schools, Northville, Mich.
MacVicar, Robert, Vice-President, Oklahoma State University, Stillwater, Okla.
Madden, Richard, Chm., Grad. Study, San Diego State Col., San Diego, Calif.
Maddox, Clifford R., 15816 Marshfield Ave., Harvey, Ill.
Madison, Thurber H., Sch. of Music, Indiana University, Bloomington, Ind.
Madore, Normand William, 17684 Manderson, Detroit, Mich.
Magary, James F., Panama Canal Zone Co., Div. of Schls., Balboa Heights, C.Z.
Magers, Norma E., Principal, Byford Elementary School, Chicago, Ill.
Magoon, Mayo M., Principal, Framingham High School, Framingham, Mass.
Magoon, Thomas M., 9521 Woodley Ave., Silver Spring, Md.
Maher, Trafford P., Dir., Dept. of Educ., St. Louis Univ., St. Louis, Mo.

Mahler, Clarence A., Dept. of Psych., Oregon State College, Corvallis, Ore.
Mailey, James H., Sch. of Educ., Southern Methodist University, Dallas, Tex.
Malan, Russell, Superintendent of Schools, Harrisburg, Ill.
Malik, Anand, University of Idaho, Moscow, Idaho
Maline, Rev. Julian L., S. J., 892 West Boston Blvd., Detroit, Mich.
Mallory, Berenice, U.S. Office of Education, Washington, D.C.
Malmquist, Eve, State School for Educ. Research, Linköping, Sweden
Malone, James J., Principal Sumner Elementary School, Chicago, Ill.
Malone, James W., Superintendent, Diocesan Schools, Youngstown, Ohio
Maloney, Genevieve A., 3077 Parkside Rd., Columbus, Ohio
Maloney, Marguerite L., Asst. Dir. of Elem. Educ., City Schls., St. Paul, Minn.
Maloof, Mitchell, P.O. Box 285, North Adams, Mass.
Manley, Francis J., Frontier Central School, Hamburg, N.Y.
Manley, Wesley, Elem. Consult., Div. of Instruction, Berkeley, Mich.
Mann, J. P., Supt. of Schools, Appleton, Wis.
Mann, V. S., Box 266, State College, Miss.
Manney, Agnes A., Tchrs. Col., University of Cincinnati, Cincinnati, Ohio
Manning, Duane, Arizona State College, Tempe, Ariz.
Manning, Walton, Sch. of Educ., University of Miami, Coral Gables, Fla.
Manolakes, George, Sch. of Educ., New York University, New York, N.Y.
Mantor, Lyle E., Chm., Div. of Soc. Sci., State Tchrs. College, Kearney, Neb.
Manuel, Herschel T., University of Texas, Austin, Tex.
Mapes, Cecil S., District Superintendent of Schools, Chatham, N.Y.
Mapes, Elmer S., Superintendent of Schools, East Weymouth, Mass.
Marc-Aurele, Paul, 162 Marois Blvd., Laval-des-Rapides, Montreal, Quebec, Canada
Marchetti, Jerome J., Dean, Col. of Arts & Sci., St. Louis Univ., St. Louis, Mo.
Margolin, Mrs. Edythe, 12013 Rose Ave., Los Angeles, Calif.
Margolis, Herman R., Principal, Goodrich Elem. School, Chicago, Ill.
Margolis, Isidor, Yeshiva University, New York, N.Y.
Marinaccio, Anthony, Superintendent of Schools, Kankakee, Ill.
Mark, Mrs. Retha D., Edmunds High School, Sumter, S.C.
Markarian, Robert E., Springfield College, Springfield, Mass.
Markey, Ruth, 6038 Canal Blvd., New Orleans, La.
Markle, David H., Dir., Evening Div., Ohio Northern University, Ada, Ohio
Marks, Sallie B., 3133 Connecticut Ave., Washington, D.C.
Marksberry, Mary Lee, Blairstown, Mo.
Marquis, Norwood, School of Educ., Miami University, Oxford, Ohio
Marrinan, Edward L., Jr., 2067 Ferncliff Ave., Dayton, Ohio
Marsden, W. Ware, 2217 West 5th St., Stillwater, Okla.
Marsh, Kathleen H., Asst. Prin., Chaney School, Detroit, Mich.
Marshall, Daniel W., Dept. of Educ., Tufts University, Medford, Mass.
Marshall, Donald H., College of Agric. & Mechanic Arts, Mayaguez, Puerto Rico
Marshall, Mrs. Lorene E., 721 Capitol Ave., Sacramento, Calif.
Marshall, Thomas O., 2 Davis Court, Durham, N.H.
Marshall, Wayne P., Nebraska State College, Kearney, Neb.
Martens, Mrs. Freda R. H., "Woodlands," Ruby, N.Y.
Martin, Mrs. Alice L., Principal, Canty School, Chicago, Ill.
Martin, Miss Clyde, 2511 Enfield Rd., Austin, Tex.
Martin, Clyde V., Div. of Educ., Long Beach State College, Long Beach, Calif.
Martin, Dorothy L., 120 George St., Mt. Prospect, Ill.
Martin, Edwin D., Dir. of Research, Public Schools, Houston, Tex.
Martin, Elaine, 608 S. Norwood Ave., Green Bay, Wis.
Martin, George B., Salem Public Schools, Salem, Ore.
Martin, Harry E., Principal, Lima Senior High School, Lima, Ohio
Martin, Howell C., Principal, High School, Chamblee, Ga.
Martin, Ignatius A., Supt. of Diocesan Schls., Lafayette, La.
Martin, John Henry, Supt., Wayne Twp. Schools, Wayne, N.J.
Martin, Judson P., Dean, Bemidji State College, Bemidji, Minn.
Martin, Millicent V., Inst. of Home Econ., Univ. of Illinois, Urbana, Ill.
Martin, R. Lee, State Univ. Teachers College, Oswego, N.Y.

Martin, Vibella, 3348 Paradise Dr., Tiburon, Calif.
Martin, W. Howard, University of Connecticut, Storrs, Conn.
Martin, W. Plunkett, New Orleans Baptist Theol. Seminary, New Orleans, La.
Martin, William I., Jr., 900 Echo Lane, Glenview, Ill.
Martini, Angiolina A., 2524 Benvenue Ave., Berkeley, Calif.
Martinson, Ruth A., Long Beach State College, Long Beach, Calif.
Martorana, S. V., Div. of High. Educ., U.S. Office of Education, Washington, D.C.
Marzolf, Stanley S., Illinois State Normal University, Normal, Ill.
Massey, William J., No. 2 Pine St., Orono, Me.
Masters, Harry V., President, Albright College, Reading, Pa.
Mathews, C. O., Dept. of Educ., Ohio Wesleyan University, Delaware, Ohio
Mathews, Mrs. Ruth, Principal, Clardy Elem. School, El Paso, Tex.
Mathias, C. Wilber, State Teachers College, Kutztown, Pa.
Mathiasen, O. F., Dept. of Educ., Antioch College, Yellow Springs, Ohio
Mathis, Claude, Sch. of Educ., Northwestern University, Evanston, Ill.
Mathis, Russell, 1306 South Anderson St., Urbana, Ill.
Matricaria, D. Anthony, 73 Howard Ave., Ansonia, Conn.
Matthew, Eunice Sophia, 860 West End Ave., New York, N.Y.
Matthews, J. W., Principal, Central High School, Little Rock, Ark.
Matthews, R. D., Dept. of Educ., Univ. of Pennsylvania, Philadelphia, Pa.
Matthews, W. B., County Supt. of Schools, Cape May Court House, N.J.
Mattila, John, 702 Main St., Woodland, Calif.
Mattila, Mrs. Ruth Hughes, 2702 East Drachman, Tuscon, Ariz.
Matulis, Anthony S., Principal, High School, Taylor Center, Mich.
Matzner, G. C., Eastern Illinois University, Charleston, Ill.
Mauck, Mrs. R. I., 623A East South Broadway, Lombard, Ill.
Maucker, James William, President, Iowa State Tchrs. College, Cedar Falls, Iowa
Maurer, Robert L., Kellogg-Voorhis Campus, State Polytech. Col., Pomona, Calif.
Maurer, Wesley C., Supervising Principal, Public Schools, Minneapolis, Minn.
Mauth, Leslie J., Ball State Teachers College, Muncie, Ind.
Maw, Wallace H., Sch. of Educ., University of Delaware, Newark, Del.
Maxwell, Ida E., Box 34, Cheyney, Pa.
May, Robert E., Southwestern Louisiana Institute, Lafayette, La.
Mayfield, L. B., Superintendent, School District 549C, Medford, Ore.
Mayhew, Lewis B., Box 391, East Lansing, Mich.
Mayo, Jane A., 2606 Wolfe Street, Little Rock, Ark.
Mayse, Hartley Ellis, Riverview Intermediate School, Pittsburg, Calif.
Maziarz, Rev. Edward A., Dean, St. Joseph's College, Collegeville, Ind.
Mazurkiewicz, Albert J., Lehigh University, Bethlehem, Pa.
Mazyck, Harold E., Jr., Prairie View A. & M. College, Prairie View, Tex.
McAdam, J. E., State University of Iowa, Iowa City, Iowa
McAllister, David, Arkansas Polytechnic College, Russellville, Ark.
McArthur, L. C., Jr., Supt., Beaufort County Sch. Dist. 1, Beaufort, S.C.
McBirney, Ruth, Boise Junior College, Boise, Idaho
McBride, James H., Superintendent of Schools, Norwalk, Ohio
McBride, William B., Hughes Hall, Ohio State University, Columbus, Ohio
McBride, William E., Principal, Farragut High School, Chicago, Ill.
McBrier, Mrs. Vivian F., District of Columbia Tchrs. Col., Washington, D.C.
McBryde, Elizabeth, Principal, Emerson Elementary School, Detroit, Mich.
McCain, Paul M., President, Arkansas College, Batesville, Ark.
McCallister, J. M., 8100 South Blackstone Ave., Chicago, Ill.
McCallister, Mabel, 9120 Bristol Ave., Overland, Mo.
McCann, Thomas W., 43 Ashley St., Bridgeport, Conn.
McCarthy, Mary C., San Francisco Unified Sch. Dist., San Francisco, Calif.
McCarthy, Mrs. Muriel L., Supv. Principal, Elem. Schools, Lewiston, Me.
McCarthy, Raymond G., 52 Hillhouse Ave., New Haven, Conn.
McCartin, Rev. William B., Supt. Catholic Schools, Tucson, Ariz.
McCartney, Hilda, 2729 Rodloy Ave., Long Beach, Calif.
McCarty, Donald James, Dept. of Educ., Univ. of Chicago, Chicago, Ill.
McCarty, Henry R., Texas Technological College, Lubbock, Texas
McClean, Donald E., 171 Lucero Way, Menlo Park, Calif.

McClellan, James, Teachers College, Columbia University, New York, N. Y.
McClendon, LeRoy, 313 East Austin, Nacogdoches, Tex.
McClintock, James A., Drew University, Madison, N.J.
McCluer, V. C., Supt. of Schools, Ferguson, Mo.
McClure, L. Morris, Col. of Educ., University of Maryland, College Park, Md.
McClurkin, W. D., George Peabody College for Teachers, Nashville, Tenn.
McClusky, F. D., Sch. of Educ., University of Calif., Los Angeles, Calif.
McClusky, Howard Y., Univ. of Michigan, Ann Arbor, Mich.
McCollom, Elinor C., 619 Ridge Ave., Evanston, Ill.
McConnell, Gaither, 254 Pine Street, New Orleans, La.
McConnell, T. R., Sch. of Educ., University of California, Berkeley, Calif.
McCook, T. Joseph, Superintendent of Schools, Springfield, Mass.
McCormick, Chester A., Col. of Educ., Wayne University, Detroit, Mich.
McCormick, George W., Vice-Prin., Stockton Unified Sch. Dist., Stockton, Calif.
McCracken, Robert A., Ball State Teachers College, Muncie, Ind.
McCrary, James W., Jr., East Texas State Tchrs. College, Commerce, Tex.
McCreight, Russell W., Teachers College, University of Nebraska, Lincoln, Neb
McCrimmon, James M., Div. of Genl. Studies, Univ. of Illinois, Urbana, Ill.
McCue, Robert E., 739 Perry St., Davenport, Iowa
McCuen, Theoron L., Supt., Kern County Union High School, Bakersfield, Calif.
McCullough, Constance M., San Francisco State College, San Francisco, Calif.
McCurdy, Charles M., Principal, Lake Shore High School, Belle Glade, Fla.
McDavit, H. W., Supt., South Orange-Maplewood Schls., South Orange, N.J.
McDermith, C. W., Superintendent of Schools, Passaic, N.J.
McDermott, John C., St. John's University, Brooklyn, N.Y.
McDermott, Leon A., Central Michigan College, Mt. Pleasant, Mich.
McDonald, Louis Rogers, Principal, Woodruff Senior High School, Peoria, Ill.
McDougall, W. D., Chm., Div. of Elem. Educ., Univ. of Alberta, Edmonton, Alba.
McFaddin, Genora, Memphis State College, Memphis, Tenn.
McFarland, John W., Superintendent of Schools, Amarillo, Texas
McFeaters, Margaret M., Prin., Freedom Area Joint Schools, Freedom, Pa.
McGarry, Francis B., State Teachers College, East Stroudsburg, Pa.
McGee, R. T., Principal, Mesa School, Los Alamos, N.M.
McGehee, Elise, 2343 Prytania St., New Orleans, La.
McGhehey, Marion A., Sch. of Educ., Indiana University, Bloomington, Ind.
McGinnis, Frederick A., Chm., Div. of Educ., Wilberforce Uni., Wilberforce, Ohio
McGinnis, James H., Knoxville College, Knoxville, Tenn.
McGlasson, Maurice A., Sch. of Educ., Indiana University, Bloomington, Ind.
McGrail, Rev. Vincent J., S.J. Headmaster, Xavier High School, New York, N.Y.
McGrath, Earl J., Institute of Higher Educ., 525 West 120th St., New York, N.Y.
McGregor, William C., Principal, Savala Elem. School, El Paso, Tex.
McGuire, J. Carson, Col. of Educ., Univ. of Texas, Austin, Tex.
McIlvaine, Franklin, State Teachers College, Lock Haven, Pa.
McInerney, George K., Principal, Public School 100, Queens, N.Y.
McIntosh, William Ray, Superintendent of Schools, Rockford, Ill.
McIntyre, Richmond E., Principal, J. F. Gunn Elem. Sch., Burlington, N.C.
McIsaac, John S., Geneva College, Beaver Falls, Pa.
McKean, Robert, Sch. of Educ., Indiana University, Bloomington, Ind.
McKee, W. J., University of North Carolina, Chapel Hill, N.C.
McKenna, F. Raymond, Eastern Illinois State College, Charleston, Ill.
McKenney, James L., 2658 South Bentley Ave., Los Angeles, Calif.
McKeough, M. J., St. Norbert College, West DePere, Wis.
McKillop, Anne S., Teachers College, Columbia University, New York, N.Y.
McKim, Margaret G., Teachers College, Univ. of Cincinnati, Cincinnati, Ohio
McKinley, Mrs. Elva, 219 Oak St., Fond du Lac, Wis.
McKinley, S. Justus, President, Emerson College, Boston, Mass.
McKinney, F. J. D., Tennessee State University, Nashville, Tenn.
*McKinney, James, Chm., Bd. of Trustees, American School, Chicago, Ill.
McKune, Esther J., State University Teachers College, Oneonta, N.Y.
McLaren, Dallas C., 3240 Manoa Rd., Honolulu, Hawaii
McLaughlin, Kenneth F., 871 North Madison, Arlington, Va.

McLaughlin, Vincent J., School of Educ., Fordham Univ., New York, N.Y.
McLaughlin, William J., Prin., D. A. Harmon Jr. H.S., Hazelton, Pa.
McLean, Mary Cannon, 620 Union St., Springfield, Mass.
McLeary, Ralph D., Superintendent of Schools, Jackson, Mich.
McLendon, Jonathon C., Dept. of Educ., Duke University, Durham, N.C.
McMahan, F. J., St. Ambrose College, Davenport, Iowa
McMahan, John Julia, New Mexico Col. of A. & M., State College, N.M.
McMahon, Mrs. G. F., Prin., Bennett Elementary School, Chicago, Ill.
McManamon, Father James, Quincy College, Quincy, Ill.
McManus, M. H., Principal, Ben Milam Elem. School, El Paso, Tex.
McManus, Robert P., State University Teachers College, Oswego, N.Y.
McManus, Very Rev. Msgr. Wm. E., Supt., Catholic Schools, Chicago, Ill.
McMaster, Blanche E., Elem. Supervisor, Public Schools, Bristol, Conn.
McMath, James G., Box 3912, Odessa, Tex.
McMillan, William Asbury, Dean, Bethune-Cookman College, Daytona Beach,
    Fla.
McMillan, William R., New York City Community College, Brooklyn, N.Y.
McMinn, Mrs. Jean H., 19215 Orangepath, Glendora, Calif.
McMullen, Charles B., Dean, State Tchrs. College, Bridgewater, Mass.
McMurtrey, Violet, 3365 Southwest 103rd St., Beaverton, Ore.
McNair, J. Stuart, State University Teachers College, Plattsburgh, N.Y.
McNally, Crystal, 428 South Broadway, Wichita, Kan.
McNally, Harold J., Teachers College, Columbia University, New York, N.Y.
McNally, Wayne W., Prin., Nathan Bishop Junior High School, Providence, R.I.
McNealy, James L., Huston-Tillotson College, Austin, Tex.
McNiel, Joe B., Superintendent, Public Schools, Wichita Falls, Tex.
McNutt, C. R., 6511 Frontier Dr., Springfield, Va.
McNutt, Franklin H., Woman's Col., Univ. of North Carolina, Greensboro, N.C.
McPheeters, Alphanso A., Dean, Clark College, Atlanta, Ga.
McPherson, Virgil L., 904 East Mayfair Ave., Orange, Calif.
McPherson, W. N., Superintendent of County Schools, Greenville, Ohio
McRae, Louie James, Principal, East Highland School, Dothan, Ala.
McSharry, John T., Principal, Ivy Junior High School, Newark, N.J.
McSwain, E. T., Sch. of Educ., Northwestern University, Evanston, Ill.
*Mead, Arthur R., 1719 Northwest 6th Ave., Gainesville, Fla.
Meadows, Audine L., Principal, Rogers Elementary School, Wichita, Kan.
Meadows, J. H., Texas Western College, El Paso, Tex.
Mease, Clyde D., Superintendent of Schools, Humboldt, Iowa
Meder, Elsa M., Houghton Mifflin Co., Boston, Mass.
Meer, Samuel J., 1304 Dahlia Lane, Wantagh, N.Y.
Meier, Frederick A., President, State Teachers College, Salem, Mass.
Melby, Ernest O., Sch. of Educ., Michigan State University, East Lansing, Mich.
Mellott, Malcolm E., Editor-in-Chief, John C. Winston, Philadelphia, Pa.
Melvin, Keith L., Dean, Peru State College, Peru, Neb.
Mendenhall, C. B., Ohio State University, Columbus, Ohio
Mendoza, Romulo Y., Bureau of Public Schools, Manila, Philippines
Menge, Carleton P., University of New Hampshire, Durham, N.H.
Menge, J. W., College of Educ., Wayne Univ., Detroit, Mich.
Merchant, Francis, Head, Div. of Humanities, Bishop College, Marshall, Tex.
Mercille, Mrs. Margaret G., Sch. of Educ., Indiana University, Bloomington, Ind.
Meredith, Cameron W., Northwestern University, Evanston, Ill.
Merenda, Peter F., 285 Huxley Ave., Providence, R.I.
Merideth, Howard V., Sch. of Educ., Northwestern University, Evanston, Ill.
Merkhofer, Beatrice E., 222 South Macomb St., Tallahassee, Fla.
Merrill, Myrtle, Michigan State University, East Lansing, Mich.
Merritt, C. B., Col. of Educ., University of Arizona, Tucson, Ariz.
Merry, Mrs. R. V., Morris Harvey College, Charleston, W.Va.
Mersand, Joseph, Eng. Dept., Jamaica High School, Jamaica, N.Y.
Mershon, M. B., Asst. Supt., Erie County Schools, Erie, Pa.
Merwin, Jack C., Sch. of Educ., Syracuse University, Syracuse, N.Y.
Metcalf, Harold H., Supt., Bloom Twp. High School, Chicago Heights, Ill.

Metzner, Jerome, 67-12 Yellowstone Blvd., Forest Hills, N.Y.
Metzner, William, Prin., John B. Stetson Junior High School, Philadelphia, Pa.
Meyer, A. R., Director of Elem. Education, Independence, Mo.
Meyer, Ammon B., Elementary School Principal, Fredericksburg, Pa.
Meyer, Charlotte, Elementary Supervisor, Public Schools, Decatur, Ill.
Meyer, George A., Tchrs. Col., University of Hawaii, Honolulu, Hawaii
Meyer, Mrs. Marie, Douglass College, Rutgers University, New Brunswick, N.J.
Meyer, Pauline, County Superintendent of Schools, Petersburg, Ill.
Meyer, Warren G., 5829 Portland Ave. So., Minneapolis, Minn.
Meyer, William T., Dean, Div. of Grad. Stud., Adams State Col., Alamosa, Colo.
Meyers, C. E., Sch. of Educ., University of So. Calif., Los Angeles, Calif.
Meyers, Max B., 324 East 59th St., Brooklyn, N.Y.
Michael, Lloyd S., Superintendent, Evanston Township High School, Evanston, Ill.
Michaelis, John U., Sch. of Educ., Univ. of California, Berkeley, Calif.
Micheels, William J., Col. of Educ., Univ. of Minn., Minneapolis, Minn.
Michie, James K., Superintendent of Schools, Hibbing, Minn.
Mickelson, John M., Sch. of Educ., Temple University, Philadelphia, Pa.
Middleton, C. A., Iowa State Teachers College, Cedar Falls, Iowa
Middleton, Mildred, Carroll Co. Curric. Coord., Coon Rapids, Iowa
Miles, Arnold A., 11500 Hamilton Ave., Detroit, Mich.
Miles, Logan T., Dir. of Instruction, Public Schools, Mill Valley, Calif.
Miles, Matthew B., Horace Mann-Lincoln Inst., Columbia Univ., New York, N.Y.
Miles, Mrs. V. G., Baylor Station, Belton, Tex.
Miles, Vaden W., Physics Dept., Wayne University, Detroit, Mich.
Milheim, Robert P., 17 East Spring St., Oxford, Ohio
Millard, C. V., Div. of Educ., Michigan State College, East Lansing, Mich.
Miller, Benjamin, Supv., Day Elementary School, Bronx, N.Y.
Miller, Carroll H., Colorado A. & M. College, Ft. Collins, Colo.
Miller, Carroll L., College of L.A., Howard Univ., Washington, D.C.
Miller, Charles, Vice-Prin., McKinley Elem. School, Newark, N.J.
Miller, David, Principal, Thos. Jefferson High School, Port Arthur, Tex.
Miller, Elmer H., Principal, Hazel Park High School, Hazel Park, Mich.
Miller, Frank M., Superintendent of Schools, Johnstown, Pa.
Miller, Helen R., 11410 Charest, Hamtramck, Mich.
Miller, Henry, Sch. of Educ., City College, New York, N.Y.
Miller, Howard G., North Carolina State College, Raleigh, N.C.
Miller, Ingrid O., Edina-Morningside Senior High School, Edina, Minn.
Miller, Ira E., Eastern Mennonite College, Harrisonburg, Va.
Miller, John L., Superintendent of Schools, Great Neck, N.Y.
Miller, Lyle L., Chm., Guid. & Spec. Educ., Univ. of Wyoming, Laramie, Wyo.
Miller, Maurice William, Principal, Riordan High Schol, San Francisco, Calif.
Miller, Mrs. Mildred T., Supervisor, City Schools, Mooresville, N.C.
Miller, Paul A., 200 Wendell Terrace, Syracuse, N.Y.
Miller, Paul A., Superintendent of City Schools, Minot, N.D.
Miller, Ralph, Superintendent of Schools, Georgetown, Ill.
Miller, Ross, West Point, Ga.
Miller, Ruth, Sch. of Music, Baylor University, Waco, Tex.
Miller, Ward I., Supt., Board of Public Educ., Wilmington, Del.
Millhollen, Lloyd F., Acting Supt., School Dist. No. 4, Eugene, Ore.
Milliamson, Florence J., 73 Chillicothe St., Cedarville, Ohio
Milligan, Glenn E., Psychologist, Bd. of Educ., Columbus, Ohio
Milligan, Phyllis E., 712 Fairlawn Dr., Columbus, Ohio
Milligan, Scott, Superintendent, Longview School Dist. No. 122, Longview, Wash.
Millikin, R. M., 301 South State St., Geneseo, Ill.
Milling, Euleas, 227 North Spring St., Concord, N.C.
Mills, Forrest L., Racine Public Library, Racine, Wis.
Mills, Henry C., University of Rochester, Rochester, N.Y.
Mills, William H., Univ. Elem. Sch., University of Michigan, Ann Arbor, Mich.
Milner, Bessie, Principal, East Ward School, Gulfport, Miss.
Milner, Ernest J., Sch. of Educ., Syracuse University, Syracuse, N.Y.
Miner, George D., Superintendent of Schools, Richmond, Calif.

Miniclier, G. E., Principal, Washington High School, St. Paul, Minn.
Minkler, F. W., Director of Education, Lansing, Ontario, Canada
Minnis, Roy B., U.S. Office of Education, Washington, D.C.
Minock, Daniel F., John A. Sutter Junior High School, Los Angeles, Calif.
Minogue, Mildred M., Prin., Armstrong Elem. School, Chicago, Ill.
Minor, Gordon M., Prin., Crocker Highlands Elem. School, Oakland, Calif.
Miranda, Luis O., Dir., Sec. Educ., Ministry of Education, Panama, R.P.
Misner, Paul J., Superintendent of Schools, Glencoe, Ill.
Mitchell, B. F., Louisiana State Univ., Baton Rouge, La.
Mitchell, Donald P., 58 Woodridge Rd., Wayland, Mass.
Mitchell, Edward C., Vice-President, Morris Brown College, Atlanta, Ga.
Mitchell, Eva C., Hampton Institute, Hampton, Va.
Mitchell, Frank W., University of Otago, Dunedin, New Zealand
Mitchell, Guy Clifford, Dept. of Educ., Mississippi College, Clinton, Miss.
Mitchell, Margaret, 900 Howard St., Corona, Calif.
Mitchell, Mrs. Louis H., Home Econ. Dept., Indiana University, Bloomington, Ind.
Mitchell, T. W., Principal, East Junior-Sen. High School, Duluth, Minn.
Mitchell, William R., Olivet College, Olivet, Mich.
Mitzel, Harold E., Div. of Tchr. Educ., 535 E. 80th St., New York, N.Y.
Moe, Richard D., Dir., Tchr. Educ., Waldorf College, Forest City, Iowa
Moffatt, Maurice P., Montclair State Tchrs. College, Montclair, N.J.
Moffitt, J. C., Superintendent of Schools, Provo, Utah
Molenkamp, Alice, Dir. of Elem. Education, White Plains, N.Y.
Moll, Boniface E., St. Benedicts College, Atchison, Kan.
Molyneaux, Mary L., Principal, H. C. Frick School, Pittsburgh, Pa.
Monell, Ira H., Principal, Lafayette School, Chicago, Ill.
Monell, Ralph P., Superintendent, Public Schools, Canon City, Colo.
Mongon, John E., Supt., Burlington County Schools, Mount Holly, N.J.
Monroe, Charles R., Dean, Wilson Junior College, Chicago, Ill.
*Monroe, Walter S., 211 South Castanya Way, Menlo Park, Calif.
Monsen, Robert W., 232 N. McPherrin Ave., Monterey Park, Calif.
Montgomery, George, Prin., West Philadelphia High School, Philadelphia, Pa.
Montgomery, John, President, Mitchell College, Statesville, N.C.
Montgomery, John F., President, Greenbrier College, Lewisburg, W. Va.
Montoya, Mary E., Principal, Fairmede School, San Pablo, Calif.
Mooney, Ross L., Col. of Educ., Ohio State University, Columbus, Ohio
Moore, Cecil L., Principal, L. L. Campbell School, Austin, Tex.
Moore, Clyde B., Stone Hall, Cornell University, Ithaca, N.Y.
Moore, Fletcher, Dept. of Fine Arts, Elon College, N.C.
Moore, Harold E., Sch. of Educ., University of Denver, Denver, Colo.
Moore, H. Kenton, Arkansas A. & M. College, College Heights, Ark.
Moore, James H., Principal, Elem. School, Riverton, Wyo.
Moore, Orville F., Nebraska State Teachers College, Wayne, Neb.
Moore, Parlett L., Coppin State Teachers College, Baltimore, Md.
Moore, R. E., Superintendent of Schools, Tuscumbia, Ala.
Moore, Robert Ezra, Lab. School, San Francisco State Col., San Francisco, Calif.
Moore, W. J., Dean, Eastern Kentucky State College, Richmond, Ky.
Moorhead, Sylvester A., Sch. of Educ., Univ. of Mississippi, University, Miss.
Moose, Mrs. Natica M., 2926 W. Oxford St., Philadelphia, Pa.
Moran, Leona, 408 Aberdeen Ave., Battle Creek, Mich.
Moreau, Rev. Jules L., Seabury-Western Theological Seminary, Evanston, Ill.
Morehead, Charles G., North Carolina State College, Raleigh, N.C.
Morgan, Barton, Dept. of Educ., Iowa State College, Ames, Iowa
Morgan, Roland R., Supt. of Schools, Mooresville, N.C.
Morgan, William E., President, Principia College, Elsah, Ill.
Moriarty, Mary J., State Teachers College, Bridgewater, Mass.
Morlan, G. C., Head, Dept. of Educ., Abilene Christian Col., Abilene, Tex.
Morley, Franklin P., 929 North 15th St., DeKalb, Ill.
Morris, Frank E., Emeritus Prof. of Philos., Connecticut Col., New London, Conn.
Morris, K. N., Dept. of Educ., University of Auckland, Auckland, New Zealand

Morris, Lee M., Superintendent, Public School Dist. 152, Harvey, Ill.
Morris, Mrs. Marjorie S., 7107 Andasol Ave., Van Nuys, Calif.
Morris, M. B., Superintendent of Schools, Uvalde, Tex.
Morris, Merva R., Col. of Educ., University of Utah, Salt Lake City, Utah
Morrison, D. A., Administrator, East York Bd. of Educ., Toronto, Ont.
Morrison, Gaylord D., Colorado State College of Educ., Greeley, Colo.
Morrison, J. Cayce, 13 Cherry Tree Rd., Loundonville, N.Y.
Morrison, Leger Roland, 16 Brown St., Warren, R.I.
Morrison, Robert H., Dean, Sch. of Educ., Seton Hall University, Newark, N.J.
Morrissey, John T., Principal, Fairview School, Milwaukee, Wis.
Morrow, Mrs. Carmon O., Principal, Elem. School, Ft. Lauderdale, Fla.
Morse, Horace T., Dean, Gen. Col., Univ. of Minnesota, Minneapolis, Minn.
Mort, Paul, Teachers College, Columbia University, New York, N.Y.
Morton, Clifford M. H., Principal, Phyllis Wheatley School, Louisville, Ky.
Morton, R. L., Ohio University, Athens, Ohio
Mosbo, Alvin O., Colorado State College, Greeley, Colo.
Moseley, S. Meredith, Principal, Dillard High School, Fort Lauderdale, Fla.
Moser, William G., Supt.-Prin., Penn-Delco Joint School, Chester, Pa.
Mosher, Frank K., Dist. Prin., Liverpool Central Schls., Liverpool, N.Y.
Mosier, Earl E., 28 Woodhampton Drive, Trenton, N.J.
Moss, Roy B., Dir., Audio-Visual Center, Grambling, La.
Moss, Theodore C., 88 Sixth Ave., Oswego, N.Y.
Mother Adelaide Marie, Educ. Supv., Our Lady of the Lake College, San
    Antonio, Tex.
Mother Margaret Burke, Pres., Barat Col. of the Sacred Heart, Lake Forest, Ill.
Mother Mary Aimee Rossi, San Diego Col. for Women, San Diego, Calif.
Mother Mary Benedetta, Prin., Villa Cabrini Academy, Burbank, Calif.
Mother Mary Benjamin, President, Immaculate College, Chicago, Ill.
Mother M. Benedict, Chm., Educ. Dept. Marymount College, Tarrytown, N.Y.
Mother M. Fidelma, Educ. Dept., Marymount College, New York, N.Y.
Mother M. Gonzaga, President, Blessed Sacrament College, Cornwells Heights,
    Pa.
Mother M. Gregory, Dean, Marymount School, Los Angeles, Calif.
Mother Mary Inez, Dept. of Educ., Holy Family College, Manitowoc, Wis.
Mother Mary McQueeny, Duchesne College, Omaha, Nebr.
Mother St. Lawrence, Librarian, Rosemont College, Rosemont, Pa.
Mother M. Rose Gertrude, Molloy Catholic Col. for Women, Rockville Centre,
    N.Y.
Motyka, Agnes L., 6311 Utah Ave., N.W., Washington, D.C.
Moyer, James Herbert, Dept. of Educ., Penn. State Univ., University Park, Pa.
Mozzi, Lucille M., Asst. Dir., Read. Clinic, Univ. of Chicago, Chicago, Ill.
Muck, Mrs. Ruth E. S., State Univ. College for Teachers, Buffalo, N.Y.
Mudge, Evelyn L., Head, Dept. of Educ., Hood College, Frederick, Md.
Mudge, John, Asst. Dist. Supt., Public Schools, Santa Maria, Calif.
Mueller, Herman J., 229 N. Merrill St., Willows, Calif.
Mulhern, John D., 58 Sheldon St., Milton, Mass.
Mulhern, Joseph C., S.M., Chm., Educ. Dept., Spring Hill College, Mobile, Ala.
Muller, Philippe, Prof. a l'Universite, Neuchatel, Switzerland
Mulliner, John H., 1561 Winnetka Ave., Northfield, Ill.
Mulrooney, Thomas W., Dir., Child Devel. & Guid., Pub. Schls., Wilmington, Del.
Mulroy, Mary D., Principal, South Shore High School, Chicago, Ill.
Mulry, Verna. Dir. of Reading, Waukesha H.S., Waukesha, Wis.
Munro, Paul M., Superintendent of Schools, Lynchburg, Va.
Muns, Arthur C., Superintendent of Schools, 222 S. Main St., Sycamore, Ill.
Munson, Alfred W., Stroud Union School Dist., Stroudsburg, Pa.
Munster, Rev. T., 2219 N. Kenmore Ave., Chicago, Ill.
Muntyan, Bozidar, Col. of Educ., University of Florida, Gainesville, Fla.
Muntyan, Milosh, Sch. of Educ., Michigan State University, East Lansing, Mich.
Murdoch, Mrs. Ruth, Washington Missionary College, Takoma Park, Wash-
    ington, D.C.
Murnane, Patrick J., Principal, Newburyport High School, Newburyport, Mass.

Murphy, A. A., Superintendent, Clarion County Schools, Clarion, Pa.
Murphy, A. C., Asst. Dir., Ext. Bureau, University of Texas, Austin, Tex.
Murphy, Donald J., Central Washington Col. of Education, Ellensburg, Wash.
Murphy, Forrest W., Dean, Sch. of Educ., Univ. of Mississippi, University, Miss.
Murphy, Helen A., Sch. of Educ., Boston University, Boston, Mass.
Murphy, Mrs. Jeannie Dean, 1960 West Seventy-ninth St., Los Angeles, Calif.
Murphy, John A., 21-10 33rd Road, Long Island City, N.Y.
Murray, Lessie L., Col. of Educ., University of Florida, Gainesville, Fla.
Murray, Robert E., 1916 South Sig Hill Drive, Kirkwood, Mo.
Murray, Thomas. Dept. of Educ., Sam Houston State Tchrs. Col.. Huntsville, Tex.
Mushtaq, Ahmed, Research Trng. & Prod. Centre, Jamia Millia, Jamianagar, New Delhi, India
Muzzall, Ernest L., Cen. Wash. College of Education, Ellensburg, Wash.
Myers, Mrs. Emma G., Orangeville, Columbia County, Pa.
Myers, Veronica A., Principal, Public School 152, New York, N.Y.

Nafziger, Mary K., Dept. of Educ., Goshen College, Goshen, Ind.
Nagel, Wilma I., Supv., Elem. Educ., School Department, Warwick, R.I.
Nagy, O. Richard, Principal, Carteret School, Bloomfield. N.J.
Nahm, Helen, Sch. of Nursing, Univ. of California, San Francisco, Calif.
Nahshon, Samuel, 1730 Penn Ave., North, Minneapolis, Minn.
Nakosteen, Mehdi, Indian Hills, Colo.
Nance, Mrs. Afton Dill, State Dept. of Education, Sacramento. Calif.
Nardelli, Robert, Prin., Campus Lab. Sch., State College, San Diego, Calif.
Nasgowitz, Mildred, Wisconsin State College, Oshkosh, Wis.
Nash, John J., Anniston Senior High School, Anniston, Ala.
Naslund, Robert A., Sch. of Educ., Univ. of Southern Calif., Los Angeles, Calif.
Nason, Doris E., Dept. of Educ., Univ. of Connecticut, Storrs, Conn.
Nassau, Dorothy P., Pedagogical Library, Bd. of Educ., Philadelphia, Pa.
Nasser, Sheffield, Coord., Special Services, County Schools, Sarasota, Fla.
Nasution, Sorimuda, Djalan Dr. Radjiman 17, Bandung, Indonesia
Nault, William H., Educ. Div.. Field Enterprises, Inc., Chicago, Ill.
Naus, Grant, Coord. of Music, Central Elem. Schools, Coronado, Calif.
Neale, Daniel C., Burton Hall, University of Minnesota, Minneapolis, Minn.
Neale, Gladys E., Macmillan Company of Canada, Toronto, Ont.
Nees, Ruth, Principal, Carl Conlee School, Las Cruces, N.M.
Neiderhiser, F. J., Superintendent of Schools, McClure, Ohio
Nelligan, William J., Dean, Sch. of Educ., St. John's Univ., Jamaica, N.Y.
Nelson, Carl Bertil, State Univ. Teachers College, Cortland, N.Y.
Nelson, Earl E., 611 College Ave., Northfield, Minn.
Nelson, Florence A., Sch. of Educ., Univ. of South Carolina, Columbia, S.C.
Nelson, Harvey D., Superintendent of Schools, Tuscaloosa, Ala.
Nelson, John M., Dir., Tchr. Educ., Grinnell College, Grinnell, Iowa
Nelson, Rev. John T., C.M., St. John's Prep. School, Brooklyn, N.Y.
Nelson, Kenneth G., U.S. Navy Pers. Res. Field Activity, Washington, D.C.
Nelson, M. J., Iowa State Teachers College, Cedar Falls, Iowa
Nelson, N. P., State Teachers College, Oshkosh, Wis.
Nelson, Mrs. Osceola W., Chm., Eng. Dept., Frederick School, New Orleans, La.
Nelson, Pearl Astrid, Sch. of Educ., Boston University, Boston, Mass.
Nelson, Sylvia, 415 West Eighth St., Topeka, Kan.
Nelson, Willard H., Inst. for Res. on Except. Children, Univ. of Illinois, Urbana, Ill.
Nemzek, Claude L., Chm., Educ. Dept.. Univ. of Detroit, Detroit, Mich.
Nerbovig, Marcella, Northern Illinois University, DeKalb, Ill.
Nesbit, Daun Wilbur, State Teachers College, Millerville, Pa.
Nesi, Carmella, Principal, Junior High School 7, Bronx, N.Y.
Netsky, Martin G., Sch. of Medicine, Wake Forest Col., Winston-Salem, N.C.
Neuber, Margaut A., Pennsylvania State University, University Park, Pa.
Neubert, Richard G., Supv. of Music, Public Schools, White Plains, N.Y.
Neuner, Elsie Flint. Dir. of Instruction. Dept. of Educ., New Rochelle, N.Y.
Neuwien, R., Superintendent of Schools, Stamford, Conn.

Nevison, Myrne B., Burton Hall, University of Minnesota, Minneapolis, Minn.
Newcomer, Leland B., Asst. Supt., Covina School Dist., Covina, Calif.
Newenham, R. L., Superintendent of Schools, Zion, Ill.
Newfield, Max, Principal, James Madison High School, Brooklyn, N.Y.
Newman, Herbert M., Education Dept., Brooklyn College, Brooklyn, N.Y.
Newman, Louis, 223 North Highland Ave., Merion, Pa.
Newsom, Herman A., P.O. Box 3912, Odessa, Tex.
Newsome, George L., University of Bridgeport, Bridgeport, Conn.
Newton, W. L., 2640—24th Ave., Meridian, Miss.
Nicholas, William T., 609 Nevada St., Susanville, Calif.
Nicholson, Alice, 1009 E. Hatton St., Pensacola, Fla.
Nicholson, Lawrence E., Harris Teachers College, St. Louis, Mo.
Niehaus, Philip C., Sch. of Educ., Dusquesne University, Pittsburgh, Pa.
Nietz, John A., University of Pittsburgh, Pittsburgh, Pa.
Nigg, William J., Superintendent of Schools, Litchfield, Minn.
Nikoloff, Nicholas, 528 West Kerr St., Springfield, Mo.
Niland, William P., Dir., Coalinga College, Coalinga, Calif.
Nisonger, Herschel W., Dir., Bur. Educ. Res., Ohio State Univ., Columbus, Ohio
Nixon, Clifford L., William J. Bryan University, Dayton, Tenn.
Nixon, John E., Sch. of Educ., Stanford University, Stanford. Calif.
Nixon, Ruth, William Jennings Bryan University, Dayton, Tenn.
Noah, Dennis P., Dept. of Educ., Louisiana State Univ., Baton Rouge, La.
Noar, Gertrude, 225 Adams St., Brooklyn, N.Y.
Noe, Clarence R., Exec. Dean, Eureka College, Eureka, Ill.
Noll, Frances E., 1810 Taylor St., N.W., Washington, D.C.
Noll, Victor H., Sch. of Educ., Michigan State Univ., East Lansing, Mich.
Norcross, Claude E., 14 Roosevelt Circle, Palo Alto, Calif.
Nordberg, H. Orville, Dept. of Educ., Sacramento State Col., Sacramento, Calif.
Norem, Grant M., State Teachers College, Minot, N.D.
Norford, Charles A., Sch. of Educ., Univ. of Virginia, Charlottesville, Va.
Norman, Wade C., 5619 Maxwell Ave., Affton, Mo.
Norris, Forbes H., Supt. of Schls., Braircliff Manor, Westchester Co., N.Y.
Norris, Ralph C., Supt., Polk County Schools, Des Moines, Iowa
Norris, Robert B., Central Bucks Joint Schools, Doylestown, Pa.
Norrix, Loy, Superintendent of Schools, Kalamazoo. Mich.
Norsworthy, E. M., Asst. Supt., Fayette County Schls., Lexington, Ky.
Norton, Rev. Edward, S.V.D., 4940 South Greenwood Ave., Chicago, Ill.
Norton, Helen R., Dept. of Educ., Gallaudet College, Washington, D.C.
Norton, John K., Teachers College, Columbia University, New York, N.Y.
Norton, Joseph A., Monterey Union High School, Monterey, Calif.
Nosal, Walter S., Dir., Dept. of Educ., John Carroll Univ., Cleveland, Ohio
Nugent, Rugh G., Principal, School No. 14, Troy, N.Y.
Nunnally, Nancy, 5916 Monticello Ave., Cincinnati, Ohio
Nutter. H. E., Head, Materials of Instruc., Univ. of Florida, Gainesville, Fla.
Nye, Robert E., Sch. of Music, University of Oregon, Eugene, Ore.
Nystrom, J. W., Jr., 10 Turner Dr., Chappaqua, N.Y.

Oberholtzer. Kenneth E.. Supt. of Schools, Denver, Colo.
Obourn, L. C., Superintendent, Public Schools, East Rochester, N.Y.
O'Brien, Cyril C., Marquette University, Milwaukee, Wis.
O'Brien, Francis J., Superintendent of Schools, North Andover, Mass.
O'Brien, James F., Principal, Clay Senior High School, Oregon, Ohio
O'Brien, John W., 24 Dartmouth Circle, Swarthmore, Pa.
O'Brien, Mae, State Univ. College for Teachers, Buffalo, N.Y.
O'Connor, Clarence D., Lexington Sch. for the Deaf, New York, N.Y.
O'Connor, John D., Teaching Principal, Hampshire, Ill.
O'Connor, Mrs. Marguerite O., Northern Illinois State Tchrs. Col., DeKalb, Ill.
O'Donnell, Beatrice, Michigan State University, East Lansing, Mich.
O'Donnell, John F., 2 Watkins Ave., Oneonta, N.Y.
O'Donnell, Roy C., Free Will Baptist College, Nashville, Tenn.
O'Farrell, Rev. John J., S.J., Loyola University, Los Angeles, Calif.

Ofchus, Leon T., Dept. of Educ. Psych., Wayne Univ., Detroit, Mich.
Ogden, J. Gordon, Jr., Dept. of Educ., Florida Southern College, Lakeland, Fla.
Ogilvie, William K., Northern Illinois University, DeKalb, Ill.
O'Hara, Rev. Charles M., Marquette University, Milwaukee, Wis.
O'Hare, Mary Rita, Manhattanville Col. of the Sacred Heart, Purchase, N.Y.
O'Hearn, Mary, 1060 High Street, Dedham, Mass.
Ohlsen, Merle M., Col. of Educ., Univ. of Illinois, Urbana, Ill.
Ojemann, R. H., Child Welfare Res. Sta., State Univ. of Iowa, Iowa City, Iowa
O'Keefe, Timothy, College of St. Thomas, St. Paul, Minn.
Olander, Herbert T., University of Pittsburgh, Pittsburgh, Pa.
Olbon, Charles, Supt., West Paterson Pub. Schls., West Paterson, N.J.
*Oldham, Mrs. Birdie V., Principal, Rochelle Elem. School, Lakeland, Fla.
Olea, Mrs. Maria, Prin., Dita School, Dita, Cuenca, Butangas, Philippines
O'Leary, Maurice J., Superintendent, Public Schools, Springfield, Vt.
O'Leary, Timothy F., Asst. Supt. of Catholic Schools, Boston, Mass.
Olivas, Romeo A., 1135 Judson Ave., Evanston, Ill.
Oliver, Albert Irving, Jr., Sch. of Educ., Univ. of Pennsylvania, Philadelphia, Pa.
Oliver, George J., Dept. of Educ., Col. of William and Mary, Williamsburg, Va.
Oliver, Stanley C., Southwest Missouri State College, Springfield, Mo.
Olmsted, M. D., Coord., Sec. Educ., Public Schools, Tonawanda, N.Y.
Olphert, Warwick Bruce, University of Melbourne, Melbourne, Victoria, Australia
Olsen, George L., 1921 Harper St., Newberry, S.C.
Olsen, Hans C., Jr., Mankato State College, Mankato, Minn.
Olsen, Hans C., Eastern Illinois State College, Charleston, Ill.
Olsen, Marion G., Principal, Public School 84, Buffalo, N.Y.
Olson, Hazel, USOM to La Paz, Bolivia, c/o Mail Rm., State Dept., Washington,
    D.C.
Olson, Norma M., 1207 So. Linden Ave., Park Ridge, Ill.
Olson, Ove S., Chm., Dept. of Educ., Wisconsin State Col., Superior, Wis.
Olson, R. A., Ball State Teachers College, Muncie, Ind.
Olson, Robert G., Editor, Summy-Birchard Pub. Co., Evanston, Ill.
Olson, Willard C., Dean, Sch. of Educ., Univ. of Mich., Ann Arbor, Mich.
O'Malley, Sarah, 1130 Washington Blvd., Oak Park, Ill.
O'Mara, Arthur P., Principal, Lane Tech. High School, Chicago, Ill.
O'Mara, J. Francis, 29 Snowling Rd., Uxbridge, Mass.
O'Neill, John J., State Teachers College, Boston, Mass.
O'Neill, Leo W., Jr., Col. of Educ., Univ. of Maryland, College Park, Md.
Oppenheimer, J. J., University of Louisville, Louisville, Ky.
Oppleman, Dan L., Central Washington College of Education, Ellensburg, Wash.
Ore, Malvern L., Chm., Div. of Tchr. Educ., Huston-Tillotson Col., Austin, Tex.
Orear, Margaret Louise, Asst. Supt., City Schools, Bellflower, Calif.
Ormsby, Lelia Ann, Sacramento State College, Sacramento, Calif.
Ormsby, Walter M., District Superintendent of Schools, Patchogue, N.Y.
O'Rourke, J. Mel, Principal, Englewood High School, Chicago, Ill.
Orr, Beryl, Principal, Lincoln Elementary School, Middletown, Ohio
Orr, Louise, 925 Crockett St., Amarillo, Tex.
Ort, Mrs. Lorrene Love, Bowling Green State University, Bowling Green, Ohio
Orton, Don A., Col. of Educ., University of Utah, Salt Lake City, Utah
Osborn, Jesse, 3436 Longfellow Blvd., St. Louis, Mo.
Osborn, John K., Central State College of Education, Mt. Pleasant, Mich.
Osborn, Wayland W., Dept. of Public Instruction, Des Moines, Iowa
Oster, John, Superintendent of Elementary Schools, New Lenox, Ill.
Ostrander, Raymond H., Supt. of Schools, Mineola, N.Y.
Ostwalt, Jay H., Box 144, Davidson, N.C.
Osuch, A. E., Newton Bateman Elem. School, Chicago, Ill.
O'Sullivan, Maurice J., Asst. Superintendent of Schools, Jersey City, N.J.
O'Sullivan, Nona R., 340 West St., Randolph, Mass.
Osuna, Pedro, Dist. Supt., Yuba College, Marysville, Calif.
Oswalt, Edna R., Head, Dept. of Spec. Educ., Kent State Univ., Kent, Ohio
Oswalt, William W., Jr., Read. Supv., Lehigh County Schools, Allentown, Pa.
Otterman, Lois M., New Haven State Teachers College, New Haven, Conn.

Otto, Henry J., University of Texas, Austin, Tex.
Ottoson, Rev. Joseph Wm., Soderville, Minn.
Overstreet, George T., Retired Prin., Burnett High School, Terrell, Tex.
Owen, Dottie Pearl, Elem. Supv., Jefferson County Schools, Birmingham, Ala.
Owen, Jason C., Louisiana Polytechnic Institute, Ruston, La.
Owen, Mary E., Editor, *The Instructor*, Dansville, N.Y.
Owens, Henry G., 13 Clarendon Ave., Sans Souci, Greenville, S.C.
Owens, Norma F., Nursing Educ., New York University, New York, N.Y.
Owings, Ralph S., Mississippi Southern College, Hattiesburg, Miss.
Ozdil, Ilhan, Ankara Caddesi 50, Pendik-Istanbul, Turkey

Pace, C. Robert, Chm., Dept. of Psych., Syracuse University, Syracuse, N.Y.
Packer, C. Kyle, 807 Lincoln Place, Niagara Falls, N.Y.
Padget, Mattie Bell, Principal, Elementary School, Carlsbad, N.M.
Pagan, Keith A., Bethany Nazarene College, Bethany, Okla.
Page, Carroll C., 527 North Main St., Fostoria, Ohio
Page, Ellis B., Eastern Michigan College, Ypsilanti, Mich.
Paine, H. W., Inst. of Inter-Amer. Aff., Amer. Emb., Balboa, Canal Zone
Painter, Fred B., Superintendent, Brighton School Dist. 1, Rochester, N.Y.
Paisley, Robert S., 5177 Park Ave., Bethel Park, Pa.
Palliser, G. C., Post Office Box 1525, Wellington, New Zealand
Palmer, Albert, Dept. of Educ., Macalester College, St. Paul, Minn.
Palmer, Anne M. H., Los Angeles State College, Los Angeles, Calif.
Palmer, Frank J., 208 Church Street, North Syracuse, N.Y.
Palmer, Mrs. Glea, P.O. Box 812, Florence, Ore.
Palmer, James B., Ginn and Company, Boston, Mass.
Palmer, John C., Dir. of Guidance, Public Schools, Concord, Mass.
Palmer, Josephine S., State Teachers College, New Paltz, N.Y.
Palmer, Lulu, State Department of Education, Montgomery, Ala.
Papsidero, Joseph, 205 Adclare Rd., Rockville, Md.
Paquin, Laurence G., Board of Education, Glastonbury, Conn.
Park, Maxwell G., Definance College, Definance, Ohio
Parke, Margaret B., 430 West 118th St., New York. N.Y.
Parker, Clyde, Asst. Supt. of Schools, Oak Park, Ill.
Parker, Edna, Florida State University, Tallahassee, Fla.
Parker, Floyd O., 1469 Ann St., Montgomery, Ala.
Parker, James R., Principal, Glidden School, DeKalb, Ill.
Parker, Marjorie H., District of Columbia Teachers Col., Washington, D.C.
Parker, Olin G., 1212 Roach St., Salina, Kan.
Parkinson, Daniel S., Research Asst., Univ. of Wisconsin, Madison, Wis.
Parkinson, E. L., 180 Keyes Rd., Christchurch, New Zealand
Parks, Ethel, Route 2, Calhoun, Mo.
Parkyn, George W., Dir., N. Z. Council for Educ. Research, Willington, New
   Zealand
Parmelee, Elizabeth, Headmistress, Calhoun School, New York, N.Y.
Parr, Kenneth E., Box 1348, Tapline, Beirut, Lebanon
Parry, O. Meredith, Principal, William Penn Senior High School, York, Pa.
Parsey, John M., Res. Dir., Natl. Project in Agric. Commun., East Lansing, Mich.
Parsons, Elmer E., President, Central College, McPherson, Kan.
Parsons, Robert G., Supt., Wilson Sch. Dist. 24, Arlington Heights, Ill.
Parsons, Seth H., Dept. of Educ., New Mexico Highlands Univ., Las Vegas, N.M.
Parton, Daisy, Dept. of Educ., Univ. of Alabama, University, Ala.
Partridge, Deborah C., Queens College, Flushing, N.Y.
Pascoe, David D., LaMesa-Spring Valley School Dist., LaMesa, Calif.
Pasricha, Bal Rama, National Defence Academy, Clement Town, Dehra Dun, U.P.
   India
Passow, A. Harry, Teachers Col., Columbia Univ., New York, N.Y.
Paster, G. Nicholas, Dir., Stud. Activ., Roosevelt Univ., Chicago, Ill.
Patch, Robert B., Superintendent of Schools, Marion, Mass.
Pate, Mildred, East Carolina College, Greenville, N.C.
Pate, Vi Martin, Holy Name College, Spokane, Wash.

Patrick, Robert B., Pennsylvania State University, University Park, Pa.
Patt, Jack M., San Jose State College, San Jose, Calif.
Pattee, Howard Hunt, P.O. Box 1211, Los Altos, Calif.
Patterson, Gordon E., 2 Park St., Boston, Mass.
* Patterson, Herbert, Oklahoma A. & M. College, Stillwater, Okla.
Pattison, Mattie, Dept. of Home Econ., Iowa State College, Ames, Iowa
Patton Earl D., 204 Gregory Hall, University of Illinois, Urbana, Ill.
Paul, Fred O., 2600—17th Street S.E., Canton, Ohio
Paul, Marvin S., 5934½ North Pauline Ave., Chicago, Ill.
Paulsen, Gaige B., Dean, University College, Athens, Ohio
Paulson, Alice T., Principal, High School, Blue Earth, Minn.
Pauly, Frank R., Dir. of Res., Board of Educ., Tulsa, Okla.
Pavel, Harriet, Greeley Vocational School, Chicago, Ill.
Pax, Rev. Walter, Brunnerdale Seminary, Canton, Ohio
Payne, Donald T., Methodist Mission, International P.O. Box 1182, Seoul, Korea
Payne, W. K., President, Savannah State College, Savannah, Ga.
Payne, Walter L., Lyons Township Junior College, La Grange, Ill.
Paynovich, Nicholas, 210 Ocatillo Ave., Ajo, Ariz.
Peabody, Ada Isabel, Westminster College, New Wilmington, Pa.
Peachman, Marguerite C., Principal, Watterson-Lake Schools, Cleveland, Ohio
Peacock, A. E., Supt. of Schools, Moose Jaw, Sask.
Pearson, Jim, 4355 Grand Blvd., Montreal, Quebec, Canada
Pearson, John C., Principal, Deer Path School, Lake Forest, Ill.
Pearson, Millie V., Oklahoma A. & M. College, Stillwater, Okla.
Pease, Clarence I., 3119—34th Place, Des Moines, Iowa
Pease, Mrs. Marion O., College of the Pacific, Stockton, Calif.
Peccolo, Charles, Superintendent of Schools, Wray, Colo.
Pedigo, Louise, Lynchburg College, Lynchburg, Va.
Peel, J. C., Dean, Florida Southern College, Lakeland, Fla.
Peiffer, Paul D., 5902 Old Jonestown Road, Harrisburg, Pa.
Peister, Ronald, Dir. of Music, Aurora High School, Aurora, Neb.
Pell, Richard E., University Apts., E-104, Bloomington, Ind.
Pella, Milton O., Univ. High School, Univ. of Wisconsin, Madison, Wis.
Pelton, Frank M., Univ. of Rhode Island, Kingston, R.I.
Penn, Floy L., Mt. Lebanon Public Schools, Pittsburgh, Pa.
Pennetta, Gerardo, 172 Harrison St., Bloomfield, N.J.
Penta, A. H. Della, Superintendent of Schools, Lodi, N.J.
Perdew, Philip W., University of Denver, Denver, Colo.
Perlmutter, Oscar W., St. Xavier College, Chicago, Ill.
Perlson, Philip, University of Wisconsin-Milwaukee, Milwaukee, Wis.
Pernecky, John M., Dept. of Music, Michigan State Univ., East Lansing, Mich.
Perny, Allen R., 2405—7th Ave. West, Bradenton, Fla.
Perrin, Porter G., Dept. of English, Univ. of Wash., Seattle, Wash.
Perry, Elizabeth W., 7 Harvard Ave., Brookline, Mass.
Perry, James Olden, Dept. of Educ., Texas Southern University, Houston, Tex.
Perry, W. D., University of North Carolina, Chapel Hill, N.C.
Persky, Mrs. Blanche, 45 Tennis Court, Brooklyn, N.Y.
Peters, Frank R., 194 Northridge Road, Columbus, Ohio
Peters, Jon S., State Dept. of Education, Sacramento, Calif.
Peters, Mary Magdalene, Asst. Supt. of Instruction, Ontario, Calif.
Petersen, Clarence E., Dir. of Curriculum, City Schools, Redwood City, Calif.
Petersen, Fred J., University of South Dakota, Vermillion, S.D.
Peterson, A. I., Supv. of Indian Education, Bemidji, Minn.
Peterson, Aaron Dean, R.R. No. 2, Villa Ridge, Godfrey, Ill.
Peterson, Basil H., President, Orange Coast College, Costa Mesa, Calif.
Peterson, C. H., Principal, Chas. Houston Elem. School, Alexandria, Va.
Peterson, Carl H., Principal, Esmond School, Chicago, Ill.
Peterson, Elmer T., Col. of Educ., State Univ. of Iowa, Iowa City, Iowa
Peterson, Evelyn F., Dir. of Elem. Educ., Waterloo, Iowa
Peterson, Laurine, University of Dubuque, Dubuque, Iowa
Peterson, LeRoy, Sch. of Educ., University of Wisconsin, Madison, Wis.

Peterson, Miriam E., Dir., Div. of Libraries, Public Schools, Chicago, Ill.
Petroski, Joseph J., Superintendent, School Union 56, Somersworth, N.H.
Pettersch, Carl A., State Teachers College, Danbury, Conn.
Petterson, Mrs. Muriel, Supv. of Lib., County Schools, San Luis Obispo, Calif.
Pettinga, R. C., Prin., North Fourth St. Christian School, Paterson, N.J.
Pettiss, J. O., Dept. of Educ., Louisiana State Univ., Baton Rouge, La.
Petty, Mary Clare, Col. of Educ., University of Oklahoma, Norman, Okla.
Petzold Robert G., Sch. of Music, University of Wisconsin, Madison, Wis.
Pezzullo, Thomas J., Asst. Supt., Johnston School Dept., Johnston, R.I.
Pfau, John M., Chicago Teachers College, Chicago, Ill.
Phaneuf, Paul H., Superintendent of Public Schools, Dracut, Mass.
Phay, John E., Bur. of Educ. Res., Univ. of Mississippi, University, Miss.
Phearman, Leo T., Long Beach State College, Long Beach, Calif.
Phelps, Norman F., Music Dept., Ohio State University, Columbus, Ohio
Phelps, Roger P., Music Dept., Mississippi Southern College, Hattiesburg, Miss.
Philips, Herbert A., Prin., Deep Creek Elem. School, Portsmouth, Va.
Phillips, A. J., Exec. Secy., Mich. Educ. Assn., Lansing, Mich.
Phillips, Cecil D., Iowa State Teachers College, Cedar Falls, Iowa
Phillips, Claude Anderson, Switzer Hall, Univ. of Missouri, Columbia, Mo.
Phillips, Murray G., 5 Target Lane, Lewittown, N.Y.
Phillips, Paul, 253 James Drive, Havertown, Pa.
Phillips, Thomas A., 203 East Park St., Marquette, Mich.
Philp, William A., P.O. Box 965, Mt. Union Station, Alliance, Ohio
Phinney, Mrs. Myrtle, Capitol Hill Senior High Schol, Oklahoma City, Okla.
Piazza, Frank, Asst. Superintendent, Board of Education, Bridgeport, Conn.
Picchiotti, Natalie, Prin., Schley School, Chicago, Ill.
Piekarz, Josephine A., Sch. of Educ., New York University, New York, N.Y.
Pierce, Arthur E., Superintendent, Hanover School Dist., Hanover, N.H.
Pierce, Raymond K., 81 Thimbleberry Lane, Levittown, Pa.
Pierce, Paul R., Dept. of Educ., Purdue University, Lafayette, Ind.
Pierson, Leroy R., Portland State Extension Center, Milwaukie, Ore.
Pierson, Mildred B., Principal, School No. 135, Baltimore, Md.
Pietz, Emil T., 4444 Irving St., Denver, Colo.
Pike, Carroll Milton, Jr., Northern Illinois University, DeKalb, Ill.
Pikunas, Justin, Psych. Dept., University of Detroit, Detroit, Mich.
Pilch, Mrs. Mary M., Mechanical Arts High School, St. Paul, Minn.
Pinckney, Paul W., Principal, Oakland High School, Oakland, Calif.
Pinkston, Dow G., 105 East Madison St., Yates Center, Kan.
Pitkin, Royce S., President, Goddard College, Plainfield, Vt.
Pitt, Rt. Rev. Msgr., Sec., Catholic School Board, Louisville, Ky.
Pittenger, Priscilla, San Francisco State College, San Francisco, Calif.
Pittman, DeWitt Kennieth, Prin., E. Mecklenburg Sr. High Schl., Matthews, N.C.
Pitts, Clara L., 1705 Kenyon St., N.W., Washington, D.C.
Plana, Juan F., Province Inspector of Prim. Inst., Camaguey, Cuba
Plantz, Nina, Principal, East Street School, Hicksville, N.J.
Pledger, Maud Myrtice, East Texas State Tchrs. Col., Commerce, Tex.
Plimpton, Blair, Superintendent of Schools, Park Ridge, Ill.
Pliska, Stanley Robert, Norfolk Div., Col. of William and Mary, Norfolk, Va.
Plog, Edward L., 6 Park Pl., Poughkeepsie, N.Y.
Plooster, Mrs. Beverly W., Box 293, Lakefield, Minn.
Plotnick, Morton, 21860 Beverly St., Oak Park, Mich.
Plucker, O. L., Superintendent of Schools, Independence, Mo.
Plumb, Valworth R., Div. of Educ., Duluth Br., Univ. of Minn., Duluth, Minn.
Plummer, Violin Gustavius, Oakwood College, Huntsville, Ala.
Podesta, Victor J., Asst. Superintendent of Schools, Plainfield, N.J.
Podlich, William F., Jr., Arizona State College, Tempe, Ariz.
Poehler, W. A., President, Concordia College, St. Paul, Minn.
Pogue, Graham, Dir. of Stud. Tchng., Ball State Tchrs. Col., Muncie, Ind.
Pohl, Rudolph G., Rt. No. 3, Box 94, Sherwood, Ore.
Polansky, Leon, 33-47 Fourteenth St., Long Island City, N.Y.
Polglase, Robert J., Vice-Prin., Bloomfield Junior High Sch., Bloomfield, N.J.

Pollak, William A., 1908 West Hood Ave., Chicago, Ill.
Pollard, Chiles Thompson, Superintendent of Schools, Sayville, L.I., N.Y.
Polley, Mrs. Victoria Z., Principal, Evershed School, Niagara Falls, N.Y.
Polychrones, James Z., 3208 North Halsted St., Chicago, Ill.
Pond, Millard Z., Superintendent of Schools, Burlington, Iowa
Ponton, Ruth V., 400 Second St., Alexandria, Va.
Poole, Albert E., 214 N. Washingfiton Circle, Lake Forest, Ill.
Poor, Gerald L., Central Michigan College, Mt. Pleasant, Mich.
Porter, F. W., Supt. of Schools, Greenfield, Mass.
Porter, R. H., Steck Company, Austin, Tex.
Potter, Donald G., 2500 Goss St., Boulder, Colo.
Potter, Muriel, Michigan State Normal College, Ypsilanti, Mich.
Potter, Willis N., College of the Pacific, Stockton, Calif.
Potthoff, Edward F., Col. of Educ., Univ. of Illinois, Urbana, Ill.
Potts, John F., President, Voorhees Junior College, Denmar, S.C.
Poulos, Thomas H., Michigan School for the Deaf, Flint, Mich.
Pound, Clarence A., Purdue University, Lafayette, Ind.
Pounds, Ralph L., Teachers Col., University of Cincinnati, Cincinnati, Ohio
Pourchot, Leonard L., 2780 Aster St., Pueblo, Colo.
Powell, Mrs. Ruth Marie, Tennessee State A. & I. Univ., Nashville, Tenn.
Powell, Mrs. Virginia L., Prin., Garfield-Buchanan Schls., Steubenville, Ohio
Powers, Francis P., Sch. of Educ., Boston College, Chestnut Hill, Mass.
Powers, Fred R., Superintendent, Amherst Schools, Amherst, Ohio
Prater, Juanita, Principal, Jackson Elementary School, Little Rock, Ark.
Pratt, L. Edward. Sch. of Educ., Southern Methodist University, Dallas, Tex.
Prentis, Roy C., State College Board, 41 Sherburne Ave., St. Paul, Minn.
Preston, Eleonora Marie, Los Angeles State College, Los Angeles, Calif.
Preston, Ralph C., Sch. of Educ., Univ. of Penn., Philadelphia, Pa.
Prestwood, Elwood L., 426 Righters Mill Rd., Gladwyne, Pa.
Pricco, Ernest, Principal, Melrose Park School, Melrose Park, Ill.
Price, Arthur H., San Jose State College, San Jose, Calif.
Price, Mrs. Franklin H., Principal, Adaire-Chandler Schools, Philadelphia, Pa.
Price, R. Holleman, University of Mississippi, University, Miss.
Price, Robert Diddams, Teachers College, Univ. of Cincinnati, Cincinnati, Ohio
Price, Ruth Evert, Language Arts Collaborator, Public Schools, Philadelphia, Pa.
Pridgeon, James M., P.O. Box 907, Chula Vista, Calif.
Prior, John J., St. John's University, Jamaica, N.Y.
Pritchard, Ruth B., 2205 Park Ave., Des Moines, Iowa
Pritzkan, Philo T., Dir., Curric. Center, Univ. of Connecticut, Storrs, Conn.
Privett, Zollie W., Principal, Elementary School, Center Moriches, N.Y.
Proctor, Bernard S., Central State College, Wilberforce, Ohio
Proctor, Ralph W., Superintendent of Schools, South Braintree, Mass.
Procunier, Robert W., 6850 East Prairie Road, Lincolnwood, Ill.
Profit, Gus F., Elementary Coordinator, Public Schools, Denver, Colo.
Prouse, Peter, 2201 Ridge Ave., Evanston, Ill.
Prudham, W. M., Prin., Collegiate and Vocational Inst., Owen Sound, Ont.
Prutzman, Stuart E., Superintendent of County Schools, Jim Thorpe, Pa.
Pugh, Sterling B., Prin., Washington School, New Rochelle, N.Y.
Pugno, Lawrence, San Jose State College, San Jose, Calif.
Pulliam, A. Lloyd, Knox College, Galesburg, Ill.
Pulsifer, Walter T., Sup. Massachusetts School Union 62, West Boylston, Mass.
Purdy, Norman E., Principal, Blue Ash School, Blue Ash, Ohio
Purdy, Ralph D., Dept. of Educ., Miami University, Oxford, Ohio
Puryear, R. W., Pres., Florida Normal and Indust. Mem. Col., St. Augustine, Fla.
Putnam, John F., Peabody College, Nashville, Tenn.
Pygman, C. H., Superintendent, School Dist. No. 89, Maywood, Ill.
Pyron, Mrs. Kate, Salem College Library, Winston-Salem, N.C.

Quall, Alvin B., Dean, Whitworth College, Spokane, Wash.
Quanbeck, Martin, Dean, Augsburg College, Minneapolis, Minn.
Quanbeck, Thor H., Augustana College, Sioux Falls, S.D.

Quarles, Mrs. Joyce, 3700 Sacramento Ave., El Paso, Tex.
Quick, Otho J., Northern Illinois University, DeKalb, Ill.
Quish, Bernard A., Prin., Phoebe Apperson Hearst School, Chicago, Ill.

Rabban, Meyer, Dir., The Windword School, White Plains, N.Y.
Rabin, Bernard, Bowling Green State University, Bowling Green, Ohio
Rabin, Marvin J., Dept. of Music, University of Kentucky, Lexington, Ky.
Radhakrishna, K. S., Hindustani Talimi Sangh., Sevagram, Wardha, M.P., India
Ragan, William B., Dept. of Educ., University of Oklahoma, Norman, Okla.
Ragsdale, Ted R., Southern Illinois University, Carbondale, Ill.
Rahn, Lloyd N., Siepert Hall, Bradley University, Peoria, Ill.
Ramer, Earl M., University of Tennessee, Knoxville, Tenn.
Ramsey, Grover C., Box 895, San Antonio, Tex.
Ramsey, J. W., Principal, Superior-Maitland School, Northfork, W.Va.
Ramseyer, John A., Ohio State University, Columbus, Ohio
Ramseyer, Lloyd L., President, Blufften College, Blufften, Ohio
Rand, E. W., Southern University, Baton Rouge, La.
Randall, Edwin H., Western State College, Gunnison, Colo.
Randall, Rachel, R.R. No. 6, Box 186, Kalamazoo, Mich.
Randall, William M., Dean, Wilmington College, Wilmington, N.C.
Randolph, Victor, Southern Illinois University, Carbondale, Ill.
Rankin, Earl F., Jr., University of Kansas City, Kansas City, Mo.
Rankin, George R., South Division High School, Milwaukee, Wis.
Rankin, Paul T., Asst. Supt. of Schools, Detroit, Mich.
Ranney, Harriet, Upper Iowa University, Fayette, Iowa
Rappaport, David, 2747 Coyle Ave., Chicago, Ill.
Rappaport, Mary B., State Education Department, Albany, N.Y.
Rasche, William F., Dir., Milwaukee Vocational School, Milwaukee, Wis.
Rasmussen, Elmer M., Dean, Dana College, Blair, Neb.
Rasmussen, Glen R., Univ. of Michigan Ext. Service, Flint, Mich.
Rattigan, Bernard T., Catholic University of America, Washington, D.C.
Raubinger, F. M., Commissioner of Educ., State Dept. of Educ., Trenton, N.J.
Rausch, Richard G., Principal, Webster Hill School, West Hartford, Conn.
Rawson, K. O., Superintendent of Schools, Clintonville, Wis.
Ray, Ethel, Dept. of Educ., Western Illinois State College, Macomb, Ill.
Ray, Rolland, Col. of Educ., State Univ. of Iowa, Iowa City, Iowa
Reade, I. D., Jr., Superintendent, Hingham Public Schools, Hingham, Mass.
Reals, Willis H., Dean, Univ. Col., Washington University, St. Louis, Mo.
Rear, Leslie V., Superintendent of Schools, Salem Drive, Whippany, N.J.
Reas, Herbert D., Act. Dean, Sch. of Education, Seattle Univ., Seattle, Wash.
Reaugh, William L., Superintendent of Schools, Dolton, Ill.
Red, S. B., University of Houston, Houston, Tex.
Reddy, Anne L., Principal, Savannah Country Day School, Savannah, Ga.
Reddel, William D., 2101 West Missouri St., Midland, Tex.
Rediger, Henry J., Principal, Lakewood Lutheran Schools, Lakewood, Ohio
Reed, Bernard W., Industrial Relations Center, 975 East 60th St., Chicago, Ill.
Reed, Donald G., 2028 Sixth St., Madison, Ill.
Reed, Duane E., 193 North Eureka St., Columbus, Ohio
Reed, Earl J., Asst. Supt., School Dist. 122, Longview, Wash.
Reed, Helen M., 324 Hapton Court, Lexington, Ky.
Reed, Lorena M., 2358 Seabury Ave., Terre Haute, Ind.
Reed, Lula B., County Supt. of Schools, Red Oak, Iowa
Reed, Richard Y., University of Miami, Coral Gables, Fla.
Rees, Helen E., Educ. Center, Smith College, Northampton, Mass.
Reeves, Floyd W., Michigan State University, East Lansing, Mich.
Reeves, Mrs. Miriam G., State Department of Education, Baton Rouge, La.
Reeves, Wilfred, Prin., Roosevelt School, Olympia, Wash.
Rehage, Kenneth J., Dept. of Educ., University of Chicago, Chicago, Ill.
Reichert, Stephen B., Jr., Pasadena City College, Pasadena, Calif.
Reid, C. E., Jr., 6225 No. Circuit Drive, Beaumont, Tex.
Reid, Charles H., Jr., 2527 Columbine Dr., Durango, Colo.

Reid, L. Leon, Sch. of Educ., University of Virginia, Charlottesville, Va.
Reiffel, Mrs. Sophie M., Principal, Von Steuben High School, Chicago, Ill.
Reifsnyder, Rev. John A., 9 East 12th St., Covington, Ky.
Reilley, Albert G., Asst. Supt. of Schools, Framingham, Mass.
Reinhardt, Emma, Eastern Illinois State College, Charleston, Ill.
Reinhardt, Mrs. Lorraine, Sch. of Educ., Northwestern University, Evanston, Ill.
Reinke, Ralph L., Concordia Teachers College, River Forest, Ill.
Reiter, Mrs. Anne, 51 Buchanan Place, Bronx, N.Y.
Reiter, M. R., Superintendent of Schools, Morrisville, Pa.
Reitze, Arnold W., 3 Lienau Place, Jersey City, N.J.
Reller, Theodore L., Sch. of Educ., University of California, Berkeley, Calif.
Remmers, Herman, Purdue University, Lafayette, Ind.
Remon, Marion E., Dir. Elem. Educ., Public Schools, Melrose, Mass.
Rempel, P. J., State College of Washington, Pullman, Wash.
Renard, John N., Oxnard Union High School, Oxnard, Calif.
Renke, W. W., 507 Waid Ave., Muncie, Ind.
Renouf, Edna M., Prin., Scenic Hills School, Springfield, Pa.
Resek, E. Frederick, Principal, Bridge Elem. School, Chicago, Ill.
Reuter, George S., Jr., Amer. Fed. of Tchrs., 28 E. Jackson Blvd., Chicago, Ill.
Reuther, Carolyn A., Sch. of Educ., University of Wisconsin, Madison, Wis.
Reuwsaat, Emily A., 503½ Byron St., Mankato, Minn.
Reynolds, Mrs. Dorothy S., Supv. Tchr., Dept. of Instruction, Denver, Colo.
Reynolds, Helen, Sch. of Educ., New York University, New York, N.Y.
Reynolds, James W., Col. of Educ., University of Texas, Austin, Tex.
Reynolds, Maynard C., University of Minnesota, Minneapolis, Minn.
Rhoads, Jonathan E., Provost, Univ. of Pennsylvania, Philadelphia, Pa.
Rhodes, J. Clark, Col. of Educ., Univ. of Tennessee, Knoxville, Tenn.
Rhodes, L. H., Principal, Central Elem. School, Alamogordo, N. M.
Ricciardi, Richard S., Dept. of Educ., 100 Reef Rd., Fairfield, Conn.
Rice, Arthur H., Mang. Editor, *Nation's Schools*, Chicago, Ill.
Rice, James G., Stephens College, Columbia, Mo.
Rice, J. C., Superintendent of Schools, Elkhart, Ind.
Rice, Ralph Samuel, Supv. Prin., North Hills Joint Schls., Pittsburgh, Pa.
Rice, Roy C., Dept. of Educ., Arizona State College, Tempe, Ariz.
Rice, Theodore D., 33963 North Hampshire, Livonia, Mich.
Richards, Eugene, 2450 West Rice St., Chicago, Ill.
Richards, Henry M. M., Dean of Faculty, Muhlenberg Col., Allentown, Pa.
Richardson, John S., Ohio State University, Columbus, Ohio
Richardson, L. S., University of Houston, Houston, Tex.
Richardson, Orvin T., Prof. of Educ., Washington Univ., St. Louis, Mo.
Richardson, Thomas H., 540 West 122nd St., New York, N.Y.
Richey, Herman G., Dept. of Educ., University of Chicago, Chicago, Ill.
Richman, Seymour, 14 East Cheshire Pl., Staten Island, N. Y.
Riday, George E., Alderson-Broaddus College, Philippi, W. Va.
Rider, Chester G., Superintendent of Schools, Concord, Ark.
Ridgway, Helen A., State Dept. of Educ., Hartford, Conn.
Riedel, Mark T., 210 South Edgewood, La Grange, Ill.
Riegle, H. Edgar, Supt. Gettysburg Joint Sch. Sys. High School, Gettysburg, Pa.
Riegel, Samuel A., Prin., Biddle Street Area School, West Chester, Pa.
Riehm, Carl L., 1306 Fisherman Rd., Norfolk, Va.
Riethmiller, Gorton, President, Olivet College, Olivet, Mich.
Rigby, Avard A., Brigham Young Univ. Laboratory School, Provo, Utah
Riggle, Earl L., Muskingum College, New Concord, Ohio
Riggs, Edwon L., 2802 E. McDowell St., Phoenix, Ariz.
Righter, Charles L., Fairmont State College, Shinnston, W. Va.
Rikkola, V. John, Dept. of Educ., State Teachers College, Salem, Mass.
Riley, Miriam, Principal, R. L. Hope School, Atlanta, Ga.
Rinott, Moshe, Dir., Dept. of Education, Haifa, Israel
Risinger, Robert G., Col. of Educ., University of Maryland, College Park, Md.
Risk, Thomas M., University of South Dakota, Vermillion, S.D.
Ritchie, Harold L., Prin., Memorial School, North Haledon, N.J.

Ritchie, Harold S., Asst. Superintendent of Schools, Paterson. N.J.
Ritscher, Richard C., Danbury State Teachers College, Danbury, Conn.
Ritsema, Louise, 231 Wildwood, Ann Arbor, Mich.
Ritter, Paul J., Western Carolina College, Cullowhee, N.C.
Ritter, William E., 2910 East State St., Sharon, Pa.
Rivard, Thomas L., Superintendent of Schools, Chelmsford, Mass.
Rivlin, Harry N., Div. of Tchr. Educ., 535 East 80th St., New York, N.Y.
Roach, Hildred Elizabeth, Tuskegee Institute, Ala.
Robbins, Edward T., Supt., Alamo Heights School Dist., San Antonio, Tex.
Robbins, Irving, Queens College, Flushing, N.Y.
Robbins, Miriam E.. 1800 Como Ave., S.E., Minneapolis, Minn.
Robbins, Rintha, Office of County Supt. of Schools, Madera, Calif.
Roberson, James A., Prin., Lamar and Valley View Schools, Abilene, Tex.
Roberts, Dodd Edward, Oakland County Schools, Pontiac, Mich.
Roberts, Ralph M., Box 1198, University, Ala.
Roberts, J. B., Head. Dept. of Educ., West Texas State College, Canyon. Tex.
Robinson, Alice L., Supv., Library Service, Bd. of Educ., Frederick, Md.
Robinson, Cliff, 1020—18th Ave., East, Eugene, Ore.
Robinson, Edward C., Principal, First Ave. Intermediate School, Arcadia, Calif.
Robinson, H. E., 205 East 31st St., Austin, Tex.
Robinson, Mrs. Helen M., Dept. of Educ., Univ. of Chicago, Chicago, Ill.
Robinson, Patricia A., Child Develop. Lab., Univ. of Illinois, Urbana, Ill.
Robinson, Richard R., Superintendent of Schools, Trenton, N.J.
Robinson, Roy E., Superintendent of Schools, Ferndale, Mich.
Robinson, Thomas L., Alabama State College, Montgomery, Ala.
Robinson, William McK.. Western State College, Kalamazoo, Mich.
Robinson, Willie, Prin., Hannah J. Mallory Junior High School, Goodwater, Ala.
Robison, W. L., Dir. of Instruction, City Schools, Norfolk, Va.
Roblee, Dana B., 5510—24th Avenue, Washington, D.C.
Rodgers, John O., Dept. of Educ., Southwestern University, Georgetown, Tex.
Rodriguez-Diaz, M., Alfred University, Alfred, N.Y.
Roeder, Jesse N., Supt. of Schools, Palmerton, Pa.
Roenigk, Elsie Mae, R.D. No. 1, Cabot, Pa.
Roeper, George A., Headmaster, City and Country School, Bloomfield Hills, Mich.
Roff, Rosella Zuber, 4410 South 148th St., Seattle, Wash.
Rogers, Elbert E., Principal, Carver School, Columbia, S.C.
Rogers, J. Lloyd, Southwestern Texas State Teachers College, San Marcos, Tex.
Rogers, John D., Prin., Mt. Lebanon Elem. Schools, Pittsburgh, Pa.
Rogers, Virgil M., Dean, Sch. of Educ., Syracuse University, Syracuse, N.Y.
Rogers, William R., San Jose State College, San Jose, Calif.
Rogosin, H. R., 3822 Evans, Hollywood, Calif.
Rohan, William, Asst. Prin., Columbus School, Chicago, Ill.
Rohrbach, Q. A. W., Pres., State Teachers College, Kutztown, Pa.
Rolfe, Howard C., 1140 Pleasant Hill Road, Sebastopol, Calif.
Rollins, William B., Jr.. 7772 Otto Street, Downey, Calif.
Rollins, Willis R., 15 Rose Brook Rd., West Hartford, Conn.
Romano, Louis, 1701 East Capitol Dr., Shorewood, Wis.
Rondinella, Orestes R., 1415—70th St., Brooklyn, N.Y.
Ronshaugen, Raydon P., Asst. Headmaster, Kent School, Kent, Conn.
Rooney, Edward B., Exec. Dir., Jesuit Educ. Assn., New York, N.Y.
Rose, Ervin, 117 West 13th St., New York, N.Y.
Roseberry, Minnie, Box 545, Flagstaff, Ariz.
Rosebrock, Allan F., State Department of Education, Trenton, N.J.
Rosecrance, Francis C., Dean, Col. of Educ., Wayne State Univ., Detroit, Mich.
Rosen, Signey, Col. of Educ., University of Illinois, Urbana, Ill.
Rosenberg, Samuel, Bureau of Jewish Education, Savannah, Ga.
Rosenbluh, Benjamin J., Principal, Central High School, Bridgeport, Conn.
Rosenlof, George W., Dean of Admissions, Univ. of Nebraska, Lincoln, Neb.
Rosenstein, Pearl, Principal, Barnard Lab. School, New Haven, Conn.
Rosenthal, Alan G., 26 Leslie Pl., New Rochelle, N.Y.

Rosenzweig, Celia, Principal, Stone School, Chicago, Ill.
Rossmiller, Richard, Educ. Bldg., University of Wisconsin, Madison, Wis.
Roster, Arlene A., Long Beach State College, Long Beach, Calif.
Roswell, Florence G., City College Education Clinic, New York, N.Y.
Roth, Bernard, 180 East 163rd St., Bronx, N.Y.
Roth, Bernice, Northern Illinois University, DeKalb, Ill.
Roth, Julian B., Los Angeles State College, Los Angeles, Calif.
Rothenberg, William, Jr., 144-26 Seventy-fifth Road, Flushing, N.Y.
Rothney, John W. M., Dept. of Educ., Univ. of Wisconsin, Madison, Wis.
Rothstein, Jerome H., San Francisco State College, San Francisco, Calif.
Rothwell, Angus B., Superintendent of Schools, Manitowoc, Wis.
Roush, Jean R., 711 South 2nd Ave. West, Newton, Iowa
Rousseve, Charles B., Principal, Johnson Locett School, New Orleans, La.
Rowland, Albert L., 10 Surrey Rd., Melrose Park, Philadelphia, Pa.
Rowland, Loyd W., Dir., Louisiana Assoc. for Mental Health, New Orleans, La.
Rowland, Sydney V., Temple University, Philadelphia, Pa.
Rozema, John R., Superintendent of Public Schools, Garfield, N.J.
Rubie, Harry C., 1130 Fifth Ave., Chula Vista, Calif.
Rubinstein, Samuel R., 309 Avenue C, Apt. 3C, Stuyvesant Town, N.Y.
Rubke, Walter C., 6325 Camden St., Oakland, Calif.
Ruch, Claud C., 1456 Oak Ave., Evanston, Ill.
Ruch, Mary A. R., RFD 1, Box 33, Tower City, Pa.
Ruckman, Stanley V., Oregon College of Education, Monmouth, Ore.
Ruddell, Arden K., Sch. of Educ., University of California, Riverside, Calif.
Rudman, Herbert C., Col. of Educ., Michigan State Univ., East Lansing, Mich.
Rudolf, Kathleen Brady, Monroe High School, Rochester, N.Y.
Rugen, Mabel E., University of Michigan, Ann Arbor, Mich.
Rugg, Harold, Woodstock, N.Y.
Rugh, Douglas, Teachers College of Connecticut, New Britain, Conn.
Rugh, Dwight, International Com. of YMCA, 291 Broadway, New York, N.Y.
Rule, Philip, Superintendent, School District No. 11, LaJunta, Colo.
Rulon, Phillip J., Peabody House, 13 Kirkland St., Cambridge, Mass.
Ruman, Edward L., Dept. of Tchg., Iowa State Tchrs. College, Cedar Falls, Iowa
Rumsey, Mary H., Hannibal-LaGrange College, College Heights, Hannibal, Mo.
Rung, Wilbur K., Senior High School, Altoona, Pa.
Runyan, Charles S., Marshall College, Huntington, W. Va.
Rusch, Reuben R., State University Teachers College, Oneonta, N.Y.
Rush, Mrs. Alice Foster, P.O. Box 2815, University Sta., Gainesville, Fla.
Rushdoony, Haig A., 901 Santa Lucia Ave., San Bruno, Calif.
Russel, John H., University of Denver, Denver, Colo.
Russell, David H., Sch. of Educ., University of California, Berkeley, Calif.
Russell, Earle S., Superintendent of Schools, Windsor, Conn.
Russell, Edward J., Superintendent of Schools, Pittsfield, Mass.
Russell, James L., Dean, Grad. Div., West Texas State College, Canyon, Tex.
Russell, James W., Northwestern Univ., 450 East Ohio St., Chicago, Ill.
* Russell, John Dale, 29 Washington Square West, New York, N.Y.
Russell, Karlene V., State Department of Education, Montpelier, Vt.
Russell, Robert D., Sch. of Educ., Stanford University, Stanford, Calif.
Russo, Anthony J., 20 Summer St., Providence, R.I.
Rutan, Harold Duane, Missouri Valley College, Marshall, Mo.
Rutledge, James A., University of Nebraska, Lincoln, Neb.
Rux, David Alan, Wisconsin State College, Oshkosh, Wis.
Ryan, Carl J., Dean, Tchrs. Col., Athenaeum of Ohio, Cincinnati, Ohio
Ryan, Margaret R., 23-22 Thirty-sixth St., Long Island City, N.Y.
Ryan, W. Carson, Dept. of Educ., Univ. of North Carolina, Chapel Hill, N.C.
Rye, Howard H., Illinois State Normal University, Normal, Ill.
Rzepka, Louis, Harvard Graduate Sch. of Education, Cambridge, Mass.

Sabik, Adolph J., Principal, Franklin School, East Chicago, Ind.
Sachs, Moses B., Congregation B'Nai Abraham, St. Louis Park, Minn.
Sack, Marion J., 5326 North Camac St., Philadelphia, Pa.

Sailer, Agnes, 705 Norton Road, Alexandria, Va.
Salen, George P., 300 Hollowood Dr., West Lafayette, Ind.
Salinger, Herbert E., 2933 Sunrise Dr., Napa, Calif.
Salmons, George B., Plymouth Teachers College, Plymouth, N.H.
Salsbury, Jerome C., Dir. of Curric., Board of Educ., Bloomfield, N.J.
Salser, G. Alden, Principal, Mayberry School, Wichita, Kan.
Salten, David G., Supt. of Schools, Long Beach, N.Y.
Saltz, Martin, Read. Specialist, Regional School Dist. No. 8, Hebron, Conn.
Samson, Gordon E., Chm., Dept. of Educ., Fenn College, Cleveland, Ohio
Samson, Ruth D., 432 S. Curson Ave., Los Angeles, Calif.
Samuels, R. L., Principal, Grove Avenue School, Barrington, Ill.
Sand, Ole, Dept. of Educ., Wayne University, Detroit, Mich.
Sanders, Dannetta M., Hunter College, 695 Park Ave., New York, N.Y.
Sanders, Richard H., 10639 Drew St., Chicago, Ill.
Sanderson, Arnold T., Principal, High School, Worthington, Minn.
Sanderson, Jesse O., Superintendent of Schools, Raleigh, N.C.
Sandilos, J. C., West Windsor Twp. Board of Education, Dutch Neck, N.J.
Sando, Wilbur B., Dean, Div. of Educ., Bethel College, Mishawaka, Ind.
Sandron, Leo, 5820 Montgall Ave., Kansas City, Miss.
Sansone, A. R., Principal, Kelly High School, Chicago, Ill.
Sarafian, Armen, Coord. of Sec. Educ., City Schools, Pasadena, Calif.
Sarner, David S., Div. of Sec. Educ., Temple University, Philadelphia, Pa.
Sartain, Harry W., Dir. of Curric. & Research, Roseville Schls., St. Paul, Minn.
Satterfield, Martha A., 40 North Summit Ave., Gaithersburg, Md.
Sattler, Wilhelmina F., 1260 E. 84th St., Cleveland, Ohio
Sauer, Dorothy V., Principal, Reavis School, Chicago, Ill.
Saunders, Alden C., Superintendent of Schools, Foster Center, R.I.
Sausjord, Gunnar, Div. of Educ., San Francisco State Col., San Francisco, Calif.
Sauvain, Walter H., Dept. of Educ., Bucknell University, Lewisburg, Pa.
Savage, Tom K., Austin Peay State College, Clarksville, Tenn.
Sawin, Ethel, Beal High School, Shrewsbury, Mass.
Sax, Gilbert, 1789 Alvira St., Los Angeles, Calif.
Sayed, Fath-elbad, Audio-Visual Dept., Ministry of Education, Cairo, Egypt
Saylor, Charles F., Superintendent of Schools, New Wilmington, Pa.
Saylor, Galen, Dept. of Educ., University of Nebraska, Lincoln, Neb.
Scanlan, William J., Consultant, Teacher Recruitment Project, St. Paul, Minn.
Scanlon, Kathryn I., Sch. of Educ., Fordham University, New York, N.Y.
Schaadt, Lucy G., Cedar Crest College, Allentown, Pa.
Schaaf, Pearl R., State Department of Education, Lincoln, Neb.
Schaefer, Frances M., 7937 Paxton Ave., Chicago, Ill.
Schaefer, Robert J., Chm., Dept. of Educ., Washington Univ., St. Louis, Mo.
Schaibly, Colon L., Admin. Asst., Waukegan Twp. High School, Waukegan, Ill.
Schardein, Raymond C., 711 Missouri Ave., Columbia, Mo.
Scharf, Louis, 570 Lefferts Ave., Brooklyn, N.Y.
Schelske, A. H., Principal, Campus Lab. School, State College, St. Cloud, Minn.
Schenke, Lahron H., Dept. of Educ., Drury College, Springfield, Mo.
Schiffilea, Doris, Mount St. Mary's College, Los Angeles, Calif.
Schiffley, Caroline, Principal, A. C. Moore School, Columbia, S.C.
Schlappich, Leon N., State Teachers College, Mansfield, Pa.
Schlegel, Miriam A., Dept. of Educ., Juaniata College, Huntington, Pa.
Schlichting, Harry F., University of Tulsa, Tulsa, Okla.
Schmidt, Rev. Austin G., Dir., Loyola University Press, Chicago, Ill.
Schmidt, L. G. H., Headmaster, Tech. Sch., Roseberg, New South Wales
Schmidt, Ralph L. W., Box 7703, University Station, Baton Rouge, La.
Schmidt, William S., County Superintendent of Schools, Upper Marlboro, Md.
Schmitt, Irvin H., 4808 South Thirtieth St., Arlington, Va.
Schmitt, John A., Educ. Psychologist, Public Schools, Ithaca, N.Y.
Schmitt, Marvin J., 523 North Kenilworth Ave., Oak Park, Ill.
Schnabel, Robert V., Asst. Supt. of Educ., Lutheran Church, Fort Wayne, Ind.
Schneider, Bernhard W., Superintendent of Schools, Rutherford, N.J.
Schnell, Fred, Principal, Jefferson School, Sheboygan, Wis.

Schneyer, J. Wesley, Read. Clinic, Univ. of Pennsylvania, Philadelphia, Pa.
Schnitzen, Joseph P., Dir., Student Pers., Texas A. & I. College, Kingsville, Tex.
Schoeller, Arthur W., Wisconsin State College, Milwaukee, Wis.
Schoolcraft, Arthur A., West Virginia Wesleyan College, Buckhannon, W.Va.
Schooler, Virgil E., Indiana University, Bloomington, Ind.
Schooling, Herbert W., Superintendent of Schools, Webster Groves, Mo.
Schott, M. S., Central Missouri State College, Warrensburg, Mo.
Schreiber, Herman, 80 Clarkson Ave., Brooklyn, N.Y.
Schroeder, Marie L., 3125 N. Spangler St., Philadelphia, Pa.
Schrupp, M. H., San Diego State College, San Diego, Calif.
Schueler, Herbert, Dept. of Educ., Queens College, Flushing, N.Y.
Schumann, Victor, 3355 North 23rd St., Milwaukee, Wis.
Schuller, Charles F., Michigan State University, East Lansing, Mich.
Schultz, Frank G., South Dakota State College, Brookings, S.D.
Schultz, Frederick, Box 931, G.P.O., New York, N.Y.
Schunert, Jim R., San Diego State College, San Diego, Calif.
Schutz, Richard E., Arizona State College, Tempe, Ariz.
Schutz, Seymour, 246 West End Ave., New York, N.Y.
Schuyler, Helen K., Kansas State Tchrs. College, Pittsburg, Kan.
Schwanholt, Dana B., Valparaiso University, Valparaiso, Ind.
Schwartz, Alfred, Dept. of Educ., Drake University, Des Moines, Iowa
Schwartz, William P., Principal, Caton School, Brooklyn, N.Y.
Schwarz, A. R., Chm., Dept. of Educ., North Central Col., Naperville, Ill.
Schwarzenberger, Alfred J., Jefferson School, Medford, Wis.
Scobey, Mary Margaret, San Francisco State College, San Francisco, Calif.
Scofield, Alice Gill, San Jose State College, San Jose, Calif.
Scott, Cecil Winfield, Rutgers University, New Brunswick, N.J.
Scott, Frances Aliene, State Dept. of Education, Charleston, W. Va.
Scott, Guy, Larned State Hospital, Larned, Kan.
Scott, Helen Elizabeth, Rhode Island College of Education, Providence, R.I.
Scott, Hester, Principal, Westside School, Niles, Mich.
Scott, Jeanne E., Central Missouri State College, Warrensburg, Mo.
Scott, Myrtle J., 100 Mira Mar, Long Beach, Calif.
Scott, Owen, College of Educ., University of Georgia, Athens, Ga.
Scott, Walter E., Supt., Tantasqua Regional School Dist., Sturbridge, Mass.
Scott, Walter W., Supt. of Schools, Holland, Mich.
Scritchfield, Floyd C., University of Denver, Denver, Colo.
Scrivner, Perry D., Dept. of Educ., Southwestern University, Memphis, Tenn.
Seagoe, May V., Sch. of Educ., University of California, Los Angeles, Calif.
Seaman, Marguerite, State Teachers College, Towson, Md.
Searles, Warren B., 467 Central Park West, New York, N.Y.
Sears, J. B., Professor Emeritus of Educ., Stanford University, Stanford, Calif.
Seaton, Donald F., Supt. of Schools, Boone, Iowa
Seay, Maurice F., Kellogg Foundation, Battle Creek, Mich.
Sechler, Hazel, 800 West Eighth St., Silver City, N.M.
Secrist, Chester C., 1315 Middle-Bellville Rd., Mansfield, Ohio
Sederberg, Charles H., 3905 Xenwood Ave. South, St. Louis Park, Minn.
Seedor, Marie M., 1401 Lincoln Ave., Prospect Park, Pa.
Seeds, Corinne A., 1416 Holmby Ave., Los Angeles, Calif.
Segner, Esther F., Women's Col., Univ. of North Carolina, Greensboro, N. C.
Seifert, George G., 11305 Hessler Road, Cleveland, Ohio
Self, David, Supt., Butler County Board of Education, Greenville, Ala.
Selleck, E. R., Supt. of Schools, Dist. 98, Berwyn, Ill.
Semmler, Albert E., 2906 Whitney Ave., Hamden, Conn.
Sentman, Everette E., Editor-in-Chief, United Educators, Inc., Lake Bluff, Ill.
Serge, Henrietta E., New Haven State Teachers College, New Haven, Conn.
Serviss, Trevor K., L. W. Singer Co., Syracuse, N.Y.
Seubert, Eugene E., Dept. of Educ., Washington Univ., St. Louis, Mo.
Seville, George C., 134 Newcomb Road, Tenafly, N.J.
Sexton, John M., Principal, Northeast High School, St. Petersburg, Fla.
Sexton, Wray E., 23 Hoffman St., Maplewood, N.J.

Seyfert, Warren C., Milwaukee Country Day School, Milwaukee, Wis.
Shack, Jacob H., Asst. Supt., Curr. Div., Board of Educ., Brooklyn, N.Y.
Shackson, Lee, Music Dept., Otterbein College, Westerville, Ohio
Shafer, Robert E., Col. of Educ., Wayne State University, Detroit, Mich.
Shaftel, Fannie R., Sch. of Educ., Stanford University, Stanford, Calif.
Shales, J. M., Ball State Teachers College, Muncie. Ind.
Shane, Harold G., Sch. of Educ., Northwestern University, Evanston, Ill.
Shankman, Mrs. Florence, 20 Garner St., South Norwalk, Conn.
Shannon, Gail, Col. of Educ., University of Oklahoma, Norman, Okla.
Shannon, MacRae, Principal, Ottawa Twp. High School, Ottawa, Ill.
Shaplin, Judson T., 182 Upland Rd., Cambridge, Mass.
Shappelle, Rev. James, 5440 Moeller Ave., Norwood, Ohio
Shattuck, George E., Prin., Norwich Free Academy, Norwich, Conn.
Shaw, Archibald B., Supt. of Schools, Scarsdale, N.Y.
Shaw, M. Luelle, Principal, Broadmoor Elementary School, Miami, Fla.
Shea, James T., Dir. of Research, School Dist., San Antonio, Tex.
Shea, William K., Inspector of Separate Schools, Ottawa, Ont.
Sheehan, Rosemary, Prin., Woodrow Wilson Jr. High School, Tulsa. Okla.
Sheldon, Muriel. Supv. of Counseling. Div. of Sec. Educ., Los Angeles, Calif.
Shelton, Nollie W., Supt., Camden County Schools, Camden, N. C.
Shepard, Robert H., Spicer Memorial College, Kirkee, Poona, India
Shepard, Samuel, Jr., Dir., Elem. Educ., Board of Education, St. Louis, Mo.
Shepherd, Gerald Q., Dept. of Educ., Los Angeles State Col., Los Angeles, Calif.
Sherer, Lorraine, University of California. Los Angeles. Calif.
Sheridan, Marion C., Head. Eng. Dept., High School. New Haven, Conn.
Sherman, Neil, Supv., Upper Elem. Grades, Dist. No. 1, Phoenix, Ariz.
Shinaberry, Charles G., Box 177, Slippery Rock. Pa.
Shipka, Emil, Dir. of Business, Ind. Sch. Dist. No. 2, Coleraine, Minn.
Shipp, Donald E., Principal, Waller Elementary School, Bossier City, La.
Shoberg, T. C., Superintendent, Community High School, Woodstock, Ill.
Shoemaker, F. L., 15 Woodside Dr., Athens, Ohio
Shoemaker, Francis, Teachers College, Columbia University, New York, N. Y.
Shoemaker, M. H., 730 North Lincoln, Hastings, Neb.
Sholund, Milford, Gospel Light Press, Glendale, California
Shores, J. Harlan, Col. of Educ., University of Illinois, Urbana, Ill.
Short, James E., Western Montana College of Education, Dillon, Mont.
Short, Richard R., Superintendent, Public Schools, Hastings, Neb.
Shreve, Robert H., Principal, Arrowhead High School, Hartland, Wis.
Shultz, Robert R., Drake University, Des Moines, Iowa
Shy, P. R., 570 Lane Ave., Jackson, Tenn.
* Sias. A. B., Professor Emeritus. Ohio University, Athens, Ohio
Sica, Morris G., P.O. Box 443, New Paltz, N.Y.
Sickles, F. J., 296 Livingston Ave.. New Brunswick, N.J.
Siderman, S. M., Barber School, Highland Park, Mich.
Siebert, Mrs. Edna M., Principal, Kelvyn Park High School, Chicago, Ill.
Siebrecht. Elmer B., 3019 Queen Anne Ave., Seattle, Wash.
Siegel, Mrs. Beatrice, 5761 Hillview Park Ave., Van Nuys, Calif.
Sieswerda, David E., Principal, Jackson School, Phoenix, Ariz.
Siewers, Karl, 5383 N. Bowmanville Ave., Chicago, Ill.
Silas, Gordon, Director, Teacher Educ., Roanoke College. Salem. Va.
Silver, Herbert, Principal, Treasure Island Elem. School, Miami Beach. Fla.
Silverman, Jacob E., Act. Principal, Public School No. 6, New York, N.Y.
Silvern, Leonard Charles, 1128 Tigertail Rd., Los Angeles, Calif.
Silvey, Herbert M., Bur. of Research, Iowa State Tchrs. Col., Cedar Falls, Iowa
Simmons, Patricia C., Whittier College, Whittier. Calif.
Simmons, Robert E., Principal, Edison Elementary School, Lima, Ohio
Simms, Naomi, Dept. of Educ.. Kent University, Kent, Ohio
Simon, Donald L., Principal. High School, Bloomington, Ind.
Simon, Eric, Sherman, Conn.
Simons, Aubrey H., Asst. Superintendent, Unified School Dist., Pomona, Calif.
Simpson, David J., Principal, Thomas Holme School, Philadelphia, Pa.

Simpson, Mrs. Ellen J., 1640 South Valley St., Kansas City, Kan.
Simpson, Ray H., Col. of Educ., University of Illinois, Urbana, Ill.
Simpson, Robert J., Public Schools, St. Clair, Mich.
Sims, H. H., Superintendent of Schools, Bristow, Okla.
Sims, Harold W., 305 West 94th Pl., Chicago, Ill.
Sims, Verner M., Col. of Educ., University of Alabama, University, Ala.
Singletary, James D., Dean, Maryland State College, Princess Anne, Md.
Singleton, Carlton M., Col. of Educ., State Univ. of Iowa, Iowa City, Iowa
Singleton, Gordon G., 2104 Gorman Ave., Waco, Tex.
Singleton, Ira C., Teachers Col., University of Cincinnati, Cincinnati, Ohio
Singleton, Stanton J., Col. of Educ., University of Georgia, Athens, Ga.
Sininger, Harlan, New Mexico Highlands Univ., Las Vegas, N.M.
Sires, Ely, 5018 LaCrosse Lane, Madison, Wis.
Sisson, S. Hull, Nebraska Wesleyan University, Lincoln, Neb.
Sister Ann Augusta, S.M.D., 400 The Fenway, Boston, Mass.
Sister Agnes Cecilia, Principal, Nazareth Academy, Rochester, N.Y.
Sister Agnes Marie Smith, Brescia College, Owensboro, Ky.
Sister Anna Clare, College of St. Rose Library, Albany, N.Y.
Sister Anne Martina, 314 Houston Ave., Crookston, Minn.
Sister Barbara Geoghegan, Supv. of Schools, Mount St. Joseph, Ohio
Sister Celine, Dean, Mother Celine House of Studies, Port Chester, N.Y.
Sister Clara Francis, Nazareth College, Louisville, Ky.
Sister Clare Mary, Xavier University, New Orleans, La.
Sister Conchessa, College of St. Benedict Library, St. Joseph, Minn.
Sister Digna Birmingham, College of St. Scholastica, Duluth, Minn.
Sister Dorothea, Prin., Shrine of the Little Flower High School, Royal Oak, Mich.
Sister Dorothy Marie Riordan, College of St. Elizabeth, Convent Sta., N.J.
Sister Helen Jean, Webster College, Webster Groves, Mo.
Sister Irene Elizabeth, 52 Main St., Concord, Mass.
Sister Justa McNamara, St. Joseph College, Emmitsburg, Md.
Sister Magdalen Marie, Siena Heights College, Adrian, Mich.
Sister Margaret Mary O'Connell, Pres., Col. of Notre Dame, Baltimore, Md.
Sister Marie Claudia, Barry College, Miami Shores, Fla.
Sister M. Adelbert, 3837 Secor Rd., Toledo, Ohio
Sister Mary Agnes Hennessey, R.S.M., Mount Mercy College, Cedar Rapids, Iowa
Sister Mary Alexander, B.V.M., 6363 Sheridan Rd., Chicago, Ill.
Sister Mary Alma, Dean, St. Mary's College, Notre Dame, Ind.
Sister M. Angela Betke, Cantalician Center for Children, Buffalo, N.Y.
Sister Mary Assumpta, President, Madonna College, Livonia, Mich.
Sister Mary Bartholomew, Principal, Lauralton Hall School, Milford, Conn.
Sister Mary Basil, Good Counsel College, White Plains, N.Y.
Sister Mary Benedict Phelan, President, Clarke College, Dubuque, Iowa
Sister Mary Bernice, St. John College, Cleveland, Ohio
Sister M. Brideen Long, Holy Family College, Manitowoc, Wis.
Sister Mary Celestine, R.S.M., President, College Misericordia, Dallas, Pa.
Sister Mary Christine Beck, Sacred Heart Junior College, Belmont, N.C.
Sister M. Clarissima, O.S.F., St. Joseph Convent, Milwaukee, Wis.
Sister M. Clotile, Dunbarton College, Washington, D.C.
Sister Mary Consuela, Immaculata College, Immaculata, Pa.
Sister Mary de Lourdes, St. Joseph College, West Hartford, Conn.
Sister Mary Dolores, College of St. Francis, Joliet, Ill.
Sister Mary Dorothy, Queen of Apostles Library, Harriman, N.Y.
Sister Mary Edwina, F.S.S.J., 5286 South Park Ave., Hamburg, N.Y.
Sister Mary Elaine, R.S.M., College of St. Mary, Omaha, Neb.
Sister M. Felicitas, Immaculata College, Dayton, Ohio
Sister Mary Florita, Community Supv., Nazareth Motherhouse, Rochester, N.Y.
Sister Mary Fridian, St. Francis College, Fort Wayne, Ind.
Sister Mary Gabrielle, Nazareth College, Nazareth, Mich.
Sister Mary Helen, Principal, St. Peter-St. Vincent Schls., Keokuk, Iowa
Sister Mary Hugh, Fontbonne College Library, St. Louis, Mo.
Sister Mary Hyacinth, Our Lady of Sorrows Convent, Ladysmith, Wis.

Sister Mary Imeldine, Marylhurst College, Marylhurst, Ore.
Sister Mary Imeldis Lawler, Cardinal Stritch College, Milwaukee, Wis.
Sister Mary Innocentia, Sch. Sisters of Notre Dame, Milwaukee, Wis.
Sister Mary Irmina Saelinger, Villa Madonna College, Covington, Ky.
Sister Mary James, Mt. St. Vincent College, Rockingham, Nova Scotia
Sister Mary Janet, Catholic University of America, Washington, D.C.
Sister Mary Joachim, O.S.B., Benedictine Heights College, Tulsa, Okla.
Sister M. Josephina, President, Xavier University, New Orleans, La.
Sister Mary Josephine McDermott, Rosary College, River Forest, Ill.
Sister Mary Judith, Briar Cliff College, Sioux City, Iowa
Sister Mary Judith, O.B.S., Principal, Holy Cross High School, Covington, Ky.
Sister Mary Justinia, Notre Dame Convent, Milwaukee, Wis.
Sister Mary Kathleen, Mt. St. Agnes College, Baltimore, Md.
Sister Mary Lauriana Gruszczynski, Madonna College, Livonia, Mich.
Sister M. Laurina, Vice-Pres., Mount Mary College, Yankton, S.D.
Sister Mary Lawrence, Dean, Mary Manse College, Toledo, Ohio
Sister M. Leonarda, St. Mary of the Springs, Columbus, Ohio
Sister Mary Leonella, Sisters of the Holy Cross, Provincial House, Ogden, Utah
Sister Mary Liguori, Mercyhurst College, Erie, Pa.
Sister Mary Lourdes, St. Mary-of-the-Woods Col., St. Mary-of-the-Wood, Ind.
Sister Mary Lucienne, Prin., McDonnell Mem. High School, Chippewa Falls, Wis.
Sister Mary Lucille, President, Mercy College, Detroit, Mich.
Sister Mary Madeline, Mt. Angel College, Mt. Angel, Ore.
Sister M. Matthew, Sacred Heart Dominican College, Houston, Tex.
Sister Mary Merici, Ursuline College, Louisville, Ky.
Sister Mary Muriel, Dean, Marian College, Fond du Lac, Wis.
Sister M. Muriel Gallagher, Mount Mercy College, Pittsburgh, Pa.
Sister Mary Muriel Hogan, Ottumwa Heights College, Ottumwa, Iowa
Sister Mary Natalie, Principal, Lauralton Hall, Milford, Conn.
Sister Mary Olivia. Dean, Marian College, Indianapolis, Ind.
Sister M. Petrine, 1205 Louisiana Ave., New Orleans, La.
Sister Mary Priscilla, Notre Dame College, Cleveland, Ohio
Sister Mary Regis, St. Peter's High School, Pittsburgh, Pa.
Sister Mary Regis, Immaculate Heart College, Los Angeles, Calif.
Sister M. Rita Gertrude, Prin., Towson Catholic High School, Towson, Md.
Sister M. Ronalda, Dir., St. Francis Sch. of Nursing, Evanston, Ill.
Sister Mary Rose Agnes, Our Lady of Cincinnati College, Cincinnati, Ohio
Sister M. Rose Alice, St. Paul's Priory, St. Paul. Minn.
Sister M. Roselyn, Prin., Sisters of Christian Charity, LeMars, Iowa
Sister Mary of St. Michael, College of the Holy Names, Oakland, Calif.
Sister M. Suzanne Walz, Principal, Cathedral High School, Superior, Wis.
Sister Mary Teresa Francis McDade, St. Joseph Convent, Dubuque, Iowa
Sister Mary Theodine, Viterbo College, LaCrosse, Wis.
Sister M. Theodore, Educ. Dept., Dominican College. Racine, Wis.
Sister Mary Thomas, Chm., Dept. of Educ., Sacred Heart College, Wichita, Kan.
Sister Mary Vianney, St. Xavier College, Chicago, Ill.
Sister Mary Vincent Therese, St. Joseph's College for Women, Brooklyn, N.Y.
Sister Mary William, President, Col. of St. Catherine, St. Paul, Minn.
Sister Mary Zeno, Notre Dame College, St. Louis, Mo.
Sister Maureen, College of Great Falls, Great Falls, Mont.
Sister Rosemarie Julie, College of Notre Dame, Belmont, Calif.
Sister St. Mary Caroline, Notre Dame College. Staten Island, N.Y.
Sitz, Herbert A., Martin Luther College, New Ulm, Minn.
Sizemore, Robert A., Col. of Educ., University of Toledo, Toledo, Ohio
Skaggs, Albert E., Jr., Oregon Education Assn., Portland, Ore.
Skaggs, Darcy A., 3699 N. Holly Ave., Baldwin Park, Calif.
Skalski, John M., Sch. of Educ., Fordham University, New York, N.Y.
Skard, Aase Gruda, Fiellyn 2 Lvsaker, Norway
Skatzes, D. H., Maysville School, South Zanesville, Ohio
Skawski, John, Asst. Superintendent of Schools, Ithaca, N.Y.
Skelly, F. Clark, Dean of Instr., State Tchrs. College, Lock Haven, Pa.

Skelton, Claude N., Asst. Prin., Soldan-Blewett High School, St. Louis, Mo.
Skibbens, Charles P., 4705 Grace St., Schiller Park, Ill.
Skipper, Mrs. Dora Sikes, Florida State University, Tallahassee, Fla.
Skogsberg, Alfred H., Principal, Bloomfield Junior High School, Bloomfield, N.J.
Skonberg, Mrs. Madelon B., 2601 Sunnyside Ave., Chicago, Ill.
Skretting, J. R., Florida State University, Tallahassee, Fla.
Slater, Rosalie, 101 Lorita Way, Hanford, Calif.
Sletten, R. Signe, Supv., Lab. Sch., State Tchers. Col., Mankato, Minn.
Sletten, Theresa C., 933 Lincoln Blvd., Santa Monica, Calif.
Sletten, Vernon, Sch. of Educ., Montana State University, Missoula, Mont.
Sligo, Joseph R., Steelcraft Apts., East State St., Athens, Ohio
Sloan, Paul W., Junior High School, Bowling Green, Ohio
Slobetz, Frank, State Teachers College, St. Cloud, Minn.
Smaage, Leon, Superintendent, Algonquin School, Des Plaines, Ill.
Small, Mrs. Turie E. Thornton, 554 South Campbell St., Daytona Beach, Fla.
Smallenburg, Harry W., Dir. of Research & Guid., County Schls., Los Angeles, Calif.
Smedstad, Alton O., Superintendent, Elementary Schools, Hillsboro, Ore.
Smith, A. Edson, Supt., East Alton-Wood River High School, Wood River, Ill.
Smith, Ara K., Prin., Elston Jr. High School, Michigan City, Ind.
Smith, B. Othanel, Dept. of Educ., Univ. of Ill., Urbana, Ill.
Smith, C. A., 7220 Lindell Ave., St. Louis, Mo.
Smith, Calvin S., 5705 South 1700 West, Murray, Utah
Smith, C. C., Principal, Reinhardt Elem. School, Dallas, Tex.
Smith, Denis C., University of British Columbia, Vancouver, B.C.
Smith, Dora V., 201 Burton Hall, University of Minnesota, Minneapolis, Minn.
Smith, Emmitt D., 2619—4th Ave., Canyon, Tex.
Smith, Garmon B., Chm., Dept. of Educ. and Psych., Austin Col., Sherman, Tex.
Smith, Gerald R., 7 Keeler St., Huntington, L.I., N.Y.
Smith, Hannis S., Minnesota Department of Education, St. Paul, Minn.
Smith, Henry P., Fraser Hall, University of Kansas, Lawrence, Kan.
Smith, H. Hayes, 326 Tower Dr., East Alton, Ill.
Smith, Ida T., Col. of Educ., Oklahoma State University, Stillwater, Okla.
Smith, J. Brabner, 2610 Walnut Ave., Evanston, Ill.
Smith, J. Edward, Regional Supt., Central Bucks Joint Schls., Doylestown, Pa.
Smith, John Allan, Paramount Unified School Dist., Paramount, Calif.
Smith, Lawrence J., Central Michigan College, Mt. Pleasant, Mich.
Smith, L. E., Principal, Technical Intermediate School, El Paso, Tex.
Smith, Leon O., Superintendent of County Schools, Omaha, Neb.
Smith, Leslie F., 705 N. Killingsworth, Portland, Ore.
Smith, Lloyd L., Col. of Educ., State University of Iowa, Iowa City, Iowa
Smith, Lloyd N., Dept. of Educ., Indiana State Teachers Col., Terre Haute, Ind.
Smith, Marion L., 239 Olympia St., Ferguson, Mo.
Smith, Margaret L., Principal, Bayview Elem. School, Ft. Lauderdale, Fla.
Smith, Mary Alice, State Teachers College, Lock Haven, Pa.
Smith, Menrie M., Route 4, Hamilton, Ala.
Smith, Nila B., Sch. of Educ., N.Y. Univ., Washington Square, New York, N.Y.
Smith, Paul E., Asst. Supt. of Schools, Rochester, N.Y.
Smith, Paul M., Principal, Jasper-Alamitos School, Heber, Calif.
Smith, Philip John, 37A Hobbs Ave., Dalkeith, Western Australia
*Smith, Raymond A., Sch. of Educ., Texas Christian Univ., Fort Worth, Tex.
Smith, Robert L., 310 Park St., Whittier, Calif.
Smith, Russell B., Dept. of Educ., Marshall College, Huntington, W.Va.
Smith, Sara E., Dept. of Educ., Western Maryland College, Westminster, Md.
*Smith, Stephen E., East Texas Baptist College, Marshall, Tex.
Smith, T. O., Superintendent, City Schools, Ogden, Utah
Smith, Vernon G., Winchester Rd., New London, Conn.
Smith, W. Holmes, El Camino College, Calif.
Smith, Walter D., Dept. of Psych., Florida State Univ., Tallahassee, Fla.
Smotherman, T. Edwin, Stetson University, DeLand, Florida
Snader, Daniel W., Col. of Educ., Univ. of Illinois, Urbana, Ill.

Snader, L. H., Supt., Port Allegany Union Schl. Dist., Port Allegany, Pa.
Snarr, Otto W., Jr., Supv., Extension Classes, Univ. of Wyoming, Laramie, Wyo.
Snarr, Mrs. Ruth G., County Supt. of Schls., Montgomery City, Mo.
Snider, Glenn R., Col. of Educ., University of Oklahoma, Norman, Okla.
Snider, Hervon L., Sch. of Educ., University of Idaho, Moscow, Idaho
Snider, Robert C., 5023 "V" St., N.W., Washington, D.C.
Snyder, Agnes, Adelphi College, Garden City, N.Y.
Snyder, E. Grant, Principal, West View School, Rockford, Ill.
Snyder, George R., Bowling Green State University, Bowling Green, Ohio
Snyder, Hartley D., San Jose State College, San Jose, Calif.
Snyder, Harvey B., Dept. of Educ., Pasadena College, Pasadena, Calif.
Snyder, Jerome R., 2103 W. Louisiana, Midland, Tex.
Snyder, Ruth C., 1217 Walnut St., Utica, N. Y.
Snyder, Walter E., Oregon College of Education, Monmouth, Ore.
Snyder, Wayne T., 4247 Bellefontaine Ave., Kansas City, Mo.
Soares, Anthony T., Eastern Illinois University, Charleston, Ill.
Soboleski, Anita B., P.O. Box 76, Niagara Falls, N.Y.
Socher, E. Elona, 1415 Clearview St., Philadelphia, Pa.
Soeberg, Mrs. Dorothy, Los Angeles State College, Los Angeles, Calif.
Soles, Stanley, San Francisco State College, San Francisco, Calif.
Solomon, Ruth H., Albany Study Center for Learn. Disabilities, Albany, N.Y.
Sommers, Mildred, Dept. of Instr., Bd. of Educ., Jackson, Mich.
Sommers, Wesley S., 705 East Wilson Ave., Menomonie, Wis.
Sonstegard, Manford A., Iowa State Teachers College, Cedar Falls, Iowa
Sorenson, A. Garth, University of California, Los Angeles, Calif.
Sorenson, Helmer E., Oklahoma A. & M. College, Stillwater, Okla.
Southall, Maycie, George Peabody College for Teachers, Nashville, Tenn.
Southerlin, W. B., State Educational Finance Comm., Columbia, S.C.
Sowards, G. Wesley, Sch. of Educ., Stanford University, Stanford, Calif.
Sowers, Mrs. Mildred L., Supv. of Elem. Schools, Ellicott City, Md.
Spain, Charles R., Superintendent of Schools, Albuquerque, N.M.
Spalding, Willard B., Genl. Ext. Div., Oregon Syst. of Higher Educ., Portland, Ore.
Spalke, E. Pauline, Lawrence Road, Salem Depot, N.H.
Sparling, Edward J., President, Roosevelt University, Chicago, Ill.
Spaulding, Meaunena S., Macalester College, St. Paul, Minn.
Spaulding, Seth, Burma Translation Society, Rangoon, Burma
Spaulding, William E., Vice-Pres., Houghton-Mifflin Co., Boston, Mass.
Spear, William G., 7233 West Lunt Ave., Chicago, Ill.
Speight, Robert L., East Texas Baptist College, Marshall, Tex.
Spence, Morris E., 1320—14th St., Des Moines, Iowa
Spence, Ralph B., Teachers College, Columbia Univ., New York, N.Y.
Spencer, E. M., Dept. of Educ., Fresno State College, Fresno, Calif.
Spencer, Peter L., Harper Hall, Claremont Colleges, Claremont, Calif.
Sperber, Robert I., Admin. Asst. to Supt. of Schools, Westfield, N.J.
Sperry, Mrs. Florence, Los Angeles State College, Los Angeles, Calif.
Spieseke, Alice W., Teachers College, Columbia University, New York, N.Y.
Spinola, A. R., Principal, Denville School No. 1, Denville, N.J.
Spitler, F. C., Supv., Baldwin-Whitehall Elementary Schools, Pittsburgh, Pa.
Spitz, Thomas A., Sch. of Educ., City College, New York, N.Y.
Spitzer, Herbert, Univ. Elem. Sch., State Univ. of Iowa, Iowa City, Iowa
Spring, William B., 1919 Manhattan Ave., Palo Alto, Calif.
Springer, Robert L., 139 Bromleigh Rd., Stewart Manor, Garden City, N. Y.
Springman, John H., Superintendent of Schools, Glenview, Ill.
Sprowles, Lee, University of Georgia, Athens, Ga.
Squire, James, 45 El Gavilan, Orinda, Calif.
Staake, Paul C., President, Webber College, Babson Park, Fla.
Staats, Pauline G., Principal, Charles Hay Elem. School, Englewood, Colo.
Stabler, Ernest, Wesleyan University, Middletown, Conn.
Stack, Eileen C., Principal, DuSable High School, Chicago, Ill.
Stack, Mrs. Thelma D., University of Wisconsin-Milwaukee, Milwaukee, Wis.
Stackhouse, Henry A., 347 Argyle, Burlington, Iowa

Stahlecker, Lotar, Kent State University, Kent, Ohio
Stahly, Harold L., 2721 Westbrook Ave., Indianapolis, Ind.
Staiger, Ralph C., Dir., Read. Clinic, Mississippi Southern Col., Hattiesburg, Miss.
Staiger, Roger P., Alumni Association, Ursinus Col., Collegeville, Pa.
Stalnaker, John M., 1075 Elm St., Winnetka, Ill.
Stanford, Madge, 2707 Exposition Ave., Austin, Tex.
Stanley, W. O., Col. of Educ., University of Illinois, Urbana, Ill.
Staple, Flora M., University of Minnesota, Duluth Branch, Duluth, Minn.
Stapleton, Edward G., Superintendent of County Schools, Towson, Md.
Starner, Norman Dean, Wyalusing, Pa.
Statler, Charles R., University of Wichita, Wichita, Kan.
Stauffer, Richard F., Principal, Horton Watkins High School, St. Louis, Mo.
Stauffer, Russell G., Dir., Read. Clinic, Univ. of Delaware, Newark, Del.
Steadman, E. R., 277 Columbia, Elmhurst, Ill.
Stecklein, John Ellsworth, 211 Burton Hall, Univ. of Minn., Minneapolis, Minn.
Stedman, Edith, 1000 University Ave., S.E., Minneapolis, Minn.
Steel, Wade A., Superintendent, Leyden High School, Franklin Park, Ill.
Steele, Herbert L., Pres., Eastern Montana Col. of Education, Billings, Mont.
Steele, Lysle H., Beloit College, Beloit, Wis.
Steelhead, Bert F., Dean, Metropolitan University, Glendale, Calif.
Steeves, Frank L., State Teachers College, Paterson, N.J.
Steffens, Mrs. Dorothy R., Box 261, Sandy Spring, Md.
Steg, Mrs. Doreen C., 4114 Fountain Green, Lafayette Hill, Pa.
Stegall, Alma L., Dept. of Educ., Virginia State College, Petersburg, Va.
Stegeman, William H., Dir. of Res., Educ. Center, City Schls., San Diego, Calif.
Steigelman, Mrs. Vivian R., 1544 Oxford St., Berkeley, Calif.
Stein, Michael W., New Lebanon School, Byram, Conn.
Steinberg, Paul M., Hebrew Union School of Education, New York, N.Y.
Steinberg, Walter F., Principal, Luther High Schol, Chicago, Ill.
Steinberg, Warren L., 4418 Corinth Ave., Culver City, Calif.
Steinbeisser, Donna Marie, 116 Center St., Wolf Point, Mont.
Steinemann, Kathryn P., Minster Public Schools, Minster, Ohio
Steinhauer, Milton H., Sch. of Educ., Rutgers Univ., New Brunswick, N.J.
Steininger, Earl W., 508 Sixth Ave., N.E., Independence, Iowa
Steinkellner, Robert H., So. Ill. Univ. Residence Center, East St. Louis, Ill.
Steinmetz, Kathryn E., 4257 North Tripp Ave., Chicago, Ill.
Stellhorn, A. C., Lutheran Schools, St. Louis, Mo.
Stephens, J. M., Dept. of Educ., Johns Hopkins Univ., Baltimore, Md.
Stephens, John F., Prin., Lab. Sch., Black Hills Tchrs. Col., Spearfish, S.D.
Stern, Elliot, 418 Sterling St., Brooklyn, N.Y.
Sternberg, William N., Prin., Public School 73, Bronx, New York, N.Y.
Stetson, G. A., Superintendent of Schools, West Chester, Pa.
Steuber, Alfred C., Principal, Raymond Elem. School, Chicago, Ill.
Steucek, Regina, Director, Elementary Education, Fairfield, Conn.
Steudler, Mary M., Teachers College of Connecticut, New Britain, Conn.
Stevens, Glenn Z., Pennsylvania State University, University Park, Pa.
Stevens, Grace Adams, Thiel College, Greenville, Pa.
Stevens, J. H., Principal, Holloway High School, Murfreesboro, Tenn.
Stevens, Paul C., 202 North Maple St., Rapid City, S.D.
Stevens, Paul E., Route 5, Box 434, Mount Vernon, Wash.
Stevens, Phyllis W., Psych. Dept., Queens College, Charlotte, N.C.
Stewart, C. E., Principal, Grant School, Ferndale, Mich.
Stewart, Frederick H., Prin., I. A. Sheppard School, Philadelphia, Pa.
Stewart, Glen C., 415 Harvard Ave., Alma, Mich.
Stibal, Willard O., Dir., Campus School, East Mont. Col. of Educ., Billings, Mont.
Stickler, W. Hugh, Dir., Educ. Res., Florida Sta. Univ., Tallahassee, Fla.
Stiemke, Eugenia A., Valparaiso University, Valparaiso, Ind.
Stienstra, Clifford C., Principal, High School, Fertile, Minn.
Stier, Lealand D., Dept. of Educ., Santa Barbara Coll., Goleta, Calif.
Stiles, Mrs. Cordelia L., Supv., Elementary Schools, Charlotte, N.C.
Stinson, Almeda, Bethel College, McKenzie, Tenn.

Stirzaker, Norbert A., University of Mississippi, University, Miss.
Stoddard, George D., 37 Washington Square West, New York, N.Y.
Stoke, Stuart M., Head, Educ. Dept., Mount Holyoke Col., South Hadley, Mass.
Stokes, Maurice S., Savannah State College, Savannah, Ga.
Stokes, Rembert, President, Wilberforce University, Wilberforce, Ohio
Stollberg, Robert, San Francisco State College, San Francisco, Calif.
Stolurow, Lawrence M., 809 Dodds Drive, Champaign, Ill.
Stone, Chester D., Superintendent of Schools, Metlakatla, Alaska
Stone, David R., Dept. of Educ., Utah State University, Logan, Utah
Stone, Gladys, Supt., Monterey County Schools, Salinas, Calif.
Stone, Paul T., Dean, Huntingdon College, Montgomery, Ala.
Stonebraker, W. Chester, Principal, Green School, Dist. 5, Roseburg, Ore.
Stonehocker, D. Doyle, Dean, Junior College, Burlington, Iowa
Stoneman, Mrs. Nora C., Principal, Lincoln School, Wickliffe, Ohio
Stonen, Helen F., Queens College, Flushing, N.Y.
Stordahl, Kalmer E., 323 Martha's Road, Alexandria, Va.
Stottler, Richard Husted, University of Maryland, College Park, Md.
Stoughton, Robert W., Consultant, State Dept. of Educ., Hartford, Conn.
Stout, Homer C., Principal, Lincoln Elementary School, El Reno, Okla.
Stout, Irving W., Arizona State College, Tempe, Ariz.
Stout, John Blaine, Dean, Northwestern State College, Alva, Okla.
Stoutamire, Albert L., 754 El Dorado, Tallahassee, Fla.
Stover, Burd D., Principal, Greenacres School, Scarsdale, N.Y.
Strain, Mrs. Sibyl M., 300 Allendale Rd., Pasadena, Calif.
Strand, Helen A., Luther College, Decorah, Iowa
Strand, William H., Sch. of Educ., Stanford University, Stanford, Calif.
*Strang, Ruth, Teachers College, Columbia University, New York, N.Y.
Stratemeyer, Florence, Teachers College, Columbia University, New York, N.Y.
Stratton, Vinton S., 195 South Mayfair Ave., Daly City, Calif.
Strawe, Walter V., Principal, Lowell School, Chicago, Ill.
* Strayer, George D., Teachers College, Columbia University, New York, N.Y.
Strayer, George D., Jr., Col. of Educ., Univ. of Washington, Seattle, Wash.
Strauch, Arnold, Elon College, P.O. Box 726, Elon College, N.C.
Straus, Albert, 3356 East First St., Long Beach, Calif.
Strebel, Jane D., Board of Educ. Library, Minneapolis, Minn.
Strem, Bruce E., 222 West Gardner Street, Long Beach, Calif.
Streng, Alice, University of Wisconsin-Milwaukee, Milwaukee, Wis.
Strawn, Norland W., Superintendent of Schools, Tucumcari, N.M.
Strehlau, Marguerite W., Child Study Dept., Vassar College, Poughkeepsie, N.Y.
Strickland, C. G., Sch. of Educ., Baylor University, Waco, Tex.
* Strickler, Robert E., 3823 Cleveland Ave., St. Louis, Mo.
Stringfellow, Mrs. D. E., Supv. Principal, Elem. Schools, Moultrie, Ga.
Stroker, Kenneth, Supt., Elementary Schools, West Chicago, Ill.
Strom, Ingrid M., 404 South Fess St., Bloomington, Ind.
Stroud, J. B., State University of Iowa, Iowa City, Iowa
Stuart, Alden T., Superintendent of Schools, Patchogue, L.I., N.Y.
Stuart, Mrs. Thelis B., Prin., Highland View Elem. School, Silver Spring, Md.
Stubbs, G. T., Oklahoma A. & M. College, Stillwater, Okla.
Stuenkel, Walter W., President, Concordia College, Milwaukee, Wis.
Stumpf, W. A., Box 6126 College Station, Durham, N.C.
Sturgeon, Paul H., 185 St. Cornelius Lane, Florissant, Mo.
Sturke, Ralph C., Superintendent of Schools, Attleboro, Mass.
Suddendorf, Sidney, 512—5th St., S.W., Rochester, Minn.
Sugden, W. E., Supt. of Schools, River Forest, Ill.
Sullivan, Helen Blair, Sch. of Educ., Boston University, Boston, Mass.
Sullivan, Ruth E., 1107 Kenwyn St., Philadelphia, Pa.
Sun, Huai Chin, Chm., Grad. Div. of Educ., Bishop College, Marshall, Tex.
Sur, William Raymond, 320 Clarendon Rd., East Lansing, Mich.
Suskowitz, Min, 185-28 Chelsea St., Jamaica, N.Y.
Sutherland, Margaret, Col. of Educ., Univ. of California, Davis, Calif.
Suttell, Lloyd, Col. of Educ., Univ. of Puerto Rico, Rio Piedros, Puerto Rico

Sutton, Elizabeth, 557 Beverly Court, Tallahassee, Fla.
Sutton, Mrs. Grace L., Principal, Ridgeway Elem. School, White Plains, N.Y.
Swann, Mrs. A. Ruth, Booker T. Washington High School, Norfolk, Va.
Swann, Reginald L., Teachers Col. of Conn., New Britain, Conn.
Swanson, Herbert L., Principal, City Schools, Manhattan Beach, Calif.
Swanson, J. Chester, Sch. of Educ., University of California, Berkeley, Calif.
Swartout, S. G., State Teachers College, Brockport, N.Y.
Swartz, David J., Asst. Supt. of Schls., Div. of Hous., Brooklyn, N.Y.
Swearingen, Mildred, Florida State Univ., Tallahassee, Fla.
Swenson, Esther J., Col. of Educ., Univ. of Alabama, University, Ala.
Swertfeger, Floyd F., Longwood College, Farmville, Va.
Swift, Frederic Fay, Hartwick College, Oneonta, N.Y.
Swift, Leonard F., Tchrs. Col., Univ. of Cincinnati, Cincinnati, Ohio
Swindall, Willington, Principal, Palmdale School, Phoenix, Ariz.
Swinton, Mrs. Sylvia P., Chm., Div. of Educ., Allen University, Columbia, S.C.
Sylla, Ben A., Field Secy., Illinois Assn. of School Boards, Chicago, Ill.

Taba, Hilda, San Francisco State College, San Francisco, Calif.
Tadelman, Joseph J., Kelly High School, Chicago, Ill.
Tadena, Tomas, Col. of Educ., Univ. of the Philippines, Quezon City, Philippines
Tag, Herbert G., University of Connecticut, Storrs, Conn.
Tait, Arthur T., 5523 Rumsey Dr., Riverside, Calif.
Tajima, Yuri, 1918 North Bissell St., Chicago, Ill.
*Tallman, Russell W., 2024 Avalon Road, Des Moines, Iowa
Tamura, Kunihiko, Meguro Gakuen High School, Tokyo, Japan
Tan, Hasan, Gazi Egitim Enstitüsü, Ankara, Turkey
Tanger, Fred, Supt., Media Borough School Dist., Media, Pa.
Tangretti, Mrs. Alberta, Baldwin-Wallace College, Berea, Ohio
Tannenbaum, Abraham, Teachers College, Columbia University, New York, N.Y.
Tanner, Daniel, San Francisco State College, San Francisco, Calif.
Tanner, B. William, 5241 Melvin Dr., Toledo, Ohio
Tanner, Wilbur H., Northwestern State College, Alva, Okla.
Tanruther, E. M., Indiana State Teachers College, Terre Haute, Ind.
Tanzi, Edmund A., Headmaster, Winnacunnet High School, Hampton, N.H.
Tarver, K. E., Principal, John P. Odom School, Beaumont, Tex.
Tassin, Rev. Anthony, Dean, St. Joseph's Abbey, St. Benedict, La.
Taylor, Bob E., State Dept. of Vocational Education, Phoenix, Ariz.
Taylor, Charles C., 604 Skyline Dr., Carbondale, Ill.
Taylor, Charles H., Superintendent of Schools, Midland Park, N.J.
Taylor, George Allen, 905 West Margate Tr., Chicago, Ill.
Taylor, Harold, President, Sarah Lawrence College, Bronxville, N.Y.
Taylor, Kenneth I., Leyden Community High School, Franklin Park, Ill.
Taylor, L. O., 4314 Dodge St., Omaha, Neb.
Taylor, Marvin, Div. of Educ., Queens College, Flushing, N.Y.
Taylor, M. Ruth, Principal, Hillcrest Schools, Drexel Hill, Pa.
Taylor, Marvin J., 527 Somerville Dr., Pittsburgh, Pa.
Taylor, Rev. Paul L., Barber-Scotia College, Concord, N.C.
Taylor, Roy H., Principal, Ingalls Elem. School, Wichita, Kan.
Taylor, Ted, Principal, Franklin School, Phoenix, Ariz.
Taylor, Wayne, 1402 Northridge, Austin, Tex.
Taylor, William H., Superintendent of Schools, Vicksburg, Mich.
Tead, Ordway, 49 East Thirty-third St., New York, N.Y.
Tegner, Olaf H., Head, Dept. of Educ., Pepperdine College, Los Angeles, Calif.
Teigen, B. W., President, Bethany Lutheran College, Mankato, Minn.
Telfer, Harold E., Central Michigan College, Mt. Pleasant, Mich.
Tempero, Howard E., Tchrs. Col., University of Nebraska, Lincoln, Neb.
Temple, F. L., Dept. of Educ., University of Alabama, University, Ala.
Templeton, Robert G., 10 Channing St., Cambridge, Mass.
Templin, Mildred C., Inst. of Child Welfare, Univ. of Minn., Minneapolis, Minn.
Tenney, Charles D., Vice-President, Southern Illinois University, Carbondale, Ill.
Tenny, John W., 7745 Pinehurst, Dearborn, Mich.
Tharrington, Bruce H., Superintendent of Schools, Mount Airy, N.C.

Theurer, Lloyd M., Supt., Cache County School Dist., Logan, Utah
Thevaos, Deno G., Pennsylvania State University, University Park, Pa.
Thies, Mrs. Emily P., University of Massachusetts, Amherst, Mass.
Thoman, Mary E. M., 3155 Dover Dr., Boulder, Colo.
Thomann, Don F., Dept of Educ., Ripon College, Ripon, Wis.
Thomas, Arnold, Lake Forest College, Lake Forest, Ill.
Thomas, Cleveland A., Principal, Francis W. Parker School, Chicago, Ill.
Thomas, Donald R., 38B University Houses, Madison, Wis.
Thomas, Dorothy B., Principal, Forbes Elem. School, Pittsburgh, Pa.
Thomas, George Isaiah, Superintendent of Schools, North Arlington, N.J.
Thomas, Harold P., Head, Dept. of Educ., Lehigh Univ., Bethlehem, Pa.
Thomas, J. A., Drawer 760, Smithers, B.C., Canada
Thomas, Mary Antonia, Principal, Haines Elementary School, Chicago, Ill.
Thomas, R. Murray, Dept. of Educ., State Teachers College, Brockport, N.Y.
Thomas, Robert E., University School, Carbondale, Ill.
Thomas, Ruth H., N. Y. State Col. of Home Econ., Cornell Univ., Ithaca, N.Y.
Thomas, Ruth M., Dir., Div. of Educ., Central State College, Wilberforce, Ohio
Thomas, Wade F., Pres., Santa Monica City College, Santa Monica, Calif.
Thompson, Mrs. Annie B., 705 Apple St., Burlington, N.C.
Thompson, Anton, 715 Locust Ave., Long Beach, Calif.
Thompson, Charles H., Dean, Graduate School, Howard Univ., Washington, D.C.
Thompson, Elton Noel, San Jose State College, San Jose, Calif.
Thompson, Emmett C., Sacramento State College, Sacramento, Calif.
Thompson, Franklin J., Peik Hall, Univ. of Minnesota, Minneapolis, Minn.
Thompson, James H., 135 Larkins St., Findlay, Ohio
Thompson, John D., Dir. of Curric., Public Schools, Seminole, Tex.
Thompson, Mrs. Louise J., Virginia State College, Petersburg, Va.
Thompson, Orrin G., Supt., Public Schools, Elgin, Ill.
Thompson, Ralph H., Western Washington College of Educ., Bellingham, Wash.
Thompson, Ray, Counselor-Trainer, North Carolina College, Durham, N.C.
Thomson, Proctor, Pitzer Hall, Claremont Men's College, Claremont, Calif.
Thornblad, Carl E., 627 North Kellogg St., Galesburg, Ill.
Thorndike, Robert L., Teachers College, Columbia University, New York, N.Y.
Thorne, Edmund H., Supt. of Schools, West Hartford, Conn.
Thorngate, J. H., Vice-Principal, Senior High School, Eau Claire, Wis.
Thornton, James W., Jr., San Jose State College, San Jose, Calif.
Thorp, Mary T., Dir., Henry Barnard School, Providence, R.I.
Thorpe, Louis P., University of Southern California, Los Angeles, Calif.
Threlkeld, Archie L., Jamaica, Vt.
Thursby, Ruth, Principal, El Cerrito School, Corona, Calif.
Thurston, Edmund W., Superintendent of Schools, Westwood, Mass.
Thyberg, Clifford S., Superintendent, West Covina Sch. Dist., West Covina, Calif.
Tidrow, Joe, Box 457, Andrews, Tex.
Tidwell, Robert E., Stillman College, Tuscaloosa, Ala.
Tiedeman, Herman R., Illinois State Normal University, Normal, Ill.
Tiffany, Burton C., Asst. Supt., Chula Vista City Schls., Chula Vista, Calif.
Tillinghast, Charles C., Ridgefield Road, Wilton, Conn.
Timko, Irene H., Principal, John Barry Elem. School, Chicago, Ill.
Tingle, Mary J. Col. of Educ., Univ. of Georgia, Athens, Ga.
Tinglof, Mrs. Mary, Los Angeles City Board of Education, Los Anegles, Calif.
Tink, Albert K., Northern Illinois State University, DeKalb, Ill.
Tinker, Miles A., University of Minnesota, Minneapolis, Minn.
Tipton, Elis M., Mariposa County Schools, Mariposa, Calif.
Tireman, L. S., Educ. Dept., Univ. of New Mexico, Albuquerque, N.M.
Toalson, Frank B., Superintendent of Schools, Dodge City, Kan.
Tobin, Alexander, 1145 Medway Rd., Philadelphia, Pa.
Todd, G. Raymond, R.D. No. 3, Bethlehem, Pa.
Tolbert, Donald R., Lincoln University, Jefferson City, Mo.
Toles, Caesar F., Dir., Bishop Junior College, Dallas, Tex.
Tollinger, William P., Superintendent, Wilson Borough Schls., Easton, Pa.
Tomaszewski, Edward J., Frederick County Schools, Frederick, Md.

Tomlinson, H. E., Principal, Twentieth Street School, Los Angeles, Calif.
Toomey, Charles B., Dean, Boston College Intown, Boston, Mass.
Toops, Herbert A., Dept. of Psych., Ohio State University, Columbus, Ohio
Topetzes, Nick John, Marquette University, Milwaukee, Wis.
Topp, Robert F., Dept. of Educ., Univ. of California, Santa Barbara, Calif.
Torbet, David P., Butler University, Indianapolis, Ind.
Torchia, Joseph, State Teachers College, Millersville, Pa.
Torkelson, Gerald M., Pennsylvania State University, University Park, Pa.
Torrey, Robert D., Tamalpois Union High School Dist., Larkspur, Calif.
Totten, W. Fred, Pres., Flint Jr. College, Flint, Mich.
Townsend, Arthur V., Principal, Bedford High School, Bedford, Pa.
Townsend, Loran G., Dean, Col. of Educ., Univ. of Missouri, Columbia, Mo.
Townsend, Virgil L., Kathleen High School, Kathleen, Fla.
Townsend, Wes. A., Glendale Union High School Dist. 205, Glendale, Ariz.
Trabue, M. R., Col. of Educ., University of Kentucky, Lexington, Ky.
Tracy, Edward, Supt., Easton-Forks & Easton Area Jt. Sch. Sys., Easton, Pa.
Tracy, Elaine M., Dept. of Educ., St. Olaf College, Northfield, Minn.
Traeger, Carl, Principal, Senior High School, Oshkosh, Wis.
Trask, Corridon F., Jr., Greenfield High School, Greenfield, Mass.
Trautwein, Marvin E., Augsburg College, Minneapolis, Minn.
Travelstead, Chester C., Col. of Educ., Univ. of New Mexico, Albuquerque, N.M.
Travis, Vaud A., Chm., Dept. of Educ., Northwestern State Col., Tahlequa, Okla.
Traxler, Arthur E., Educational Records Bureau, New York, N.Y.
Traxler, Howard W., 1206—65th St., Des Moines, Iowa
Traynor, Rev. Vincent, St. Gregory's College, Shawnee, Okla.
Treacy, John P., 2111 North Fifty-ninth St., Milwaukee, Wis.
Tremaine, Donahue L., Roosevelt University, Chicago, Ill.
Trescott, B. M., Kirk Lane, Media, Pa.
Tressler, Robert Millard, 823 Main St., Rockwood, Pa.
Triggs, Frances O., 419 West 119th St., New York, N.Y.
Trione, Verdon, Psych. Consult., Mendocino County Schls., Ukiak, Calif.
Triptow, Richard F., St. Patrick High School, Chicago, Ill.
Tronsberg, Josephine, University of Pittsburgh, Pittsburgh, Pa.
Troth, Harold Ray, Principal, McKinley Occupational School, Dayton, Ohio
Troupe, Carolyn H., Principal, Blow-Terrace Elem. School, Washington, D.C.
Trow, William Clark, School of Educ., Univ. of Mich., Ann Arbor, Mich.
Troxel, O. L., Colorado State College of Education, Greeley, Colo
Troxel, Vernon, Sch. of Educ., University of Kansas, Lawrence, Kan.
Truitt, John W., Michigan State University, East Lansing, Mich.
Trump, J. Lloyd, Col. of Educ., Univ. of Illinois, Urbana, Ill.
Tsugé, Haruko, 5570 Tsujido, Fujisawa, Kanagawa, Japan
Tucker, David W., 1613—32nd Ave., Sacramento, Calif.
Tudyman, Al, Dir. Spec. Educ., Oakland Public Schools, Oakland, Calif.
Tulley, George, 2148 South High St., Denver, Colo.
Turansky, Isadore, 106 Smalley Rd., Syracuse, N.Y.
Turner, C. Adam, Western Illinois State College, Macomb, Ill.
Turner, Howard, Southern Louisiana Institute, Lafayette, La.
Turner, Rex Allwin, Pres., Alabama Christian Col., Montgomery, Ala.
Turner, Mrs. Sara Booker, Tougaloo College, Tougaloo, Miss.
Turner, Winston E., 150 Rhode Island Ave., N.W., Washington, D.C.
Tuttle, Caroline, Principal, Kenilworth School, Phoenix, Ariz.
Twombly, John J., Northern Illinois State College, DeKalb, Ill.
Tydings, R. N., Hobbs Municipal Schools, Hobbs, N.M.
Tyler, Charles M., Asst. Superintendent of Education, Oxnard, Calif.
Tyler, Fred T., Sch. of Educ., Univ. of California, Berkeley, Calif.
Tyler, I. Keith, Ohio State University, Columbus, Ohio
Tyler, Ralph W., 202 Junipero Serra Blvd., Stanford, Calif.
Tyler, Robert, Southwestern State College, Weatherford, Okla.
Tyrrell, Rev. Francis M., Immaculate Conception Seminary, Huntington, N.Y.
Tyson, George R., Ursinus College, Collegeville, Pa.

Ulmer, T. H., Superintendent, Hartsville Area Schls., Hartsville, S. C.
Ulrich, Foster G., Superintendent of County Schools, Lebanon, Pa.
Umberger, Willis H., State Department of Education, Hartford, Conn.
Umstattd, J. G., University of Texas, Austin, Tex.
Underwood, Mrs. Anna, Fairview High School, Fairview, Okla.
Underwood, Helen B., 1920 Nadrona, Napa, Calif.
Underwood, William J., 116 Madison St., Lee's Summit, Mo.
Unger, Dorothy Holberg, 99 Lawton Road, Riverside, Ill.
Unruh, Adolph, Dept. of Educ.. Washington University, St. Louis, Mo.
Urben, Walter E., Longwood College, Farmville, Va.
Urquhart, Margaret, Superintendent Dist. V Public Schools, Chicago, Ill.

Vakil, K. S., 119 Marzbanabad, Andheri, Bombay, India
Valentine, E. A., Jr., 2081 Lakeshore Dr., Klamath Falls, Ore.
Van Bodegraven, Paul, Dept. of Music Educ., New York Univ., New York, N.Y.
Van Bruggen, John A., Dept. of Educ., Calvin College, Grand Rapids, Mich.
Van Campen, Marion, Head, Elem. Educ. Dept., Kent State Univ., Kent, Ohio
Vander Horck, Karl J., Col. of Educ., Univ. of Minnesota, Minneapolis, Minn.
Vanderlinden, J. S., Superintendent, Dawson Consolidated Schls., Dawson, Iowa
VanderMeer, A. W., Pennsylvania State University, University Park, Pa.
Vanderpool, J. Alden, 1125 West Sixth St., Los Angeles, Calif.
Vander Werf, Lester S., Dean, Col. of Educ., Northeastern University, Boston,
  Mass.
Van Loan, W. L., Supt. of Schools, Corvallis, Ore.
Van Luven, Elizabeth A., 7110 Hawthorne St., Hyattsville, Md.
Van Nastrand, M. Eugene, State Teachers College, St. Cloud, Minn.
Van Ness, Carl C., Vice-Pres., Appleton-Century-Crofts Co., New York, N.Y.
Van Ness, Paul H., Prin., Central Ave. and Warren St. Schls., Newark, N.J.
Vannorsdall, H. C., Superintendent of County Schools, Bryan, Ohio
Van Ormer, Edward B., Pennsylvania State University, University Park, Pa.
Van Patter, Vernon E., Chm., Dept. of Educ., Wisconsin State Coll., Superior, Wis.
Van Putten, M. W., Superintendent of Schools, Eveleth, Minn.
Van Steenwyk, Linda, 1454 Union St., Allentown, Pa.
Van Vrancken, Charles, Principal, Elementary School, Ponchatoula, La.
Van Wagenen, Marvin J., University of Minnesota, Minneapolis, Minn.
Van Zanten, Mrs. Hazel, 4822 Division Ave., Grand Rapids, Mich.
Van Zwoll, James A., University of Maryland, College Park, Md.
Varn, Guy L., Supt., City Schools, Columbia, S.C.
Vasey, Hamilton G., Superintendent of Schools, Fargo, N.D.
Vaughan, Verdry D., Supv., Kendall School for Deaf, Washington, D.C.
Veltman, Peter, Wheaton College, Wheaton, Ill.
Verseput, Robert F., Dover High School, Dover, N.J.
Vett, John George, State University Teachers College, New Paltz, N.Y.
Vickers, Robert C., 1130 Halpin, Cincinnati, Ohio
Vickery, Verna L., Box 289, College Station, Hammond, La.
Vickery, William E., National Conf. of Christians and Jews, New York, N.Y.
Vikner, Carl Filip, Gustavus Adolphus College, St. Peter, Minn.
Villano, George R., 1274 Logan St., Denver 3, Colo.
Villemain, Francis T., 417 A Eighteenth St., Brooklyn, N.Y.
Vincent, Harold S., Superintendent of Schools, Milwaukee, Wis.
Vincent, Kenneth L., Principal, MacArthur School, Fort Leavenworth, Kan.
Vineyard, Jerry J., Superintendent of Schools, Arkansas City, Kan.
Vislay, Patricia Jean, 1937 Greenfield Ave., Los Angeles, Calif.
Vitalo, Nicholas F., Jr., 1513 Marine Pkwy., Brooklyn, N.Y.
Voelker, Paul H., Asst. Dir.. Special Educ.. Public Schls., Detroit, Mich.
Vogan, Mrs. Edwina, 1605 Howze St., El Paso, Tex.
Voigt, Virginia E., Seton Hall University, South Orange, N. J.
Voirol, Eula C.. 4927 Bell Ave., Kansas City. Mo.
Vonk, Paul Kenneth, University of Miami Branch, Coral Gables, Fla.
Voorhies, William T., Indiana University, Bloomington, Ind.

Vopni, Sylvia, Col. of Educ., University of Washington, Seattle, Wash.
Vorce, M. Barrett, Principal, Lee M. Thurston High School, Detroit, Mich.
Vosburgh, William T., 135 Smalley Rd., Syracuse, N.Y.
Votava, Arthur J., 5401 South Nordica Ave., Chicago, Ill.
Votaw, Daniel C., 3535 Sterne St., San Diego, Calif.
Voydat, Mitchell L., San Juan College, Farmintgon, N.M.
Vredevoe, Lawrence E., Sch. of Educ., Univ. of California, Los Angeles. Calif.
Vroman, Clyde, Dir. of Admissions, Univ. of Michigan, Ann Arbor, Mich.

Wachowski, Chester, Principal, Fisher School, Detroit, Mich.
* Waddell, C. W., 1365 Midvale Ave., Los Angeles. Calif.
Wade, D. E., 26 Clarke Dr., East Northport, N.Y.
Waggoner. Sherman G.. Teachers College of Conn.. New Britain Conn
Wagner, Robert W., Head, Dept. of Cinema, Univ. of So. Calif., Los Angeles,
    Calif.
Wagner. Carl E., 7421 Zephyr Place. Maplewood, Mo.
Wahle, Roy, Asst. Supt., Bellevue Schools, Bellevue, Wash.
Waid, Guy, Principal, High School, Carlsbad, N.M.
Waimon, Morton D., Northern Illinois University, DeKalb, Ill.
Waine, Sidney I., 842 44th St., Brooklyn, N. Y.
Wainscott, Carlton O., 301 Hawthorne, Abilene, Tex.
Walby, Grace S., 293 Polson Ave., Winnipeg, Manitoba, Canada
Walcott, Fred G., Univ. High School. Univ. of Michigan. Ann Arbor, Mich
Walden, C. C., Principal, Forest Hill School, Amarillo, Tex.
Waldron, Margaret L., St. Mary-of-the-Woods. Ind.
Waldschmidt, Carl L., Concordia Teachers College, River Forest, Ill.
* **Walker. E. T., Bigfork, Mont.**
Walker, John S., Principal, West View School, Muncie, Ind.
Walker, K. P., Supt. of Schools, Jackson, Miss.
Walker, Peter, 41-933 Laumilo Road, Wainamala, Oahu, T.H.
Walker, Stanley E., Principal, William Penn Senior High School, Harrisburg, Pa.
Wall, G. S., Dept. of Educ., Stout State College, Menomonie, Wis.
Wall, Sandy A., Sch. of Educ., Texas Christian Univ., Forth Worth, Tex.
Wall, William Michael, 540 Cordova St., Winnipeg, Manitoba. Canada
Wallace, Donald G., Dean, Col. of Educ., Drake University, Des Moines, Iowa
Wallace, Elsie H., Florida State University, Tallahassee, Fla.
Wallace, Morris S., Dept. of Educ., Texas Tech. College, Lubbock, Tex.
Wallar, Gene A., San Jose State College, San Jose. Calif.
Wallen, Carl J., 416 Santa Barbara Ave., Daly City, Calif.
Walling, Mrs. Isabel G., 4217 So. 17th St., Minneapolis, Minn.
Walsh, J. Hartt, Dean, Col. of Educ., Butler University, Indianapolis, Ind.
Walsh, John J., Chm., Grad. Dept. of Educ., Boston College, Boston, Mass.
Walsh, Michael F., Commissioner of Educ., 205 Benefit St., Providence, R.I.
Walsh, Michael J., 1830 Bayshore, Palo Alto, Calif.
Walter, Mildred M., Iowa State Teachers College, Cedar Falls, Iowa
Walter, Raymond L., Box 201, Millbrook, Ala.
Walter. Robert B.. Chief Deputy Supt., County Schools, Los Angeles, Calif.
Walters, Everett L., Wisconsin State College, La Crosse, Wis.
Walters, Maxine Oyler. Principal, John Burroughs School, Columbus. Ohio
Walther, Herbert K., USOM/Education, Box 32, Navy 150 FPO, San Francisco,
    Calif.
Walton, Eugene W., 503½ West 7th St., Cedar Falls, Iowa
Walvoord, Anthony C., Box 2845, University Hill Sta., Denton, Tex.
Wampler, W. Norman. Supt. of Schools, Bellflower, Calif.
Wang, Martin Iver, 2508 Vuelte Grand Ave., Long Beach, Calif.
Wantling, Dale, Dean, Grad. Schl., Univ. of Tennessee, Knoxville, Tenn.
Ward, Mrs. Annie W., University of Tennessee, Knoxville, Tenn.
Ward, John Henry, Texas College. Tyler, Tex.
Ward, Virgil S., School of Educ., University of Virginia, Charlottesville, Va.
Wardeberg, Helen. 108 Stone Hall. Cornell University, Ithaca, N.Y.
Ware, Kay, 1400 Jamaica Court, Kirkwood, Mo.

Warner, Doris E., Principal, Cayuga Drive School, Niagara Falls, N.Y.
Warner, Robert Dale, Westchester Christian Church, Los Angeles, Calif.
Warren, John S.. Dir.. Teacher Educ., Hendrix College, Conway, Ark.
Warren, Majl Michel, Azusa College, Azusa, Calif.
Warren, Richard B., Superintendent of Schools, Muskegon, Mich.
Warrick, Lida P., Supv. of Music, City Schools, Kansas City, Mo.
Warriner, Clell C., Principal. Okmulgee High School. Okmulgee, Okla.
Warriner, David A., Jr., Michigan State University, East Lansing, Mich.
Warwick, Raymond, Principal, Public School, Riverton, N.J.
Washburne, Carleton W., Brooklyn College, Brooklyn, N.Y.
Washington, Booker T., Principal. Williston Ind. School. Wilmington, N.C.
Washington, Walter, President, Utica Inst. Junior College, Utica Institute, Miss.
Washington, Mrs. J. Mae, 2301 Eleventh Ave., Bessemer, Ala.
Wasson, Margaret, 3705 University Blvd., Dallas, Tex.
Wasson, Roy J., Superintendent of Schools, Colorado Springs, Colo.
Wassum, Sylvesta M., Music Dept., University of California, Los Angeles, Calif.
Waterman, Floyd T., Baker Elementary School, Great Neck, N.Y.
Waters, E. Worthington, Maryland State College, Princess Anne, Md.
Watkins, Ralph K.. University of Missouri, Columbia, Mo.
Watkins, Thomas W., Supv. Principal, South Lehigh Sch. Dist., Coopersburg, Pa.
Watkius, Ray H., Decatur Baptist College, Decatur, Tex.
Watson, C. Hoyt, President, Seattle Pacific College, Seattle, Wash.
Watson, David Roland, Elm Place School, Highland Park, Ill.
Watson, Jack M., Indiana University, Bloomington, Ind.
Watson, Mary R., Elem. Supervisor, Cobre Consolidated Schools, Bayard, N.M.
Watson, N. E., Supt., Northfield Twp. High School. Northbrook. Ill.
Watson, Norman E., Asst. Supt., Orange Coast College, Costa Mesa, Calif.
Watson, William C., 29 Woodstock Rd., Mt. Waverley, Victoria, Australia
Watts. B. C.. School of Educ.. Southern Methodist Univ., Dallas, Tex.
Watt, John Steward, Col. of Educ., University of Akron, Akron, Ohio
Wattenberg, William W., Wayne University, Detroit, Mich.
Watts. Morrison L.. Dept. of Educ., Prov. of Alberta, Edmonton, Alba.
Way, Gail W., 1232 Henderson St., Chicago, Ill.
Waxwood. Howard B., Jr., Principal, Witherspoon School, Princeton, N.J.
Weaver, David Andrew, 2619 Brown St.. Alton, Ill.
Weaver, David O.. 3033 John Marshall Dr., Arlington, Va.
Weaver, Edward K., Sch. of Educ., Atlanta University, Atlanta, Ga.
Weaver, Gladys C., Dept. of Educ., Juniota College, Huntingdon, Pa.
Weaver, Harold D., Dept. of Educ., Delaware State College, Dover, Del.
Weaver, J. Fred. Sch. of Educ., Boston Univ.. Boston. Mass.
Weaver, John E., Washington Missionary Col., Takoma Park, Washington, D.C.
Weaver, P. C., Pennsylvania State University, University Park, Pa.
Webb, Holmes, Principal, Tyler High School, Tyler, Tex.
Webber, Frank Clarence, 635 Locust St., Kalamazoo, Mich.
Webber, Warren L., Cedarville College, Cedarville, Ohio
Weber, Clarence A., Sch. of Educ., Univ. of Conn., Storrs, Conn.
Weber, Mrs. Martha Gesling, Bowling Green State Univ., Bowling Green, Ohio
Weber, Robert A.. R. 3, Arcadia. Columbia, S.C.
Webster, Gloria M., Roseville Union High School, Roseville, Calif.
Weddington, Rachel T., Merrill-Palmer School, Detroit, Mich.
Wedul, Melvin O., Div. of Educ. & Psych., State College, Winona, Minn.
Weeks, James S., Eastern Michigan College, Ypsilanti, Mich.
Weeks, Mrs. Lexine H., Box 153, Tuskegee Institute, Ala.
Wegener, Frank C., 1916 Montair Ave., Long Beach, Calif.
Wegrzyn, Helen A., 5240 W. Newport Ave.. Chicago, Ill.
Wehner, Freda, 470 Algoma Blvd., Oshkosh, Wis.
Wehrer, Charles S., Jr., Ohio Northern University, Ada, Ohio
Weibaker, Charles R.. Tchrs. Col., University of Cincinnati. Cincinnati, Ohio
Weinrich, Ernest F., Board of Cooperative Educ. Services, Huntington, N.Y.
Weintraub. Sam. University of Illinois, Champaign, Ill.
Weisberg, Mrs. Patricia H., 9411 South Pleasant Ave., Chicago, Ill.

Weisiger, Louise P., Dir. of Research, Public Schools, Richmond, Va.
Weiss, George D., Supv., Stud. Tchg., State Teachers College, Kutztown, Pa.
Weiss, Morris H., Principal, Public School 215, Brooklyn, N.Y.
Weiss, Robert M., University of Michigan, Flint College, Flint, Mich.
Welcenbach, Frank J., Principal, Trombly School, Grosse Pointe, Mich.
Welch, Carolyn M., 830 Chauncey Rd., Penn Valley, Narberth, Pa.
Welch, Cornelius A., Dean, Sch. of Educ., Bonaventure Col., Bonaventure, N.Y.
Welch, Eleanor W., Illinois State Normal University, Normal, Ill.
Weldon, J. Elmer, Georgetown College, Georgetown, Ky.
Wellck, Arthur Albert, University of New Mexico, Albuquerque, N.M.
Welling, Helen F., 333 East McWilliams St., Fond du Lac, Wis.
Welsh, Walter C., Sch. of Ind. Art, New York, N.Y.
Wendt, Adeline M., 251 Birmingham St., St. Paul, Minn.
Wendt, Paul R., Audio-visual Aids, Southern Illinois Univ., Carbondale, Ill.
Wenger, Roy E., Kent State University, Kent, Ohio
Wenrich, Esther M., Director, Elementary Education, Langhorne, Pa.
Wente, Walter H., Concordia Senior College, Fort Wayne, Ind.
Wentz, Howard A., Supv. Prin., Nether Providence Sch. Dist., Wallingford, Pa.
Wernick, Leo J., 2040 West Adams St., Chicago, Ill.
Wesley, Charles H., Pres., Central State College, Wilberforce, Ohio
Wesley, Edgar B., Box 1201, Los Altos, Calif.
Wesley, Willena, Principal, Fairport Elem. School, Dayton, Ohio
West, Allan M., Exec. Secy., Utah Education Assn., Salt Lake City, Utah
West, Mrs. Lorraine W., Bakersfield Center, Fresno State College, Bakersfield, Calif.
West, William H., Superintendent, County Schools, Elizabeth, N.J.
Westbrook, Charles H., 17 Towana Rd., Richmond, Va.
Westlund, Hildur L., 920 N. 22nd St., Superior, Wis.
Westover, Frederick L., Box 1553, University, Ala.
Wetmore, Joseph N., Ohio Wesleyan University, Delaware, Ohio
Wetter, Allen H., Superintendent of Schools, Philadelphia, Pa.
Weyer, F. E., Dean, Hastings College, Hastings, Neb.
Whayland, Charles W., Prin., Glen Burnie High School, Glen Burnie, Md.
Wheat, H. G., Col. of Educ., West Virginia University, Morgantown, W.Va.
Wheat, Leonard B., Southern Illinois University, Alton, Ill.
Wheeler, Eldon G., East Alton-Wood River Com. High School, Wood River, Ill.
Wheeler, Joseph A., Principal, Benjamin Franklin School, Miami, Fla.
Wheeler, Mrs. Olive Boone, Box 818, Austin 64, Tex.
Whelan, James F., Chm., Dept. of Educ., Loyola University, New Orleans, La.
Whigham, E. L., School Administration Bldg., Wilmington, Del.
Whipple, Carl E., Superintendent, Sch. Dist. of Warren Borough, Warren, Pa.
Whipple, Gertrude, Wayne University, Detroit, Mich.
Whisler, H. M., 292 East Broadway, Danville, Ind.
Whitaker, Mrs. Nell M., Principal, Burleson School, El Paso, Tex.
Whitcomb, Charles L., Superintendent of Schools, Haverhill, Mass.
White, Byron J., State Teachers College, New Paltz, N.Y.
White, D. V., Jr., 2812 Kinney Dr., Walnut Creek, Calif.
White, George L., Harcourt, Brace & Co., New York, N.Y.
White, Mrs. Helen B., P.O. Box 144, Tujunga, Calif.
White, J. B., Dean. Col. of Educ., University of Florida, Gainesville, Fla.
White, James E., Dept. of Educ., Canisius College, Buffalo, N.Y.
White, John C., Principal, Edison School, Mesa, Ariz.
White, Kenneth B., Dean of Instr., State Teachers Col., Paterson, N.J.
White, Kenneth E., Central Michigan College, Mt. Pleasant, Mich.
White, Nathan L., 1008 Willora Road, Stockton, Calif.
White, Vern A., Psychologist, Alvord School Dist., Arlington, Calif.
Whitehead, Willis A., 15900 Kinsman Road, Shaker Heights, Ohio
Whitelaw, John B., Glen Hills, Rockville, Md.
Whitney, Gilbert A., Northwest Missouri State College, Maryville, Mo.
Whitney, John D., Harris Teachers College, St. Louis, Mo.
Whittaker, John W., Lemoyne College, Memphis, Tenn.

Whittier, C. Taylor, Supt., Montgomery County Schools, Rockville, Md.
Wickes, Mrs. Una S., Counselor, Pasadena High School, Pasadena, Calif.
Wickstrom, Rod A., Vice-Prin., Public School System, Saskatoon, Sask., Canada
Wickstrum, Adrian M., Panhandle A. & M. College, Goodwell, Okla.
Wiebe, Elias, Upland College, Upland, Calif.
Wiebe, Joel A., 3374 Mayfair Drive South, Fresno, Calif.
Wiens, Ben J., Registrar, Tabor College, Hillsboro, Kan.
Wier, J. B., P.O. Box 1, Carrollton, Ala.
Wiersma, Jack, 12319—104th St., Edmonton, Alba., Canada
Wiggin, Gladys A., Col. of Educ., University of Maryland, College Park, Md.
Wiggin, Richard G., Supervisor of Art, Public Schools, Arlington, Va.
Wikel, Patricia S., 4077 Toledo Ave. South, St. Louis Park, Minn.
Wilburn, D. Banks, Dean, Tchrs. Col., Marshall College, Huntington, W. Va.
Wilcox, A. Hardy, Registrar, University of Corpus Christi, Corpus Christi, Tex.
Wilkerson, H. Clifton, 542 Market St., Platteville, Wis.
Wilks, William T., State Teachers College, Troy, Ala.
Willard, Robert L., Utica College, Utica, N.Y.
Willey, Lawrence V., Jr., Grad. Sch. of Educ., Harvard Univ., Cambridge, Mass.
Williams, Beatrice, State Teachers College, St. Cloud, Minn.
Williams, Byron B., University of Rochester, Rochester, N.Y.
Williams, Catharine M., Bur. of Educ. Res., Ohio State Univ., Columbus, Ohio
Williams, Charles C., North Texas State College, Denton, Tex.
Williams, Chester Spring, Col. of Educ., Univ. of Oklahoma, Norman, Okla.
*Williams, Claude L., 2457 E. 73rd St., Chicago, Ill.
Williams, Cyrus P., 903 Peach St., El Campo, Tex.
Williams, E. B., Principal, Stoner Hill School, Shreveport, La.
Williams, Fannie C., 1633 St. Bernard Ave., New Orleans, La.
Williams, Fountie N., Principal, Broadway School, Clarksburg, W.Va.
Williams, Frederick Allen, Dean, Grad. Sch., A. & T. College, Greensboro, N.C.
Williams, G. A., Principal, Walnut Hill High School, Shreveport, La.
Williams, Mrs. Geneva B., Claflin College, Orangeburg, S.C.
Williams, Harold A., 406 East Torrance Road, Columbus, Ohio
Williams, Howard Y., Jr., Dir., St. Paul Read. Clinic, St. Paul, Minn.
Williams, J. Post, Tulare County Supt. of Schls., Visalia, Calif.
Williams, Jacob T., Principal, Carver High School, Gadsden, Ala.
Williams, James Harry, Asst. Prin., Armstrong High School, Richmond, Va.
Williams, John D., Long Beach State College, Long Beach, Calif.
Williams, Mrs. Lois, 200 North 18th St., Montebello, Calif.
Williams, Malcolm D., Sch. of Educ., Tennessee A. & I., Univ., Nashville, Tenn.
Williams, Meta F., 13 Fieldstone Dr., Hartsdale, N.Y.
Williams, Nat. Supt. of Schools, Lubbock, Tex.
Williams, Richard H., Princial, Burlingame High Schol, Burlingame, Calif.
Williams, W. Gloria, Principal, Brownell Elementary School, Chicago, Ill.
Williams, W. Morris, San Francisco Unified Sch. Dist., San Francisco, Calif.
Williams, Wilbur A., Registrar, Moorhead State College, Moorhead, Minn.
Williamson, Mrs. Eva D., Sch. of Educ., University of South Carolina, Columbia, S.C.
Williamson, Walter W., 1820 Cromwood Road, Baltimore, Md.
Willis, Benjamin C., General Supt. of Schools, Chicago, Ill.
Wills, Benjamin G., 1550 Bellamy St., Santa Clara, Calif.
Willson, Gordon L., Supt. of Schools, Baraboo, Wis.
Wilson, David H., Lodi, N.Y.
Wilson, Frank T., Hunter College, New York, N.Y.
Wilson, George D., Kentucky State College, Frankfort, Ky.
Wilson, Gilbert M., Sch. of Educ., Boston University, Boston, Mass.
Wilson, Herbert B., 29 Skyline Dr., Daly City, Calif.
Wilson, Irwin A., Westmont College, Santa Barbara, Calif.
Wilson, J. A. R., Santa Barbara College, Goleta, Calif.
Wilson, Joseph L., P.O. Box 669, Tuscaloosa, Ala.
Wilson, Lytle M., Geneva College, Beaver Falls, Pa.
Wilson, Merle A., Dir., Elementary Education, Public Schls., Des Moines, Iowa

Wilson, Walter E., Pluckemin, N.J.
Wilson, William G., Superintendent Dist. 14 Schools, Chicago, Ill.
Wiltse, Earl W., Supt. of Schools, Grand Island, Neb.
Winchell, Karl F., Exec. Secy., Wyoming Educ. Assn., Cheyenne, Wyo.
Winslow, Robert B., Superintendent of Schools, Milford, Conn.
Winston, Bertha H., Ralph Waldo Emerson Elem. School, Chicago, Ill.
Winston, Ethna B., Elizabeth City State Tchrs. Col., Elizabeth City, N.C.
Winter, Stephen S., Col. of Educ., Univ. of Minnesota, Minneapolis, Minn.
Wise, Joseph M., 108-14 65th Rd., Forest Hills, N.Y.
Wiseman, Rex M., Principal, Pasadena Academy, Pasadena, Calif.
Witherington, Henry C., 86 Beechwood Dr., Jackson, Tenn.
Witt, Paul W. F., Teachers College, Columbia University, New York, N.Y.
Witte, Cyril M., Dept. of Educ., Loyola College, Baltimore, Md.
Witter, Sanford C., Superintendent of Schools, Lead, S.D.
Witty, Paul A., School of Educ., Northwestern University, Evanston, Ill.
Witucki, Lillian Geden, 18649 Harlow Ave., Detroit, Mich.
Wixon, John L., Contra Costa Junior College, El Cerrito, Calif.
Wixted, William G., Hunter College, New York, N.Y.
Wochner, Raymond E., Arizona State College, Tempe. Ariz.
Woelfel, Norman, Dir., Tchg. Aids Lab., Ohio State University, Columbus, Ohio
Woellner, Robert C., Dir., Voc. Guid. & Plac., Univ. of Chicago, Chicago, Ill.
Woestehoff, Orville W., Supv. Principal, Holmes School, Oak Park, Ill.
Wolbrecht, Walter F., 316 Parkwood, Kirkwood, Mo.
Wolf, Lloyd L., 605 North McLean, Lincoln, Ill.
Wolfe, Josephine B., Gen. Supv., Elementary Education, Gary, Ind.
Wolfe, W. D. Superintendent of Schools. Lawrence, Kan.
Wolff, Mrs. Kate, Asst. to Dean, Bard College, Annandale-on-Hudson, N.Y.
Wolfram, Donald J., Dean, Alma White College, Zarephath, N.J.
Wolinsky, Gloria F., Hunter College, Flushing, N.Y.
Wolk, Mrs. Samuel J. B., 420 East 23rd St., New York, N.Y.
Wong, William T. S., Principal, R. L. Stevenson Intermed. Schl., Honolulu,
    Hawaii
Woo, K. K., 563 Tenth Ave., San Francisco, Calif.
Wood, C. B., 3923 W. 11th Ave., Vancouver, B.C., Canada
Wood, Crispin M., 1024 Elmwood, Lincoln, Neb.
Wood, Ernest R., Dean, Rocky Mountain College, Billings, Mont.
Wood, Harold R., Principal, Allen Street School, Lansing, Mich.
Wood, Mrs. Helen Cowan, Fresno County Schools, Fresno, Calif.
Wood, Joseph E., Prin., Glenfield Junior High School, Montclair, N.J.
Wood, Roi S., Superintendent of Schools, Joplin, Mo.
Wood, W. Clement, Head, Dept. of Educ., Ft. Hays Kan. State Col., Hays, Kan.
Wood, W.H., Chm., Dept. of Educ., E. M. College, Berrien Springs, Mich.
Woodard, C. T., Dean, Sch. of Educ., Louisiana Polytechnic Inst., Ruston, La.
Woodard, Prince B., Tchrs. Col., Temple University, Philadelphia, Pa.
Woodburn, John H., Johns Hopkins University, Baltimore, Md.
Woodhull, James E., Voc. Educ. Dept., Colorado A. & M. Coll., Fort Collins, Colo.
Woodruff, Asahel D., Dean, Col. of Educ., Brigham Young Univ., Provo, Utah
Woodruff, Olive, Kent State University, Kent, Ohio
Woodruff, Mrs. Vieva L., Supv. Teacher, City Schools, Elizabethton, Tenn.
Woods, Robert K., Wisconsin State College, Platteville, Wis.
Woodside, J. Barnes, Supt. of Schools, Willoughby, Ohio
Woodson, C. C., Principal, Carver High School, Spartanburg, S.C.
Woodward, Myrle A., 124 High Rock Lane, Westwood, Mass.
Woodworth, Denny, Col. of Educ., Drake University, Des Moines, Iowa
Woodworth, I. R., Dept. of Educ., Sacramento State College, Sacramento, Calif.
Woody, Thomas, Sch. of Educ., University of Pennsylvania, Philadelphia, Pa.
Woofter, J. A., 412 South Union St., Ada, Ohio
Woolcock, Mrs. Doris L., Psychologist, Nassau County Schls., Garden City, N.Y.
Woolf, Kenneth A., Supt., Hunterdon County Schools, Flemington, N.J.
Woollatt, Lorne H., Dir. of Research, Public Schools, Baltimore, Md.
Wooton, Flaud C., Dept. of Educ., Univ. of California, Los Angeles, Calif.

Wotring, Clayton W., Cedar Crest College, Allentown, Pa.
Wozencraft, Marian, Fenn College, Cleveland, Ohio
Wozniak, John M., Chm., Dept. of Educ., Loyola University, Chicago, Ill.
Wray, Mabel E., Principal, Flagg Street School, Worcester, Mass.
Wrenn, C. Gilbert, Buton Hall, Univ. of Minnesota, Minneapolis, Minn.
Wright, C. O., Exec. Secy., Kansas State Tchrs. Assn., Topeka, Kan.
Wright, Mrs. Eleanore B., Elem. Supv., Public Schools, Little Silver, N.J.
Wright, Elizabeth T., Packer Collegiate Institute, Brooklyn, N.Y.
Wright, John R., San Jose State College, San Jose, Calif.
Wright, Nelle B., General Supv. of Curriculum, Public Schools, Tallahassee, Fla.
Wright, Mrs. Roberta Peddy, Dept. of Educ., A. & I. State Col., Nashville, Tenn.
Wright, William Francis, Prin., John Adams Jr. High Schl., Albuquerque, N.M.
Wrightstone, J. Wayne, Dir., Bureau of Educ. Res., Bd. of Educ., Brooklyn, N.Y.
Wronski, Stanley P., Col. of Educ., Michigan State Univ., East Lansing, Mich.
Wubben, Horace J., President, Mesa County Junior Col., Grand Junction, Colo.
Wyeth, E. R., San Fernando State College, Northridge, Calif.
Wynne, John P., Head, Dept. of Educ., State Tchrs. College, Farmville, Va.

Yaple, Graydon W., Dean of Faculty, Wilmington College, Wilmington, Ohio
Yates, J. W., St. Cloud State College, St. Cloud, Minn.
Yauch, Wilbur A., Head, Dept. of Educ., Northern Illinois University, DeKalb, Ill.
Yeager, Paul M., Principal, Sheridan School, Allentown, Pa.
Yntema, Otto, Div. of Field Serv., Western Michigan Col., Kalamazoo, Mich.
Young, Albert T., Jr., School Psychologist, Falls Church, Va.
Young, Mrs. Aurelia Norris, Jackson State College, Jackson, Miss.
Young, Charles W., Bowling Green State University, Bowling Green, Ohio
Young, Doris, Col. of Educ., Michigan State University, East Lansing, Mich.
Young, Francis Allan, State College of Washington, Pullman, Wash.
Young, Harold L., Central Missouri State College, Warrensburg, Mo.
Young, Horace A., Jr., Texas Southern University, Houston, Tex.
Young, J. E. M., Macdonald College, Province of Quebec, Canada
Young, Jesse E., 6000 Jay St., Sacramento, Calif.
Young, John J., Superintendent of Schools, Mishawaka, Ind.
Young, Keneth G., Dir. of Curric., Siskiyou County Schls., Yreka, Calif.
Young, Kenneth E., University of Alaska, College, Alaska
Young, Lloyd P., President, Keene Teachers College, Keene, N.H.
Young, William E., Dir., Div. of Elem. Educ., State Educ. Dept., Albany, N.Y.
Youngblood, Chester E., Supv. Prin., Los Fresnos Prim. School, Los Fresnos, Tex.
Yourd, John L., 1104—2nd Ave., Fargo, N.D.
Yuhas, Andrew J., Prin., Roberts and Morrow Schools, Pittsburgh, Pa.
Yuhas, Theodore F., Prin., Campus Sch., State Tchrs. Col., Mankato, Minn.
Yunghans, Ernest E., R.R. 7, Wayne Ter., Fort Wayne, Ind.

Zaeske, Arnold, St. Cloud State College, St. Cloud, Minn.
Zahn, D. Willard, Dean, Tchrs. Col., Temple University, Philadelphia, Pa.
Zahorsky, Mrs. Metta, 2211 Valleywood Dr., San Bruno, Calif.
Zakrzewski, Aurelia R., Cooley High School, Detroit, Mich.
Zastrow, Joyce, University of Minnesota, Minneapolis, Minn.
Zawadski, Bohdan, Dept. of Psych., City College of New York, New York, N. Y.
Zbornik, Joseph J., 3219 Clarence Ave., Berwyn, Ill.
Zeddies, Leslie, Concordia Teachers College, River Forest, Ill.
Zeiler, E. J., Superintendent of Schools, Whitefish Bay, Wis.
Zellers, Everett C., University of Minnesota, Minneapolis, Minn.
Zellner, Aubrey, Dept. of Educ., St. John's Univ., Collegeville, Minn.
Zim, Herbert S., Box 34, Tavernier, Fla.
Zimmerman, Mrs. Alice B., 4801 Indianapolis Blvd., East Chicago, Ind.
Zintgraff, Paul E., Superintendent of County Schools, San Diego, Calif.
Zintz, Miles V., 3028 Marble Ave., N.E., Albuquerque, N.M.
Zion, Leela C., 2550 San Miguel Dr., Walnut Creek, Calif.
Zipper, Joseph H., 2306 Parade St., Erie, Pa.

INFORMATION CONCERNING THE NATIONAL SOCIETY FOR THE STUDY OF EDUCATION

1. PURPOSE. The purpose of the National Society is to promote the investigation and discussion of educational questions. To this end it holds an annual meeting and publishes a series of yearbooks.

2. ELIGIBILITY TO MEMBERSHIP. Any person who is interested in receiving its publications may become a member by sending to the Secretary-Treasurer information concerning name, title, and address, and a check for $6.00 (see Item 5).

Membership is not transferable; it is limited to individuals, and may not be held by libraries, schools, or other institutions, either directly or indirectly.

3. PERIOD OF MEMBERSHIP. Applicants for membership may not date their entrance back of the current calendar year, and all memberships terminate automatically on December 31, unless the dues for the ensuing year are paid as indicated in Item 6.

4. DUTIES AND PRIVILEGES OF MEMBERS. Members pay dues of $5.00 annually, receive a cloth-bound copy of each publication, are entitled to vote, to participate in discussion, and (under certain conditions) to hold office. The names of members are printed in the yearbooks.

Persons who are sixty years of age or above may become life members on payment of fee based on average life-expectancy of their age group. For information, apply to Secretary-Treasurer.

5. ENTRANCE FEE. New members are required the first year to pay, in addition to the dues, an entrance fee of one dollar.

6. PAYMENT OF DUES. Statements of dues are rendered in October for the following calendar year. Any member so notified whose dues remain unpaid on January 1, thereby loses his membership and can be reinstated only by paying a reinstatement fee of fifty cents.

School warrants and vouchers from institutions must be accompanied by definite information concerning the name and address of the person for whom membership fee is being paid. Statements of dues are rendered on our own form only. The Secretary's office cannot undertake to fill out special invoice forms of any sort or to affix notary's affidavit to statements or receipts.

Cancelled checks serve as receipts. Members desiring an additional receipt must enclose a stamped and addressed envelope therefor.

7. DISTRIBUTION OF YEARBOOKS TO MEMBERS. The yearbooks, ready prior to each February meeting, will be mailed from the office of the distributors, only to members whose dues for that year have been paid. Members who desire yearbooks prior to the current year must purchase them directly from the distributors (see Item 8.)

8. COMMERCIAL SALES. The distribution of all yearbooks prior to the current year, and also of those of the current year not regularly mailed to members in exchange for their dues, is in the hands of the distributor, not of the Secretary. For such commercial sales, communicate directly with the University of Chicago Press, Chicago 37, Illinois, which will gladly send a price list covering all the publications of this Society. This list is also printed in the yearbook.

9. YEARBOOKS. The yearbooks are issued about one month before the February meeting. They comprise from 600 to 800 pages annually. Unusual effort has been made to make them, on the one hand, of immediate practical value, and, on the other hand, representative of sound scholarship and scientific investigation.

10. MEETINGS. The annual meeting, at which the yearbooks are discussed, is held in February at the same time and place as the meeting of the American Association of School Administrators.

Applications for membership will be handled promptly at any time on receipt of name and address, together with check for $6.00 (or $5.50 for reinstatement). Applications entitle the new members to the yearbook slated for discussion during the calendar year the application is made.

5835 Kimbark Ave.
Chicago 37, Illinois

NELSON B. HENRY, *Secretary-Treasurer*

xcix

PUBLICATIONS OF THE NATIONAL SOCIETY FOR THE STUDY OF EDUCATION

NOTICE: Many of the early Yearbooks of this series are now out of print. In the following list, those titles to which an asterisk is prefixed are not available for purchase.

Distributed by
THE UNIVERSITY OF CHICAGO PRESS, CHICAGO 37, ILLINOIS
1959